STANFORD

Home of Champions

BY

GARY MIGDOL

FOREWORD BY BILL WALSH

SPORTS PUBLISHING

a Division of Sagamore Publishing

Director of production, book layout: Susan M. McKinney
Book and dust jacket design: Michelle R. Dressen

ISBN: 1-57167-116-1

Printed in the United States.

SPORTS PUBLISHING
a Division of
Sagamore Publishing
804 N. Neil
Champaign, IL 61820
www.sagamorepub.com

To my wife, partner and best friend, Julie,
who gives me life every day.
To my beautiful twin daughters, Robin and Erin,
who make me realize what life is truly all about.

And to the spirit of Leland Stanford Junior University,
organized 1891.

CONTENTS

ACKNOWLEDGMENTS

Now I know what's it like for an Academy Award winner who has 30 seconds to thank everyone who should be recognized. There's simply not enough time—or space in my case—to tell everyone how much I appreciate their support, their assistance and their generosity in helping me finish such a monumental project.

I find myself thinking of all the people who have made it possible for me to write this book, of all the people who went out of their way to help me find a photo, or research a fact, or who simply took time out of their day to talk to me about a great Stanford team or player. I'll do my best in this space to thank them from the bottom of my heart, knowing full well that it will fall short of expressing my sincere gratitude. For without them, and their kindness, I could not have written this book.

While several people assisted me along this journey, there is only one person who not only provided me with great support and encouragement for this project, but who inspired me on a daily basis—my wife, Julie. She was there for me when I asked her to proofread copy, to update portions of the book, to read a passage, offer an opinion.

I wish to extend a very special and heartfelt "Thank you" to my good pal, Bob Murphy, who himself is an encyclopedia of Stanford sports knowledge. I have learned so much about Stanford University and college athletics from Murph that I cannot ever say "Thanks" too much.

I would also like to acknowledge the tremendous support and effort given to me by three of Stanford's greatest coaches: track coach Payton Jordan, tennis coach Dick Gould and football coach Bill Walsh.

To the Stanford Athletic coaching staff, I say "Thank you" on two fronts. One, you are collectively the best coaching staff in America and have given your fans much to cheer about. Secondly, you have been a great help to me in compiling the information needed to put this book together, particularly baseball coach Mark Marquess, women's tennis coach Frank Brennan, women's swimming coach Richard Quick, football coach Tyrone Willingham, men's basketball coach Mike Montgomery, and women's basketball coach Tara VanDerveer.

The Stanford Athletic Department has been very supportive of this project and I must thank them, including Athletic Director Ted Leland, Senior Associate Athletic Director Cheryl Levick and Associate Athletic Director Jon Denney.

My staff in the Media Relations Office has put up with me for the past year and I couldn't have done it without their tremendous support. I particularly wish to thank Debbie Kenney, Beth Goode, Scott Leykam, Darci Bransford, and the rest of our staff and student-assistants. And of course, the incomparable Sam Goldman.

There were two other books written on Stanford Athletics by two of my predecessors: *The Color of Life is Red* by the late Don Leibendorfer and *Stanford Sports* by Gary Cavalli. Both books provided me with excellent resources and background information on Stanford's great athletic heritage. Other books that I used for research included *Great Moments in Stanford Sports* by Pete Grothe, *Down on The Farm* by Fred Merrick and *The Big Game* by John Sullivan.

I also wish to thank the staff at the Stanford University Archives for their patience and assistance, photographers David Madison and David Gonzalez for their wonderful cover photos, the United States Olympic Committee, U.S. Swimming, USA Track and Field, USA Basketball and of course, Mike Pearson from Sagamore Publishing for giving me the opportunity to write this book.

Finally, I wish to acknowledge the people who mean the most to me: my family. My wife and soulmate, Julie, for being a great mom and friend while I spent countless days and nights in front of my computer during this past year; my twin daughters Erin and Robin, the loves of my life; my parents, Irv and Sylvia; my three sisters—Marcie, Randie and Laurie—and their families; and our dear friends, Susan and Julie. You're the best.

FOREWORD

Stanford University is recognized as the preeminent athletic program in the country. It has a record unparalleled in collegiate athletics and it establishes Stanford as "the best overall program in the United States" for both men's and women's athletics.

During my career in athletics, I have been associated with some of the greatest teams and greatest players in the history of football. I have been a part of organizations that have won Super Bowl championships, but also have finished last in the league and have experienced the ultimate highs and lows that come with being in the arena.

I have also been fortunate enough to have learned from some of the legends of football. My first college coaching job was, shall I dare say, at the University of California under Marv Levy from 1960-62. That led to my first of three stints at Stanford. I was hired in 1963 by the great John Ralston to join his staff at Stanford. This was my introduction to Stanford and there wasn't a more dynamic person to work for during that time than Coach Ralston.

After leaving Stanford in 1966, I worked for Al Davis with the Oakland Raiders, Paul Brown with the Cleveland Browns and Tommy Prothro with the San Diego Chargers. I was then 45-years-old and anxious to become a head coach. Then, in 1977, Athletic Director Joe Ruetz selected me at Stanford. I was again brought back to a place that was very special to me, that truly inspired me.

And, many years later, when given an opportunity to return to coaching at Stanford in 1992, I knew that if I was to ever resume my coaching career, it would be at Stanford. It was a privilege. The unique environment, the quality of student-athletes, the commitment to being the best on the athletic field and in the classroom set a standard for the nation.

I vividly recall our incredible come-from-behind Bluebonnet Bowl victory over Georgia in 1978. That victory rivaled our dominance over Penn State in the 1993 Blockbuster Bowl. Our win over Notre Dame in 1992 ranks with any Super Bowl victory that I have experienced. Also, our wins over nationally ranked Colorado in 1993 and Washington in '94 would be as high on my list as any regular season NFL game.

There is a dimension that exists at Stanford that is one of a creative spirit, an assertive nature and, in a sense, the willingness to search the unknown. This spirit, by the nature of the school's vision and the atmosphere that has existed from its very origins, has created an environment in which people challenge themselves by seeking alternative avenues, sometimes original ways, to reach even higher goals and set higher standards.

In the Athletic Department, the locker rooms and even in the coaches' offices, there is a central theme that enhances accomplishment. This theme is totally energized, people are connected and universally committed to doing the very best they can on the athletic field and in sharing their success with each other, the University and community. I have experienced my ultimate gratification and satisfaction in the camaraderie, mutual commitment, sacrifice and personal relationships while a member of the Athletic Department at Stanford University.

I believe the Stanford coaching staff to be the finest in the nation and in *Stanford: Home of Champions* you'll find this to be well documented. The successes at Stanford cross through every sport and transcend what would normally be considered a successful program into one in which students, faculty, administration, campus community and alumni can take pride in this marvelous representative intercollegiate program. It is also a point of pride internationally for a great academic institution to produce the finest athletes in the world and do it in a thoroughly honest way.

Home of Champions is an appropriate title to a book that allows all of us to relive the great spirit of Stanford Athletics and the many, many inspiring men and women who have helped make Stanford University the finest overall athletic program in the nation.

—Bill Walsh

1891-92

·· AMERICA'S TIME CAPSULE ··

- September 22, 1891: A presidential proclamation opened 900,000 acres of Indian land in Oklahoma.
- December 29, 1891: Thomas A. Edison received a patent for wireless telegraphy for a "means of transmitting signals electronically ... without the use of wires."
- January 1, 1892: Ellis Island in upper New York became the receiving station for immigrants.
- June 7-11, 1892: The Republican National Convention nominated President Benjamin Harrison for reelection and Whitelaw Reid of New York for the vice presidency.
- June 21-23, 1892: The Democrats nominated Grover Cleveland of New York for president and Adlai Ewing Stevenson of Illinois for vice president.

STANFORD MOMENT

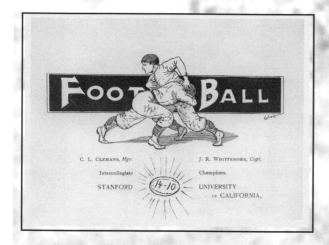

First Big Game Played on March 19, 1892

California had been playing football for over 10 years when they met their new rivals from Stanford in the first Big Game on March 19, 1892. Cal came into the game with a 4-1 record, while Stanford was 2-1 following wins over Hopkins Academy and Berkeley Gym and a loss to the Olympic Club. Stanford surprised the stronger and more experienced Bears by jumping out to a 14-0 lead at halftime (touchdowns were worth four points, PATs two in these days). The first touchdown in Big Game history was scored by Stanford's Carl Clemens, who took a handoff from Paul Downing on a reverse and raced the final 45 yards into the end zone. Clemens scored the second TD of the game, again on a 45-yard run, and John Whittemore scored later in the second quarter. Whittemore also added one conversion to give Stanford a commanding lead. Cal's defense stiffened in the second half and their offense scored two TDs and one conversion, but it still fell short as Stanford upset the Bears 14-10 in the first intercollegiate football game in Stanford history.

A SHORT TIME after the opening registration at Stanford in 1891, talk began about organizing the Cardinals' first football team. A group of students interested in playing football called on John R. Whittemore to spearhead the process. Whittemore, a senior transfer student from Washington University in St. Louis, had played football at Washington and knew the game. He was asked to organize a team and serve as its captain. Whittemore immediately went to work, devising plays and coaching the team. After three months of practice, he decided the team was ready for some competition. After learning of the challenge by California, Whittemore decided to line up a series of practice games before taking on the more experienced Bears. The game of football had come to Stanford University.

Stanford Stat . . .

Word of Stanford University forming a football team reached Berkeley, and California manager Roy Gallagher issued a verbal challenge to Stanford to meet in a game on Thanksgiving Day, 1891. John R. Whittemore, Stanford's player-coach, knew there was no way he could get his fledgling team ready to face Cal by Thanksgiving. The first game was later scheduled for March 19, 1892.

STANFORD LIST

FOOTBALL PLEDGE

In order to be a member of the 1892 Stanford football team, all candidates had to take a pledge and promise to conform to the following training rules:

1. To abstain absolutely from the use of tobacco and alcoholic drinks
2. To retire regularly not later than 10:30 p.m.
3. Not to rise before 6:30 a.m.
4. To obey implicitly and regularly the call of the manager for cross country running, gymnasium practice, and field practice
5. To abstain absolutely from eating between meals.

Stanford LEGEND

Herbert Hoover

Herbert Hoover was Stanford's first football manager in 1892. (Stanford University News Service)

While Herbert C. Hoover was never an athlete at Stanford, his role as the football team's manager and the series of events leading up to the first intercollegiate football game in Stanford history are legendary. Hoover, later to become the 31st President of the United States, had printed 10,000 tickets for the 15,000-seat Haight Street baseball grounds in San Francisco. However, when the overflow crowd kept filling up the stadium, Hoover, with no printed tickets left, was forced to collect coins at the gate and put them in empty wash tubs, boxes and anything else he could get. When the team captains were on the field and the referee asked for the ball, there was one small problem. No one remembered to bring the ball!! An owner of a local sporting goods store who was in the stadium set off on horseback to get a ball. The game was delayed almost an hour until a football arrived. "I did not see the game," Hoover said. "After the game, the California manager and I retired to a hotel with our money, now transferred to grain bags, and sat up most of the night counting it. I had never seen $30,000 before. We were well financed for the next season."

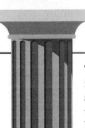

STANFORD LORE

The University opened as a fully coeducational institution, charging no tuition, with 559 students and 15 faculty members, on October 1, 1891. From the beginning, the University operated under the major-subject system with electives rather than the more common rigid curriculum of classical studies. "Ours is the youngest of the universities, but it is heir to the wisdom of all the ages, and with this inheritance it has the promise of a rapid and sturdy growth," said new President David Starr Jordan on Opening Day.

1892-93

- **August 4, 1892:** Andrew J. Borden and his second wife, Abby, were murdered with blows from an ax in their Massachusetts home, beginning one of the most intriguing murder cases in U.S. history.
- **October 5, 1892:** While attempting to rob a bank, the notorious Dalton Gang was virtually wiped out in Coffeyville, Kansas.
- **November 8, 1892:** Grover Cleveland unseated incumbent Benjamin Harrison to win election as President of the United States.
- **January 4, 1893:** President Cleveland granted amnesty to violators of the Anti-polygamy Act of 1882 with the stipulation that they observe the law henceforth.
- **June 14, 1893:** The city of Philadelphia observed the first Flag Day by displaying flags over every public building in the city.

1892 Football Team. (Stanford Archives)

STANFORD MOMENT

Stanford-Cal Battle to 10-10 tie in Second Big Game

Still reeling after being beaten by Stanford in the first Big Game in the spring of 1892, California was eager to get another chance against Stanford and was pressing to schedule a second game. An agreement was made to play on December 17, 1892 with the following four games to be played each Thanksgiving. With Walter Camp as its first football coach, Stanford jumped out to a 6-0 halftime lead and led 10-4 before Cal scored the final six points to earn a 10-10 tie with Stanford. After Carl Clemans gained 40 yards on a double-reverse, Stanford's H.A. Walton scored the game's first touchdown (four points) and Martin Kennedy added the conversion (two points). Cal's first TD made the score 6-4, but an impressive 80-yard drive in four plays by Stanford stretched the lead to 10-4. Clemans scored the touchdown on a 40-yard run. Cal's Loren Hunt scored on a 20-yard run with less than eight minutes to play and the subsequent conversion tied the score at 10-10. A unique feature of this game was that both coaches—Camp from Stanford and Thomas McClung of Cal—were also the officials, alternating between referee and umpire. There were no substitutions in the game as all 22 men played the entire game.

Stanford SPOTLIGHT

BASEBALL was the second sport to field a team at the young Leland Stanford Junior University in the spring of 1892. Stanford defeated Cal 13-6 on April 23, 1892 in the first intercollegiate baseball game in school history. The following season, Stanford won 11 of the 12 games it played, including winning all three games vs. California. Captained by catcher Harry Walton, Stanford beat Cal 12-6, 10-6 and 12-4. The games were played at Haight Street Grounds in San Francisco, Piedmont Grounds in Oakland and Cycler's Park in San Jose. Walton became the first player to hit a home run in a Stanford-Cal game when he connected in game two of the series. The only game Stanford lost in 1893 was a one-run decision against the Oakland Pros.

Stanford Stat . . .

The first intercollegiate track meet in Stanford history was held on April 22, 1893 vs. California at the old Olympic Club Grounds in San Francisco. California dominated the meet, winning 10 of the 14 events, and beat Stanford 91-35. Stanford did not have a coach and was handled by an Executive Track Committee composed of R.E. Maynard, Scott Calhoun and Jackson E. Reynolds.

STANFORD LIST

BEST WON-LOSS RECORDS BY STANFORD FOOTBALL COACHES

(minimum three seasons; excluding rugby)

COACH	W-L-T	.PCT
1. James Lanagan, 1903-05	23-2-4	.862
2. Glenn S. "Pop" Warner, 1924-32	71-17-8	.781
3. Walter Camp, 1892, 1894-95	12-3-3	.750
4. John Ralston, 1963-71	55-36-3	.588
5. Bill Walsh, 1977-78, 92-94	34-24-1	.585
6. Chuck Taylor, 1951-57	40-29-2	.577
7. C.E. "Tiny" Thornhill, 1933-39	35-25-7	.574
8. Jack Christiansen, 1972-76	30-22-3	.573

Stanford LEGEND

Walter Camp

Walter Camp is considered the Father of American Football.
(Stanford Athletic Dept.)

After a very successful entry into intercollegiate football in 1891 and the first Big Game in the spring of 1892, Stanford set out to find itself a football coach for the '92 season. James Whittemore, Stanford's team captain and player-coach in '91, wrote a letter to Yale's famous coach, Walter Camp, and asked Camp to recommend a coach for Stanford. Camp's reply was quite a surprise. He volunteered himself to be Stanford's coach, but only after the Yale season had ended. Camp, generally considered to be the "father of American football," was an outstanding halfback at Yale who earned seven football letters from 1876-1882. He played in the first Harvard-Yale game in 1876 and led his team to a record of 30-1-6 during his playing days. Camp served at Yale, as he did at Stanford, as an unpaid coach. He was one of the founders of the Intercollegiate Football Association and is credited with creating the line of scrimmage, 11-man team, signal calling and the QB position. Camp coached at Stanford in 1892, returned to the East Coast in 1893, then came back to coach at Stanford in 1894 and '95. His three-year record on The Farm was 12-3-3.

STANFORD LORE

Leland Stanford Sr. died at his Palo Alto home on July 21, 1893 at the age of 69. His casket was borne to the mausoleum. Shortly thereafter, Leland Jr.'s casket (he died of typhoid on March 13, 1884) was moved from a temporary tomb to the mausoleum. Stanford's death threw the University into a severe financial crisis.

1893-94

·· AMERICA'S TIME CAPSULE ··

- **September 16, 1893:** The Cherokee Strip, purchased from the Cherokee Indians in 1891, was opened for land rush settlement. Some 100,000 people converged on the area located between Kansas and Oklahoma.
- **October 13, 1893:** U.S. yacht *Vigilant* successfully defended the America's Cup by defeating the British challenger *Valkyrie*.
- **January 8, 1894:** A fire at the Chicago World's Colombian Exposition destroyed virtually all the buildings and caused an estimated $2 million in damage.
- **May 11, 1894:** The famous Pullman labor strike began at the Pullman railroad car plant in Chicago. It was declared over on August 3, 1894.
- **June 16, 1894:** George Case and Dutch Carter of Yale University were the first baseball players to employ the squeeze play in an intercollegiate game between Yale and Princeton.

STANFORD MOMENT

1893 Football Team (Stanford Archives)

Stanford Makes Claim as Pacific Coast Champions

Stanford was 4-0-1 when it headed up to Washington and Oregon to play four games against teams representing the Northwest. When it was over, on January 1, 1894, Stanford had won all four games by an aggregate score of 154-0 and had laid claim as champions of the Pacific Coast. Stanford defeated Tacoma 48-0, Port Townsend 50-0, Washington 40-0 and the Multnomah Athletic Club of Portland 18-0.

It was the longest trip ever taken by a football team in the country. Stanford played all of its games away from campus, including four in San Francisco, one in San Jose and four in the Northwest. The top players for Stanford included Paul Downing, William Harrelson, H.A. Walton, Louis Whitehouse and Claud Downing.

STANFORD'S BASEBALL TEAM played just two intercollegiate games during the 1894 season, beating California on both occasions. Stanford scored six runs in the first inning of the first game, played on April 13 at Stanford, and went on to defeat Cal 15-11. The two teams met again on April 21 in Berkeley, and again Stanford's big bats prevailed in an 11-7 victory. During the summer of '94, Stanford traveled north for a 22-game schedule against teams from Washington and Oregon and compiled an 18-4 record. Stanford's big hitters included H.T. Dyer (.484), Abraham Lewis (.454) and C.W. Davey (.414).

Stanford Stat . . .

California beat Stanford 90-36 in the second intercollegiate field day held in Berkeley. Seven intercollegiate and two Pacific Coast records were broken. Stanford's David Brown won the mile run in a Coast record time of 4:49.4.

STANFORD LIST

STANFORD'S BOWL MVP'S

1925 Rose Bowl	Ernie Nevers
1928 Rose Bowl	Cliff Hoffman
1936 Rose Bowl	Jim "Monk" Moscrip
	Keith Topping
1941 Rose Bowl	Pete Kmetovic
1971 Rose Bowl	Jim Plunkett
1972 Rose Bowl	Don Bunce
1977 Sun Bowl	Guy Benjamin
	Gordy Ceresino
1978 Bluebonnet Bowl	Steve Dils
	Gordy Ceresino
1986 Gator Bowl	Brad Muster
1991 Aloha Bowl	Tommy Vardell
1993 Blockbuster Bowl	Darrien Gordon
1995 Liberty Bowl	Kwame Ellis
1996 Sun Bowl	Chad Hutchinson
	Kailee Wong

Stanford LEGEND

C.D. "Pop" Bliss

C.D. "Pop" Bliss led Stanford to football prominence. (Stanford Archives)

When Walter Camp returned to the East Coast after just one season as Stanford's head football coach, C.D. "Pop" Bliss, a famous halfback from Yale, was called on to coach the team in 1893. Bliss came to Stanford with an agenda of fixing the ails of the Stanford football team. "The tackling generally is weak and the center men are slow and awkward. The quarterback is slow passing the ball while the tackles overrun their men," he said prior to the season. But Bliss apparently corrected the faults. His Stanford team went 8-0-1 with the only blemish on their record being a 6-6 tie with California in the third Big Game. Stanford so dominated its opponents that it outscored them 284-17 in the nine games, which included seven shut-outs. Walter Camp returned to Stanford to coach the 1894 team, ending Bliss' brief one-year stay as Stanford's head coach. But his success during the '93 season put Stanford on the map as one of the powerful teams on the West Coast.

STANFORD LORE

The U.S. Government filed a $15 million claim on May 10, 1894 against the Stanford estate, bringing probate procedures to a halt. The suit asked liquidation of loans made for construction of the Central Pacific Railroad, even though the loans were not due. Mrs. Stanford was again advised to close the University, but again she said "No."

1894-95

- August 8, 1894: The United States' government officially recognized the Hawaiian Republic.
- August 27, 1894: A predominately Democratic Congress passed the first graduated income tax law. It was declared unconstitutional by the Supreme Court the following year.
- December 22, 1894: The United States Golf Association (USGA) was formed at a meeting of five golf clubs from New York, Massachusetts, Rhode Island and Chicago.
- February 24, 1895: The revolt of Cuba against Spain broke out, causing President Cleveland to call on U.S. citizens to avoid giving aid to the insurgents.
- July 4, 1895: Katherine Lee Bates, a Wellesley College professor, published "America the Beautiful" in the *Congregationalist*, a church publication.

STANFORD MOMENT

Stanford's 1894 team beat Cal 6-0 in the Big Game.
(Stanford Archives)

Blocked Punt Leads to Big Game Victory

After two consecutive ties, both Stanford and Cal had pressure to bring home a victory in the fourth Big Game. But on Thanksgiving Day, 1894, Stanford won the game 6-0 on an unusual play that netted the game's only touchdown. Cal was attempting to surprise Stanford by punting on first down to try to establish better field position. But Stanford guard Charlie Fickert broke through the line and blocked Wolf Ransome's punt. Stanford's Guy Cochran then outran Ransome to the ball, inadvertently kicked it in the end zone where he fell on it for the game's lone touchdown. Cal thought it had a touchdown later in the game, but a controversial call by the referee disallowed it. *"A Fluke Glorifies the Cardinal"* wrote the *San Francisco Chronicle* the following day. Nevertheless, Stanford extended its Big Game undeafeated streak to four.

THE STANFORD BASEBALL TEAM, led by captain H.T. Dyer, won six of seven games in 1895, including two more victories over California. Stanford ran its winning streak over Cal to seven after 14-8 and 11-4 wins. In the two games with Berkeley, Stanford pounded out 33 hits. Infielder Abe Lewis had five hits, including a triple, in game two. Stanford's Billy McLaine, who was later elected captain of the 1896 team, was the winning pitcher in both games.

Stanford Stat . . .

Stanford played its first football game on campus in 1894 when it defeated Reliance Club 20-0. Earlier in the season, the Reliance Club had beaten Stanford twice. Also, 1894 featured Stanford's first two intersectional games vs. the University of Chicago. Stanford lost the first game in San Francisco 24-4, but won the second game played in Los Angeles 12-0.

STANFORD LIST

ALL "OLDTIMERS" FOOTBALL TEAM (1891-1940)

E	Monk Moscrip	1933-5
T	Bob Reynolds	1933-35
G	Chuck Taylor	1940-42
C	Vic Lindskog	1940-41
G	Bill Corbus	1931-33
T	Bruno Banducci	1940-42
E	Jim Lawson	1922-24
QB	Frankie Albert	1939-41
HB	Ernie Nevers	1923-25
HB	Bobby Grayson	1933-35
HB	Norm Standlee	1938-40
HB	Phil Moffatt	1929-31
P	Frankie Albert	1939-41
PK	Dink Templeton	1915-17, '19-20

Stanford LEGEND

Charlie Fickert

Charlie Fickert was named Stanford head football coach in 1901. (Stanford Archives)

He was known as a devastating blocker who had the ability to pull halfbacks through defenders. As a guard on the Stanford football team from 1894-97, Charlie Fickert had the reputation as one of the toughest men on the team. He gained the respect of his teammates through his relentless display of blocking and, in 1896, he was named the team captain. In his first Big Game in 1894, Fickert was credited with blocking a punt which was picked up by a Stanford teammate and taken into the end zone for the game's only touchdown. His four Stanford teams outscored Cal 60-6 while posting a 3-0-1 record vs. the Bears. Fickert later became the first Stanford alumnus to be named head football coach, a position he held in 1901. In his only season as the head coach, Fickert led the Cardinal to the first Rose Bowl game ever played on January 1, 1902 vs. Michigan.

STANFORD LORE

On May 29, 1895, the first group of students to complete a full four years of study at Stanford University graduated. Known as the Pioneer Class, the group included future United States President Herbert Hoover. In June of '94, George Hall Ashley was awarded the first Ph.D. He came to Stanford after receiving his undergraduate degree from Cornell to study geology under John Casper Branner.

1895-96

- October 4, 1895:   Newport (Rhode Island) Golf Club hosted the first U.S. Open golf tournament.
- January 4, 1896:   Utah became the 45th state in the Union.
- April 6, 1896:   The first modern Olympic Games opened in Athens, Greece.
- April 23, 1896:   The first public showing of a moving picture was presented in New York City.
- June 4, 1896:   Assembly of the first Ford automobile was completed by Henry Ford in Detroit.

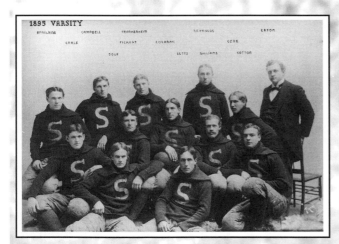

Stanford and Cal tied 6-6 in the 1895 Big Game.
(Stanford Athletic Dept.)

STANFORD MOMENT

Third Big Game Tie in Five Years

Walter Camp, coaching in his third Big Game, brought an undefeated Stanford team (4-0) to face a California squad that was 3-1 on the season but had still not beaten Stanford. The game was played on November 28, 1895 in front of a small (approximately 10,000) crowd at Central Park in San Francisco. Wet and windy weather conditions accounted for the lowest turnout since the first Big Game. While accounts of the events vary as to who scored for Stanford, what is known is that Stanford scored the first touchdown of the game, added the conversion and led 6-0. Whether it was Bill Campbell or Guy Cochran to get in the end zone, there seems to be no consensus. Cal captain Eddy Sherman scored the Bear's touchdown on a four-yard run late in the game and Wolf Ransome added the conversion to knot the score at 6-6. It was the third tie in five Big Games, but Stanford had still not lost to their new rivals from Berkeley.

AFTER BEING BEATEN badly in its first three intercollegiate track and field meets against California, Stanford won a *moral* victory by earning a 56-56 tie with the Bears in 1896. Stanford had hired their first coach, W.M. Hunter, in 1894, but by the '96 season he had already departed. Without a head coach during the 1896 season, Stanford managed to win seven events against the more talented and experienced Bears. Freshman John Burton scored 16 points for Stanford. He won the 440-yard run and the broad jump and placed second in the 100 and 220-yard dash.

Stanford Stat . . .

The first intercollegiate women's basketball game was played with California in the San Francisco Armory on April 4, 1896. Stanford won the game 2-1. Backboards had not yet been introduced. Women were involved in athletics since the inception of the University, but not necessarily encouraged to participate. Even so, the women decided on their own to enter competition. Men were not allowed to attend the first basketball game.

STANFORD LIST

MEDAL COUNT OF STANFORD ATHLETES AT SUMMER OLYMPIC GAMES

Year	Site	Gold	Silver	Bronze	Total
1908	London	0	0	0	0
1912	Stockholm	0	0	1	1
1920	Antwerp	12	3	1	16
1924	Paris	12	3	6	21
1928	Amsterdam	4	0	0	4
1932	Los Angeles	2	4	5	11
1936	Berlin	1	1	0	2
1948	London	1	1	0	2
1952	Helsinki	1	0	0	1
1956	Melbourne	5	2	0	7
1960	Rome	7	2	0	9
1964	Tokyo	5	2	1	8
1968	Mexico City	1	3	3	7
1972	Munich	1	2	2	5
1976	Montreal	5	2	0	7
1980	Moscow	Boycott			
1984	Los Angeles	5	8	1	14
1988	Seoul	8	6	3	17
1992	Barcelona	10	4	5	19
1996	Atlanta	16	1	1	18

Stanford LEGEND

Guy Cochran

Guy Cochran was one of Stanford's first great football players. (Stanford Archives)

A four-year letterman from 1892-95, Guy Cochran was one of the early stars on the Stanford football team. Named captain of the 1895 team, Cochran played left tackle and punted, among other chores, for the Cardinal. In the 1894 Big Game with Cal, it was Cochran who outran the Bears' Wolf Ransome, picked up the loose ball after the blocked punt, and scored the game's only touchdown in a 6-0 Stanford victory. A year later in the '95 Big Game, Stanford and Cal played to a 6-6 tie. While reports differ on the events of the game, some claim that it was Cochran who scored Stanford's touchdown, giving his team an early 6-0 lead. In his four years at Stanford, Cochran helped his team compile a 20-3-4 overall record.

STANFORD LORE

By unanimous decision, on March 2, 1896, the U.S. Supreme Court rejected the federal government's claims against the Stanford estate. As the financial crisis that threatened the University's existence was eased by the court verdict, pandemonium broke out on campus. Students painted the campus U.S. Post Office Stanford red, which President Jordan said greatly improved its appearance.

1896-97

•• AMERICA'S TIME CAPSULE ••

- July 11, 1896: The Democratic National Convention nominated William Jennings Bryan of Nebraska for presidency.
- October 1, 1896: The Federal Post Office established rural free delivery.
- November 3, 1896: William McKinley won the U.S. presidency in a landslide.
- March 17, 1897: Bob Fitzsimmons defeated "Gentleman Jim" Corbett for the world heavyweight boxing title.
- April 19, 1897: John McDermott won the first Boston Marathon in a time of two hours, 55 minutes, and 10 seconds.

The 1896 club routed Cal, 20-0 in the Big Game.
(Stanford Archives)

STANFORD MOMENT

Stanford Wins First Rout in Big Game History

The first five Big Games had been close contests—three of them ending in ties—but Big Game No. 6 would end up a 20-0 rout by Stanford on November 26, 1896. An overflow crowd of 15,000 jammed Central Park to witness the annual intercollegiate football game that was vastly becoming a Bay Area tradition. Stanford built a 10-0 lead in the first half and was never seriously threatened by the Bears all afternoon. Steuart Cotton capped a 60-yard, 16-play drive by scoring the game's first TD on a short run. Three minutes later, freshman quarterback Chet Murphy punted to Cal on the Bear's 15-yard line, but when the Cal safety dropped the ball, Stanford's Jack Rice fell on it in the end zone for the touchdown and a 10-0 halftime lead. Stanford added two more TDs in the second half to finish the scoring. Murphy scored on a 17-yard run and Cotton culminated another long Stanford drive by going over from the three.

FOR THE first time since baseball was played at Stanford in 1892, the university had a head coach—W.A. Lange. He guided the '97 team to a 3-3 record, which included losing two of three games to California, the first time ever that the Bears had won the season series from Stanford. The first game of the Cal series was a wild 14-13 Stanford victory that was highlighted by 13 Cal errors, seven by the shortstop. In game two, Stanford committed nine errors to none for Cal as the Bears snapped their eight-game losing streak to Stanford with a 15-11 decision. Cal pounded Stanford for 20 hits and 20 runs in a 20-9 win to take the season series for the first time.

Stanford Stat . . .

In February, 1897, Stanford and Cal drew up a pact that outlined some basic rules of eligibility. Among the new regulations adopted were the limitation of athletes to four years of competition in one sport, establishment of a minimum number of hours of classroom work for an athlete to be eligible and a ruling that students of other institutions would be ineligible to compete for either university.

STANFORD LIST

STANFORD FOOTBALL NCAA POST-GRADUATE SCHOLARSHIP WINNERS

1965	Joe Neal
1966	Terry DeSylvia
1968	John Root
1971	John Sande III
1972	Jackie Brown
1974	Randy Poltl
1975	Keith Rowen
1976	Gerald Wilson
1977	Duncan McColl
1981	Milt McColl
1984	John Bergren
1985	Scott Carpenter
1986	Matt Soderlund
1987	Brian Morris
1988	Doug Robison
1995	David Walker
1996	Marlon Evans

Stanford ❧ LEGEND ❧

Steuart Cotton

Steuart Cotton was captain of the 1897 football team.
(Stanford Archives)

When Harry P. Cross took over as Stanford's head football coach in 1896, one of his first moves was to switch Steuart Cotton from tackle to fullback. Cotton, who was chosen team captain for the 1897 squad, proved to be one of the most prolific backs in Big Game history. He was the starting fullback on Stanford's '96 and '97 teams, which beat Cal 20-0 and 28-0. In those two games, Cotton scored five touchdowns, which remains today among the best ever in Big Game annals. A four-year letterman (1894-97), Cotton scored twice in '96 and a Big Game record three times in the '97 contest.

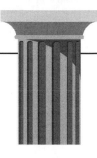

STANFORD LORE

In the summer of 1897, Jane Stanford sailed to London with the intention of selling her jewels to help bolster University finances. Upon arrival, however, she had difficulty finding buyers because Queen Victoria's Diamond Jubilee was in progress and the city was teeming with royalty who were well fixed for jewels. Later, she gave the gems to the Trustees, who used them to endow a half-million-dollar Jewel Fund for the purchase of library books.

1897-98

- September 21, 1897: In response to a letter from young Virginia O'Hanlon, a New York Sun editorial declared, "Yes, Virginia, there is a Santa Claus."
- July 2, 1897: A coal miners' strike put 75,000 men out of work in Pennsylvania, Ohio and West Virginia.
- February 15, 1898: An explosion destroyed the battleship Maine, killing 260 crew members.
- April 24, 1898: The United States declared war on Spain, and the Spanish-American War begins.
- June 1, 1898: Congress passed the Erdman Arbitration Act, making government mediation in railroad disputes legitimate.

STANFORD MOMENT

Stanford shut out Cal for the second consecutive season, beating the Bears 28-0 in 1897. (Stanford Archives)

Stanford Scores Back-to-Back Shutouts in Big Game

Only once in Big Game history has Stanford scored back-to-back shutout victories over California; in 1896 and '97. On November 25, 1897, one year after blanking Cal 20-0 in the '96 Big Game, Stanford pulled the trick again, this time beating the Bears 28-0. With new head coach George H. Brooke, Stanford scored three touchdowns in the first half and two more in the second to completely dominate the Bears in the most lopsided win in the seven-year history of the Big Game. Captain Steuart Cotton led the charge for Stanford as he scored three touchdowns while Forrest Fisher and Jack Daly also added touchdowns for Stanford. A crowd of 15,000 witnessed the beating in Recreation Park in San Francisco.

Stanford SPOTLIGHT

AFTER LOSING the season series to Cal the year before, Stanford was anxious to get back on the diamond to face their rivals from across the bay. The Bears won the first game of the series 7-3, but with stars like Chet Murphy, team captain Bert Lougheed and George Beckett leading the way, Stanford came back to win the final two games 12-2 and 6-5. Beckett, who pitched all three games vs. Cal in 1897, again pitched all three games while batting cleanup in the first two games. The schedule in 1898 was an abbreviated one and only the three games with Cal were considered intercollegiate contests. Thus, Stanford officially finished the 1898 campaign with a 2-1 record.

Stanford Stat . . .

The first seven Big Games were in the record book and Stanford, the upstart university in Palo Alto, had still not lost a football game to California. Stanford was 4-0-3 through the first seven Big Games, including winning three and tying one while outscoring the Bears 60-6 in the last four Big Games (1894-1897).

STANFORD LIST

LARGEST MARGIN OF VICTORY FOR STANFORD IN THE BIG GAME

Year	Margin	Final Score
1930	41	41-0
1926	35	41-6
1914	28	36-8
1897	28	28-0
1987	24	31-7
1996	21	42-21
1981	21	42-21
1968	20	20-0
1978	20	30-10
1992	20	41-21
1896	20	20-0
1942	19	26-7
1946	19	25-6
1955	19	19-0

Stanford LEGEND

Jack Sheehan

Jack Sheehan became Stanford's baseball coach in 1898. (Stanford Archives)

One of the early pioneers for the Stanford baseball program was John F. "Jack" Sheehan, class of 1895. Sheehan was the starting center fielder on Stanford's first four baseball teams from 1892-95, including being selected the team captain in 1894. Sheehan returned to the Stanford baseball program in 1898 and '99 and became the school's second baseball coach. He went one-for-four with three stolen bases in Stanford's first baseball game on April 23, 1892—a 13-6 win over California. Sheehan's two teams went 2-1 in 1898 and 0-2-2 in '99. After Stanford had lost the series to Cal for the first time in 1897, Sheehan got Stanford back on track in '98 by taking the series from Cal two games to one.

STANFORD LORE

As the Spanish-American War began in April of 1898, Stanford men enlisted in the California Militia. Thirty-eight were sent to the Philippines, two of whom were killed in action. The conflict ignited President Jordan's mission as an advocate of world peace.

1898-99

- **August 1, 1898:** The United States estimated that 4,200 servicemen fighting in Cuba suffered from yellow fever or typhoid.
- **November 8, 1898:** Rough Rider Teddy Roosevelt was elected governor of New York.
- **December 10, 1898:** A peace treaty was signed in Paris by United States and Spain, ending the Spanish-American War.
- **February 14, 1899:** Congress approved the use of voting machines for federal elections.
- **June 9, 1899:** Jim Jeffries knocked out Bob Fitzsimmons for the world heavyweight boxing title.

STANFORD MOMENT

Stanford's seven-year unbeaten streak vs. Cal ended in 1898. (Stanford Archives)

Stanford Suffers First Big Game Loss

The Bears took out seven years of Big Game frustration on Stanford on November 24, 1898. With Cal students displaying signs on campus that read "Remember the Maine! To Hell With Stanford!" the Bears were serious about finally beating Stanford. And that they did. Cal entered the game with a 6-0-2 record, including seven shutouts, while Stanford was 5-2-1. The previous two years had seen Stanford win 20-0 and 28-0, and Cal wanted revenge in the worst way. A crowd of over 20,000 jammed Recreation Park and watched the Bears win their first Big Game by a score of 22-0. Stanford's only scoring threat came when Chet Murphy caught his own bad punt that had gone straight up in the air and raced downfield towards the end zone, only to be caught at the Cal 25 yard line. The Bears, however, were in complete control of this game throughout the day.

Stanford SPOTLIGHT

THE AXE made its first appearance on April 13, 1899 at a rally held at Stanford to whip up spirit for the upcoming Stanford-Cal baseball series. Stanford students used the Axe to vigorously decapitate a straw man dressed in blue and gold. At the baseball game the following day, Stanford student Billy Erb and his classmates used the Axe to chop off lengths of prominently displayed blue and gold ribbons. During a post-game brawl, Cal students grabbed the Axe and headed off to Berkeley. To better conceal the Axe, the handle was cut off and the remaining blade was safely brought back to Berkeley. Cal's capture of the Axe caused furor on both campuses. Two law professors from each school were asked to meet and rule on final ownership. The ruling was unanimous in Cal's favor—the Axe was a prize by reason of conquest. The Axe remained in Berkeley until April 3, 1930. (see 1929-30 for more on the saga of the Axe).

Stanford Stat . . .

Harry P. Cross, a great center for Yale University in his playing days and Stanford's head football coach in 1896, returned to Stanford in 1898 to coach the football team. Cross had replaced Walter Camp in 1896 and guided Stanford to a 2-1-1 record and a 20-0 win over Cal in the Big Game. After a year's absence, Cross came back to coach Stanford to a 5-3-1 record in '98.

STANFORD LIST

STANFORD'S PAC-10 CHAMPIONSHIPS BY SPORT

148 total

Men's Swimming	36
Men's Tennis	15
Baseball	13
Football	11
Men's Water Polo	11
Women's Swimming	11
Women's Tennis	10
Men's Golf	8
Women's Basketball	8
Men's Basketball	7
Women's Volleyball	5
Men's Track and Field	3
Women's Soccer	3
Women's Cross Country	3
Men's Cross Country	2
Men's Gymnastics	2

Stanford LEGEND

Samuel Hardy

Stanford's Sanuel Hardy played against his brother, Sumner, on the Cal team. (Stanford Archives)

For two years, 1899 and 1900, Stanford and Cal played tennis matches that were nicknamed "the civil war" because the star players on each team were brothers— Samuel Hardy of Stanford and Sumner Hardy of California. In 1899, Samuel led Stanford to a 2-1 win over Cal (only three matches were played: two in singles, one in doubles) by defeating his brother Sumner in both singles and doubles. The following year, Sumner turned the tables and beat Samuel in singles, but Samuel teamed with Fred Schneider to win the doubles match over Sumner and his partner. Stanford's William P. Roth won the other singles match in 1900, giving Stanford a second straight tournament win over California.

STANFORD LORE

"Plug Ugly" was inaugurated by the Junior Class in October, 1898. It started as an outdoor play which lampooned the seniors and somehow evolved into a physical contest in which the juniors battered the seniors with their traditional headgear, plug hats hardened with coats of paint. When injuries became excessive, authorities stopped the brawls in 1915.

1899-1900

- **October 14, 1899:** William McKinley became the first President to ride in an automobile.
- **November 21, 1899:** Vice President Garret Hobart died. New York Governor Theodore Roosevelt was nominated as Hobart's replacement. Roosevelt first declined the nomination, but later relented at the Republican National Convention.
- **March 14, 1900:** Congress standardized the gold dollar as the unit of monetary value in the United States.
- **May 14, 1900:** Carrie Nation began her anti-liquor campaign.
- **July 4, 1900:** The Democratic Party nominated William Jennings Bryan of Nebraska as its presidential candidate.

STANFORD MOMENT

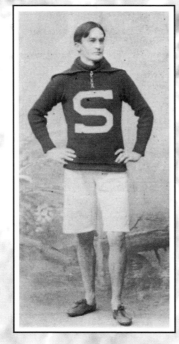

Captain H.J. Boyd and his Stanford teammates hosted the Big Meet on April 21, 1900. (Stanford Archives)

Stanford Hosts Cal in First Big Meet on Campus

The first Big Meet with California to be held on the Stanford campus took place on April 21, 1900. Although the Bears won another lopsided meet over Stanford, this time by a score of 84-33, the event was significant as not only the first Big Meet held at Stanford, but the first track meet of any kind on campus. Five of the previous seven Big Meets had been held in San Francisco with the other two held on the California campus in Berkeley (1984, 1899). From this point on, the meets alternated between the two campuses.

Stanford SPOTLIGHT

THE 1899 SEASON of Stanford football was the first disappointing year for the young University. Under the direction of new head coach Burr Chamberlain, a Yale All-American center, Stanford suffered its first losing season by going just 2-5-2, including a 30-0 loss to Cal in the most lopsided Big Game to date. Stanford entered the season with an inexperienced team and a schedule that called for five games against the Olympic Club. Stanford lost three and tied two vs. the Olympic Club while scoring just 10 points in the five games. It would be another 37 years—in 1936—until Stanford would suffer another losing season.

Stanford Stat . . .

STANFORD LIST

RHODES SCHOLARSHIP RECIPIENTS

Name	Sport	Year
Robert Brown	Track	1931
Jay Knapp	Water Polo	1933
Tom Killifer	Baseball	1938
Sandy Tatum	Golf	1942
Scott Matheson	Tennis	1972
Victoria Donaldson	Crew	1989
Kim Grose	Sailing	1990
Cory Booker	Football	1992
Bob Sternfels	Water Polo	1992

Stanford LEGEND

Chet Murphy

Chet Murphy earned a total of nine varsity letters in three sports. (Stanford Archives)

Chet Murphy is recognized as the first great all-around athlete in Stanford history. Not only was he a star football player and captain of the 1899 team, but he was also a standout baseball player and track performer. He earned a total of nine varsity letters in those three sports and established himself as one of Stanford's great athletes of his time. He was a four-year letterman in football (1896-99), three-year letterman in baseball and a two-time letterman in track. He was Stanford's starting quarterback as a freshman and sophomore in Stanford's two Big Game routes over Cal in 1896 (20-0) and '97 (28-0). Murphy was also Stanford's punter and kicker as well as the team's top punt return specialist. As team captain in 1899, Murphy suffered a broken rib and had not practiced with the team until the week prior to the Big Game. "My condition is not as serious as I thought and I have little fear of being put out of the game," Murphy told the *San Francisco Examiner*. "At any rate I am in it until I am carried out." He left the game before halftime. "Captain Murphy, fighting with the desperation of a gladiator, was finally so nearly in a state of collapse, that he was forced to withdraw," wrote the *San Francisco Chronicle*.

STANFORD LORE

Classes were dismissed on January 19, 1900 and students pitched in to move the University's 45,000-volume library from the Inner Quad to the new Thomas Welton Stanford Library. A younger brother of Leland Stanford, Thomas, donated his inheritance from Leland's estate for construction of the library.

1900-01

- September 8, 1900: A hurricane ravaged Galveston, Texas, killing 6,000 people and causing property damages of $20 million.
- November 6, 1900: William McKinley won the presidency for a second term.
- January 10, 1901: A well near Beaumont, Texas struck oil, the first evidence of oil from that region.
- March 3, 1901: The United States Steel Corporation was incorporated in New Jersey.
- June 15, 1901: Willie Anderson won the U.S. Open golf tournament.

STANFORD MOMENT

The 1900 football team won seven games, the second most wins by a Stanford team. (Stanford Archives)

Stanford Beats Cal in Defensive Struggle

Stanford's 5-0 win over California on November 29, 1900 not only halted the Bear's modest two-game winning streak over Stanford, but it gave Stanford its seventh win of the season, the second most wins by a Cardinal team. During the 1900 campaign, Stanford began playing the University of Oregon and San Jose Normal (now San Jose State University), two teams who to this day continue to be one of Stanford's great rivals. In the Big Game, although some say California outplayed Stanford in a hard-fought defensive struggle, it was Stanford who converted the game's only field goal—worth five points—in the waning moments. California had already missed three field goals and Stanford was 0-for-2 when Bill Traeger kicked the first field goal ever made in an intercollegiate game in California to give Stanford the win.

DR. FRANK ANGELL, a faculty member at Stanford, was an early proponent of athletics and it was through his influence and dedication that the athletic program at Stanford survived the early years. Angell wrote, "Under the present constitution, there ought to be an advisory board made up in part of members chosen for at least four years, and in part of undergrads, perhaps the Student Body President and captains of the athletic teams who should outline an athletic policy and choose coaches to carry out the policies adopted." More than a decade later, Stanford President Dr. Ray Lyman Wilbur established the Board of Athletic Control, of which Dr. Angell was a member.

Stanford Stat . . .

A unique pair of games occurred during the 1900 season between Stanford and San Jose Normal. With Fielding Yost serving as head coach at Stanford and as one of three coaches at San Jose, it was Yost vs. Yost when Stanford and San Jose Normal (now San Jose State University) met for the first time. Stanford won both games, 35-0 and 24-0, in the first of what is now a 52-game series.

STANFORD LIST

STANFORD FOOTBALL SUCCESS (DECADE BY DECADE)

Decade	W	L	T	.PCT
1891-1899	36	14	8	.690
1900-1909	73	16	8	.794
1910-1919	64	14	2	.813
1920-1929	68	22	6	.740
1930-1939	57	32	11	.625
1940-1949	39	28	2	.580
1950-1959	50	47	4	.515
1960-1969	46	51	3	.475
1970-1979	70	40	4	.632
1980-1989	44	65	2	.405
1990-1996	44	36	2	.549
Totals	591	365	53	.612

Stanford LEGEND

Fielding H. "Hurry Up" Yost

Fielding Yost coached Stanford to a 7-2-1 record in 1900. (Stanford Archives)

At the turn of the century, Stanford departed from its practice of hiring ex-Yale stars to coach the football and picked one of the bright, young coaches in the nation in Fielding H. Yost, later to be given the nickname "Hurry Up." Yost, a graduate of Lafayette College in Easton, Pennsylania, had earned All-America honors in 1896 as a member of Lafayette's national championship team that went 12-0. From 1897-99, Yost had great success coaching three schools to a combined record of 24-4-1. He went 7-1-1 as coach at Ohio Wesleyan in 1897, 7-3 at Nebraska in '98 and 10-0 at Kansas in 1900. In his one year at Stanford, Yost led his club to a 7-2-1 record. But Yost did more than simply coach at Stanford in 1900. He also coached a San Francisco high school in the morning and worked with San Jose Normal (now San Jose State University) at night under gas lights. Following his one year at Stanford, Yost went on to become a legendary coach at the University of Michigan. He brought his "point-a-minute" Wolverines out west on January 1, 1902 to face Stanford in the first Rose Bowl game.

STANFORD LORE

President Jordan asked political activist and sociology Professor Edward A. Ross to resign in November. Ross complied, but announced to the press that he was dismissed from the faculty on the arbitrary orders of Jane Stanford, over the supposed opposition of Jordan. The University was embarrassed by the public reaction to Ross's claim that his academic freedom had been abridged.

1901-02

•• AMERICA'S TIME CAPSULE ••

- September 2, 1901: A few weeks before becoming president, Theodore Roosevelt was credited with saying, "Speak softly and carry a big stick."
- September 6, 1901: President McKinley was shot as he attended a reception in Buffalo. He died of his wounds eight days later.
- September 14, 1901: Forty-two-year-old Theodore Roosevelt took the presidential oath of office, becoming the 26th President of the United States.
- May 12, 1902: Nearly 140,000 United Mine Workers went on strike.
- May 20, 1902: Four years after the end of the Spanish-American War, Cuban independence was achieved.

The first Rose Bowl game on January 1, 1902 pitted Stanford against Michigan. (Stanford Media Relations)

STANFORD MOMENT

Stanford Plays Michigan in First Rose Bowl

Former Stanford head coach Fielding Yost brought his "point-a-minute" Michigan Wolverines to Pasadena to face Stanford in the inaugural Rose Bowl, held January 1, 1902 at Tournament Park. Yost, who was Stanford's head coach the previous year, had turned Michigan into the most powerful team in the country in 1901. The Wolverines were 10-0 heading into the Rose Bowl and had outscored their opponents by an amazing 501-0 tally. Stanford, on the other hand, was 3-1-2 and was coming off a 2-0 loss to California in the Big Game. Michigan's Willie Heston rushed for 170 yards on 18 carries while fullback Neil Snow scored five touchdowns en route to Michigan's 49-0 victory. One question that remains unanswered is why Stanford was chosen to play in the Rose Bowl instead of Cal, which was 7-0-1 and had just beaten Stanford in the Big Game.

FROM 1890 TO 1901, a variety of sports events had been held as a climax to the Tournament of Roses celebration in Pasadena. But, the idea of a post-season East-West college football game was instituted on January 1, 1902 with Michigan being selected to represent the east vs. the west representative, Stanford. The game was played at Tournament Park, which had a seating capacity of 1,000. However, it is estimated that an overflow crowd of 8,500 showed up for the game and surrounded the playing field. Because tournament officials became disenchanted with football as part of their program after the Stanford-Michigan debacle, the game was dropped. Professional chariot racing replaced the football game. The Rose Bowl, however, returned to Pasadena on January 1, 1916 and has been played annually ever since.

Stanford Stat . . .

Walter Rose, a Stanford student, was credited with raising the question of amateur status of athletes after he and his teammates, who advertised themselves as "The Stanford Football Team" received $12 for participating in a game against a team in San Jose. When it became evident that the amateur rules would be enforced, the concept of expenses was rapidly and freely developed.

STANFORD LIST

STANFORD IN THE ROSE BOWL

January 1, 1902	Michigan 49, Stanford 0
January 1, 1925	Notre Dame 27, Stanford 10
January 1, 1927	Stanford 7, Alabama 7
January 1, 1928	Stanford 7, Pittsburgh 6
January 1, 1934	Columbia 7, Stanford 0
January 1, 1935	Alabama 29, Stanford 13
January 1, 1936	Stanford 7, SMU 0
January 1, 1941	Stanford 21, Nebraska 13
January 1, 1952	Illinois 40, Stanford 7
January 1, 1971	Stanford 27, Ohio State 17
January 1, 1972	Stanford 13, Michigan 12

Stanford LEGEND

William K. Roosevelt

William Roosevelt starred for Stanford in the 1902 Rose Bowl. (Stanford Archives)

The second cousin of U.S. President Theodore Roosevelt, William K. Roosevelt rose to legendary status after his gutsy effort in the 1902 Rose Bowl vs. Michigan. A two-time letterwinner, Roosevelt, a freshman guard in 1901, reportedly told a teammate early in the game that he had "felt something break in my leg." Roosevelt, however, continued playing. "With his leg fractured he continued playing the best quality of football for another 10 minutes, giving way to a substitute only after having received additional injuries which made it impossible for him to play," according to reports. Actually, Roosevelt had suffered broken ribs during the contest and was unable to continue.

STANFORD LORE

A 100-foot high sandstone Memorial Arch at the entryway to the Outer and Inner Quadrangles was completed on July 9, 1902. A 12-foot high frieze depicting "The March of Civilization" was carved into its parapet. Senator and Mrs. Stanford were depicted on horseback charting the route of the Central Pacific.

1902-03

- October 11, 1902:   Lawrence Auchterlonie won the U.S. Open golf tournament.
- November 4, 1902:   In congressional elections, the Republicans maintained their Senate majority over the Democrats, 57-33.
- January 22, 1903:   A 99-year lease was signed by the United States and Columbia giving America sovereignty over a canal zone in Panama.
- July 4, 1903:   President Roosevelt sent a message around the world and back in 12 minutes through the use of the first Pacific communications cable.
- August 8, 1903:   Great Britain defeated the United States to capture tennis' Davis Cup.

STANFORD MOMENT

Cal Scores Another Shutout in Big Game

For the fourth time in the last five seasons, Stanford was shutout by Cal and lost the Big Game—this time by a final score of 16-0. Stanford began the season impressively with five consecutive wins, but even though they entered the Big Game undefeated and untied, so did Cal. The Bears had outscored their opponents 104-0 and were considered favorites before the game. Played before a record crowd of 20,000 at San Francisco's Richmond Field on November 8, the Bears proved they were the superior team. With Cal's star running back Warren "Locomotive" Smith out of the game after being ruled ineligible, his replacement, Bobby Sherman, got himself in the Big Game record book by returning a punt 105 yards for touchdown. Cal led 5-0 at half and 11-0 after Sherman's punt return as Stanford never mounted a serious threat to overtake the Bears.

Stanford LEGEND

Carl L. "Clem" Clemans

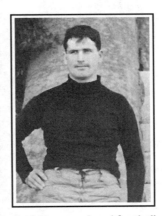

Carl Clemans, head football coach for the 1902 season. (Stanford Archives)

Considered to be one of the great fullbacks in Stanford football history, Carl L. "Clem" Clemans, a star player on Stanford's first two teams in 1891 and '92, became Stanford's eighth head football coach and sixth in the last six years. Clemans was the team manager in 1891 and team captain in '92. He scored the first two touchdowns in Big Game history when on March 19, 1892, he scored on two 45-yard runs. In the second Big Game on December 17, 1892, Clemans scored his third Big Game touchdown on a 40-yard run. As head coach in 1902, Clemans' team won its first five games, then lost a 16-0 decision to Cal before finishing the season 6-1 after beating Utah.

STANFORD LORE

Memorial Church, built by Jane Stanford in honor of her late husband, was dedicated on January 25, 1903. The ceremony included 14 clergy of various faiths to emphasize the founders' nondenominational stance. A month later, on February 22, Ethel Rhodes and William Armfield Holt, both members of the class of 1902, were married in the first wedding ceremony to be held there.

- October 13, 1903:   The Boston Red Stockings defeated the Pittsburgh Pirates in baseball's first World Series.
- December 17, 1903:   Orville and Wilbur Wright made their first successful flight in a crude flying machine at Kitty Hawk, North Carolina.
- January 4, 1904:   The Supreme Court ruled that Puerto Ricans are not aliens and must not be refused admission into the United States.
- June 1, 1904:   President Theodore Roosevelt was nominated as the Republican candidate at the national convention in Chicago.
- July 6, 1904:   The Democrats convened in St. Louis to nominate Alton Parker for president.

STANFORD MOMENT

Undefeated Stanford Settles for Tie in Big Game

Under hew head coach James Lanagan, Stanford compiled a record of 7-0-2 in its first nine games before facing California at a sold out Richmond Field in San Francisco on November 12, 1903. Stanford had not allowed a single point prior to the Big Game, outscoring opponents by an astonishing 175-0. Stanford held a 6-0 lead with less than a minute to play in the game, but had to settle for a 6-6 tie. The Stanford TD came on a 45-yard quarterback reverse by Louis "Dutch" Bansbach, who only made it in the end zone after teammate Walter Sprott threw a beautiful block. Cal's only score—the only points scored against Stanford the entire season—came on a blocked punt. Orval Overall was set to punt from the Stanford 12-yard line when Cal's Heine Heitmuller broke through the line, blocked the punt and fell on it in the end zone for a TD. The extra point gave the Bears a 6-6 tie.

Stanford LEGEND

Norman Dole

Norman Dole set a world record in the pole vault in 1904. (Stanford Archives)

It may have taken Stanford University 10 years to beat California in a track meet, but once it did, Stanford became one of the country's top producers of track and field superstars and world record holders. The first person to be thrust onto the national stage was Norman Dole, who in 1904 set a world record by registering a 12-1 8/25 in the pole vault. Although this was Dole's fifth year of competition, he had already made a reputation for himself in the west by twice setting coast intercollegiate records of just under 12 feet. After Dole set his world record, two other Stanford athletes—Leland Scott in 1910 and Bill Miller in 1932—also set new world records in the pole vault.

STANFORD LORE

On March 31, 1904, the trustees adopted the Articles of Organization of the Faculty in an attempt to curb the power of the presidency. The Articles were written by trustee and faculty committees with concurrence of President Jordan. They created the Academic Council of assistant, associate, and full professors to give the faculty a stronger voice in University governance.

1904-05

- October 8, 1904:   Automobile racing as an organized sport began with the Vanderbilt Cup race on Los Island, New York.
- October 27, 1904:   The first section of New York City's subway system was opened to the public.
- November 8, 1904:   Theodore Roosevelt was reelected president of the United States, defeating Alton Parker by nearly two million votes.
- April 17, 1905:   The Supreme Court found a New York state law that limited maximum hours for workers unconstitutional, ruling that such a law interfered with the right to free contract.
- May 5, 1905:   Boston's Cy Young threw baseball's first-ever perfect game, retiring 27 consecutive Philadelphia Athletic batters.

STANFORD MOMENT

Stanford posted its seventh shutout of the season in the 1904 Big Game—an 18-0 victory over California.
(Stanford Archives)

Stanford Shuts Out Bears 18-0 in Big Game

Stanford Coach James Lanagan did not like giving up points. His team had recorded 10 shutouts in 11 games in 1903 and, by the time the '04 Big Game was played on November 12, Stanford had registered six shutouts in its first eight games. Big Game No. 14 would be another shutout for Lanagan's team as Stanford beat the Bears 18-0 for their first Big Game victory in four years. After a scoreless first half, Stanford overpowered Cal in the second half by scoring three touchdowns on long drives. Wilfred Dole, Alexander Chalmers and Milo Weller all scored touchdowns for Stanford. "There was no question, or fluke or chance about that victory," reported the *San Francisco Examiner*. "The better team won."

SINCE ITS INCEPTION IN 1892, the Big Game remains today as one of the great traditions in college football history. The series began on March 19, 1892 at the Haight Street Grounds in San Francisco before an overflow crowd of 20,000. The first 14 games were played at four different locations in San Francisco: Haight Street Grounds, Central Park, Recreation Park and Richmond Park. On November 12, 1904, the Big Game moved to Berkeley and an agreement was made to play the Big Game on alternate campuses each year. The first Big Game at Stanford was played on November 11, 1905 at the Stanford Campus Field. Stanford Stadium hosted its first Big Game on November 19, 1921. The first Big Game played at Cal's Memorial Stadium occurred on November 24, 1923.

Stanford Stat . . .

Although there was concern from both schools about playing the first Big Game on campus rather than in San Francisco, their worries proved to be groundless. The 14th Big Game was played on November 12, 1904 before 21,500 in Berkeley—the largest crowd in the series' history. The game proved to be a huge success financially, with both schools splitting a $20,000 profit.

Stanford ❧ LEGEND ❧

James F. Lanagan

James Lanagan coached football, rugby and baseball on The Farm. (Stanford Archives)

One of the most popular and respected coaches of his time, James F. "Jimmy" Lanagan was the first Stanford coach to coach more than one sport. He graduated from Stanford in 1900 after having played on the baseball team for four years (1897-1900), earning a letter in his final two seasons. Even though he had never played football, Lanagan was named Stanford's head coach in 1903, a position he held for six seasons. Known as an inspirational leader, Lanagan led Stanford to an 8-0-3 record in 1903. The season included 10 shutouts in 11 games with the only points scored on Stanford all season coming in a 6-6 tie with Cal in the Big Game. Lanagan's 1905 football squad became the first undefeated, untied team in Stanford history as they chalked up a perfect 8-0 record. Lanagan coached American football at Stanford his first three years (1903-05), but when the University dropped football in favor of rugby, Lanagan remained as the school's rugby coach for three more years (1906-08). His six-year record stands at an impressive 49-10-5. Lanagan also served as Stanford's baseball coach in 1906 and '07. His two-year record was 19-19-2.

STANFORD LIST

SITE AND ATTENDANCE OF THE FIRST 13 BIG GAMES
All Were Played in San Francisco

March 19, 1892	Haight Street Grounds	20,000
December 17, 1892	Haight Street Grounds	20,000
November 30, 1893	Haight Street Grounds	18,000
November 29, 1894	Haight Street Grounds	15,000
November 28, 1895	Central Park	10,000
November 26, 1896	Central Park	15,000
November 25, 1897	Recreation Park	15,000
November 24, 1898	Recreation Park	20,000
November 30, 1899	Richmond Field	14,600
November 29, 1900	Richmond Field	19,000
November 28, 1901	Richmond Field	18,500
November 8, 1902	Richmond Field	20,000
November 4, 1903	Richmond Field	14,600

STANFORD LORE

While vacationing in Hawaii, Jane Stanford died on February 28, 1905. Initial reports theorized that Mrs. Stanford was poisoned, but a second autopsy declared probable cause of death to have been a rupture of the coronary artery. On March 24, an overflow crowd of 6,000 filled Memorial Church for the funeral.

1905-06

- September 22, 1905:   Willie Anderson won his third consecutive U.S. Open golf tournament championship.
- October 14, 1905:   The New York Giants defeated the Philadelphia Athletics to win baseball's second World Series.
- February 23, 1906:   Tommy Burns won the world heavyweight boxing title.
- April 7, 1906:   The first successful transatlantic wireless transmission was made from New York City to a receiving station in Ireland.
- April 18, 1906:   A massive earthquake rocked the San Francisco Bay Area as more than 500,000 were left homeless.

The first football game played at Stanford occurred on November 11, 1905. *(Stanford Archives)*

STANFORD MOMENT

First Football Game Played at Stanford

Although there was concern whether the bleachers would be ready in time, the first football game played at Stanford did proceed on November 11, 1905 with Stanford completing an 8-0 season with a 12-5 victory over Cal in the Big Game. The new Stanford Field, as it was called, was made possible by a group called the Training House Corporation, brought together for the sole purpose of constructing a training house and athletic fields at Stanford. After raising some $10,000 through student fees and investments, the corporation proceeded with construction on a tract of 40 acres provided by the University Board of Trustees. Drs. Frank Angell and Charles B. Wing are credited with leading the early fight to build a strong athletic program.

IN JAMES LANAGAN'S third season as Stanford's head football coach, his troops completed the first undefeated, untied season in school history. In fact, the only other undefeated, untied team in school history is the 1940 team coached by Clark Shaughnessey. But in 1905, Lanagan's squad proved to be the best team on the coast. Stanford outscored its opponents 138-13, had five shutouts and beat Cal in the Big Game. It was also the year that Stanford began playing USC. Only Cal has played more football games with Stanford that the Trojans. And in 1905, USC was just another victim of the great Stanford defense as it dropped a 16-0 decision.

Stanford Stat . . .

The Great San Francisco Earthquake on April 18, 1906 severely affected the athletic program at Stanford. The Big Meet with Cal was canceled as was the third game of the three-game baseball series with Cal. There were no tennis matches held in 1906 due to the earthquake and several other athletic activities were limited or canceled.

STANFORD LIST

ALL-TIME PAC-10 CHAMPIONSHIPS WON BY SCHOOL

USC	186
Washington	160
UCLA	157
Stanford	148
California	97
Oregon	64
Oregon State	48
Washington State	37
Arizona State	33
Arizona	24

Stanford ❦ LEGEND ❦

E.W. "Dad" Moulton

E.W. Moulton was track coach for 10 seasons.
(Stanford Archives)

Stanford University had been competing against California in track for 10 years and had not won a Big Meet. But, when E.W. "Dad" Moulton was named head coach in 1903, the fortunes of the Stanford track and field program immediately looked brighter. Moulton, nicknamed "Dad" because of his popularity on campus, not only beat Cal in his first Big Meet in '03, but he went on to coach 12 seasons (1903-13, 1916), compile a dual meet record of 27-10 and put Stanford on the map as a program that produces Olympians and world-class athletes. Moulton coached some of the great early track stars in the United States, including pole vault world record holder Norman Dole, 1908 U.S. Olympians Sam Bellah and John O. Miller—Stanford's first two Olympians—and world record holders Leland Scott (pole vault) and George Horine (high jump, 1912 Olympian). Moulton changed Stanford from a struggling track and field program to one of the country's most respected.

STANFORD LORE

The Great San Francisco Earthquake hit the Bay Area on April 18, 1906, causing severe damage on campus. Two people were killed and an estimated $2 million in damage to the University was reported. The brand new library and gymnasium were completely destroyed and a Memorial Arch at the front of the Quad fell and was never replaced. Memorial Church sustained heavy damage, but was rebuilt without its tall steeple, and some unreinforced wings of the Museum collapsed and were never replaced. Classes were dismissed and Commencement postponed to September. Classes resumed in the fall.

1906-07

- October 14, 1906: The Chicago White Sox beat the Chicago Cubs to win the third World Series.
- November 9, 1906: Theodore Roosevelt became the first President to travel abroad, journeying to Panama to inspect the progress of the Panama Canal.
- December 24, 1906: Reginald Fessenden made the first known radio broadcast of voice and music from his Branch Rock, Massachusetts experiment station.
- February 20, 1907: President Roosevelt signed the Immigration Act of 1907, restricting immigration by Japanese laborers.
- March 21, 1907: U.S. Marines were sent to Honduras to quell a political disturbance.

STANFORD MOMENT

Rugby Replaces Football at Stanford

Despite the fact that neither coach James Lanagan nor any of his players knew anything about rugby prior to the 1906 season, Stanford managed to put together a 6-2-1 season and defeat Cal in the Big Game. Prior to the season, Lanagan made a trip to Vancouver, British Columbia and spent the summer trying to gather as much knowledge as he could about rugby. Stanford students were encouraged by the news that rugby was "any man's game" and turned out in record numbers to try out for the 1906 team. Among the top players were Captain "Stump" Stott, Bill Pemberton, George Presley and Kenny Fenton.

Stanford's first rugby team in 1906 compiled a 6-2-1 record and defeated Cal in the Big Game. (Stanford Archives)

Stanford LEGEND

John O. Miller

John O. Miller earned a spot on the 1908 U.S. Olympic team. (Stanford Archives)

In 1905, coach Dad Moulton unveiled a talented, young middle distance runner named John O. Miller, who would be one of the cornerstones of the up-and-coming track program Moulton was building. Miller won two events in his first Big Meet in '05—the quarter-mile and mile— and went on to earn the distinction as one of the finest middle distance runners in school history. In 1908, he and teammate Sam Bellah were named to the United States Olympic Team, becoming the first Stanford athletes to be named Olympians. Unfortunately, Miller, who was to run the 400-meters and 800-meters at the London Olympics, suffered an injury prior to the Games and was unable to attend.

STANFORD LORE

Automobiles were permitted on campus for the first time in April, 1907. However, the automobiles could only travel on a new service road constructed through the Arboretum. It wasn't until 1914 that horseless carriages were allowed to use Palm Drive.

1907-08

- September 12, 1907: The Lusitania, the world's largest steamship, completed its maiden voyage between Ireland and New York.
- October 12, 1907: The Chicago Cubs swept the World Series from the Detroit Tigers.
- November 16, 1907: Oklahoma became the 46th state in the union.
- December 6, 1907: Three hundred sixty-one miners were killed in a West Virginia coal mine explosion.
- May 10, 1908: Mother's Day was first celebrated.

STANFORD MOMENT

Stanford Beats USC in First Track Meet

The first track meet between Stanford and USC still stands today as the widest margin of victory. The inaugural meet between Stanford and the Trojans in 1908 ended with a lopsided 104-18 victory for Stanford. Stanford won the first 22 meets of the series with USC before the Trojans closed the gap to four points—67 1/3-63 1/3—in 1926. Beginning in 1933, the tide had turned. USC dominated the series for the next 40 years.

The 1908 track team defeated USC in the inaugural meeting between the two schools. *(Stanford Archives)*

Stanford ❧ LEGEND ❧

Sam Bellah

Sam Bellah was Stanford's first two-time Olympian. *(Stanford Archives)*

Not only was Sam Bellah the first Stanford Olympian—along with teammate John O. Miller—but he also has the distinction of being Stanford's first two-time U.S. Olympian. Both Bellah and Miller competed at the 1908 Games in London as the first two Stanford Olympians. But Bellah, a world-class pole vaulter, became the school's first two-time Olympian by competing at the 1912 Olympic Games. Bellah placed sixth in London in 1908 and seventh at Stockholm four years later with a vault of 12-3 3/5, a distance that would have won gold in 1908. Bellah was a star freshman on the Stanford track team in 1907 and was later named captain of the 1911 squad.

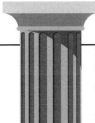

STANFORD LORE

In an effort to curb a perceived problem of excessive drinking by male students, the Academic Council unanimously adopted a resolution to ban liquor from Encina Hall, fraternity houses and other student residences. The actions taken by the university were in response to a February 5, 1908 incident in which a drunken student, returning home from a saloon, entered the wrong house in Palo Alto and was mistaken for a burglar and shot to death.

1908-09

•• AMERICA'S TIME CAPSULE ••

- October 1, 1908: The Model T was introduced by Henry Ford.
- November 3, 1908: William Howard Taft was elected President of the United States.
- April 6, 1909: Robert Peary reached the North Pole.
- July 12, 1909: Congress proposed an amendment to authorize a national income tax.
- July 27, 1909: Orville Wright set a flight-duration record of just more than one hour.

STANFORD MOMENT

Stanford's five-man relay team helped Stanford beat Cal 66-56 in the 1909 Big Meet. (Stanford Archives)

Stanford Wins 1909 Big Meet

One of the great track meets in the history of the Stanford-Cal rivalry occurred on April, 17, 1909 in Berkeley. While Stanford won the meet 66-56, the outcome remained in doubt until John O. Miller, Bill Wyman and Leland Scott nailed down the victory on the final two events of the meet. Stanford led 56-52 heading into the five-man relay and needed a win to secure at least a tie. Cal led by 15 yards after the first three legs, but Miller cut the lead to five yards after the fourth leg, and Wyman raced ahead of the Bears to win the relay and assure Stanford of a tie. The final event, the pole vault, was won by Stanford's Scott, giving the Cardinals the 10-point margin of victory.

IN ITS THIRD SEASON of playing rugby instead of football, Stanford coach James Lanagan guided his troops to a 12-2 record, which stands today as the most single season wins in school history. Stanford won the first seven games of the 1908 season before losing an 11-3 decision to Vancouver. A 12-3 victory over California in the Big Game gave Stanford its fifth straight win over the Bears. Stanford won three games against Vancouver in Canada, but lost the season finale to the world famous Australian Wallabies. After the season, Lanagan bid farewell to Stanford after having coached six seasons and chalking up a school record 49 wins.

Stanford Stat . . .

The Stanford varsity crew won the Pacific Coast championship on May 29, 1909 when it defeated the University of Washington. The race was held before a crowd estimated at 25,000 at the Washington Regatta held on Lake Washington in Seattle. Stanford trailed at the two-mile bunting, but came from behind at the end of the race to overtake Washington and make their claim as the best on the Pacific Coast.

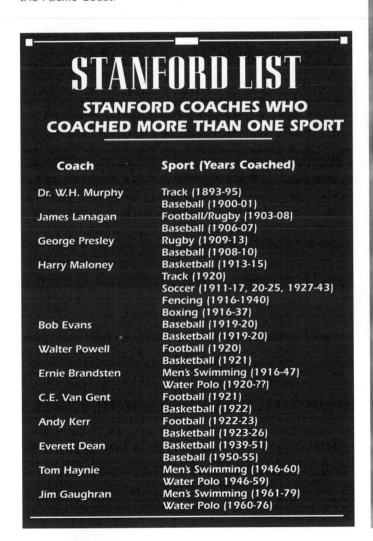

STANFORD LIST

STANFORD COACHES WHO COACHED MORE THAN ONE SPORT

Coach	Sport (Years Coached)
Dr. W.H. Murphy	Track (1893-95)
	Baseball (1900-01)
James Lanagan	Football/Rugby (1903-08)
	Baseball (1906-07)
George Presley	Rugby (1909-13)
	Baseball (1908-10)
Harry Maloney	Basketball (1913-15)
	Track (1920)
	Soccer (1911-17, 20-25, 1927-43)
	Fencing (1916-1940)
	Boxing (1916-37)
Bob Evans	Baseball (1919-20)
	Basketball (1919-20)
Walter Powell	Football (1920)
	Basketball (1921)
Ernie Brandsten	Men's Swimming (1916-47)
	Water Polo (1920-??)
C.E. Van Gent	Football (1921)
	Basketball (1922)
Andy Kerr	Football (1922-23)
	Basketball (1923-26)
Everett Dean	Basketball (1939-51)
	Baseball (1950-55)
Tom Haynie	Men's Swimming (1946-60)
	Water Polo 1946-59)
Jim Gaughran	Men's Swimming (1961-79)
	Water Polo (1960-76)

Stanford ❧ LEGEND ❧

George Presley

George Presley went 30-8-1 in four years as rugby coach.
(Stanford Archives)

In what had become a common practice on The Farm, George Presley, a former star athlete, was named to a head coaching position at Stanford after his playing days. In the early 1900s, Presley was one of the top student-athletes on campus. He was an infielder on the baseball team from 1905-07 and was named team captain as a senior in '07. He also played one year of rugby in 1906. Following his graduation, Presley was chosen by then-rugby coach James Lanagan to be his field coach, a position he held in 1907 and '08. When Lanagan departed after the 1908 season, Presley stepped in to become the school's head rugby coach. His teams won their first eight games in 1908—seven by shutout—and finished the year 8-1. His four-year record stands at 30-8-1, an impressive winning percentage of .782. While coaching rugby, Presley was also Stanford's head baseball coach from 1908-10. He was the first Stanford baseball coach to remain in that position for more than two seasons. His 30 career victories remains today as the sixth highest in school history.

STANFORD LORE

After complaints by local residents about the drunk and disorderly conduct of students, a California state law was enacted in March of 1909 that forbid the sale of alcohol within a mile and a half of the boundaries of Stanford University and the University of California. The new law, however, was not taken seriously by students, saloon keepers or city supervisors as drinking in dorms and fraternities increased.

1909-10

- October 16, 1909: The Pittsburgh Pirates defeated the Detroit Tigers in the sixth World Series.
- February 6, 1910: The Boy Scouts of America organization was chartered by Chicago publisher William Boyce.
- March 16, 1910: Auto racer Barney Oldfield set a land speed record of 133 miles per hour.
- June 19, 1910: Spokane, Washington became the first city to celebrate Father's Day.
- July 4, 1910: Jack Johnson successfully defended his world heavyweight boxing championship against Jim Jeffries.

STANFORD MOMENT

Stanford's undefeated season was ruined after a 19-13 loss to Cal.
(Stanford Archives)

Stanford Settles for 8-1 Record After Losing the Big Game

First-year head coach George Presley had led his team to a perfect 8-0 record, had registered seven shutouts and outscored the opposition 220-3 heading into the 19th Big Game with California. The Bears, however, were also enjoying an outstanding season, evidenced by their 10-1-1 pre-Big Game record. A crowd of 13,000 on November 9, 1909 at the Stanford Field on campus witnessed the Bears ruin Stanford's undefeated season by posting an impressive 19-13 win, ending Stanford's five-game winning streak over Cal. The Bears took a 19-10 lead at halftime and controlled the game in the second half, despite not scoring. "I have no excuses to offer for the loss of the game. The better team won," said Presley following the game.

FOR THE SECOND CONSECUTIVE SEASON, Stanford's track and field team compiled an undefeated dual meet season, this time winning a school-record six meets in one year. Stanford defeated USC twice in 1910, 74-47 and 93-29, the Olympic Club 77 2/3-43 1/3, Brigham Young University 63-33, Colorado 71 1/2-50 1/2 and California in the Big Meet 66 2/5-55 3/5. Stanford went on to tie Notre Dame for first place in the Western Conference meet at Champaign, Illinois, thus concluding perhaps the finest track and field season to date. Leland Scott, who set the world record in the pole vault, and freshman George Horine, a future world record holder in the high jump, were the catalysts of the team.

Stanford Stat . . .

Four months after winning the Pacific Coast championship, crew was dropped as a varsity sport on September 9, 1909. Due to a financial deficit and because of the limited facilities which Stanford offered to boating, the Executive Committee deemed it advisable to drop crew as an intercollegiate sport. Afterwards, the Lagunita Boating Club was formed.

STANFORD LIST

BIGGEST FOOTBALL VICTORIES (POST WORLD WAR II)

Margin	Year	Opponent	Score
54	1949	Hawaii	74-20
54	1981	Oregon State	63-9
53	1975	Army	67-14
50	1991	Cornell	56-6
49	1949	San Jose State	49-0
49	1969	Washington State	49-0
48	1950	San Francisco	55-7
48	1968	San Jose State	68-20
47	1970	Washington State	63-16
45	1946	Idaho	45-0

Stanford LEGEND

Leland Scott

Leland Scott set a world record in the pole vault in 1910. (Stanford Archives)

Leland Stanford "Lee" Scott was a great two-sport athlete in track and baseball at Stanford from 1907-10. While he earned three letters in baseball from 1907-09, it was on the track and field team that Scott gained international fame. In 1910, as a senior and team captain of the Stanford track and field team, Scott reached 12-10 7/8 on the pole vault in a dual meet with the University of Colorado in Boulder—setting a new world record. It was the second world record ever for a Stanford athlete. Oddly enough, the first world record also came in the pole vault in 1904 when Norman Dole went 12-1 8/25 to set the record. Scott was a major force behind the success of the Stanford track and field team. In his final two seasons, Stanford won all 10 dual meets, beat Cal twice and placed second and tied for first in the Western Conference meet.

STANFORD LORE

Thorstein Veblen, an associate professor of economics, resigned after three years at Stanford when requested to do so by President Jordan. Although his professional views were unorthodox, it was his extramarital arrangements that got him into trouble. "Dr. Jordan does not approve of my domestic arrangements. Nor do I," said Veblen.

1910-11

•• AMERICA'S TIME CAPSULE ••

- November 8, 1910: In congressional elections, the Democratic party took control of Congress for the first time in 16 years.
- November 14, 1910: The first successful attempt of a naval aircraft launching from the deck of a warship was made off the cruiser Birmingham.
- March 25, 1911: One hundred forty-six persons perished in a New York City industrial fire.
- May 11, 1911: The Supreme Court ordered Standard Oil dissolved because it violated the antitrust law.
- May 30, 1911: Ray Harmon won the first Indianapolis 500 automobile race.

STANFORD MOMENT

For the second consecutive season, Stanford entered the Big Game undefeated but lost to California in the season finale. *(Stanford Archives)*

Deja Vú For Unbeaten Stanford

For the second consecutive season, George Presley brought his undefeated and untied Stanford rugby team into the Big Game, only to lose once again to the Bears. Stanford had outscored its first seven opponents 183-0, but the Bears could do one better. Cal was 10-0, had scored 248 points and came into the game as the decided favorite. Three thousand extra seats had to be brought in to California Field to accommodate the overflow crowd of 23,000 on November 12, 1910. Led by Ben Erb and Jim Arrell, Stanford jumped out to a 6-0 lead. But Cal scored on its next three possessions, led 15-6 at the half and cruised to a 25-6 victory. Presley could take solace in the fact that Stanford was 15-0 against everyone except the Bears over the last two seasons, but 0-2 in the Big Game.

THE BIG GAME reached an all-time high in 1910 when 23,000 fans jammed California Field to witness the 20th meeting between the two schools. An additional 3,000 bleacher seats had to be brought in and tickets were selling for inflated prices outside the stadium. Several thousand fans, unable to get tickets, attempted to scale the fence but were beaten back by police. When the final numbers were in, both teams split a record $45,000. The 1910 Big Game is also recognized as being the first intercollegiate game to use card stunts.

Stanford Stat . . .

The starting leftfielder on the 1911 Stanford baseball team was Knight Starr Jordan, son of David Starr Jordan, Stanford University's first president. Jordan was Stanford president from its inception in 1891 until 1913.

Stanford ❧ LEGEND ❧

Zebulon Alexander "Zeb" Terry

Zeb Terry went on to a major league baseball career. (Stanford Athletics)

Zebulon "Zeb" Terry has the distinction of being the first great baseball player to don a Stanford uniform. While there were talented players before Terry's arrival in 1911, none showed the kind of ability that led Terry a very long and successful career in the Major Leagues. He was Stanford's starting shortstop from 1911-14 and was elected team captain in both 1913 and '14. He was the catalyst for the 1913 team that went 15-5-1 and was considered the school's best team to that point. Following his Stanford career, Terry played seven seasons in the Major Leagues with the Chicago White Sox, Boston Braves, Pittsburgh Pirates and Chicago Cubs. He sported a .260 career batting average in the big leagues.

STANFORD LIST

WORLD RECORD PERFORMANCES BY STANFORD TRACK ATHLETES FIELD EVENTS ONLY

Year	Athlete	Event	Mark
1904	Norman Dole	Pole Vault	12-1 8/25
1910	Leland Scott	Pole Vault	12-10 7/8
1912	George Horine	High Jump	6-7
1925	Glen Hartranft	Discus	157-1 5/8
1930	Harlow Rothert	Shot Put	52-1 5/8
1930	Eric Krenz	Discus	167-5 3/8
1932	Bill Miller	Pole Vault	14-1 7/8
1934	John Lyman	Shot Put	54-1
1950	Bob Mathias	Decathlon	8,042 pts.
1952	Bob Mathias	Decathlon	7,887 pts. (old scoring system)
1953	Bud Held	Javelin	263-10
1955	Bud Held	Javelin	266-2 1/2
1956	Bud Held	Javelin	270-0
1976	Terry Albritton	Shot Put	71-8 1/2

STANFORD LORE

Lewis M. Terman joined the School of Education faculty in the fall of 1910. One of the founders of educational psychology, Terman published an intelligence scale known as the "Stanford-Binet" in 1916. It later became the universally adopted IQ test. His son, Frederick E. Terman, became Provost at Stanford years later.

1911-12

·· AMERICA'S TIME CAPSULE ··

- October 26, 1911: The American League's Philadelphia Athletics defeated the New York Giants to win the World Series.
- November 10, 1911: Andrew Carnegie established the Carnegie Corporation with an endowment of $125 million.
- February 14, 1912: Arizona was admitted to the Union as the 48th state.
- April 15, 1912: About 1,500 persons were killed when the British liner Titanic struck an iceberg and sank off the coast of Newfoundland.
- July 22, 1912: The Olympic Games came to a close in Stockholm, Sweden. Among the American gold medal winners was decathlete Jim Thorpe.

STANFORD MOMENT

Horine Becomes First Stanford Olympic Medalist

Two Stanford athletes competed in the 1912 Olympic Games in Stockholm, Sweden: George Horine in the high jump and Sam Bellah in the pole vault. Horine, of course, became Stanford's first Olympic medalist when he took the bronze in the high jump. Although he had broken the world record twice during the 1912 track season, Horine had an off day in Stockholm and did not reach his world record mark of 6-7. Bellah, who became the first Stanford athlete to compete in the Olympic Games in London in 1908, finished seventh in the pole vault in Stockholm with a vault of 12-3 3/5. Ironically, that vault would have won the gold in London. Since the 1912 Olympics, Stanford athletes have won gold in every Olympiad from Antwerp in 1920 to Atlanta in 1996.

PERHAPS THE GREATEST ATHLETE in the early days of the Stanford crew program was Frank L. "Husky" Guerena, a coxswain of the 1909, 1911 and 1912 eights. Guerena was a member of the Coaching Committee during his final two years of competition. The committee consisted of a group of oarsmen who acted as volunteer coaches after the loss of Dan Murphy, Stanford's first coach. In 1914, Guerena became Stanford's official coach, a position he held until 1917. Guerena was also a longtime member of the Board of Athletic Control.

One of the great athletes on the Stanford crew was Frank Guerena, a coxswain on the 1909, 1911, and 1912 eights. He was Stanford's head coach from 1914-17. (Stanford Archives)

44

Stanford Stat . . .

Soccer made its debut as a minor sport during the 1911-12 season. Behind the coaching of Harry Maloney, who would coach Stanford for most of the next 30 years, the Cardinal won all three games it played with California by scores of 6-2, 2-1 and 4-2. The following year, Stanford took two of three from the Bears.

STANFORD LIST

FOOTBALL PLAYERS WHO WERE MULTIPLE FIRST-TEAM ALL-CONFERENCE SELECTIONS

Sam Morley, end	1952-53
Paul Wiggin, tackle	1955-56
Chris Burford, end	1958-59
Marv Harris, guard	1962-63
Gene Washington, wide receiver	1967-68
Don Parish, linebacker	1968-69
Bob Moore, wide receiver	1969-70
Jim Plunkett, quarterback	1969-70
Jeff Siemon, linebacker	1970-71
Rod Garcia, placekicker	1972-73
Randy Poltl, defensive back	1972-73
Alex Karakazoff, guard	1975-76
Tony Hill, wide receiver	1975-76
Duncan McColl, linebacker	1975-76
Darrin Nelson, running back	1977-78, 80-81
Gordy Ceresino, linebacker	1977-78
Ken Margerum, wide receiver	1978-80
John Elway, quarterback	1980, 1982
Vaughn Williams, defensive back	1981-82
Brad Muster, running back	1985-86
Bob Whitfield, offensive tackle	1990-91
Glyn Milburn, running back	1990, 1992
Ron George, linebacker	1991-92

Stanford LEGEND

George Horine

George Horine developed the "western roll." (Stanford Archives)

It is said that what George Horine began in his back yard as a teenager changed the face of high jumping forever. Horine, a member of Stanford's track team from 1910-13, indeed is credited with developing a technique that was the forerunner to what was commonly called the Western Roll, or the belly-roll. Because of the layout of his backyard, Horine was forced to approach the bar from the left instead of the right, which had been his former style. When he came to Stanford as a freshman in 1910, coach Dad Moulton ordered him to abandon his new technique and adopt a more traditional style. In 1911, Horine jumped 6'-4" to equal a 24-year old collegiate record. But as a junior in 1912, Horine reverted back to his old style. First he broke the collegiate record of 6-4 3/4, then he broke the world record with a jump of 6-6 1/8. At the Olympic Trials a few weeks later, Horine set another record by becoming the first man to jump 6-7. At the Olympic Games in Stockholm, Horine did not have his best day and had to settle for the bronze. He became the first Stanford athlete to win an Olympic medal.

STANFORD LORE

One of Dr. Jordan's longtime friends, President Theodore Roosevelt, visited the Stanford campus in 1912, the same year as Roosevelt's Bull Moose Party mishap. Roosevelt planted a sequoia tree at Stanford and took a drive with Jordan across the Santa Clara Valley. Jordan reported that Roosevelt, a naturalist, was especially interested in the sparrows and warblers in roadside thickets.

1912-13

•• AMERICA'S TIME CAPSULE ••

- October 14, 1912: Presidential candidate Theodore Roosevelt was shot in an assassination attempt in Milwaukee, Wisconsin.
- October 16, 1912: The Boston Red Sox won the ninth annual baseball World Series over the New York Giants.
- November 5, 1912: Democrat Woodrow Wilson won the U.S. presidency in a landslide victory.
- May 31, 1913: The Seventeenth Amendment, providing for the popular election of U.S. senators, went into effect.
- July 28, 1913: The U.S. won the Davis Cup tennis challenge for the first time in 11 years.

STANFORD MOMENT

Paul McKee was one of Stanford's top sprinters. He won a runoff in the 1913 Big Meet with Cal to give Stanford the win. *(Stanford Archives)*

McKee Wins Runoff; Stanford Wins Big Meet

A crowd of 7,200 in Berkeley witnessed what many considered to be the most climactic finish in the history of the Big Meet. Stanford's Paul McKee, who earlier in the meet won the 100-yard dash, and Cal's Fui Wood were locked in a controversy surrounding the 220-yard dash. In those days, each team picked one judge. After Stanford's Cap Campbell won the 220, the Stanford judge picked McKee as the second place finisher while the Cal judge said Wood placed second. After an hour debate, Cal accepted Stanford's challenge to have a runoff between McKee and Wood to determine the second place finisher. The Stanford contingent wondered why the Bears would accept such a challenge. If the results had remained and McKee and Wood were determined to have tied, the Bears would have won the meet 61 4/5 to 60 1/5. But, after McKee beat Wood by more than three feet in their runoff, Stanford wound up winning the meet 61 1/5 to 60 4/5. "That runoff between McKee and Wood was a beautiful and unforgettable sight," said Dink Templeton, who would later be named Stanford's head track coach in 1921.

WITH CAPTAIN ZEB TERRY leading the way, the 1913 Stanford baseball team established itself as the school's best to date and one of the top teams during the first half-century of Stanford baseball. The team finished the season with a 15-5 overall record, including victories of 9-4 and 4-3 over California in the Big Series. The 15 wins was the highest single-season total in school history and it was not until 1931 that Stanford would win more than 15 games in a season. The '13 team had little depth with only 10 players earning letters. But, it was the quality of players that counted. Along with Terry, who played shortstop, Stanford was led by 1B Tom Workman, 2B Louis Cass, 3B Pete McCloskey, LF A.G. Halm, CF Walter Argabrite, RF Heinie Beeger, C Babe Dent and P Ray Maple. The 1913 team also established the Most Valuable Player Award, which to this day is still presented in honor of the team of 1913.

Stanford Stat . . .

In his final game as Stanford's rugby coach, George J. Presley avoided losing the Big Game for the fourth year in a row —but just barely. Presley's four-year record was an impressive 30-8-1, but it was 0-3-1 against California. On November 9, 1912, Stanford and Cal battled to a 3-3 tie, thus avoiding sending Presley off with another loss to the Bears.

STANFORD LIST

COACHES IN THE STANFORD ATHLETICS HALL OF FAME

Coach	Sport	Years Coached
Ernie Brandsten	Men's Swimming	1916-47
John Bunn	Men's Basketball	1931-38
Everett Dean	Men's Basketball	1939-51
	Baseball	1950-55
Dutch Fehring	Baseball	1956-67
Dick Gould	Men's Tennis	1967-present
Tom Hayne	Men's Swimming	1948-60
Payton Jordan	Men's Track & Field	1957-79
Harry Maloney	Multiple Sports	1912-43
John Ralston	Football	1963-71
Clark Shaughnessy	Football	1940-41
Chuck Taylor	Football	1951-57
Dink Templeton	Men's Track & Field	1921-39
Eddie Twiggs	Men's Golf	1932-48
Glenn "Pop" Warner	Football	1924-32

Stanford LEGEND

Henry Wilfred "Harry" Maloney

Harry Maloney coached six sports for a total of over 70 years. (Stanford Athletics)

He didn't lead Stanford to any national championships or bowl games. He didn't produce Olympians or All-Americans either. But what Henry Wilfred "Harry" Maloney did achieve during his 40-plus years as a Stanford employee was the recognition as one of the university's truly great coaches who gave of himself to countless student-athletes who were fortunate to be touched by him. Maloney first came to Stanford in 1908 and during his career he held more positions than perhaps any person in the history of Stanford Athletics. He was the head coach of six sports for an aggregate total of more than 70 years. Maloney's first love was the so-called "minor" sports as they were called during his era. He was the head coach of the Stanford soccer program for 29 years between 1912-43, the fencing program for 22 years between 1916-40 and the boxing program for 19 years between 1916-37 (his service in all three sports was not continuous as he was forced to take short breaks). He also coached track and field for one year (1920), wrestling and rugby. Maloney also served as the Director of Minor Sports and trainer during his tenure. The current soccer stadium at Stanford bears his name, "Harry Maloney Field," as a tribute to one of the school's all-time great coaches and contributors to Stanford athletics.

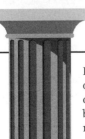

STANFORD LORE

Dr. David Starr Jordan, the first president of Stanford University, announced at commencement exercises on May 19, 1913 that he was relinquishing his duties as university president in order to assume the new office of Chancellor of the University. Jordan also announced that geologist John Casper Branner would become the university's second president. Branner accepted the job with the understanding that he would retire in two years when he reached the age of 65.

1913-14

- **October 11, 1913:** The Philadelphia Athletics defeated the New York Giants to capture the 10th annual World Series.
- **December 23, 1913:** President Woodrow Wilson reformed the American banking system by establishing the Federal Reserve System.
- **April 22, 1914:** Mexico severed diplomatic relations with the United States.
- **May 7, 1914:** A congressional resolution established the second Sunday in May to be celebrated as Mother's Day.
- **August 15, 1914:** Australia defeated the United States to win the Davis Cup tennis challenge.

STANFORD MOMENT

Basketball was officially recognized as a major sport at Stanford in 1914. (Stanford Archives)

Men's Basketball Makes Debut on March 18, 1914

Although it had been played on campus since the early 1900s, basketball was not officially recognized as a major sport at Stanford until March 18, 1914 when Stanford met St. Ignatius (now USF) in the school's first-ever intercollegiate men's basketball game. Sixty men tried out for the new team, which came as a surprise to university personnel. Stanford's first coach, the legendary Harry Maloney, led his team to a respectable 7-5 record. Stanford had joined the newly-formed intercollegiate conference which included California, Nevada, St. Mary's, St. Ignatius and College of the Pacific (now UOP). Stanford won the opener over St. Ignatius, 22-20, and came back to win their second game—also against St. Ignatius—by a score of 37-14. Stanford, however, lost both its games against California.

STANFORD ENDED A FIVE-YEAR DROUGHT in the Big Game by defeating Cal 13-8 on November 8, 1913, before 18,000 fans at Stanford Field and another 3,000 outside the stadium who were unable to get tickets. Stanford had lost three and tied one in the previous four Big Games, but this time it was Danny Carrol and Charlie Austin who refused to let Cal battle back from a 10-point deficit late in the game. "Carrol was in the best form that he has ever shown on the Stanford Field. Austin, at first five, proved equally indispensable to the team," wrote the *Stanford Daily*. Stanford beat USC a week after the Big Game to give first-year head coach Floyd Brown an 8-3 record.

Stanford Stat . . .

Stanford followed its 15-5 record in 1913 with a 12-6-3 mark in 1914, giving the baseball program an all-time high of 27 wins in consecutive seasons. Six members off the talented '13 team were back for the 1914 season, including two-time team captain Zeb Terry. It would take almost 20 years before Stanford put together consecutive seasons of more than 27 wins. In 1930 and '31, Stanford chalked up 28 wins.

STANFORD LIST

ALL-TIME WINNINGEST BASEBALL COACHES IN STANFORD HISTORY

Coach	W-L-T	PCT.
Mark Marquess, 1977-97	853-453-4	.653
Ray Young, 1968-76	326-161-3	.668
Dutch Fehring, 1956-67	290-162-4	.640
Harry Wolter, 1923-43, 1946-49	265-304-5	.466
Everett Dean, 1950-55	125-83-4	.599

Stanford LEGEND

Rick Templeton

Rick Templeton later became Stanford's head track coach. (Stanford Archives)

He was considered a great competitor and a great leader—an athlete who led by example. For Rick Templeton, the art of competition meant never stop battling. He exemplified those traits not only as a member of Stanford's track and field team in 1913 and 1915, but also as Stanford head coach in 1917 and '18. As an athlete, Templeton's events included the high jump, long jump and low hurdles. The older brother of Dink, who held the head coaching position at Stanford from 1921-39, Rick was a gifted athlete who helped Stanford win all eight dual meets in which he competed, including two over California. As a coach, Rick's teams went 4-0 in dual meets with two more victories over the Bears. Along with his brother Dink, the Templeton brothers helped form the great Stanford track and field tradition which began when Rick first arrived in 1913.

STANFORD LORE

Memorial Church was reopened on October 5, 1913 following repair of extensive damage due to the 1906 earthquake. Maurizio Camerino of Salviati studios in Venice, Italy, returned to California after the earthquake to supervise reconstruction of the mosaics he had finished in 1905. This time, however, the Church was rebuilt around a steel skeleton.

1914-15

- **October 13, 1914:** The National League's Boston Braves completed their sweep of the Philadelphia Athletics to win baseball's World Series.
- **January 25, 1915:** Alexander Graham Bell placed the first successful transcontinental telephone call from New York City to San Francisco.
- **February 8, 1915:** D.W. Griffith's famous motion picture, "Birth of a Nation" opened in Los Angeles.
- **April 5, 1915:** Jess Willard defeated Jack Johnson in 23 rounds to win the world heavyweight boxing title.
- **May 7, 1915:** A German submarine sank the British steamship Lusitania and nearly 1,200 drown.

STANFORD MOMENT

Rick Templeton's 22-foot broad jump gave Stanford a 62-60 win in the 1915 Big Meet.
(Stanford Archives)

Templeton's Jump Gives Stanford Big Meet Victory

If the Big Meet of 1913 was considered the most exciting meet to date, the 1915 edition may have it beaten. At least in the minds of some. Stanford coach Cap Campbell was saving his new 440 sensation—Ed Beal—to run the anchor leg of the relay. Sure enough, the meet was so close that the final relay would decide the winner. Cal's anchor leg was Jimmy Todd, who had been sick during the meet. Campbell felt that Todd, in his condition, could not beat Beal on that final leg. After the first three legs, Stanford held a 20-yard lead and it looked as though Beal would easily secure the win. But, Todd pulled off the upset by coming from behind to overtake Beal and win the relay for Cal. As the Cal rooting section began celebrating their victory, Stanford's Rick Templeton argued that he had one broad jump left. For 15 minutes, the crowd stood still awaiting Templeton's final jump. He had to beat 21 feet, 11 inches to place third and give Stanford the additional points it needed to win the meet. Templeton's jump just cleared the 22-foot mark, thus giving Stanford an improbable 62-60 victory.

Stanford SPOTLIGHT

THE BEST RUGBY TEAM at Stanford was the 1914 squad that went 10-0, outscored its opponents 228-43 and defeated Cal in the Big Game 26-8. It was the first undefeated, untied team at Stanford since Jim Lanagan's 1905 team. It would take another 12 years before Stanford would come up with another undefeated season (10-0-1 in 1926) and 26 years before Clark Shaughnessy led Stanford to an unbeaten, untied season (10-0 in 1940). The Big Game drew a record crowd of 26,000 to California Field and even though the Bears entered the game with a 13-0 record, they were no match for the talented Stanford team.

Stanford Stat . . .

Stanford finished 3-6 in their second season of intercollegiate basketball. The three wins came against U.C. Davis and two vs. College of the Pacific. Stanford lost two games to California, giving the Bears a 4-0 record in two seasons vs. the young Stanford team.

STANFORD LIST

PLAYERS AND COACHES

Listed below are the seven former Stanford players who later became the school's head football coach.

Name	Years Played	Years as as Head Coach
Charles Fickert	1894-98	1901
Carl Clemans	1892	1902
George Presley	1906	1909-12
Floyd Brown	1907-11	1913-16
Jim Wylie	1914-15	1917
Chuck Taylor	1940-42	1951-57
Paul Wiggin	1954-56	1980-83

Stanford LEGEND

Reginald E. "Reg" Caughey

Reg Caughey won eight varsity letters at Stanford. (Stanford Archives)

Talk about being a great all-around athlete, Reginald E. "Reg" Caughey is the definition of the term. He participated in five sports at Stanford, won eight letters and made the 1920 United States Olympic Team. He first wore a Stanford uniform as a freshman guard on the 1915 basketball team. Although he did not earn a letter that season, Caughey did earn letters as a member of the basketball team in 1916 and 1919. He earned one letter each in baseball, football and swimming and three more in track and field. Caughey competed in the shot put at the 1920 Antwerp Games, but did not win a medal. Following his playing days, Caughey remained active in Stanford Athletics as a member of the Board of Athletic Control and the chairman of the Stanford Athletic Council.

STANFORD LORE

The Men's Clubhouse and the Women's Clubhouse were dedicated in February, 1915. The purpose of the two buildings was to help promote informal and social contact among students, faculty and alumni and become headquarters for student body activities. A third building, the Stanford Union, which includes dining and dormitory facilities, was completed in 1922.

1915-16

- October 13, 1915:   The Boston Red Sox won the World Series from the Philadelphia Phillies.
- December 10, 1915:   The millionth Model T rolled off Ford's assembly line in Detroit.
- March 9, 1916:   Legendary Mexican bandit "Pancho" Villa led 1,500 guerrillas across the border, killing 17 Americans in New Mexico.
- June 30, 1916:   Charles Evans won the U.S. Open golf tournament.
- August 4, 1916:   The United States purchased the Virgin Islands from Denmark for $25 million.

STANFORD MOMENT

Stanford lost its first intercollegiate swim meet to Cal in 1916.
(Stanford Archives)

Four Sports Make Their Debuts

Four sports made their debuts in 1916 while another, men's basketball, was given "major" status. The basketball program, which was about to begin its third season, was made a major sport at Stanford on January 26, 1916. Four other "minor" sports began play this year, including wrestling, boxing, fencing and swimming. The first recorded wrestling match occurred on April 8, 1916 when Stanford met Cal. Eleven days later, on April 19, 1916, fencing and boxing were made minor sports. Boxing continued at Stanford as a minor sport until it was made a major sport in 1964. It was abandoned as an intercollegiate sport in 1970. Coach Ernie Brandsten lost the first swimming meet in Stanford history in 1916 as California won the meet 41-27.

Stanford SPOTLIGHT

THE BIG GAME has had only two interruptions in its 104-year history (1892-1996)—from 1915-18 and again from 1943-45 due to World War II. The first interruption was due to a disagreement between the two schools over freshman eligibility. California had been arguing for more than a decade that freshman should not be able to compete on the varsity level. Stanford's position was that incoming freshman needed 15 units of college level work to gain admittance, and therefore should be able to play. On January 1, 1915, a five-year agreement between the two schools had expired and when neither school would budge on its position, athletic relations were severed. The Big Game did not return until the 1919 season.

Stanford Stat . . .

Swimming was added as a sport to the Women's Athletic Association in 1916 and an added emphasis was placed on interclass competition a short time later. The women were provided with a pool of their own in 1916, the same time Greta and Ernie Brandsten came to The Farm. Ernie, of course, took over the men's program while Greta, a former Olympic diving champion, took over the women's program.

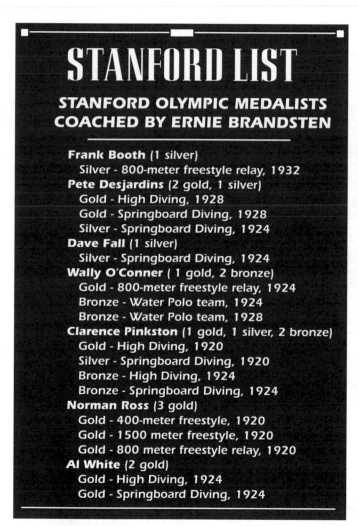

STANFORD LIST

STANFORD OLYMPIC MEDALISTS COACHED BY ERNIE BRANDSTEN

Frank Booth (1 silver)
   Silver - 800-meter freestyle relay, 1932
Pete Desjardins (2 gold, 1 silver)
   Gold - High Diving, 1928
   Gold - Springboard Diving, 1928
   Silver - Springboard Diving, 1924
Dave Fall (1 silver)
   Silver - Springboard Diving, 1924
Wally O'Conner (1 gold, 2 bronze)
   Gold - 800-meter freestyle relay, 1924
   Bronze - Water Polo team, 1924
   Bronze - Water Polo team, 1928
Clarence Pinkston (1 gold, 1 silver, 2 bronze)
   Gold - High Diving, 1920
   Silver - Springboard Diving, 1920
   Bronze - High Diving, 1924
   Bronze - Springboard Diving, 1924
Norman Ross (3 gold)
   Gold - 400-meter freestyle, 1920
   Gold - 1500 meter freestyle, 1920
   Gold - 800 meter freestyle relay, 1920
Al White (2 gold)
   Gold - High Diving, 1924
   Gold - Springboard Diving, 1924

Stanford ☙ LEGEND ❧

Ernie Brandsten

Ernie Brandsten's athletes won 10 Olympic medals in diving and five in swimming. (Stanford Archives)

One of the truly great swimming and diving coaches in American history is Stanford's own Ernie Brandsten, who in the 1920s and 30s produced national and Olympic champions at a phenomenal rate. Consider the facts: Brandsten-coached Stanford divers won 10 Olympic medals, including five golds, in the Olympic Games of 1920, '24, and '28 while Brandsten-coached Stanford swimmers won four golds and one silver in Olympic competition. He was the head coach of the United States Diving teams at four consecutive Olympic Games (1924, '28, '32, '36) and was Stanford's head swimming and diving coach for 31 years (1916-47). Brandsten, Stanford's first swimming and diving coach, had a dual meet record of 95-30, including a 26-5 mark against California. Brandsten, whose first love was diving, also produced several national and AAU swimming champions on The Farm, including John McKelvey, Austin Clapp, Ted Wiget and Emmet Cashin. His wife, Greta, won an Olympic gold medal in diving in 1912 as a member of the Swedish Team.

STANFORD LORE

Dr. Ray Lyman Wilbur, class of '96, was formally inaugurated as the third president in Stanford University history on January 22, 1916 in Memorial Church. Wilbur, who was the Dean of the School of Medicine for 13 years, moved quickly to "bring a number of things into the open." At his inauguration, Wilbur was linked from Stanford to a party of alumni in New York City through a transcontinental telephone call, which was very new technology at the time.

1916-17

•• AMERICA'S TIME CAPSULE ••

- September 30, 1916: The New York Giants' 26-game winning streak, baseball's longest ever, was halted by the Boston Braves.
- November 7, 1916: Woodrow Wilson was reelected president of the United States.
- February 3, 1917: The United States severed diplomatic relations with Germany due to increased submarine warfare.
- March 2, 1917: The Jones Act made Puerto Rico a U.S. territory.
- April 2, 1917: President Wilson requested a declaration of war against Germany.

STANFORD MOMENT

The 1916-17 Stanford basketball team finished with an 8-8 record.(Stanford Archives)

Basketball Takes On a More Prominent Role

With basketball now a major sport at Stanford, the 1916-17 schedule was the most ambitious to date with games against USC, California, Washington State and the Oregon Athletic Club (now Oregon State University). It was to be a preview of the Pacific Coast Conference (now the Pacific-10 Conference), which Stanford would join a year later. Stanford, which was a member of the California Nevada League, finished the season with an 8-8 record. While Stanford defeated USC twice this season, it lost two games apiece to Cal, Washington State and Oregon Athletic Club. Russell Wilson, formerly of Whittier College, a perennial basketball power at the time, was brought in to coach the team. One of his pupils, C.E. Righter, went on to become Stanford's first all-conference basketball player in 1920.

NEWLY APPOINTED UNIVERSITY PRESIDENT Dr. Ray Lyman Wilbur created the Board of Athletic Control, which came into existence in February, 1917. Prior to the B.A.C., athletics had been under faculty supervision, but managed by the Associated Students. This system was not working and by 1917, the ASSU was essentially bankrupt and the Trustees had to loan the B.A.C. $15,000 to cover the debt. The B.A.C. was responsible for maintaining athletic buildings, equipment and fields, appointing coaches and trainers and controlling funds for and from athletic events. Receipts from football games financed construction of Stanford Stadium, Branner Hall, Old Pavilion, Women's Gym, the Golf Course and Clubhouse and the expanded Men's Gym. The Board of Athletic Control remained in existence until Stanford returned to intercollegiate athletics after World War II, in 1946, when it was replaced by the Stanford Athletic Council.

Stanford Stat . . .

Coach Ernie Brandsten led his Stanford swim team to its first-ever dual meet victory—a 34-33 win over Cal in its second season of competition. Brandsten would lose to Cal the following two years before turning the tables to beat the Bears for 17 consecutive seasons.

Stanford ❧ LEGEND ❧

Ken Lilly

Ken Lilly was a four-sport letterman at Stanford.
(Stanford Athletics)

In an era that included World War I and the introduction of several new sports at Stanford, Ken Lilly stood apart from the rest as one of the school's all-time great all-around athletes. During his time, Lilly starred in baseball, football, basketball and track, earning eight varsity letters in all. After playing on the 1917 baseball squad, Lilly assumed the role of player-coach in 1918 after team captain Mush Stevens joined the Army and there was no one else to coach the team. In an abbreviated season due to World War I, Lilly and his teammates won just once in the four game series with California and ended the season with a 1-3 record. It is said that one day in the spring of 1918, Lilly sprained his ankle in a 13-inning baseball game in the morning and came back in the afternoon to win the 100-yard dash in the Big Meet vs. California, helping Stanford beat Cal 70-52.

STANFORD LIST

ALL-TIME PACIFIC-10 CONFERENCE PASSING LEADERS

1.	Steve Stenstrom, Stanford, 1991-94	10,911
2.	Erik Wilhelm, Oregon State, 1985-88	9,393
3.	John Elway, Stanford, 1979-82	9,349
4.	Jake Plummer, Arizona State, 1993-96	8,626
5.	Rob Johnson, USC, 1991-94	8,472
6.	Bill Musgrave, Oregon, 1987-90	8,343
7.	Danny O'Neil, Oregon, 1991-94	8,301
8.	Rodney Peete, USC, 1985-88	8,225
9.	Troy Taylor, California, 1986-89	8,126
10.	Jack Thompson, Washington State, 1975-78	7,818

STANFORD LORE

The United States' entry into World War I in April, 1917 brought about severe changes on campus. Athletic and social events were curtailed, some faculty members volunteered for active duty, doctors and nurses at the Medical School formed a Naval Base Hospital unit, half of the male students were enrolled on campus in the Students' Army Training Corps, which led to active duty, and a call from the Red Cross for educated women to serve in France was answered by 14 Stanford women.

1917-18

·· AMERICA'S TIME CAPSULE ··

- October 15, 1917: The Chicago White Sox defeated the New York Giants to win the World Series.
- November 3, 1917: U.S. forces engaged in its first World War I battle in Europe.
- December 18, 1917: The U.S. Constitution's 18th amendment was passed, outlawing the manufacture and sale of alcoholic liquors.
- May 15, 1918: Airmail service began between New York City and Washington D.C.
- June 25, 1918: American forces halted the Germans in the Battle of Belleau Wood in France.

Jim Wylie was Stanford's head rugby coach in 1917. (Stanford Archives)

STANFORD MOMENT

World War I Hits Stanford Athletics

The impact of World War I took its toll on the athletic programs at Stanford. Limited schedules in rugby, baseball, track and many other sports became commonplace. Several of Stanford's best basketball players missed the 1917-18 season due to the War. Stanford played only one game of rugby in 1917, beating Santa Clara in the Big Game, 15-11. When the series with Cal stopped following the 1914 season, the Big Game became the Stanford-Santa Clara matchup. Jim Wylie, former Stanford and New Zealand star, was the coach in 1917. The Stanford baseball team played just three games during the 1918 season while the track and field team competed in just one dual meet.

DESPITE THE LOSS of star players C.E. Righter and Bob Pelouze to World War I, Stanford finally broke through and defeated Cal in basketball 22-18 on February 14, 1918. The win snapped an eight-game losing streak against the Bears and gave Stanford its first-ever win over Cal in basketball. Although Stanford lost the next two games to Cal during the '17-18 campaign, the Cardinal managed to finish the season with an impressive 11-4 record. Captain Schwarzy Schwarzenbeck led the team along with Dale Butt, Everts Moulton, Fred Williamson and Bill Hood.

Stanford Stat . . .

The roots of the Pacific-10 Conference go back to December 15, 1915 when the Pacific Coast Conference (PCC) was founded at a meeting at the Oregon Hotel in Portland, Oregon. Original membership consisted of the University of California, the University of Washington, the University of Oregon and Oregon State College (now Oregon State University). Washington State University was accepted into the conference in 1917 and Stanford University joined in 1918.

Stanford LEGEND

R. Lindley Murray

R. Lindley Murray was Stanford's first great tennis player. (Stanford Archives)

The list of all-time great tennis players at Stanford University reads like a who's who in collegiate tennis. It all started in 1917 when R. Lindley Murray first made his mark on the national scene by winning the National Patriotic Tournament (which was the equivalent of the national championship) over Nat Niles. Murray, whose father and four other siblings all attended Stanford, came back in 1918 to beat the great Bill Tilden to capture the National Championship and earn the nation's number-one ranking. Murray was team captain of Stanford's 1913 tennis team and also a member of the Cardinal's track team. He graduated from Stanford in 1913 with a degree in chemistry and, a year later, earned his Master's degree in chemical engineering. His ranking rose to number four in 1914 and 1916, but it wasn't until his back-to-back national titles in 1917-18 that Lin Murray established himself as one of the great tennis players of his era. He was inducted into the International Tennis Hall of Fame in 1958.

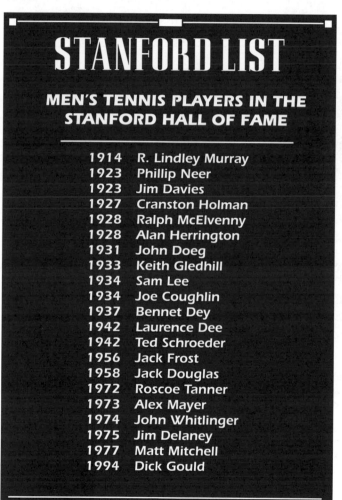

STANFORD LIST

MEN'S TENNIS PLAYERS IN THE STANFORD HALL OF FAME

1914	R. Lindley Murray
1923	Phillip Neer
1923	Jim Davies
1927	Cranston Holman
1928	Ralph McElvenny
1928	Alan Herrington
1931	John Doeg
1933	Keith Gledhill
1934	Sam Lee
1934	Joe Coughlin
1937	Bennet Dey
1942	Laurence Dee
1942	Ted Schroeder
1956	Jack Frost
1958	Jack Douglas
1972	Roscoe Tanner
1973	Alex Mayer
1974	John Whitlinger
1975	Jim Delaney
1977	Matt Mitchell
1994	Dick Gould

STANFORD LORE

The first official residence of the University president, the Knoll, was completed in June of 1918. San Francisco architect Louis C. Mullgardt designed the residence for President Wilbur and his family. It was described as a "many-chimneyed three-story house in Spanish Gothic style."

1918-19

•• AMERICA'S TIME CAPSULE ••

- November 9, 1918: Kaiser Wilhelm II of Germany was abdicated.
- November 11, 1918: World War I ended on the 11th hour of the 11th day of the 11th month.
- January 29, 1919: The 18th Amendment to the Constitution was ratified, prohibiting transportation and sale of alcoholic beverages.
- June 11, 1919: Walter Hagen won the U.S. Open golf tournament.
- July 4, 1919: Jack Dempsey won the world heavyweight boxing title with a technical knockout against defending champion Jess Willard.

STANFORD MOMENT

Baseball Team Ends Five-Year Drought

After losing the season series to Cal for five consecutive years, the Stanford baseball team finally ended the drought in 1919 by beating the Bears twice in their two-game series. The effects of World War I were still being felt in 1919 and Stanford was forced to play a limited schedule once again (they played just three games in 1918). Stanford went 6-2 in their eight-game season, but most celebrated were 5-3 and 5-2 victories over the Bears. Not since the great 1913 team had Stanford won a season series from Cal. Bob Evans, who tripled as Stanford's head coach for baseball, football and basketball, took over the baseball head coaching position after it remained vacant during the 1918 campaign.

Captain of the 1919 baseball team, Hugh Galloway, led the Cardinal to its first series victory over Cal in five years. (Stanford Archives)

THE RECORD BOOKS INDICATE that Stanford played an "unofficial" schedule in 1918, losing all four games it played by an aggregate score of 242-8. The games, which were no more than scrimmages, were American football games played by a group of Student Army Training Corps (SATC) personnel stationed at Stanford. In fact, some of the players were not Stanford university students. Lt. A.H. Badenoch was pressed into service as a volunteer coach. Although some of the players knew little or nothing about American football, they had a good time learning. For the record, Stanford lost to Mare Island 80-0, Mather Field 72-0, USC 25-8 and California 67-0. None of the four games are counted in the Stanford record book.

Stanford Stat . . .

Bob Evans made his debut as a head coach in 1918-19, leading the men's basketball team to a 9-3 record. Evans, however, was busy wearing three hats over the next two seasons. Following the 1918-19 basketball season, Evans was the head coach of the Stanford baseball team for two years (1919, 1920), the football team in 1919 and the basketball team for a second year in 1919-20. All totaled, he went 17-6 in basketball, 16-13 in baseball and 4-3 in football.

STANFORD LIST

STANFORD UNIVERSITY PRESIDENTS

Dr. David Starr Jordan	1891-1913
Dr. John Casper Branner	1913-1915
Dr. Ray Lyman Wilbur	1916-1943
Dr. Donald B. Tresidder	1943-1948
Dr. J.E. Wallace Sterling	1949-1968
Dr. Kenneth S. Pitzer	1968-1970
Dr. Richard W. Lyman	1970-1980
Dr. Donald Kennedy	1980-1992
Dr. Gerhard Casper	1992-present

Stanford 🌿 LEGEND 🌿

Feg Murray

Feg Murray won a bronze medal at the 1920 Olympic Games. (Stanford Athletics)

Frederick Seymour "Feg" Murray, a three-year letterman on the Stanford Track and Field team from 1914-16 and a team captain as a senior in '16, was one of the nation's top sprinters and hurdlers during his time. He was one of seven Stanford track athletes who competed at the 1920 Olympic Games in Antwerp and one of three to come home with a medal. Murray, whose brother R. Lindley Murray was one of Stanford's all-time great tennis players, earned a bronze medal in the 110-meter hurdles. At the Intercollegiate Association of Amateur Athletes of America (IC4A) meet in 1916, Murray captured the spotlight by winning both low hurdle events. He was the head coach of the Stanford track program in 1919, and following his competitive days, Murray served with the American Expeditionary Forces in France. He later joined the Metropolitan Newspaper Service as a sports cartoonist.

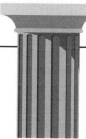

STANFORD LORE

In the spring of 1919, Board of Trustee member Herbert Hoover presented President Wilbur with a $50,000 check to set up the collection of materials documenting war, revolution and communism. These papers were the basis for the Hoover War Collection, later the Hoover War Library and finally the Hoover Institution on War, Revolution and Peace. Propaganda leaflets, newspapers, government documents and periodicals were sent to the U.S. beginning in 1921 on ships that had taken food to Europe.

1919-20

- September 26, 1919: President Wilson suffered a stroke during a national tour.
- April 20, 1920: The Olympic Games began in Antwerp, Belgium.
- May 14, 1920: The Socialist Party nominated Eugene V. Debs of Indiana for the presidency for the fifth time, while Debs was serving a 10-year prison sentence.
- July 3, 1920: Bill Tilden won the men's singles title at the Wimbledon tennis championships.
- July 5, 1920: The Democratic Party nominated Gov. James M. Cox of Ohio for the presidency and Franklin D. Roosevelt of New York for the vice presidency.

STANFORD MOMENT

American football returned to Stanford in 1919 after a 14-year hiatus. Stanford finished the season with a 4-3 record and a 14-10 loss to Cal.
(Stanford Archives)

Football Returns to The Farm

After a 14-year hiatus, American football returned to Stanford for the 1919 season. Stanford President Ray Lyman Wilbur approved the plans of the Board of Athletic Control to bring football back to campus for the first time since 1905. With the end of World War I—and Stanford's 14-year absence from football—the 1919 season has to be considered a successful one. M.C. "Bob" Evans, a relative unknown, was selected to be the team's head coach in '19. His team finished with a 4-3 record and a 14-10 loss to Cal in the Big Game. It was the first Big Game since 1914 when the two teams played rugby and the first Big Game in football since Stanford's 12-5 victory on November 11, 1905. Rugby stars Danny Carroll and Dink Templeton made a successful transition to football and helped bring the spirit of football back to The Farm.

STANFORD'S ILLUSTRIOUS HISTORY in Olympic competition began in 1912 when track star George Horine won a bronze medal in the high jump. But at the 1920 Games in Antwerp, Belgium, Stanford athletes won an unprecedented 16 medals, including 12 golds, and put Stanford on the map as a university that produces Olympic champions. Seven members of the U.S. gold medal-winning rugby football team hailed from Stanford, including Morris Kirksey, who also won a gold and silver in track. Swimmer Norman Ross won three gold medals, and diver Clarence Pinkston won a gold and silver. As well as Stanford did in 1920, the 1924 Games in Paris saw Stanford athletes take home 21 medals, 12 of which were gold.

Stanford Stat . . .

Stanford put an amazing seven athletes on the United States Olympic Track team in 1920, winning one gold, two silver and one bronze medal in the process. Morris Kirksey led the way with one gold (400-meter relay) and one silver medal (100-meter dash), John Norton won a silver (400-meter hurdles) and Feg Murray took a bronze medal (110-meter high hurdles). Other Stanford track Olympians in 1920 were Dink Templeton, Reg Caughey, Herc Bihlman and Flint Hanner.

STANFORD LIST

MEN'S SWIMMING WORLD RECORD HOLDERS FROM STANFORD

Name	Event	Year (s) Record Broken
Norman Ross	200m free	1916
Norman Ross	400m free	1919, 1921
Norman Ross	800m free	1920
George Harrison	400m IM	1960, 1968
Dick Roth	400m IM	1964
Greg Buckingham	200m IM	1966, 1967
Brian Job	200m breast	1970
John Hencken	200m breast	1972, '73, '74
John Hencken	100m breast	1972, '73, '74, '76
Mike Bruner	200m fly	1976
John Moffet	100m breast	1984
Pablo Morales	100m fly	1984, 1986
Jeff Rouse	100m back	1991, 1992

Stanford LEGEND

Norman Ross

Norman Ross won three gold medals at the 1920 Olympic Games. (Stanford Archives)

Stanford's first great swimmer was Norman Ross, a Portland, Oregon native who won three gold medals at the 1920 Olympic Games in Antwerp. Ross, who trained at Stanford under Ernie Brandsten, took home gold medals at in the 400-meter freestyle, 1,500-meter freestyle and the 800-meter freestyle relay. Ross burst on to the international scene in 1919 when he won five events at the Inter-Allied Games in Paris. In his career, Ross set 13 world records at international distances and won 18 AAU championships. After graduating from Stanford, Ross attended Northwestern Law School. At a swim meet in Honolulu, Ross met and then married a Hawaiian princess. He went into the music business after his swimming career and became the country's first classical disc jockey, known to millions as "Uncle Normie." Ross was decorated by Gen. Pershing during World War I and served as an aide to Gen. Doolittle in World War II.

STANFORD LORE

Salinas native John Steinbeck decided to attend Stanford because of its free tuition. In the fall of 1919, he received a "C" in freshman English. Steinbeck, who supported himself and lived in Encina Hall and various modest rooms in Palo Alto, dropped out of Stanford in 1921, reentered as a journalism major in 1923 and dropped out again in 1925. In 1975, the University Libraries acquired the manuscripts of his *Cannery Row* as its four millionth book.

1920-21

- September 28, 1920: Eight members of the Chicago White Sox were indicted on charges of taking bribes to throw the 1919 World Series.
- November 2, 1920: Warren Harding was elected president of the United States in a landslide margin.
- November 2, 1920: Radio station KDKA in Pittsburgh broadcast the results of the presidential election for the first time in history.
- November 20, 1920: President Woodrow Wilson was awarded the Nobel Peace Prize in recognition of his efforts to promote world peace through the League of Nations.
- July 2, 1921: Jack Dempsey successfully defended his heavyweight boxing title against George Carpentier.

STANFORD MOMENT

C.E. Righter was the first Stanford basketball player to earn All-Pacific Coast Conference honors. (Stanford Athletics)

Righter Leads Hoops Team Over Cal

Led by Cornelius Erwin C.E. Righter, Stanford took two of three from Cal in 1921 to record its second straight season series victory over the Bears. After winning just one of the first 13 games with Cal from 1914-1919, Righter and his teammates managed to beat the Bears four times in five meetings in 1920 and 1921. Stanford went 23-6 in those two seasons and Righter was twice named to the All-Pacific Coast Conference teams in 1920 and '21, thus becoming the first Stanford basketball player to earn all-conference honors. Righter, who earned seven varsity letters at Stanford—four in basketball and three in football—was a member of the United States' gold medal-winning rugby team at the 1920 Olympic Games in Antwerp.

THE BIG GAME in 1920 was a milestone in Stanford football history on two fronts: it was the worst Big Game loss in history and the second worst defeat to date for a Stanford football team. The Bears, en route to an undefeated season, trounced Stanford 38-0 in front of 27,700 at Berkeley, the largest crowd of the 26 Big Games played to date. The only football game that was more one-sided was Stanford's 49-0 loss to Michigan in the 1902 Rose Bowl. The Bears finished the 1920 season 9-0, beat Ohio State 28-0 in the Rose Bowl and outscored their opponents 510-14. Stanford was in its second season of football after taking a 14-year break and was still in the rebuilding stages. The Cardinals finished the season with a 4-3 record for coach Walter Powell with wins over St. Mary's, Santa Clara, Washington and Oregon. But 1920 was Cal's year. The Bears led just 10-0 at halftime of the Big Game, but scored often and early in the second half to secure the lopsided victory.

Stanford Stat . . .

When Dink Templeton arrived to coach the Stanford Track and Field team in 1921, the fortunes of the program immediately took off. In his first season, Templeton coached his first NCAA champion, beginning a string of outstanding national-caliber athletes who would train under Templeton. Flint Hanner threw the javelin 191-2 1/4 in 1921 to win the NCAA title, the first in Stanford history. Under Templeton (1921-39), Stanford athletes won 21 individual NCAA titles.

STANFORD LIST

STANFORD'S MEN'S TRACK WORLD RECORD HOLDERS (INDIVIDUAL RUNNING EVENTS ONLY)

Name	Event	Year Record Broken
Morris Kirksey	100-yard dash	1921
Bud Spencer	400-meter dash	1928
Ben Eastman	440-yard dash	1932
Ben Eastman	880-yard run	1932
Gus Meier	120-yard high hurdles	1933
Sam Klopstock	120-yard high hurdles	1935
Clyde Jeffrey	100-yard dash	1940
Paul Moore	1320-yard run	1940
Ernie Cunnliffe	1000-yard run	1961

Stanford LEGEND

Morris Kirksey

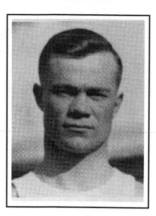

Kirksey is one of two Americans who have won two gold medals in two different sports. (Stanford Athletics)

Morris Marshall Kirksey has the distinction of being just one of four men and one of two Americans who have won Olympic gold medals in two different sports. Kirksey, one of the great sprinters of his time, won two gold medals and one silver medal at the 1920 Games in Antwerp. He won one of his golds as a member of the U.S. rugby team and the other as a member of the 400-meter relay team. Kirksey, who in 1921 set a world record in the 100-yard dash at 9.6, won a silver medal in Antwerp in the 100-meter dash. He also competed in the 200-meter run in Antwerp, but did not make the finals. Kirksey went on to earn a medical degree from St. Louis Medical College. He then served for 25 years as a staff psychiatrist for the State Department of Corrections in California, working at San Quentin and Folsom prisons.

STANFORD LORE

Lewis M. Terman received funding in the summer of 1921 to begin a lifelong study of 1,528 gifted children. The children chosen, often referred to as "Termites" had IQs ranging from 135-200. Although Terman died in 1956, the study continued by Profs. Robert and Pauline Sears. After six decades, the study concluded that exceptionally intelligent children grow up to be more successful, better satisfied and more productive than average people. However, the gifted seem to have as many emotional difficulties as the rest of the population.

1921-22

·· AMERICA'S TIME CAPSULE ··

- September 8, 1921: Margaret Gorman of Washington, D.C. won the title of the first Miss America.
- October 5, 1921: The first radio coverage of the World Series was carried by a wireless station set up at the Electrical Show in New York and station WJZ in New Jersey.
- November 11, 1921: The "Unknown Soldier" of World War I was buried at Arlington National Cemetery.
- February 21, 1922: An explosion on the airship Roma killed 34 of its 45-man crew.
- February 27, 1922: The Nineteenth Amendment to the Constitution, providing for women's suffrage, was declared constitutional by a unanimous decision of the Supreme Court.

STANFORD MOMENT

Stanford Stadium opened November 19, 1921 when Stanford hosted Cal in the 27th Big Game. (Stanford News Service)

Stanford Stadium Opens on November 19, 1921

Initially sparked by a feud with the University of California to see which school could complete a new football facility sooner, Stanford Stadium opened its doors on November 19, 1921 when 62,740 jammed the new 60,000 seat stadium to witness the 27th Big Game. Although Cal spoiled Stanford's dedication of its new facility by winning the game 42-7, it was nevertheless a historical moment in Stanford athletic history. The stadium was built in four-and-a-half months at a cost of $211,000. Its original seating capacity of 60,000 made it second only to the Yale Bowl. An additional 10,200 seats were added in 1925 and by 1927, 14 additional rows of seats were added, bringing the capacity to its present day total of 85,500.

GLENN "TINY" HARTRANFT was an Olympian, world record holder, NCAA champion and a member of Stanford's first NCAA championship team. Hartranft, originally from Aberdeen, South Dakota, was a member of the U.S. Olympic Track and Field team at the '24 Games in Paris. There, he won a silver medal in the shot put and placed sixth in the discus. In 1925, he set a world record in the discus with a throw of 157-1 5/8. Hartranft, who competed on the Stanford track team from 1922-25, was a major reason why Stanford captured its first-ever NCAA team championship in 1925. He set a new NCAA record in winning the shot put and placed second in the discus.

Stanford Stat . . .

The Old Pavilion was completed on January 13, 1922 and dedicated that night with an all-university free dance and celebration. The Pavilion, at the time, was the largest facility exclusively for basketball in the United States. The following night, January 14, the first official basketball game was played at the Old Pavilion with Stanford beating College of the Pacific 30-21.

STANFORD LIST

HISTORICAL EVENTS HELD AT STANFORD STADIUM

August 12, 1928
Herbert Hoover's acceptance speech following nomination to run for president

July 1-2, 1960
United States Olympic Track and Field Trials

July 21-22, 1962
USA-U.S.S.R Track Meet

July 29-August 6, 1984
Eight Olympic soccer matches

January 20, 1985
Super Bowl XIX (San Francisco 49ers vs. Miami Dolphins)

June 20-July 10, 1994
Six World Cup Soccer matches

Stanford LEGEND

Philip Neer

Phillip Neer was the first non-Ivy League player to win the NCAA tennis championship. (Stanford Athletics)

Philip Neer placed his name in the Stanford record book in 1921 and '22 as the school's first NCAA singles tennis champion and the first doubles champion along with his partner, Jimmie Davies. In 1921, Neer became the first player from the West to ever win the NCAA singles championship, thus breaking the stranglehold Ivy League schools had on the tournament. Two years later, Neer and Davies won the NCAA doubles title, once again blunting the domination held by the eastern universities since the tourney's inception in 1883. Neer was voted into the Stanford Athletic Hall of Fame in 1923.

STANFORD LORE

The main building of the Stanford Union was completed in 1922. Two other buildings which composed the Union—the Men's Clubhouse and Women's Clubhouse—were completed in 1915. This project was the first to seek substantial funding from alumni. However, because of Stanford's image as a well-to-do university, the process was slow. Today, the buildings are occupied by administrative offices and known as the Old Union.

1922-23

·· AMERICA'S TIME CAPSULE ··

- October 4, 1922: Famed sportswriter Grantland Rice reported the first radio play-by-play coverage of the World Series.
- October 8, 1922: John McGraw's New York Giants won their second consecutive World Series title against the New York Yankees.
- March 13, 1923: Motion pictures with sound were first demonstrated in New York City.
- July 15, 1923: Golf amateur Bobby Jones won the U.S. Open.
- August 2, 1923: President Warren Harding died of an embolism while recovering from an attack of ptomaine poisoning.

STANFORD MOMENT

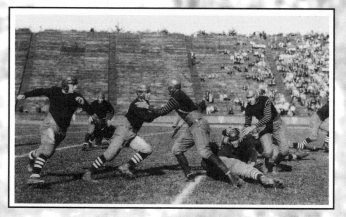

Pop Warner's Pitt team came to Stanford in 1922 to play Stanford's first intersectional game in 18 years. Pitt won the game 16-7. *(Stanford Athletics)*

Warner's Pitt Team Beats Stanford

Anxious to see how his two assistants—Andy Kerr and Tiny Thornhill—were doing at Stanford, Pittsburgh coach Pop Warner, who agreed to remain at Pitt and fulfill his obligation through the 1923 season before taking over the Stanford program, brought his team West for an intersectional game at the new Stanford Stadium. The Panthers easily won the game 16-7 (they led 16-0 before Stanford scored a late TD) in front of a sparse crowd of just 6,000 on December 20, 1922. It was Stanford's first intersectional game in 18 years and the first such game in Stanford Stadium. Because the game was played so late in the year, the issue of lost class time and commercialism caused a bit of controversy.

THE MOST DECORATED of Ernie Brandsten's Stanford divers was Clarence Pinkston, a four-time Olympic medalist. Pinkston, from Wichita, Kansas, won one gold, one silver and two bronze medals at the 1920 and '24 Olympic Games. He took home a gold medal at the '20 Games in Antwerp in platform diving and a silver in springboard. Four years later in Paris, Pinkston won bronze medals in both platform and springboard. A five-time AAU platform champion, Pinkston married 1924 Olympic platform champion Betty Becker and coached her to a gold medal at the 1928 Games in Amsterdam.

Stanford Stat . . .

Prior to the 1922 season, Leland Cutler, a member of the Board of Athletic Control, convinced the great "Pop" Warner to come west and coach the Stanford team. Warner, however, had two years to go on his contract at the University of Pittsburgh and was emphatic about finishing his commitment to Pitt. "I'll send you two good men who will do a great job of laying the foundations for the future— Andy Kerr and Tiny Thornhill," Warner said. Kerr coached Stanford in 1922 and '23 before Warner took over in 1924.

STANFORD LIST

STANFORD COACHES IN THE COLLEGE FOOTBALL HALL OF FAME

Coach	At Stanford	Elected
Walter Camp	1892, '94-95	1951
Fielding Yost	1900	1951
Andy Kerr	1922-23	1951
Glenn "Pop" Warner	1924-32	1951
Clark Shaughnessy	1940-41	1968
Chuck Taylor	1951-57	1984
John Ralston	1963-71	1994

Stanford LEGEND

Andy Kerr

Andy Kerr was head football coach in 1922-23 and head basketball coach from 1923-26. (Stanford Archives)

Andy Kerr's contribution to Stanford athletics goes far beyond his two-year stint as head football coach (1922-23) and four-year reign as head men's basketball coach (1923-26). Kerr came to The Farm in 1922 as a fill-in until "Pop" Warner arrived in 1924. A former member of Warner's staff at Pittsburgh, Kerr was sent to Stanford by Warner to coach the football team along with Tiny Thornhill. Known as a perfectionist and tough task-master, Kerr's orders were to install the "Warner System," complete with the double-wing attack, tricky reverses, multiple ball-handling and pulling lineman. By Warner's instructions, Kerr was always mindful that he was building for the future. His team went 4-5 in 1922 and improved to 7-2 in '23. Those two years, however, laid the groundwork for perhaps the greatest era of Stanford football. Over the next 12 years, Stanford won 96 football games and played in six Rose Bowls. Kerr, who compiled a 42-18 record in four years as Stanford's basketball coach, was inducted into the College Football Hall of Fame in 1951.

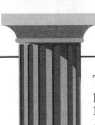

STANFORD LORE

Though former Stanford University President Dr. Ray Lyman Wilbur had stopped his medical practice and teaching seven years earlier, he was called in as a consultant when U.S. President Warren G. Harding fell critically ill in July of 1923 in San Francisco. A battery of physicians could not prevent Harding's death, however.

1923-24

- **September 14, 1923:** Jack Dempsey retained his heavyweight boxing crown with a second-round knockout of Luis Angel Firpo, the "Wild Bull of the Pampas."

- **January 25, 1924:** The first Winter Olympics were held in Chamonix, France, as the Americans finished fourth in the unofficial team standings.

- **June 30, 1924:** The Teapot Dome oil leasing scandal indicted several oil company presidents on charges of bribery and conspiracy to defraud the United States.

- **July 21, 1924:** Life sentences were given to Nathan Leopold and Richard Loeb for the highly publicized murder of Bobby Franks.

- **July 27, 1924:** At the Summer Olympics in Paris, France, the U.S. took first place in the unofficial team standings with 45 gold medals.

STANFORD MOMENT

Track Team Finishes Third at Nationals

In his fourth year as Stanford's head track coach, Dink Templeton brought his team to a near national championship at the 1924 Intercollegiate 4A Meet at Harvard University. With the meet apparently over and Stanford out in front by four points, coaches, athletes and reporters crowded around to give congratulations. No one was aware that the results of the hammer throw, held on another field, hadn't come in yet. When they did, however, it was Yale University who took first and second place in the hammer throw, propelling itself to first place and sending Stanford to third. The final tally read Yale 28 points, Pennsylvania 27 and Stanford 24 1/2. Half-miler Bill Richardson and weight-man Tiny Hartranft followed the '24 season with a berth on the United States Olympic Team. Hartranft took second in the shot and sixth in the discus at the Olympics while Richardson took fifth in the 800-meter run.

THE 1924 OLYMPIC GAMES in Paris had Stanford athletes on the medal stand 21 times—an amazing number by anyone's count. Stanford student-athletes accounted for 12 gold medals, three silver medals and six bronze. The U.S. gold medal winning rugby team had nine Stanford athletes on its squad while the bronze medal-winning water polo team had four Stanford athletes. Divers Al White (two gold medals), Clarence Pinkston (two bronze), Pete Desjardins (one silver) and Dave Fall (one silver) led a Stanford-dominated U.S. diving team.

Pete DesJardins (left) and Dave Fall both won medals in Olympic competition. *(Stanford Athletics)*

Stanford Stat . . .

Dave Fall won a silver medal at the 1924 Olympic Games in Paris in springboard diving, helping Stanford divers secure a record six medals. Fall, the 1924 National Junior Champion off the 1-meter board, graduated from Stanford in '24 and went on to a fine law career. Shortly before his death in 1964, Fall was appointed a district court judge in California.

STANFORD LIST

TODAY'S TOP EIGHT AWARD WINNERS
(Presented to the nation's top eight student-athletes annually)

1977	John Hencken	Swimming
1983	John Elway	Football
1987	Jon Louis	Gymnastics
1987	John Moffet	Swimming
1991	Ed McCaffrey	Football
1995	Lea Loveless	Swimming
1996	Jenny Thompson	Swimming

Stanford LEGEND

Al White

Al White won two gold medals in diving at the 1924 Olympic Games in Paris (Stanford Athletics)

Al White was not only the first person (man or woman) to capture both diving titles in Olympic competition, he was also a Lt. Colonel in the Army during World War II, an accomplished gymnast and a member of a touring U.S. basketball team during World War I in Europe. But White is best known for his accomplishments on the diving board. At the 1924 Olympic Games in Paris, White, as a 29-year-old Stanford graduate and war veteran, won two gold medals in springboard and platform diving, thus becoming the first person to ever win both diving events in Olympic competition. White was also captain of Stanford's 1921 gymnastics team that won the Pacific Coast Championship. As a World War I serviceman, White toured inter-allied Europe in 1919 with the U.S. basketball team. Two of his teammates were pentathlon world record holder Fred Thompson and Dr. James Naismith, who invented the game of basketball.

STANFORD LORE

An innovative and ground-breaking required freshman course, "Problems of Citizens" was introduced in the fall of 1923. The course was taught by a variety of faculty members as a team with History Prof. Edgar Eugene Robinson as director. It was designed to examine "the fundamental, political, social and economic problems of the American people." In 1935, the class evolved into the "History of Western Civilization."

1924-25

- October 10, 1924: The Washington Senators, led by pitcher Walter Johnson, defeated the New York Giants four games to three in the World Series.
- November 4, 1924: Calvin Coolidge was re-elected president of the United States, defeating Democrat John Davis.
- January 5, 1925: Mrs. William B. Ross was inaugurated governor of Wyoming, becoming the first woman governor in U.S. history.
- July 21, 1925: Tennessee teacher John Scopes was convicted for teaching the theory of evolution to his students. Scopes was defended by Clarence Darrow and Dudley Field Malone.
- August 24, 1925: Helen Wills and Bill Tilden successfully defended their singles titles at the U.S. Lawn Tennis Championships.

STANFORD MOMENT

Ernie Nevers vs. the Four Horsemen

In one of the classic matchups of all-time, the Four Horsemen of Notre Dame defeated Ernie Nevers and Stanford 27-10, in the 1925 Rose Bowl. *(Stanford Archives)*

One of the classic matchups in college football history took place on January 1, 1925 when Stanford coach Pop Warner and his star player, Ernie Nevers, went up against Knute Rockne and the "Four Horsemen" of Notre Dame. When it was over, the Fighting Irish had a 27-10 victory, a 10-0 season and a national championship, while Stanford ended its season at 7-1-1. Nevers, Stanford's All-American two-way star, turned in one of the greatest performances in the school's history. Not only did he play all 60 minutes in the game, but he rushed for 114 yards, more yardage than the Four Horsemen combined, despite having his ankles bandaged so tightly that the circulation was almost completely shut off. Nevers could barely walk. Elmer Layden was the star Horseman as he scored three touchdowns to lead the Irish. Layden intercepted two of Nevers' passes and returned them 78 and 70 yards for touchdowns.

ANY LIST of great Big Games is sure to include the 1924 contest played in front of 77,000 fans at Cal's Memorial Stadium. Stanford entered the game with a perfect 7-0 record while the Bears were an impressive 7-0-1. Cal was also a heavy favorite to beat Pop Warner's team, which was decimated by injuries, including one to the great Ernie Nevers. The Bears held a 20-6 lead with 14 minutes to play and seemed on their way to their sixth-straight Big Game victory. Reserve quarterback Ed Walker was summoned to replace Jim Kelley for Stanford. He promptly hit end Ted Shipkey on a 20-yard TD pass to bring Stanford within a touchdown at 20-13. Stanford got the ball back on their own 19-yard line with less than three minutes to play. After moving inside Cal territory, Walker struck again, this time hitting Murray Cuddeback for a 34-yard TD with just a few seconds remaining in the game. Stanford had fought back for a 20-20 tie.

Stanford Stat . . .

Led by Biff Hoffman (discus), Tiny Hartranft (shot put) and Hugo Leisner (120 high hurdles), Stanford's team of just six athletes captured the NCAA Track and Field Championship, the first NCAA title in any sport in school history. Hoffman, Hartranft and Leisner each won NCAA titles in their events. The other three members of Stanford's championship squad included Ted Miller (440-yard run), Bill Richardson (880-yard run) and Tommy Work (high jump).

STANFORD LIST

POP WARNER'S CAREER RECORD

Years	School	Record
1895-99	Iowa State	22-12-1
1895-96	Georgia	7-4
1897-98, 1904-06	Cornell	36-13-3
1899-1903, 1907-14	Carlisle Indian School	
		114-42-8
1915-23	Pittsburgh	60-12-4
1924-32	Stanford	71-17-8
1933-38	Temple	31-18-9
TOTALS		341-118-33 (.727)

Note: Warner coached two teams each season from 1895-99.

Stanford
LEGEND

Glenn "Pop" Warner

Glen "Pop" Warner was 71-18-8 in nine years as Stanford's head coach.
(Stanford Athletics)

The legend that was Glenn Scobey "Pop" Warner began his nine-year stay at Stanford in 1924 and helped put Stanford on the map as one of the premier college football programs in the nation. Warner, who compiled a 71-17-8 (.781) record at Stanford, is one of the great college football coaches of all-time. During his nine years at Stanford, his teams won three Pacific Coast Championships, one national championship (1926) and participated in three Rose Bowls. In his first season on The Farm in 1924, Warner and his double-wing attack propelled Stanford to a 7-1-1 overall record, a PCC championship and a trip to the Rose Bowl. The highlight of Warner's career at Stanford occurred in 1926 when his team put together a 10-0-1 record and won the unofficial national championship. The only blemish on that record was a 7-7 tie vs. Alabama in the Rose Bowl. Warner is credited by football historians with inventing the single and double wing offensive attacks, the reverse play, crouching start, huddles between plays, numbers for players, headgear and various hidden ball plays. He coached two of the greatest players in college football history in Ernie Nevers at Stanford and Jim Thorpe at Carlisle Indian School. Warner is the all-time winningest coach in college football history with a career record of 341-118-33.

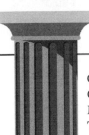

STANFORD LORE

On May 15, 1925, the School of Engineering was organized. Born from the departments of Civil Engineering, Mechanical Engineering, Electrical Engineering and Mining and Metallurgy, the School of Engineering became a reality. The school's first dean was Theodore J. Hoover.

1925-26

- September 3, 1925: The U.S. Army dirigible Shenandoah was wrecked in a storm near Ava, Ohio, killing 14 people.
- October 15, 1925: Baseball's World Series was won by the Pittsburgh Pirates in seven games over the Washington Senators.
- March 7, 1926: The American Telephone and Telegraph Company successfully demonstrated the first transatlantic radiotelephone conversation between New York City and London.
- May 9, 1926: Rear Admiral Richard Byrd made the first successful flight over the North Pole.
- August 6, 1926: Nineteen-year-old Gertrude Ederle of New York City became the first woman to swim the English Channel.

STANFORD MOMENT

The great Ernie Nevers rushed for 117 yards and two touchdowns in his final Big Game in 1925. (Stanford Athletics)

Nevers Leads Stanford to Big Game Victory

In his final game at Stanford, All-American fullback Ernie Nevers rushed for 117 yards and two touchdowns to lead his team to a 27-14 victory, November 21, 1925 in front of 74,200 at Stanford Stadium. The win was Stanford's first over Cal in the last seven meetings and the first since the 1914 season But on this day, it was Nevers, once again, who stole the show. He scored Stanford's final two touchdowns—from four yards and one yard out—to put his team ahead 27-7 in the fourth quarter. "It will be a long time before Cal wins another Big Game," said Stanford coach Pop Warner following the game. Despite fielding a young and inexperienced team, Warner had guided his 1925 club to a 7-2 record, including an 82-0 victory over UCLA in the first meeting with one of Stanford's oldest rivals.

MANY CONSIDER Wally O'Connor to be the greatest U.S. water polo player of all time. He wasn't a bad swimmer either. O'Connor was Stanford's first NCAA swimming champion, winning the 220-yard freestyle and 440-yard freestyle at the 1926 NCAA Championships. But it was as a water polo player that O'Connor is best remembered. He was a member of the United States Olympic water polo team five times and competed in four Olympic Games (he made the 1940 team, but the war in Europe prevented the Games from being held). He won a bronze medal in both the 1924 and 1932 Olympics and was also a member of the U.S. team in 1928 and 1936. He was a member of the color guard that accompanied the U.S. flag bearer at the '36 Games in Berlin. O'Connor won one gold medal in Olympic competition, as a member of the U.S. 800-meter freestyle relay team at the '24 Games in Paris.

Stanford Stat . . .

From 1923 to 1927, Stanford and California severed relations in the boxing ring because of differing opinions on the racial issue. The controversy was not confined to Stanford and Cal, however. It was being discussed at both the professional and amateur levels and even in some political circles. The question at hand was, "Would racial relations be harmed by clashes between white men and black men in the boxing ring?"

STANFORD LIST

STANFORD FOOTBALL ALL-CENTURY TEAM (1891-1991)

OFFENSE

QB	Jim Plunkett
HB	Ernie Nevers, Darrin Nelson
E	James Lofton, Gene Washington
TE	Bill McColl
OT	Blaine Nye, Bob Reynolds
OG	George Buehler, Chuck Taylor
C	Vic Lindskog
PK	Rod Garcia

DEFENSE

DL	Pat Donovan, Garin Veris, Pete Lazetich, Paul Wiggin
LB	Gordy Ceresino, David Wyman, Jeff Siemon
DB	Toi Cook, Dick Horn, Randy Poltl, Benny Barnes
P	Frankie Albert
Coach: John Ralston	

Stanford LEGEND

Ernie Nevers

Ernie Nevers is considered one of the best college football players of all time.
(Stanford Athletics)

To this day, Ernie Nevers' name will top any list of the greatest college football players of all time. He was Stanford's All-American fullback in 1925 and has been called the greatest football player and athlete in Stanford University history. Nicknamed "Sweede" or "Big Dog" by his teammates, Nevers legend grew from his phenomenal athletic talent and his intense toughness. One example of this was the 1925 Rose Bowl vs. the Four Horsemen of Notre Dame when Nevers played all 60 minutes and carried the ball 34 times for 114 yards. He had broken both ankles during the season and, just 10 days before the game, had one of his casts taken off. His ankles were bandaged so tightly and he could barely walk, but Nevers would not let that slow him down. From 1923-25, Nevers' teams went 21-5-1. In 1962, he was named the greatest college player of all time by *Sports Illustrated*. He was also named to the NCAA's All-Time All-America team in 1969. Pop Warner, who coached both Nevers and the great Jim Thorpe, chose Nevers as the greatest college player of all time.

STANFORD LORE

The Graduate School of Business opened on September 30, 1925 with 16 students. Stanford alum Herbert Hoover, Secretary of Commerce in the Coolidge cabinet, said business should be taught on par with such professions as engineering, law and medicine. It was Hoover's desire to halt the flow of Stanford graduates who traveled East seeking business education and careers.

1926-27

- **September 18, 1926:** Nearly 400 people were killed and 6,000 injured as a hurricane swept through Florida and other Gulf states.
- **September 23, 1926:** Challenger Gene Tunney defeated boxing champ Jack Dempsey in a 10-round heavyweight title fight in Philadelphia.
- **April 7, 1927:** Television was demonstrated for the first time in New York City, as Secretary of Commerce Herbert Hoover, a Stanford alum, was seen and heard from his office in Washington D.C.
- **May 20, 1927:** Aviator Charles Lindbergh took off from Long Island, New York for Paris, France in his monoplane, The Spirit of St. Louis. He successfully landed 33 1/2 hours later.
- **August 2, 1927:** President Calvin Coolidge declined renomination for a second term.

STANFORD MOMENT

Stanford-Alabama Tie in Rose Bowl

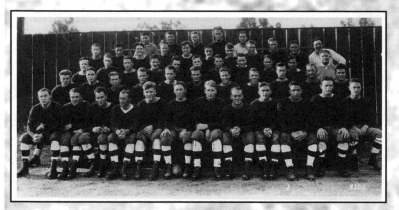

The 1926 Indians tied Alabama 7-7 in the Rose Bowl before a record crowd on 57,417. (Stanford Athletics)

In a game that pitted two undefeated teams, Stanford (10-0) and Alabama (9-0) battled to a 7-7 tie in Pasadena on January 1, 1927 before a Rose Bowl-record crowd of 57,417. Stanford scored an early touchdown and dominated play throughout much of the game, but a last-minute TD by the Crimson Tide forced the tie. Stanford scored in the first quarter when quarterback George Bogue hit Ed Walker for a 20-yard TD pass play. Stanford had numerous chances to score, but couldn't find a way to put more points on the board. Late in the game, Alabama's Clark Pearce blocked a Frankie Wilton punt to put the Crimson Tide at the Stanford 14-yard line. Five plays later, Alabama scored a TD with less than a minute to play to tie the game. Stanford outgained Alabama 311 total yards to 92, but had to settle for a tie and a final season record of 10-0-1 for coach Pop Warner.

THE 1926 FOOTBALL SEASON has to be considered perhaps the greatest season in Stanford history. Pop Warner's club breezed through the regular season, winning all 10 of its games, before settling for a 7-7 tie with Alabama in the Rose Bowl. Still, Stanford was awarded the Rissman National Trophy, emblematic of the top college football team in America. During the year, Stanford outscored its opponents 268-73, including a 41-6 win over Cal in the Big Game, Stanford's most lopsided Big Game victory to date. Stars of the '26 club included All-American end Ted Shipkey, Biff Hoffman, George Bogue, Dick Hyland, Ed Walker, and captain Fred Swan.

Stanford Stat . . .

Clarita Hunsberger was the first female athlete in Stanford history to compete in the Olympic Games. A 1927 Stanford graduate, Hunsberger competed in the 1928 Olympic Games in Amsterdam, finishing fourth in the platform diving competition.

STANFORD LIST

STANFORD FOOTBALL FIRST-TEAM ALL-AMERICANS (PRE-WWII)

Year	Player	Position
1924	Jim Lawson	End
1925	Ernie Nevers	Fullback
1926	Ted Shipkey	End
1928	Seraphim Post	Guard
1928	Don Robesky	Guard
1930	Phil Moffat	Halfback
1932-33	Bill Corbus	Guard
1934	Bob Reynolds	Tackle
1934	Bones Hamilton	Tackle
1934-35	Bobby Grayson	Fullback
1934-35	Monk Moscrip	End
1940	Hugh Gallarneau	Halfback
1940-41	Frankie Albert	Quarterback
1942	Chuck Taylor	Guard

Stanford LEGEND

Ted Shipkey

All-American Ted Shipkey played all 60 minutes in the 1925 and 1927 Rose Bowl games. (Stanford Athletics)

The arrival of Pop Warner in 1924 signaled a new era in Stanford football. Along with innovative offenses and a system matched by no other team in America, Warner also produced seven All-Americans in his nine-year tenure on The Farm. Receiver Ted Shipkey became Warner's third Stanford All-American in 1926 following Jim Lawson (1924) and Ernie Nevers (1925). Shipkey, who played all 60 minutes in Stanford's 1925 Rose Bowl matchup with Notre Dame and the '27 Rose Bowl vs. Alabama, was a three-year letterman from 1924-26. He scored Stanford's only touchdown in the '25 Rose Bowl on a seven-yard reception. In the 1927 Rose Bowl (a 7-7 tie with Alabama), Shipkey carried the ball twice on end-arounds, caught five passes and recovered two fumbles while playing outstanding defense. During his three years as a letterman, Shipkey's teams went 24-3-1, appeared in two Rose Bowls and won one national championship.

STANFORD LORE

The Harris J. Ryan High-Voltage Laboratory for the study of power transmission opened on September 17, 1926. Over 300 guests at the opening watched a demonstration of six 2,100,000-volt flashovers in air between electrodes 20-feet apart. Professor Ryan and his associates solved many problems of long-distance power transmission, including those of the lines connecting the Hoover Dam on the Colorado River with Los Angeles.

1927-28

- September 30, 1927:   Babe Ruth slugged his record-setting 60th home run for the New York Yankees.
- October 6, 1927:   The world's first talking motion picture, "The Jazz Singer", starring Al Jolson using the sound-on-film process, was released.
- November 13, 1927:   The Holland Tunnel, America's first underwater tunnel, was opened to traffic, linking New Jersey to Manhattan.
- May 5, 1928   Amelia Earhart became the first woman to fly an airplane across the Atlantic.
- July 30, 1928:   George Eastman demonstrated the world's first color motion pictures at Rochester, New York.

STANFORD MOMENT

First Rose Bowl Victory

For the third time in four years, Pop Warner's team was selected to represent the Pacific Coast Conference in the Rose Bowl. This time, however, Stanford came away with its first Rose Bowl victory in school history by defeating Warner's former team, Pittsburgh, 7-6 in front of 65,000 in Pasadena. Stanford's Frankie Wilton, who a year earlier had his punt blocked in the Rose Bowl against Alabama, got a chance to redeem himself. He began the game, however, by getting further into Warner's doghouse. Wilton's fumble was scooped up by the Panther's Jimmy Hagen and returned 20-yards for a touchdown. Fortunately for Stanford, the extra point failed. In the third quarter, on a fourth-and-goal from

Pop Warner led his team to its third Rose Bowl in four years, but this time Stanford took home a victory by defeating Pittsburgh 7-6. It was Stanford's first-ever Rose Bowl victory. *(Stanford Athletics)*

the Pitt two yard line, Stanford's Biff Hoffman took a screen pass and raced straight for the goal line. Just before he reached the end zone, Hoffman was hit and fumbled the ball. The ball bounced left, directly to Wilton, who took it away from three Pitt players and then streaked in for the score. Hoffman kicked the extra point and Stanford had its first Rose Bowl win.

TWO OF THE GREATEST TRACK AND FIELD ATHLETES who ever donned a Stanford uniform enjoyed storybook years in 1928. Bud Spencer set the world record in the 400-meter dash (47.0) and was a member of the world-record setting 1600-meter relay team (3:14.2) and the world record mile relay team (3:13.4). After winning the NCAA title in the 440-yard dash in a world-best time of 47.7, Spencer went on to capture an Olympic gold medal at the 1928 Games in Amsterdam as a member of the U.S. 1600-meter relay team. While Bob King did not set any world records, he nevertheless won an Olympic gold medal in the high jump at the Games in Amsterdam and placed first in the NCAA championship with a personal best of 6-6 5/8.

Stanford Stat . . .

Dink Templeton's track team won its second NCAA championship in 1928 as five individuals all won their events. Winning NCAA titles were Bud Spencer in the 440-yard dash, Ward Edmonds in the pole vault, Eric Krenz in the discus, Harlow Rothert in the shot put and Robert King in the high jump. Stanford scored an NCAA-meet record 72 points to bring home the second national championship in school history.

STANFORD LIST

STANFORD ATHLETES WHO HAVE WON AT LEAST TWO OLYMPIC GOLD MEDALS IN INDIVIDUAL EVENTS

Name (gold medals)

Sport	Event	(year)
Norman Ross (2)		
Swimming	400-meter freestyle	(1920)
	1,500-meter freestyle	(1920)
Al White (2)		
Diving	Platform diving	(1924)
	Springboard diving	(1924)
Pete DesJardins (2)		
Diving	Platform diving	(1928)
	Springboard diving	(1928)
Bob Mathias (2)		
Track	Decathlon	(1948)
	Decathlon	(1952)
John Hencken (2)		
Swimming	200-meter breaststroke	(1972)
	100-meter breaststroke	(1976)
Janet Evans (4)		
Swimming	400-meter freestyle	(1988)
	800-meter freestyle	(1988)
	400-meter I.M.	(1988)
	800-meter freestyle	(1992)

Stanford LEGEND

Pete DesJardins

Pete DesJardins won two gold medals at the 1928 Olympic Games in Amsterdam. (Stanford Athletics)

Born in St. Pierre, Manitoba, Canada, Pete DesJardins began diving as a small boy in Miami Beach, then migrated to Stanford to train under Ernie Brandsten. After winning two gold medals and one silver medal in two Olympics, DesJardins continued to dive professionally well into his 50s. He won his first medal—a silver in the springboard event—at the 1924 Games in Paris. After training with Brandsten, DesJardins went to the 1928 Games in Amsterdam and came away a double-gold medalist in both platform and springboard. He was rather fortunate to win the platform event, however. Farid Simiaka, an Egyptian diver who attended UCLA, was on the victory stand with his national anthem playing when the decision was reversed. Four of the five judges had placed DesJardins ahead of Simiaka and, under the rules, the gold medal went to DesJardins. Following his competitive career, DesJardins, an economics major at Stanford, began performing in a Miami water show with Johnny Weissmuller and with the Billy Rose Aquacades.

STANFORD LORE

Stanford alum Herbert Hoover, after receiving the Republican Party's nomination for President of the United States, delivered his formal acceptance speech at Stanford Stadium on August 12, 1928 in front of an estimated 90,000. The entire ceremony was broadcast on radio from coast to coast.

1928-29

- October 9, 1928:   The St. Louis Cardinals were swept in four straight games by the New York Yankees at the World Series.
- November 6, 1928:   Stanford alum Herbert Hoover, the football manager in 1892, was elected President of the United States in a landslide victory over Alfred Smith.
- May 16, 1929:   "Wings" was selected as the best picture of the year at the first Academy Awards.
- June 30, 1929:   Bobby Jones won the U.S. Open golf tournament over runner-up Al Espinosa.
- July 5, 1929:   Helen Wills won the women's singles title at the Wimbledon tennis championship in England for the third consecutive year.

Biff Hoffman, captain of the 1928 Indians, saw his team come back from a 13-0 deficit to tie Cal 13-13 in the Big Game. *(Stanford Athletics)*

STANFORD MOMENT

Stanford Erases 13-0 Deficit to Tie Cal in Big Game

In a game many consider to be one of the finest Big Games in history, Stanford came back from a 13-0 halftime deficit to score a touchdown in the final minute of play and tie Cal 13-13 before 82,000 at Memorial Stadium in Berkeley. Trailing 13-0 at the half, Stanford coach Pop Warner decided to bench several of his veteran players and go with a younger squad who "might breathe new life into our sputtering attack." Len Frentrup took over for Frank Wilton and Bill Simkins replaced captain Biff Hoffman in the backfield. Simkins scored on a short run to bring Stanford within a touchdown at 13-7. The Cardinal mounted a final drive beginning at the Cal 34-yard line following a 21-yard punt return by Frentrup. On a fourth-and-10 from the Bear's 24-yard line with less than a minute to play, Simkins hit Frentrup in the end zone for a 24-yard game-tying TD. Cal's Frank Fitz blocked the extra point and the game ended in a 13-13 tie.

THE POWER OF COLLEGE FOOTBALL was beginning to change and Stanford, led by Pop Warner, was at the forefront. When Warner moved west to Stanford from Pittsburgh in 1924, it sent a signal that college football in the west was about to close the gap with the east. And in 1928, Warner took his Stanford team to Yankee Stadium on December 1 to face Army in a much-publicized game that drew a sellout crowd of over 86,000. After spending three days and four nights on a train from San Francisco to New York, Stanford arrived in New York prepared to play an Army team that had lost just one game all season to Notre Dame. A one-sided Cadet victory was the talk of the town. In what many consider to be the greatest exhibition of Warner's offense, Stanford proceeded to shutout Army 26-0 and stun the college football world. "This was the day which I had long awaited," said Warner. "My Stanford team had come back to the East and conquered the best that the East had to offer. Now, I knew that the Cardinal football program had truly arrived and deserved to be considered among the elite of college football."

Stanford Stat . . .

Ward Edmonds is the only athlete in Stanford history to win the NCAA championship in the pole vault. While Stanford has had pole vaulters who have set world records and won Olympic gold medals, Edmonds remains as the only one to win an NCAA title. He won the 1928 championship with a vault of 16-6 1/4 in helping Stanford win its first NCAA team title. A year later, Edmonds tied for the NCAA championship with a vault of 13-8 7/8. "My own favorite of all come-through athletes was Skinny Ward Edmonds," said his coach at Stanford, Dink Templeton.

STANFORD LIST

GREAT BIG GAME FINISHES

November 22, 1947—Cal won 21-18 on a Jackie Jensen to Paul Keckley 80-yard TD pass with less than 3:00 to play.

November 18, 1972—Cal won 24-21 on the game's final play —an 8-yard TD pass from Vince Ferragamo to Steve Sweeny.

November 23, 1974—Stanford won 22-20 on a Mike Langford 50-yard field goal in the game's final seconds.

November 20, 1976—Stanford recovered a Cal fumble on the two-yard line with 1:31 remaining and trailing 24-19. Ron Inge scored the game-winning TD moments later, giving Stanford a 27-24 victory.

November 20, 1982—"The Play." Cal's infamous five-lateral play on the final kickoff resulted in a controversial TD that gave the Bears a 25-20 win.

November 19, 1988—Stanford's Tuan Van Le blocked a field-goal attempt with four seconds to play to preserve a 19-19 tie.

November 17, 1990—Stanford scored nine points in the final 12 seconds to win 27-25. John Hopkins hit the game-winning field goal as time ran out.

Stanford LEGEND

Seraphim Post
Don Robesky

The best guard tandem in college football in 1928 was Seraphim Post (top) and Don Robesky, both named All-Americans. (Stanford Athletics)

Together they formed the best guard-tandem in college football in 1928. Seraphim "Dynamite" Post and Don Robesky were the heart-and-soul of the Stanford line, one of the main reasons why Pop Warner's team went 8-3-1 in '28. Both Post and Robesky were considered consensus All-Americans in 1928. Every All-America team chosen that year included either Post or Robesky. "How can I choose between them," Warner would say. "They are both deserving of All-America recognition." Post and Robesky were Stanford's first All-American linemen and the fourth and fifth football players in school history to be honored as All-Americans. "Robesky and Post were undoubtedly the two best guards I ever saw play," said Warner.

STANFORD LORE

Herbert Hoover, class of 1895, was at his campus home on November 6, 1928 when he heard the news that he had been elected the 31st President of the United States. Hoover defeated democratic candidate Alfred E. Smith in a landslide victory. Hoover won 444 electoral votes to Smith's 87. Following the news of Hoover's election, students and others, led by John Philip Sousa and his band, marched to Hoover's campus home, now known as the Lou Henry Hoover House, to pay tribute to the new president-elect.

•• AMERICA'S TIME CAPSULE ••

- October 29, 1929: A record 16,410,000 shares were traded for whatever they would bring, signaling the beginning of the American Depression.
- November 29, 1929: Lt. Commander Richard E. Byrd completed the first flight over the South Pole.
- March 13, 1930: The planet Pluto was identified from an observatory in Flagstaff, Arizona.
- June 7, 1930: Gallant Fox captured horse racing's Triple Crown with a victory at the Belmont Stakes.
- June 12, 1930: Germany's Max Schmeling defeated Jack Sharkey to win the world heavyweight boxing championship.

The Immortal Twenty-One

STANFORD MOMENT

On the evening of April 3, 1930, the legend of the Immortal Twenty-one was born. The Stanford Axe, which was captured by the University of California on April 15, 1899 following a baseball game, had been kept in Berkeley for 31 years. Attempt after attempt by Stanford students to regain it proved frustrating. Then, along came the Immortal Twenty-one. The Axe was kept in a bank vault and taken out only for Cal's annual Axe Rally. At around 7:00 p.m. following the rally, the Axe was being taken from an armored car to the bank when two Stanford students, posing as photographers, released a shot of flashlight powder with a blinding flash that temporarily blinded the Cal custodian who held the Axe. Stanford student Howard Avery then wrestled the Axe away from the custodian, tossed it to Bob Loofbourow who got into a car driven by Jim Trimingham and headed to Palo Alto. Other members of the Immortal Twenty-one, posing as Cal students, led search parties in the wrong direction. When the Immortal Twenty-one returned to campus, the celebration began. Classes were canceled for two days and the University presented each member of the Immortal Twenty-one with a block "S" letter.

Stanford SPOTLIGHT

Eric Krenz was an NCAA champion, a world record holder and an Olympian.
(Stanford Athletics)

ERIC KRENZ AND HARLOW ROTHERT
teamed in the shot put and discus to give Stanford the most formidable duo in the weight events in the country. Together, Krenz and Rothert dominated the shot and discus at the intercollegiate level. Krenz won an NCAA championship, set a world record and earned a spot on the 1928 United States Olympic Team. Krenz won the discus (149-2) at the 1928 NCAA championship in leading Stanford to the team title for the second time in four years. He finished fourth at the '28 Olympics in Amsterdam in the shot put. In 1930, he set a world record by throwing the discus 167-5 3/8. Krenz and Rothert still stand today as Stanford's greatest duo in the shot and discus.

Stanford Stat . . .

The Stanford Golf Course was formally opened on January 1, 1930. When the Board of Athletic Control authorized Athletic Director Al Masters to build the course, Masters hired golf architect William P. Bell, best known as the architect of the Pebble Beach Golf Course. Original cost of the course was approximately $160,000 and subsequent additions of the pro shop and clubhouse brought the overall total to $240,000. Preliminary work began in 1927 and although there was some casual play in 1929 before its completion, the grand opening occurred on New Year's Day, 1930.

STANFORD LIST

STANFORD UNIVERSITY ATHLETIC FACILITIES' OPENING DATES

Facility	Year Opened
Stanford Stadium	1921
Stanford Golf Course	1930
Sunken Diamond	1931
Roble Gym	1932
Maples Pavilion	1969
deGuerre Pool Complex	1974
Varsity Hockey Field	1983
Harry Maloney Field	1988
Stanford Tennis Stadium	1989
Burnham Pavilion	1989
Ford Center	1990
Arrillaga Family Sports Center	1994

Stanford LEGEND

Harlow Rothert

Harlow Rothert is the only athlete in school history to earn three letters in four sports. (Stanford Athletics)

Harlow Rothert's resume is quite impressive. His claim as one of the truly great all-around athletes in the nation during his era is hard to argue. Consider the facts: Rothert was a nine-time letterman at Stanford as he earned three letters each in football, basketball and track from 1928-30. He was a two-time member of the United States' Olympic Track team (1928, 1932) and a silver medalist in the shot put at the '32 Games in Los Angeles. Rothert set a world record in the shot put in 1930 with a toss of 52-1 5/8. He won the NCAA title in the shot put for three consecutive seasons (1928-30) and was a member of Stanford's 1928 NCAA championship team. In basketball, Rothert became the first player in school history to be named First-Team All-American. In his spare time, Rothert was a halfback and fullback for Pop Warner's Stanford teams of 1928-30. His three football teams compiled a record of 26-6-2. Perhaps no athlete in the history of Stanford University has accomplished more in three different sports than the legendary Harlow Rothert.

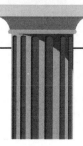

STANFORD LORE

Following the theft of the Axe by the Immortal Twenty-one on April 3, 1930, the Axe remained in a bank vault for two years because of fears of rioting if it appeared in public. After three years of negotiating, the presidents of the two student bodies agreed that the Axe would be a trophy given to the winner of the Big Game. The Axe has been stolen at least eight times since 1930, but none that rival the drama of the Immortal Twenty-one.

1930-31

·· AMERICA'S TIME CAPSULE ··

- **September 30, 1930:** Bobby Jones became the first player to capture golf's Grand Slam when he won the U.S. Amateur tournament.

- **December 11, 1930:** The powerful Bank of the United States closed in New York City due to the depressing economic crisis.

- **January 7, 1931:** The President's Emergency Committee for Unemployment Relief announced that between four and five million Americans were out of work.

- **March 3, 1931:** President Herbert Hoover, Stanford class of 1895, signed a congressional act making "The Star Spangled Banner" the USA's national anthem.

- **May 1, 1931:** The Empire State Building, the world's tallest building, opened in New York City.

STANFORD MOMENT

Indians Crush Cal 41-0 in Big Game

Harlow Rothert ran for three second-half touchdowns as Stanford handed California the largest Big Game defeat in series history, 41-0, in front of 82,000 at Memorial Stadium in Berkeley on November 30, 1930. Stanford led just 6-0 at the intermission, but 22 unanswered points in the third quarter put the Indians well out of reach of the struggling Bears. Rothert, who did not play in the first half, rushed the ball 19 times for a game-high 88 yards and three touchdowns. He also passed for one TD, that coming on a 63-yarder to All-American Phil Moffat. The win pushed Stanford's record to 8-1-1 and extended the Indians' unbeaten string vs. Cal to seven games (5-0-2 since 1923). The Indians concluded the season with a 14-7 win over Dartmouth and ended the 1930 campaign with an impressive 9-1-1 record.

TWO OF THE FINEST PERFOR-MANCES in Stanford athletic history were turned in during the spring of 1931: Keith Gledhill's NCAA singles championship in tennis and the Indians' mile relay team setting a new world record. Gledhill became the second Stanford tennis player to win the NCAA singles crown (the other was Philip Neer in 1921). He teamed with Joseph Coughin to win the 1932 NCAA doubles title and followed that achievement by winning the National Doubles Championship in '32 and the Australian Open doubles title in '33. Stanford's mile relay team of Maynor Shove, Abe Hables, Ike Hables and Ben Eastman set the world record in 1931 with a time of 3:12.6.

In 1931, Keith Gledhill became the second Stanford tennis player to win the National Singles Championship. Gledhill also won the doubles title in 1932. (Stanford Athletics)

Stanford Stat . . .

Celebrating the completion of Sunken Diamond, Harry Wolter put together his finest baseball team in 1931 as he led the Indians to an 18-5 overall record and a 15-3 mark in the California Intercollegiate Baseball Association, giving Stanford its first conference title in baseball. Sunken Diamond was created in the large pit which remained after dirt was borrowed for construction of an addition to Stanford Stadium. Right-handed pitcher Dan Johnson was the team's top player as he hurled 110 of the 205 innings pitched by Stanford during the entire season. He also won 12 of the 15 CIBA victories, including all three vs. California.

STANFORD LIST

STANFORD'S ALL-PRO NFL TEAM

Name	Pro Bowls	Year (s)
Frankie Albert	1	1951
Bruno Banducci	1	1955
John Brodié	2	1966, '71
Chris Burford	1	1962 (AFL)
Pat Donovan	4	1980-83
John Elway	6	1987, '88, '90, '92, '94, '95
Hugh Gallarneau	1	1942
Tony Hill	3	1979, '80, '86
Brian Holloway	3	1984-86
James Lofton	8	1979, '81-86, '92
Glyn Miburn	1	1996
Blaine Nye	2	1975, '77
Hamp Pool	2	1940, '42
Jeff Siemon	4	1974, '76, '77, '78
Norm Standlee	2	1942, '51
Gene Washington	4	1970-73
Paul Wiggin	2	1966, '68

Stanford LEGEND

Phil Moffat

Phil Moffat's name appears in the Stanford record book for rushing, interceptions and punt returns. (Stanford Athletics)

One of the most versatile players in Stanford history, Phil Moffat's name peppers the Stanford record books in rushing, punt returns and interceptions. While he was a First-Team All-American as a half-back in 1930, Moffat excelled as a punt returner and defensive back as well. His 5.9 career yards per carry average (193 carries, 1,139 yards, 12 TDs) is an all-time Stanford record. He is also the school record holder with 20 career interceptions, and his nine interceptions in 1930 is tied for the Stanford season record. Moffat's 41 punt returns in 1930 and his 13 returns vs. Dartmouth the same year still stand today as Stanford records. He had 72 punt returns in his career for 718 yards and a 10.0 average—all three of which are still listed on the school's all-time top-10 charts. Moffat, who starred at Stanford from 1929-31, was selected to Stanford's "All-Oldtimers" Team.

STANFORD LORE

The ASSU Executive Committee officially adopted the Indian as a symbol for Stanford on November 25, 1930 following an emotional Big Game Rally. The Indian symbol first appeared in 1923 by former football player Dr. Tom Williams, class of '97. Recent excavation of Indian archeological sites in the campus area, combined with the image of this symbol as the conqueror of bears and other animal mascots, led to its popularity among alumni and the news media. The school color, "Cardinal," continued to symbolize Stanford as well.

1931-32

·· AMERICA'S TIME CAPSULE ··

- **October 25, 1931:** The George Washington Bridge, connecting Manhattan with New Jersey across the Hudson River, was opened to traffic.
- **March 1, 1932:** Charles A. Lindbergh, Jr., 20-month-old son of the famous aviator, was kidnapped from his home at Hopewell, New Jersey.
- **May 20, 1932:** Amelia Earhart became the first woman to cross the Atlantic in a solo flight when she landed near Londonderry, Ireland, 2,026 1/2 miles from her starting point in Harbor Grace, Newfoundland.
- **July 2, 1932:** Franklin Roosevelt accepted the Democratic party's nomination for president, and announced his plan for a "new deal."
- **August 14, 1932:** The United States won the unofficial team championship at the Summer Olympic Games in Los Angeles by claiming 16 gold medals.

STANFORD MOMENT

Bill Miller's first victory in the pole vault came at the most opportune time: the 1932 Olympic Games. *(Stanford Athletics)*

Bill Miller Wins Olympic Gold

Bill Miller picked a great time to win his first major event. He was a world-record holder and a contender to win a medal at the 1932 Olympic Games in Los Angeles, but Miller had never won a major title. At the U.S. Olympic Trials, Miller's best vault of 14-1 1/4" placed him second to Bill Graber's mark of 14-4 1/4". At the Olympics three weeks later, Graber could only manage a fourth place finish while Miller won the gold with a best of 14-1 3/4". He set a world-record in 1932 in the pole vault by clearing 14-1 7/8". Previous to the '32 Games, Miller's best finish was a three-way tie for first at the 1932 Intercollegiate 4A Championships. Miller followed three of the world's great pole vaulter who also attended Stanford: Two-time Olympian Sam Bellah and former world-record holders Norman Dole and Leland Scott.

HEC DYER was another great track athlete in Dink Templeton's stable at Stanford. Dyer won a gold medal at the 1932 Olympic Games in Los Angeles as a member of the U.S. 4x100 relay team. Dyer ran the third leg of the United States' sprint relay team that set world records in both the heats and finals. While at Stanford, Dyer posted a personal best in the 100-yard dash of 9.6, a mark he set in a dual meet against USC in April of 1930.

Stanford Stat . . .

Although the Indian football team finished the season with a respectable 7-2-2 record, it was the worst mark in Pop Warner's eight seasons on The Farm. Stanford went scoreless in four games—and they went 0-2-2 in those contests. For the fourth straight season, the Indians lost to USC and for the first time in Warner's tenure, Stanford lost the Big Game to Cal. Scoreless ties with Washington and the Olympic Club left a bitter taste with Stanford faithful and set the stage for grumbling among alumni and Warner's critics.

STANFORD LIST

STANFORD'S OLYMPIC MEDALISTS IN TRACK AND FIELD

Year	Name	Event	Medal
1912	George Horine	High Jump	Bronze
1920	Morris Kirksey	100m	Silver
		400m Relay	Gold
1920	John Norton	400m Hurdles	Silver
1920	Feg Murray	100m Hurdles	Bronze
1924	Glen Hartranft	Shot Put	Silver
1928	Bob King	High Jump	Gold
1928	Bud Spencer	1600m Relay	Gold
1932	Ben Eastman	400m	Silver
1932	Bill Miller	Pole Vault	Gold
1932	Hec Dyer	400m Relay	Gold
1932	Harlow Rothert	Shot Put	Silver
1932	Henry Laborde	Discus	Bronze
1936	Gordon Dunn	Discus	Silver
1948	Bob Mathias	Decathlon	Gold
1952	Bob Mathias	Decathlon	Gold
1964	Dave Weill	Discus	Bronze
1996	Chryste Gaines	400m Relay	Gold

Stanford LEGEND

Ben Eastman

Bill Eastman was one of the best middle distance runners in Stanford history. (Stanford Athletics)

Benjamin Bangs Eastman, or "Blazin' Ben" as he was called, is without doubt one of the greatest track stars in the history of Stanford University. A tall, lanky, even awkward-looking athlete who wore glasses, Eastman proved to be the best half-miler of his era, a world record holder and an Olympic silver medalist. As a Stanford freshman in 1930, Eastman, from Burlingame High School, ran a 48.4 in the 440 and opened the eyes of not only coach Dink Templeton, but the entire track world. So far ahead of his time was Eastman that the 48.4 he ran in 1930 stood as a Stanford freshman record for 35 years. The following year, Blazin' Ben came of age. In an eight-day period in 1931, Eastman helped Stanford set a world record in the mile relay with a time of 3:12.6, then equaled Ted Meredith's 15-year-old record of 47.4 in the 440-yard dash. In 1932, Eastman shattered the 440 record by a full second as he ran an astonishing 46.4 at Stanford Stadium in a dual meet against the Los Angeles Athletic Club. Later that year, he set another world record with a 1:49.8 in the 880. At the 1932 Olympic Games in Los Angeles, Eastman took the silver medal in the 400-meters, finishing second to the great Bill Carr. Eastman continued his running and world-record breaking prowess after the '32 Games, setting world records in the 500-meters, 600-yards, 800-meters and 880-yards. He retired after the 1936 Olympic Trials.

STANFORD LORE

Chancellor Emeritus David Starr Jordan, Stanford's University's first president, died in his campus home on September 19, 1931 at the age of 80. Jordan became Stanford's first president in 1891, when the University first opened its doors, and held that position until 1913. He is largely credited with helping mold the University from its beginning. "There is only one David Starr Jordan," Jane Stanford said many years earlier.

1932-33

- November 8, 1932: In a landslide victory over Stanford alum Herbert Hoover, Franklin Roosevelt was elected president of the United States.
- March 12, 1933: The first fireside chat, a radio address to the entire nation, was delivered by President Roosevelt. His subject was the reopening of the nation's banks.
- March 13, 1933: United States banks reopened across the country following a prolonged depression.
- June 16, 1933: The Banking Act of 1933 was passed by Congress, establishing the Federal Bank Deposit Insurance Corporation.
- July 6, 1933: Babe Ruth hit a home run in major league baseball's first All-Star game, as the American League defeated the National League, 4-2.

STANFORD MOMENT

Warner Resigns After Eight Seasons

Amid reports that he was annoyed by certain Stanford alumni and frustrated by Stanford's academic requirements, legendary coach Pop Warner resigned on December 5, 1932 to accept the head coaching position at Temple University. Following the Indians' 6-4-1 season—the worst record for a Warner-coached team in nine seasons on The Farm—Dr. Thomas A. Storey, head of Stanford's physical education department and Al Masters, graduate manager, denied Warner was going to quit. "We are wholly satisfied with Mr. Warner's season," Storey said. But, shortly after those remarks, Warner announced his resignation. He said he had no fault to find with the Stanford administration or student body, but he blamed some alumni in Los Angeles for suggesting a change be made. His final record at Stanford was 71-17-8.

HE WAS CALLED the "Baby-Faced Assassin" because of his relentless assault on the opposition on both sides of the ball. For three seasons (1931-33), Bill Corbus made his claim as one of the greatest lineman in college football. He was twice named First-Team All-American—in 1932 and '33—and became Stanford's first two-time All-American in football. A native of Vallejo, California, Corbus, who played guard, also doubled as the Indian's placekicker. He was a senior on Tiny Thornhill's first team in 1933—the year the "Vow Boys" began their dominance. Corbus kicked two field goals in the fourth quarter in Stanford's 13-7 win over USC before 90,000 at the L.A. Coliseum in 1933 when the Vow Boys won their first of three straight from the Trojans. He was elected to the National Football Foundation College Football Hall of Fame in 1957.

Bill Corbus, nicknamed the "Baby-Faced Assassin" was a first-team All-American in 1932 and '33. (Stanford Athletics)

Stanford Stat . . .

Henri Laborde and Gus Meier each won NCAA titles in leading the Indians to a third-place finish at the 1933 NCAA Track and Field Championships. Laborde won a silver medal at the 1932 Olympic Games in Los Angeles in the discus and followed up that performance by winning the discus at the '33 NCAA's with a throw of 163-3 3/4. Meier won the NCAA title and set a world record in the 120-yard high hurdles with a time of 14.2.

STANFORD LIST

STANFORD FOOTBALL COACHES WHO BECAME NFL HEAD COACHES

Coach	At Stanford	NFL Team
Frankie Albert	1939-41	San Francisco 49ers
Monte Clark	1993-94	San Francisco 49ers, Detroit Lions
Rod Dowhower	1977-79	Baltimore Colts
Denny Green	1977-78, 80, 89-91	Minnesota Vikings
Ray Handley	1972-73, 79-83	New York Giants
Norb Hecker	1972-78	Atlanta Falcons
Jim Mora	1967	New Orleans Saints
John Ralston	1963-71	Denver Broncos
Clark Shaughnessy	1940-41	Los Angeles Rams
George Seifert	1972-74, 77-79	San Francisco 49ers
Dick Vermeil	1965-68	Philadelphia Eagles, St. Louis Rams
Bill Walsh	1963-64, 77-78, 92-94	San Francisco 49ers
Mike White	1964-71	Oakland Raiders
Paul Wiggin	1980-83	Kansas City Chiefs

Stanford LEGEND

John Doeg

John Doeg won the 1930 U.S. Open Singles Championship and twice won the U.S. Open Doubles title. (Stanford Athletics)

Although he played tennis at Stanford for just one season in 1929, John Doeg went on to earn the reputation as one of the finest left-handed players of his era. Following his season on The Farm, Doeg captured several tennis championships, including the 1930 U.S. Open singles title and the 1929 and '30 U.S. Open Doubles titles with his partner, George Lott. Doeg and Lott were also finalists in the doubles competition at the 1930 Wimbledon Championships. Doeg was a member of the 1930 U.S. Davis Cup team. At Stanford in 1929, Doeg went undefeated during the season in both singles and doubles and won the Pacific Coast Conference singles championship. He was named to the Stanford Athletic Hall of Fame in 1931 and the Collegiate Tennis Hall of Fame in 1992.

STANFORD LORE

Trustees adopted a resolution on May 11, 1933, to remove the limit of 500 women students who were permitted to enroll at Stanford. The new resolution, which came about at the height of the Great Depression, was due in part to increase income from tuition. The Trustees provided that the number of women should be "substantially the same proportion" as existed when Mrs. Stanford set the limit in 1889. With post-World War I enrollment increases, the ratio of females to males had dropped to 14 percent. Within a year of the limit being dropped, the enrollment of women doubled.

1933-34

- December 5, 1933:   Prohibition in the United States was repealed when Congress adopted the 21st Amendment.
- May 23, 1934:   Dr. Wallace Carothers of DuPont Laboratories developed a synthetic fiber called nylon.
- June 6, 1934:   The Securities Exchange Act was signed by President Roosevelt, providing for the creation of the Securities and Exchange Commission.
- July 16, 1934:   The first general strike in U.S. history took place in San Francisco as an expression of support for the striking 12,000 members of the International Longshoremen's Association.
- July 22, 1934:   John Dillinger, America's public enemy number one, was shot and killed in Chicago by FBI agents.

STANFORD MOMENT

The "Vow Boys" lost their first Rose Bowl game on January 1, 1934. (Stanford Athletics)

"Vow Boys" Drop 7-0 Decision to Columbia in Rose Bowl

In the first of three consecutive Rose Bowl appearances, the "Vow Boys" could not overcome a muddy and sloppy field, eight fumbles and the Columbia Lions as they lost a 7-0 decision in Stanford's fifth trip to the Rose Bowl in school history. While Stanford entered the game with an 8-1-1 record and were considered a two-touchdown favorite, too many mistakes and the Lions' hidden-ball play, know as KF79, were enough to give the visitors from the East the win. Stanford was led by such greats as fullback Bobby Grayson, who ran for 152 yards on 27 carries, tackle Robert "Bones" Hamilton, who played all 60 minutes of the 1934, '35 and '36 Rose Bowl games, two-time All-American guard Bill Corbus, and quarterback Frank Alustiza. Columbia scored the game's only touchdown on a 17-yard run by Al Barabas, who used a hidden-ball maneuver to run untouched into the end zone. Stanford fumbled the ball away eight times, including four inside the Lion's 10-yard line, on a wet and muddy Rose Bowl turf that had been subjected to 12 inches of rain during the two days leading up to the game. The Pasadena Fire Department had to pump water off the field to make it playable for the game.

DINK TEMPLETON'S TRACK TEAM won its third NCAA championship in 1934 at the Los Angeles Coliseum as Stanford defeated both USC and LSU to win the title. Stanford had two individual champions at the NCAA's: Sammy Klopstock in the 120 hurdles (14.4) and Gordon Dunn in the discus (162-7). Jimmy Wilson, injured most of his four-year career, added 12 crucial points to the Indian's cause by placing third in both the 100-yard dash and 220-yard dash. The meet was decided in the pole vault when Stanford's Bud Deacon, who was not enjoying a particularly good season, cleared 14 feet on his final attempt to give the Indians all the points they would need to win the national title.

Stanford Stat . . .

On April 21, 1934, Stanford shot putter Johnny Lyman placed his name in the track history books by becoming the first athlete to break the 54-foot barrier in the shot put. His put of 54 feet, 1 inch not only helped Stanford beat Cal 81-50 in the Big Meet— Stanford's 11th consecutive win over the Bears—but it broke the world record and gave Lyman a place in track and field history. Unfortunately for Lyman, his record was broken just two weeks later by an LSU shot putter named Jack Torrance.

STANFORD LIST

DINK TEMPLETON'S RECORD OF SUCCESS (1921-39)

11 of 19 teams ranked in top four
71-25-2 dual meet record

NCAA Championships (3): 1925, 1928, 1934

NCAA Runner-up (3): 1937, 1938, 1939

NCAA Third Place (3): 1933, 1935 (tie), 1936

NCAA Fourth Place (2): 1929, 1930

Stanford LEGEND

Dink Templeton

Dink Templeton won three NCAA championships in 19 years as the Indians' head track coach. (Stanford Athletics)

The labels used to describe Richard Lyman "Dink" Templeton included controversial, colorful, fiery, brilliant, gravel-voiced and perfectionist. He was also described as perhaps the greatest track and field coach of his era, a man who produced winners, Olympic champions and team championships. For Dink Templeton knew of only one method of coaching— and that was to work, work, work. He thrived on challenging the track and field establishment, introducing unorthodox techniques and convincing his athletes that they could accomplish things they never believed possible. A rugby, track and football player at Stanford, Templeton earned a gold medal as a member of U.S. Olympic Rugby Team at the 1920 Games in Amsterdam. He also placed fourth in the long jump at the '20 Games. Following his graduation from Stanford, where he earned a law degree, Templeton became the Indians head track coach in 1921 at the age of 24. In 19 years at the helm (1921-39), Templeton's teams won three NCAA team championships, finished second three times and placed among the nation's top four 11 times. His athletes won 22 national individual titles, set 16 world records and won nine Olympic medals. After leaving Stanford in 1939, Templeton worked as a radio broadcaster and a journalist while coaching at the Olympic Club in San Francisco.

STANFORD LORE

After losing several games to USC, the freshman football team of 1932 vowed to never again lose to the Trojans—and they never did. During their first season on the varsity in 1933, the "Vow Boys" traveled to the Los Angeles Coliseum and defeated a USC team that had won 27 consecutive games and were the defending national champions. The 13-7 victory over the Trojans almost did not take place. The train carrying the Stanford players to Los Angeles was delayed for five hours in Salinas by a washout. Stanford did arrive, however, sleepless, and one hour before kickoff.

1934-35

- October 9, 1934:   Dizzy Dean and the St. Louis Cardinals won the World Series over the Detroit Tigers.
- December 9, 1934:   The New York Giants won the NFL championship by beating the Chicago bears 30-13.
- May 6, 1935:   The Works Progress Administration (WPA) began operation, giving jobs to millions of Americans.
- May 24, 1935:   More than 20,000 fans at Cincinnati's Crosley Field watched their Reds beat the Philadelphia Phillies in baseball's first-ever night game.
- August 14, 1935:   President Roosevelt signed the Social Security Act, establishing payment of benefits to senior citizens.

STANFORD MOMENT

"Vow Boys" Reach Second Straight Rose Bowl

The "Vow Boys" reached their second straight Rose Bowl, but lost 29-13 to Alabama. (Stanford Athletics)

Tiny Thornhill led the "Vow Boys" to a second straight Rose Bowl appearance and another outstanding regular season, but once again Stanford finished the year with a loss in the Rose Bowl, this time 29-13 to Alabama and its great passing combination of Dixie Howell and Don Hutson. While establishing itself as one of the top teams in college football, Stanford entered the Rose Bowl having given up just two touchdowns all season and had outscored its opponents 211-14. Bobby Grayson put Stanford on top 7-0 in the first quarter on a one-yard run as the Indians capitalized on a Crimson Tide fumble. From that point on, it was all Alabama. A 22-point second quarter put the game out of reach. Howell completed nine-of-12 passes for 160 yards and one touchdown—that coming on a 59-yard completion to Hutson—while also running for two more TDs from five and 67 yards out. Hutson caught six passes for 164 yards and two touchdowns. Stanford finished the season with a 9-1-1 record and left the "Vow Boys" with just one more chance to win in the Rose Bowl.

ONE OF THE original "Vow Boys," James. H. "Monk" Moscrip was a star end on both offense and defense as well as the placekicker for Stanford from 1933-35. He played in all three Rose Bowl games and was an integral part of the "Vow Boys'" three-year record of 25-4-2. Moscrip was twice named a consensus All-American as an end and, in 1985, he was named to the National Football Foundation Hall of Fame. During the 1935 season, with the "Vow Boys" attempting to get their third straight invitation to the Rose Bowl, Moscrip's placekicking was responsible for a three-game stretch during which time the Indians beat Washington 6-0, Santa Clara 9-6 and USC 3-0. Those three wins allowed the "Vow Boys" to reach their ultimate goal—a victory in the Rose Bowl. Stanford defeated SMU 7-0 on January 1, 1936 in Pasadena as Moscrip and fellow defensive end Keith Topping were named the game's Most Valuable Players after shutting down the vaunted SMU offense.

Stanford Stat . . .

Sam Klopstock set a world record in the 120-yard high hurdles in 1935 of 14.1, highlighting a season which saw Stanford place third in the national championships after winning it all a year earlier. During the 1934 season, which saw Stanford win its third national championship, Klopstock won the high hurdles in a time of 14.4.

STANFORD LIST

FOOTBALL TWO-TIME ALL-AMERICANS

Bill Corbus, guard	1932-33
Bobby Grayson, fullback	1934-35
Monk Moscrip, end	1934-35
Frankie Albert, quarterback	1940-41
Bill McColl, end	1950-51
Paul Wiggin, tackle	1955-56
Pat Donovan, defensive end	1973-74
Ken Margerum, flanker	1979-80
John Elway, quarterback	1980, 1982
Bob Whitfield, offensive tackle	1990-91

Stanford ❧ LEGEND ❧

Bobby Grayson

One of the most famous "Vow Boys" was Bobby Grayson, who rushed for 1,547 yards in 1933, '34, and '35. (Stanford Athletics)

Ernie Nevers was considered the best athlete of his time and the best who had ever played for Stanford University. But even Nevers was awestruck by the ability of Grayson. "He is the best back I've ever seen, and I've seen a lot of backs," Nevers said of Grayson. Indeed, the names Nevers and Grayson will forever be remembered as the greatest running backs in Stanford football history during the pre-WWII era and two of the best to ever wear the Stanford uniform. Grayson, a member of the infamous "Vow Boys," was the heart and soul of his Stanford teams. He finished his career with 1,547 yards rushing and 18 touchdowns, which remain today among the best in school history. Grayson played in three Rose Bowl games, gaining 299 yards rushing on 69 carries, including a 152-yard performance in the '34 Rose Bowl and a 119-yard rushing day in the '35 Rose Bowl. He was twice named a consensus All-American and, in 1951, became the second Stanford athlete elected to the National Football Foundation Hall of Fame.

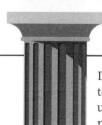

STANFORD LORE

Dr. Harry B. Reynolds, '96, suggested to President Wilbur the formation of Stanford Associates to help raise money for the university. At the time of its founding, Stanford was the richest university in the world for a short period of time. The myth persisted that the university didn't need any help. But, the value of the endowment had dropped due to inflation after World War I and the Depression. The Associates' first appeal to alumni brought in $35,000.

1935-36

- **September 8, 1935:** Powerful Louisiana politician Huey Long was assassinated in the corridor of the state capitol in Baton Rouge.
- **November 9, 1935:** The Committee for Industrial Organization (CIO) was established by John L. Lewis.
- **February 16, 1936:** At the Winter Olympics in Germany, the U.S. won two gold medals and placed fifth in the unofficial team scoring after Norway, Germany, Sweden and Finland.
- **June 12, 1936:** Kansas governor Alf Landon and Col. Frank Knox of Illinois were nominated by the Republican National Convention as its candidates for president and vice president.
- **August 16, 1936:** The Summer Olympic Games, featuring American track star Jesse Owens, ended in Berlin, Germany.

The "Vow Boys" got together for a reunion a few years after their three-straight Rose Bowl appearances. (Stanford Athletics)

STANFORD MOMENT

Third Time a Charm for "Vow Boys"

The "Vow Boys" had accomplished everything they had set out to—everything that was a part of their vow. The only goal that was left undone was winning the Rose Bowl. On January 1, 1936, the Indians gave the "Vow Boys" a fitting end to their storied careers by defeating powerful SMU 7-0 in the Rose Bowl. The Mustangs were a perfect 12-0 entering the game and their offense, led by quarterback Bobby Wilson, was considered one of the most potent in all of college football. The Indians scored what turned out to be the game's only touchdown in the first quarter on a one-yard run by quarterback Bill Paulman. After Paulman had quick-kicked to the Mustangs, defensive ends Keith Topping and Monk Moscrip downed the ball at the SMU 10-yard line. The Mustangs were forced to punt back to Stanford a short time later, giving the Indians the ball on the SMU 42-yard line. A 23-yard pass play from Bones Hamilton to James Coffis put the Indians on the 19-yard line and, a few plays later, Paulman got into the end zone for the TD. Moscrip and Topping were named the game's Most Valuable Players for their defensive efforts in limiting SMU to just 38 yards rushing and 105 passing on 11-of-31. It was a fitting end for one of college football's legendary teams—Stanford University's "Vow Boys."

THE 1935-36 STANFORD MEN'S BASKETBALL TEAM gave Indian fans a glimpse of what lay ahead. A young sophomore named Angelo "Hank'" Luisetti burst onto the national scene and helped put Stanford basketball on the map by leading the '35-36 team to a 22-7 overall record—to date the most single-season wins in school history. Luisetti, who earned the first of three-straight First-Team All-America honors, was the great all-around player and scorer sixth-year head coach John Bunn was looking for to add to his talented supported cast, which included point guard Dinty Moore and center Art Stoefen. The Indians won the Southern Division of the Pacific Coast Conference before beating Washington, winner of the PCC Northern Division, to claim the conference championship. Although the Huskies had beaten Stanford twice earlier in the season, this time it was the Indians who handed out a pair of losses. Luisetti, who led the team with a 14 point average, scored 32 in Stanford's 60-39 win over Washington in game one. In the second game, Stanford claimed the PCC title with a 48-38 win.

Stanford Stat . . .

At the age of 13 years, 267 days, Margorie Gestring became the youngest woman in history to win an Olympic gold medal. At the 1936 Berlin Games, Gestring captured the gold in the spring-board diving event, beating both teammate Katherine Rawls and defending champion Dorothy Poynton-Hill. Gestring, who later attended Stanford University, won eight AAU national titles from 1935-40.

STANFORD LIST

"VOW BOYS" RECORD OF SUCCESS

- 25-4-2 overall record from 1933-35
- First team ever to play in three consecutive Rose Bowls
- Finished 8-2-1 in 1933, 9-1-1 in '34 and 8-1 in '35
- Five members named First-Team All-Americans
- Five members elected to National Football Foundation Hall of Fame
- Undefeated in three games vs. USC
- Recorded 20 shutouts in 31 games
- Outscored opponents 476-99

Stanford LEGEND

The "Vow Boys"

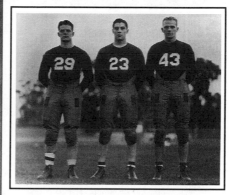

The "Vow Boys": Bones Hamilton, Monk Moscrip, and Alf Brandin.
(Stanford Athletics)

The legend of the "Vow Boys" began in the fall of 1932 following the varsity's 13-0 loss to USC Two days after that loss, quarterback Frank Alustiza gathered his freshman team together and proclaimed, "They will never do that to us. We'll never lose to USC." "Let's make that a vow," shouted halfback Bones Hamilton. And they did. In the ensuing three years (1933-35), those freshman moved on to the varsity squad and not only beat USC all three times they met, but the "Vow Boys" compiled a 25-4-2 overall record and became the first team to play in three consecutive Rose Bowls. Five of the "Vow Boys" went on to earn All-America honors, including Bobby Grayson, Monk Moscrip, Bob "Horse" Reynolds, Hamilton and Bill Corbus. The "Vow Boys'" first victory over USC in 1933 is one of the most memorable in Stanford football history. After enduring train problems and a sleepless night during their trip to Los Angeles, the "Vow Boys" arrived at the L.A. Coliseum less than an hour before kickoff. A second-quarter touchdown by Grayson and two fourth-quarter field goals by Corbus gave Stanford a 13-7 win over the Trojans, which not only stunned the crowd of 95,000, but it snapped USC's 27-game winning streak. After being frustrated in their previous two Rose Bowls, the "Vow Boys" finally brought home a Rose Bowl winner in their final game together, defeating SMU 7-0 on January 1, 1936.

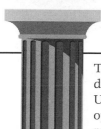

STANFORD LORE

The Class of '36 initiated a plan for students to contribute at least $1 to the Stanford Fund during their senior year. The funds would help provide "for continued growth of the University." Also assets of the University were increased after the Trustees obtained a court opinion that the Stanford Trust allow investments of endowment funds in common stocks and real estate instead of exclusively in bonds and mortgages.

1936-37

•• AMERICA'S TIME CAPSULE ••

- **November 3, 1936:** Franklin Roosevelt was elected president of the United States in a crushing victory over Republican Alf Landon.

- **May 6, 1937:** The dirigible Hindenburg burst into flames at Lakehurst, New Jersey, marking the virtual end of lighter-than-air transportation.

- **May 12, 1937:** Americans listened to the coronation of King George IV of England in radio's first world-wide broadcast.

- **May 27, 1937:** The Golden Gate Bridge in San Francisco was dedicated.

- **June 5, 1937:** Jockey Charles Kurtsinger rode War Admiral to victory at the Belmont Stakes, thus winning horse racing's Triple Crown.

Hank Luisetti and his teammates changed the game of basketball on December 30, 1936. (Stanford Athletics)

STANFORD MOMENT

Luisetti Forever Changes the Game of Basketball

On December 30, 1936, Stanford University, led by All-American Hank Luisetti, changed the way the game of basketball was played. Never before had so many seen what those "westerners" from Stanford were doing on the basketball court. The one-handed shot, a fast-break attack and the zone defense were just some of the innovations John Bunn's Stanford teams were introducing to the world. On this night in New York's Madison Square Garden, Luisetti and his mates were to face powerful Long Island University under legendary coach Clair Bee. LIU, the reigning champions of eastern basketball, had won 43 straight games and did not consider Stanford a threat to break the streak. But, in front of a standing-room-only crowd of 17,263, Stanford stunned LIU, 45-31, behind the 15-point effort of Luisetti. The game of basketball would never be the same and Luisetti became a national figure. Players from all over the country began shooting with one hand. "That night we changed the game around," Luisetti was quoted as saying. "I got credit for the one-handed shot. I'm sure someone else did it before me, but I did it in Madison Square Garden. Anytime you do something in New York, everyone hears about it."

FOR THE SECOND STRAIGHT SEASON, Stanford continued to ride on the shoulders of Hank Luisetti. Now a junior, Luisetti averaged 17.1 points per game in leading Stanford to a 25-2 record and the unofficial Helms National Championship. Luisetti, who was named First-Team All-American and the nation's Player of the Year, was surrounded by a supporting cast that included all-conference guard Bryan "Dinty" Moore and Howie Turner. Stanford won its first 14 games before losing a 42-39 decision at USC. The only other blemish on the record was a 44-31 loss to California in the third-to-last game of the year. The 25-2 record established by the '36-37 team stands today as the best single-season mark in school history.

94

Stanford Stat . . .

With Stanford head track coach Dink Templeton nearing the end of his coaching career, a group of four Indian sprinters gave Dink the last of his wonderful string of world records. On March 15, 1937 at the West Coast Relays in Fresno, California a team of four Indian sprinters stole the spotlight in the 880-yard relay. When the race was over, Stanford had not only beaten an outstanding team from USC, but Jimmy Kneubuhl, Ray Malott, Stan Hiserman and Jack Weiershauser had set a new world record with a time of 1:25.00. Led by that stunning relay, Stanford went on to capture the team title at the West Coast Relays.

STANFORD LIST

BEST MEN'S BASKETBALL RECORDS OF ALL-TIME
(min. 15 wins)

Year	Record	Winning Percentage
1936-37	25-2	.926
1941-42	28-4	.875
1937-38	21-3	.875
1940-41	21-5	.808
1920-21	15-3	.833
1988-89	26-7	.788
1935-36	22-7	.759
1955-56	18-6	.750
1996-97	22-8	.733
1961-62	16-6	.727
1995-96	19-9	.689
1994-95	19-9	.689
1951-52	19-9	.689
1948-49	19-9	.689

Stanford ❦ LEGEND ❦

Claude "Tiny" Thornhill

Coach Tiny Thornhill led the "Vow Boys" to three consecutive Rose Bowls.
(Stanford Athletics)

Claude "Tiny" Thornhill, named on January 6, 1933 to replace the legendary Pop Warner as Stanford's football coach, spent seven seasons at the helm (1933-39) of the Indian football program. As coach of the "Vow Boys," Thornhill led his team to three consecutive Rose Bowl appearances, the only football coach in school history to accomplish that feat. In his first season at the helm, his team went 8-2-1 and lost 7-0 to Columbia in the Rose Bowl. He went 9-1-1 in his second year and again led his team to Pasadena, this time losing to Alabama 29-13. But in his third year—the last for the "Vow Boys"—Thornhill's team went 8-1 and defeated SMU 7-0 in the Rose Bowl. Thornhill may have been a victim of his early success. In his first three seasons at Stanford, his teams went 25-4-2, went to three Rose Bowls and won one. After the "Vow Boys" graduated following the 1935 season, Thornhill could never live up to the expectations that Stanford fans had been accustomed to with the "Vow Boys". His final four teams went 10-21-5 and in 1939, following a 1-7-1 season, Thornhill resigned as Stanford's head coach. Still, his seven-year record of 35-25-7 and three Rose Bowl appearances are unmatched in Stanford history.

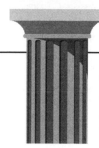

STANFORD LORE

In March, 1937, brothers Russell and Sigurd Varian and physics professor William W. Hansen began the collaboration that led to discovery of the klystrom tube, which generated high-power microwaves. The tube made commercial air navigation safer, made airborne radar possible during World War II, opened the field of world-wide communication by satellites and led to a variety of high-energy particle accelerators useful in medicine and in nuclear physics.

·· AMERICA'S TIME CAPSULE ··

- December 12, 1937: The Chicago Bears lost the NFL championship game to the Washington Redskins, 28-21.
- April 10, 1938: The German army occupied and annexed Austria.
- May 2, 1938: Thornton Wilder's "Our Town" won a Pulitzer Prize for drama.
- June 25, 1938: President Franklin Roosevelt signed the Wage and Hours Act, raising the minimum wage for workers engaged in interstate commerce from 25 cents to 40 cents per hour.
- July 1, 1938: Don Budge and Helen Wills Moody captured the Wimbledon tennis titles.

STANFORD MOMENT

Stanford Golf Team Begins Five-Year Dynasty with 1938 NCAA Championship

Under head coach Eddie Twiggs, 1938 was the beginning of a five-year dynasty for Stanford's golf program. During this time, Stanford won four NCAA team championships and numerous regional and conference titles. But it was in June of 1938 in Louisville, Kentucky, that Twiggs' team made history. Never before had a team west of Michigan won the NCAA golf championship. The Indians, however, shot 601 in the 36-hole tournament to beat runnerup Oklahoma by eight strokes. Stanford's talented foursome included John Wallace, who shot 148, Art Doering (150), Bill Boyd (151) and Brown Cannon (152). Two other members of the team, Al Hyman and Jim Rea, both competed in the tournament, but their scores of 167 did not count as only the low four scores were tallied to make the team totals.

Head basketball coach John Bunn led Stanford to the 1942 NCAA Championship with star player Hank Luisetti as his top weapon. (Stanford Athletics)

ONE COULD SAY John Bunn had two coaching careers as Stanford's basketball coach—a five-year pre-Hank Luisetti Era and the incomparable three years with Luisetti. Bunn was named the Indians' head coach in 1931 on a recommendation from Kansas coach Dr. Forrest "Phog" Allen, one of the most respected coaches in the nation. When Stanford athletic director Al Masters asked Allen for a candidate, the reply was swift in favor of Bunn. During his first five years at Stanford (1931-35), Bunn chalked up a rather unspectacular 41-70 overall record. But when Luisetti came aboard beginning with the 1935-36 season, Bunn's Indian teams took off. From 1936-38, Bunn led Stanford to 68 wins in 80 games, a school-record 25 victories and the Helm's National Championship in 1936-37. With Luisetti at the controls, Stanford went 22-7 in 1935-36, 25-2 in '36-37 and 21-3 in '37-38. Following his retirement from coaching after the '38 season, Bunn was named the Dean of Men at Stanford.

Stanford Stat . . .

Although the 1938 track season was not one of the best in Stanford history, the year enjoyed by sprinter Ray Malott has to be considered one of the finest ever. Malott, who came to Stanford as a half-miler, became one of the best quarter-milers in the world in 1938. Prior to the season, Malott was a member of Stanford's 1937 world record 880-yard relay team. As a senior in '38, Malott won every quarter-mile race he entered, which included a two-month trip through Europe during the summer. He capped his collegiate career by winning the NCAA title in the 440-yard dash in a time of 46.8.

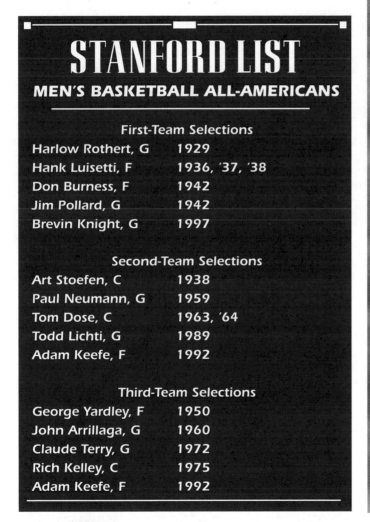

STANFORD LIST

MEN'S BASKETBALL ALL-AMERICANS

First-Team Selections

Harlow Rothert, G	1929
Hank Luisetti, F	1936, '37, '38
Don Burness, F	1942
Jim Pollard, G	1942
Brevin Knight, G	1997

Second-Team Selections

Art Stoefen, C	1938
Paul Neumann, G	1959
Tom Dose, C	1963, '64
Todd Lichti, G	1989
Adam Keefe, F	1992

Third-Team Selections

George Yardley, F	1950
John Arrillaga, G	1960
Claude Terry, G	1972
Rich Kelley, C	1975
Adam Keefe, F	1992

Stanford LEGEND

Angelo "Hank" Luisetti

Angelo "Hank" Luisetti was named All-American for three years and the player of the year for two seasons.
(Stanford Athletics)

He was dubbed the first "modern" basketball player—the first to shoot one-handed and on the run, the first to dribble and pass behind his back and the first to switch positions in game situations. Angelo "Hank" Luisetti was considered the greatest basketball player of his era, a man who revolutionized the game of basketball and a player who was clearly superior to his contemporaries in every facet of the game—shooting, dribbling, passing, defending and rebounding. Luisetti almost single-handedly put Stanford basketball on the map. In his three seasons (1936-38), he was a three-time First-Team All-American and a two-time college basketball Player of the Year. He set the school single-game scoring record in 1938 when he scored 50 points against Duquesne. His teams posted a three-year record of 68-12, including a 25-2 mark and the Helms national championship in 1936-37. He was selected to the Naismith Memorial Hall of Fame and the Helms Foundation Hall of Fame. Despite his honors, Luisetti is remembered more for the way he changed the game than for his individual greatness. Following graduation, Luisetti played two years of AAU basketball and two years with St. Mary's Pre-Flight before World War II. While serving in the Navy in November of 1944, he was stricken with spinal meningitis which ended his playing career, thus preventing fans from seeing the greatest player of his era play professional basketball.

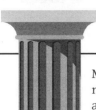

STANFORD LORE

Memorial Hall was dedicated on October 24, 1937, 18 years after it was first conceived as a memorial to Stanford's 77 dead from World War I. It was built with funds from students, alumni, trustees and faculty. The new building housed a large and little theater, radio broadcasting facilities and the Department of Drama. The names of those killed in World War II, the Korean conflict and the war in Vietnam were added later.

1938-39

- October 9, 1938: The New York Yankees defeated the Chicago Cubs in four straight games for the World Series title.
- October 30, 1938: American radio listeners panicked as Orson Welles staged his play, "War of the Worlds."
- June 8, 1939: King George VI and Queen Elizabeth of Great Britain visited President Roosevelt at the White House.
- June 12, 1939: Byron Nelson captured the U.S. Open golf tournament championship.
- June 28, 1939: The Pan American Airways airliner "Dixie Clipper" began regular transatlantic passenger service.

STANFORD MOMENT

Warren Berl leads Stanford to NCAA Golf Championship

Warren Berl turned in one of the finest individual seasons in Stanford golf history in 1939 as he led the Indians to their second straight NCAA championship while establishing himself one of the school's all-time greats. In '39, Berl became the first golfer in school history to win the conference championship. At the NCAA Championships, his 36-hole total of 147 not only led the team, but it placed him second in the nation and helped the Indians win the team title by two strokes over Northwestern. Berl was also a member of Stanford's 1941 NCAA championship team.

Stanford LEGEND

Pete Zagar

When talk turns to the best two-sport athletes at Stanford, the name Pete Zagar must be included. For three years, Zagar was a star tackle on the football team (1936-38) as well as the best discus thrower in the nation. He is one of only three athletes in Stanford history to have won three NCAA individual track championships. Zagar, a native of New Mexico, won the NCAA title in the discus in 1937 with a throw of 156-3. He bettered his marks in repeating as the NCAA discus champion in 1938 (162-3 1/4) and '39 (164-0 1/4). During those three years, Zagar helped the Indians finish second as a team in the NCAA Championships. In football, Zagar played tackle on the three teams that followed the Vow Boys. Following graduation, Zagar served in the U.S. Army during World War II.

 # STANFORD LORE

The School of Education building, made possible with funds given by Dean and Mrs. Ellwood Cubberley, was dedicated on November 12, 1938. Shortly after his arrival at Stanford in 1898, President Jordan appointed Cubberley head of the department. Despite a peak annual salary of $8,000, Cubberley gave the University stocks and bonds totaling $367,000 following his retirement in 1933. Later contributions to the University brought his gift total to $772,000. Cubberley died in 1941.

1939-40

- September 3, 1939: The nations of France and Great Britain declared war on Germany, while President Roosevelt said that the United States would remain neutral.
- December 10, 1939: The Green Bay Packers defeated the New York Giants, 27-0, to win the NFL championship.
- March 30, 1940: Indiana won its first NCAA basketball title, beating Kansas, 60-42.
- May 6, 1940: John Steinbeck won a Pulitzer prize for his book, *The Grapes of Wrath*.
- May 15, 1940: The first successful helicopter flight in the United States took place.

STANFORD MOMENT

Track team places second at NCAA's

After Dink Templeton had retired following the 1939 track season, Al Masters, then the General Manager of the Board of Athletic Control, hired Templeton's longtime assistant, Bill Ellington to take over the reigns for the 1940 season. Ellington enjoyed a fine year in his only season as the Indians head man, leading Stanford to a 3-1 dual meet record, a first place finish at the West Coast Relays, a second place showing at the conference meet and a second place finish at the NCAA Championships. Ellington's squad set three world records in 1940, including Clyde Jeffrey in the 100-yard dash, the mile relay team and Paul Moore's phenomenal run in the 1320. Moore, a junior college transfer from Fullerton, California, set his world record with a time of 2:58.7. Ellington, however, was not hired back for the 1941 season. Franklin "Pitch" Johnson coached the Indians from 1941-43.

Stanford 🦅 LEGEND 🦅

Clyde Jeffrey

Clyde Jeffrey was the last of the great sprinters who ran for the Indians and gained worldwide recognition as one of the best of his time. First came Morris Kirksey in the early 1920s, then Bud Spencer later in the decade, and then "Blazin'" Ben Eastman in the early 1930s. Jeffrey, who won the NCAA championship in 1939 in the 220-yard dash, appeared on the world stage in 1940 when he tied the world record in the 100-yard dash at 9.4 and was a member of the world-record setting mile relay team (3:10.5). Jeffrey became the third man in history to run 9.4 in the 100-yard dash. He teamed with Charles Shaw, Ernie Clark and Craig Williamson to break the mile relay record.

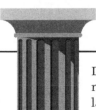

STANFORD LORE

During the summer of 1939, Charles Lindbergh paid a secret visit to Stanford to inspect the research work of professor Durand and others in the Daniel Guggenheim Aeronautic laboratory. He and the faculty in aeronautics discussed aviation in general over lunch at the Stanford Union.

1940-41

•• AMERICA'S TIME CAPSULE ••

- September 16, 1940: Congress passed the Selective Service Act, requiring all men between the ages of 20 and 36 to register for the armed services.
- November 5, 1940: Franklin Roosevelt defeated Republican Wendell Willkie for a second term as president.
- December 8, 1940: The Chicago Bears beat the Washington Redskins 73-0 in the NFL Championship game.
- June 22, 1941: Germany invaded the U.S.S.R.
- July 17, 1941: Joe DiMaggio's incredible baseball hitting streak of 56 consecutive games was ended by the Cleveland Indians.

STANFORD MOMENT

The "Wow Boys" went 10-0 in 1940 and defeated Nebraska 21-13 in the Rose Bowl. (Stanford Athletics)

"Wow Boys" Beat Nebraska in 1941 Rose Bowl

There were skeptics in the football world who, before the 1941 Rose Bowl game between Stanford and Nebraska, were not convinced of this new style of offensive football called the "T" Formation. But after the second-ranked "Wow Boys" had beaten seventh-ranked Nebraska 21-13, the critics were silenced. Although Clark Shaughnessy and his Stanford team had been using the "T" from the outset of the 1940 season, it is this Rose Bowl game that is considered the clincher that convinced football pundits that the "T" was the offense of the future. Stanford's backfield of QB Frankie Albert, halfbacks Pete Kmetovic and Hugh Gallarneau and fullback Norm Standlee scored all three touchdowns for the Indians, gained 254 yards rushing and helped bring Stanford its first undefeated season since Pop Warner's 1926 team. Shaughnessy would later call this backfield one of the greatest of all-time in American football. "The 1941 Rose Bowl game was an important one in the course of football," Shaughnessy said. "because that was the game that sold the "T" Formation to college football. Everybody accepted the "T" after the game. That's why I contend that it was one of the most important games of modern football," he said.

Stanford SPOTLIGHT

STANFORD'S third NCAA championship in golf in four years further established the Indians under coach Eddie Twiggs as the nation's top program. The '41 team shot 580 during the 36-hole NCAA Championship in Columbus, Ohio to win the title. This team was perhaps the most talented of all of Twiggs' teams. All-time greats Warren Berl and Bud Finger, members of the 1939 championship team, teamed with another all-time great, Bud Brownell, and Dee Replogle in 1941. At the NCAA's, Brownell led the way for Stanford by shooting 143, followed by Finger at 144, Berl had 146 and Replogle shot 147. Brownell won the conference title in 1941 and placed second at the NCAA Championships. The following year, on November 26, 1941, Brownell set the Stanford Course record by shooting 63 and cementing his name as one of the school's all-time great golfers.

Stanford Stat . . .

He was called a mad scientist and eccentric, obsessed with football strategy. He was recognized as changing the face of football, of revolutionizing the game as never before. You see, Clark Shaughnessy gave us the T-Formation and after its debut on September 28, 1940, football would never be the same. Shaughnessy coached at Stanford for just two seasons, 1940 and '41, but his impact was felt for years to come. He inherited a team that had gone 1-7-1 in 1939, but in his two years the Indians went 16-3, including 10-0 in 1940 and a Rose Bowl win. "He started a whole new era in coaching," said 1940 team member Pete Kmetovic.

STANFORD LIST

STANFORD PLAYERS IN THE NATIONAL FOOTBALL FOUNDATION HALL OF FAME

Player	At Stanford	Year Elected
Ernie Nevers, fb	1923-25	1951
Bobby Grayson, fb	1933-35	1955
Frankie Albert, qb	1939-41	1956
Bill Corbus, g	1931-33	1957
Bob Reynolds, t	1933-35	1961
Bones Hamilton, hb	1933-35	1972
Bill McColl, e	1949-51	1973
Hugh Gallarneau, fb	1938-41	1982
Chuck Taylor, g	1940-42	1984
Monk Moscrip, rb	1933-35	1985
John Brodie, qb	1954-56	1986
Jim Plunkett, qb	1968-70	1989
Chris Burford, e	1956-59	1995

Stanford ✽ LEGEND ✽

Frankie Albert

Frankie Albert was a two-time All-American first-round NFL draft choice, NFL Pro Bowl player and the head coach of the San Francisco 49ers. (Stanford Athletics)

There can be no argument that one of the true legends of Stanford University is Frankie Albert, quarterback of the undefeated "Wow Boys," two-time All-American, first-round NFL draft pick, member of the National Football Foundation Hall of Fame, NFL Pro Bowl player and former head coach of the San Francisco 49ers.

Albert played tailback in Stanford's single-wing offense in 1939 as a sophomore, but when rookie head coach Clark Shaughnessy moved Albert to quarterback in his "T-Formation," Albert and the Indians catapulted to the top of the college football map. The "Wow Boys" turned a 1-7-1 team of 1939 into a 10-0 squad in 1940 that won the conference title and beat Nebraska in the Rose Bowl. Albert was named All-American and finished third in the Heisman Trophy balloting. The next year, Albert was again named All-American and was fourth in the Heisman balloting. In the 1942 NFL draft, the Chicago Bears made Albert their first-round draft pick. Albert, however, signed a professional football contract with the San Francisco 49ers of the All-American Football Conference in 1946. He was named the league's co-MVP in 1948 with Otto Graham. Albert finished his pro career with the Calgary Stampeeders in 1953. He served as the 49ers radio-TV broadcaster in 1954, was named an assistant coach in 1955 and became the Niner's head coach in 1956. Albert coached only three seasons (1956-58), compiling a record of 19-16-1. Indeed, the great Frankie Albert will always be synonymous with the legends of Stanford University.

STANFORD LORE

The University opened its 50-year celebration on Founder's Day, March 9, 1941. President Wilbur spoke in appreciation of the Stanfords, followed by the traditional march to the Stanford Mausoleum and a concert featuring the debut of a work written for the occasion. From June 16-20, a symposium, "The University and the Future of America," and an academic convocation featured speakers on education, science, civilization and the war in Europe.

1941-42

- December 7, 1941: About 3,000 Americans lost their lives when the Japanese attacked Pearl Harbor, Hawaii.
- December 8, 1941: Congress declared war on Japan.
- December 11, 1941: Germany and Italy declared war against the United States and Congress adopted a resolution recognizing a state of war.
- April 8, 1942: America bombers, under the command of Maj. Gen. James Doolittle, conducted a successful air raid on Tokyo.
- June 6, 1942: The Battle of Midway ended with the U.S. gaining an important victory over the Japanese. The Japanese lost 275 ships and 4,800 men as the U.S. repulsed an attempt to seize the island.

One of the greatest teams in Stanford athletic history—the 1942 NCAA champion basketball team. *(Stanford Athletics)*

STANFORD MOMENT

Stanford Wins NCAA Basketball Championship

At a time when any basketball player over six feet tall was considered a "big man," the 1942 Stanford team proved to be the giants of their time. Averaging 6'4" and led by five players from San Francisco-area high schools, Stanford hit paydirt in 1942 by defeating Dartmouth to win the school's only NCAA championship in men's basketball. The fivesome that were the heart-and-soul of the team included 6'5 1/2" C Ed Voss, 6'5" F Jim Pollard, 6'3" F Don Burness, 6'3" G Bill Cowden and 6'4" G Howie Dallmar. Stanford proved in 1942 that a big team could not only rebound, but run the floor, shoot with accuracy and play tough defense. Stanford, which finished the season 28-4, beat Oregon State in a three-game series to advance to the NCAA Western Regional Finals in Kansas City. Stanford was without the services of Burness in the Regionals because he had suffered a sprained ankle against Oregon State. Still, the Indians beat Rice and Colorado to reach the title game. In the championship game, Pollard did not dress due to the flu and Burness tried but couldn't continue to play on his ankle. Nevertheless, Stanford, led by tournament MVP Dallmar, beat Dartmouth 53-38 for the title. After expenses, Indian coach Everett Dean brought home a check for $93.75.

ONE OF THE BEST DUOS in Stanford basketball history was Jim Pollard and Don Burness of the 1942 NCAA championship team. Burness and Pollard, the Indians' starting forwards in '42, were named First-Team All-Americans, the third and fourth players in Stanford history to be so honored. Burness was considered the quarterback of the team, one of the great passers in college basketball. Pollard, of course, went on to a great professional basketball career with the Minneapolis Lakers. Nicknamed the "Kangaroo Kid," Pollard averaged over 13 points per game while playing eight seasons with the Lakers. His Laker teams won six championships during his eight seasons. He became head coach of the Lakers 1960 and was elected to the Naismith Memorial Basketball Hall of Fame in 1977.

Stanford Stat . . .

After an undefeated 1940 season, the Indians entered the '41 football season with hopes of another Rose Bowl appearance. But, the loss of several key players to graduation and some injuries prevented the Indians from a repeat performance. Quarterback Frankie Albert was again named First-Team All-American, but he was minus fullback Norm Standlee and halfback Hugh Gallarneau, who had both graduated, and injuries to key players Pete Kmetovic and Vic Lindskog proved costly. Stanford won its first two games, then lost 10-0 at Oregon State, the first loss in 13 games under Clark Shaughnessy. The Indians finished the year 6-3 after losing their final two games to Washington State and California.

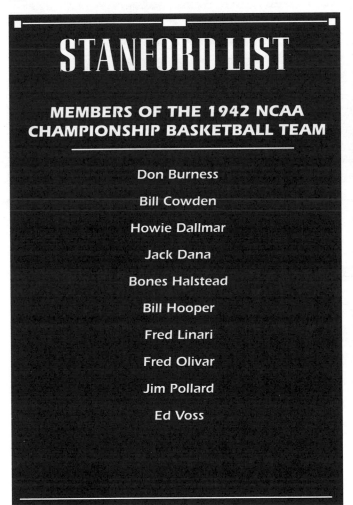

STANFORD LIST

MEMBERS OF THE 1942 NCAA CHAMPIONSHIP BASKETBALL TEAM

Don Burness

Bill Cowden

Howie Dallmar

Jack Dana

Bones Halstead

Bill Hooper

Fred Linari

Fred Olivar

Jim Pollard

Ed Voss

Stanford LEGEND

Frank "Sandy" Tatum

Frank Tatum won the individual title at the 1942 NCAA golf championships and led the Indians to the team title. (Stanford Athletics)

Frank "Sandy" Tatum was the epitome of a true college student-athlete: a championship golfer, outstanding student and campus leader. His list of accomplishments goes far beyond that day in 1942 when he won the NCAA golf championship while leading his team to the co-championship with LSU. Tatum, who shot 142 at the Notre Dame Golf Course to become Stanford's first NCAA golf champion, set standards few college athletes have equaled. He was elected Phi Beta Kappa and later was named a Rhodes Scholar. After a successful career in the Navy, Tatum graduated from the Stanford Law School and practiced law in San Francisco for many years. He became a member of the University's Board of Trustees years later as well as president of the United States Golf Association. After Stanford won the 1941 NCAA golf title, the Athletic Department revealed it did not have the necessary funds to send the '42 team to Notre Dame for the NCAA's. Tatum was undaunted. He went to Stanford President Ray Lyman Wilbur and asked permission to raise the funds for the trip. As fate would have it, Tatum and his teammates raised the money and went to Notre Dame and promptly captured the NCAA title with Tatum himself winning the individual crown.

STANFORD LORE

The University's golden anniversary year observance continued on October 1, 1941 with a lighthearted family celebration on the date on which the University first opened its doors. A dramatic recreation on the Inner Quad of the Opening Day ceremonies highlighted the day with faculty members playing the part of Leland and Jane Stanford, David Starr Jordan and other dignitaries. A sound and light show of Stanford history was performed by Charles K. Field, Class of '95.

1942-43

- November 15, 1942: The U.S. scored a major victory in a naval engagement off Guadalcanal, preventing Japanese reinforcements from reaching the island.
- December 1, 1942: Nationwide gasoline rationing went into effect.
- January 14, 1943: The Casablanca Conference opened in Morocco, attended by President Franklin Roosevelt and other Allied officials.
- May 5, 1943: Postmaster Frank Walker inaugurated a postal-zone numbering system to speed up mail delivery.
- July 19, 1943: More than 500 Allied planes bombed Rome.

STANFORD MOMENT

Marchie Schwartz Named Head Football Coach

Marchie Schwartz took over the reins of the Stanford football program in 1942 and endured two of the most difficult periods in Stanford football history—the prewar and postwar eras. An All-American halfback at Notre Dame, Schwartz came to Stanford as an assistant coach under Clark Shaughnessy in 1940 and '41. His first team went 6-4 in 1942, but World War II interrupted play in '43 and '44 and Schwartz returned to private business in the Midwest. He was lured back to Stanford in 1946 and remained as head coach until he resigned following the 1950 season. In six years as head coach, Schwartz compiled a record of 28-28-4.

Stanford LEGEND

Chuck Taylor

No one has had more of an impact on the Stanford Athletic Department than Chuck Taylor. He was a player, coach and athletic director at Stanford who for over 30 years had a profound impact on the fortunes of the Stanford athletic program. Taylor is perhaps best known for having been a player, coach and athletic director in the Rose Bowl, one of only two people in the history of college football who can make that claim. Taylor was a member of Clark Shaughnessy's "Wow Boys" team of 1940 that beat Nebraska in the Rose Bowl, and as a senior Taylor was chosen First-Team All-American as a guard. He was an assistant coach at Stanford in 1948 and '49 and in 1951, he was named head coach. In his rookie season, his team went 9-2 in '51 and played Illinois in the Rose Bowl. Taylor was named the nation's Coach of the Year. He compiled a 40-29-2 record in seven years as head coach (1951-57). His third and fourth trips to the Rose Bowl occurred in 1971 and '72 as athletic director when coach John Ralston's teams won back-to-back Rose Bowls. Taylor was Stanford's A.D. from 1963-71. In 1984, Taylor was named to the National Football Foundation Hall of Fame.

STANFORD LORE

In April of 1943, Stanford began receiving its first quota of soldier-students for the Army Specialized Training Program (ASTP), a federal program designed to use college and university faculties to train specialists for the military. By June, almost 2,400 soldiers were registered with the number increasing to 2,900 by October.

1943-44

- September 8, 1943: Italy surrendered unconditionally to the Allied powers. German troops there fought on.
- December 24, 1943: General Dwight D. Eisenhower was appointed Supreme Commander of Allied forces for the European invasion.
- March 6, 1944: U.S. pilots dropped 2,000 tons of bombs on Berlin.
- June 6, 1944: More than 4,000 ships, 3,000 planes and four million Allied troops began the Normandy invasion.
- August 25, 1944: Paris was liberated as the Germans surrendered to the French.

STANFORD MOMENT

Intercollegiate Sports Canceled Due to WWII

The announcement came in August that Stanford would not be fielding a football team for the 1944 season due to World War II. In October, it was disclosed that Stanford had notified its opponents that their games would be canceled in all sports. Some thought that Stanford might field teams in all sports except football, because fewer men are needed to complete a team in sports such as basketball, baseball and tennis. But the decision stood to drop all intercollegiate sports for the 1944-45 academic year. While football took two dozen men to field a team, wrote *The Stanford Daily*, basketball took less than a dozen and baseball would need about a dozen. "Surely there are a dozen men interested in baseball," wrote *The Daily*, "out of which might come another Mel Ott." The track and tennis teams had some of the top athletes on the West Coast on campus, including middle distance runner Johnny Fulton and tennis star Bob Forbes. "From here, it looks as though Stanford would be missing a good opportunity in not using their talents," wrote *The Daily*.

Stanford LEGEND

Everett Dean

No coach in Stanford history has won two national championships in two different sports, but Everett Dean came closer than anyone. He was Stanford's basketball coach from 1939-51 and it was his Fab Five who went to Kansas City in March of 1942 and took home Stanford's only NCAA championship in men's basketball. Dean also coached the Indian baseball team from 1950-55 and in 1953, he took the most talented team ever at Stanford to the College World Series, but had to settle for a fifth place finish. In 11 seasons at the helm of the basketball program, Dean's teams went 167-120, including 28-4 in the '42 championship season. In baseball, his first team in 1950 produced a league championship and was two close losses away from the College World Series. Dean got his team to the College World Series in 1953 - the first in school history— while chalking up a school-record 29 wins. His six-year record as baseball coach was an impressive 125-83-4. Dean is a member of the Stanford Athletic Hall of Fame.

 ## STANFORD LORE

Because of World War II, less than half of those scheduled to receive degrees were on hand for commencement exercises on July 2, 1944. Of the 760 graduates, 412 received their diplomas in absentia. Not a single graduate of the Medical School was able to take time off from hospital work for the ceremony.

1944-45

- **November 7, 1944:** Franklin Roosevelt was re-elected president of the United States for a record fourth term.
- **December 16, 1944:** The last major German offensive of World War II—the Battle of the Bulge—began.
- **April 12, 1945:** President Franklin Roosevelt died in Warm Springs, Georgia, on the 83rd day of his fourth term at the age of 63. He was succeeded by Harry S. Truman.
- **May 8, 1945:** The Germans unconditionally surrendered, ending the European phase of World War II.
- **August 6, 1945:** The city of Hiroshima, Japan, was destroyed by the first atomic bomb to be used in war. Nine days later, the Japanese surrendered to the Allies.

STANFORD MOMENT

Students Invited to USC-Cal Game in Berkeley

For the second straight year, the events of World War II forced university administrators to cancel all intercollegiate sports at Stanford. At many other schools, however, intercollegiate sports continued uninterrupted. When the University of California met USC in football, Stanford students were invited to travel to Berkeley and attend the game. And the football-starved students on The Farm turned out in big numbers. Over 1,200 Stanford students took the train to Berkeley to sit in a special Stanford section. Students were involved in the halftime card stunts and the 70-member Stanford Band was also asked to perform at the intermission. "Admission to the card section can be obtained only by wearing white shirts or sweaters. Rain or shine, the requirement holds, as coats will be removed for card stunts between the halves," wrote *The Stanford Daily*.

Stanford ❦ LEGEND ❦

Harry Wolter

Only two coaches in Stanford history have coached their sport longer than Harry Wolter coached the Indian baseball team. For 26 seasons, Wolter led the fortunes of the baseball program. A former major leaguer, Wolter first coached Stanford in 1916, then again from 1923-43 and 1946-49. He won 277 games in his career, which ranks fourth among Stanford baseball coaches. Wolter played major league baseball for seven seasons, four of which were with the New York Yankees from 1910-13. He played in 588 major league games, hit 12 home runs, drove in 167 runs and sported a career batting average of .270. One of the finest teams on The Farm was Wolter's 1931 California Intercollegiate Baseball Association champions. Stanford went 18-5 overall and 15-3 in CIBA play in '31. The 18 wins set a school record for most wins in a season.

STANFORD LORE

The surrender of Japan in August of 1945 unleashed a flood of veterans returning to campuses under the GI Bill. The resulting need for additional classroom and dormitory space had been anticipated by Stanford President Donald Tresidder. Aside from immediate needs, newly appointed Director of Planning Eldridge Spencer initiated long-term planning of campus lands and buildings.

1945-46

- September 2, 1945: Japan signed the formal document of surrender aboard the U.S.S Missouri in Tokyo Bay.
- February 15, 1946: Scientists developed the world's first electronic digital computer in Philadelphia.
- March 23, 1946: The NCAA basketball championship was won by Oklahoma A&M, which defeated California 52-35.
- July 2, 1946: African-Americans voted for the first time in Mississippi primaries.
- July 4, 1946: President Harry Truman proclaimed Philippine independence.

STANFORD MOMENT

Athletic Programs Return

After a two-year layoff due to the World War II, the athletic programs at Stanford and throughout the nation were returning to their prewar status in 1945-46. While the Indian football team played an unofficial schedule in '45 as they began the process of getting players for the team, other sports were in full swing, including basketball, track, baseball, swimming, tennis and golf. Eddie Twiggs' golf team highlighted the year by winning their fifth national championship since 1938. This time, the foursome of Frank McCann, Bob Rosburg, Jack Shuler and Bob Cardinal led Stanford to a 36-hole total of 619 at the Springdale Golf Course in New Jersey, five strokes better than runnerup Michigan.

Stanford LEGEND

Ted Schroeder

Frederick R. "Ted" Schroeder was one of the most accomplished tennis players that Stanford University has ever produced. He was not only a dominant college player, but Schroeder enjoyed an outstanding professional career that included the Wimbledon singles championship in 1949. He capped his Stanford career in 1942 by winning the NCAA singles and doubles crowns, both against fellow teammates. Schroeder won the U.S. Open singles title later that year, beating Frank Parker. Schroeder teamed with Jack Kramer to win the U.S. Open doubles championships in 1940, '41 and '47. He reached the pinnacle of his career in 1949 when he won the singles title at the prestigious Wimbledon Championships. Schroeder was a member of the United States' Davis Cup teams five times, from 1946-48 and again in 1950 and '51. He was elected to the Stanford Hall of Fame in 1942 and the Collegiate Tennis Hall of Fame in 1983.

STANFORD LORE

To honor a wish that his wife had expressed before her death, Herbert Hoover gave to Stanford their campus home atop San Juan Hill for use as the official residence of the University president. Completed in 1921, the home was designed in "early international style" by Mrs. Hoover with help from Stanford Art Prof. Arthur B. Clark and his son, Birge Clark.

1946-47

- April 11, 1947: Jackie Robinson made his debut with the Brooklyn Dodgers as major league baseball's first black player.
- April 16, 1947: Some 500 persons died in a ship explosion at Texas City, Texas.
- June 5, 1947: The Marshall Plan for reconstruction of Europe was proposed at Harvard University by Secretary of State George C. Marshall.
- June 23, 1947: Despite President Truman's veto, the controversial Taft-Hartley Labor Act was passed by Congress.

STANFORD MOMENT

Football Returns to Stanford

After a three-year layoff due to World War II, football returned to Stanford in the fall of 1946. Marchie Schwartz, who coached the Indians before the war in 1942, was persuaded to return from the Midwest and take over the head coaching position once again. His team was comprised mostly of returning veterans and young men who had not played football for two or three years. Still, Schwartz led his team to a respectable 6-3-1 record, which included a 25-6 win over Cal in the Big Game. Stanford began the season with easy wins over Idaho (45-0) and San Francisco (33-7), but a 26-6 loss to UCLA ended the mild winning streak. The three losses came at the hands of UCLA, USC and Washington with a tie against Oregon State.

Stanford LEGEND

Eddie Twiggs

Eddie Twiggs was hired in 1932 by Stanford Athletic Director Al Masters to take over the reins of the Stanford golf program. For the next 15 years, Twiggs proceeded to produce five NCAA team championships, seven of nine Pacific Coast Conference Southern Division titles and several of the top golfers in Stanford history. His teams also won three Pacific Coaster Intercollegiate Golf Association titles. Twiggs, who was a successful railroad representative and outstanding amateur golfer when he was tabbed by Masters to head the Indian program in 1932, led his team to NCAA titles in 1938, 1939, 1941, 1942 and 1946. Two of his pupils, Bud Finger and Sandy Tatum, are still regarded today as two of the best golfers to ever play for Stanford.

 # STANFORD LORE

Campus station KSU (now KZSU) had its premiere broadcast on January 6, 1947. The station's first signal went to student residences via wires strung through University steam tunnels. Doodles Weaver '36, later a famous Hollywood comedian-actor, put on the first show. Initially, the station operated from 7-11 p.m. Sunday through Thursday out of a studio in Stanford Village.

1947-48

- October 14, 1947: Captain Chuck Yeager piloted the world's first supersonic aircraft.
- December 5, 1947: Heavyweight boxing champion Joe Louis earned a split decision over "Jersey Joe" Walcott.
- March 8, 1948: The Supreme Court ruled that religious education in public schools was a violation of the First Amendment.
- May 3, 1948: James Michner's *Tales of the South Pacific* and Tennessee Williams' *A Streetcar Named Desire* earned Pulitzer prizes.
- August 16, 1948: Babe Ruth, baseball's greatest player, died of cancer.

STANFORD MOMENT

Winless Stanford Almost Pulls off Big Game Upset

In a classic Big Game in 1947, Stanford went into the game with an 0-8 record and as decided underdogs against the 8-1 Bears. The Indians took an 18-14 lead midway through the fourth quarter when quarterback Don Campbell hit Bob Anderson on an 11-yard touchdown pass. With 3:14 remaining in the game, the Bears, which entered the game ranked sixth in the nation, took over on their own 20-yard line with one more chance at victory. On a third-down play, Cal fullback Jackie Jensen took a pitch from QB Dick Erickson and began running right when he stopped and threw a wobbly pass to Paul Keckley, who promptly caught the ball at the 40 and raced the final 60 yards to the end zone to complete an 80-yard touchdown play. The Bears won 21-18 and sent Stanford's season to a close with an 0-9 record. The 85,000 fans who jammed Stanford Stadium witnessed what is still considered one of the greatest Big Games of all-time.

Stanford LEGEND

Bud Held

Bud Held came to Stanford from Los Angeles as a pole vaulter, but by the time he graduated, he had won three NCAA titles in the javelin and was on his way to becoming the world's best. Held won NCAA javelin championships in 1948, '49 and '50, joining the great Harlow Rothert and Pete Zagar as the only three-time NCAA track champions in school history. Following his Stanford days, Held broke the first of his six American javelin throw records in 1951 with a 249-8 effort. Two years later, he became the first American to hold the world record when he threw 263-10. He set another world record in 1955 with a throw of 268-2. Held was ranked number one in the world on three occasions (1951, 1953, 1955) and number one in the U.S. seven times. He competed in the 1952 Olympics in Helsinki, but finished ninth after suffering an injury to his shoulder. Held established a personal best of 270-0 in 1956, but missed qualifying for his second Olympic team by one inch.

STANFORD LORE

President Donald B. Tresidder died of a heart attack while on a trip to New York on January 28, 1948. Education Prof. Alvin C. Eurich, who had been named academic vice president by Tresidder in May, 1944, served as acting president. Eurich announced in November, 1948 that he would leave Stanford to become CEO of the State University of New York.

1948-49

- November 2, 1948:   In a major political upset, Harry Truman defeated Thomas Dewey for the U.S. presidency.
- December 15, 1948:   Former State Department official Alger Hiss was indicted by a federal grand jury on two counts of perjury.
- April 4, 1949:   NATO was formed when the North Atlantic Treaty was signed in Washington, D.C.
- April 20, 1949:   Cortisone, the hormone promised to bring relief to rheumatoid arthritis sufferers was discovered.
- July 2, 1949:   Former Stanford tennis star Ted Schroeder won the men's singles title at the Wimbledon tennis championships.

STANFORD MOMENT

All-American Ken Rose scored Stanford's only touchdown in the 1948 Big Game. (Stanford Athletics)

Undefeated Bears Edge Stanford 7-6 in Big Game

Undefeated Cal, led by their All-American running back Jackie Jensen, entered the 1948 Big Game as three touchdown favorites over the 4-5 Indians. The 81,000 fans that turned out at Cal's Memorial Stadium saw Jensen rush for a Big Game record 170 yards on just 19 carries as the Bears narrowly beat the upstart Indians 7-6 to advance to the Rose Bowl. For Stanford, the 1948 season was a vast improvement from its 0-9 record in 1947, but it still wasn't a strong enough team to beat the powerful Bears in the first one-point decision in Big Game history. Cal scored its touchdown in the first quarter on a two-yard run by Jack Swaner, capping a 12-ply, 59-yard touchdown. The extra point was added by the Bears' Jim Cullom, who later in the game blocked Stanford's extra point to preserve the lead for Cal. Stanford's touchdown came in the second half when Jackie Jensen fumbled on the Bear's 22-yard line and Stanford's Bill DeYoung recovered to give the Indians great field position. Four plays later, quarterback Tom Shaw connected with Ken Rose on an 11-yard touchdown play, pulling Stanford within a point. But, Cullom's blocked extra point prevented Stanford from tying the game. The game started in a frightening manner when, on the first play, Stanford's Don Campbell was knocked out. Play was stopped for 15 minutes while Campbell was treated. He was taken by ambulance to the nearby hospital where it was determined that he suffered a concussion and would recover.

IN 13 SEASONS as Stanford's swimming coach (1948-60), Tom Hayne further established Stanford University as national power. His teams went 84-9 in dual meet competition, including a string of 54 consecutive victories from 1950-58. Hayne's teams won 11 of 13 conference championships and finished among the top-10 in the nation on 10 occasions. Two of his top swimmers were Robin Moore, world record holder and NCAA champion in the 50-free, and George Harrision, Olympic gold medalist and NCAA champion. Hayne's teams went 24-0 vs. Cal, 13-0 vs. UCLA and 11-2 vs. USC.

Stanford Stat . . .

Basketball coach Everett Dean put together his best team in 1948-49 since the '42 NCAA championship club. Stanford went 19-9, including taking four of five from California. Guard Dave Davison led the team in scoring and was an All-Pacific Coast Conference Southern Division selection. Junior George Yardley, who would later become an outstanding professional player, was one of the bright young players on the '48-49 squad.

STANFORD LIST

MULTIPLE NCAA TRACK CHAMPIONS

Name	Event	Years
Ward Edmonds	Pole Vault	1928, 1929
Harlow Rothert	Discus	1928, 1929, 1930
Pete Zagar	Discus	1937, 1938, 1939
Bud Held	Javelin	1948, 1949, 1950
Dave Weill	Discus	1962, 1963
Carol Cady	Shot Put	
	/Discus	1983, 1984

Stanford LEGEND

George Yardley

George Yardley followed his Stanford career with a seven-year NBA career that included six All-Star games. (Stanford Athletics)

"George Yardley was a scoring machine," says basketball Hall of Famer Dolph Schayes. "He had an unstoppable jump shot," adds another basketball great, Bill Sharman. Indeed, Yardley knew how to put the ball in the hole. After playing three seasons on the Indian varsity (1948-50), Yardley went on to a professional career that landed him in the Naismith Basketball Hall of Fame in 1996. As a senior at Stanford in the '49-50 season, Yardley broke Hank Luisetti's Pacific Coast Conference record by scoring 237 points in the 12-game PCC schedule. He averaged 11.5 points per game during his college days, but it was as a pro that Yardley blossomed. For three years after his Stanford graduation, where he earned both a bachelor's and master's degree, Yardley played for an AAU team. He then started a seven-year NBA career in 1953-54 with the Fort Wayne and Detroit Pistons and the Syracuse Nationals. He was named to six straight NBA All-Star games, led the Pistons to the 1955 NBA Finals and was named First-Team All-NBA in 1957-58 after leading the league with a 27.8 scoring average. Yardley became the first player in NBA history to surpass 2,000 points in a single season in '57-58, breaking George Mikan's record.

STANFORD LORE

J.E. Wallace Sterling, director of the Huntington Library and Art Gallery, former Caltech professor and Stanford Ph.D., took over as the University's fifth president on April 1, 1949. At a press conference on his first day, he told newsmen, "Communism is a real menace and its facts should be taught, but not by Communists."

·· AMERICA'S TIME CAPSULE ··

- October 9, 1949:   The New York Yankees beat the Brooklyn Dodgers to win baseball's World Series.
- October 24, 1949:   The United Nations headquarters were dedicated in New York.
- January 31, 1950:   President Truman authorized development of the hydrogen bomb.
- April 23, 1950:   George Mikan led the Minneapolis Lakers over the Syracuse Nationals to win the first National Basketball Association championship.
- June 27, 1950:   President Truman ordered U.S. armed forces to Korea to help South Korea repel the North Korean invasion.

In his six years as Stanford's head coach, Marchie Schwartz put together his best team in 1949. *(Stanford Athletics)*

STANFORD MOMENT

Marchie's Best Season

The 1949 season proved to be the best in Marchie Schwartz' six-years as Stanford's head football coach. The Indians, led by a group of sophomores that included quarterback Gary Kerkorian and end Bill McColl, went 7-3-1 in '49, losing only to Michigan, UCLA and Cal in the Big Game. All seven of Stanford's wins were by 20 points or more while five of the team's seven victories were by over 40 points, including a 63-0 win over Idaho, 74-20 over Hawaii, 49-0 over San Jose State, 44-0 over Harvard and 40-0 at Washington. The 366 points scored not only set a record at that time, but it is a record that still stands today. Kerkorian did not start the season opener against San Jose State, but made his debut as the Indian starter the following week against Harvard. As a senior two years later, Kerkorian was a First-Team All-American and regarded as one of the great Stanford quarterbacks of all-time. After winning its first two games by scores of 49-0 and 44-0, Stanford lost its next two games to Michigan 27-7 and UCLA 14-7. A 40-0 win over Washington—the largest margin of victory for Stanford in series history—and a 27-7 win over Oregon State put the Indians back in the Rose Bowl race. The Indians, who played just three road games in 1949, beat USC in Los Angeles 34-13 and swamped Idaho 63-0 leading up to the Big Game against the undefeated Bears. A Stanford win would have given it the inside track to the Rose Bowl, but the Bears came up big with a 33-14 win and earned the trip to Pasadena.

CHARLES "BUD" FINGER was a fixture at the Stanford Golf Course from 1938, when he first arrived on The Farm as a freshman on the golf team, to 1981, when he died at his home in Los Altos. In between, Finger was a player and coach on the Stanford golf team, then the course manager and head PGA professional at the Stanford Golf Course. Finger was a member of two NCAA championship teams (1939, 1941) while playing for the legendary Eddie Twiggs. Finger succeeded Twiggs as head coach in 1948, a position he held for 29 years until his retirement in 1976. As a coach, Finger's team won one NCAA title (1953), placed among the nation's top-10 16 times and won 12 conference championships. He was named manager of the Stanford Golf Course and Driving Range and Head PGA Professional at the Course following his retirement from coaching in '76.

Stanford Stat . . .

When he began classes at Stanford in the Fall of 1949, Bob Mathias was already considered the greatest athlete in the world. After all, at the age of 17 he won the Olympic gold medal in the decathlon at the 1948 Games in London. Mathias competed on the Stanford freshman track team in the spring of 1950. He averaged nearly 18 points per meet and set four Stanford freshman records (shot, discus, high hurdles and pole vault). When Stanford beat Cal 74-57 in the frosh track meet on May 6, 1950, Mathias accounted for 28 points. Later in the year, he set a world record in the decathlon with 8,042 points

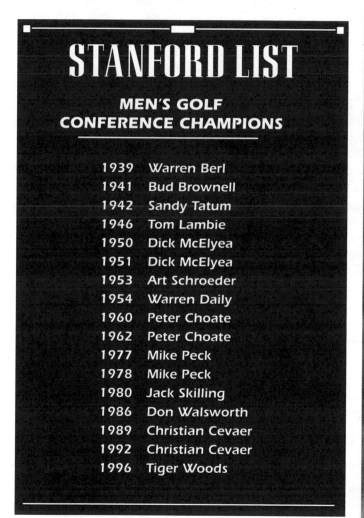

STANFORD LIST

MEN'S GOLF
CONFERENCE CHAMPIONS

1939	Warren Berl
1941	Bud Brownell
1942	Sandy Tatum
1946	Tom Lambie
1950	Dick McElyea
1951	Dick McElyea
1953	Art Schroeder
1954	Warren Daily
1960	Peter Choate
1962	Peter Choate
1977	Mike Peck
1978	Mike Peck
1980	Jack Skilling
1986	Don Walsworth
1989	Christian Cevaer
1992	Christian Cevaer
1996	Tiger Woods

Stanford LEGEND

Bill McColl

Two-time All-American Bill McColl earned his M.D. while playing professional football with the Chicago Bears. (Stanford Archives)

What Bill McColl accomplished on the playing field is reason enough to include him as one of the legends of Stanford athletics. But it is his achievements off the field that distinguish him from all others. You see McColl, a consensus First-Team All-American football player in 1950 and '51, not only starred as a college and professional football player, but he took advantage of his educational opportunities so that he could benefit mankind. After eight seasons with the Chicago Bears from 1952-59, Dr. Bill McColl - he earned his M.D. from the University of Chicago while playing pro football - dedicated his life to helping the suffering people in the mission fields of Korea. He served as a medical missionary in Korea and also at the Ae Rak Won Leprosarium from 1962-64. When he returned to the U.S., McColl established a private practice in orthopedic surgery in southern California. He was one of college football's best players in '50 and '51. He set new Pacific Coast Conference records in 1950 for receptions (39) and receiving yardage (671). In 1951, he registered 42 receptions for 607 yards and seven touchdowns while finishing fourth in the balloting for the Heisman Trophy. He was elected to the National Football Foundation Hall of Fame in 1973. Two of McColl's sons, Duncan ('77) and Milt ('81) played football at Stanford.

STANFORD LORE

Con Home Day, an annual clean-up by students of the Convalescent Home ground, was renamed San McDonald Day in May of 1950. McDonald, who became caretaker of athletic property in 1907 and was later named the Superintendent of Athletics Buildings and Grounds, had headed the crew and run the barbecue since the event was started in 1922. Sam McDonald Road, named in his honor, runs adjacent to Stanford Stadium.

1950-51

- September 26, 1950: U.S. troops recaptured Seoul, the capital of South Korea.
- December 24, 1950: The NFL Championship was won by the Cleveland Browns, who defeated the Los Angeles Rams, 30-28.
- February 26, 1951: Congress adopted the 22nd Amendment to the U.S. Constitution, stipulating that no person may be elected to the presidency for more than two terms.
- April 11, 1951: President Truman relieved Gen. Douglas MacArthur of his post as supreme commander.
- June 25, 1951: The Columbia Broadcasting Company (CBS) presented television's first commercial color broadcast.

STANFORD MOMENT

Stanford Ties Undefeated Cal in Big Game

Pappy Waldorf's Cal Bears were 9-0 and headed to a third straight Rose Bowl when they were dubbed two touchdown favorites over the 5-3-1 Indians. But Stanford, healthy for the first time all season, battled Cal to a 7-7 tie in one of the hardest fought Big Games in history. After a scoreless first half, the Bears struck first in the third quarter when running back Pete Schabarum busted up the middle for 31 yards and touchdown. Schabarum fumbled later in the third quarter, allowing Stanford to gain possession deep in Cal territory. Six plays later, on a third-and-goal play from the six, QB Gary Kerkorian hit Boyd Benson on a six-yard touchdown pass play, knotting the score at 7-7 early in the fourth quarter. Stanford had a TD nullified later in the period when Kerkorian hit Bob White for an apparent 28-yard touchdown, but the referees called offensive pass interference, negating the score. In the waning moments of the game, Bill McColl dropped back from his end position, took a lateral from Kerkorian and uncorked a 66-yard pass to speedster Bob Bryan. The ball looked to be on target, but it just went off Bryan's fingertips at the Cal 10-yard line. Kerkorian set a Big Game record by completing 17-of-30 passes for 217 yards.

Stanford SPOTLIGHT

One of Stanford's great female swimmers, Sharon Geary was an alternate on the 1952 United States Olympic Swimming Team (Stanford Athletics)

IN THE 1950s, women's athletics on the college level did not exist. While men's athletics were being offered in a variety of sports, women were relegated to club teams and intramurals. The top female athletes did not have the opportunity to train and compete against other college athletes. Such was the case for Sharon Geary, a talented swimmer who, as a student at Stanford, was one of the best in the nation in her events. In 1950, Geary was a star on the United States Pan-American Games team. She won the 100-meter freestyle and was a member of the U.S. winning 300-meter medley relay and 400-meter freestyle relay teams. A member of Stanford's class of '54, Geary went on to capture the United States championships in the 100-meter outdoor and 200-yard indoor in 1951. She was an alternate for the U.S. in the 4x100 freestyle relay at the 1952 Olympic Games in Helsinki.

Stanford Stat . . .

Eddie Tucker played basketball at Stanford for two seasons in 1951 and '52 and was one of the school's most prolific scorers during this time. But Tucker, a transfer from Compton Junior College, gained notoriety off the court as well as Stanford's first African-American athlete. He became the third Stanford basketball player—behind Hank Luisetti and George Yardley—to score more than 400 points in a single season. His 427 points during the '51-52 campaign not only led the Pacific Coast Conference, but it was second in Stanford history to Luisetti's 465 points. Although he played at Stanford just two seasons, Tucker left as the school's sixth-leading scorer of all-time with 791 points.

STANFORD LIST

LONGEST COACHING TENURES ON THE FARM

Below are the longest coaching tenures for those who have coached intercollegiate sports at Stanford (through 1996-97 season):

Name, Sport	No. of Years	Years Coached
Dick Gould, Men's Tennis	31	1967-97*
Ernie Brandsten, Men's Swimming	31	1916-47+
Bud Finger, Men's Golf	29	1948-76
Harry Wolter, Baseball	26	1916, '23-49+
Payton Jordan, Men's Track	23	1957-79
Mark Marquess, Baseball	21	1977-97*
Howie Dallmar, Men's Basketball	21	1955-75
Dante Dettamanti, Men's Water Polo	20	1977-96*
Frank Brennan, Women's Tennis	18	1980-97*
Skip Kenney, Men's Swimming	18	1980-97*
Jim Gaughran, Men's Swimming	18	1961-79
Dink Templeton, Men's Track	18	1921-39

* active through 1996-97 season
\+ did not coach in 1944-45 due to WWII

Stanford LEGEND

Bob Mathias

Bob Mathias won gold medals at the 1948 Olympic Games in London and the '52 Game in Helsinki (Stanford Athletics)

As a 17-year-old from Tulare, California, Bob Mathias became the youngest athlete ever to win a track and field gold medal in Olympic competition when he won the decathlon at the 1948 London Olympics. That was the beginning of an athletic career that ended with Mathias being considered the greatest athlete of all time. Indeed his achievements were unprecedented: back-to-back Olympic decathlon gold medalist, three-time world record holder, undefeated in 11 decathlons in which he competed and an outstanding college football player. Mathias entered Stanford in the fall of 1949, competed on the freshman track team in 1950 and the varsity from '51-53. He was also a star football player for Stanford in 1951 and '52. He is the only man ever to compete in the Olympics and the Rose Bowl in the same year (1952). His 96-yard kickoff return for a touchdown vs. USC in 1951 helped Stanford beat the Trojans 27-20 and advance to the Rose Bowl against Illinois. Later that year, Mathias set a world record and won an incredible second straight Olympic gold medal in the decathlon at the 1952 Games in Helsinki. Mathias later had a brief movie career and was a U.S. congressman from California.

STANFORD LORE

More than 300 students from 59 western colleges and universities convened at Memorial Auditorium on April 26, 1951 for the first Model United Nations conference sponsored by Stanford's Institute of International Relations. The Collegiate Council of the United Nations selected Stanford as host to acquaint citizens with the machinery for peace, and to demonstrate the limitations, potentialities and day-to-day working problems of the U.N.

1951-52

- November 10, 1951: The first transcontinental direct dial telephone service happened when a call was placed from New Jersey to California.
- December 20, 1951: A station in Idaho began producing electricity from the first atomic-powered generator.
- April 8, 1952: A presidential order prevented a shutdown of the nation's steel mills by strikers.
- July 11, 1952: Gen. Dwight Eisenhower and Sen. Richard Nixon were nominated as the presidential ticket for the Republicans.
- July 26, 1952: Illinois governor Adlai Stevenson was nominated at the Democratic National Convention as the party's presidential candidate.

STANFORD MOMENT

Stanford rookie coach Chuck Taylor led his '51 team to the Rose Bowl, where it lost a 40-7 decision to Illinois. (Stanford Athletics)

Taylor Returns to Lead Stanford to Rose Bowl

Former Stanford All-American Chuck Taylor, in his first year as head coach, took his storybook season all the way to Pasadena on January 1, 1952 as his 9-1 Indians were matched up against the University of Illinois in the Rose Bowl. Taylor, the 31-year-old rookie coach who was a guard on Stanford's last Rose Bowl team in 1941, was named the Coach of the Year by the American Football Coaches Association after turning Stanford into a national power in just his first season as head coach. Taylor utilized the passing attack like no other coach before him and is largely credited with making the forward pass a more prominent part of the game of football. With Gary Kerkorian at quarterback and Bill McColl at end, Taylor's passing attack led Stanford to nine consecutive wins to start the '51 season. After a loss in the Big Game, Stanford suffered its second straight defeat in the Rose Bowl as the Illini scored 27 points in the fourth quarter to take home an easy 40-7 win. Stanford led 7-6 at halftime and trailed just 13-7 in the fourth quarter before Illinois' scoring burst put the game out of reach. Still, Stanford finished the '51 campaign with a 9-2 record and a number-seven national ranking.

JOE CHEZ went 20-4 from 1950-52 as not only the ace of the Stanford staff, but as one of the finest pitchers in college baseball. He was twice named All-California Intercollegiate Baseball Association (CIBA) in 1950 and '52 and was an All-American selection in 1952. Chez's winning percentage of .833 is still among the top-five all-time in Stanford baseball history and his 8-1 record in 1950 is also among the best ever at Stanford. As a sophomore in '50, Chez's 8-1 record lifted Stanford to its first CIBA championship since 1931. Chez went 7-0 in conference games and his only loss was a 3-2 decision to Washington State in the Pacific Coast Conference playoffs. As a junior, Chez went 5-2 in an injury-shortened season. He came back as a senior to post a 7-1 record, including an impressive one-hit shutout over powerful USC. He also led the team in batting with a .375 average. Chez was elected to the Stanford baseball Hall of Fame in 1976.

Stanford Stat . . .

At the 1952 Olympic Games in Helsinki, Finland, Stanford had eight athletes competing representing three countries. The highlight of the Games was, of course, Stanford's Bob Mathias, who won his second straight Olympic decathlon gold medal for the U.S. Other Stanford Olympians in Helsinki included Jim Beggs, Dewey Hecht and Jim Fifer in the two-oar crew with coxswain, swimmer Sharon Geary, javelin thrower Bud Held, Carlos Bea, a member of the Cuban basketball team and Ian Reed, who competed in the discus for Australia.

STANFORD LIST

ROSE BOWL QUARTERBACKS

Name	Rose Bowl
Paul Tarpey	1902 vs. Michigan
Ed Walker	1925 vs. Notre Dame
George Bogue	1927 vs. Alabama
Spud Lewis	1928 vs. Pittsburgh
Frank Alustiza	1934 vs. Columbia
Frank Alustiza	1935 vs. Alabama
Bill Paulman	1936 vs. SMU
Frankie Albert	1941 vs. Nebraska
Gary Kerkorian	1952 vs. Illinois
Jim Plunkett	1971 vs. Ohio State
Don Bunce	1972 vs. Michigan

Stanford LEGEND

Gary Kerkorian

Gary Kerkorian was selected first-team All-American in 1951 while leading Stanford to the Rose Bowl. (Stanford Athletics)

If Frankie Albert was the first in a long line of great Stanford quarterbacks, Gary Kerkorian has to be considered the second. Kerkorian was a three-year starter for the Indians from 1949-51, earning All-America honors and leading his team to the Rose Bowl in his final season. He was the school record holder in every passing category when he left The Farm following the '51 season. Kerkorian made his first start against Harvard as a sophomore in 1949 for Marchie Schwartz's team and made his final start in the 1952 Rose Bowl for coach Chuck Taylor. In between, he re-wrote the Stanford record book. Kerkorian enjoyed his best season in 1951, when he completed 103-of-186 for 1,417 yards and seven touchdowns while also kicking extra points and field goals. "Perhaps the best thing that can be said about Stanford football is that it was fun," Kerkorian said. Following his Stanford days, Kerkorian went on to play four seasons with the Pittsburgh Steelers (1953) and Baltimore Colts (1954-56) before completing his law degree and becoming a partner in a law firm in Fresno, California.

STANFORD LORE

Estes Kefauver, seeking the democratic nomination for president, wrote to Warren G. Wonka in May of 1952, thanking him for his campaign assistance and expressing hope of meeting him personally. Wonka's name appeared often on unanswered traffic citations, as a proponent of a new Bible free of "objectionable words and corrupting ideas" and in other unexpected places. While it was never proved, some say Wonka was a mythical student.

1952-53

- September 23, 1952:   Rocky Marciano won his 43rd consecutive bout, defeating "Jersey Joe" Walcott for the world heavyweight boxing title.
- October 7, 1952:   The New York Yankees won the World Series by defeating the Brooklyn Dodgers four games to three.
- November 4, 1952:   Dwight Eisenhower defeated Adlai Stevenson for the presidency of the United States.
- January 2, 1953:   Wisconsin senator Joseph McCarthy, known for his charges of communist infiltration in various organizations, was accused by a senate subcommittee of "motivation by self-interest."
- May 4, 1953:   Author Ernest Hemmingway was awarded a Pulitzer Prize for his book, *The Old Man and the Sea.*

STANFORD MOMENT

Bob Murphy set two school records in 1953 while leading the Indians to their first-ever College World Series. (Stanford Athletics)

Stanford Advances to First College World Series

The 1953 baseball season is still remembered as one of the greatest in school history. The '53 club set a school record for most wins in a season with 29, tied for the league championship and became the first Stanford baseball team to advance to the College World Series. After going 29-15-2 during the regular season, Stanford beat Oregon State in the league playoffs to earn the right to play in Omaha. The Indians were led by a threesome of talented pitchers—Bob Murphy, Phil Page and Mike Acker, along with catcher Jack Shepard, shortstop Warren Goodrich and outfielder Chuck Essegian. In its opening game at the College World Series, Stanford lost to eventual champion Michigan, 4-0. Then, the Indians scored a 7-6 victory over Houston to set up an elimination game with Lafayette. The Indians lost a tough 4-3 decision to Lafayette to end their season, but not before it had accomplished more than any other Stanford team in Stanford history.

TWO OF THE GREATEST PLAYERS in Stanford baseball history were teammates on the 1953 College World Series team—pitcher Bob Murphy and outfielder Chuck Essegian. Murphy set two school records as the team's ace in '53 for most wins in a season with 11 and most innings pitched with 142. He was named the team's MVP. Murphy continued his relationship with Stanford by becoming the Voice of Stanford Athletics through a 30-year career broadcasting Stanford athletic events on radio and television. He was also the Sports Information Director at Stanford and the Athletic Director at San Jose State University. Essegian, meanwhile, has the distinction of being the only man to play in a Rose Bowl (1952, Stanford vs. Illinois) and a World Series (1959 with the Los Angeles Dodgers). A three-year letterman in both baseball and football, Essegian left Stanford as the school's all-time home run leader. He then went on to a career in professional baseball with the Los Angeles Dodgers.

Stanford Stat . . .

Junior running back Bill Rogers placed his name in the Stanford record book when he ran 96 yards down the right sideline at Stanford Stadium for a touchdown—the longest run from scrimmage in Stanford football history. Rogers' run helped the Indians beat Oregon State 41-28 and improve their record to 4-0. Stanford had just forced Oregon State to give up possession at the Indians' four-yard line when Rogers broke through the line on a first-down play and raced 96 yards for the touchdown.

STANFORD LIST

CAREER BATTING AVERAGE LEADERS

1. Jack Shepard, 1951-53	.362
2. David McCarty, 1989-91	.359
3. Mike Aldrete, 1980-83	.356
4. Jeffrey Hammonds, 1990-92	.353
5. A.J. Hinch, 1993-96	.351
Rick Lundblade, 1982-85	.351
7. Tom Williams, 1970-72	.349
8. Nate Olmstead, 1991-94	.344
9. Rod Boone, 1970-73	.341
10. Mike Dotterer, 1980-83	.340

Stanford LEGEND

Jack Shepard

Jack Shepard's .362 career batting average stands today as the best in school history. (Stanford Athletics)

Jack Shepard was not only one of the great baseball players to ever play on The Farm, but his contribution to the Stanford Athletic Department continued for over 40 years. As a player, Shepard was a catcher on Stanford's first College World Series team in 1953, set the school record for career batting average (.362)—which still stands today—was a three-time letterman and an All-American. He and pitcher Bob Murphy were perhaps the most formidable battery in the nation in 1953. While Shepard was hitting .379 in '53, Murphy set a school record by winning 11 games. A great athlete who could have become a great major league player, Shepard decided to leave professional baseball after four seasons with the Pittsburgh Pirates to pursue a career in management. After earning his bachelor's degree in 1953, Shepard earned a master's in 1955 and an MBA in 1957. He was active in volunteering his time to Stanford Athletics for over 40 years. He became the Chairman of the Athletic Board and was instrumental in Stanford's fund-raising efforts. Shepard died at the age of 63 in 1995.

Stanford Lore

Physics professor Felix Bloch became Stanford's first Nobel laureate on November 6, 1952. Bloch was awarded the Nobel Prize for his discovery of nuclear magnetic resonance, a powerful diagnostic tool for medicine. Bloch was named a co-recipient of the award with Edward Purcell of Harvard.

•• AMERICA'S TIME CAPSULE ••

- December 16, 1953:   A new airplane speed record was achieved by U.S. Air Force Major Charles E. Young, who flew a Bell X-1A rocket powered plane more than 1600 mph.
- February 23, 1954:   Inoculation of school children against polio began for the first time.
- March 1, 1954:   An explosion of a hydrogen bomb in the Marshall Islands exceeded all estimates of its power.
- March 10, 1954:   The first atomic power plant was planned for the Duquesne Power Co. in Pittsburgh.
- May 17, 1954:   The Supreme Court declared racial segregation in public schools unconstitutional.

Big Game Tie Knocks Stanford Out of Rose Bowl

STANFORD MOMENT

A 23-20 loss to USC two weeks before the Big Game put Stanford's Rose Bowl hopes in jeopardy, but a 21-21 tie with Cal in the Big Game closed the door on the Indians' New Year's Day plans. With All-American quarterback Bobby Garrett leading the way, Stanford built a 21-7 lead in the third quarter, but two fourth-period touchdowns by Cal allowed the Bears to forge a tie. Garrett proved he was worthy of all his post-season honors as he set up one touchdown, scored one TD, passed for another and kicked all three extra points. Cal scored first to take a 7-0 lead, but Stanford came right back and drove 68 yards for the tying score with Garrett hooking up with Sam Morley on a 10-yard TD pass. Stanford opened up a two-touchdown lead in the third quarter when Garrett led the offense on a 73-yard touchdown drive, then intercepted a Paul Larson pass and returned it 56 yards for another TD. But, the Bears scored twice in the final stanza to tie the game and eliminate Stanford from any hope of going to the Rose Bowl.

WHILE THERE HAVE BEEN many great shortstops in Stanford baseball history, some would say that Warren Goodrich, a three-year starter from 1952-54, is the best of them all. A smooth fielder with a tremendous arm, great range and an outstanding hitter, Goodrich became the third Stanford baseball player to be named All-American (1954), following Joe Chez (1952) and Jack Shepard (1953). As a sophomore in 1952, Goodrich was named the team's Most Valuable Player. In '53, he was a part of one of the great Stanford teams of all time. That team won a school-record 29 games and became the first Indian squad to advance to the College World Series. Goodrich's team in '54 went 18-12 and finished second in the conference. Only two other shortstops in Stanford baseball history have captured All-America recognition: Frank Duffy in 1967 and Roger Burnett in 1991.

Warren Goodrich is one of only three shortstops in Stanford baseball history who have earned All-America honors. (Stanford Athletics)

Stanford Stat . . .

Leo Long became the third person in Stanford track history to win the NCAA championship in the javelin. Long, who had a personal best of 235-9 3/4", won the 1954 NCAA title with a throw of 226-8 3/4". He helped Stanford to a sixth place finish in '54, marking the sixth time in an eight-year span (1947-54) that the Indians had finished among the top six teams in the nation. Prior to Long, Stanford's other two NCAA javelin champs were Flint Hanner in 1921 and three-time winner Bud Held (1948-50).

STANFORD LIST

FIRST-TEAM ALL-AMERICAN QUARTERBACKS

Player	Year (s)
Frankie Albert	*1940, *1941
Gary Kerkorian	1951
Bobby Garrett	*1953
John Brodie	*1956
Jim Plunkett	*1970
Mike Boryla	1973
Guy Benjamin	*1977
John Elway	1980, *1982

*consensus

Stanford LEGEND

Bobby Garrett

Quarterback Bobby Garrett was the first player selected in the 1954 NFL draft. (Stanford Athletics)

There have been three number-one NFL draft picks in Stanford football history: John Elway in 1983, Jim Plunkett in 1971 and Bobby Garrett in 1954. All three were quarterbacks, all three were All-Americans and all three broke several school records before they graduated. To distinguish Garrett from the other two, one need only to look at the other side of the ball where Garrett starred as a defensive back while also placekicking and punting. He was Stanford's last great two-way player. A first-team All-American quarterback as a senior in 1953, Garrett also tied a school record with nine interceptions from his safety position. He played all 60 minutes in five games in 1953— the last Stanford player to accomplish that feat. But it was as a quarterback where Garrett shined most. He threw for a school-record 17 touchdown passes in 1953, including an 84-yarder that was the longest in Stanford history at the time. He won the Pop Warner Award as the top player on the West Coast and finished fifth in the Heisman Trophy balloting. The Cleveland Browns made Garrett the number-one selection in the NFL draft, then immediately traded him to the Green Bay Packers, where he played for just one season. He spent two years in the U.S. Air Force as a second lieutenant, then played his final two seasons of professional football with the Cleveland Browns.

STANFORD LORE

The Leland Stanford Jr. Museum was reopened on May 16, 1954 after extensive refurbishing of the building and reorganization of the collections. Two special items were added to the Stanford Family section: one was a painting, the "Palo Alto Spring -1878" and the other was the gold spike that Senator Stanford drove to mark completion of the transcontinental railroad.

1954-55

·· AMERICA'S TIME CAPSULE ··

- December 2, 1954: In a vote by U.S. Senators, Sen. Joseph McCarthy was condemned for activities in his anti-communist witch hunt.
- March 19, 1955: Bill Russell led the University of San Francisco Dons over La Salle 77-63 in the NCAA basketball championship game.
- April 12, 1955: A successful polio vaccine was announced by Dr. Jonas E. Salk. Tests carried out in 44 states indicated its effectiveness against poliomyelitis.
- May 2, 1955: A Pulitzer prize was awarded to Tennessee Williams for his drama, "Cat on a Hot Tin Roof."
- May 23, 1955: The Presbyterian Church approved the ordination of women ministers.

STANFORD MOMENT

Indians Suffer Worst Defeat in Football History

After beginning the season 3-0, Chuck Taylor's Indian football team suffered back-to-back losses to Navy and UCLA by an aggregate score of 97-0. Stanford lost a 27-0 decision to the Midshipmen, then lost to the Bruins by a whopping score of 72-0, the worst defeat in the history of Stanford football. UCLA coach Red Sanders, who some say remembered Stanford's 82-0 drubbing of the Bruins in 1925, continued to run up the score right up until the final gun. The Indians threw eight interceptions—although not all of them belonged to Stanford starting quarterback John Brodie— and the Bruins' netted 218 yards on the returns. Brodie, Stanford's sophomore QB who would become a First-Team All-American as a senior, completed 21 passes for 192 yards but failed to get his team in the end zone. A week later, however, Stanford bounced back to beat Washington 13-7. The Indians then lost the final four games of the season to finish 4-6.

TWO OF THE GREATEST small players in Stanford basketball history were 5-11 Ron Tomsic and 5-8 George Selleck. Selleck got his first opportunity to shine during the '53-54 season when Tomsic suffered an injury in game seven which forced him to miss the remainder of the season. Selleck responded by finishing second in the conference in scoring. He teamed with Tomsic in the backcourt for the '54-55 campaign —the first for rookie coach Howie Dallmar—and helped Stanford to an outstanding 16-8 season. As a senior in '55-56, Selleck was the man running the team. He was named to the all-conference team while leading the Indians to an 18-6 record. He finished his career as the number-eight all-time leading scorer in Stanford history with 1,004 points.

George Selleck teamed with Ron Tomsic during the 1954-55 season to give Stanford one of the best backcourt tandems in school history. (Stanford Athletics)

Stanford Stat . . .

Three of the top seven single-game high-point performances in Stanford men's basketball history belong to Ron Tomsic. As a sophomore in 1953, Tomsic scored 38 points in a game vs. USC and 39 points vs. Bradley. As a senior in '55, he scored 40 points against USC. The only players who have scored more points in a game than Tomsic are Hank Luisetti, Tom Dose, Kimberly Belton and Claude Terry.

STANFORD LIST

MEN'S BASKETBALL
MOST POINTS SCORED IN A GAME

Player, Year	Opponent	Points
Hank Luisetti, 1937-38	Duquesne	50
Tom Dose, 1963-64	Washington State	42
Kimberly Belton, 1979-80	USC	41
Claude Terry, 1970-71	Oregon State	41
Ron Tomsic, 1954-55	USC	40
Ron Tomsic, 1952-53	Bradley	39
Ron Tomsic, 1952-53	USC	38
Tom Dose, 1963-64	UCLA	38
Art Harris, 1967-68	Oregon	37
Art Harris, 1967-68	Washington State	37

Stanford LEGEND

Ron Tomsic

Ron Tomsic graduated from Stanford as the school's all-time leading scorer, surpassing the great Hank Luisetti. (Stanford Athletics)

At 5-11 and 185 pounds, Ron Tomsic was the quintessential scoring guard. By the time he departed The Farm in 1955, Tomsic had surpassed the great Hank Luisetti as Stanford's all-time leading scorer with 1,416 points. He was named to the conference's All-Southern Division team three times (1952, '53, '55) and was a member of the 1956 United States Olympic gold medal-winning basketball team. As a sophomore in 1953, Tomsic scored a school-record 515 points while averaging 19.1 points per game. He broke Luisetti's 1938 single-season record of 465 points. Tomsic broke his own record of 19.1 points per game in 1955 when he averaged 19.3 per game. His 40-point game vs. USC in 1955, which ranks fifth on Stanford's single-game scoring list, is still one of the greatest single games in Stanford history. Following graduation, Tomsic was playing AAU ball when he made the Olympic Team. He continued to play AAU ball after the Olympics with the San Francisco Olympic Club and was eventually elected to the Helms Amateur Basketball Hall of Fame.

STANFORD LORE

Alexander Kerensky, premier of Russia before his government was overthrown by the Bolsheviks in 1917, visited the Hoover Institution to inspect the collection of documents of his regime. Pleased with the wealth of information, Kerensky returned several times through 1967 to study, write, lecture and teach seminars. He and his co-author used more than 1,400 documents from the Hoover Archives.

1955-56

- **September 21, 1955:** Rocky Marciano defeated Archie Moore to retain the heavyweight boxing title.
- **October 4, 1955:** The Brooklyn Dodgers beat their cross-town rivals, the Yankees, in Game 7 of the World Series.
- **November 25, 1955:** Racial segregation in interstate trains and buses was banned by the Interstate Commerce Commission.
- **February 6, 1956:** The University of Alabama's first black student, Autherine Lucy, was suspended, ending three days of campus violence.
- **April 19, 1956:** American actress Grace Kelly married Prince Rainier of Monaco.

Jim Fifer (top) and Duvall Hecht (bottom) won a gold medal at the 1956 Olympic Games in the pairs without coxswain event. (Stanford Athletics)

STANFORD MOMENT

Fifer, Hecht Win Olympic Rowing Gold Medal

After suffering a narrow defeat at the 1952 Olympic Games in Helsinki, Jim Fifer and Duvall Hecht returned to the '56 Olympics in Melbourne and came home with a much different result—a gold medal. The duo had competed in the coxed pairs with coxswain in Helsinki and came within one-third of a length from reaching the semifinals. After winning their first heat, both Hecht and Fifer contracted colds as they were unable to beat Germany to advance. Melbourne was a different story. The duo decided to compete in the pairs without coxswain event—a well-advised decision. They qualified for the Olympics by defeating the defending gold medalists in the Trials Finals. In Melbourne, they won every race decisively en route to winning the gold medal.

THEY WERE THE "DREAM TEAM" of their era—one of the most dominating U.S. Olympic men's basketball teams of all-time. At the 1956 Games in Melbourne, two former Stanford players were a part of the U.S. gold medal-winning basketball team—a team that won their eight games in Olympic competition by an average margin of 53.5 points. Ron Tomsic '55 and Jim Walsh '52 joined USF legends Bill Russell and K.C. Jones to form one of the great Olympic teams. Tomsic was the team's third-leading scorer, averaging 11.1 points per game, while Walsh was the team's fifth-leading scorer at 9.1 points per game. The U.S. beat the Soviet Union in the gold medal game on December 1, 1956, 89-55 as Walsh chipped in 14 points. In the semifinal game, Tomsic led the U.S. in scoring with 18 points in a 101-38 victory over Uruguay.

Stanford Stat . . .

Nancy Simons Peterson became the third female in Stanford history to capture an Olympic medal when she won a silver in the 400-meter freestyle relay at the 1956 Games in Melbourne. Peterson, who also competed in the 100-meter freestyle at the Olympics, helped set a world record in the Olympic finals, but was still two seconds behind the world-record-setting team from Australia. She followed Marjorie Gestring Bowman and Brenda Helser de Morelos as Stanford's first three female Olympic medalists.

STANFORD LIST

FIRST ROUND NFL DRAFT PICKS

Player, Position	Year	Team
Darrien Gordon, CB	1993	San Diego Chargers
Bob Whitfield, OT	1992	Atlanta Falcons
Tommy Vardell, FB	1992	Cleveland Browns
Brad Muster, FB	1988	Chicago Bears
John Elway, QB	1983	Baltimore Colts
Darrin Nelson, RB	1982	Minnesota Vikings
Brian Holloway, OT	1981	New England Patriots
James Lofton, WR	1978	Green Bay Packers
Gordon King, OT	1978	New York Giants
Greg Sampson, DT	1972	Houston Oilers
Jeff Siemon, LB	1972	Minnesota Vikings
Jim Plunkett, QB	1971	New England Patriots
Gene Washington, WR	1969	San Francisco 49ers
John Brodie, QB	1957	San Francisco 49ers
Bobby Garrett, QB	1954	Cleveland Browns
Pete Kmetovic, RB	1942	Philadelphia Eagles
Frankie Albert, QB	1942	Chicago Bears

Stanford LEGEND

John Brodie

John Brodie starred at Stanford from 1954-56, then went on to a 17-year career with the San Francisco 49ers. (Stanford Athletics)

Although Chuck Taylor's teams from 1954-56 went 14-15-1, the Indians passing attack, led by John Brodie, continued to capture headlines. A three-year starter for Stanford, Brodie put up numbers matched by few quarterbacks in the nation. As a senior in 1956, Brodie led the nation in passing (1,633 yards) and total offense (1,642 yards) and was named a consensus First-Team All-American. He was the second player chosen in the first round of the 1957 NFL draft by the San Francisco 49ers. Brodie wound up playing all 17 of his professional seasons with the 49ers, earning All-Pro honors and becoming one of the all-time 49er greats. During his three years as Stanford's starting QB, Brodie threw for 3,594 yards, which set a school record at that time and was still among Stanford's top-10 over 40 years later. After his pro football career ended, Brodie, who was a member of Stanford's varsity golf teams, began a career in broadcasting and as a professional golfer on the Senior Tour. He was elected to the National Football Foundation College Hall of Fame in 1986.

STANFORD LORE

On January 30, 1956, the first use in Western Hemisphere of a linear accelerator for treatment of cancer took place at the Stanford Medical School. The patient was a boy, already blind in one eye, whose sight was saved when the machine removed tumors from his remaining eye. The use of medical accelerators spread to hospitals throughout the world.

1956-57

- October 8, 1956: Don Larsen of the New York Yankees hurled the first perfect game in World Series history.
- November 4, 1956: Political demonstrations against Communist rule in Hungary led to a surprise attack by Soviet Armed forces, resulting in the death of 32,000 persons.
- November 6, 1956: Dwight Eisenhower defeated Illinois governor Adlai Stevenson in the presidential election.
- January 21, 1957: NBC carried the first nationally televised videotaped broadcast, a recording of the presidential inauguration ceremonies.
- July 2, 1957: Surgeon General Leroy Burney reported that a link between cigarette smoking and lung cancer had been established.

STANFORD MOMENT

Valli's Record-Breaking Performance Not Enough in Big Game

Lou Valli, a 176-pound junior halfback from San Jose set a Stanford and Big Game-rushing record in the 1956 Big Game when he carried the ball 23 times for 209 yards. Stanford, which lost its last four games of the '56 season to finish 4-6 overall, fell to Cal 20-18. Valli had gained a modest 419 yards in nine games leading up to the Big Game, but his record-breaking effort at Cal was still not enough to overcome Joe Kapp and the Bears. Stanford had its chances, however, to win the game. Although Stanford missed all three extra-point attempts—the difference in the game—the Indians still had opportunities to add to their 18 points. Quarterback John Brodie had one touchdown pass called back due to a penalty and the Indians were stopped at the Cal seven-yard line on another occasion. Valli's 209-yard effort remained a Stanford single-game record until Darrin Nelson's 211-yard game in 1977. Valli's Big Game rushing record remains intact today.

Lou Valli's Big Game record 209 yards rushing was not enough as Cal beat Stanford 20-18. (Stanford Athletics)

THE INDIAN FOOTBALL TEAM in 1956 was very much alive in the Rose Bowl race after beating USC 27-19 to run its Pac-8 record to 3-0 and its overall mark to 4-2. But, Stanford lost its final four games all to conference opponents to finish the year 4-6. Three of those losses came by a total of four points and all were attributed to missed extra points. Despite the offensive firepower from All-American quarterback John Brodie and running back Lou Valli, Stanford could not overcome its missed extra points in suffering those three tough defeats. After the USC win, Stanford lost a 14-13 decision to UCLA and a 20-19 contest to Oregon State in successive weeks. A 34-13 loss to Washington preceded a 20-18 Big Game loss to Cal when the Indians failed to convert three extra points. Brodie was named a consensus First-Team All-America while defensive tackle Paul Wiggin earned All-America honors for the second straight year.

Stanford Stat . . .

Catcher Ralph Holding was the fourth Stanford baseball player to earn All-America recognition, following Joe Chez, Jack Shepard and Warren Goodrich. Holding was a three-year letterman from 1956-58 who, in '58, led the team in hitting with a .358 average while being named All-American. His teams won 24 games in 1956 and 23 in '58 - the second and third most victories in a season by a Stanford team. Holding is a member of the Stanford baseball Hall of Fame.

STANFORD LIST
PLAYERS AND COACHES

Below is a list of those who were both student-athletes and head coaches at Stanford (since 1920).

Coach, Sport	Player	Head Coach
Howie Dallmar, Basketball	1940-43	1955-75
Bud Finger, Golf	1938-41	1948-76
Jim Gaughran, Swimming	1951-54	1961-79
Dick Gould, Tennis	1957-60	1967-present
Mark Marquess, Baseball	1966-69	1977-present
Chuck Taylor, Football	1939-42	1951-57
Dink Templeton, Track	1917-20	1921-39
Paul Wiggin, Football	1953-56	1980-83
Ray Young, Baseball	1953-56	1968-76
Jack Weierhauser, Track	1934-37	1946-56

Stanford LEGEND
Paul Wiggin

A two-time first-team All-American, Paul Wiggin returned to the Farm as head coach from 1980-83. (Stanford Athletics)

Paul Wiggin was 18 years old in the fall of 1953 when he first arrived on the Stanford campus. After being recruited out of Manteca High School, Indian head coach Chuck Taylor told Wiggin he would have to go to junior college before he could get into Stanford. "I was being recruited heavily by everyone," recalls Wiggin. "But Stanford stuck out in my mind. I've made a few great decisions in my life and Stanford University was clearly one of them." Wiggin spent the 1952 season at Modesto Junior College, then transferred to Stanford. He was forced to sit out the '53 season due to an injury, but he came back to become a three-year starter as a defensive tackle from 1954-56. Wiggin earned All-America and All-Pacific Coast Conference honors in 1955 and '56 and went on to an 11-year career in the NFL with the Cleveland Browns. He played in three world championship games with the Browns and was a member of the Browns' 1964 NFL title club which beat Baltimore 27-0. Wiggin coached in the NFL for 12 years, including being the head coach of the Kansas City Chiefs from 1975-77. He returned to Stanford in 1980 as the 27th head football coach in school history. A member of Stanford's All-Century Team, he returned to the NFL after his four-year reign as Stanford's head coach ended in 1983.

STANFORD LORE

William Shockley, a lecturer in electrical engineering, was named co-winner of the 1956 Nobel Prize in physics in October. He and his two colleagues invented the transistor at Bell Laboratories in 1948. Shockley became a controversial figure years later because of his theories that blacks are genetically inferior.

1957-58

- September 25, 1957: President Eisenhower sent 1,000 Army paratroopers to Little Rock, Arkansas to enforce the desegregation of Central High School.
- October 4, 1957: The Soviet Union launched Sputnik I, the first Earth satellite.
- October 10, 1957: The Milwaukee Braves beat the New York Yankees in Game 7 of the 54th World Series.
- January 31, 1958: Explorer I, the first U.S. Earth satellite, was launched from Cape Canaveral, Florida.
- March 25, 1958: Sugar Ray Robinson regained the world middleweight boxing title for an unprecedented fifth time, defeating Carmen Basilio.

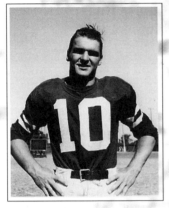

QB Jack Douglas scored the winning touchdown in Stanford's 14-12 Big Game victory. (Stanford Athletics)

STANFORD MOMENT

Stanford Wins Big Game After Taylor Announces Resignation

Just as Cal's Pappy Waldorf had done the year before, Stanford's Chuck Taylor announced two days before the Big Game that he would retire following the game. His team responded with a 14-12 victory before a crowd of over 91,000 at Stanford Stadium. An immensely popular coach and player on The Farm, Taylor assumed a newly created position of Assistant Athletic Director the next year. Entering the 60th meeting between Stanford and Cal, the Indians had a modest 5-4 record while the Bears were a dreadful 1-9. Stanford had suffered a key injury early in the season when star running back Lou Valli was lost for the season, but Chuck Shea filled in capably and was the league's leading ground gainer heading into the Big Game. He gained 155 yards and scored the game's first touchdown on a nine-yard run. The TD was set up by a 40 yard punt return by the Indian's Jeri McMillian. Cal scored in the second quarter to close the gap, but the Indian's Joel Freis blocked the extra point as Stanford took a 7-6 lead into the locker room. The Indians put together a 10-play, 73-yard drive in the third quarter to take a 14-6 lead. Quarterback Jack Douglas scored the TD on a one-yard run. The Bears' second touchdown came on a 41-yard pass play from QB Joe Kapp to Steve Glagoia in the fourth quarter, but once again the extra point was blocked—this time by the Indian's Eric Protiva. A Big Game victory was a fitting end to Chuck Taylor's coaching career.

JON A. "JACK" DOUGLAS will forever be the answer to the following trivia question, "Who is the only athlete in Stanford history to play quarterback on the football team and compete for the United States' Davis Cup team in tennis?" A rare two-sport athlete in football and tennis, Douglas earned six varsity letters on The Farm, three in football (1955-57) and three in tennis (1956-58). As a football player, he was the team's starting quarterback in 1957, completing 78-of-146 for 957 yards and nine touchdowns. As a tennis player, Douglas' three Stanford teams all placed in the top-10 nationally with the '58 club finishing second to USC. At the NCAA tennis tournament in 1958, Douglas won six singles matches and four doubles matches to help Stanford finish number-two. He went on to become a member of the U.S. Davis Cup Team on three occasions: 1958, '61, '62.

Stanford Stat . . .

Senior running back Chuck Shea set a Stanford single season rushing record in 1957 as he gained 840 yards on 163 carries while scoring eight touchdowns. Shea's record stood for seven years until Ray Handley gained 936 yards in 1964. Still, Shea's 1957 season ranks among the best in school history. He became the first player in school history to gain over 1,000 yards in all-purpose running when he totaled 1,155 yard in 1957. He also led the team with a 24.7 average on kickoff returns.

STANFORD LIST

WINNINGEST MEN'S BASKETBALL COACHES

Coach	At Stanford	Wins
Howie Dallmar	1955-75	264
Mike Montgomery	1987-present	204
Everett Dean	1939-51	167
John Bunn	1931-38	108
Dick DiBiaso	1976-81	70
Tom Davis	1982-86	58
Andy Kerr	1923-26	42
Bob Burnett	1952-54	41
Husky Hunt	1927-30	40

Stanford LEGEND

Howie Dallmar

Howie Dallmar is truly one of the legends of the Stanford basketball program. (Stanford Athletics)

His name will forever be synonymous with Stanford basketball— a legend as a player and coach stamped firmly in the history of Stanford Athletics. Born in San Francisco, Howie Dallmar is the quintessential "local boy makes good" story. He attended Lowell High School in San Francisco, then spent one year at Menlo College before transferring to Stanford in 1941. As a sophomore at Stanford, he was a starting guard on the Indians' 1942 NCAA championship team. After helping Stanford beat Dartmouth for the national title, he was named the Most Valuable Player of the '42 tournament. After serving in World War II, Dallmar played two seasons in the NBA with the Philadelphia Warriors. As a rookie, he ranked fourth in the NBA in assists. He was an all-NBA selection in his second year after leading the league in assists and ranking 11th in scoring. Dallmar retired from the NBA to take a job at the University of Pennsylvania as head basketball and baseball coach, where he compiled a six-year record in basketball of 105-51. Dallmar returned to Stanford as head basketball coach in 1955 and spent the next 21 years at the helm of the program he helped put on the map. He retired from coaching in 1975 after winning one league championship and recording a 264-264 record. His 27-year college coaching record of 369-315 made him one of the winningest coaches of his time.

STANFORD LORE

Sixteen wooden boxes, held under seal for 31 years at the Hoover Institution by agreement with the secret donor, were opened in November of 1957. The boxes revealed the files of the Paris office of the Russian czar's secret police. Basil Maklakoff, last pre-Communist ambassador to France, signed a statement that he had burned the entire file. Instead, he shipped it to the Hoover War Library in 1926. Experts described the information as a "mother lode of knowledge of the crucial years leading to the overthrow of the Romanovs in March 1917."

1958-59

•• AMERICA'S TIME CAPSULE ••

- **September 30, 1958:** Arkansas Gov. Orval Faubus defied the Supreme Court's ruling against racial segregation in public schools.
- **January 3, 1959:** President Dwight Eisenhower proclaimed Alaska the 49th state.
- **February 3, 1959:** Rock-and-roll stars Buddy Holly and Richie Valens died in an airplane crash.
- **March 21, 1959:** The University of California defeated West Virginia 71-70 to win the NCAA basketball championship.
- **May 28, 1959:** The U.S. Army launched two monkeys into space. They were recovered unhurt from the Caribbean Sea after a 300-mile-high flight.
- **August 21, 1959:** Hawaii was admitted to the union as the 50th state.

STANFORD MOMENT

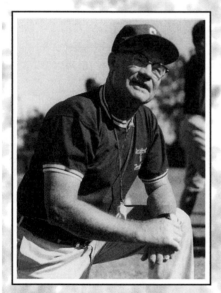

"Cactus Jack" Curtice began his five-year tenure as Stanford's head football coach in 1958.
(Stanford Athletics)

Taylor Resigns; "Cactus Jack" Takes Over

Chuck Taylor had made it known to Athletic Director Al Masters that he did not want to be a coach all his life. At the end of the 1957 season, Taylor decided the time was right to resign as head coach after seven years and a 40-29-2 overall record. His replacement came with glowing credentials, but his five-year stint was anything but glowing. Jack Curtice, who had tremendous success at Utah, West Texas State and Texas Western, was named to succeed Taylor in 1958. He was colorful and witty and folksy and he brought with him a reputation for a wide-open offense. But "Cactus Jack" got off to a slow start as the Indians' head man and never really recovered. He lost his first three games by a combined score of 98-13 and finished his first season with just two wins in 10 games. He went 3-7 in 1959 and 0-10 in 1960 and, after three years, his record stood at 5-25. Curtice resigned after the 1962 season with a five-year record of 14-36.

ONE OF THE GREAT FLOOR LEADERS in Stanford basketball history was Paul Neumann, who started for Howie Dallmar's teams from 1957-59. Neumann joined Stanford's "400" club in 1959 by scoring over 400 points en route to being named Second-Team All-American and First-Team All-Pacific Coast Conference. He was only the sixth basketball player in school history to earn All-America recognition. Neumann was captain of the '58-59 team that went 15-9 and tied with UCLA for third place in the conference. He left Stanford with 997 career points, which placed him fifth on the school's all-time list. Neumann went on to a fine professional career with Syracuse, Philadelphia and San Francisco.

Stanford Stat . . .

George Harrison won an NCAA swimming championship for Stanford in 1959, then went on to the 1960 Olympic Games in Rome to capture a gold medal as part of the U.S. 800-meter freestyle relay team. Harrison, whose specialty was the individual medley, won the NCAA title in the 200-yard IM in '59 in a time of 2:06.70. He set two world records in the 400-meter IM in 1960, but because this was not an Olympic event, he was forced to turn to the 200-meter free, which he won at the Trials Finals. In Rome, Harrison swam the leadoff leg on the U.S. 800-meter freestyle relay team which won the gold and set a new world record.

STANFORD LIST

SEASON RECEPTION LEADERS

	Name, year	Receptions
1.	Brad Muster, 1985	78
2.	Gene Washington, 1968	71
3.	Vincent White, 1982	68
4.	Justin Armour, 1994	67
	Darrin Nelson, 1981	67
6.	Chris Walsh, 1991	66
7.	Glyn Milburn, 1990	64
8.	Chris Burford, 1959	61
	Greg Baty, 1985	61
	Brad Muster, 1986	61
	Ed McCaffrey, 1990	61

Stanford LEGEND

Chris Burford

In 1959, Chris Burford led the nation and tied the NCAA record by registering 61 receptions. (Stanford Athletics)

In 1959, there was no better passing combination in college football than Stanford's Dick Norman to Chris Burford. As a quarterback, Norman led the nation in passing with 1,963 yards and his favorite target was Burford at tight end, who led the nation and tied an NCAA record by hauling in 61 passes. Burford was also the national leader in receiving yards with 757. Those numbers earned him First-Team All-America honors and a place among the greatest tight ends college football had ever seen at that time. A two-time first-team All-Pacific 8 selection, Burford's greatest game at Stanford may have been his last. The Big Game of 1959, a 20-17 California win, saw Norman complete an NCAA-record 34-of-39 for 401 yards. Twelve of those completions for 115 yards and one TD went to Burford, who was playing in his final game in a Stanford uniform. Burford had an outstanding junior season as well, tying a school record with 45 receptions. He left Stanford as the school's number-five receiver with 107 receptions and began a professional career with the Kansas City Chiefs. Burford played eight seasons with the Chiefs (1960-67) and was an All-AFL pick in 1961. In 1995, he became the 13th player in Stanford history to be elected to the National Football Foundation College Hall of Fame. Burford earned his law degree while playing pro football and has enjoyed a successful practice in his own law firm of Burnhill, Morehouse and Burford.

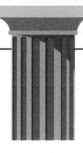

STANFORD LORE

Scientists from the University and Stanford Research Institute announced in August, 1959, plans to construct the world's second largest dish antenna in the foothills—as tall as a 15-story building—for the study of upper atmosphere physics. Scientists also announced that the 150-foot dish will be funded by the Air Force and include a high-powered transmitter valued at more than $1 million, which will make it possible to bounce signals off the Sun, Moon, Mars and Venus.

1959-60

- September 15, 1959: Soviet Premier Nikita Khrushchev arrived in the United States for meetings with President Eisenhower.
- October 15, 1959: The Nobel Prize in Physiology of Medicine was awarded Arthur Kornberg of Stanford University and Severo Ochoa of NYU for their joint work on the chemistry of heredity.
- January 4, 1960: The United Steel Workers and the nation's steel companies agreed on a wage increase to settle a six-month-long strike.
- February 11, 1960: Jack Parr, protesting NBC censorship of one of his jokes the night before, walked off his late-night television show.
- May 1, 1960: A United States U-2 reconnaissance plane was shot down inside the U.S.S.R, causing Soviet Premier Khrushchev to cancel a planned summit meeting in Paris.

Skip Face gave Stanford a 17-14 lead in the 1959 Big Game after kicking a 25-yard field goal, but Cal came back to win 20-17. *(Stanford Athletics)*

STANFORD MOMENT

Norman's Sets Three NCAA Records in Big Game Loss

It remains one of the greatest single-game performances in Stanford football history. Junior quarterback Dick Norman placed his name in the record book after completing 34-of-39 passes for 401 yards in Stanford's 20-17 loss to California in the Big Game. Norman broke NCAA records for most passes completed (34), yards gained passing (401) and completion percentage (.872). He also helped tight end Chris Burford tie an NCAA record for most receptions in a season. Burford caught 12 passes in the Big Game to raise his season total to 61. Cal led 14-0 before Norman marched his team on two long third quarter drives to tie the scored at 14-14. Skip Face booted a 25-yard field goal midway through the final period to put Stanford on top 17-14. Cal marched 64 yards on their next possession for the go-ahead TD, but missed the extra point. Norman, with time running out, drove his team to the Bear's 10-yard line with seconds remaining in the game. Stanford coach Jack Curtice elected to go for the win instead of game-tying field goal. On the game's final play, Norman took the snap and ran around right end to the five yard line, but time ran out and Stanford was not able to run another play.

OVER 125,000 PEOPLE came to Stanford Stadium on July 1-2, 1960 to watch the United States Track & Field Trials in what was, and still is, the best attended Trials in U.S. history. It was a glorious time for track and field in the U.S. and the Trials epitomized the popularity of the sport, especially in the Bay Area. World records were broken by Don Bragg in the pole vault (15-9 1/4") and John Thomas in the high jump (7-3 3/4"), but the highlight of the Trials for the local fans were three Bay Area collegians who all earned a spot on the Olympic Team. Stanford's Ernie Cunnliffe took the third and final spot in the 800-meters as his 1:47.5 narrowly edged out the fourth place finisher. Ray Norton from San Jose State won the 100-meters (10.4) and 200-meters (20.5) while Cal's Jack Yerman took first in the 400-meters. "Al Masters, who had a great love for track and field and the Olympic movement, told me to put in a bid to host the 1960 Olympic Trials," recalls longtime Stanford track coach Payton Jordan of his Athletic Director. "We went for it and got it. It was a glorious two-day event," he said.

Stanford Stat . . .

A three-year letterman in basketball from 1958-60, John Arrillaga became the team captain and leading scorer during the '59-60 campaign and earned All-Pacific 8 Conference honors in the process. His 894 career points ranked him among the school's all-time top-10 in 1960. A prominent builder and real estate developer in the San Francisco Bay Area, Arrillaga has been a major influence in the construction of many buildings on the Stanford campus, including the Arrillaga Family Sports Center, home of the Stanford Athletic Department, and named for his family.

STANFORD LIST

WOMEN'S SWIMMING WORLD RECORD HOLDERS
(individual events only)

Name	Event (s)	Year(s) Record Broken
Janet Evans	400m freestyle	1987, 1988
	800m freestyle	1987,1988,1989
	1500m freestyle	1987, 1988
Jo Harshbarger	800m freestyle	1972, 1974
	1500m freestyle	1973
Linda Jezek	200m backstroke	1978
Claudia Kolb	100m breaststroke	1964
	200m IM	1966,1967,1968
	400m IM	1967, 1968
Sharon Stouder	100m butterfly	1964
	200m butterfly	1964
Jenny Thompson	100m freestyle	1992
Chris Von Saltza	400m freestyle	1960
	200m backstroke	1958

Stanford LEGEND

Chris Von Saltza

Chris Von Saltza won three gold medals and one silver as a 16-year-old at the 1960 Olympics. (Stanford Athletics)

She was only 16 years old when she arrived in Rome for the 1960 Olympic Games. Already a two-time world record holder, Chris Von Saltza surprised no one by taking home three golds and one silver medal in four swimming events, concluding one of the most dominating performances of any woman in Olympic competition. Von Saltza, a San Francisco native, had won five gold medals at the 1959 Pan American Games and had just become the first American woman to break the five-minute barrier in the 400-meter freestyle when she clocked a world record time of 4:44.5 at the 1960 Olympic Trials. She took home gold medals in the 400-meter free, 400-meter freestyle relay and 400-meter medley relay while earning a silver in the 100-meter free. Von Saltza, who won 19 AAU titles while swimming for the Santa Clara Swim Club, retired from swimming after the '60 Games and entered Stanford, where she majored in Asian history. She accompanied the 1968 United States Olympic Team to Mexico City as an assistant coach/chaperone. Von Saltza's four-medal Olympic performance in 1960 still ranks today as one of the great individual efforts in U.S. Olympic history.

STANFORD LORE

The Stanford Medical Center, a $27 million complex, was dedicated on September 17, 1959. The Stanford School of Medicine moved from San Francisco to the new complex, which included clinics and a 420-bed hospital. Having the Medical School on campus helped interrelate medical studies and research with other academic disciplines.

1960-61

•• AMERICA'S TIME CAPSULE ••

- September 26, 1960: Sen. John Kennedy and Vice-President Richard Nixon participated in the first of a series of televised presidential campaign debates.
- October 13, 1960: Bill Mazeroski of Pittsburgh slammed a game-winning home run against the New York Yankees to give the Pirates the World Series championship.
- November 8, 1960: John F. Kennedy was elected president of the United States in a narrow victory over Richard Nixon.
- April 17, 1961: Nearly 2,000 CIA-trained anti-Castro Cuban exiles landed at the Bay of Cochinos in Cuba, in what came to be known as the Bay of Pigs invasion.
- May 5, 1961: Alan Shepard made a successful flight aboard the Project Mercury capsule Freedom Seven to become the first American in space.

A member of the Olympic Track team in 1960, Ernie Cunnliffe set a world record in the 1,000-meter run in 1961. (Stanford Athletics)

STANFORD MOMENT

Cunnliffe Sets World Record in 1,000-Yard Run

Ernie Cunnliffe was no doubt one of the best distance runners Stanford has ever produced. Like so many of Payton Jordan's athletes, Cunnliffe was a world-record holder, an Olympian and an NCAA All-American. In 1961, after graduation from Stanford, Ernie set a new world record in the 1,000-yard run (indoors). Prior to setting the record, he was a member of the 1960 United States Olympic Track team that competed in Rome. At the Olympic Trials in 1960—held at Stanford Stadium—Cunnliffe held a big lead in the 800-meter run with two laps to go. But he was forced to hold on at the end as two runners passed him and one more was right on his side. After the judges examined the photo-finish, they ruled that Cunnliffe had indeed finished third to earn the final spot on the Olympic team. During his Stanford days, Cunnliffe twice earned All-America honors—in 1959 and '60—in the 880-yard run and set six school records, four individual events and two relays. His school records in the 880-yard run and 800-meters still stand today as testimony to his claim as one of Stanford's all-time great distance runners.

BILL "SKIP" FACE did more than simply carry the ball from his running back position. During his three seasons (1958-60), Face kicked field goals and extra points, caught passes out of the backfield, returned kickoffs and punts and set records as the team's most prolific scorer. He left Stanford as the school's record holder for most points in a game (27), in a season (100) and in a career (176) and most touchdowns scored in a season (11). Face broke single-season records in '59 by scoring 100 points and scoring 11 touchdowns. He also led the team in rushing, kickoff returns and punt returns. Against Oregon State in '59, Face set a Stanford record by accounting for 27 points. He scored three touchdowns, kicked one field goal and four extra points and scored on a two-point conversion. His season record of 100 points remained for 32 years until Tommy Vardell scored 120 in 1991. Face and Vardell remain the only players in Stanford history to score 100 points in a season.

Stanford Stat . . .

Since Stanford began playing football in 1891, there have been only two winless seasons: 0-9 in 1947 and 0-10 in 1960. Jack Curtice's team scored just 111 points during the 1960 campaign while being held to 10 points or less in all but three games. Stanford began the year at Washington State and led 14-0 at the half, but the Cougars scored 15 unanswered points in the second half for a 15-14 victory. Stanford's only other close game of the year was a 25-21 loss to Oregon State.

STANFORD LIST

MOST SEASON POINTS IN FOOTBALL

	Name, Year	Points
1.	Tommy Vardell, 1991	120
2.	Skip Face, 1959	100
3.	Darrin Nelson, 1981	96
4.	Vincent White, 1982	92
5.	Tommy Vardell, 1990	84
6.	John Hopkins, 1988	82
7.	Eric Abrams, 1995	81
8.	Eric Abrams, 1992	79
9.	Mark Harmon, 1982	78
	Brad Muster, 1986	78
	Glyn Milburn, 1992	78

Stanford LEGEND

Dick Norman

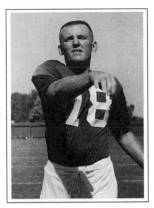

Dick Norman left Stanford as the school's all-time leader in yards passing and total offense. (Stanford Athletics)

Despite the fact that Dick Norman was the starting quarterback for two teams in 1959 and '60 that went 3-17, he nevertheless established passing numbers never before seen in college football. Norman's 1959 totals of 1,963 yards passing and 2,018 yards in total offense were far and away the best in the nation. No one was within 300 yards of him. He left Stanford following the 1960 season as the school record holder in yards passing (3,737) and total offense (3,654)—which also ranked among the best in college football history. Norman will forever be remembered for his 1959 Big Game, when he set three NCAA records by completing 34-of-39 for 401 yards. His numbers went down during Stanford's 0-10 season in 1960 as he lost his top four receivers from the '59 club, but he still managed to throw for 1,057 yards. Norman was selected in the 1960 NFL draft by the Chicago Bears and the 1961 AFL draft by the Oakland Raiders. He played just one season of professional football (1961) with the Bears.

STANFORD LORE

The red brick building that Senator Stanford built in 1886 as part of his winery operation was converted in January, 1961 to accommodate a bank, restaurant and other tenants. The building was most recently used as a cow barn and to stable bulls as part of an artificial insemination program. The new tenants became part of the Stanford Shopping Center complex.

1961-62

- October 1, 1961: Roger Maris of the New York Yankees hit his 61st home run, breaking Babe Ruth's single-season record.
- February 10, 1962: Jim Beatty became the first American to break the four-minute mile indoors, registering a time of 3:58.9 in Los Angeles.
- February 20, 1962: Astronaut John Glenn became the first American to orbit the Earth, circling the globe three times aboard Friendship 7.
- March 2, 1962: Wilt Chamberlain of the Philadelphia Warriors became the first NBA player to score 100 points in a game.
- August 5, 1962: Actress Marilyn Monroe, 36, died in her Los Angeles home of an apparent overdose of sleeping pills.

The 1962 U.S.-U.S.S.R. track meet is considered by some to be the greatest track meet of all time.
(Stanford Athletics)

STANFORD MOMENT

The Greatest Track Meet of All Time

It has been called the greatest track meet of all time. For two days in July, 1962, the Cold War stopped and all eyes were focused on Stanford Stadium, site of the U.S.-U.S.S.R. track meet. What began as a way to help the budget deficit in the Stanford University Athletic Department ended as an historical event of tremendous proportions. It was more than a track meet. It was East vs. West, the Reds vs. the Red, White and Blue, Communism vs. Democracy. "It was a wonderful moment," said Payton Jordan, Stanford's track coach and organizer of the event. "It had more value than any Olympics I've ever been to. We'll never see it again. It was a one-time thing," he said. The idea for the meet began when Stanford Athletic Director Al Masters, facing a $100,000 budget deficit, asked Jordan if a track meet could generate some revenue. "Do you think we can get the Russians here?" Masters said to Jordan. And Jordan did the rest. Highlights on the field included Soviet high jumper Valeriy Brumel breaking his own world record; 1960 Olympic triple gold medalist Wilma Rudolph winning the women's 100-meters and future NFL star Bob Hayes winning the men's 100-meters. But the real highlight of the event occurred at the end. As the two teams were leaving the field during the closing ceremonies, American and Soviet men and women began putting arms around each others shoulders, slipping arm through arm and generally embracing one another. The 81,000 fans in attendance stood and cheered. Many were in tears. They realized that they had just witnessed something special.

DAVE WEILL joined an elite group of Stanford discus throwers by becoming the sixth athlete in school history to win the NCAA title in this event. Previously, five athletes had won seven NCAA individual discus titles. Weill won back-to-back NCAA championships in 1962 and '63 and was a three-time All-American (1961-63). He went on to win a bronze medal at the 1964 Olympic Games in Tokyo. Weill had a knack for finishing third, however. He placed third three times at the AAU Championships, was third at the '64 U.S. Olympic Trials and third in Tokyo. His best performance came in 1967 when he threw 206-7 1/2" at the Sacramento Invitational Meet. He placed third. Weill, at 6-7 and 270, helped Stanford to their best national finish as a team under Payton Jordan. His 1962 team placed second at the NCAA Championships and in '63, Stanford finished third.

Stanford Stat . . .

Howie Dallmar's men's basketball team began a string of six consecutive winning seasons in 1961-62 as the Indians finished with an impressive overall record of 16-6. Stanford, which ran off a string of seven straight wins, went 6-0 vs. Cal and USC, but could muster just one win in three games with UCLA, which won the AAWU league championship ahead of Stanford. Sophomore center Tom Dose, destined to be one of the great players in Stanford history, made his debut on the varsity but it was forward John Windsor, an All-League selection, who was leader of the '61-62 Indians.

STANFORD LIST

STANFORD'S HEAD OLYMPIC COACHES

Name, Sport	Olympic Year (s)
Ernie Brandsten, Diving	1924, 1928, 1932, 1936
Austin Clapp, Water Polo	1948
George Haines, Swimming	1980
Brooks Johnson, Track	1984 (women's team only)
Payton Jordan, Track	1968
Skip Kenney, Swimming	1996 (men's team only)
Mark Marquess, Baseball	1988
Richard Quick, Swimming	1988, 1996 (women's team only)
Fred Sturm, Men's Volleyball	1992, 1996
Tara vanDerveer, W Basketball	1996

Stanford LEGEND

Payton Jordan

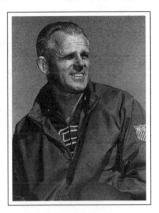

Payton Jordan was Stanford's head track & field coach from 1957-79 and the head coach for the 1968 U.S. Olympic Track team. (Stanford Athletics)

Payton Jordan first tasted success in track and field running a race as a young boy in southern California. He was a great college athlete at USC, became a world-renowned track and field coach during his 23 years as Stanford's head man (1957-79), and was the head coach of the 1968 United States Olympic Track team. Jordan also coordinated and promoted the 1960 U.S. Olympic Trials and the 1962 USA-USSR Track Meet at Stanford Stadium and became a world-record holder in numerous events in the over-50 and over-60 classification. As an athlete at USC, Jordan captained the track team, played rugby and was a halfback on the 1938 Trojan football team which defeated Duke in the '39 Rose Bowl. He came to Stanford in 1957 and began a long and storied career. His best two teams at Stanford were in 1962 and '63 when his troops finished third and second, respectively, at the NCAA Championships. His Stanford athletes won six individual NCAA titles, broke five world records and earned All-America honors 29 times. He was lauded for a tremendous success in putting on the 1962 USA-USSR Track Meet at Stanford Stadium. But the highlight of coaching career came in 1968 when he was the head coach of the U.S. Olympic Team in Mexico City. That team won more Olympic medals and established more records than any other team in history. Jordan set five world records in the sprints in the over-50 classification and four world records in the over-60 classification. He is recognized today as one of the innovators of track and field and a leader in developing champions.

STANFORD LORE

Robert Hofstadter was awarded the Nobel Prize for physics on November 2, 1961, for his research on the structure of atomic nuclei. His findings were based on experimental data obtained from the Mark III accelerator. He obtained accurate measurements of the density distributions of electric charge for protons and neutrons in the nucleus of the atom.

1962-63

•• AMERICA'S TIME CAPSULE ••

- Ocotber 1, 1962: James Meredith, escorted by U.S. marshals, became the first black to attend classes at the University of Mississippi. Two men were killed in the ensuing mob violence.
- October 22, 1962: President Kennedy addressed the nation on television regarding the Cuban missile crisis. The missile bases were dismantled by the Soviet Union 11 days later.
- May 7, 1963: The communications satellite Telstar 2 was launched from Cape Canaveral, Florida, and began relaying television signals between the United States and Europe.
- June 26, 1963: President Kennedy spoke to a crowd of more than one million adjacent to the Berlin Wall in Germany.
- August 28, 1963: Dr. Martin Luther King presented his "I have a dream" speech to a crowd of 200,000 from the steps of the Lincoln Memorial in Washington, D.C.

STANFORD MOMENT

Stanford tied for the league championship in 1962-63 with All-American Tom Dose (l) leading the way. Here, Dose is presented his All-America certificate by head coach Howie Dallmar (r). (Stanford Athletics)

Men's Hoops Team Ties for League Championship

Not since the 1942 NCAA championship had Stanford finished among the elite in college basketball or won a league title. But in 1962-63, with 6-8 junior center Tom Dose leading the way, Stanford earned the co-championship of the Athletic Association of Western Universities and finished the season ranked 10th in the country with a 19-9 overall record. Stanford won two of three in league play over Cal and UCLA and its 7-5 AAWU record tied the Bruins for the league title. Dose became the first Stanford player to average 20 points a season as he broke the school's single season scoring mark with 520 points. Co-captains Don Clemetson (12.5 points per game) and Darrell Sutherland (6.6 ppg) teamed with rugged Clayton Raaka (eight rebounds per game) and Dose to form the most talented team on The Farm since Howie Dallmar's '42 championship club.

TOM DOSE was the first great big man in Stanford basketball history. He is one of only two players who averaged in double digits in both points (19.2) and rebounds (10.1) during their Stanford career (the other is Rich Kelley). Dose earned Second-Team All-America and First-Team All-AAWU honors in both 1963 and '64. He became the first player ever to average 20 points and 10 rebounds in a season in 1963 and was a major factor in Stanford's winning the league championship that season. Dose owns two of the top eight single-game high scoring efforts at Stanford, both coming during the '63-64 season. He had 38 against UCLA and 42—second highest behind Hank Luisetti's 50-point game in 1938—against Washington. But perhaps his best game came during the '62-63 season when he grabbed 20 rebounds and scored 29 points against Oregon State and their 7-1 center Mel Counts. Dose left Stanford as the school's all-time leader in points scored (1,441) and rebounds (755).

Stanford Stat . . .

Jim Lonborg was Stanford's top pitcher in 1962 and '63, setting a school record with 114 strikeouts in 109.1 innings pitched in 1963. In two seasons, Lonborg struck out 211 in 203 innings of work, a ratio that made professional baseball teams covet the hard-throwing right-hander. He eventually signed with the Boston Red Sox and in 1967, Lonborg went 22-9, led his team to the American League pennant title, won the Cy Young Award and tossed a one-hitter vs. the St. Louis Cardinals in the World Series.

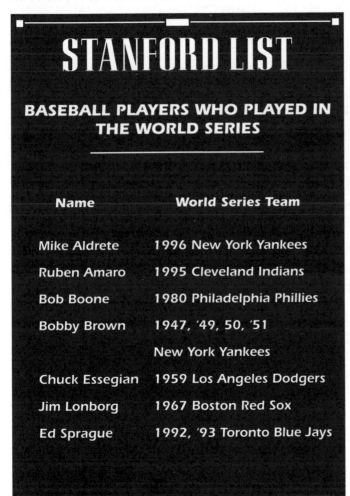

STANFORD LIST

BASEBALL PLAYERS WHO PLAYED IN THE WORLD SERIES

Name	World Series Team
Mike Aldrete	1996 New York Yankees
Ruben Amaro	1995 Cleveland Indians
Bob Boone	1980 Philadelphia Phillies
Bobby Brown	1947, '49, 50, '51 New York Yankees
Chuck Essegian	1959 Los Angeles Dodgers
Jim Lonborg	1967 Boston Red Sox
Ed Sprague	1992, '93 Toronto Blue Jays

Stanford LEGEND

Larry Questad

Larry Questad was an NCAA champion, a world-record holder, an Olympian and All-American. (Stanford Athletics)

While he may not have gotten the recognition that he deserved, make no mistake about it, Larry Questad was one of the great sprinters in the world during his era and perhaps the greatest sprinter to ever wear a Stanford uniform. He was an NCAA champion, a world record holder, an Olympian and an All-American. Questad, from Livingston, Montana, won the NCAA championship as a sophomore in 1963 in the 100-yard dash and placed second in the 220 to eventual Olympic champion Henry Carr. Three of the school records he set in '63 still stand today: 100-yard dash (9.3), 220-yard dash (20.6) and 200-meter dash (20.5). His 100-meter time in 1964 of 10.2 also stands today as the school record. Questad anchored Stanford's 440-yard relay team in 1965 that set a new world record of 39.7. He made his big splash on the world stage in 1968 when he became the first person ever to run the 100-meters in 10.0 and the 200-meters in 20.28. No one before had ever shown that kind of speed in both events. He qualified for the 1968 U.S. Olympic team but finished sixth in Mexico City in the 200-meters. Still, Questad had made his stamp on the sprint events—one that will last forever.

STANFORD LORE

NASA announced in January, 1963, that genetics Professor Joshua Lederberg and associates would design instruments to search for microscopic life on other planets. Lederberg, who in 1958 won the Nobel Prize for his work in genetics, coined the term "exobiology" to describe his interest in the possibility of life on other planets. Later, he helped start SUMEX/AIM (Stanford University Medical Experimental Computer/Artificial Intelligence in Medicine).

1963-64

- **October 2, 1963:** Pitcher Sandy Koufax of the Los Angeles Dodgers set a World Series record by striking out 15 New York Yankees in the opening game.
- **November 22, 1963:** President John F. Kennedy was killed by an assassin's bullet in Dallas, Texas.
- **November 24, 1963:** Lee Harvey Oswald was shot and killed by Jack Ruby while in the custody of the Dallas police.
- **February 7, 1964:** The Beatles arrived in New York City for an appearance on the Ed Sullivan Show.
- **February 25, 1964:** Challenger Cassius Clay defeated Sonny Liston for the world heavyweight boxing title.
- **July 2, 1964:** The Civil Rights Act of 1964 was signed by President Lyndon Johnson.

STANFORD MOMENT

Steve Thurlow's touchdown helped the Indians win the 1963 Big Game. *(Stanford Athletics)*

Big Game Delayed Following Kennedy Assassination

The 66th Big Game, scheduled to be played on November 23, 1963, was delayed one week while the country mourned the assassination of President John F. Kennedy. A day before the game, Kennedy was shot to death in Dallas, Texas and the country was sent into shock. The Big Game was played on November 30 and over 82,000 fans filled Stanford Stadium to watch the Indians beat Cal, 28-17. Both bands, in honor of the slain President, played a tribute to Kennedy. The game pitted Stanford, with a 2-7 record and coached by first-year head man John Ralston, against the 4-4-1 Bears, coached by Marv Levy. Ralston, who replaced Jack Curtice, concluded the worst season of his nine-year Stanford career. But, a Big Game win over Cal salvaged some pride. The game was tied at 3-3 at the intermission and, after an exchange of third-quarter touchdowns, Cal assumed a 10-9 lead after Stanford failed to make its two-point conversion attempt. The Bears took a 17-9 lead when Tom Blanchfield returned a punt 69 yards for a TD. Stanford, however, scored 19 unanswered points to secure the win. Ken Babajian capped a 74-yard drive by scoring from a yard out, then Braden Beck added a field goal to give Stanford an 18-17 lead. Steve Thurlow's five-yard TD run and another Beck field goal rounded out the scoring.

AS A FRESHMAN on Stanford's women's tennis team, Jane Albert, daughter of Stanford's great quarterback Frankie Albert, won the national collegiate singles championship, defeating teammate Julie Heldman to become the first Stanford woman to win the national singles title. As a senior in 1967, Albert teamed with Julie Anthony to win the national doubles title. Albert was the first and is currently one of only four women at Stanford to win both the national singles and doubles championships. In '64, Heldman was the top-seeded player in the tournament and was on her way to winning the singles title until Albert staged a comeback. Heldman won the first set, 10-8, and was leading in the second set when Albert fought back to win the set, 7-5. Albert won the third and decisive set, 6-3, to claim the title. Albert retired from tennis following the '67 season.

Stanford Stat . . .

Stanford won its first national championship in water polo in 1963 after compiling an overall record of 20-2. At the time, the national champion was decided by a vote of the nation's coaches, not by a national tournament. Still, Stanford dominated the sport in 1963 and won the first of many national titles in the sport of water polo. Jim Gaughran, who took over the program in 1960, relied on stars George Stransky, a member of the 1964 U.S. Olympic water polo team, Marty Hull, an NCAA champion swimmer for Stanford, and Don Buehler.

STANFORD LIST

TWO-SPORT ATHLETES

Stanford has produced some of the best two-sport athletes in NCAA history. Below are just some of the top two-sport athletes in Stanford history who gained national recognition in one of their sports while excelling in the other.

Name	Sports
John Brodie	football / golf
Mike Dotterer	football / baseball
Jack Douglass	football / tennis
Toi Cook	football / baseball
John Elway	football / baseball
Kristin Folkl	volleyball / basketball
Chad Hutchinson	football / baseball
James Lofton	football / track
Bob Mathias	football / track
Mark Marquess	football / baseball
Darrin Nelson	football / track
Ernie Nevers	football / baseball

Stanford LEGEND

Sharon Stouder Clark

Sharon Stouder Clark is a three-time Olympic gold medalist. *(Stanford Archives)*

At the age of 15, Sharon Stouder made Olympic history in Tokyo at the 1964 Games by winning three gold and one silver medal. A native of Glendora, California, Stouder took home gold in the 100-meter butterfly, as a member of the U.S. 400-meter free relay and 400-meter medley relay and a silver in the 100-meter free. In the process, she set a world record in the 100 fly and helped her two U.S. relay teams each set world records. Although she won three golds, it was her silver medal- winning swim in the 100 free that may have been her most spectacular. She finished just a touch behind Olympic legend Dawn Fraser of Australia—just 0.4 seconds off the pace—and became only the second woman in history to swim the 100 meters in under 1:00. Stouder began swimming at age three and by the time she was eight she began winning gold medals in age-group competition. She won her first national age-group event at age 12, and at 14 she was a gold medalist at the Pan American Games. After her Olympic performance, she was named the World Woman Swimmer of the Year. Stouder, who attended Stanford after her gold medal-winning effort in Tokyo, is a member of the International Swimming Hall of Fame.

STANFORD LORE

Civil rights leader Dr. Martin Luther King Jr. made the first of his two visits to Stanford University on April 23, 1964. Dr. King, who returned to Stanford in 1967, the year before he was assassinated in Memphis, spoke to an overflow crowd in Memorial Auditorium.

1964-65

- September 27, 1964: The Warren Commission on the assassination of John Kennedy reported that there was no conspiracy and that Lee Harvey Oswald alone was responsible for the shooting.
- November 3, 1964: Lyndon Johnson defeated Barry Goldwater in the presidential election.
- March 8, 1964: The first United States combat forces landed in South Vietnam to guard the U.S. Air Force base at Da Nang.
- March 21, 1965: A five-day civil rights march from Selma to Montgomery, Alabama, began with 3,200 marchers led by Dr. Martin Luther King, Jr.
- June 5, 1964: Astronaut Edward White successfully completed a 20-minute walk in space, the first by an American.

STANFORD MOMENT

Stanford's 1965 world-record setting relay team (left to right): Larry Questad, Bob McIntyre, Dale Rubin, Eric Frische. (Stanford Archives)

Stanford Quartet Sets World Record

The consensus at the West Coast Relays in Fresno, California in May of 1965 was that Stanford's 440-yard relay team had one great sprinter and three who ranged from "good to adequate." But what the Indian quartet did have was the "flip-flop" downward pass, a new innovation in track involving the exchange of the baton in relay events. Under Payton Jordan, Stanford utilized this new method of passing, something the track world had never seen before, and changed the way relays were run forever. The Indian foursome of Eric Frische, Dale Rubin, Bob McIntyre and the great Larry Questad used the "flip-flop" exchange to break the world record in the 440-yard relay, running the event in 39.7 at the West Coast Relays in Fresno. While only Questad could be considered a world-class sprinter, the record was largely due to the perfection of the "flip-flop." Wrote Bert Nelson of *Track & Field News*: "It is only fitting that Stanford, which achieved the most perfect series of exchanges I have seen in 30 years of relay watching, was rewarded with the world record. Each exchange achieved maximum advantage and it was a beautiful sight indeed. With such perfection it was inevitable that the record would fall." After the world record, the "flip-flop" became commonplace.

Stanford SPOTLIGHT

WILLIAM "DUTCH" FEHRING holds the distinction of being the only person in Stanford history to coach a Stanford team in the Rose Bowl and the College World Series. Although he was an assistant football coach for 17 years (1949-66), Fehring is best known for being Stanford's head baseball coach for 12 seasons, from 1956-67. He was an assistant football coach on Chuck Taylor's staff in 1951 when the Indians played Illinois in the '52 Rose Bowl. As head baseball coach, Fehring led Stanford to the College World Series in 1967, setting school records for most wins in a season (36) and best winning percentage (.909, 36-6-1). By the time he retired from coaching following the '67 College World Series, Fehring had chalked up a 290-162-4 (.640) record and was the winningest baseball coach in school history. A nine-time letterman in football, basketball and baseball at Purdue University, Fehring led Stanford to 11 winning seasons in his 12-year stint as head baseball coach. Many consider his 1967 squad, which finished third at the College World Series, to be one of the best in school history.

Stanford Stat . . .

Bob Stoeker became the seventh—and last—Stanford discus thrower to win the NCAA championship when his throw of 183-7 1/4" gave him the 1965 title. Stoeker, a two-time All-American in the discus in '65 and '66, left Stanford with the second-best mark in school history. His 189-1" trailed only the 195-2" record set by Dave Weill. Stoeker, who came to Stanford as the national prep record holder and two-time California prep champion with a toss of over 196 feet, was also a fine shot putter for Stanford.

STANFORD LIST

LONGEST WINNING STREAKS

Sport	Streak	Years
Women's Tennis	76	1988-91
Women's Swimming	58	1988-96
Water Polo	51	1985-87
Men's Swimming	46	1982-87
Water Polo	39	1980-82
Men's Tennis	38	1995-96
Women's Volleyball	27	1991
Women's Basketball	25	1996-97
Men's Basketball	17	1938-39
Baseball	18	1996
Football	18	1904-06
Men's Volleyball	10	1990, '93, '94

Stanford LEGEND

Pete Middlekauf

Pete Middlekauf hit .349 in 1965 and was a first-team All-American.
(Stanford Ahtletics)

As a junior in 1965, Stanford first baseman Pete Middlekauf earned First-Team All-America honors and First-Team All-California Intercollegiate Baseball Association recognition after leading his team to a school-record 32 wins. Middlekauf, a local prep player at Los Altos high School, became the fifth Stanford baseball player to earn All-America honors. He hit .349 in 1965 with two home runs, 31 RBI and a school-record 18 doubles. His team went 32-13 and came within a game of advancing to the College World Series. In the District-8 Tournament, Stanford won two of three from San Fernando Valley State, but two consecutive losses to Washington State eliminated the Indians from post-season play. Middlekauf was called "the best defensive first baseman in Stanford history" by his coach, Dutch Fehring, who also said Middlekauf's defensive prowess was among the best he had seen in 31 years as a college coach. During the '65 season, Middlekauf joined an elite group of players who hit a home run over the right field fence at Sunken Diamond—a feat he accomplished against Santa Clara. A three-year letterman from 1964-66, Middlekauf was drafted by the Kansas City Athletics following the 1965 season, but he returned to Stanford in 1966 for his senior season and to finish his degree in history. His '66 club went 26-12-1, but failed to earn a trip to post-season play. Still, Middlekauf, named MVP of the 1965 team, must be remembered as one of the great baseball players of all-time on The Farm.

STANFORD LORE

Electrical engineering Prof. John Linvill invented the Optacon during the fall of 1964. The Optacon is a reading machine for the blind that can translate any printed page into a kind of "electronic braille." His 12-year-old daughter, Candace, who is blind, tested the device.

1965-66

- September 9, 1965: Sandy Koufax of the Los Angeles Dodgers pitched a perfect game against the Chicago Cubs. Koufax struck out 14 in a 1-0 victory.
- January 31, 1966: President Lyndon Johnson announced that American pilots had resumed their bombing raids on North Vietnam after a 38-day hiatus in hopes of furthering peace negotiations.
- April 28, 1966: The Boston Celtics beat the Los Angeles Lakers in game seven of the NBA championship series, enabling coach Red Auerbach to retire with his eighth successive title.
- June 8, 1966: The National and American football leagues merged, effective in 1970, setting up a Super Bowl game between the league champions.
- August 6, 1966: Demonstrations against the Vietnam War were held across the country on the anniversary of the atomic bombing of Hiroshima in 1945.

STANFORD MOMENT

Greg Buckingham was a world-record holder, an NCAA champion and a silver medal winner at the 1968 Olympic Games. *(Stanford Athletics)*

Buckingham Sets Swimming World Record

Greg Buckingham, a junior on the Stanford men's swim team, set a world record in the 200-meter individual medley on August 21, 1966 at the U.S. Senior Nationals. Buckingham, who broke two other world records during his career, starred on Stanford's 1967 NCAA championship team and was a member of the 1968 United States Olympic Team. He broke his own world record in the 200 IM in 1967 at the same U.S. Senior National Meet and, at the '68 Senior Nationals, be broke the world record in the 400-meter IM. At Stanford, Buckingham was one of the heroes of the school's first NCAA team title in men's swimming. He won two events—the 200 and 500-yard freestyle—in NCAA and American record-setting time, helped the Indians win the 800 freestyle relay in American record time and placed second in the 1650 free. Following his Stanford career, Buckingham earned a spot on the '68 Olympic Team in Mexico City. He won a silver medal in the 200 IM and just missed out on a medal in the 400 IM as he placed fourth.

FROM 1964-66, Jim Hibbs was not only one of Stanford's top baseball players, but he was among the best in the country. He led the team in batting (.351), home runs (five) and RBI (27) as a sophomore in 1964 and gained All-CIBA honors. He came back in 1965 to hit .303 and drive in 26 runs as Stanford won a school-record 32 games and advanced to postseason play. He was again named All-CIBA. Hibbs became the third Stanford catcher to earn All-America honors when he put together another outstanding season as a senior in 1966, hitting a school-record 11 home runs and driving in 41 runs while sporting a .331 batting average. In 1964, following his sophomore season, Hibbs was selected to play on the United States Olympic baseball team. In 20 games with team USA, Hibbs was the team's leading hitter with a .379 batting average.

Stanford Stat . . .

From the 1952 Olympic Games in Helsinki to the '72 Munich Games, Stanford was represented on every United States men's rowing team. While several Stanford athletes have won Olympic rowing medals, so too have the Stanford crews had success both nationally and internationally. In 1966, the Stanford men's crew, considered the finest in school history, won the four without coxswain and placed third in two other events at the nationals. The foursome included 1964 Olympic gold medalist Kent Mitchell, '68 silver medalist Larry Hough and '64 bronze medalist Dick Lyon. Hough later won two world titles in the pairs competition.

STANFORD LIST

TOP-10 RUSHERS IN STANFORD HISTORY

Name	At Stanford	Career Rushing Yards
1. Darrin Nelson	1977-81	4,033
2. Brad Muster	1984-87	2,940
3. Glyn Milburn	1990-92	2,178
4. Mike Mitchell	1993-96	1,849
5. Tommy Vardell	1988-91	1,789
6. Ray Handley	1963-65	1,768
7. Anthony Bookman	1994-96	1,723
8. Vincent White	1979-82	1,689
9. Jon Volpe	1987-90	1,674
10. Bill Tarr	1953-55	1,593

Stanford LEGEND

Ray Handley

Ray Handley gained 1,795 yards rushing and left the Farm as the school's all-time leading rusher. (Stanford Athletics)

It has been over 30 years since Ray Handley wore a Stanford football uniform, but his name still appears in the Cardinal record book as one of the school's all-time leaders in career rushing and single season rushing. A First-Team All-American in 1964, Handley's tenure on The Farm did not stop following his graduation in 1966. He returned to Stanford on two occasions as an assistant coach, first under John Ralston from 1971-73, then under Rod Dowhower and Paul Wiggin from '79-83. But it was as a Stanford running back that Handley first made his mark. He gained 936 yards on 197 carries—both school records—in 1964 en route to earning First-Team All-America and First-Team All-Pac 8 Conference honors. He gained 654 yards rushing in 1965, giving him 1,795 career rushing yards and making him the school's all-time leading rusher. He held both records until Darrin Nelson broke them in 1977 (season) and '78 (career). Today, Handley still ranks sixth in school history in both single season and career rushing. He returned to Stanford as a graduate assistant in 1971 before becoming linebackers coach in '72-73. In 1979, after stints at Air Force and Army, Handley returned to Stanford under Dowhower as linebackers coach. He was elevated to associate head coach under Wiggin in 1982 and '83. Handley culminated his coaching career by being named head coach of the New York Giants in 1991, where he remained for two seasons (1991-92). A member of the Stanford Athletic Hall of Fame, Handley was the fifth Stanford running back—and first since 1940—to earn All-America honors.

STANFORD LORE

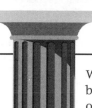

What started out as a protest against University involvement in Selective Service testing broadened into a three-day sit-in related to the Vietnam War. From May 19-21, 1966, 15 students occupied the President's Office and attacked the faculty and administration on their decision making. Thirty-six students were charged with violating the Fundamental Standard and placed on probation for a year.

1966-67

- October 13, 1966: U.S. bombers made their heaviest air strike of the war on North Vietnam.
- November 11, 1966: The last mission of the Gemini space series was launched as astronauts Jim Lovell and "Buzz" Aldrin successfully rendezvoused with an Agena target vehicle.
- January 15, 1967: The Green Bay Packers defeated the Kansas City Chiefs in the first-ever Super Bowl, 35-10.
- March 25, 1967: Sophomore center Lew Alcindor led UCLA to the NCAA basketball championship over Dayton, 79-64.
- July 23, 1967: Forty-three people were killed in Detroit as the worst race riot in U.S. history erupted.

The 1967 Stanford men's swimming team won the NCAA championship. (Stanford Athletics)

STANFORD MOMENT

Stanford Wins First NCAA Men's Swimming Championship

Led by Greg Buckingham, Dick Roth and Mike Wall, Stanford ended the four-team monopoly in men's swimming by winning the 1967 NCAA team championship on March 25 at Michigan State University in East Lansing, Mich. Prior to the meet, only four teams—USC, Yale, Ohio State and Michigan—had ever won the NCAA men's swimming title. But Stanford, which had placed among the top-10 18 times in the program's history, won the meet's final race—the 800-yard freestyle relay—to outpoint USC 275-260 and win the title. Head coach Jim Gaughran, in his seventh season, gained a bit of revenge against a Trojan team that had defeated Stanford at the conference meet and tied Stanford 52-52 in a dual meet, the only blemish on the Indians' 10-0-1 dual meet record. Buckingham and Roth both won two individual titles and were members of Stanford's American record-setting 800 freestyle relay team. Buckingham set NCAA and American records in winning the 200 free and 500 free. He also placed second in the 1650 free. Roth won the 200 and 400 individual medleys and took sixth in the 200 backstroke. Wall, who swam a leg on the 800 freestyle relay, placed third in the 1650 free, fifth in the 200 free and sixth in the 500 free. Moments after winning the championship, every member of the Stanford team was wearing a T-shirt with the inscription, "Stanford U. 1967 NCAA Swimming Champions," given to them by a longtime supporter confident they would win the title.

THE BEST BASEBALL TEAM to date in school history was the 1967 club, which established a school-record winning percentage of .849 after compiling a 36-6-1 overall mark. Led by sophomore All-American first baseman Mark Marquess, who hit a school-record .404, and pitcher Sandy Vance (11-0, 1.53 ERA), Stanford won the Pacific-8 Conference championship with a 10-1 record, beat Fresno State in a three-game series in the District-8 Tournament and advanced to the College World Series for the second time in school history. The Indians won their first two games in Omaha, but lost two of the next three to settle for a third place tie—the best national finish ever for Stanford. Along with Marquess, who was named the team's MVP, catcher Mike Schomaker and second baseman Frank Duffy also earned All-America recognition. Vance was the ace of staff that sported a team ERA of 1.96. Frank Klinger (4-0, 1.31), Rod Poteete (5-1, 1.48), Don Rose (5-2, 2.84) and Daro Quiring (5-2, 2.82) joined Vance to form perhaps the greatest pitching staff ever on The Farm.

Stanford Stat . . .

Head coach John Ralston improved to 4-0 in the Big Game and Stanford won a record sixth straight over Cal as the Indians defeated the Bears 13-7 in the 69th Big Game. Stanford's six-game winning streak over the Bears from 1961-66 is the longest in series history. Only 58,000 showed up at Berkeley's Memorial Stadium as a driving rainstorm kept many fans at home. Touchdowns by John Root and Greg Broughton put Stanford on top 13-0 in the second quarter and a late Cal TD made the score 13-7 at the half. But, as field conditions worsened, neither team was able to score in the second half.

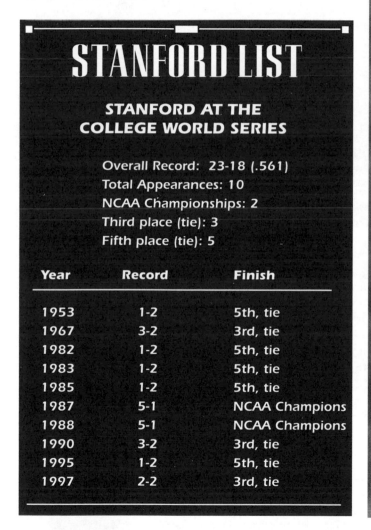

STANFORD LIST

STANFORD AT THE COLLEGE WORLD SERIES

Overall Record: 23-18 (.561)
Total Appearances: 10
NCAA Championships: 2
Third place (tie): 3
Fifth place (tie): 5

Year	Record	Finish
1953	1-2	5th, tie
1967	3-2	3rd, tie
1982	1-2	5th, tie
1983	1-2	5th, tie
1985	1-2	5th, tie
1987	5-1	NCAA Champions
1988	5-1	NCAA Champions
1990	3-2	3rd, tie
1995	1-2	5th, tie
1997	2-2	3rd, tie

Stanford LEGEND

Dick Roth

Dick Roth broke the world record and won the Olympic gold medal in the 400-IM at the 1964 Olympic Games. (Stanford Athletics)

He was a 17-year-old high school junior competing in the 1964 Olympic Games in Tokyo. The night before he was to swim in the Olympic final in the 400-meter individual medley, Dick Roth had an attack of appendicitis. After insisting that surgeons delay an operation to allow him to swim in the final, Roth went out and swam to Olympic glory by capturing the gold medal and shattering his own world record by more than three seconds. A year after that remarkable feat, Roth enrolled at Stanford, where he went on to become one of the great swimmers in school history and a hero on Stanford's first NCAA championship team in 1967. Together with Greg Buckingham, Roth helped give Indian coach Jim Gaughran his only NCAA title by winning two individual events, one relay and finishing sixth in his other race. Roth won NCAA titles in the 200 and 400 individual medley events and was a member of Stanford's American record-setting 800-yard free relay team. Roth, winner of six AAU outdoor IM titles, set his first world record on July 31, 1964 as he swam the 400-meter IM in 4:48.6. But, at the Tokyo Olympics, the day after an appendicitis, Roth improved his world-record time to 4:45.4, a mark that would last four years.

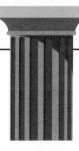

STANFORD LORE

In a campus forum on February 20, 1967, U.S. Vice-President Hubert Humphey defended American involvement in Vietnam. Many students and faculty wore white armbands to show their concern for peace in Vietnam. Following his remarks, 240 students and faculty quietly walked out to protest. Anti-war demonstrators shouted as Humphrey left and some tried unsuccessfully to impede his departure.

1967-68

- October 2, 1967: Thurgood Marshall was sworn in as the United States' first black Supreme Court justice.
- December 31, 1967: The Oakland Raiders won the AFL championship by defeating the Houston Oilers 40-7.
- January 23, 1968: North Korea seized the Navy Intelligence ship U.S.S. Pueblo off its coast. Its crew of 83 was released on December 23.
- April 4, 1968: Dr. Martin Luther King Jr. was assassinated by a sniper at the Lorraine Motel in Memphis, Tennessee, setting off a week of rioting in several urban black neighborhoods.
- June 5, 1968: Presidential candidate Robert Kennedy was fatally shot in Los Angeles after delivering a speech to acknowledge his victory in the California primary.

STANFORD MOMENT

1968 U.S. Olympic Head Coach Payton Jordan with Stanford high jumper Peter Boyce, also a member of the '68 Olympic Team.
(Stanford Athletics)

Jordan Leads U.S. Olympic Track Team

It was a time of political unrest and racial divide—a signature of American history during the 1960s. The 1968 Olympic Games in Mexico City, in its celebration of the best athletes in the world, could not keep the political arena out of the Games. But for Payton Jordan, Stanford's head track coach and head coach of the U.S. Olympic Track team, the '68 Olympic Games went far beyond the political statement made by Americans Lee Evans and Jimmy Hines on the medal stand. "I will always think of how lucky I was to be given the honor of coaching the 1968 U.S. Olympic Track and Field Team," says Jordan. "We were fortunate to have the team chemistry that brought out the best performances by our men and women. I am very proud that, through all the adversity, our team turned in what some say is the best performance by any Olympic team in history," he said. Indeed, the pundits who make that claim might be right. Consider that in 1968, Jordan's team saw Bob Beamon's 29-2 1/2" long jump, one of the greatest athletic achievements of all-time, Al Oerter win his fourth consecutive gold medal in the discus, Evans and Hines setting world records and winning the 400-meters and 100-meters, respectively, Jim Ryun's legendary battle with Kenya's Kip Keino in the 1,500, Bob Seagren's gold medal in the pole vault and Dick Fosbury winning gold in the high jump with the "Fosbury Flop."

FOR THREE SEASONS, Stanford's Art Harris was not only one of the school's most prolific scorers, but one of best pure shooters in the Pac-8 Conference. Harris, from Jordan High School in Los Angeles, averaged 17.2 points per game from 1966-68, second best ever at Stanford to date and still among the best all-time on The Farm. As a senior in 1967-68, Harris scored a then-school record 540 points. His 20.7 points-per-game average that season was second only to Tom Dose's 20.8 average. Harris was a First-Team All-Pac-8 selection as a sophomore in 1965-66 after scoring over 18 points per game in league play. He was a Second-Team All-Conference choice in '67-68 when he scored more than 20 points in 15 of Stanford's 25 games. Two of his games—a 37-point effort vs. Oregon and another 37-point game against Washington State—are still among the top single-game scoring efforts in Stanford history. A member of the Stanford Athletic Hall of Fame, Harris went on to a professional career in the NBA with the Seattle Super Sonics and Phoenix Suns.

Stanford Stat . . .

Not only was Stanford represented by Payton Jordan as the U.S. track coach, but six Stanford athletes on the 1968 United States Olympic Team won a total of seven medals: one gold, three silver and three bronze. The gold medal went to decathlon champion Bill Toomey, who went the University of Colorado as an undergraduate, but received a master's in education from Stanford in 1964. Larry Hough won a silver in rowing while four Stanford swimmers also won medals in Mexico City, including John Ferris, Greg Buckingham, Mitch Ivey and Brian Job.

STANFORD LIST

MOST STRIKEOUTS PER NINE INNINGS

Name	At Stanford	Average
1. Steve Dunning	1969-70	10.74
2. Sandy Vance	1967-68	9.84
3. Phil Keller	1968-70	9.83
4. Scott Weiss	1988-91	9.63
5. John Mason	1964	9.36
6. Jim Lonborg	1962-63	9.35
7. Darryl Sutherland	1061-63	9.24
8. Rod Poteete	1967-69	9.16
9. Jason Middlebrook	1994-96	9.12
10. Rick Deitz	1983-85	8.93

Stanford LEGEND

Sandy Vance

Sandy Vance compiled a 17-3 record in two seasons on the Stanford baseball team. (Stanford Athletics)

The only word to describe Sandy Vance's two-year varsity career at Stanford University is dominant. Plain and simple. He was virtually unhittable during the 1967 and '68 seasons. When they had the chance to sign him to a professional contract, the Los Angeles Dodgers didn't miss it. He was such a dominant collegiate pitcher that the only challenge left for him was the major leagues. His numbers will likely never be matched in Stanford history. In two seasons, he was 17-3 with a 1.70 ERA, 179 strikeouts in 163.2 innings of work and an opponent batting average of just .174. That's right. He allowed opponents only 107 hits in 615 at bats. His 1967 season will forever be remembered as one of the greatest in school history. He went 11-0 with a 1.53 ERA, struck out 94 in 86.1 innings and had an opponent batting average of .165. Vance was Stanford's top pitcher on the '67 team that set a school record by finishing with a 36-6-1 overall record and a trip to the College World Series. He wasn't too shabby in '68 either. He went 6-3 with a 1.86 ERA, 85 strikeouts in 77.1 innings. Vance left Stanford after his junior season to sign a professional contract with the Los Angeles Dodgers, who made him their second-round draft choice. During his rookie season in 1970, Vance went 7-7 with a 3.13 ERA. He would last just one more year in baseball, however, as arm injuries forced him to retire.

STANFORD LORE

An overflow crowd of 2,400 attended a noon service in Memorial Church on April 5, 1968 for slain civil rights leader Dr. Martin Luther King Jr., who was assassinated the previous day. In the late afternoon, more than 2,000 members of the Palo Alto and East Palo Alto communities staged a silent walk from downtown Palo Alto to the steps of the Quad to hear a tribute to King by B. Dave Napier, dean of the chapel.

1968-69

- November 5, 1968: Republican Richard Nixon won the presidential election, beating Hubert Humphrey by only 500,000 votes.
- May 15, 1969: People's Park in Berkeley, California was attacked by police and National Guardsmen. Five days later a National Guard helicopter dropped a stinging chemical powder on demonstrators.
- July 16, 1969: U.S. space capsule Apollo 11 landed on the moon at 4:17 p.m. EDT. Astronaut Neil Armstrong became the first person to set foot on the moon.
- July 18, 1969: Senator Edward Kennedy was involved in an auto accident on Chappaquiddick Island, Massachusetts, resulting in the death of his passenger, Mary Jo Kopechne.
- August 15, 1969: The Woodstock Music and Art Fair began, drawing a crowd estimated at nearly a half million people.

STANFORD MOMENT

After an All-America career at Stanford, Tom Watson went on to become one of the greatest golfers of all time. (Stanford Athletics)

Golf Legend Tom Watson Earns All-America Honors

Stanford unveiled its new phenom in 1969—a sophomore from Kansas City, Missouri named Tom Watson. What followed in the ensuing years was the birth and maturation of one of the all-time legends of the sport. Watson won the 1969 NCAA driving championship with a drive of 298 yards and earned the first of his three consecutive Second-Team All-America honors. He placed fifth at the 1970 NCAA Championships and sixth at the '71 NCAA's and was named Second-Team All-America both years. Watson, who graduated from Stanford in 1971 with a degree in psychology, turned professional in the fall of '71. By 1973, he was in the top-60 in earnings and by '74, he was in the top-10. As a professional, Watson's resume is matched by few in the history of the sport. He won his first major, the British Open, in 1975. His first championship at the Masters occurred in 1977 when he beat Jack Nicklaus in what some consider to be one of the greatest head-to-head battles in golf history. Watson has won 33 PGA Tour championships through the '97 season, including five British Opens ('75, '77, '80, '82, '83), two Masters ('77, '81) and one U.S. Open (1982 at Pebble Beach). Watson, a five-time member of the U.S. Ryder Cup Team, was the top money winner on the tour for five years, including four in a row from 1977-80. Still active on the PGA Tour, Watson's spot in the Hall of Fame is waiting for him once he concludes his competitive career.

BOB BOONE came to Stanford as a third baseman/pitcher who had turned down an offer to play professional baseball after high school. Four years later, Boone graduated from Stanford University in 1969 with a degree in psychology, then began a pro career that would establish him as one of the all-time greats. Boone was a three-year letterman and Stanford's starting third baseman from 1967-69. He went 9-1 as a pitcher his senior season had a sparkling ERA of 1.27. But as a professional, Boone was converted to catcher. He played 19 years in the major leagues (1972-90), was a member of the 1980 World Series champion Philadelphia Phillies and his 2,264 games set an all-time record for most games played by a catcher. Boone earned First-Team All-Pac 8 honors in '68 and '69 as a third baseman. In the major leagues, he had a career batting average of .254 while playing for the Phillies (1972-81), California Angels (1982-88) and Kansas City Royals (1989-90). His family roots are legendary: his father, Ray, played in the big leagues for 13 years (1948-60) and won one world championship with the 1948 Cleveland Indians. His son, Bret, played college baseball at USC and is currently in the major leagues. Following his playing days, Bob went into the coaching ranks and became a major league manager for the Kansas City Royals.

Stanford Stat . . .

Sophomore quarterback Jim Plunkett made his debut in 1968, giving Indian faithful a glimpse of what was to come. Plunkett broke the school's single season passing record by throwing for 2,156 yards, a record he would break in each of the ensuing two seasons. His team finished 6-3-1, beat Cal 20-0 in the Big Game and lost to USC and UCLA by a field goal apiece. Although Stanford lost a tough 27-24 decision to the Trojans, the Indians gave notice that it was a team on the rise. Stanford lost again to USC 26-24 in 1969, but in 1970, Plunkett and his teammates hit paydirt by beating USC for the first time in 13 years and winning the Pac-8 Conference championship.

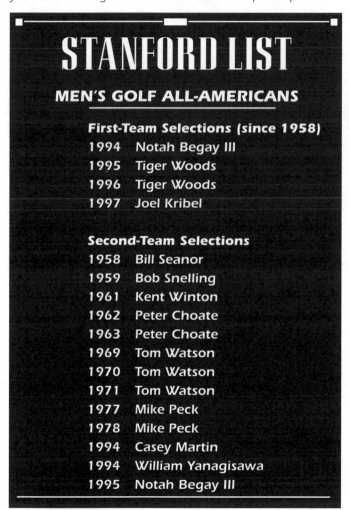

STANFORD LIST

MEN'S GOLF ALL-AMERICANS

First-Team Selections (since 1958)

1994	Notah Begay III
1995	Tiger Woods
1996	Tiger Woods
1997	Joel Kribel

Second-Team Selections

1958	Bill Seanor
1959	Bob Snelling
1961	Kent Winton
1962	Peter Choate
1963	Peter Choate
1969	Tom Watson
1970	Tom Watson
1971	Tom Watson
1977	Mike Peck
1978	Mike Peck
1994	Casey Martin
1994	William Yanagisawa
1995	Notah Begay III

Stanford LEGEND

Gene Washington

Gene Washington set records for receptions, receiving yards and receiving touchdowns. (Stanford Athletics)

A shoulder injury during his sophomore season in 1966 may have been just what the doctor ordered for Gene Washington. With his shoulder ailing, Washington asked head coach John Ralston to switch him from quarterback to wide receiver. And the rest, as they say, is history. In 1967, Washington led Stanford in receptions with 48 and receiving yardage with 585. But in 1968, with Jim Plunkett at quarterback, Washington re-wrote the Stanford record book. He caught 71 passes for 1,117 yards and eight touchdowns—all three school records—and he finished his collegiate career with a Stanford record 122 receptions for 1,785 yards. A two-time First-Team All-Pacific 8 Conference selection, Washington was the 16th pick overall in the first round of the 1969 NFL Draft by the San Francisco 49ers. For the next nine seasons (1969-77), Washington became one of the best receivers in the NFL while breaking 49er records for most TD receptions (59) and most receiving yards (6,664). He caught 372 passes for San Francisco and was named to the Pro Bowl on four occasions. In 1970, Washington set career-bests in receptions (53), receiving yards (1,100) and touchdowns (12). "From the first day I stepped foot on the Stanford campus as a high school student, I fell in love with the university," says Washington. "And I've felt that way ever since." Following his football career, Washington worked as a color commentator for NBC and ESPN and was a sports anchor for television stations in Los Angeles and San Francisco. He is currently working at the NFL office in New York.

STANFORD LORE

Several hundred protesters, objecting to classified and war-related research on campus, occupied the Applied Electronics Laboratory on April 9, 1969. They also called for greater control over the Stanford Research Institute. The occupation lasted nine days and ended less than two hours before a deadline imposed by the Stanford Judicial Council.

1969-70

·· AMERICA'S TIME CAPSULE ··

- September 22, 1969:   Willie Mays of the San Francisco Giants hit his 600th career home run, becoming only the second major leaguer other than Babe Ruth to reach that plateau.
- November 16, 1969:   More than 450 Vietnam villagers were slain by a U.S. infantry unit in what would be known as the My Lai massacre.
- March 18, 1970:   The first major postal workers' strike began in the United States.
- April 29, 1970:   U.S. and South Vietnamese troops invaded Cambodia.
- May 4, 1970:   Four Kent State University students were killed by National Guard troops during an anti-war demonstration.

Steve Dunning struck out 18 batters on two occasions during the 1970 season. *(Stanford Athletics)*

STANFORD MOMENT

Dunning Strikes Out 18 Trojans Twice

It had never been done before and it has never been done since. And Steve Dunning did it twice in 1970. What's more, he did it both times against perennial power USC. What the junior from San Diego did was strike out an amazing 18 batters in game on two occasions. In fact, striking out batters was what Dunning did best, especially in 1970. He had an outstanding sophomore season in 1969 when he went 4-4 with a 2.40 ERA and 70 strikeouts and 71 and one-third inning. He also threw a no-hitter on March 7, 1969 vs. Cal Poly Pomona, striking out 13 batters in the process. But in 1970, Dunning was spectacular. He went 13-2, had a 1.83 ERA and struck out 144 batters in just 108 innings of work. He set school records for wins and strikeouts and became one of the most sought-after players in the nation by professional baseball. Dunning's 144 strikeouts was a Stanford record for 20 years and is still number three on Stanford's all-time single season strikeout list. Dunning was selected in the first round of the 1970 Major League Baseball Draft by the Cleveland Indians. He pitched seven seasons in the major leagues for five teams.

THERE'S THE 10-YARD TOUCHDOWN PASS from Jim Plunkett in the 1971 Rose Bowl, or the 96-yard TD pass play against Washington State in 1970—the longest pass play in Stanford history—or the crucial TD catch against Washington in 1970 that gave Stanford a 29-22 victory, clinching the Rose Bowl berth. Take your pick. They're all vintage Randy Vataha, one of the most exciting and popular players to ever play on The Farm. He was Jim Plunkett's favorite receiver in 1969 and '70, a big-play specialist who gave Stanford fans some of the greatest moments in school history. Vataha, just 5-10 and 175, caught 83 passes for 1,535 yards, 11 touchdowns and an impressive 18.5 yards per catch average. In the '71 Rose Bowl, Vataha caught six passes for 51 yards, but it was his last one that will forever be remembered. The Indians held a slim 20-17 lead when Plunkett and Vataha hooked up on a 10-yard scoring pass with 8:18 remaining in the game, giving Stanford a comfortable 27-17 advantage. Vataha played seven seasons in the NFL, six with the New England Patriots, after his Stanford career. "There's no question," Vataha said, "that the highlight of my football career was the 1971 Rose Bowl."

Stanford Stat . . .

In 1968 and '69, Don Parish was the man in the middle of the Stanford defense. Never before had a player made as many tackles as the 284 Parish made in those two years. While he graduated a year before Stanford made it to Pasadena for back-to-back Rose Bowls, Parish helped pave the way for the Indian defense. He was named First-Team All-Pacific-8 Conference in both 1968 and '69 and was a First-Team All-America selection following the '69 season. Parish, the first linebacker in Stanford history to be named All-American, concluded his career as one of the school's all-time great defensive players.

STANFORD LIST

STANFORD BASEBALL FIRST-ROUND DRAFT PICKS
(the Major League Baseball Draft began in 1965)

Player, Position	Year	Team
Steve Dunning, P	1970	Cleveland Indians
Jack McDowell, P	1987	Chicago White Sox
Ed Sprague, 3B	1988	Toronto Blue Jays
Mike Mussina, P	1990	Baltimore Orioles
Stan Spencer, P	1990	Montreal Expos
David McCarty, 1B	1991	Minnesota Twins
Jeffrey Hammonds, CF	1992	Baltimore Orioles
Rick Helling, P	1992	Texas Rangers
Willie Adams, P	1993	Oakland A's
Kyle Peterson, P	1997	Milwaukee Brewers

Stanford LEGEND

John Ralston

John Ralston was named Stanford's coach of the century. (Stanford Athletics)

When Stanford University chose its All-Century Football team in 1991, John Ralston was selected as the school's Coach of the Century. And for good reason. During his nine-year tenure on The Farm, Ralston led the Indians to heights never before known. Sure, Stanford had played in the Rose Bowl before Ralston's arrival in 1963, but never before had Stanford won back-to-back Rose Bowls. And it was some 13 years since Stanford had defeated USC and UCLA in the same season, a feat Ralston would accomplish in both '70 and '71. With his Heisman Trophy winning quarterback, Jim Plunkett, leading the way, Ralston's 1970 Stanford team upset undefeated Ohio State 27-17 in the '71 Rose Bowl. The following year, Ralston again led his team to the Pac-8 Championship and a trip to Pasadena, this time coming home with a thrilling 13-12 victory over Michigan. Legendary status was thrust upon Ralston after a nine-year record of 55-36-3 on The Farm. His success at Stanford led the Denver Broncos to make Ralston their head coach and general manager in 1972. Ralston led the Broncos to their first winning season in franchise history in 1973 and was named the UPI AFC Coach of the Year. He spent five years in Denver, compiling a 34-33-3 record. Ralston's storied career has earned him a spot in the College Football Hall of Fame, the Stanford Athletic Hall of Fame, the Rose Bowl Hall of Fame and the Bay Area Sports Hall of Fame. His career in athletics spanned five decades, from his first college coaching job in 1956 as an assistant at Cal to his final head coaching job at San Jose State, where he retired following the 1996 campaign. He is a true legend of the game of football.

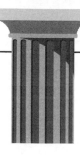

STANFORD LORE

The year 1970 was marked by a change from passive resistance to outbursts of violence between demonstrators and sheriff's deputies. The worst battles were set off by President Richard Nixon's announcement on April 29 of the U.S. invasion of Cambodia. A day-long sit-in at the Old Union erupted into a battle between several hundred rock-throwing demonstrators and more than 200 club-wielding police. Sixteen demonstrators were arrested, a dozen protesters and 30 officials were injured. The next night was a virtual repeat as officers and demonstrators surged back and forth across the central campus.

1970-71

·· AMERICA'S TIME CAPSULE ··

- November 8, 1970:   Tom Dempsey of the New Orleans Saints kicked an NFL-record 63-yard field goal.
- December 23, 1970:   The World Trade Center was topped in New York City to become the world's largest building.
- January 25, 1971:   Charles Manson and three of his followers were convicted of the 1969 murders of actress Sharon Tate and six others.
- March 29, 1971:   William Calley was convicted of the murder of 22 South Vietnamese people at My Lai.
- July 30, 1971:   Astronauts David Scott and Jim Irwin became the fourth American space team to explore the moon's surface, making their tour in a four-wheeled lunar rover.

Stanford played in its first Rose Bowl game in 19 years on January 1, 1971. (Stanford Archives)

STANFORD MOMENT

Plunkett Leads Indians to Rose Bowl Victory

Led by their Heisman Trophy-winning quarterback, Stanford stunned the college football world on January 1, 1971 with its 27-17 upset win over previously unbeaten Ohio State. The Indians, who were making their first appearance in Pasadena since 1952, entered the game with an 8-3 record and were prohibitive underdogs against the 9-0 Buckeyes. Plunkett was named the game's Most Valuable Player after passing for 265 yards and one TD on 20-of-30. He led his team on a 59-yard, five-play drive to open the game. Running back Jackie Brown capped the drive with a four-yard plunge, giving Stanford a 7-0 lead less than five minutes into the game. It was 10-0 Stanford in the first quarter before two John Brockington one-yard touchdown runs put Ohio State on top 14-10 at the half. Brockington rushed for 101 yards on the day and Buckeye quarterback Rex Kern gained 129 yards as OSU compiled 380 rushing yards vs. the Indian defense. But in the second half, Stanford's defense, led by tackle Dave Tipton and linebacker Jeff Siemon, allowed just one field goal to Ohio State while Plunkett and Co. tallied 17 points. Stanford took the lead for good early in the fourth quarter when Brown scored his second TD of the game, this one from a yard out to give Stanford the lead 20-17. It capped a masterful 13-play, 80-yard drive in which Plunkett went five-for-five for 69 yards. After Kern was intercepted on OSU's next possession by Jackie Schultz, Plunkett and flanker Randy Vataha connected on a 10-yard scoring play to put the Indians ahead 27-17. Stanford had not only pulled off the upset, but it recorded its first Rose Bowl win in 30 years.

THE LEGEND OF THE THUNDERCHICKENS began as a inside joke, but wound up being a part of Stanford football lore. Before the 1970 season, several members of the Stanford defense thought that a nickname would be appropriate. After all, the USC defense called themselves the "Wild Bunch," so why not a nickname for the Stanford defense? "(Pete) Lazetich said there was this motorcycle gang in Montana named the Thunderchickens," said Dave Tipton, a charter member of the Thunderchickens and current Stanford assistant football coach. "Plus, he said that I looked like a chicken running up and down the field. It started out as a joke, but once the media got hold of it, and we won a few Rose Bowls, it just took off," said Tipton. The Thunderchickens lasted two seasons, 1970 and '71. In 1970, the defensive line of Larry Butler, Greg Sampson, Bill Alexander, Jody Graves, Tipton and Lazetich comprised the Thunderchickens. In 1971, Tipton graduated and was replaced by Roger Cowan on the defensive line, but by this time the linebackers had been added to the group. "It was a catchy name, we won some Rose Bowls and we were pretty good," said Tipton. "We didn't make a big deal of it, but the media sure did." The Thunderchickens were more than "pretty good." Sampson (1st round, 1972), Lazetich (2nd round, 1972) and Tipton (4th round, 1971) all played in the NFL.

Stanford Stat . . .

A two-time member of the United States Olympic swimming team, Brian Job was the first Stanford swimmer to be a dominate performer in NCAA competition. Job, from Warren, Ohio, won a bronze medal in the 200-meter breaststroke at the '68 Games in Mexico City. He was a member of the 1972 Olympic team as well, but did not win any medals. During his career at Stanford (1970-73), Job won five NCAA individual titles and was a member of two championship relay teams. He won the NCAA title in the 200 breast from 1970-72, the 100 breast in '70-71 and was a member of Stanford's NCAA winning 400 medley relay team in 1970 and '71. He was the school's all-time record holder for points scored in NCAA championships with 116. Job received an engineering degree from Stanford.

STANFORD LIST

TOP-10 FINISHERS IN HEISMAN TROPHY BALLOTING

Year	Player	Position	Place
1940	Frankie Albert	QB	4th
1940	Norm Standlee	FB	7th
1941	Frankie Albert	QB	3rd
1951	Bill McColl	TE	4th
1953	Bobby Garrett	QB	5th
1956	John Brodie	QB	7th
1969	Jim Plunkett	QB	8th
1970	Jim Plunkett	QB	1st
1977	Guy Benjamin	QB	6th
1981	Darrin Nelson	RB	6th
1982	John Elway	QB	2nd
1992	Glyn Milburn	RB	9th

Stanford LEGEND

Jim Plunkett

Jim Plunkett led the Indians to a 27-17 Rose Bowl victory over Ohio State in 1971. (Stanford Athletics)

Following the 1969 season Jim Plunkett made a decision that would forever change his life and the history of the Stanford football program. Plunkett, who had just thrown for 2,673 yards and 20 touchdowns and finished eighth in the Heisman balloting, decided to return to Stanford in 1970 for his senior season instead of turning pro. And the rest, as they say, is history. He won the Heisman Trophy in 1970, led Stanford to its first Pac-8 Championship and Rose Bowl appearance in 19 years and its first Rose Bowl win in 30 years and went on the become the number-one pick in the '71 NFL Draft. Plunkett completed 191-of-358 for 2,715 yards and 18 touchdowns during his Heisman season, finishing his career with 7,887 career yards in total offense, which was not only a Stanford record but an NCAA record. In the '71 Rose Bowl vs. Ohio State, Plunkett earned MVP honors after completing 20-of-30 for 265 yards and one TD. His pro football career lasted 16 seasons and included two Super Bowl victories and one Super Bowl MVP honor. Plunkett was the first pick in the '71 draft by the New England Patriots and earned NFL Rookie of the Year honors after his first pro season. But injuries over the next several years limited his effectiveness and after the 1978 season, it appeared his career might be over. He was picked up by the Oakland Raiders and suddenly his career was thriving. He led the Raiders to the 1981 world championship after a 27-10 win over Philadelphia in Super Bowl XV, where he was named the game's MVP. Three years later, Plunkett quarterbacked the L.A. Raiders to a 38-9 triumph over Washington in Super Bowl XVIII. A member of the College Football Hall of Fame, Plunkett's number 16 was retired by Stanford in 1991.

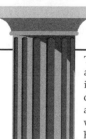

STANFORD LORE

The Computation Center was seized by students on February 10, 1971 during 12 hours of confrontation and violence aimed at shutting down the University and protesting the recent U.S. invasion of Laos. There were 12 arrests and 10 injuries. During a noon rally in White Plaza, Associate Prof. H. Bruce Franklin said protesters should "begin to shut down the most obvious machinery of the war, such as the Computer Center." Students vacated the building in the late afternoon when 80-100 sheriff's deputies arrived. Later that evening, eight members of the Free Campus Movement were assaulted by 15-30 persons and the 16-year-old son of a professor was shot in the thigh while standing near the headquarters of the FCM.

1971-72

- September 13, 1971: A prison riot at Attica State Correctional Facility in New York ended, an uprising that claimed 43 lives.

- December 10, 1971: The nomination of Stanford graduate William H. Rehnquist to the Supreme Court was approved by the Senate.

- February 21, 1972: President Richard Nixon began his historic visit to mainland China.

- May 26, 1972: Soviet secretary Leonid Brezhnev and President Nixon signed a treaty on antiballistic missile systems.

- June 17, 1972: Police arrested five men involved in a burglary of Democratic Party headquarters, beginning the famed Watergate affair.

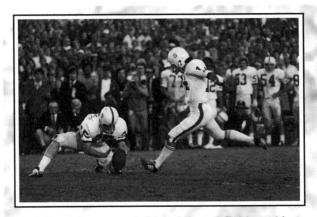

Rod Garcia's game-winning 31-yard field goal in the 1972 Rose Bowl gave Stanford a 13-12 victory. (Stanford Athletics)

STANFORD MOMENT

Garcia's Kick Lifts Stanford to Second Straight Rose Bowl Win

Quarterback Don Bunce and the famous "Thunderchickens" gave Stanford coach John Ralston his second consecutive Rose Bowl victory in a thrilling come-from-behind win over Bo Schembechler's previously undefeated Michigan Wolverines. Stanford, for the second straight season, came into the game with an 8-3 record and played the undefeated Big-10 champs—this time the 11-0 Wolverines. And, once again, the underdog Indians pulled out a win. Bunce, named the game's Most Valuable Player, completed 24-of-44 for 290 yards, including a five-for-five effort on Stanford's final drive of the game. But it was the Indian defense that held the mighty Michigan offense to just 12 points, enabling Stanford to pull out the win. Down 12-10 after a Michigan safety with 3:18 remaining in the game, it looked as though the Big-10 champs would go home with the win. But, after the Wolverines were forced to punt after gaining possession on the safety, Stanford had one last chance to put up a score. And Bunce and the rest of the offense did not disappoint. Stanford took over on their own 22-yard line with 1:48 remaining in the game. Bunce hit on five consecutive passes, moving Stanford to the Michigan 17-yard line with 22 seconds remaining. Two plays, three yards gained and two timeouts later, the Indian's Rod Garcia entered the field to attempt a game-winning 31-yard field goal. With 12 seconds left in the game, Garcia's field goal went through the uprights, giving Stanford its second straight Rose Bowl win.

CLAUDE TERRY was what you call a "pure shooter." By the time he graduated from Stanford with a degree in economics following the 1972 season, he was the most prolific scorer in Stanford basketball history. He left Stanford as the school record holder in career points (1,566), career points per game (20.6), season points (544 in 1971) and season points per game (21.2, 1971-72), among others. His 20.6 career average stands today as the best in school history. He was named First-Team All-Pac 8 and Third-Team All-America following his senior season. Terry was the team's leading scorer for three straight years, averaging 19.6 as a sophomore in '69-70, 20.9 his junior year and 21.2 as a senior. He scored 41 points vs. Oregon State his junior season, the third highest single-game total to date in school history. He also scored 36 points in a game on two occasions, one during his junior year and one during his senior year. Terry played six seasons in the NBA with Atlanta, Denver and Buffalo before injuries forced him from the game. He was head coach at Cal State Stanislaus and Seattle Pacific University. Terry is now the Associate Pastor of World Outreach for the First Baptist Church in Modesto, California.

Stanford Stat . . .

He had just one season in the sun, one year where everything he had worked towards came together, where all his dreams, somehow, came true. Sure, Don Bunce had to wait until Jim Plunkett's storied career was over, but in 1971 Bunce made the most of his only season as Stanford's starting quarterback. He passed for 2,265 yards and 13 TDs, led the Indians to another Pac-8 championship and a second straight date in the Rose Bowl. He was the 1972 Rose Bowl MVP after leading his team to a stunning 13-12 win over undefeated Michigan. Bunce played one year of professional football in Canada, then left the game for medical school. A general orthopedic surgeon at the Palo Alto Medical Clinic, Bunce was Stanford's team physician for the football program for many years.

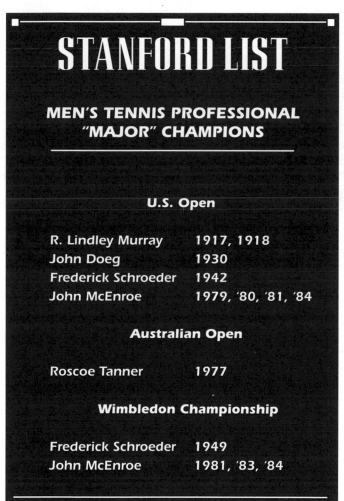

STANFORD LIST

MEN'S TENNIS PROFESSIONAL "MAJOR" CHAMPIONS

U.S. Open

R. Lindley Murray	1917, 1918
John Doeg	1930
Frederick Schroeder	1942
John McEnroe	1979, '80, '81, '84

Australian Open

Roscoe Tanner	1977

Wimbledon Championship

Frederick Schroeder	1949
John McEnroe	1981, '83, '84

Stanford LEGEND

Roscoe Tanner

The Stanford men's tennis dynasty began when Roscoe Tanner arrived on the team. (Stanford Athletics)

Ask men's tennis coach Dick Gould when his program took its first step toward building the dynasty that it is today and he'll tell you that it was the day Roscoe Tanner decided to come to Stanford to play tennis. Tanner was Gould's first major recruit, the first bonafide star who could help turn a good program into national champions. Tanner was a three-time All-American from 1970-72, one of the truly great collegiate players of his time. Although Tanner and Gould never won the national title together, they built the foundation for future success. Tanner's three Stanford teams finished fifth in 1970 and '71 and second in '72. But Stanford proceeded to win its first NCAA championship in 1973 and six titles in the next nine years. The dynasty was now in full swing. Tanner was an NCAA singles finalist in 1970 and '71; NCAA doubles champion in 1972 and NCAA doubles finalist in 1970. He went on to a very successful career on the professional tennis tour. Tanner was annually among the top-15 ranked players in the world in the mid to late '70s. He won the 1977 Australian Open and was a finalist at the 1979 Wimbledon Championship, losing to Bjorn Borg in the finals. He was a semifinalist at Wimbledon in 1975 and '76 and a quarterfinalist in 1980. At the U.S. Open, Tanner was a semifinalist in 1974 and '79 and a quarterfinalist in 1972 and '80. He was also a member of the United States' Davis Cup Team from 1975-77 and again in 1981. Tanner is a member of the Stanford Athletic Hall of Fame and the Collegiate Tennis Hall of Fame.

STANFORD LORE

The ASSU Senate voted 18-4 on March 2, 1972, in favor of President Lyman's recommendation that the "Indian" be discontinued as the University mascot. In 1930, the Indian image had joined the color cardinal red to symbolize Stanford athletic spirit, but growing concern for the use of a stereotyped racial image brought increasing criticism from Native American students and staff and other members of the Stanford community. The Indian was again rejected in 1975 by the ASSU Senate, 18-1, and by the student body by more than 2-1.

1972-73

- November 7, 1972: The Republican Party enjoyed its greatest landslide victory with the re-election of President Richard Nixon.
- December 18, 1972: Paris peace negotiations reached an impasse and full-scale bombing of North Vietnam was resumed by American pilots.
- January 22, 1973: An agreement to end the war in Vietnam was signed in Paris by representatives of the United States and North and South Vietnam.
- June 9, 1973: Secretariat, called the greatest racehorse ever, won the Belmont Stakes and became the ninth Triple Crown winner.
- July 16, 1973: The existence of the Watergate tapes was revealed.

STANFORD MOMENT

Stanford Loses Big Game on Final Play

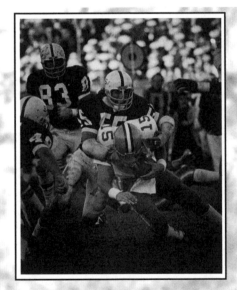

Gordon Riegel scored on a 71-yard interception return, but Cal won the 1972 Big Game 24-21. (Stanford Athletics)

On a rain-soaked Memorial Stadium field in Berkeley, the 1972 Big Game entered the record book as one of the classic matchups between Stanford and Cal. The 68,000 fans who braved the weather conditions witnessed a 24-21 Bears' victory on the game's final play. Stanford led 21-18 when Cal took over on their own 38-yard line with 1:13 remaining in the game. The Bears drove to the Cardinal eight-yard line with three seconds left on the clock and had an easy field-goal attempt to tie the game. But Cal coach Mike White decided for forgo the tie. He wanted the win. "I never thought about going for a tie. This game means too much," White said. On the game's final play, Cal freshman quarterback Vince Ferragamo hit wide receive Steve Sweeney for the touchdown. The extra point was never attempted because the fans poured onto the field in celebration of Cal's victory. Stanford, which finished the year with a 5-5 record, had taken a 14-3 lead when linebacker Gordon Riegel intercepted a Ferragamo pass and raced 71-yards for a touchdown with eight seconds left in the half. Cal assumed an 18-14 lead in the fourth quarter, but Stanford got the lead back at 21-18 with 3:42 remaining in the game when Reggie Sanderson scored on a three-yard run. The Bears, however, were not quite done scoring.

THE NCAA MEN'S TENNIS championship that had eluded Stanford and head coach Dick Gould became a reality in 1973 as Alex Mayer led the Cardinal its first-ever national title. Stanford won the title, held at Princeton University, by scoring 33 points, five better than runner-up USC's total of 28. Mayer, a three-time All-American, was the catalyst for the Cardinal. He became the fourth Stanford athlete to win the NCAA singles crown. He also teamed with Jim Delaney to win the doubles title for the second straight year. Mayer and Roscoe Tanner had won the '72 NCAA doubles championship. For Gould, the title was the culmination of seven years of labor in building the Cardinal program. His teams had finished in the top eight the previous four years, including second in 1972. "It was an obsession with me at first to win the national championship," Gould said. "I really felt it could be done here at Stanford." And who would argue with Gould? His teams won six of nine NCAA championships from 1973-81 and 15 of 25 from '73-97.

Stanford Stat . . .

Stanford's 880-yard relay team set a new world indoor record of 1:27.4 in a meet held in Pocatello, Idaho. The Cardinal foursome of Ken Curl, John Kessel, Matt Hogsett and John Anderson surprised many, even themselves, with the record. While the four runners were all talented, competitive and capable of turning in such performances, a world record was not expected from this group. "I think we were all a bit stunned," said Stanford head coach Payton Jordan. "We knew we could run with anybody in the world, but until we did it, we were a bit unsure. We had a great night, got hot and became world record holders. We were all thrilled to death by the race," said Jordan.

STANFORD LIST

MEN'S TENNIS THREE-TIME FIRST-TEAM ALL-AMERICANS

Player	All-America Years
Roscoe Tanner	1970, 1971, 1972
Alex Mayer	1971, 1972, 1973
Jim Delaney	1972, 1973, 1974, 1975
Bill Maze	1976, 1977, 1978
Matt Mitchell	1976, 1977, 1978
Scott Davis	1981, 1982, 1983
Dan Goldie	1984, 1985, 1986
Jim Grabb	1984, 1985, 1986
Patrick McEnroe	1986, 1987, 1988
Jeff Tarango	1987, 1988, 1989
Alex O'Brien	1989, 1990, 1991, 1992
Jason Yee	1990, 1991, 1992
Chris Cocotos	1992, 1993, 1994
Paul Goldstein	1995, 1996, 1997

Stanford LEGEND

Alex Mayer

Alex Mayer won the NCAA singles and doubles titles and led Stanford to its first men's tennis championship.
(Stanford Athletics)

If Roscoe Tanner was the first of Dick Gould's great tennis recruits, Alex "Sandy" Mayer was the second. He came to Stanford from Flushing, New York, the year after Tanner came to The Farm from Tennessee. Mayer earned All-America honors for three straight seasons from 1971-73 and was the key player on Stanford's first NCAA championship team in '73. He won the NCAA doubles title with Tanner in 1972 and helped the Cardinal place second in the team competition. A year later, however, Mayer won college tennis' version of the triple crown. He won the NCAA singles title, teamed with Jim Delaney to win the doubles crown and led his team to the championship, the first in school history. Mayer left Stanford during the 1974 season and in June of '74, he turned professional. His world ranking rose to number seven in 1982. He was a semifinalist at Wimbledon in 1983 and a quarterfinalist in '78, he won the Wimbledon doubles title in 1975 with Vitas Gerulaitis and the French Open doubles crown in 1979 with fellow Stanford graduate Gene Mayer. In 1982, Mayer was named the Comeback Player of the Year by *Tennis* Magazine. A member of the Stanford Athletic Hall of Fame, Mayer was elected to the College Tennis Hall of Fame in 1991.

STANFORD LORE

The Stanford Daily became an independent newspaper in February, 1973. Student editors discussed independence as early as 1963, but the real impetus for change was initiated by President Lyman after a columnist in 1970 advocated killing prison informants. An editorial in *The Daily* said, "there will no longer be the threat of potential censorship by the University or the Associated Students."

1973-74

•• AMERICA'S TIME CAPSULE ••

- December 6, 1973: Gerald Ford was sworn in as vice president, filling the void created by Spiro Agnew's resignation on October 10.
- February 5, 1974: Patricia Hearst was kidnapped from her California apartment by a group calling itself the Symbionese Liberation Army.
- April 8, 1974: Hank Aaron of the Atlanta Braves hit his 715th career home run, breaking Babe Ruth's legendary record.
- July 30, 1974: Three articles of impeachment were voted against President Nixon by the House Judiciary Committee.
- August 8, 1974: President Richard Nixon announced in a televised address that he would resign, with Gerald Ford sworn in as president the following day.

STANFORD MOMENT

Mike Boryla and his Cardinal teammates saw their Rose Bowl hopes end after a 27-26 loss to USC. *(Stanford Athletics)*

Heartbreaking Loss to Trojans

In a game that had Rose Bowl implications, defending Pac-8 champion USC overcame a nine-point deficit in the last 3:10, kicked a 34-yard field goal with :03 seconds remaining and denied Stanford a major upset by beating the Cardinal, 27-26, on November 10, 1973 at the L.A. Coliseum. Second-year coach Jack Christiansen saw his team's Rose Bowl hopes fade away in the haze of the Los Angeles sky as they let the Trojans score 10 points late in the game to erase a 26-17 lead. Placekicker Rod Garcia, who earlier in the game booted a school and Pac-10 record 59-yard field goal, made good on a 25-yarder with 3:10 to play to put Stanford on top by nine. The Trojans, aided by a pass interference penalty against Stanford, used only one minute off the clock to score a touchdown when quarterback Pat Haden ran it in from 10 yards out with 2:10 left in the game. Stanford, however, was forced to give the ball to USC after failing to run out the clock on its next possession. The Trojans took over on their own 30-yard line with no timeouts remaining. Two long passes from Haden to tight end Jim Obradovich, one for 24 yards, the other for 25-yards, set up the Trojans at the Cardinal 17 with just three seconds left on the clock. There, USC's Chris Limahelu booted home a 34-yard field goal to give the Trojans the win and propel them to their second straight Rose Bowl appearance. Stanford finished the season with a 7-4 record and a 5-2 reading in conference games. But a Cardinal win on this day would have changed the entire season and given Stanford a chance to return to Pasadena.

JOHN WHITLINGER is one of only three Stanford men's tennis players to capture the "triple crown." In 1974, Whitlinger won the NCAA singles championship, teamed with Jim Delaney to win the NCAA doubles crown and led Stanford to its second straight national title. (The other two "triple crown" winners are Alex Mayer in 1973 and Alex O'Brien in 1992). A member of the Cardinal's first NCAA title team in 1973, Whitlinger was named first-team All-American in 1974 and '75. After his collegiate career, he became an international touring pro for six years. He reached a world singles ranking of No. 27 and a world doubles ranking of No. 9 before leaving the tour in 1980. Whitlinger returned to Stanford in 1987 to become an assistant coach under Dick Gould, the man who recruited him to The Farm out of high school. Since his return to Stanford, Whitlinger has been a part of seven NCAA team championships. In 1986, Whitlinger's family was named the National Tennis Family of the Year. His father, sister and niece Teri, who went to Stanford along with her twin sister, Tami, are all teaching pros. Tami played on the professional tennis tour.

Stanford Stat . . .

The last world record relay in track by Stanford occurred in 1974 at Stanford Stadium when the Cardinal's mile intermediate hurdle relay team turned in a 3:37.8, becoming the sixth relay team in school history to set a world record. The team consisted of Matt Hogsett, who a year earlier was a member of Stanford's 880-yard relay team which set a world record, Dave Bagshaw, Reggie Mason and Kenny Kring. "It is very unusual to get four hurdlers to run so well and so steady and have them all come up to their potential at one time," said Payton Jordan, Stanford's track coach from 1957-79. "It was a well-earned record by four tough, gutsy athletes who went for it, and got it."

STANFORD LIST

NCAA MEN'S GYMNASTICS CHAMPIONS

Name	Year	Event
Steve Hug	1972	All-Around
Steve Hug	1973	All-Around
Steve Hug	1973	Parallel Bars
Steve Hug	1974	All-Around
Steve Hug	1974	Parallel Bars
Ted Marcy	1974	Pommel Horse
Ted Marcy	1975	Pommel Horse
Ted Marcy	1976	Pommel Horse
Jon Louis	1986	All-Around
Jair Lynch	1992	Horizontal Bar
Mark Booth	1994	Floor Exercise

Stanford LEGEND

Steve Hug

Steve Hug, a two-time Olympian, won the NCAA all-around gymnastics title three times. (Stanford Athletics)

By the time he came to Stanford University from Chatsworth High School in southern California, Steve Hug was already internationally recognized in the sport of gymnastics. He made the United States Pan-Am Team in 1967 at the age of 15 and, a year later, he was a member of the U.S. Olympic Team. After he graduated from Stanford in 1974, Hug had accomplished more than any other gymnast in school history. He won the NCAA all-around championship for three straight years (1972-74, tied for the national title in '73), won the Pacific-8 Conference all-around championship for three consecutive seasons and was the 1974 winner of the prestigious Nissen Award, presented to the nation's top collegiate male gymnast. Following the '68 Olympics in Mexico City and his high school graduation, Hug said he wanted to learn as much as he could and travel wherever he needed to go to receive the best training. That took him to Japan, where he spent more than a year studying the Japanese approach to gymnastics. Upon his return, Hug enrolled at Stanford where he became the school's all-time best male gymnast. He made his second Olympic Team in 1972 in the Munich Games and was the highest scoring all-around performer for the U.S. team. Hug, who was also a member of the U.S. World Championship team in 1970 and '74, was inducted into the USA Gymnastics Hall of Fame in 1995.

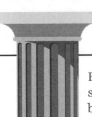

STANFORD LORE

B. Gerald Cantor, holder of the largest privately owned collection of Auguste Rodin's sculptures, announced on February 11, 1974 that a significant portion of his collection would be given to the University. In May, 1985, an outdoor Rodin sculpture garden, made possible by Cantor, opens next to the Museum.

1974-75

•• AMERICA'S TIME CAPSULE ••

- **September 8, 1974:** President Ford pardoned former President Nixon for any crimes he may have committed while in office, calling for an end to the Watergate episode.
- **October 30, 1974:** Muhammad Ali recaptured the heavyweight boxing title with an eighth-round knockout of George Foreman in Zaire.
- **February 21, 1975:** Former White House aides H.R. Haldeman and John Ehrlichman, and former attorney general John Mitchell were each sentenced to 30 months imprisonment for their roles in the Watergate affair.
- **July 5, 1975:** Arthur Ashe became the first African-American to win the men's singles title at England's Wimbledon tennis championships.
- **July 31, 1975:** Former Teamsters leader James Hoffa was reported missing.

STANFORD MOMENT

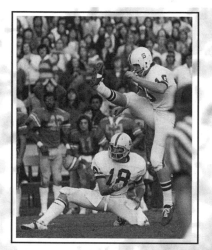

Mike Langford's 50-yard field goal on the game's final play gave Stanford a 22-20 Big Game win.
(Stanford Athletics)

Langford's Field Goal Gives Stanford Big Game Win

On November 23, 1974, Stanford and Cal waged another Big Game classic. Another incredible finish. Another unlikely outcome. Stanford, which entered the game with a 4-4-2 record and a season-long quarterback controversy, beat Cal, 7-2-1 entering the game, 22-20, on a 50-yard field goal by Mike Langford on the game's final play. Here's how events unfolded: Cal led 10-3 after three quarters. Stanford starting QB Mike Cordova was not having his best day. He had completed seven-of-21 for 93 yards and had thrown three interceptions. After one series in the fourth quarter, Cardinal head coach Jack Christiansen replaced Cordova with Guy Benjamin. Then the fireworks began. Benjamin promptly led Stanford to 16 consecutive points and a 19-10 lead with 7:36 remaining in the game after a 61-yard touchdown pass to wide receiver Tony Hill. The Bears closed to 19-13 with 4:40 to play and, on a 13-yard pass play from quarterback Steve Bartkowski to Steve Rivera, Cal retook the lead 20-19 with just 26 seconds on the clock. Jubilant Cal fans had to be restrained from tearing down the goal posts. Stanford took over at their own 19-yard line with 19 seconds left. Benjamin hit Ted Pappas on a 19-yard pass play to the Stanford 38. The next pass fell incomplete. Then, Benjamin hooked up with tight end Brad Williams, who raced 25 yards to the Cal 37 before getting out of bounds with two seconds remaining. Enter Langford. His kick went through the uprights as time ran out, giving the Cardinal a most improbable Big Game victory.

IT WAS APPROPRIATELY DUBBED the "Miracle at Maples." For two nights in January, 1975, Howie Dallmar's men's basketball team made headlines across the country after posting consecutive wins over second-ranked UCLA, 64-60, and fifth-ranked USC, 67-66. "I'll never forget after the USC game—the second one—the fans just stomping on the Maples floor doing that Beach Boy swim," said center Rich Kelley, who scored 22 points vs. UCLA and 30 the next night against the Trojans. "It was quite a weekend," he said. Stanford began its "Miracle" weekend by beating John Wooden's Bruins for the first time since 1966. The Cardinal led by as many as 13 points in the second half, but UCLA scored 11 unanswered points to cut the lead to four, 45-41, with just over 10 minutes to play`. But the Bruins could get no closer than four as Stanford held on for the win. The next night, Kelley's 30 was matched by USC's Gus Williams' 31-point effort in a game that was close throughout. Stanford led 63-62 with 1:21 to play, but USC could not get off a shot before Kelley made four straight free throws to seal the Cardinal win.

Stanford Stat . . .

As a freshman in 1975, Mike Bruner won the NCAA swimming championship in the 1650-yard freestyle. That would prove to be just the beginning for the Omaha, Nebraska native. At the 1976 Olympic Games in Montreal, Bruner took home two gold medals, winning the 200-meter butterfly and as a member of the U.S. 800-meter freestyle relay. He came back to win his second NCAA individual title at the 1977 NCAA's, this one in the 200-yard butterfly. In 1980, Bruner, at the peak of his career, qualified for 1980 United States Olympic Team in three events—the 1500-meter free, 200-meter butterfly and 400-meter free—but did not compete due to the boycott.

STANFORD LIST

MEMORABLE MEN'S BASKETBALL GAMES AT MAPLES PAVILION

1. January 5, 1989—Stanford 83, Arizona 78— Todd Lichti scores 35 for Stanford; Arizona's Sean Elliot scores 34
2. January 17 , 1975—Stanford 64, UCLA 60—Rich Kelley leads upset win over Bruins in "Miracle at Maples Part I
3. January 9, 1997—Stanford 109, UCLA 61—Cardinal gives UCLA biggest loss in school history
4. February 21, 1981—Stanford 74, UCLA 72—Three Cardinal freshmen shock Larry Brown's first Bruin team
5. January 5, 1989—Stanford 82, Arizona 74—Stanford upsets number-one ranked Wildcats
6. December 23, 1987—Stanford 116, UCLA 110 (2ot)—Todd Lichti sparks Cardinal win in double overtime
7. December 27, 1978—Stanford 75, UCLA 72—Wolfe Perry scores 34 in upset win over Bruins
8. January 28, 1980 —Oregon State 18, Stanford 16— Cardinal stall tactics almost pulls of upset over second-ranked Beavers
9. January 18, 1975 —Stanford 67, USC 66—"Miracles at Maples Part II" is complete with win over Trojans
10. December 2, 1983—North Carolina 88, Stanford 75— Record crowd turns out to see UNC's Michael Jordan.

Stanford LEGEND

Rich Kelley

The first seven-foot basketball player in school history, Rich Kelley was also one of the best ever on The Farm. (Stanford Athletics)

Three things distinguished Rich Kelley on the Stanford campus from 1973-75: he had his trademark handlebar mustache, he was seven feet tall and he was one of the best basketball players the school has ever produced. While Kelley's three Cardinal teams never won any league championships, never advanced to the NCAA Tournament and had just one winning season, Kelley managed to earn three consecutive First-Team All-Pacific-8 honors, become the school's all-time leader in rebounds and number three career scoring leader. He played at a time when John Wooden's UCLA teams dominated college basketball and received all the headlines, especially on the west coast. But that didn't seem to faze Kelley, the first seven-foot player in school history. He was a team player. He was more interested in winning games than breaking records. "Basketball is a sport that epitomizes team play," he would say. "Every player on the team is responsible for every win." Kelley graduated from Stanford as the school record holder for career rebounds with 944 and career rebounding average at 12.4. Both of those records still stand today. He scored 1,412 points and averaged 18.6 points per game, which was the third highest average in school history. During his senior season, he scored over 20 points in a game 14 times and grabbed more than 10 rebounds in a game 18 times. On March 7, 1975, the largest crowd in Maples Pavilion history—8,021—turned out to see Kelley's final game at Stanford. Following his college playing days, Kelley was drafted by the New Orleans Jazz and went on to a fine career in professional basketball.

STANFORD LORE

Three Stanford students and a Dutch research assistant were kidnapped on May 19, 1975 from the Gombe Stream Center in Tanzania, Africa by guerrillas from Zaire, who demand ransom of $460,000, arms and ammunition, and the release of political prisoners from Tanzania. After prolonged negotiation, all four were released unharmed. Students were first sent to the center three years before to study primate behavior with anthropologist Jane Goodall. No more would be sent.

•• AMERICA'S TIME CAPSULE ••

- September 5, 1975: President Gerald Ford escaped the first of two assassination attempts in a little more than two weeks. Lynette "Squeaky" Fromme was apprehended.
- September 18, 1975: A 19-month FBI search ended when Patricia Hearst was captured in San Francisco.
- October 1, 1975: Heavyweight boxing champion Muhammad Ali defeated Joe Frazier in the "Thrilla in Manilla".
- February 13, 1976: Dorothy Hamill won a gold medal in figure skating at the Winter Olympic in Innsbruck, Austria.
- July 4, 1976: The bicentennial of United States independence was celebrated.
- July 20, 1976: Viking I, launched 11 months earlier, landed on Mars.

STANFORD MOMENT

Albritton Breaks World Record in Shot Put

Terry Albritton's 71-8 1/2" shot put in 1976 set a new world record. (Stanford Athletics)

Terry Albritton came to Stanford in the fall of 1972 to play football and compete in track and field. But after one year on The Farm, Albritton decided to leave Stanford and train full time for the 1976 Olympics in the shot put. He played on the freshman football team in '72 and participated in track in '73, where he was beaten by Oregon's Mac Wilkins for the Pac-8 shot put title. He spent the next year training full-time in Southern California before moving to Hawaii, where he trained for two years. At the age of 21 at an all-comers meet in Honolulu in 1976, Albritton threw the shot 71-8 1/2" to break the world record. "I told everyone I knew to come to the meet because I was going to break the world record," he said. "There were 5,000 people there and most of them were my friends. It was that much more gratifying because I was surrounded by my friends," he said. His goal of making the Olympic Team seemed just a formality. But, at a weight lifting session six weeks before the Olympic Trials, Albritton was hurt while attempting a bench press exercise with 525 pounds. At the Trials, Albritton's still ailing shoulder limited him to a best of 67-0, which left him in fourth place and off the Olympic Team. Albritton returned to Stanford the following year and in his final season of competition for Stanford, he won the 1977 NCAA shot put title.

BOTH DUNCAN MCDONALD and Don Kardong finished their Cardinal careers in 1971, but five years later, both found themselves on the 1976 United States Olympic Track & Field team that competed in Montreal. Two of the greatest distance runners Stanford has ever produced, McDonald and Kardong each made their marks in ways that will forever be remembered. McDonald, who had as much range as any runner in school history, broke the American record in the 5,000 meters held by the legendary Steve Prefontaine. He became Stanford's first sub-4:00 miler when he ran 3:59.6 in 1970. McDonald was a talented runner who could compete in any race between the 880 and the marathon. Kardong, a two-time All-American in the three mile and cross country in 1970, is the only Stanford athlete to compete in the Olympic marathon. At the '76 Games in Montreal, Kardong placed fourth in the marathon. He still holds Stanford records in the two mile, three mile and six mile events.

Stanford Stat . . .

After leading Stanford to the NCAA water polo championship in 1976—the first in school history—two-time All-American goalie Chris Dorst joined the U.S. National Team and began training for the 1980 Olympic Games. Four years of training up to six hours per day were shattered when the boycott of the Moscow Games was announced. "It made me feel bitter. I said, OK, that part of my life is over." Dorst then attended the Stanford Business School and quit water polo altogether. But, four years later, Dorst would return to the U.S. team and become a member of the 1984 team that won a silver medal in Los Angeles. "It was everything I ever wanted in athletics," he says of the '84 Games.

STANFORD LIST

MEN'S SWIMMING OLYMPIC GOLD MEDALISTS

Name	Olympic Year (s)	Gold Medal (s)
Norman Ross	1920	400 free, 1500 free
Wally O'Connor	1924	800 free relay
George Harrison	1960	800 free relay
Paul Hait	1960	400 medley relay
John Hencken	1972	200 breast
	1976	100 breast, 400 medley relay
Mike Bruner	1976	200 fly, 800 free relay
Pablo Morales	1984	400 medley relay
	1992	100 fly, 400 medley relay
Jay Mortenson	1988	400 medley relay
Jeff Rouse	1992	400 medley relay
	1996	100 back, 400 medley relay
Joe Hudepohl	1992	400 free relay
	1996	200 free relay
Kurt Grote	1996	400 medley relay

Stanford LEGEND

John Hencken

John Hencken won five Olympic medals, including three golds, while breaking the world record 12 times. (Stanford Athletics)

John Hencken did not begin his swimming career dreaming of Olympic gold. It was not in his mind that one day the National Anthem would be played in his honor while the entire nation watched on television. No, John Hencken began swimming as therapy to recover from an operation that removed a growth behind his knee. The Cupertino (California) High School graduate who began swimming as therapy wound up winning three Olympic gold medals, one silver and one bronze while breaking the world record 12 times. He also won five NCAA championships for Stanford and 10 AAU titles. As an 18-year-old school graduate, Hencken won a gold and bronze medal at the 1972 Olympic Games in Munich. He won gold in the 200-meter breaststroke and bronze in the 100-meter breast. At the 1976 Games in Montreal, Hencken won gold medals in the 100-meter breast and the 400-meter medley relay and a silver in the 200-meter breast. He broke the world record in the 100 breast for the seventh time while taking the gold in Montreal. He had already broken the world record in the 200 breast five times prior to the Montreal Games. At Stanford, Hencken won the NCAA championship in the 100-yard breaststroke three times (1973, '75, '76) and the 200-yard breast on two occasions (1974, '75). His 118 points in NCAA championship competition was the school's all-time best following his final season in 1976. A top scholar-athlete, Hencken received an NCAA post-graduate scholarship after graduating from Stanford with an engineering degree.

STANFORD LORE

After two-and-a-half years of study, Stanford's men's and women's intercollegiate athletic programs were merged under a new Department of Athletics, Physical Education and Recreation. Athletic scholarships for women were inaugurated. On June 21, 1975, Title IX of the Educational Amendments of 1972 became law. It read, "No person shall, on the basis of sex, be excluded from participation in, be denied the benefits of, or be subjected to discrimination under any education program or activity receiving Federal financial assistance."

1976-77

- September 12, 1976:   Jimmy Connors joined Chris Evert as U.S. Open tennis champions.
- November 2, 1976:   Jimmy Carter defeated incumbent Gerald Ford in the presidential election.
- December 14, 1976:   ABC-TV aired Barbara Walters' first special, featuring interviews with Jimmy Carter and Barbra Streisand.
- January 17, 1977:   A 10-year halt on capital punishment ended in the U.S. when Gary Gilmore was executed by a Utah firing squad.
- July 28, 1977:   The trans-Alaska pipeline went into full operation.
- August 10, 1977:   New York City police arrested David Berkowitz as the Son of Sam killer.

STANFORD MOMENT

An Emotional Big Game Win For Cardinal

In his final game as Stanford's head coach, Jack Christiansen was carried off the field after a Big Game victory. (Stanford Athletics)

The day before the 79th Big Game on November 20, 1976, Stanford Athletic Director Joe Ruetz announced that Jack Christiansen had been fired. Though Christiansen had been under scrutiny by alumni who were not pleased with his handling of the quarterback situation the past two years, Christiansen remained a popular figure among his players. He was carried out onto the field by his players for his final game—one that would end as memorably as it began. With quarterbacks Guy Benjamin and Mike Cordova alternating, Stanford jumped out to a 9-0 lead. Cordova capped an 80-yard drive when he hit Tony Hill on a 28-yard touchdown pass. The Bears scored 10 straight points and took a 10-9 lead at the intermission, but 10 consecutive third-quarter points by Stanford gave them the lead, 19-10, heading into the final stanza. Cal scored two TDs—the last one with five minutes left in the game—to assume a 24-19 lead. Stanford, forced to punt with 2:25 remaining, pinned the Bears back on their own two-yard line. On Cal's first-down play, quarterback Joe Roth pitched to Markey Crane, who handled the toss cleanly and headed up field. But, as Crane reached the line of scrimmage, the ball squirted loose, right into the hands of Stanford's Duncan McColl. Stanford had the ball on the Bears' two-yard line with 2:20 to play. Three plays later, Ron Inge scored from the one and, after a two-point conversion, Stanford held a 27-24 lead with 1:31 left in the game. As the game ended, Stanford players once again carried Christiansen off the field. Tears of joy and sadness were flowing from the Cardinal's now ex-coach and from most of his players in the locker room. "I've never played a game where I wound up crying at the end," said Cordova. "I think every guy, every person and every coach started crying when Coach told us he was finished." Christiansen, who never had a losing season in five years as Stanford's head coach, had a 30-23-3 record on The Farm.

THE MEN'S TENNIS DYNASTY that coach Dick Gould was building was in full swing in 1977 as his team not only won the NCAA team championship—the third in five years—but Matt Mitchell, a sophomore from nearby Gunn High School in Palo Alto, won the NCAA singles title. Mitchell became the sixth Stanford men's tennis player and third in five years to win the singles crown. "All I did was go out and hit a few balls," Mitchell said following the singles final. Mitchell did more than just hit a few balls. He beat UCLA's Tony Graham in the title match 6-4, 1-6, 6-3, 6-4 on May 30, 1977 at the University of Georgia in Athens. Mitchell wound up playing at Stanford for three seasons (1976-78), earning All-America honors each year and leading the Cardinal to NCAA team championship in 1977 and '78. During his senior season in 1979, Mitchell announced he was leaving The Farm to turn pro. "It was the toughest meeting I've ever had to deal with," Mitchell said after telling his coaches and teammates that he was leaving Stanford for the professional ranks. Mitchell, who followed his brother, Mark, to Stanford, was inducted in the Stanford Tennis Hall of Fame.

Stanford Stat . . .

The streak that has now lasted 21 years began in 1976-77 when two Stanford teams won NCAA championships: water polo and men's tennis. Since then, Stanford has won at least one NCAA team title every year for the past 21 years—a record unmatched in collegiate athletic history. In '76-77, the Cardinal water polo team won its first national championship after compiling a 20-2 overall mark. Dick Gould's men's tennis program was now among the pre-eminent programs in the country in 1977 after his squad won its third title in five years. Led by NCAA singles champion Matt Mitchell, the Cardinal beat Trinity (Texas) 5-4 in the final match.

STANFORD LIST

STANFORD BASKETBALL IN THE NBA DRAFT
(the NBA draft began in 1947)

Player	Year	Round	Team
Kimberly Belton	1980	2	Phoenix Suns
Mike Bratz	1977	3	Phoenix Suns
Art Harris	1968	2	Seattle SuperSonics
Keith Jones	1984	6	Los Angeles Lakers
Adam Keefe	1992	1	Atlanta Hawks
Rich Kelley	1975	1	New Orleans Jazz
Brevin Knight	1997	1	Cleveland Cavaliers
Todd Lichti	1989	1	Denver Nuggets
Jim Pollard	1947	1	Minneapolis Lakers
John Revelli	1984	4	Los Angeles Lakers
Claude Terry	1972	*	Denver Nuggets (ABA)

* specific rounds not announced

Stanford LEGEND

Mike Bratz

As a senior in 1976-77, Mike Bratz led Stanford in scoring, assists and steals and was named first-team All-Pac 8. (Stanford Athletics)

After leading Allan Hancock College to the 1974 California State Junior College championship, Mike Bratz transferred to Stanford and became one of the school's all-time best basketball players. In three years on The Farm, Bratz set Stanford records for career assists with 281 and season assists with 132 in 1975-76 as a junior. He ended his Cardinal career among the best in school history in scoring, field goal percentage, free- throw percentage and assists. As a senior in '76-77, Bratz led the team in scoring (19.6 ppg), assists (113) and steals (59) and was named First-Team All-Pacific-8 Conference. But the individual accolades and records did not matter as much to Bratz as winning. None of his three Stanford teams finished the season with a winning record. "I've got an unfulfilled feeling even though I am scoring more points," Bratz said in 1977. "All the points in the world couldn't ever make up for the fact that the team isn't winning." A native of Lompoc, California, Bratz scored more than 20 points in 17 of Stanford's 28 games in 1976-77 while finishing fourth in Pac-8 in scoring. "Mike has proved to be the heartbeat of both our offense and defense," said his coach, Dick DiBiaso in 1977. "He contributes both leadership and consistency on the team." Bratz, an Academic All-American as a senior, was selected in the third round of the 1977 NBA Draft by the Phoenix Suns. During his professional basketball career, Bratz played for the Cleveland Cavaliers, San Antonio Spurs, Chicago Bulls, Golden State Warriors and Sacramento Kings as well as the Suns.

STANFORD LORE

The largest display of civil disobedience in Stanford University history occurred on May 9-10, 1977 and resulted in the arrests of 294 persons—of whom 270 were students—in the Old Union. The 16-hour nonviolent, peaceful sit-in protested apartheid, United States corporate investments in South Africa, and the Board of Trustees' refusal to urge Ford Motor Co. to close its operations there. Also, the University announced its five-year drive to raise $300 million topped its goal by $4 million. The "Campaign for Stanford" was the largest single fundraising drive completed by any university.

1977-78

- September 13, 1977: The first diesel-engine automobiles were introduced by General Motors.
- February 8, 1978: Egyptian President Anwar el-Sadat began a six-day visit to the United States to hasten a Middle East peace settlement.
- February 15, 1978: Leon Spinks won a 15-round decision over Muhammad Ali to capture the heavyweight boxing title.
- June 10, 1978: Affirmed, ridden by jockey Steve Cauthen, won horse racing's Triple Crown with a victory at the Belmont Stakes.
- August 4, 1978: Evacuation of the Love Canal area of Niagara Falls, a dumping ground for toxic waste in the 1940s and '50s, began.

All-Pac-8 receiver James Lofton helped Stanford beat LSU 24-14 in the Sun Bowl. *(Stanford Athletics)*

STANFORD MOMENT

Walsh-Led Cardinal Wins Sun Bowl

First-year head coach Bill Walsh guided Stanford to its finest season since 1971 as he led the Cardinal to a 9-3 overall record, a #15 national ranking and a 24-14 win over LSU in the Sun Bowl on December 31 in El Paso, Texas. Walsh, who had been an assistant coach on The Farm in 1963 and '64, saw his team come back from a 14-10 halftime deficit and shut out the powerful LSU offense in the second half. The game pitted the explosive Cardinal passing attack, led by All-American quarterback Guy Benjamin, freshman sensation Darrin Nelson at running back, and All-Pac 8 receiver James Lofton, against the potent LSU running attack, led by their All-American running back, Charles Alexander. No one went home disappointed as Benjamin set Sun Bowl records for passing, and Alexander, with 197 yards on the ground, set the bowl record for rushing. Stanford tied the game at 7-7 early in the second quarter on a 49-yard pass play from Benjamin to Lofton. But a seven-yard run by Alexander with less than a minute to play in the first half put LSU on top 14-10 at the intermission. Enter Stanford linebacker Gordy Ceresino and the rest of the Cardinal defense. While the offense put up two TDs in the second half—on Benjamin passes to Lofton and Nelson—Ceresino and Co. were shutting down the Tigers' offense. Ceresino finished the game with 22 tackles and was named the game's Defensive MVP. Benjamin, the game's Offensive MVP, finished 23-for-36 for 269 yards, three touchdowns and no interceptions.

ANY LIST OF THE TOP 10 ATHLETES at Stanford University would have to include James Lofton, a world-class long jumper and first-round NFL draft choice. Lofton starred on both the Cardinal track and football teams during his tenure on The Farm (1975-78), then moved on to a 16-year career in the National Football League, which will undoubtedly land him in the Hall of Fame. As a senior in 1977, Lofton recorded 53 receptions for 931 yards and a school-record 12 receiving touchdowns. His performance against Washington on October 15, 1977 was the greatest single-game effort by a Stanford receiver to date. He caught 12 passes—second only to Gene Washington's 13 in 1968—for 192 yards and three touchdowns, both school records. He was named First-Team All-Pac 8 and was a first-round selection in the NFL draft by the Green Bay Packers (sixth pick overall) in 1978. His All-Pro career concluded in 1993 with Lofton as the NFL record holder for career receiving yardage (14,004) and second in receptions (764). In track, he was a three-time All-American and the 1978 NCAA champion in the long jump. His NCAA winning jump of 26-11 3/4 stands today as the school record.

Stanford Stat . . .

After finishing second in the nation for three straight years, the Cardinal women's tennis team won the first national team championship ever in women's sports at Stanford. The Cardinal men also won the NCAA title in 1978, giving Stanford the distinction of being the first school ever to win both the men's and women's championships in the same season. For the women, four players earned All-America honors: Susie Hagey, Barbara Jordan, Kathy Jordan and Diane Morrison. Stanford won the AIAW doubles crown for the third straight year, this time Kathy and Barbara Jordan defeated teammates and two-time defending champions Morrison and Hagey.

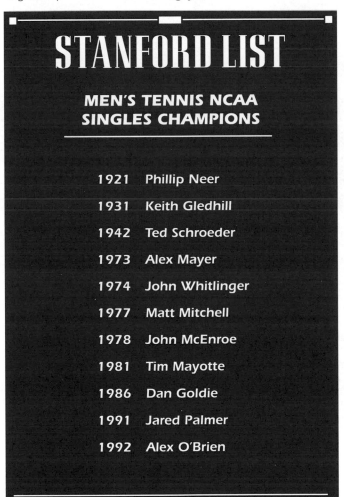

STANFORD LIST

MEN'S TENNIS NCAA SINGLES CHAMPIONS

1921	Phillip Neer
1931	Keith Gledhill
1942	Ted Schroeder
1973	Alex Mayer
1974	John Whitlinger
1977	Matt Mitchell
1978	John McEnroe
1981	Tim Mayotte
1986	Dan Goldie
1991	Jared Palmer
1992	Alex O'Brien

Stanford LEGEND

John McEnroe

He played at Stanford just one season, but John McEnroe left his mark on the men's tennis program. (Stanford Athletics)

John McEnroe was a member of the Stanford men's tennis team for just one season, then he went on to become one of the greatest tennis players of all time. But, his one year on The Farm gave Cardinal fans a glimpse of what this phenom from Douglaston, New York was all about. He was irreverent, temperamental, somewhat introverted and aloof, tenacious, competitive, admired and respected by his teammates and a Wimbledon semifinalist —all before he stepped foot on the Stanford campus for the 1978 season. In his one season on The Farm, McEnroe led the Cardinal to a perfect 24-0 dual match record in '78, won the NCAA singles championship and helped Stanford win yet another team title—the school's fourth in a six-year period. "This is the way I wanted to finish up my college career," McEnroe said after winning the NCAA title. "I'm ready for the pro tour." Since McEnroe had been a Wimbledon semifinalist in 1977— the year before he came to Stanford—there was little doubt his star would rise once on the tour. During his illustrious and sometimes infamous career, McEnroe won three Wimbledon singles championships (1981, '83, '84) and four U.S. Open singles titles (1979, '81, '83, '89). He also won five Wimbledon doubles championships and was a member of the United States Davis Cup Team 12 times. He was the number-one ranked singles player in the world from 1980-84 and the number-one ranked doubles player in the world from 1979-84 and again in 1989. "I did my darndest getting John to come to Stanford," said his Cardinal coach, Dick Gould. "But I knew he couldn't and shouldn't stay four years. He was ready to be a leading pro after a single season with us; he was a prized package waiting to be opened," Gould said.

STANFORD LORE

Physics graduate student Sally Ride, working on her Ph.D. degree, became one of the first six women named to the astronaut corps by NASA. Ride applied for the astronaut corps after reading a NASA ad in *The Stanford Daily*. In June, 1983, Ride, who also played volleyball at Stanford, became America's first woman in space. She earned bachelor's degrees in English and physics and a master's and Ph.D. in physics, all from Stanford.

1978-79

- September 15, 1978:   Muhammad Ali regained the heavyweight boxing title with a 15-round decision over Leon Spinks.
- November 18, 1978:   More than 900 people, including 211 children, were found dead in Guyana. Jim Jones, leader of a religious sect, led the group in a mass suicide by poison.
- November 27, 1978:   George Moscone and Harvey Milk, the mayor and city supervisor of San Francisco, respectively, were shot to death in City Hall by Dan White, a former supervisor.
- March 26, 1979:   Magic Johnson and Michigan State defeated Larry Bird and Indiana State in the NCAA basketball championship game at Salt Lake City.
- * March 28, 1979:   Three Mile Island, near Harrisburg, Pennsylvania, was the site of a nuclear near-disaster.

Steve Dils was named the offensive MVP after leading Stanford to a Bluebonnet Bowl victory. (Stanford Athletics)

STANFORD MOMENT

Dils Sparks Great Comeback in Bluebonnet Bowl Victory

One of the greatest comebacks in Stanford football history occurred on New Year's Eve, 1978 in the Astrodome in Houston, Texas. In his second year as head coach, Bill Walsh led his Cardinal to a second consecutive bowl game—this time vs. Georgia in the Bluebonnet Bowl. The Bulldogs led 15-0 at halftime and 22-0 early in the third quarter before Stanford mounted its comeback. Over a six-and-a-half minute span late in the third quarter and early in the fourth, the Cardinal scored 25 unanswered points to shock the Bulldogs. Offensive MVP Steve Dils, who completed 17-of-28 for 210 yards and three TDs, got things started with 6:03 left in the third period by hitting wide receiver Ken Margerum on a 32-yard TD pass play. Dils hit running Darrin Nelson on a 20-yard TD pass play with 3:57 remaining in the quarter, then hit Margerum again from 14-yards out with 1:33 in the quarter. A two-point conversion tied the score at 22-22. Placekicker Ken Naber's 24-yard field goal with 14:50 left in the game completed the comeback and put the Cardinal ahead to stay. Defensive MVP Gordy Ceresino, who accounted for 20 tackles, asserted his troops to hold tight the rest of the way.

STANFORD'S FIRST FOUR-TIME All-American women's tennis player, Susie Hagey won two AIAW national doubles championships and led the Cardinal to three second-place finishes and one AIAW championship during her Stanford career (1976-79). Hagey had two brothers and two sisters who also excelled in tennis, including her brother Chico, who was an All-American at Stanford in 1972 and '74. Susie won the AIAW doubles title with Diane Morrison in 1976 and '77 and was a part of Stanford's first AIAW national championship team in 1978. During her four-year tenure on The Farm, Hagey's teams went 48-10, won on national title (1978) and finished second her other three seasons (1976, '77, '79).

Stanford Stat . . .

For senior quarterback Steve Dils, October 21, 1978 will be one day he can tell his grandchildren about. On a day when sophomore running back Darrin Nelson eclipsed the school's career rushing record, Dils stole the show with a record-setting performance of his own. While Stanford was beating Washington State 43-27 in Pullman, Washington, Dils was completing 32-of-51 passes for 430 yards and five touchdowns. He set three school and Pac-10 records on this day: passing yards (430), total offense (438) and TD passes (five, tying four others).

STANFORD LIST

HIGHEST WOMEN'S TENNIS WORLD RANKINGS (TOP 50)

5.	Kathy Jordan	1984
18.	Kate Gompert	1987
18.	Alycia Moulton	1984
19.	Patty Fendick	1988
21.	Marianne Werdel	1987
22.	Elise Burgin	1988
26.	Meredith McGrath	1991
30.	Lele Forood	1979
35.	Debbie Graham	1993
37.	Barbara Jordan	1980
39.	Anna Ivan	1985
41.	Tami Whitlinger	1991
50.	Diane Morrison	1980

Stanford LEGEND

Kathy Jordan

Kathy Jordan was ranked 5th in the world in 1984. *(Stanford Athletics)*

While her career at Stanford may have been brief, Kathy Jordan's presence on The Farm will last a lifetime. After coming to Stanford from King of Prussia, Pennsylvania, as one of the top junior players in the world, Jordan immediately stamped her name as one of the nation's all-time great collegiate tennis players. While she stayed at Stanford just two seasons (1978-79) before joining the professional tour, the Jordan legacy will be recorded as one that was nearly flawless. As a freshman in 1978, she helped Stanford to the AIAW national championship—the first women's tennis championship in school history—won the AIAW doubles championship with her sister Barb and was a singles finalist. She followed that performance a year later by winning the AIAW singles and doubles championship and becoming the first player in history to accomplish that feat. Jordan was ranked 14th in the world as a sophomore at Stanford in 1979 and, after two great seasons on The Farm, she decided to turn pro. A month later, Jordan advanced to the round of 16 at Wimbledon. Jordan's professional career included winning doubles championships at all four Grand Slam Tournaments (U.S. Open, 1981; Wimbledon, 1980, '85; French Open, 1980; Australian Open, 1981). She rose to a number-five world ranking in 1984. Jordan was inducted into the Stanford Athletic Hall of Fame in 1995.

STANFORD LORE

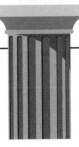

Don E. Fehrenbacher, professor of history, won a Pulitzer Prize for his book, *The Dred Scott Case: Its Significance in American Law and Politics*, on Aril 16, 1979. The prize was followed by two years a Pulitzer awarded for Prof. David M. Potter's *The Impending Crisis: 1848-1861*, published posthumously after Fehrenbacher completed and edited it. Also, economist Kenneth Arrow returned to the Stanford faculty after 11 years at Harvard, during which he received a Nobel Prize for economics in 1972.

1979-80

- September 9, 1979: Former Stanford star John McEnroe and 16-year old Tracy Austin won singles titles at the U.S. Open Tennis Championships.
- November 4, 1979: Iranian revolutionaries seized the U.S. embassy in Teheran, taking some 90 hostages, including 65 Americans.
- January 20, 1980: President Jimmy Carter announced that the U.S. Olympic Team would boycott the 1980 Summer Games in Moscow, in protest against the Soviet invasion of Afghanistan.
- February 22, 1980: The U.S. hockey team beat the heavily favored Soviet Union, 4-3, advancing to the finals where it defeated Finland for the gold medal.
- May 18, 1980: Mt. St. Helens, a volcano that had been dormant since 1857, erupted in Washington, leveling about 120 square miles of forest.

STANFORD MOMENT

Olympic Boycott Halts Dreams of 21 Stanford Athletes

John Moffett was one of 21 Stanford athletes unable to compete in the 1980 Olympics due to the U.S.-led boycott. (Stanford Athletics)

The Olympic dreams of hundred of athletes around the country were dashed in the summer of 1980 when the U.S. boycotted the Olympic Games in Moscow to protest the Soviet invasion of Afghanistan. The boycott, which was supported by 35 national sports governing bodies, affected 21 Stanford athletes who had trained for years for their Olympic moment. "It's so disappointing to work as hard as you can for the top rung of success and then have that top rung removed," said Chris Dorst, a member of the U.S. water polo team. Dorst was one of four Stanford athletes who had earned a spot on the U.S. water polo team. Seven Cardinal women swimmers, six men swimmers, one field hockey player and one member of the U.S. crew team were also scheduled to compete in Moscow. Those Stanford athletes included field hockey player Nancy White, rower Kathy Thaxton, track team members Mary Osborne (javelin) and Tony Sandoval (marathon), women swimmers Lisa Buese, Kim Carlisle, Stephanie Elkins, Linda Jezek, Libby Kinkead, Marybeth Linzmeier and Susan Rapp, men's swimmers Mike Bruner, John Hencken, John Simons, Wade Flemons (representing Canada), John Moffet and Dave Sims and water polo team members Dorst, Jody Campbell, Drew McDonald and Doug Burke. Some of the athletes had their Olympic moments at the 1984 Games in Los Angeles, but for others, their Olympic dreams were dashed when President Jimmy Carter announced his plan to lead a U.S. boycott of the 1980 Games.

Stanford SPOTLIGHT

LED BY FRESHMEN Janet Buchan and Kim Carlisle and sophomore Linda Jezek, the Stanford women's swimming team captured its first national championship in 1980 by edging Texas 629-623. Buchan and Carlisle were Stanford's top point scorers with 81 and 80, respectively, while Jezek won two events and placed second in another. But it was Stanford's superior depth that provided the margin of victory. In the final event of the meet, the 400 freestyle relay, Stanford needed a fifth-place finish to ensure the national title. When the team of Carlisle, Carol Proctor, Barb Major and Kelly Asplund came home in third, the championship was Stanford's. Buchan set a national record in winning the 400 individual medley, placed third in two events and fourth in two others. Carlisle won the 50 back and scored in six other events.

Stanford Stat . . .

The best field hockey player to ever wear a Stanford uniform was no doubt Nancy White, a four-year letterwinner from 1976-79 who had her dreams of Olympic competition shattered when the U.S. boycotted the 1980 Games in Moscow. White, the daughter of Supreme Court Justice Byron "Whizzer" White, a football All-America at Colorado, was not only Stanford's best, but one of the best in the nation. She was named All-America in 1978 and '79 and was a member of the 1980 U.S. Olympic Team. White traveled around the world competing for the U.S. National Team for three years, but never got her chance to compete in the Olympic Games. "It was a real shock," she said. "No one thought it would happen."

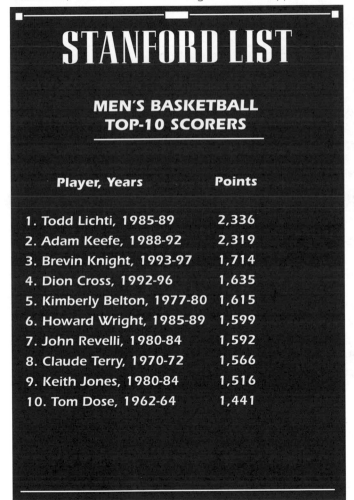

STANFORD LIST

MEN'S BASKETBALL TOP-10 SCORERS

Player, Years	Points
1. Todd Lichti, 1985-89	2,336
2. Adam Keefe, 1988-92	2,319
3. Brevin Knight, 1993-97	1,714
4. Dion Cross, 1992-96	1,635
5. Kimberly Belton, 1977-80	1,615
6. Howard Wright, 1985-89	1,599
7. John Revelli, 1980-84	1,592
8. Claude Terry, 1970-72	1,566
9. Keith Jones, 1980-84	1,516
10. Tom Dose, 1962-64	1,441

Stanford LEGEND

Kimberly Belton

Kimberly Belton graduated from Stanford as the school's all-time leading scorer and rebounder. (Stanford Athletics)

In the Bronx neighborhood that Kimberly Belton grew up in, dreaming about playing basketball and receiving a scholarship to Stanford University were incongruous. An outstanding student, the 6-7, 217-pound Belton learned how to play basketball on the playgrounds in the Bronx. When he averaged 20 points and 17 rebounds as a senior at Horace Mann High School and was named New York City's top scholar-athlete, the scholarship offers poured in. Belton wound up at Stanford, some 3,000 miles from home and a world apart from his neighborhood back in New York. Four years after arriving on The Farm, Belton rewrote the Cardinal record book, became the school's all-time leading scorer and rebounder, earned three All-Pac-8 Conference honors and was a second-round selection in the NBA draft by the Phoenix Suns. During his four years, Belton played in all 107 games from 1977-80, averaged 15.1 points and 8.9 rebounds and set 11 school records. His 1,615 points and 955 rebounds were the best in school history when Belton graduated in 1980 with a degree in communications. "What Kimberly Belton meant to the Stanford community went far beyond his statistical achievements," said his coach, Dick DiBiaso. "He always displayed great maturity as a leader when faced with adversity. For four years, Kimberly played as close to his maximum potential as possible. I cannot envision there being a better person playing basketball on the college level in the United States," he said in 1980. Belton, an Academic All-American at Stanford, went on to a successful career as a television sports producer for ABC.

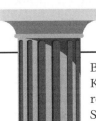

STANFORD LORE

Biologist Donald Kennedy was appointed eighth president in Stanford history on June 13, 1980. Kennedy, on leave since 1977 as Commissioner of the U.S. Food and Drug Administration, returned to Stanford in 1979 to accept the post of Vice President and Provost. He first joined the Stanford faculty in 1960, serving as chairman of Biological Sciences from 1965-72 and as chairman of Human Biology from 1974-77. He remained University President until 1992.

1980-81

- November 4, 1980: Ronald Reagan won the presidential election in a landslide over incumbent Jimmy Carter.
- November 21, 1980: More than half of America's television audience tuned in Dallas to see "Who shot J.R."
- January 20, 1981: The Iranian hostage crisis ended when Iran releases American captives who were seized at the U.S. Embassy in Teheran 14 months before.
- January 25, 1981: The Oakland Raiders won Super Bowl XV by defeating the Philadelphia Eagles 27-10. Stanford's Heisman Trophy Winner, Jim Plunkett, was named the game's Most Valuable Player.
- April 14, 1981: The space shuttle Columbia successfully touched down on Earth following a 54-hour maiden flight in space.

STANFORD MOMENT

Sophomore QB John Elway led Stanford to a 31-14 upset win over Oklahoma in Norman on September 27, 1980. (Stanford Athletics)

Elway, Cardinal Dethrone Mighty Sooners

In one of the greatest non-conference wins in Stanford football history, sophomore QB John Elway put on a show Oklahoma head coach Barry Switzer will never forget in leading the underdog Cardinal to a 31-14 upset over the Sooners on September 27, 1980 in Norman, Oklahoma. "He put on the greatest exhibition of quarterback play and passing I have ever seen on this field," Switzer said of Elway, who completed 20-of-34 for 237 yards and three touchdowns. He also ran for 95 yards (not including sacks) and scored one TD. What made the win more remarkable was the fact that Darrin Nelson did not play due to a bruised hip sustained the week before. But with Elway connecting with Ken Margerum for one TD pass from 11-yards out and Andre Tyler for two touchdown scores—from 12 and nine yards out—the Cardinal not only shut down the mighty Sooner wishbone, but its 31-0 lead midway through the third quarter proved to be too much for Oklahoma to overcome.

TO DEFINE THE CAREER OF JODY CAMPBELL is to define the term "near perfection." In four years at Stanford, Campbell not only won most of the top individual honors given to water polo players, but he led his Stanford teams to a spot in collegiate water polo history. For four years, from 1978-81, the Campbell-led Cardinal ruled the pool. During this time, Campbell and his teammates won three national championships, three conference titles and compiled a four-year record of 108-8-3—a winning percentage of .920. Campbell himself was named a First-Team All-American all four years. He was a member of three United States Olympic Water Polo teams in 1980, 1984 and 1988. Although he did not compete in the '80 Games due to the Olympic boycott, he won a silver medal in at the 1984 Games in Los Angeles.

Stanford Stat . . .

The 1980 Cardinal football team featured some of the top offensive stars in Stanford history. Leading the way was sophomore quarterback John Elway, who would become one of the greatest QBs in college football history, running back Darrin Nelson, perhaps the greatest all-purpose back in college football history and wide receiver Ken Margerum, a two-time consensus First-Team All-American. The offense generated over 432 yards and 28 points per game.

STANFORD LIST

CAREER RECEIVING YARDAGE LEADERS

1. Justin Armour, 1991-94	2,482
2. Ken Margerum, 1977-80	2,430
3. Darrin Nelson, 1977-81	2,368
4. Ed McCaffrey, 1986-90	2,333
5. Brian Manning, 1993-96	2,280
6. Emile Harry, 1981-84	2,270
7. Jeff James, 1984-87	2,265
8. Tony Hill, 1973-76	2,225
9. Mike Tolliver, 1979-83	1,825
10. Gene Washington, 1966-68	1,722

Stanford LEGEND

Ken Margerum

Ken Margerum was a two-time consensus First-Team All-American. (Stanford Athletics)

He was called a free-spirit, refreshingly unconventional, a carefree college student with a spontaneous approach to life. But, after witnessing his 38-inch vertical leap and 30 career touchdown receptions, everyone who saw him play knew that Ken Margerum was a very gifted athlete— perhaps the best receiver in Stanford football history.

While his legend was due in part to his wind surfing under the Golden Gate Bridge, skateboarding to his next class and playing catch with a Frisbee at Stanford Stadium at 3:00 in the morning, Margerum was also a Cardinal legend because of what he did during his record-breaking four-year Stanford career. By the time he graduated from Stanford with a degree in Communications, Margerum had compiled an impressive list of accolades: Two-time consensus First-Team All-American, three-time First-Team All-Pac-10 selection, Academic All-American, Stanford and Pac-10 career record holder in career touchdown receptions with 30, Stanford record holder in career receiving yardage (2,430) and the number-two receiver in Cardinal history with 141 receptions. Margerum, who teamed with quarterback John Elway and running back Darrin Nelson in 1980 to form one of the most potent offenses in school history, was chosen in the third round of the NFL draft by the Chicago Bears.

STANFORD LORE

In December, 1980, a month after his election to the U.S. presidency, Ronald Reagan, an honorary fellow of the Hoover Institution, named at least 21 Hoover scholars and Stanford professors to advisory committees. Also, the first combined heart-lung transplant in nearly 10 years was performed at the Stanford Medical Center on March 9, 1981. The patient, Mary Gohlke of Mesa, Arizona, recovered successfully. Doctors used the anti-rejection drug Cyclosporin A, which had not been available earlier when operations brought only limited success.

1980-81

•• SEASON HIGHLIGHTS ••

- Sophomore quarterback John Elway was named First-Team All-American after passing for a school and Pac-10 record 27 touchdowns in 1980. He threw six TDs in a 54-13 win over Oregon State, breaking another school and conference record.
- The Cardinal women's volleyball team recorded its best record in school history by posting a 33-18 overall mark in 1980. Stanford's ninth-place finish in the AIAW was also the best ever at Stanford.
- Stanford advanced to the NCAA baseball regionals in 1981 for the first time since 1967. The Cardinal came within one win of the College World Series, but lost a 10-2 decision to Texas in the Central Regional championship game.
- Cardinal teams won two more NCAA championships for the fourth time in the last five years. The water polo team won the 1980 title with a 28-2-1 overall record, while the men's tennis team won the '81 championship with a 20-2 mark.

Dick Gould's men's tennis team won its sixth NCAA championship in nine years in 1981 after its 5-1 win over UCLA. *(Stanford Athletics)*

STANFORD MOMENT

Cardinal Men's Tennis Team Wins Sixth NCAA Championship

The dominance of Stanford's men's tennis program under head coach Dick Gould continued on May 25, 1981 when the Cardinal defeated UCLA, 5-1, to win its sixth NCAA men's tennis team championship in the last nine years. Stanford, which finished the season with a 20-2 overall record, beat Utah, 9-0, California, 5-4, and Georgia, 7-2, before meeting with their Pac-10 rivals for the title in Athens, Georgia. After losing the first set, 7-6, Tim Mayotte, playing #1 singles for the Cardinal, came back to beat Marcel Freeman of UCLA, 6-7, 7-6 (5-1), 6-3. Mayotte's victory put Stanford on top, 3-1. Earlier in the match, Jimmy Gurfein, playing #3, won his match, 6-0, 6-3, while #6 player Jeff Arons won, 3-6, 6-1, 6-3. After Mike Falberg won his match at #4 singles, 3-6, 7-6 (5-3), 6-2, Stanford found itself one win away from the championship. Scott Bondurant, playing at #5 singles, recorded the clinching match by beating the Bruins' Bruce Brescia, 6-3, 4-6, 7-5. "I didn't know we had won it until the guys came running up and said something to me," Bondurant said. Four Cardinal players earned First-Team All-Americans honors in '81, including Mayotte, Gurfein, Bondurant and Scott Davis.

THE LIST OF ELITE TENNIS PLAYERS who have competed at Stanford is long and indeed impressive. But few can match the success of Alycia Moulton, whose list of trophies and honors are too numerous to mention here. Suffice to say, however, that her collegiate career is second to none. She was a four-time First-Team All-American, an NCAA singles champion in 1982 and an AIAW doubles champion in 1979 with Kathy Jordan and again in '81 with Caryn Copeland. Moulton was an AIAW singles finalist in 1980 and '81 and in 1982, she was a member of Stanford's undefeated 20-0 team which captured the first NCAA title in women's tennis and second ever on The Farm. She went on to play professional tennis following her Cardinal career and reached her highest world ranking of number 18 in 1984.

Stanford Stat . . .

In his fifth season at the helm of the Cardinal baseball program, head coach Mark Marquess led Stanford to its first NCAA post-season appearance in 14 years and only the fourth in school history. Stanford was led by Dave Meier, Mike Dotterer, Mike Aldrete, Bill Worden, Mike Toothman, Paul Grame, Gregg Lomnicky, Mike Sullivan and Steve Cottrell. The Cardinal finished the season 43-22 overall and 16-14 in the Pac-10, good for second place.

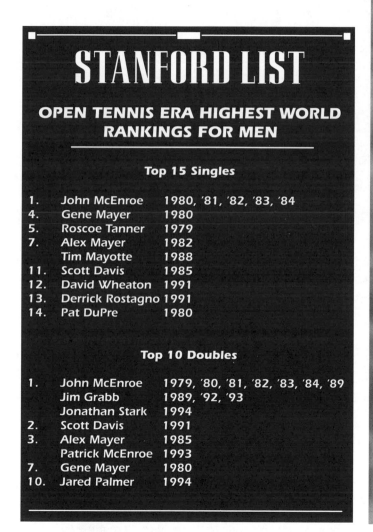

STANFORD LIST

OPEN TENNIS ERA HIGHEST WORLD RANKINGS FOR MEN

Top 15 Singles

1.	John McEnroe	1980, '81, '82, '83, '84
4.	Gene Mayer	1980
5.	Roscoe Tanner	1979
7.	Alex Mayer	1982
	Tim Mayotte	1988
11.	Scott Davis	1985
12.	David Wheaton	1991
13.	Derrick Rostagno	1991
14.	Pat DuPre	1980

Top 10 Doubles

1.	John McEnroe	1979, '80, '81, '82, '83, '84, '89
	Jim Grabb	1989, '92, '93
	Jonathan Stark	1994
2.	Scott Davis	1991
3.	Alex Mayer	1985
	Patrick McEnroe	1993
7.	Gene Mayer	1980
10.	Jared Palmer	1994

Stanford LEGEND

Tim Mayotte

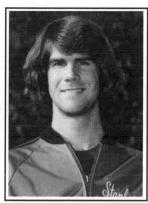

Tim Mayotte won the 1981 NCAA singles crown while leading his team to the national title. (Stanford Athletics)

When Tim Mayotte defeated Jimmy Connors as a 20-year-old college junior in the quarterfinals of the TransAmerica Open pro tournament in October of 1980, the secret of Mayotte's powerful serve and deadly volley game was no more. The next young superstar on the pro tennis tour resided at Stanford University—at least for one more year. Following that win over Connors, Mayotte proceeded to have a storybook junior season in 1981, his third and final as a Cardinal. After leading Stanford to its sixth NCAA men's tennis championship, and second in a row, Mayotte then defeated teammate Jimmy Gurfein to win the NCAA singles crown. Shortly after the victory, Mayotte decided to turn pro and forego his senior season at Stanford. "This has been like a long road for me," Mayotte said after winning the singles crown, the eighth Stanford player to do so. "As humans, I guess we want to completely finish anything we start. I really wanted this," he said. In his three years at Stanford, Mayotte led the Cardinal to a third-place finish his freshman season and back-to-back titles his sophomore and junior seasons in 1980 and '81. He was twice named a First-Team All-American, and in 1981 he was awarded the prestigious Rafael Osuna Award, presented to the collegiate tennis player who best exemplifies competitive excellence, sportsmanship and contributions to the game. As a professional, Mayotte rose to number seven in the world in 1988. He was elected to the Stanford Hall of Fame in 1994.

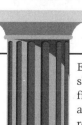

STANFORD NOTABLE

Eric Heiden established himself at the age of 21 as perhaps the greatest competitor in the history of speed skating. At the 1980 Winter Olympics at Lake Placid, N.Y., he achieved the unprecedented feat of winning five individual gold medals. Heiden, at the time a medical student, took first in the 500, 5,000, 1,000, 1,500 and 10,000 meter events, setting two Olympic marks and a world record. After the Olympics, Heiden retired from speed skating and turned to professional bicycle racing, where in 1985 he won the U.S. professional cycling championship. He returned to school to complete his M.D. from Stanford in 1991.

1981-82

- September 13, 1981: Former Stanford All-American John McEnroe won the singles championship at the U.S. Open Tennis Tournament.
- October 19, 1981: Arthur Schawlow of Stanford University and Nicolaas Bloembergen of Harvard University were awarded the Nobel Prize in physics.
- January 24, 1982: The San Francisco 49ers, behind former Stanford head coach Bill Walsh, beat the Cincinnati Bengals 26-21 to win Super Bowl XVI.
- January 8, 1982: An eight-year antitrust suit by the Justice Department ended when the American Telephone and Telegraph Company (AT&T) agreed to divest itself of its 22 Bell Telephone operating systems.
- June 25, 1982: Secretary of State Alexander Haig resigned following disagreements with President Ronald Reagan.

Mike Dotterer helped the Cardinal advance to the College World Series in 1982—the first under head coach Mark Marquess.
(Stanford Athletics)

STANFORD MOMENT

Cardinal Advances to College World Series

When the Cardinal beat Pepperdine 15-8 on May 29, 1982 in the finals of the NCAA West I Regional at Fresno State, it marked the beginning of a new era in Stanford baseball. Mark Marquess, the former Cardinal All-American first baseman in his sixth year as head coach on The Farm, had put Stanford baseball on the proverbial map. His team, which advanced to the Regionals in 1981 only to lose to Texas in the regional final, had now earned a trip to Omaha, Nebraska and the College World Series. It was the second trip to the Series in Stanford history and the first since Marquess led his 1967 club to Omaha. Led by second baseman Steve Buechele, the regional MVP, Stanford hit .377 as a team and scored 42 runs in beating Hawaii 10-5 and Fresno State 17-10 before knocking off Pepperdine. Buechele went 10-for-13 with three home runs and 13 RBI in the regional to spark the Cardinal offense. Other mainstays on the '82 club included left fielder Mike Dotterer, first baseman Mike Aldrete, third baseman Loring Davies, catcher Bob Hausladen, shortstop Bob DeCosta and pitchers Brian Mignano, Brian Myers, David Harris and Jeff Ballard. Following the 1982 season, Stanford went on to advance to the College World Series five times in the next eight years—winning two championships along the way.

KIM SCHNURPFEIL WAS A SWIMMER in San Mateo, California and Ceci Hopp was taking ballet classes and playing in tennis tournaments in Cos Cob, Connecticut in high school. When they came together at Stanford in the early 1980s, however, they turned the Cardinal women's cross country and track programs into national contenders. During their careers, both won NCAA individual titles in track and both earned All-America honors in cross country and track. Schnurpfeil broke the course and school record in cross country during her freshman season in 1979, was a finalist in the national 5,000 meter run and placed seventh in the 1980 U.S. Olympic Trials. She went on to win the 10,000 meter run at the first NCAA Women's Track and Field Championships in 1982 as a junior. Hopp, a two-time cross country All-American in 1981 and '82, won the NCAA 3,000 meter run in 1982 as a freshman in helping Stanford place fifth in the nation. With Hopp and Schnurpfeil leading the way, the Cardinal cross country team placed third in the nation in 1982 and second in '83.

Stanford Stat . . .

In an amazing display of dominance, eight former Stanford tennis players qualified for the round of 32 at the 1982 Wimbledon Championships. John McEnroe earned a spot in the finals, Tim Mayotte played in the semifinals, Gene Mayer in the quarterfinals, Nick Saviano and Roscoe Tanner made it to the round of 16 and Lloyd Bourne, Peter Rennert and Sandy Mayer played in the round of 32. No school has ever had eight former players in the round of 32 at Wimbledon.

STANFORD LIST

WOMEN'S TRACK NCAA CHAMPIONS

1982 Ceci Hopp, 3000 meters (outdoors)

1982 Kim Schnurpfeil, 10,000 meters (outdoors)

1983 Carol Cady, shot put (outdoors)

1983 Alison Wiley, 3000 meters (outdoors)

1984 Carol Cady, discus (outdoors)

1984 PattiSue Plumer, 5000 meters (outdoors)

1992 Jackie Edwards, long jump (indoors)

1992 Chryste Gaines, 55 meters (indoors)

1992 Jackie Edwards, long jump (outdoors)

1992 Chryste Gaines, 100 meters (outdoors)

Stanford LEGEND

Mark Marquess

Mark Marquess has been the school's head baseball coach since 1977. (Stanford Athletics)

Perhaps no one embodies the characteristics of Stanford University more than Cardinal head baseball coach Mark Marquess. A student-athlete at Stanford from 1966-69, Marquess played football and baseball while earning a bachelor's degree in political science and a reputation as one of the nation's best first basemen. After playing minor league baseball, Marquess was hired as Ray Young's assistant coach at Stanford in 1972. Five years later, in 1977, Marquess was named to replace Young as the Cardinal's head coach. And the rest, as they say, is history. In 21 years as the head man at Stanford, Marquess' record of success is unparalleled. He has led his teams to two NCAA championships (1987 and 1988), 15 NCAA Regional appearances, eight trips to the College World Series, seven conference championships and an overall record of 853-453-4—making him the winningest coach in Stanford baseball history. Marquess, who has been named the Pac-10 Coach of the Year six times and the national Coach of the Year on three occasions, was also the head coach of the gold medal-winning 1988 United States Olympic Baseball Team. As a baseball player, he was a First-Team All-American in 1967 and a two-time All-Pac-8 selection. His .404 batting average in 1967 still stands today as the fifth best single-season average in school history. A member of the USA Baseball Hall of Fame, Marquess continues to be one of the most respected college baseball coaches in the country.

STANFORD LORE

An interdisciplinary major in feminist studies was available to students beginning in the fall of 1981. One of the key organizers of the new major was Estelle Freedman, who won a highly publicized fight for tenure in 1983. In May of 1982, 20 years of treatment trials for Hodgkin's disease was celebrated on campus by more than 500 former patients of Dr. Henry Kaplan. Kaplan changed Hodgkin's disease from a hopeless illness to one that is more than 90 percent curable when treated early. In no other malignancy have gains been more dramatic. Kaplan died in February, 1984.

1981-82

- The Cardinal won the Big Game 42-21 in the largest margin of victory by Stanford since 1930.
- Stanford's women's cross country team placed third in the nation in the fall of '81 while the women's track team took fifth nationally in the spring of '82.
- Third-year head coach Frank Brennan led his team to a perfect 20-0 record and the first-ever NCAA championship in women's tennis in 1982. Five Stanford athletes earned All-America honors.
- The Stanford women's basketball team finished with a 19-8 record and advanced to the NCAA Tournament.
- Sophomore Marybeth Linzmeier won three NCAA swimming titles in leading the Cardinal to a second place finish at the 1982 NCAA championships.

Jody Campbell and his Cardinal teammates won the 1981 NCAA water polo championship with a 31-0 record. (Stanford Athletics)

STANFORD MOMENT

The Best Water Polo Team of All-Time

It was called the best collegiate water polo team of all-time—and for good reason. Not only did the Cardinal win its fourth NCAA championship in six years, and second in a row, but Stanford compiled a perfect 31-0 record, placed five players on the First-Team All-America squad and won each match by an average score of 13-5. When the Cardinal pounded Long Beach State 17-6 on November 29, 1981 to win the national championship, it put a fitting end to an incredible season. The 1981 Cardinal set NCAA records for most wins in a season (31), most goals in the championship match (17) and largest championship match scoring margin (11). Only three times in 31 matches in 1981 did a team come within three goals of the Cardinal while Stanford outscored its opponents 411-165. First-team All-America honors went to James Bergeson, who led the team with 82 goals, Jody Campbell (71 goals), Chris Kelsey, Alan Mouchawar and Vince Vanelli.

STANFORD UNIVERSITY has had a great tradition of student-athletes who have excelled in both baseball and football, but only one earned four varsity letters in each sport—Mike Dotterer. From the fall of 1979 to the spring of 1983, Dotterer moved from Stanford Stadium to Sunken Diamond with great ease. A running back in football and an outfielder in baseball, Dotterer finished his Cardinal career with more accolades in baseball, but turned to the NFL for his pro career. He hit .340 for baseball coach Mark Marquess, including .386 in 1981, and led the Cardinal to three straight appearances in the NCAA Regionals (1981-83) and back-to-back trips to the College World Series (1982-83) for the first time in school history. He was twice named All-American in baseball. He was drafted by the New York Yankees in baseball and the Oakland Raiders in football in 1983. His choice was the Raiders, where he played in '83 and '84 and was a part of the Raider's Super Bowl championship team in 1984.

Stanford Stat . . .

The first All-American in women's gymnastics history, Merilyn Chapman came to Stanford after having success on the international level as well as being a member of the United States National Team for two years (1977-78). As a freshman in 1982, she placed eighth in the all-around competition at the AIAW Championships, earning her All-America honors. Before competing for Stanford, Merilyn had won two national all-around titles, five regional crowns and two state championships. She was also the first American gymnast to place ahead of a Russian on Soviet soil.

STANFORD LIST

FOOTBALL FIRST-TEAM ACADEMIC ALL-AMERICANS

1970	John Sande, center
1975	Don Steverson, fullback
1976	Don Steverson, fullback
1977	Guy Benjamin, quarterback
1978	Vince Mulroy, wide receiver
1978	Jim Stephens, offensive guard
1979	Pat Bowe, tight end
1979	Milt McColl, linebacker
1979	Joe St. Geme, safety
1981	John Bergren, defensive tackle
1981	Darrin Nelson, running back
1982	John Bergren, defensive tackle
1983	John Bergren, defensive tackle
1985	Matt Soderlund, linebacker
1987	Brad Muster, running back
1990	Ed McCaffrey, wide receiver
1991	Tommy Vardell, fullback
1994	Justin Armour, wide receiver

Stanford LEGEND

Darrin Nelson

Darrin Nelson was the first player in NCAA history to rush for over 1,000 yards and catch 50 passes in a season. (Stanford Athletics)

The legend that was Darrin Nelson grew well beyond his 5-9, 185-pound frame. He was the most exciting and prolific all-purpose running back in college football during his Cardinal career and by the time he was selected in 1982 in the first round of the NFL Draft by the Minnesota Vikings, he had rewritten the Stanford record book and placed his name among the all-time greats in NCAA history. Nelson's prowess was not limited to the football field, however. While being named First-Team All-Pac-10 for four years and First-Team All-American in 1981 in football, Nelson was also an Academic All-American and a record-breaking track star for the Cardinal. In his freshman season in 1977, all Nelson did was rush for a school-record 1,069 yards, catch 50 passes and account for a school-record 1,672 yards in all-purpose running. He became the first player in NCAA history to rush for over 1,000 yards and catch 50 passes in a season —a feat he accomplished three times in his four years at Stanford. When all the numbers were in, Nelson had set Stanford records for career rushing (4,033 yards), all-purpose running (6,885), receptions (214), scoring (242 points) and touchdowns (40). He became the all-time NCAA leader in all-purpose running and earned the reputation as the "most exciting player in college football in 1981." Nelson, who finished sixth in the Heisman Trophy balloting in 1981, went on to a very successful 11-year career in the National Football League.

STANFORD NOTABLE

Sandra Day O'Connor became the first woman to sit on the United States Supreme Court when she was confirmed by the U.S. Senate on September 22, 1981. O'Connor, who earned her bachelor's degree from Stanford in 1950 and her law degree from Stanford in 1952, was nominated by President Ronald Reagan as Associate Justice of the United States Supreme Court on July 7, 1981. After her confirmation on September 22, she took the oath of office on September 25, 1981. O'Connor was a member of the Stanford University Board of Trustees from 1976-81.

1982-83

·· AMERICA'S TIME CAPSULE ··

- **December 2, 1982:** Barney Clark was the first successful recipient of an artificial heart transplant. He died on March 23, 1983.
- **March 2, 1983:** More than 125 million viewers watched the final television episode of M*A*S*H.
- **April 18, 1983:** The U.S. Embassy in Beirut, Lebanon, was almost totally destroyed by a car-bomb explosion that killed 63 people.
- **June 8, 1983:** Magic Johnson led the Los Angeles Lakers over the Philadelphia 76ers four games to two to capture the NBA Championship.
- **June 24, 1983:** Stanford graduate Sally K. Ride became the first U.S. woman astronaut in space as a member of the crew of the space shuttle Challenger in its second flight.

STANFORD MOMENT

Head Coach George Haines (left) and 1980 Olympian Marybeth Linzmeier led Stanford to the first NCAA championship in womens' swimming in 1983. (Stanford Athletics)

Cardinal Women Win First NCAA Swimming Title

Led by 1980 Olympian Marybeth Linzmeier, the Cardinal women's swimming and diving team won its first NCAA championship on March 19, 1983. After surging to a 65-point lead over defending champion Florida after the first two days of the meet, Stanford withstood a final-day charge by the Tracy Caulkins-led Gators to outscore Florida 418.5-389.5 at the University of Nebraska. Linzmeier, a member of the U.S. Olympic Team that boycotted the 1980 Games, won two individual events (500 free, 1650 free) and placed second in her other event (200 free) to lead Stanford. While Linzmeier was the only Cardinal to win an individual event, it was Stanford's depth that eventually proved too much for Florida. Other Cardinal swimmers who helped bring the championship trophy back to Stanford included Kelly Asplund, Kim Carlisle, Patty Gavin, Sherri Hanna, Libby Kinkead, Barb Major and Kathy Smith. For Cardinal head coach George Haines, who was the head coach of the 1980 U.S. Olympic Team, it was his finest moment as Stanford's head coach and one of the greatest moments in school history.

DURING ERIC HARDGRAVE'S SENIOR SEASON in 1983, he was one of the most feared hitters in college baseball. His numbers (24 home runs, 81 RBI, .360 batting average) earned him Pac-10 Player of the Year honors as well as First-Team All-American recognition. He helped the Cardinal win its first Pac-10 title since 1967 and advance to the College World Series for the second consecutive season for the first time in school history. Hardgrave, who graduated from Stanford with a degree in economics, finished his career tied for the number-one spot in career home runs with 37 and third in RBI with 150. During his four-year career (1980-83) on The Farm, he helped Stanford post a 162-81-2 overall record (.667), earn two trips to the College World Series, three straight appearances in the NCAA Regionals and one conference championship.

Stanford Stat . . .

Vincent White, named First-Team All-Pac-10 in 1982, finished his Cardinal career second to Darrin Nelson in the Stanford record book in rushing (1,689), receptions (162), touchdowns (31) and all-purpose running (4,665). His 68 receptions in '82 was the second best single-season in school history. He began the year by rushing for 97 yards and catching 11 passes for 124 yards and one TD vs. Purdue. White followed that game with a nine-reception, 152-yards and two-TD game against San Jose State, then had 11 receptions for 107 yards against Ohio State. After three games, he was the nation's leading receiver with 31 catches for 383 yards and three touchdowns.

STANFORD LIST

WOMEN'S BASKETBALL ALL-TIME TOP SCORERS

1. Kate Starbird, 1994-97	2,215	(16.9 ppg)
2. Val Whiting, 1989-93	2,077	(16.1 ppg)
3. Jeanne Ruark-Hoff, 1978-83	2,038	(17.6 ppg)
4. Trisha Stevens, 1987-91	1,649	(13.5 ppg)
5. Jennifer Azzi, 1986-90	1,634	(13.4 ppg)
6. Katy Steding, 1986-90	1,586	(12.8 ppg)
7. Anita Kaplan, 1991-95	1,509	(11.7 ppg)
8. Virginia Sourlis, 1982-86	1,449	(12.4 ppg)
9. Sonja Henning, 1987-91	1,445	(11.4 ppg)
10. Louise Smith, 1978-82	1,414	(13.1 ppg)

Stanford LEGEND

Jeanne Ruark-Hoff

Jeanne Ruark-Hoff was Stanford's all-time leading scorer and rebounder after her career concluded in 1983. (Stanford Athletics)

Before Azzi and Steding, Whiting, Henning, Starbird, VanDerveer and all the post-season accolades and team championships, there was Jeanne Ruark-Hoff, perhaps the finest Cardinal women's basketball player of her time and still among the greatest players in Stanford history. She played at a time (1979-83) when women's basketball simply did not have the visibility it has today. But the accomplishments of Ruark-Hoff, who helped the Cardinal to three postseason appearances, including the school's first NCAA Tournament berth in 1982, puts her in the elite group of Stanford women's basketball players. As a freshman in 1978-79, she averaged 21.3 points and 8.4 rebounds per game and was named First-Team All-NorCal. Her 21.3 ppg remains today as the school's single-season record for scoring average. She came back her sophomore season to post equally impressive numbers: 20.1 ppg, 10.0 rpg and a school-record 42 points in a game at North Carolina. She was again named First-Team All-NorCal. Ruark-Hoff took the 1980-81 season off after she married fellow Stanford student John Hoff in the summer of 1980. She concluded her career in 1981-82 and '82-83 as the school's all-time leader in points scored (2,038) and rebounds (908), marks that stand today among the top three in the Cardinal record book.

STANFORD LORE

The anthropology faculty voted to terminate Steve Mosher as a Ph.D. candidate on February 24, 1983, after an investigation of charges related to Mosher's field research on a Chinese commune in 1979-80. Mosher claimed his dismissal was in response to pressure from Chinese officials upset over his writing about forced abortions. After two years of publicity and formal appeals, the decision was upheld by President Donald Kennedy on September 30, 1985. Results of a February, 1982 survey, Assessment of Research-Doctorate Programs in the U.S., ranked Stanford among the top-10 in 25 different fields.

1982-83

·· SEASON HIGHLIGHTS ··

- Freshman Kim Oden led the Cardinal women's volleyball team to its first-ever Final Four appearance in 1982.
- In his first season at Stanford, Dr. Tom Davis led the men's basketball team to a 14-14 record. Guard Keith Jones was named All-Pac-10.
- Stanford compiled a 14-0 dual meet record—most ever on The Farm— won the Pac-10 championship and placed fourth in the nation in men's swimming.
- The Cardinal men's tennis team reclaimed the national championship in '83 by defeating SMU.
- After hosting the NCAA West Regional at Sunken Diamond, Stanford returned to the College World Series in 1983 for a second consecutive season.

"The Play" is one of the greatest plays in college football history. *(California Athletics)*

STANFORD MOMENT

The Greatest Play in College Football History

It is known simply as *The Play*. Home videos and highlight reels will forever include it in anthologies of the greatest plays in college football history. November 20, 1982 at California's Memorial Stadium was the site of this truly bizarre occurrence. John Elway had just led the Cardinal downfield to the Cal 18-yard line with eight seconds remaining to play. There, Stanford's Mark Harmon booted a 35-yard field goal to put the Cardinal on top, 20-19. Stanford had to kick off from their 25 after being flagged for delay of game after their sideline celebration. With four seconds left, Harmon squib-kicked the ball to the Cal 48.

The Bear's five-lateral folly began with Kevin Moen, who picked up the ball and quickly lateralled it to Richard Rodgers, who then lateralled it to Dwight Garner. Garner then shoveled the ball back to Rodgers, who then pitched it to Mariet Ford. With members of both teams now on the field, Ford was able to run down the field to the 28-yard line. Before being swallowed up by several would-be tacklers, he released the ball over his right shoulder to Kevin Moen. Moen then raced through a red sea of parting Stanford band members into the end zone, where he smashed into trombonist Gary Tyrell. After much discussion and confusion, the officials saw nothing wrong with The Play and awarded Cal the touchdown, giving the Bears a 25-20 victory. Three days later, the Pac-10 office issued a statement indicating the officials were "in error" for not throwing flags as The Play began due to the fact that Cal had only four men lined up between 10 and 15 yards away from the point of the kickoff. It was also noted that the Bears had just 10 men on the field at the start of The Play. It was the wildest, most bizarre ending to a football game, college or pro, anyone had ever seen.

ALISON WILEY was named All-American on seven occasions in track and cross country during her Cardinal career (1982-86), placing her name firmly at the top of Stanford's all-time great distance runners' list. As a freshman in 1982-83, Wiley earned All-America honors in both cross country and track, finishing ninth in the NCAA Cross Country meet and winning the NCAA 3,000 meter race at the NCAA Track championships. She was a three-time All-American in cross country while leading her team to a second-place finish for three straight seasons (1982-84). In track, Wiley not only won the 3,000 meters in 1983, but she placed second in the 5,000 and eighth in the 3,000 in 1984 and finished fifth in the 5,000 in 1986, capturing All-America honors each time.

Stanford Stat . . .

After having eight of the final 32 men's players at the '82 Wimbledon Tennis Championship, Stanford again made headlines by having four reach the quarterfinals in 1983. John McEnroe, who played at Stanford as a freshman in 1978, won the '83 Wimbledon singles title while fellow Cardinal's Tim Mayotte, Roscoe Tanner and Sandy Mayer reached the quarterfinals. Mayer (1973), McEnroe (1978) and Mayotte (1981) were all NCAA singles champions for Stanford while Tanner was an NCAA doubles champion (1972) while playing for the Cardinal.

STANFORD LIST

STANFORD PLAYERS IN THE SUPER BOWL

Name, Position	Team, Super Bowl
Barnes, Benny, CB	Dallas Cowboys, Super Bowl X, XII, XIII
Benjamin, Guy, QB	San Francisco 49ers, Super Bowl XVI
Buehler, George, G	Oakland Raiders, Super Bowl XI
Burford, Chris, TE	Kansas City Chiefs, Super Bowl I
Cook, Toi, CB	San Francisco 49ers, Super Bowl XXIX
Dalman, Chris, C/G	San Francisco 49ers, Super Bowl XXIX
Donovan, Pat, DT	Dallas Cowboys, Super Bowl X, XII, XIII
Elway, John, QB	Denver Broncos, Super Bowl XXI, XXII, XXIV
Gordon, Darrien, CB	San Diego Chargers, Super Bowl XXIX
Hill, Tony, WR	Dallas Cowboys, Super Bowl XII, XIII
Holloway, Brian, OT	New England Patriots, Super Bowl XX
Laidlaw, Scott, RB	Dallas Cowboys, Super Bowl XII, XIII
Lofton, James, WR	Buffalo Bills, Super Bowl XXV, XXVI, XXVII
Margerum, Ken, WR	Chicago Bears, Super Bowl XX
McCaffrey, Ed, WR	San Francisco 49ers, Super Bowl XXIX
McColl, Milt, LB	San Francisco 49ers, Super Bowl XVI, XIX
Nye, Blaine, OG	Dallas Cowboys, Super Bowl V, VI, X
Plunkett, Jim, QB	Oakland Raiders, Super Bowl XV
	Los Angeles Raiders, Super Bowl XVIII
Poltl, Randy, S	Minnesota Vikings, Super Bowl IX
	Denver Broncos, Super Bowl XII
Schonert, Turk, QB	Cincinnati Bengals, Super Bowl XVI, XXIII
Siemon, Jeff, LB	Minnesota Vikings, Super Bowl VIII, IX, XI
Veris, Garin, DE	New England Patriots, Super Bowl XX
Walsh, Chris, WR	Buffalo Bills, Super Bowl XXVIII
Wilbur, John, OG	Washington Redskins, Super Bowl VII

Stanford LEGEND

John Elway

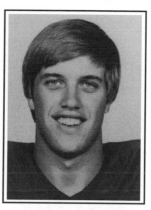

One of the greatest college quarterbacks of all time was Stanford's John Elway.
(Stanford Athletics)

If there was a top-ten list of Stanford's all-time great athletes, John Elway's name would certainly be at the top. He was, in a word, a spectacular college football player. The Elway years on The Farm (1979-82) were filled with great passes, lots of touchdowns and exciting offensive football. By the time he was a number-one selection in the NFL Draft in 1983, Elway had rewritten the Stanford and Pacific-10 Conference record books. Among many others, Elway became the school and conference leader in career passing yards (9,349), career touchdown passes (77) and career total offense (9,070). He was named First-Team All-American and First-Team All-Pac-10 in both 1980 and '82 and, in a close vote for the Heisman Trophy, Elway finished second to Herschel Walker of Georgia in 1982. One of the great two-sport athletes in school history, Elway played two years on the Cardinal baseball team and, in the summer of 1982, he signed a professional baseball contract with the New York Yankees and played with their Class A team. But his career was clearly as a football player. Elway went on to a professional football career with the Denver Broncos where he led the Broncos to three Super Bowl appearances during his career, which will undoubtedly land him in the NFL Hall of Fame.

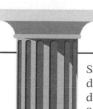

STANFORD NOTABLE

Sally Ride, the first U.S. astronaut and the first American woman in space, received her first Stanford degrees—a B.S. in Physics and a B.A. in English—in 1973. She later earned a master of science and doctorate degrees in Physics from Stanford in 1975 and '78, respectively. She flew on the 7th and 13th Space Shuttle missions in 1983 and '84, becoming the first U.S. woman in space. Ride left NASA in 1987 to join the Stanford University Center for International Security and Arms Control. In 1989, Ride became the head of the Space Institute of the University of California, San Diego.

1983-84

- **September 1, 1983:** A Soviet fighter plane was shot down by a South Korean airliner, killing all 269 people aboard.
- **October 23, 1983:** An explosive-laden truck blew up outside the U.S. Marine headquarters in Beirut, Lebanon, taking the lives of 241 Marine and Navy personnel.
- **April 2, 1984:** Federal researchers announced the identification of a virus thought to cause acquired immune deficiency syndrome (AIDS).
- **May 8, 1984:** The U.S.S.R. Olympic Committee withdrew from the 1984 Olympics, to be held at the Los Angeles Coliseum.
- **July 28, 1984:** The Summer Olympic Games began in Los Angeles, highlighted by the performances of Carl Lewis and Mary Lou Retton.

Stanford's 1984 women's tennis team is arguably the best in the history of NCAA women's tennis. [Stanford Athletics]

STANFORD MOMENT

Women's Tennis Dominates NCAA's

In the annals of NCAA collegiate women's tennis, Frank Brennan's 1984 Stanford team can be compared to the 1927 Yankees, John Wooden's UCLA basketball teams or the 1960's Bill Russell-led Boston Celtics. It was that dominant. Consider the facts: Stanford finished the season with a perfect 26-0 record, its second undefeated season in three years, won its second NCAA championship in three years, and shut out USC 6-0 in the championship match on May 23. In the first three matches prior to the championship, the Cardinal disposed of Clemson, 8-1, UCLA, 8-1 and San Diego State, 7-2. In its 26 matches, the Cardinal had 17 matches in which the opponent won one game or less and only twice in the entire season did an opponent win four games in a match. More impressively, Stanford won its 22 regular-season matches without the services of its #1 player, Elise Burgin, who was unable to play due to a back injury. Burgin was the nation's #1-ranked player in the pre-season and was among the top 50 players in the world. She returned for the NCAA's and played #5 singles for the Cardinal and won the NCAA doubles title. In the end, six Stanford players earned All-America honors, including doubles champs Burgin and Linda Gates, Leigh Anne Eldridge, Patty Fendick, Kate Gompert and Michelle Weiss.

FROM 1981-84, JOHN REVELLI, a 6-8 forward from Scarsdale, New York, and Keith Jones, a 6-1 guard from Phoenix, Arizona, gave the Cardinal an inside-outside game that opponents found difficult to match up against. Revelli was the picture of consistency. For four years, he averaged 15.9 points per game and 8.0 rebounds per game, including a 19.1 ppg average in 1982-83. He was named the Pac-10 Rookie of the Year in 1980-81 and was twice named First-Team All-Pac-10 (1981-82, 1983-84). When his Cardinal career had concluded, he was the school's number-two all-time scorer, number-three rebounder and the school record holder in field goal percentage (.591), free throws made (542) and free throws attempted (726). Revelli was drafted in the fourth round by the Los Angeles Lakers in 1984.

Stanford Stat . . .

Two of the greatest track and field athletes in school history concluded their careers in 1984: Carol Cady and PattiSue Plumer. Cady, who competed in the 1984 and '88 Olympic Games, won two NCAA events in her career (shot put in 1983, discus in '84), was named All-American five times and set a new NCAA record in the shot put. Plumer was a member of the 1988 and '92 U.S. Olympic Teams. She won one NCAA title (5,000m in 1984) and earned All-America recognition nine times, including two in cross country.

STANFORD LIST

MOST NCAA WOMEN'S SWIMMING INDIVIDUAL CHAMPIONSHIPS
(number of championships won)

9 - Jenny Thompson (1992-95)

8 - Marybeth Linzmeier (1982-85)

6 - Summer Sanders (1990-92)

6 - Jenna Johnson (1986-89)

5 - Janel Jorgensen (1990-93)

5 - Janet Evans (1990-91)

5 - Eileen Richetelli, diver (1992-95)

4 - Lea Loveless (1992-94)

3 - Susan Rapp (1984-87)

2 - Catherine Fox (1997)

Stanford LEGEND

Marybeth Linzmeier

Marybeth Linzmeier won eight individual NCAA titles and led Stanford to its first NCAA championship.
(Stanford Athletics)

By the time Marybeth Linzmeier graduated from Stanford University, she had established herself as perhaps the school's greatest female swimmer. During her Cardinal career (1982-85), Linzmeier did it all: she won eight NCAA individual events, led her team to an NCAA championship, four conference titles, a 36-3 dual meet record and earned a spot on the United States Olympic Team. Linzmeier, a middle-distance freestyler, dominated her events during her Stanford tenure. She won the 500 and 1650-yard freestyle events three straight seasons while posting NCAA titles in the 200 free twice. As a 17-year old high school senior-to-be, Linzmeier earned a spot on the 1980 U.S. Olympic Team, although she never got to compete in the Moscow Games due to the Olympic boycott. She was elected to the Stanford Hall of Fame in 1993. "You know what's so special about Marybeth?," asked George Haines, her Stanford coach. "None of the success she's ever had has affected her personality. I coached for over 30 years before I came to Stanford," Haines said. "and, like they say, you can always learn from the great athletes. I learned from Marybeth."

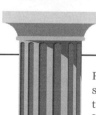

STANFORD LORE

Renovation was completed on the Red Barn on May 2, 1984, the century-old stable that is the last significant building remaining from Leland Stanford's Palo Alto Stock Farm. The Red Barn was the trotting department's training stable. In December, 1985, the barn was added to the National Register of Historic Places. On March 26, 1984, French President Francois Mitterrand visited Stanford to see the Center for Integrated Systems and attend a reception hosted by President Kennedy.

·· SEASON HIGHLIGHTS ··

- Stanford's lone football win came in game seven when the Cardinal beat Arizona 31-22 at Stanford Stadium. Stanford finished the season 1-10 and head coach Paul Wiggin was fired.
- A trio of freshmen swimmers arrived on The Farm in 1983-84 and led the Cardinal to a fourth-place finish at the NCAA's. The threesome of Pablo Morales, Jeff Kostoff and John Moffet won 21 individual NCAA titles and three team championships before they departed.
- The women's swim team placed second in the '84 NCAA championships after recording a 10-0 dual meet season and winning the conference title.
- Guard Keith Jones and center John Revelli were both All-Pac-10 selections as the men's basketball team posted a 19-12 record—the most wins on The Farm since 1951-52.
- UCLA beat Stanford 5-4 in the 1984 NCAA men's tennis championship match.

All-American Kim Oden helped Stanford finish third in the nation, the best in Stanford women's volleyball history. (Stanford Athletics)

STANFORD MOMENT

Women's Volleyball Caps Finest Season

Although the Cardinal women's volleyball team fell short in its attempt to win its first ever national championship, there was all-everything outside hitter Kim Oden congratulating her teammates for beating UOP on December 17, 1983 to give Stanford a third-place finish—the highest in school history. For head coach Fred Sturm, it was the continuation of the process of making his Cardinal squad an annual visitor to the NCAA Final Four. After Stanford beat BYU and San Diego State to reach the Final Four, the Cardinal ran into a very talented Hawaii team. The Rainbows disposed of Stanford in three games and sent the Cardinal into the consolation match with UOP. Oden, a First-Team All-American, led the charge as Stanford beat the Tigers, 7-15, 15-8, 15-11, 15-2 to take third place. Stanford finished the season with a 22-9 overall record and an 11-3 conference mark. Oden was named the Western Collegiate Athletic Association MVP while teammates Kari Rush and Diedra Dvorak were first-team selections.

WITH JOHN REVELLI patrolling the inside, Keith Jones made his living from the outside. After joining Revelli on the 1980-81 Pac-10 All-Rookie Team, Jones went on to earn First-Team All-Pac 10 honors his junior and senior seasons (1982-83, 1983-84). As a junior, he set a Stanford single-season record by scoring 553 points, a mark he broke the following year by scoring 619 points. In his last two seasons on The Farm, Jones scored in double figures 57 times in 59 games, including 27 games of scoring over 20 points. In 1983-84, Jones and Revelli became the first Stanford duo to score more than 500 points apiece (Jones 619, Revelli 501). Jones was drafted in the sixth round of the 1984 NBA Draft by the Los Angeles Lakers (the Lakers also drafted Revelli in the fourth round).

Stanford Stat . . .

For the first time in school history, Stanford finished among the top three nationally in women's cross country and track and field. The Cardinal finished second in cross country as Regina Jacobs (ninth) and PattiSue Plumer (10th) led the way. In track, Stanford placed third in the nation as Plumer (NCAA champ in 5,000m) and Carol Cady (NCAA champ in discus) spearheaded the way.

STANFORD LIST

MULTIPLE ALL-CONFERENCE MEN'S BASKETBALL SELECTIONS

C.E. Righter, 1920-21

Dinty Moore, 1935, 1937

Hank Luisetti, 1936, '37, '38

John Higgins, 1947, '48

Ron Tomsic, 1952, '53, 1955

Tom Dose, 1963, '64

Rich Kelley, 1973, '74, '75

Kimberly Belton, 1978, '79, '80

John Revelli, 1982, 1984

Keith Jones, 1983, '84

Todd Lichti, 1986, '87, '88, '89

Howard Wright, 1988, '89

Adam Keefe, 1990, '91, '92

Dion Cross, 1995, '96

Brevin Knight, 1995, 96, '97

Stanford LEGEND

Dan Goldie

Dan Goldie won one NCAA singles championship and was a member of two NCAA team championships.
(Stanford Athletics)

Well before the University of Michigan's Fab Five in men's basketball, Stanford had the "Four Freshmen" in men's tennis in 1983. Led by Dan Goldie from McLean, Virginia, the Four Freshmen —including Goldie, Jim Grabb, John Letts and Eric Rosenfeld—went 24-1 during the season, beat SMU 5-2 in the NCAA championship match and won an unexpected national championship, the seventh in school history. Goldie played three more seasons on The Farm and etched his name as one of the school's all-time greats. He was named First-Team All-American for three straight seasons. He played No. 1 for the Cardinal for three years and in 1986, he culminated his collegiate career by not only leading Stanford to its eighth NCAA team title, but he won the NCAA singles championship, becoming the ninth Stanford men's tennis player to win the title. In four years at Stanford (1983-86), Goldie led the Cardinal to two national championships, one second-place finish and an overall record of 89-16.

STANFORD NOTABLE

The son of Italian emigrants, Robert Mondavi was born in Minnesota in 1913 and grew up in Lodi, California, where he began his lifelong education in the California wine industry. Mondavi, who graduated from Stanford in 1936, spent his youth learning the wine business from his father, Cesare. Robert convinced his father to purchase the Charles Krug Winery in 1943 and for the next two decades, Robert's expertise in wine making and marketing strategies continued to grow. In 1966, the Robert Mondavi Winery was opened.

1984-85

- **November 6, 1984:** Ronald Reagan was re-elected president over Walter Mondale in the greatest Republican landslide ever.
- **February 17, 1985:** A $120 million libel suit against CBS was dropped by Gen. William C. Westmoreland, former commander of the U.S. forces in Vietnam, after 18 weeks of court testimony.
- **March 4, 1985:** The Environmental Protection Agency ordered a ban on leaded gasoline.
- **April 8, 1985:** The government of India sued the Union Carbide Corporation in connection with a plant disaster that killed 1,700 and injured as many as 200,000 others.
- **July 13, 1985:** President Reagan underwent surgery to remove a cancerous tumor from his colon.

STANFORD MOMENT

Stanford earned its first #1 ranking in baseball in 1985, partly due to All-American pitcher Jeff Ballard's 14 wins. (Stanford Athletics)

Baseball Team Earns First-Ever #1 Ranking

The 1985 season was a landmark for the Stanford baseball program. Not only did head coach Mark Marquess' club win its third-straight Pac-10 championship, earn a fifth-straight appearance in the NCAA Regionals and advance to the College World Series for the third time in four years, but the Cardinal earned its first-ever number- one national ranking. After finishing the regular season with a 43-12 overall record and an amazing 23-7 mark in the Pac-10, Stanford headed into post-season play as the nation's top-ranked team. Led by Pac-10 MVP and triple crown winner Rick Lundblade and All-Americans Jeff Ballard and Pete Stanicek, the Cardinal put together one of the best teams in school history. The Cardinal beat Oregon State, Nebraska and Pepperdine in the NCAA West Regional held at Sunken Diamond to earn another trip to the College World Series. But losses to Miami and Arkansas sandwiched by a win over Arizona eliminated Stanford from the CWS and sent the Cardinal home with a 47-15 final record and memories of a remarkable 1985 campaign.

FOR NINE YEARS, JOHN MOFFET had dreamt of hearing the *Star-Spangled Banner* played in his honor after winning a gold medal at the Olympic Games. At the age of 16, he became the youngest member of the 1980 U.S. Olympic Swimming Team. Because of the U.S. boycott of the Moscow Games, Moffet never got his chance. Four years later, as a Stanford sophomore, Moffet broke the world record in the 100-meter breaststroke at the Olympic Trials and immediately became the favorite to win the gold. In his qualifying heat at the Los Angeles Olympics on July 29, 1984, Moffet broke the Olympic record while swimming the fastest qualifying time. As he raised himself to the pool deck after his heat, he was limping and holding his right thigh. "Between the prelims and the final," remembered Moffet, "I watched all my dreams shatter before my eyes." Moffet did swim in the final that evening—finishing fifth—but his pulled thigh muscle ended his dream of Olympic gold. On the collegiate level, Moffet continued to dominate. In his Cardinal career, he won five NCAA individual titles and two relay titles while helping Stanford win back-to-back NCAA championships in 1985 and '86.

Stanford Stat . . .

Two years after his son completed a storybook career at Stanford, Jack Elway was named the Cardinal's head football coach, replacing former Stanford All-American Paul Wiggin. In his first season on The Farm in 1984, Elway's team finished 5-6, four games better than the 1-10 team of 1983. Elway, who coached Stanford from 1984-88, had his best season in 1986 when the Cardinal went 8-4 while participating in its first bowl game in eight years.

STANFORD LIST

TOP-10 HOME RUN HITTERS IN STANFORD HISTORY

1.	Paul Carey, 1987-90	56
2.	Rick Lundblade, 1982-85	42
3.	Ed Sprague, 1986-88	41
	David McCarty, 1989-91	41
5.	Eric Hardgrave, 1980-83	37
	Tom Guardino, 1975-78	37
7.	Mark Davis, 1983-86	36
8.	John Schaeffer, 1994-97	33
9	A.J. Hinch, 1993-96	31
	Dusty Allen, 1992-95	31

Stanford ❧ LEGEND ❧

Rick Lundblade

Rick Lundblade finished his career as Stanford's all-time home run leader.
(Stanford Athletics)

The list of great baseball players who have played for Stanford is quite an impressive array of talent. But, in the 104-year history of Cardinal baseball, no player has put up the kind of offensive numbers Rick Lundblade did in 1985. A first baseman from Eureka, California, Lundblade, Stanford's only Pac-10 triple crown winner, broke school records by hitting 25 home runs, drove in 92 runs, scored 80 runs and hit .408—the third best single-season batting average in school history. He was named the Pac-10 Player of the Year and All-American as he led the Cardinal to a 47-15 overall record, a Pac-10 championship and a trip to the College World Series. Lundblade was so dominant in conference play that in 30 games he hit .453 with 11 home runs and 43 RBIs. He finished his career as Stanford's all-time home run leader with 42—second best in Pac-10 history—second in RBI (200) and third in batting average (.351).

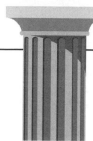

STANFORD LORE

Stanford University made professional football history when, on January 20, 1985, it became the first university to host a Super Bowl. Joe Montana led the San Francisco 49ers over Dan Marino and the Miami Dolphins 38-16 in Super Bowl XIX held at Stanford Stadium. Former Stanford head coach Bill Walsh led his 49ers to their second world championship in four years. On May 16,1984, history Prof. Clayborne Carson was selected by Coretta Scott King to edit the papers of her late husband, Martin Luther King Jr.

1984-85

- The Cardinal snapped a two-game losing skid to Cal and brought the Axe back to The Farm after a 27-10 Big Game win.
- Stanford finished second in the nation in women's volleyball after losing to UCLA in the championship match. Junior Kim Oden was named the national Player of the Year.
- For the third straight season, the Cardinal women's cross country team placed second in the nation.
- Both the men's and women's tennis teams were upset at the NCAA Championships and both had to settle for a fifth-place finish. The women entered the NCAA's with a 25-1 record.
- After a 9-19 season in '84-85, women's basketball coach Dotty McCrea was replaced by Ohio State head coach Tara VanDerveer.

The Cardinal won its first NCAA men's swimming title since 1967 and only the second in school history in 1985. (Stanford Athletics)

STANFORD MOMENT

Morales Leads Cardinal to NCAA Swimming Championship

Led by Olympians Pablo Morales, John Moffet and Jeff Kostoff, Stanford erased three straight seasons of knocking on the door by finally winning the NCAA Men's Swimming and Diving championship, the second in school history and first since 1967. Morales, who would later become the most prolific male swimmer in NCAA history, was the catalyst for a Cardinal team that beat two-time defending champion Florida, 403.5-329. Morales won three individual titles (100 fly, 200 fly, 200 IM) and was a member of Stanford's first-place 400 medley relay team. He set American records in the 100 and 200 fly, and his medley relay team, with Moffet, Dave Bottom and David Lundberg, also set an American record. Moffet came back after a serious injury he suffered at the '84 Olympics to win both the 100 and 200 breast while Kostoff set a new American record after winning the 400 IM. Two freshmen who turned in outstanding performances included Sean Murphy, who won the NCAA title in the 200 back, and Anthony Mosse, who was a finalist in two events.

IF FEW PEOPLE outside Billings, Montana heard of Jeff Ballard in 1982, they certainly knew of him by 1985, when he tied the Stanford record for most wins in a season with 14 and broke the school record for career wins with 37. During his four years on The Farm, Ballard proved to be a consistent, reliable pitcher, both as a starter and reliever, and one of the main reasons for Stanford's entrance into national prominence. He went 37-13 in his career with 12 saves (number-two all-time at Stanford), a 3.91 ERA, 315 strikeouts (Stanford record) and 428 innings pitched, a school and Pac-10 record. His Cardinal teams won or shared three Pac-10 titles, advanced to the NCAA Regionals four straight seasons and went to the College World Series three times. In 1985, when Stanford was ranked #1 in the nation in the final regular-season polls, Ballard went 14-4 with a 3.78 ERA as the team's ace. He was twice named First-Team All-Pac-10 and in '85 he was selected Second-Team All-American. Ballard went on to a career in professional baseball, which was highlighted by his 18-8 record with the Baltimore Orioles in 1989.

Stanford Stat . . .

Regina Jacobs capped her storied career at Stanford by placing fourth at the NCAA Cross Country Championships in the fall of 1984 and earning All-America honors in the spring of '85 in the 1500 meter run at the NCAA Track and Field Championships. Jacobs, a native of Los Angeles, was a six-time All-American at Stanford in track and cross country. She is also Stanford's only three-time U.S. Olympian in track having competed at the 1988 Games in Seoul, the '92 Games in Barcelona and the '96 Games in Atlanta.

STANFORD LIST

MEN'S SWIMMING TOP POINT SCORERS AT NCAA CHAMPIONSHIP MEETS

1. Pablo Morales, 1984-87	235
2. Jeff Kostoff, 1984-87	193
3. Derek Weatherford, 1991-94	184
4. Brian Retterer, 1992-95	178
5. Jeff Rouse, 1989-92	173
6. John Witchel, 1987-90	162
7. John Moffet, 1983-86	152
8. Tyler Mayfield, 1991-94	134
9. Dave Bottom, 1982-85	132
10. Kurt Grote, 1992-95	130

Stanford LEGEND

Linda Gates

Linda Gates was a four-time All-American and 1985 NCAA singles champion. (Stanford Athletics)

In four years on the Stanford women's tennis team, Linda Gates did not win all her matches and her team did not win every championship—but it was close. Her storied career has a list of achievements reserved only for those in the *legend* category. Consider this: Gates was a member of two undefeated NCAA championship teams (20-0 in 1982, 26-0 in '84), she was a four-time All-America selection, the 1985 NCAA singles champion, a two-time NCAA doubles champion (1984, 1985) and the 1985 winner of the prestigious Broderick Award as the nation's top female tennis player. Add to that her Cardinal team's record of 92-8 in dual meets during Gates' four-year tenure and what you have is perhaps the most dominate collegiate female tennis player of her time. Her world ranking rose from No. 316 to No. 66 in a seven-month period from July-December, 1986 and Gates' professional career was off and running. "Things I hoped for when I was younger are now happening," Gates said following her graduation from Stanford. "It is almost like a dream."

STANFORD NOTABLE

As a child sensation in movies of the 1930s, Shirley Temple captivated Americans with her curls, dimples and films. She starred in such movies as Little Miss Marker (1934), The Little Colonel (1935), Captain January (1936), Wee Willie Winkie (1937), Heidi (1937), Rebecca of Sunnybrook Farm (1938) and The Little Princess (1939). She retired from films in 1949 and later became active in politics. In 1969, she was a delegate to the United Nations, was the U.S. Ambassador to Ghana in 1974 and U.S. Chief of Protocol in 1976. President George Bush appointed her the U.S. Ambassador to Czechoslovakia in 1989.

1985-86

- September 9, 1985: President Reagan announced trade sanctions against South Africa to protest that country's policy of apartheid.
- September 18, 1985: A U.S. hostage in Lebanon, the Rev. Benjamin Weir, was back in the United States after 16 months in captivity.
- July 11, 1985: Nolan Ryan of the Houston Astros became the first pitcher in major league history to strike out 4,000 batters when he fanned Danny Heep of the New York Mets.
- September 11, 1985: Cincinnati's Pete Rose broke Ty Cobb's major league baseball record for hits when he collected his 4,192nd hit against San Diego.
- January 28, 1986: Seven astronauts were killed when the space shuttle Challenger exploded just 74 seconds after liftoff at Cape Canaveral, Florida.

STANFORD MOMENT

During the 1985-86 season, Stanford won four NCAA team championships, including another one by the men's tennis team.
(Stanford Athletics)

Stanford Brings Home Four NCAA Championships

The 1985-86 season was a breakthrough year in Stanford Athletics. While Cardinal teams had won at least one NCAA championship for nine straight years, the '85-'86 season proved to be a watershed year for national titles. Stanford won four NCAA championships in 1985-86—the most in the nation—and earned itself the title "Champion of Champions" for the first, but certainly not the last, time. Stanford won championships in water polo, men's swimming, women's tennis and men's tennis. It was the fifth national championship in water polo, the third in men's swimming, the fourth in women's tennis and the eighth in men's tennis. Dante Dettamanti's water polo team went 25-4 in '85, the men's swimming team completed its fourth straight undefeated dual-meet season, Frank Brennan's women's tennis team went 21-1, while Dick Gould's men's tennis team finished the year 19-5. Over the next 10 years (1985-95), Stanford teams would bring home an astonishing 36 NCAA team championships, by far the most in the nation. During this time, the Cardinal won four titles in a single year four times and an NCAA-record five championships on two occasions: 1991-92 and again in 1994-95.

WHEN TARA VANDERVEER came to Stanford in 1985-86 from Ohio State, she saw a program that had won 14 games the past two years, a near-empty Maples Pavilion and an apathetic campus community for women's basketball. But, it didn't take VanDerveer long to change all that. In her third year, VanDerveer's team was 27-5 and in her fifth season (1989-90), VanDerveer hit paydirt as she led her team to a 32-1 overall record, a second straight conference crown and the school's first-ever NCAA championship in women's basketball. More than a decade later, VanDerveer has built Stanford into one of the most respected and admired women's basketball programs in the nation. VanDerveer, who led the Cardinal to a second NCAA title in 1991-92, has guided Stanford to 10 NCAA Tournament appearances, five trips to the Final Four and two national titles. She took a leave of absence from coaching Stanford in 1995-96 to become the head coach of the 1996 United States Olympic women's basketball team where she led Team USA to a gold medal after beating Brazil 111-87.

Stanford Stat . . .

Before beginning her sophomore season at Stanford, Susan Rapp had already qualified for two United States Olympic Swimming Teams, won one silver medal (200 breast-stroke) at the 1984 Games in Los Angeles and had one NCAA individual title under her belt. Her four-year Cardinal career (1984-87) netted her three NCAA individual titles and one NCAA relay championship. She took home NCAA titles in the 200 breast in 1984 and 1987 and in the 200 IM in 1986.

STANFORD LIST

WOMEN'S TENNIS ALL-DECADE TEAM FOR 1980S

The NCAA's All-Decade team for the 1980s celebrated the first 10 years of the NCAA women's tennis competition. It was dominated by Stanford. Below are the nine members and coach of the NCAA Women's Tennis All-Decade Team:

Sandra Birch	Stanford
Patty Fendick	Stanford
Linda Gates	Stanford
Debbie Graham	Stanford
Alycia Moulton	Stanford
Lisa Spain	Georgia
Beth Herr	USC
Shaun Stafford	Florida
Frank Brennan,	Stanford

Stanford LEGEND

Jenna Johnson

Jenna Johnson was an Olympic gold medalist and six-time NCAA champion. (Stanford Athletics)

Jenna Johnson came to Stanford as a freshman in 1985-86 with two Olympic gold medals and one silver medal to her credit. At the Los Angeles Olympics, Johnson, a high school senior-to-be, took home gold medals in the 400 free relay and 400 medley relay while earning a silver in the 100 fly. For the next four years, Johnson proved to be one of the greatest female swimmers in Stanford history. Not only did Johnson help the Cardinal win the 1989 NCAA championship—the second NCAA women's swimming title in school history—but she won six NCAA individual titles and was a member of four NCAA championship relay teams. As a freshman at the 1986 NCAA's, Johnson won three individual titles (50 free, 100 free, 100 fly), placed second in another event (200 free) and was a member of Stanford's NCAA-winning 200 medley relay team which set an American record. Johnson, who also set an American record in winning the 100 fly, was named winner of the '86 Broderick Award for women's swimming, emblematic of the nation's top athlete in her sport for excellence in academics, athletics and leadership. She went on to win three more NCAA titles: 50 free in 1987, 100 free in 1987, and the 100 fly in 1989.

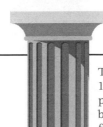

STANFORD LORE

The University celebrated the centennial of its founding on November 11, 1985. The original calligraphed 100-year-old Founding Grant was put on public display. Also, on May 7, 1986, Lucile and David Packard pledged $70 million to finance construction of the New Children's Hospital at Stanford, a facility that will be integrated with the Medical Center, but governed separately. Children's Hospital at Stanford evolved from the Stanford Home for Convalescent Children, opened in 1920.

·· SEASON HIGHLIGHTS ··

- A 22-point outburst by Cal cut Stanford's 24-0 lead to just two points, but the Cardinal hung on to post its second straight Big Game victory, 24-22.
- For the second straight season, Kim Oden, named the nation's Player of the Year, led the women's volleyball team to the championship match, this time losing to Pacific.
- Pablo Morales won three individual events and was a member of one relay winner as Stanford won its second straight men's swimming championship.
- Stanford advanced to the NCAA Regionals in baseball for the sixth straight year, but failed to make it to Omaha after losing the regional final to Oklahoma State, 3-0.
- Junior Patty Fendick and senior Dan Goldie won the NCAA women's and men's singles crowns while leading their teams to the championship.

STANFORD MOMENT

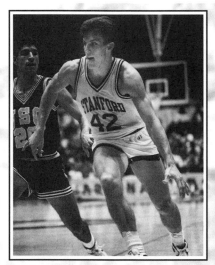

Freshman Todd Lichti helped Stanford score big wins over UCLA and Arizona. (Stanford Athletics)

Men's Hoops Scores Two Big Wins at Maples

Although the Cardinal finished the 1985-86 season with a 14-16 overall record, Stanford, behind freshman guard Todd Lichti, scored two big wins at Maples Pavilion to highlight the season. On January 23, the Cardinal beat UCLA 76-70 despite Reggie Miller's 28-point performance. Guard Novian Whitsitt scored 19 points for Stanford while Lichti added 18, 13 in the second half. "I'm exhausted, and I'm sure the players are too," said Cardinal coach Tom Davis, who resigned following the '86 campaign. Two weeks after the UCLA win, Stanford scored its biggest upset of the year, a 62-56 win over nationally-ranked Arizona on February 8. A balanced scoring attack led by Whitsitt's 13 points and Lichti's 12 and a stubborn Cardinal defense were enough to dethrone the Pac-10 leading Wildcats. Stanford built a 30-20 halftime lead that was cut to 48-46 with 5:28 remaining. But, freshman Howard Wright scored five straight points to give the Cardinal a 53-46 lead with 3:50 left to play. The lead never was reduced to fewer than five points.

Stanford SPOTLIGHT

WHEN JACK MCDOWELL was on the mound, everyone in the Stanford dugout had the same thought: We're glad he's on our side. McDowell was not only a great talent, but he was perhaps the most competitive player of his time. Even when "Black Jack" did not have his best stuff, he found a way—like all the great ones do. Case in point was on June 7, 1987 at Rosenblatt Stadium in Omaha, Nebraska. McDowell got the call to start the College World Series championship game vs. Oklahoma State. Working on two days' rest, McDowell, while giving up 12 hits and four walks in seven-plus innings of work, left the game in the eighth inning with his team ahead, 6-4. It was not vintage McDowell, but it was the McDowell competitiveness that Stanford fans had come to know and expect. He played at Stanford for three seasons (1985-87) before being a number-one selection (fifth pick overall) by the Chicago White Sox in the Major League Draft. His three-year record at Stanford was quite impressive: 35-13, 3.58 ERA, 337 strikeouts in 392.2 innings of work. He left as the school record holder for strikeouts, number-two all-time in wins and innings pitched. McDowell won the 1993 Cy Young Award while playing for the White Sox.

Stanford Stat . . .

In four years at Stanford (1984-87), swimmer Jeff Kostoff's Cardinal teams won three NCAA championships and four Pac-10 championships while compiling a dual-meet record of 39-1. Kostoff, a two-time United States Olympian, won five individual NCAA titles and his 193 points in NCAA meets is number two all-time on The Farm. He won NCAA titles in the 1650 free three times (1984, '86, '87) and the 400 IM twice (1985, '87).

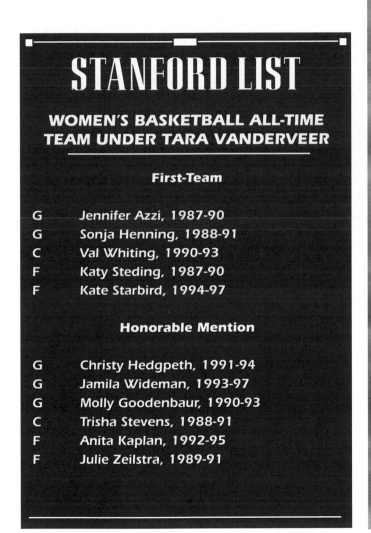

STANFORD LIST

WOMEN'S BASKETBALL ALL-TIME TEAM UNDER TARA VANDERVEER

First-Team

G	Jennifer Azzi, 1987-90	
G	Sonja Henning, 1988-91	
C	Val Whiting, 1990-93	
F	Katy Steding, 1987-90	
F	Kate Starbird, 1994-97	

Honorable Mention

G	Christy Hedgpeth, 1991-94	
G	Jamila Wideman, 1993-97	
G	Molly Goodenbaur, 1990-93	
C	Trisha Stevens, 1988-91	
F	Anita Kaplan, 1992-95	
F	Julie Zeilstra, 1989-91	

Stanford LEGEND

Kim Oden

Kim Oden is considered one of the all-time great players in NCAA women's volleyball history. (Stanford Athletics)

There are times in sports when a team or coach can point to a defining moment in their program. For the Stanford women's volleyball program, that moment was in 1982 when a freshman from Irvine, California named Kim Oden arrived on The Farm. Hailed as the top recruit in the nation, Oden, quite simply, was the catalyst for turning Stanford from a good, up-and-coming program to a national powerhouse. She was the best player of her time, indeed one of the best of all-time. She was named the Collegiate Women's Volleyball Player of the Decade for the 1980's - and for good reason. Oden was a four-time First-Team All-American (1982-85), a two-time National Player of the Year, three-time Conference Player of the Year, an Academic All-American and winner of the 1985 Broderick Award as the nation's best women's volleyball player. She led Stanford to four straight appearances in the Final Four - the first in school history - and a 100-30 overall record. The only hurdle Oden could not overcome was leading the Cardinal to the national championship. In her final two seasons, Oden and her teammates reached the title match, only to lose to UCLA in 1984 and UOP in '85. A two-time U.S. Olympian in 1988 and 1992, Oden helped build Stanford into one of the premier women's volleyball programs in the country.

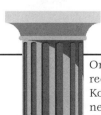

STANFORD NOTABLE

One of the most popular and respected figures in television news today is Ted Koppel, who in 1962 received a master's in mass communications research and political science from Stanford University. Koppel is the anchor and managing editor of ABC's "Nightline," one of the finest innovations in broadcast news. Koppel, who went to work for ABC News as a general correspondent in 1963 following his Stanford days, was named Nightline's anchor when the show was first broadcast in March, 1980. Koppel has won every major broadcasting award, including 25 Emmy Awards and five Peabody Awards, among others.

1986-87

·· AMERICA'S TIME CAPSULE ··

- **November 3, 1986:** The Iran-Contra affair became public when a Lebanese magazine revealed that the United States had been secretly selling arms to Iran in hopes of securing the release of hostages held in Lebanon.
- **November 22, 1986:** Twenty-year-old Mike Tyson became the youngest heavyweight boxing champion in history when he knocked out Trevor Berbick.
- **March. 19, 1987:** TV evangelist Jim Bakker admitted that he had an extramarital affair with his church secretary. He was dismissed as minister of the Assemblies of God on May 6.
- **April 12, 1987:** Larry Mize sank a 50-yard wedge shot on the second hole of a three-way playoff against Greg Norman and Seve Ballesteros to win the Masters golf tournament.
- **August 16, 1987:** A Northwest Airlines jet crashed on takeoff from the Detroit Metropolitan Airport, killing 156 of 157 passengers.

STANFORD MOMENT

Pablo Morales beat teammate Anthony Mosse to win his 11th individual title, the most in NCAA history. (Stanford Athletics)

Morales Breaks NCAA Record With 11th Career Victory

The emotions leading up to the race could be felt throughout the University of Texas Swim Center. Stanford had all but wrapped up its third-straight NCAA championship and its star pupil, Pablo Morales, had won his first two events, tying him with USC's John Naber for the most individual titles in NCAA swimming history with 10. All that was left for Morales was to win No. 11 and become the all-time NCAA leader. In order to do that, however, he would have to win the 200-yard butterfly and beat his friend and teammate Anthony Mosse, who was considered to be the only person who could beat Morales in this event. True to his reputation as a great champion, on April 4, 1987, Morales set a new NCAA and American record of 1:42.60 to beat Mosse and break the all-time record. In four years of NCAA championship competition, Morales scored 235 of a possible 240 points and won 11 of the 12 individual races he entered. He is arguably the greatest male swimmer in NCAA championship history.

FOR THE FIRST TIME IN EIGHT SEASONS—and the 14th time in school history—Stanford earned an invitation to play in a postseason bowl game. After an 8-3 regular season, the Cardinal was selected to face Clemson on December 27, 1986 in the Gator Bowl in Jacksonville, Florida. Led by All-American fullback Brad Muster and All-American linebacker David Wyman, the Cardinal advanced to a bowl game for the first time since 1978. Stanford, however, played perhaps its poorest half of the season in the Gator Bowl as Clemson built a 27-0 halftime lead and appeared on the verge of a blowout. But the Cardinal came back in the second half, and, despite playing without six starters, including starting quarterback John Paye, scored 21 unanswered points to make a game of it. Muster was named the game's Offensive MVP after rushing for 70 yards, catching four passes and scoring all three of Stanford's second-half TDs while sophomore QB Greg Ennis completed 20-of-40 for 168 yards. After yielding 27 points and 291 yards in total offense in the first half, the Cardinal defense allowed the Tigers no points and just 88 yards in the second half.

Stanford Stat . . .

For the second consecutive year, Stanford teams brought home four NCAA team championship trophies, giving it eight in the last two years. Dante Dettamanti's water polo team went 36-0 en route to winning its second straight title, Frank Brennan's women's tennis team also won the title for the second year in a row, Skip Kenney's men's swimming team won the championship for the third consecutive season while Mark Marquess won his first national title in baseball.

STANFORD LIST

BRODERICK AWARD WINNERS

The Broderick Award is presented annually to the NCAA's top female student-athlete in her sport for excellence in athletics, academics and leadership.

1978-79	Kathy Jordan	Tennis
1984-85	Linda Gates	Tennis
1985-86	Kim Oden	Volleyball
1985-86	Jenna Johnson	Swimming
1986-87	Patty Fendick	Tennis
1988-89	Sandra Birch	Tennis
1988-89	Jenna Johnson	Swimming
1989-90	Jennifer Azzi	Basketball
1989-90	Janet Evans	Swimming
1989-90	Debbie Graham	Tennis
1990-91	Bev Oden	Volleyball
1990-91	Sandra Birch	Tennis
1991-92	Summer Sanders	Swimming
1992-93	Janel Jorgensen	Swimming
1994-95	Jenny Thompson	Swimming

Stanford LEGEND

Patty Fendick

Patty Fendick concluded her Cardinal career with 57 straight dual-match wins and two NCAA singles crowns. (Stanford Athletics)

It's pretty simple to describe Patty Fendick's career at Stanford—awesome. She was without parallel during her four years on The Farm (1984-87), which ended with her winning 57 consecutive dual matches and back-to-back NCAA singles titles—the only tennis player, male or female, to accomplish that feat. Fendick, a native of Sacramento, California, became only the second player in school history to play No. 1 singles as a freshman, a role she held for four years. In her collegiate career, Fendick led the Cardinal to three NCAA team championships (1984, 1986, 1987), won back-to-back NCAA singles crowns (1986-87) and recorded a career dual-match record of 140-18, an all-time Stanford best. In her senior season, Fendick went undefeated as she won all 40 of her matches. She was so dominant in 1987 that she lost only four sets all year long. Before she graduated from Stanford, Fendick had already reached the third round at Wimbledon and the U.S. Open in both singles and doubles. A four-time All-American, Fendick rose to a world ranking of No. 19 in 1988.

STANFORD LORE

Trustees officially launched a five-year, $1.1 billion Centennial Campaign on February 10, 1987, the largest to date in higher education. A nucleus fund of $307 million already was raised. On May 14, the University announced plans to celebrate the centennial of the laying of the cornerstone on the anniversary of Leland Jr.'s birth. The Stanford Historical Society placed a bronze plaque near the cornerstone to commemorate the 100th anniversary.

1986-87

·· SEASON HIGHLIGHTS ··

- Brad Muster rushed for 1,053 yards, joining Darrin Nelson as the only running backs in Stanford history to rush for over 1,000 yards in a single season.
- Freshman Jennifer Azzi and Katy Steding, members of Tara VanDerveer's first recruiting class at Stanford, helped the Cardinal to a 14-14 record in 1986-87.
- Mike Montgomery's first Stanford team was 15-13 in '86-87. Sophomore guard Todd Lichti earned All-Pac-10 honors for the second straight season.
- Jenna Johnson won two events and Susan Rapp one as the Cardinal women's swimming team placed second at the NCAA Championships.
- Stanford won its second straight women's tennis championship and third in four years by beating Georgia 6-1 in the finals.
- The Cardinal baseball team set a new school record by posting a 53-17 mark en route to winning its first national championship.

Freshman Paul Carey provided Cardinal baseball fans with the greatest moment in Stanford baseball history. (Stanford Athletics)

STANFORD MOMENT

The Greatest Moment in Stanford Baseball History

In the 104-year history of Stanford baseball, there is one moment that stands frozen in time. The site was the College World Series in Omaha, Nebraska, Game #12 on June 5, 1987—Stanford vs. LSU in an elimination game. The winner moves on in the tournament, the loser goes home. With the game tied at 2-2 after nine innings, the Tigers came up big in the top half of the 10th as they scored three runs to take a commanding 5-2 lead and put the Cardinal on the brink of elimination. With one out in the bottom of the 10th, Ruben Amaro worked the count full then drew a walk. Toi Cook followed with another walk. Ben McDonald replaced Barry Manuel on the mound for LSU and he promptly hit Ed Sprague to load the bases. Then came Paul Carey, the national Freshman of the Year from Weymouth, Massachusetts, who had gone hitless in three at bats. In the greatest moment in school baseball history, Carey deposited a McDonald fastball over the left-field fence for a game-winning grand slam homer. Stanford went on to beat Texas, 9-3 and Oklahoma State, 9-5 the next two days to win their first-ever College World Series championship. "To realize the dream of being national champions is a very special feeling. It's something that stays with you forever," said head coach Mark Marquess.

ONE COULD ARGUE that Craig Klass was the best player on the best team in collegiate water polo history. It would be tough to disagree with that assessment. As a senior in 1986, Klass scored a school-record 87 goals (tied with teammate Erich Fischer) for a team that went 36-0—best record in college water polo history—won the national championship and outscored opponents by an average score of 14-5. Klass was named First-Team All-America three straight seasons (1984-86) and went on to compete in the 1988 and '92 Olympic Games as a member of the United States National Team. As a freshman in 1983, Klass' team finished 11-13-3, the second-worst record ever at Stanford. But in his final three seasons, his teams reached the NCAA title game all three years, winning two championships while recording an overall record of 86-9. In a sport that has produced All-Americans and Olympians at an alarming rate, Klass ranks as one of the best ever on The Farm.

Stanford Stat . . .

The Cardinal water polo team posted a perfect 36-0 record, won the NCAA championship and layed claim to being the best collegiate water polo team in the history of the sport. Stanford set a school record by scoring 487 goals while outscoring opponents by an average score of 14-5. At the NCAA's, the Cardinal punched out Air Force, Pepperdine and California by an aggregate score of 47-19. Seniors Craig Klass and Erich Fischer set school records by scoring 87 goals apiece.

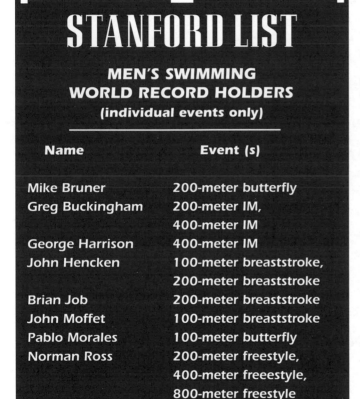

STANFORD LIST

MEN'S SWIMMING
WORLD RECORD HOLDERS
(individual events only)

Name	Event (s)
Mike Bruner	200-meter butterfly
Greg Buckingham	200-meter IM,
	400-meter IM
George Harrison	400-meter IM
John Hencken	100-meter breaststroke,
	200-meter breaststroke
Brian Job	200-meter breaststroke
John Moffet	100-meter breaststroke
Pablo Morales	100-meter butterfly
Norman Ross	200-meter freestyle,
	400-meter freeestyle,
	800-meter freestyle
Dick Roth	400-meter IM
Jeff Rouse	100-meter backstroke

Stanford ❧ LEGEND ❧

Pablo Morales

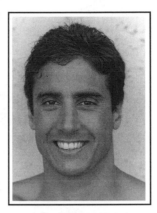

Pablo Morales is the all-time NCAA leader with 11 individual titles. (Stanford Athletics)

There are few athletes in the history of Stanford University who have impacted their sport more than Pablo Morales. He was swimming's Michael Jordan or Joe Montana—the kind of athlete who personifies greatness both on and off the playing field. Morales was an exemplary student-athlete at Stanford from 1984-87 who broke the NCAA record for most individual championships with 11, was named Academic All-American for three years and still found time to be involved in other campus and community activities. In Olympic competition, Morales' career included three gold and two silver medals and a comeback in 1992 that was one of the most talked about and heart-warming stories of the Barcelona Games. After winning one gold and two silver medals in Los Angeles in 1984, Morales failed to make the '88 Olympic Team, retired from swimming and went to Law School at Columbia University. He came out of retirement at the age of 27 after a three-year hiatus from swimming and, against all odds, won the gold medal in the 100-meter butterfly by three one-hundredths of a second. He went on to capture a second gold in Barcelona in the 400-meter medley relay. Morales, who held the world record for the 100-meter fly, led Stanford to three consecutive NCAA championships (1985-87) while winning an NCAA-record 11 events.

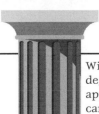

STANFORD NOTABLE

William Rehnquist earned a bachelor's and master's degree from Stanford in 1948, then completed his law degree at Stanford in 1952. He has since enjoyed a career in law and politics that culminated in his appointment as Chief Justice of the U.S. Supreme Court in September, 1986. Rehnquist enjoyed a 16-year career in private practice in Arizona before being appointed Assistant Attorney General in 1969. In October, 1971, President Richard Nixon nominated Rehnquist as Associate Justice of the Supreme Court. On June 17, 1986, President Ronald Reagan nominated Rehnquist as Chief Justice of the Supreme Court.

1987-88

- **October 1, 1987:** A severe earthquake measuring 6.1 on the Richter scale shook the Los Angeles area, killing at least eight people and injuring more than 100.

- **October 19, 1987:** The worst stock crash in the recent history of the New York Stock Exchange occurred when the Dow Jones industrial average fell 508 points.

- **November 18, 1987:** President Reagan was blamed for failing in his constitutional duty by the congressional committee report on the Iran-Contra affair.

- **February 5, 1988:** A federal grand jury in Miami indicted Panamanian General Manuel Noriega in connection with illegal drug dealings.

- **April 23, 1988:** A ban on smoking in passenger planes went into effect.

Scott Fortune shows the gold medal he won at the 1988 Olympics in Seoul, Korea *(Stanford Athletics)*

STANFORD MOMENT

Stanford Represented by 38 Athletes and Coaches at 1988 Seoul Olympics

Stanford University had an amazing 38 athletes and coaches compete at the 1988 Olympic Games in Seoul, Korea, a phenomenal number unmatched by any university in the nation. Thirty athletes and eight coaches comprised the Stanford family in Seoul. Head U.S. Olympic coaches from Stanford included Richard Quick (swimming), Mark Marquess (baseball) and Willy Cahill (judo). The 30 Cardinal athletes were found in 12 different sports, led by track and field with seven Stanford athletes, six in swimming, four in water polo, three in volleyball, two in baseball and field hockey and one each in six other sports. All totaled, Cardinal athletes won eight gold medals, six silver and three bronze medals. Baseball players Ed Sprague and Doug Robbins took home gold medals, as did men's volleyball team members Scott Fortune and Jon Root and swimmer Jay Mortenson. Future Cardinal swimmer Janet Evans—who was a member of the Stanford women's team in 1990 and '91—won a memorable three gold medals. Silver medals went to USA water polo players James Bergeson, Jody Campbell, Craig Klass and Alan Mouchawar, tennis player Tim Mayotte and swimmer Janel Jorgensen.

WHEN BRAD MUSTER RUSHED for 148 yards on 25 carries against Washington in only his fourth collegiate football game, the message was sent loud and clear. The next week he rushed for 80 yards and caught seven passes and the following week, he caught six passes and rushed 32 times for 137 yards. "Muster the ball carrier" became a familiar public address announcement at Stanford Stadium for the next three seasons. Despite missing six games during his career (1984-87) with injuries, Muster still managed to conclude his career as the school's number-two all-time leading rusher (2,940 yards) and receiver (194 receptions). His 78 receptions in 1985 still stands today as the Cardinal's single-season record and his 204 yards rushing in the 1984 Big Game vs. California is the fourth-best rushing game in school history. Chosen in the first round of the NFL Draft by the Chicago Bears, Muster went on to a seven-year career in the National Football League.

Stanford Stat . . .

Although he entered the College World Series as Stanford's No. 3 starting pitcher, senior Lee Plemel took center stage in Omaha, Nebraska and earned Most Valuable Player honors in leading the Cardinal to its second straight national championship. Plemel allowed just four earned runs in his two games, both complete game victories. He beat Fresno State 10-3 in the series opener, then came back to knock off Cal State Fullerton 4-1. Plemel led a pitching staff that had an impressive 2.38 team ERA in six games at the College World Series.

STANFORD LIST

WOMEN'S VOLLEYBALL ALL-AMERICANS

Kim Oden	1982, '83, '84, '85
Kari Rush	1983
Wendi Rush	1984, '85, '86, '87
Deidra Dvorak	1984
Bobbi Broer	1984
Teresa Smith	1986, '87
Nancy Reno	1987
Kristin Klein	1988, '89, '90, '91
Bev Oden	1989. '90, '91, '92
Carrie Feldman	1992
Cary Wendell	1993, '94, '95
Kristin Folkl	1994-95
Marnie Triefenbach	1994
Lisa Sharpley	1995-96
Kerri Walsh	1996

Stanford ❧ LEGEND ❧

Wendi Rush

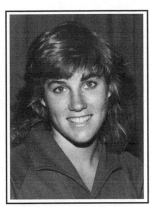

Wendi Rush led her Cardinal women's volleyball teams to four straight Final Four appearances. (Stanford Athletics)

When Wendi Rush arrived at Stanford in the fall of 1984 from Rim of the World High School in Lake Arrowhead, California, she appeared to be the perfect setter for the nation's best outside hitter, Kim Oden. She was Magic Johnson to Kareem Abdul-Jabbar, John Stockton to Karl Malone. The team of Rush to Oden would go down as one of the finest one-two combinations in the history of the sport. Together in 1984 and '85, Rush and Oden, both First-Team All-Americans each season, led Stanford to two straight appearances in the NCAA championship match, two conference titles and an overall record of 48-8. When Oden graduated after the '85 season, Rush continued to be the nation's dominant setter. She led her final two Stanford teams to the Final Four two more times and was named First-Team All-America both years. Rush's Stanford teams went to the Final Four all four years (1984-87), finished second three times and third once and had a 101-25 match record. As a freshman in 1984, Rush and Oden took Stanford to the fifth game of the championship match at UCLA, losing a heartbreaking 15-13 decision to the Bruins. A year later, the Cardinal was again in the championship match, but this time fell to UOP in four games. Rush led her teammates to their third Final Four appearance in four years in 1987, but once again settled for second after losing to Hawaii. It is no coincidence that the rise of the Stanford women's volleyball program into a national power began to take shape when Wendi Rush arrived on The Farm.

STANFORD LORE

Santa Clara County Superior Court Judge Conrad Rushing on November 19, 1987 issued a preliminary injunction allowing Stanford athletes, except football and men's basketball players, to compete without submitting to drug testing. Because the NCAA's mandatory drug testing program, as it is administered, violates California and U.S. constitutions, Rushing said, "there is no evidence of a compelling need to engage in drug testing student-athletes." The injunction had been sought by two Stanford athletes: Jennifer Hill of the women's soccer team and Barry McKeever of the football team.

1987-88

- Stanford won three more NCAA championships in 1987-88, bringing the number of national team titles in the last three years to 11.
- An 82-yard TD pass from QB Brian Johnson to FL Walter Batson highlighted Stanford's lopsided 31-7 victory in the 90th Big Game.
- Cardinal tennis teams once again each won the NCAA title. The women finished 27-2 and took the title for the third consecutive season and fourth in the last five years while the men finished 27-1 en route to their ninth championship.
- Mike Montgomery's men's basketball team advanced to postseason play for the first time since the 1942 NCAA championship season. The Cardinal finished the year 21-12—the first 20-win season since '42—and played in the National Invitational Tournament.
- In her third season at Stanford, Tara VanDerveer led the Cardinal to a 27-5 record and a trip to the NCAA tournament. Stanford advanced to the round of 16 after winning its first NCAA tournament game.

Stanford won its second straight NCAA College World Series championship in 1988. (Stanford Athletics)

STANFORD MOMENT

Baseball Team Repeats as College World Series Champions

Stanford University made history on June 11, 1988, by becoming only the third team in college baseball annals to capture back-to-back national championships. The Cardinal, which entered the College World Series seeded seventh in the eight-team field, beat Pac-10 rival Arizona State 9-4 in the first nationally televised title game on CBS. "I honestly didn't think it was possible for us or any other team to win back-to-back championships," said Cardinal head coach Mark Marquess. "There were times during the year where we could have quit, but we just kept telling ourselves to keep working hard and maybe something good will happen—and it did," he said. In order to get to the title game, Stanford had to beat Fresno State, Miami and Cal State Fullerton twice. In the championship game, freshman pitcher Stan Spencer was the recipient of an early 8-0 Cardinal lead after three innings. Stanford jumped all over ASU starter Rusty Kilgo for five first-inning runs. Ed Sprague's two-run homer and Brian Johnson's two-run double keyed the inning. Spencer worked seven innings before giving way to ace reliever Steve Chitren, who allowed just one hit in two innings and was again on the mound when Stanford was crowned College World Series champions.

HIS STORY IS ONE OF FAME AND FORTUNE. After an All-American season at Stanford in 1987 as a junior, Scott Fortune decided to stop out of school in 1988 to train with the United States Men's Volleyball Team. He made the Olympic Team as the only collegian and went to the 1988 Games in Seoul as the first middle blocker off the bench by Team USA. In the gold medal match vs. the Soviet Union, the U.S. held a two-games-to-one advantage and led 14-8 in the fourth game when Fortune entered the match. "Russia overpassed," he explained. "I couldn't believe it. I happened to be the middle blocker and the ball was coming right to me." Fortune proceeded to slam the ball back at the Soviets as the U.S. won 15-8 and clinched the gold medal. He came back to Stanford for his senior season in 1989 and was again named First-Team All-American as he led the Cardinal to its first-ever NCAA championship match, where it lost to UCLA in four games. Still, it was the best season in Stanford men's volleyball history.

Stanford Stat . . .

Katie Connors was Stanford's first great national-caliber diver. She captured six Pac-10 championships and earned All-America honors nine times in her Cardinal career (1987-90). When she was a finalist in all three diving events at the 1989 NCAA Championships, she became only the second diver in NCAA history to final on all three boards. Connors helped lead Stanford to the 1989 NCAA championship.

STANFORD LIST

MOST NCAA DIVISION I TEAM TITLES, BY COACH

Name, School	Sport	No. of Titles
Dave Williams, Houston	Men's Golf	16
Al Scates, UCLA	Men's Volleyball	16
Dick Gould, Stanford	Men's Tennis	15
Dan Gable, Iowa	Wrestling	15
Anson Dorrance, North Carolina	Women's Soccer	14
Willy Schaeffler, Denver	Skiing	13
Dean Cromwell, USC	Men's Track	12
John McDonnell, Arkansas	Men's Indoor Track	12
Richard Quick, Stanford/Texas	Women's Swimming	11
Mike Peppe, Ohio State	Men's Swimming	11
E.C. Gallagher, Oklahoma State	Wrestling	11

Stanford LEGEND

Dick Gould

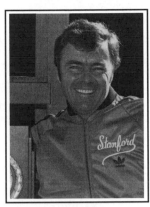

Dick Gould has built Stanford into one of the most respected programs in any sport in NCAA history. (Stanford Athletics)

In 31 years as Stanford's head men's tennis coach, Dick Gould has built a program that is admired and respected as one of the best in any sport in NCAA history. Gould, a 1960 graduate of Stanford, became the Cardinal's head coach in 1967. Since that time, he has produced 15 NCAA team championships, eight NCAA singles champions, four doubles champions and a list of former players that reads like a Who's Who in professional tennis. Forty-four of his players have earned All-America honors while his teams have finished among the top five nationally 25 times in the last 28 years. It is an incredible list of achievements that is unparalleled in college athletics. Individually, Gould has been honored by every known tennis organization, including being named the conference Coach of the Year and national Coach of the Year several times as well as the Coach of the Decade for the 1980s. Since winning his first NCAA title in 1973, Gould has directed Stanford to 15 championships in the last 25 years. John McEnroe, Roscoe Tanner, Tim Mayotte, Gene Mayer and Alex Mayer are just some of the tennis greats who have been coached by Gould.

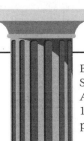

STANFORD NOTABLE

Born July 23, 1936 in Sacramento, California, Anthony Kennedy earned his bachelor's degree from Stanford University in 1958. Thirty-years later, on February 18, 1988, Kennedy took the oath of office as an Associate Justice of the United States Supreme Court. Kennedy's first judicial appointment occurred in 1975 when President Gerald Ford nominated him to the U.S. Court of Appeals for the Ninth Circuit, a position he held until 1988 when President Ronald Reagan nominated Kennedy to the Supreme Court.

1988-89

•• AMERICA'S TIME CAPSULE ••

- September 29, 1988: NASA launched its first manned space flight in 32 months, carrying a $100 million communications satellite.
- November 8, 1988: Vice President George Bush defeated Governor Michael Dukakis of Massachusetts in the presidential election.
- January 22, 1989: The San Francisco 49ers defeated the Cincinnati Bengals, 20-16, in Super Bowl XXIII. Joe Montana passed for a record 357 yards as the 49ers won their third Super Bowl title under former Stanford coach Bill Walsh.
- March 24, 1989: The oil tanker Exxon Valdez struck a reef in Prince William Sound, Alaska, leaking more than a million barrels of crude oil into water.
- August 10, 1989: President Bush nominated Army General Colin Powell to be chairman of the Joint Chiefs of Staff. Powell became the first African-American to hold the nation's highest military post.

STANFORD MOMENT

Co-captains of Stanford's 1989 women's swimming champion-ship team: Jenna Johnson (left) and Susan Lenth. (Stanford Athletics)

Cardinal Women Win Second NCAA Swimming Championship

Under first-year head coach Richard Quick, who had won the previous five NCAA titles as head coach at the University of Texas, Stanford used its depth to outdual the Longhorns and take home their second NCAA team championship and third national title in women's swimming in school history (the 1980 team won the AIAW national championship). "I'm not sure we had the best swimmers in the meet, but I am sure we are the best team in the country," said Quick moments after the Cardinal won the title on March 18, 1989. "And I mean that in the truest sense of the word. This was a total team effort," he said. Only senior Jenna Johnson (100 fly) and sophomore Michelle Griglione (400 IM) won individual NCAA championships. But, Stanford placed second, third or fourth 12 times during the three-day meet and had at least two finalists in nine of the 13 events. Those who were finalists in at least two events included Aimee Berzins (50 free, 100 free), Dede Trimble (100 back, 200 back), Michelle Donahue (100 back, 200 back), Jill Johnson (100 breast, 200 breast), Susan Lenth (100 breast, 200 breast), Barb Metz (500 free, 1650 free), Susannah Miller (200 back, 200 IM) and diver Katie Connors, who finalled on all three boards.

KATY STEDING was an integral part of the metamorphosis of the Stanford women's basketball program from 1987-90. A three-time First-Team All-Pac-10 player, Steding not only left Stanford No. 3 on the all-time scoring list with 1,586 points (12.8 points per game) and No. 2 all-time in rebounding (864), but she left The Farm after having helped Stanford win its first-ever NCAA championship in women's basketball in 1989-90. Steding was part of Tara VanDerveer's first recruiting class in 1986-87. That team went 14-14 and did not make the NCAA Tournament. In the three subsequent seasons, however, Stanford finished 27-5 (round of 16 in NCAA Tournament), 28-3 (round of eight) and 32-1 in '89-90 in winning the NCAA title. Steding went on to play professional basketball in Japan and Spain before earning a spot on the 1996 United States Olympic Team.

Stanford Stat . . .

Jay Mortenson won three individual NCAA titles for Stanford, including the 100 fly in 1989 as he led the Cardinal to a second-place finish at the NCAA Championship. Mortenson, from Madison, Wisconsin, also was a member of Stanford's American record-setting 200 medley relay team at the '89 NCAA's. He won a gold medal at the 1988 Olympics in Seoul as a member of the United States' 400-meter medley relay team.

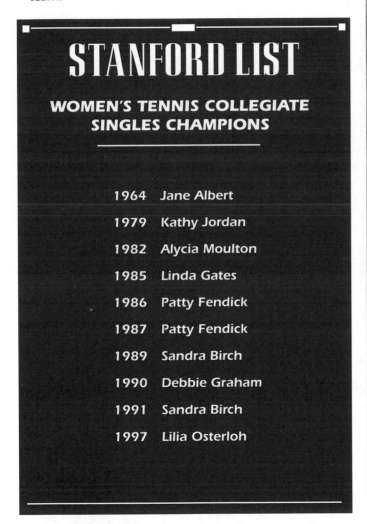

STANFORD LIST

WOMEN'S TENNIS COLLEGIATE SINGLES CHAMPIONS

1964	Jane Albert
1979	Kathy Jordan
1982	Alycia Moulton
1985	Linda Gates
1986	Patty Fendick
1987	Patty Fendick
1989	Sandra Birch
1990	Debbie Graham
1991	Sandra Birch
1997	Lilia Osterloh

Stanford LEGEND

Sandra Birch

Sandra Birch won two NCAA singles crowns and four team championships. (Stanford Athletics)

There is no female tennis player in Stanford University history that accomplished more and won more championships—both team and individual—than Sandra Birch. A native of Huntington Bay, New York, Birch was a major reason the Cardinal dynasty was in full swing during her four year career (1988-91). The condensed version of her Stanford tennis resume includes two NCAA singles crowns, four NCAA team championships, First-Team All-America honors for four consecutive years, two-time winner of the Broderick Award for tennis, two undefeated seasons and an overall team record of 111-3. She won her first NCAA singles title as a sophomore in 1989, then came back as a senior in '91 to win her second singles championship, joining Patty Fendick as Stanford's only two-time NCAA singles champion. Birch was a part of Stanford's back-to-back 29-0 seasons in 1989 and 1990. In fact, beginning in 1988 and continuing to 1991, Stanford put together a 76 dual match winning streak. In a program that can truly call itself a dynasty-winning six straight NCAA championships from 1986-91—it will be difficult for another Cardinal tennis player to match the accomplishments of Sandra Birch.

STANFORD LORE

A 1989 study by the University's Committee on Minority Issues found that, despite substantial interracial contact in close and casual friendships and dating, undergraduates still perceive racial tensions and feel social distance from each other. Among 100 recommendations, the report urged adding 30 minority faculty, doubling minority Ph.D. enrollment and undergraduate courses focused on minorities, and establishing an ethnic studies requirement for graduation. The study was headed by History Associate Prof. Albert Camarillo.

1988-89

·· SEASON HIGHLIGHTS ··

- Three more NCAA team championships were won in 1988-89: women's swimming, men's tennis, women's tennis.
- Tuan Van Le blocked a 20-yard field goal attempt by Cal in the last four seconds to preserve a 19-19 Big Game tie.
- Stanford completed the best season in women's basketball history by finishing 28-3 overall, 18-0 in winning the Pac-10 championship, and reaching the round of eight in the NCAA tournament. The Cardinal ranked fourth in the final *Associated Press* poll.
- Junior Jennifer Azzi became the first women's basketball player in school history to earn First-Team All-America honors.
- Sophomore Sandra Birch won the NCAA women's tennis singles championship while leading her team to a perfect 29-0 dual meet record and the NCAA title.

Howard Wright helped Stanford post a 26-7 overal record and advance to the NCAA Tournament for the first time in 47 years.
(Stanford Athletics)

STANFORD MOMENT

Men's Hoops Team Advances to NCAA Tournament

Despite the fact that it took 47 years to return to the NCAA Men's Basketball Tournament and despite the fact that the Cardinal was upset in an 80-78 first-round loss to Sienna, 1988-89 will always be remembered as one of the great seasons in Stanford history. Seniors Todd Lichti (20.1 points per game) and Howard Wright (14.5 points, 6.9 rebounds per game) were the catalysts for a team that featured seniors Eric Reveno at center and Terry Taylor at point guard, sophomore Andrew Vlahov at forward and key reserve Adam Keefe, then just a freshman. The Cardinal, which compiled an impressive 26-7 overall record and 15-3 in the Pac-10, finished the season ranked No. 12 by UPI and No. 13 by AP in the final national polls, the highest finish by a Stanford team since the 1962-63 team was No. 10. The 26 wins was the second most in school history, trailing only the 28-4 record of the 1942 NCAA championship team—the only other Stanford team to advance to the tournament. During the season, Stanford beat UCLA twice in three meetings, including a memorable 84-75 win at Maples Pavilion and a 95-86 victory in the Pacific-10 Conference Tournament. An 11-game winning streak highlighted a 23-game stretch in which the Cardinal went 21-2. Even an upset loss in the NCAA's cannot diminish the accomplishments of Mike Montgomery's '88-89 Cardinal.

HOWARD WRIGHT made an immediate impact when he joined the Cardinal for the 1985-86 season. As a freshman, he started 27 of the team's 32 games, averaged 9.7 points, a team-leading 6.3 rebounds and recorded 41 blocked shots, one shy of the school record. Over the next three seasons, Wright was a fixture in the Cardinal lineup as he and teammate Todd Lichti started 94 consecutive games to form one of the great one-two duos in Stanford history. Wright, a two-time First-Team All-Pac-10 selection in 1988 and '89, finished his career as the school's No. 3 scorer (1,599 points) and rebounder (860) and his 121 blocked shots set a new Cardinal record. Together with Lichti and Co., Wright put Stanford basketball on the national map in 1988-89 as the Cardinal went 26-7 and finished the year ranked No. 12 and 13 in the two national polls.

Stanford Stat . . .

Sophomore Jon Volpe broke Darrin Nelson's 11-year-old record by rushing for 220 yards on 29 carries vs. Washington on October 29, 1988 in Seattle. Although the Cardinal lost a heartbreaking game 28-25 to the Huskies, Volpe stole the show with his performance. His longest run was a career-high 68 yards. Nelson set the previous record of 211 yards vs. San Jose State in 1977.

STANFORD LIST

MIKE MONTGOMERY'S ALL-TIME TEAM (1987-97)

First-Team

F	Howard Wright,	1986-89
F	Andrew Vlahov,	1988-91
C	Adam Keefe,	1989-92
G	Todd Lichti,	1986-89
G	Brevin Knight,	1994-97

Second-Team

F	Andy Poppink,	1992-96
F	Eric Reveno,	1985-89
C	Tim Young,	1995-97
G	Dion Cross,	1993-96
G	Terry Taylor,	1985-89

Stanford LEGEND

Todd Lichti

Todd Lichti is the only Cardinal men's basketball player to be named first-team All-Pac-10 four consecutive seasons. (Stanford Athletics)

The first great Stanford basketball player was Hank Luisetti, who was a three-time First-Team All-American from 1936-38 and two-time College Basketball Player of the Year in 1937 and '38. Forty years after Luisetti played his first game at Stanford, Todd Lichti took his place as the next great Cardinal basketball player. A 6-4 shooting guard from Concord, California, Lichti not only rewrote the Stanford record book, but he became the first and only Cardinal men's basketball player to be named First-Team All-Pac-10 for four consecutive seasons (1986-89). In his four seasons, Lichti averaged 17.2, 17.6, 20.1, and 20.1 points per game, making him the all-time leading scorer in school history with 2,336 points—a career average of 18.8. But there was more to Lichti than points. Much more. He could go left. He could go right. He could shoot the outside jumper or drive to the basket. He was the ultimate team player, a great competitor who was relentless in his drive to become a great basketball player. Todd Lichti had many great games and many Stanford victories can be attributed directly to his presence on the court. He scored 30 points in his eighth collegiate game vs. Seton Hall. He had 35 points, 27 in the second half, as a senior in 1989 in a Stanford upset of nationally-ranked Arizona. And in between, he put together a career many consider to be second only to Hank Luisetti in Stanford history.

STANFORD NOTABLE

Phil Knight earned his MBA from Stanford in 1962 and two years later began Blue Ribbon Sports with a $500 investment matched by his co-founder and former coach Bill Bowerman. Knight sold shoes out of the back of a station wagon, continued to practice as a C.P.A. and taught at Portland State University until 1969. The Cortez, the first shoe to appear under the NIKE brand, arrived in 1972. Since then, Knight has turned NIKE into the world's number-one sports and fitness company. His master's work at Stanford provided the outline for the business that would become NIKE.

1989-90

- **September 21, 1989:** Hurricane Hugo ravished Charleston, South Carolina, causing more than a billion dollars in damages.
- **October 17, 1989:** An earthquake measuring 6.9 on the Richter scale hit the San Francisco Bay Area, killing more than 60 people. A World Series game between the Oakland A's and San Francisco Giants at Candlestick Park was halted due to the quake.
- **February 28, 1990:** Black nationalist Nelson Mandela met with President Bush just two weeks after having spent 27 years in prison in South Africa.
- **May 31, 1990:** Mikhail Gorbachev met with President Bush in a Washington Summit.
- **August 7, 1990:** American troops, responding to the crisis in the Middle East, left for Saudi Arabia as Operation "Desert Storm" began.

STANFORD MOMENT

Mike Mussina was a starting pitcher on Stanford's 1990 baseball team that won a school-record 59 games.
(Stanford Athletics)

Baseball Team Wins School Record 59 Games

The 1990 Cardinal, it can be argued, was the most talented in school history. No, it didn't win the national title like the '87 and '88 teams, but after winning a school-record 59 games and breezing through the tough Pac-10 Southern Division with a 24-6 mark, Stanford finished third at the College World Series despite playing its worst baseball of the season. After winning all four games at the NCAA West Regional (held at Sunken Diamond), Stanford entered the College World Series as the top-seeded team. But, once there, the Cardinal struggled. Stanford hit just .216 as a team, had its top home run hitter go hitless in 17 at bats, had its All-American pitcher Stan Spencer unable to pitch a second game due to an injury and had its other star pitcher, Mike Mussina, get roughed up in his two starts. Still, with a star-studded team of RF Paul Carey, CF Jeffrey Hammonds, 1B David McCarty and SS Troy Paulsen, among others, the Cardinal managed to reach the semifinal game on June 8, 1990, where it lost 5-1 to eventual NCAA champion Georgia. Five players off the 59-12 team of 1990 made it to the major leagues, including Mussina, Hammonds, Carey, McCarty and pitcher Brian Sackinsky.

SHE WAS AT STANFORD for three years from 1989-91 and the disappointment of losing on the tennis court was one aspect of college life she rarely had to experience. That's because Debbie Graham was a great tennis player in a great program with other great players. Life was indeed good for Graham, a lanky six-footer from Fountain Valley, California. She went 73-2 in dual matches, a Stanford best, won the 1990 NCAA singles championship and was a part of three national championship teams. Her first two teams in 1989 and '90 each went 29-0 while her '91 team was *only* 26-1, bringing her three-year team record to 84-1. In 1990, Graham also reached the NCAA doubles finals with her partner, Sandra Birch, and was named winner of the Broderick Award as the nation's top female tennis player.

Stanford Stat . . .

Freshman Jeffrey Hammonds hit .355 and stole a school-record 48 bases in leading the Cardinal to a 59-12 overall record and a trip to the College World Series.

Hammonds was named First-Team All-American, First-Team All-Pac-10 and the NCAA Freshman of the Year in 1990. He also put together a school-record 37-game hitting streak. Following his junior season in 1992, Hammonds was a first-round draft choice by the Baltimore Orioles.

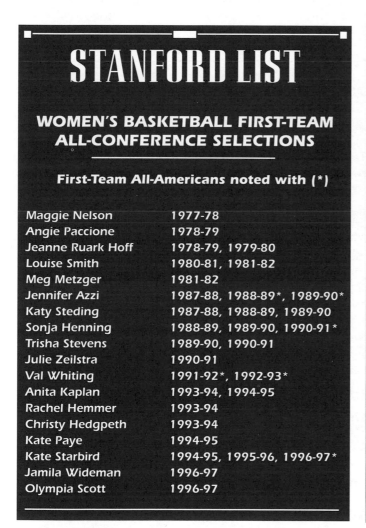

STANFORD LIST

WOMEN'S BASKETBALL FIRST-TEAM ALL-CONFERENCE SELECTIONS

First-Team All-Americans noted with (*)

Maggie Nelson	1977-78
Angie Paccione	1978-79
Jeanne Ruark Hoff	1978-79, 1979-80
Louise Smith	1980-81, 1981-82
Meg Metzger	1981-82
Jennifer Azzi	1987-88, 1988-89*, 1989-90*
Katy Steding	1987-88, 1988-89, 1989-90
Sonja Henning	1988-89, 1989-90, 1990-91*
Trisha Stevens	1989-90, 1990-91
Julie Zeilstra	1990-91
Val Whiting	1991-92*, 1992-93*
Anita Kaplan	1993-94, 1994-95
Rachel Hemmer	1993-94
Christy Hedgpeth	1993-94
Kate Paye	1994-95
Kate Starbird	1994-95, 1995-96, 1996-97*
Jamila Wideman	1996-97
Olympia Scott	1996-97

Stanford ⚜ LEGEND ⚜

Jennifer Azzi

Jennifer Azzi was named the NCAA Player of the Year in 1990. (Stanford Athletics)

The history of success that has become commonplace—even expected—by the Cardinal women's basketball team can be traced back to two people: head coach Tara VanDerveer and a 5-9 guard from Oak Ridge, Tennessee named Jennifer Azzi. Little did anyone know that when Azzi decided to attend Stanford for the 1986-87 season, the fortunes of the program were about to turn. In a word, Azzi became the greatest player in Stanford women's basketball history. She was the school's first women's basketball All-American (she was honored twice in 1989 and 1990), the first NCAA Player of the Year award winner (1990), the first NCAA Final Four MVP recipient (1990) and the leader of Stanford's first NCAA championship team in 1990. "Jennifer Azzi is not only one of the great basketball players in Stanford history, but she is one of my favorite people," said VanDerveer. Azzi concluded her career as the school's all-time leader in assists (751) and steals (271), No. 2 in scoring (1,634 points) and No. 10 in rebounding (476 rebounds). She started 122 of Stanford's 124 games during her four-year career (1987-90) and, in her final three seasons, she led the Cardinal to an overall record of 87-9. Azzi played professional basketball overseas and is currently playing in the ABL. She was a member of the 1996 United States Olympic Women's Basketball Team which brought home the gold medal.

STANFORD LORE

The hands of the clock in the Clock Tower stopped at 5:04 p.m. on October 17, 1989 when the Loma Prieta earthquake shook Northern California, causing severe damage throughout the Bay Area and on the Stanford campus. No deaths or serious injuries on campus were reported, but repair of buildings, likely to take at least three or four years to complete, was estimated at $170 million. Among the most severely damaged were Memorial Church, Language and Geology Corners, Green Library West Wing, Museum, Business School, Quad arcades and seven Row Houses.

1989-90

·· SEASON HIGHLIGHTS ··

- Stanford continued its assault on NCAA team championships by winning three more in '89-90, giving it 17 in a five-year span.
- John Hopkins' 37-yard field goal on the game's final play completed an astonishing comeback against Oregon and gave first-year head coach Denny Green his first Stanford win. The Cardinal trailed the Ducks 17-0 before scoring 18 points in the final 7:19.
- Sophomore Adam Keefe averaged 20 points per game as the Cardinal men's basketball team advanced to the NIT.
- Freshman Janet Evans was named the NCAA Swimmer of the Year after winning three events at the NCAA Championships.
- The women's tennis team completed its second straight 29-0 dual meet season and wins the NCAA title for the fifth straight year.
- Dick Gould's men's tennis team championship was Stanford's 11th in the last 18 years.

Sonja Henning (left) and Trisha Stevens with President George Bush after the 1990 NCAA championship. *(Stanford Athletics)*

STANFORD MOMENT

Cardinal Beats Auburn For First NCAA Women's Hoops Championship

Led by All-American and NCAA Player of the Year Jennifer Azzi, Stanford concluded the finest season in school history by defeating Auburn 88-81 on April 1, 1990 in Knoxville, Tennessee, to win the first-ever national championship in women's basketball for Stanford University. Azzi, named the Final Four MVP, sparked a 14-2 run in the second half to bring the Cardinal from three points down to a nine-point lead—a lead that never fell below six for the remaining 14 minutes of the game. Azzi finished with 17 points and five assists while guard Sonja Henning led the team in scoring with 21 points, including seven clutch free throws in the final 1:27. Katy Steding had 18 points on six three-pointers, and seven rebounds while Trisha Stevens chipped in with 16 points and 10 rebounds. The Cardinal began the year by winning its first 20 games, then suffered an 81-78 loss at Washington before winning the final 12 games and finishing with a 32-1 record—the best in school history. Stanford averaged 92 points per game and scored over 100 points in a game on 10 occasions. Their average margin of victory was an astonishing 26 points per game.

THE CARDINAL WOMEN'S SOCCER PROGRAM began as a varsity sport in 1984, but it wasn't until the arrival of Julie Foudy in 1989 that Stanford made its mark on the national scene. A 5-6 midfielder from Laguna Nigel, California, Foudy was Stanford's first true superstar in women's soccer. She was named First-Team All-American for four consecutive years (1989-92) and in 1991, she not only led the Cardinal to a 17-2 overall record, but she was named the National Player of the Year. Foudy joined the United States National Team following her playing days at Stanford and in 1996 she competed in Atlanta as a member of the U.S. Olympic women's soccer team.

Stanford Stat . . .

Nick Bravin not only became the top fencer in Stanford history, but he was the country's top contender at the 1992 and 1996 Olympic Games. A three-time NCAA individual foil champion, Bravin won NCAA titles in 1990, '92 and '93. He was awarded the Al Masters Trophy as the top student-athlete at Stanford in 1993.

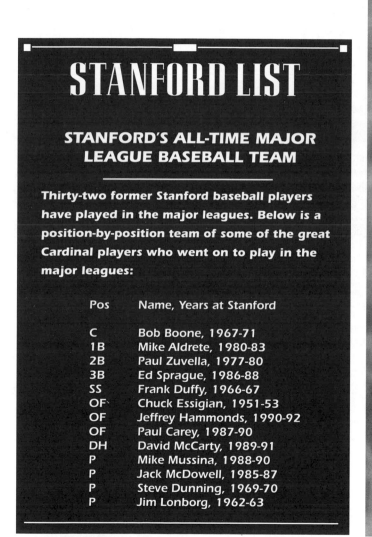

STANFORD LIST

STANFORD'S ALL-TIME MAJOR LEAGUE BASEBALL TEAM

Thirty-two former Stanford baseball players have played in the major leagues. Below is a position-by-position team of some of the great Cardinal players who went on to play in the major leagues:

Pos	Name, Years at Stanford
C	Bob Boone, 1967-71
1B	Mike Aldrete, 1980-83
2B	Paul Zuvella, 1977-80
3B	Ed Sprague, 1986-88
SS	Frank Duffy, 1966-67
OF	Chuck Essigian, 1951-53
OF	Jeffrey Hammonds, 1990-92
OF	Paul Carey, 1987-90
DH	David McCarty, 1989-91
P	Mike Mussina, 1988-90
P	Jack McDowell, 1985-87
P	Steve Dunning, 1969-70
P	Jim Lonborg, 1962-63

Stanford LEGEND

Paul Carey

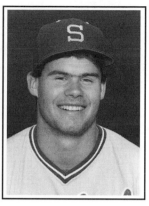

Paul Carey set five school records and was twice named All-America. (Stanford Athletics)

It was the shot heard 'round The Farm. Paul Carey, a freshman right fielder from Weymouth, Massachusetts, had just hit a 10th inning, grand-slam home run vs. LSU in the 1987 College World Series to give Stanford a 6-5 victory and propel him into legendary status in Stanford annals. It will always be remembered as one of the great moments in Stanford University sports history. For Carey, though, it was simply the most important hit of a spectacular college career. For four years (1987-90), Carey roamed right field at Sunken Diamond, hit more home runs than any player in school and conference history and was a member of three of the best Cardinal teams of all-time, including two national championship teams. A four-year starter, Carey set five school records (games played, at bats, home runs, RBI, hits) and was among the top-10 all-time in nine of 11 offensive categories. He was a two-time All-American and two-time All-Pac-10 selection, the 1987 NCAA Freshman of the Year and the MVP of the 1987 College World Series. Following Carey's grand slam in the '87 series, the Cardinal went on to beat Oklahoma State for its first NCAA title. The next season, Carey's team beat Arizona State in the championship game for its second consecutive national crown. As a senior in 1990, Carey led his team to a school record 59 wins and another trip to the College World Series. In 268 games for the Cardinal, Carey had a career batting average of .337 with 56 home runs and 220 RBI.

STANFORD NOTABLE

One of the popular fiction authors of our time, Scott Turow spent five years at Stanford as a Fellow in the Stanford University Creative Writing Center (1970-72) and as a creative writing teacher from '72-75. His first three novels were all #1 on the *New York Times* bestseller list, including *Presumed Innocent* (1987), *Burden of Proof* (1990) and *Pleading Guilty* (1993). His fourth novel, *The Laws of our Fathers* (1996), was purchased for a feature film by Universal Pictures. *Presumed Innocent* was made into a major motion picture while *Burden of Proof* was an ABC-TV miniseries.

1990-91

- November 8, 1990: President George Bush doubled U.S. forces in the Persian Gulf region to nearly a half million troops.
- January 16, 1991: U.S. and allied planes attacked Iraq's communications systems and chemical weapons plants.
- February 27, 1991: The United States and allied forces claimed an overwhelming victory, pushing back the Iraqi army
- March 3, 1991: Los Angeles policemen stopped and beat African-American motorist Rodney King, and an observer recorded the event on videotape.
- June 12, 1991: Michael Jordan led the Chicago Bulls to their first-ever NBA championship, beating the Los Angeles Lakers four games to one.

STANFORD MOMENT

"Touchdown" Tommy Vardell scored four TDs in Stanford's 36-31 win over Notre Dame.
(Stanford Athletics)

Stanford Stuns Number-One Ranked Notre Dame

The headline in the *USA Today* simply read "Stun-ford." That said it all. The Cardinal, off to a 1-3 start, beat #1 ranked and unbeaten Notre Dame in South Bend in one of the greatest upsets in school history. Led by quarterback Jason Palumbis, "Touchdown" Tommy Vardell, All-American receiver Ed McCaffrey and all-purpose back Glyn Milburn, Stanford battled back from a 24-7 deficit, scored the go-ahead TD with 36 seconds remaining in the game and held on for dear life as it literally stunned the college football world with a 36-31 victory. When the Irish took a 17-point second-quarter lead after QB Rick Mirer's second TD pass of the game, it looked as though top-ranked Notre Dame was well on its way to another lopsided win. But, the Cardinal scored a touchdown and two-point conversion before the end of the half to cut the lead to 24-15. Vardell, who scored four TDs on the day, all on one-yard runs, got his first to cap an impressive 10-play, 80-yard drive. Vardell's second score cut the Irish lead to 24-22 in the third period and suddenly Stanford was back in the game. Rodney Culver, who rushed for 104 yards, scored from a yard out to put the Irish up 31-22. Notre Dame, which fumbled three times on the day, muffed its second punt of the game and once again, Stanford was in business with good field position. A 43-yard Palumbis to McCaffrey pass set up Vardell's third one-yard TD, cutting the lead to 31-29. The Cardinal finally took the lead when Vardell capped a 62-yard drive with his fourth one-yard TD plunge. Milburn's eight-yard reception on a third-and-eight and Palumbis' run on fourth-and-two kept the drive alive. Mirer, however, completed two, 20-yard passes and had two attempts at the end zone from the Stanford 23. On the game's final play, Irish tight end Derek Brown dropped the game-winning touchdown pass and Stanford players and coaches had something special to celebrate.

IN ONE OF THE GREATEST GAMES in school history, the Cardinal scored nine points in the final 12 seconds to pull out a 27-25 victory in the 93rd Big Game. Although Glyn Milburn set a Pac-10 record with 379 all-purpose yards, it was the final minute of play that will forever mark this game. Quarterback Jason Palumbis hit receiver Ed McCaffrey in the corner of the end zone on a 19-yard TD pass play with 12 seconds left, pulling the Cardinal within a point at 25-24. Stanford head coach Denny Green elected to go for two and the win rather than a kick to tie. This time, however, Palumbis could not connect with McCaffrey and when the two-point try failed, Cal fans poured onto the field in a wild celebration. What followed is Big Game lore. The Bears were penalized 15 yards for unsportsmanlike conduct, allowing Stanford to kick off from midfield. Kevin Scott recovered the on-sides kick for Stanford at the 37-yard line with nine seconds left. On the ensuing play, Cal was called for roughing the passer—a 15-yard penalty—putting the ball on the Bears' 22-yard line and giving Stanford's John Hopkins a 37-yard field goal attempt to win the game. Hopkins kick was true and Cardinal fans celebrated much like the Cal fans had just 12 seconds before.

Stanford Stat . . .

Not only was Bob Whitfield one of the greatest offensive tackles to play at Stanford, but he was also one of the most colorful. At 6-7 and 300 pounds, Whitfield became a symbol for comic relief during his three years at Stanford. "I don't run around with a clown suit on," he said in 1991, "but I like to keep the tension loose." Whitfield, who played every down as a freshman in 1989, started all 34 games during his three-year Stanford career. He was twice named First-Team All-American and All-Pac-10 Conference. As a junior in '91, Whitfield was a finalist for both the Outland Trophy and Lombardi Award. He left Stanford following his junior season and was the eighth pick in the first round of '92 NFL Draft by the Atlanta Falcons.

STANFORD LIST

WOMEN'S TENNIS MOST DUAL MATCH WINS IN A CAREER

	Name	Years	Career Record
1.	Teri Whitlinger	1988-91	101-6
2.	Lisa Green	1987-90	93-17
3.	Heather Willens	1990-93	91-14
4.	Sandra DeSilva	1994-97	88-15
5.	Amy Chiminello	1992-96	87-9
6.	Laxmi Poruri	1991-94	84-11
7.	Patty Fendick	1984-87	77-11
	Sandra Birch	1988-91	77-15
9.	Katie Schlukebir	1994-97	75-26
10.	Debbie Graham	1989-91	73-26
11.	Kylie Johnson	1989-92	72-13
12.	Stephanie Savides	1984-87	69-28
13.	Linda Gates	1982-85	68-19
14.	Kim Shasby	1992-96	67-27
15.	Leigh Anne Eldridge	1984-87	62-10

Stanford ❦ LEGEND ❦

Janet Evans

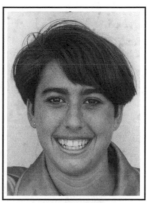

An American Olympic legend, Janet Evans won five NCAA titles during her two years on The Farm. (Stanford Athletics)

She was America's Sweetheart after the 1988 Olympic Games in Seoul, Korea. The petite 17-year-old from Placentia, California, winner of three gold medals and holder of three world records, became an instant celebrity after her phenomenal performance in Seoul. Before her senior year at El Dorado High School, Janet Evans won gold medals in the 400-meter freestyle in world record time, the 400-meter individual medley in American record time and the 800-meter freestyle in Olympic record time. She became a household name. After the Olympics, there were offers for commercial endorsements, parade appearances and even marriage proposals from strangers. Despite all the attention and certain financial gain, Evans decided instead to attend Stanford. In two seasons on The Farm (1990-91), Evans won five NCAA individual events and two relay events while setting two more American records. As a freshman in '90, she was named the NCAA Female Swimmer of the Year. Evans left Stanford following the 1991 season to concentrate on training for the 1992 Olympics. She made the U.S. team once again, this time taking a gold in the 800-meter free and a silver in the 400-meter free in Barcelona. Evans made her third U.S. Olympic Team in 1996, but failed to win a medal. Still, her three Olympic appearances, four gold medals and one silver medal and magnetic smile will remain a part of Olympic lore forever. During her storied career, Evans won the 1989 Sullivan Award as the nation's top amateur athlete after being a finalist in '87 and '88, was named the U.S. Swimmer of the Year in both 1987 and '88 and was the World Swimmer of the Year in 1989.

STANFORD LORE

Stanford President Donald Kennedy announced his resignation on July 29, 1991. Kennedy, who was named the university president in August, 1980, said he would step down from his post in August, 1992. "At present we are talking too much about our problems and too little about our opportunities," Kennedy said in a letter to University trustees. Kennedy's resignation came in the midst of the university's embroilment with the federal government on reimbursement for the indirect cost of research. The university had withdrawn more than $1.3 million in charges over the last decade that it said were errors.

1990-91

·· SEASON HIGHLIGHTS ··

- Wide receiver Ed McCaffrey was named First-Team All-America after recording 61 receptions for 917 yards and eight TDs during the 1990 season.
- Five years after her sister Kim was named National Player of the Year for Stanford, sophomore Bev Oden was named the nation's top women's volleyball player in 1990.
- The Cardinal women's soccer team finished the season 15-3-1 and advanced to the NCAA Tournament for the first time in school history.
- Sophomore Jared Palmer won the NCAA singles championship, becoming the 10th men's tennis player in Stanford history to win the singles title.
- Senior Sandra Birch won her second NCAA singles championship while leading Stanford to the national team title for the sixth consecutive season.

Stanford won the 1991 NIT Championship after beating Oklahoma, 78-2. (Stanford Athletics)

STANFORD MOMENT

Men's Hoops Wins NIT Championship

After finishing the regular season 15-13 overall and 8-10 in the Pac-10, Mike Montgomery's men's basketball team received an invitation to play in the NIT. Five games later, with a home win over Houston, road wins at Wisconsin and Southern Illinois and victories over Massachusetts and Oklahoma in New York, Stanford took home the NIT championship trophy. "We played probably the best basketball during the five-game stretch leading up the NIT championship game that we have since I've been here," said Montgomery following the title game with Oklahoma, which Stanford won 78-72. "Unselfish, focused, intense, together, are all words that come to mind." All five Cardinal starters scored in double figures against the Sooners, including 22 by senior guard Kenny Ammann, 14 points and 11 rebounds by forward Andrew Vlahov, 13 points and 13 boards by Deshon Wingate and 12 points and eight rebounds by All-American Adam Keefe, who was named the MVP of the NIT. On the road to Madison Square Garden for the NIT Finals, Keefe, as he was all season, was the Cardinal's focal point. He scored 33 in Stanford's second NIT game at Wisconsin and 24 at Southern Illinois and against UMass in the NIT semifinal. Stanford became the 13th school in NCAA history to win both the NCAA (1942) and NIT championships. "I can't tell you what this means to us," said Montgomery. "This just kicks down another barrier for Stanford basketball. I think it means that we can win a national championship of sorts—that we can come to Madison Square Garden and play with some of the best teams in the country."

HER NAME IS SYNONYMOUS WITH TENNIS. The Whitlinger's, tennis Family of the Year in 1986, know a little something about tennis. Teri and her twin, Tami, were both All-Americans at Stanford and their uncle, John, was a Stanford All-America and an assistant coach to Dick Gould for the Cardinal men's team. Teri and Tami arrived at Stanford in 1988 as two of the top junior players in the country. Tami left Stanford for the pro tour after two seasons, but Teri remained and compiled a list of accomplishments that may never be matched again. During her four years on The Farm (1988-91), Teri was a four-time All-American, an NCAA doubles champion and a member of four consecutive NCAA team championships. Her career dual match record of 101-6 is not only an astonishing feat, but it set a school record for career dual match victories. Teri's four Cardinal teams won 111 matches and lost just three and had an NCAA-record dual match winning streak of 76 from '88-91. Two of her teams—1989 and '90—went 29-0 en route to dominating the sport. In 1990, she teamed with Meredith McGrath to win the NCAA doubles title.

Stanford Stat . . .

In 1987-88, Tara VanDerveer was in the process of molding her women's basketball program into one of the nation's elite. Sonja Henning may have been the final piece to the puzzle. She was the quintessential point guard to complement shooting guard Jennifer Azzi and forwards Katy Steding and Trisha Stevens. In the four years that followed, VanDerveer's mission was complete. Stanford advanced to the NCAA Tournament four straight seasons, won one national championship and made two trips to the Final Four. Henning, who graduated as the school's season and career assist leader, became the second Cardinal women's basketball player to earn First-Team All-America honors, which she did in 1990-91. She was also a three-time First-Team All-Pac-10 performer.

STANFORD LIST

The Voice of Stanford Athletics, Bob Murphy, has been broadcasting Stanford football games for over 30 years. Below is his list of the top-10 Stanford football games of all-time (listed chronologically):

- **November 22, 1947**   California 20, Stanford 18
"A Rose Bowl-bound Cal team is almost upset by winless Stanford"
- **November 10, 1951**   Stanford 27, USC 20
"This game marked the resurgence of the Stanford football program."
- **November 7, 1970**   Stanford 29, Washington 22
"Jim Plunkett probably won the Heisman after this game."
- **January 1, 1971**   Stanford 27, Ohio State 17
"Stanford upsets one of the great Ohio State teams of all-time in the Rose Bowl."
- **January 1, 1972**   Stanford 13, Michigan 12
"Who will ever forget Don Bunce's performance or Rod Garcia's kick?"
- **November 23, 1974:**   Stanford 22, California 20
"Mike Langford's 50-yard field goal on the game's final play was unbelievable."
- **December 31, 1978**   Stanford 25, Georgia 22
"One of the greatest comebacks in Stanford history."
- **November 20, 1982**   California 25, Stanford 20
"The Play will live forever....."
- **November 17, 1990**   Stanford 27, California 25
"So many things happened in the final minute....."
- **December 31, 1996**   Stanford 38, Michigan State 0
"The greatest performance by any Stanford team in a bowl game."

Stanford LEGEND

David McCarty

David McCarty was named the NCAA Player of the Year in 1991.
(Stanford Athletics)

David McCarty became the second Stanford baseball player ever to be named the national Player of the Year in 1991, joining 1970 recipient Steve Dunning. A 6-5 first baseman from Houston, "Tex" had entered his junior year in 1991 as a legitimate pro prospect, but not one that was projected to be a first-round draft pick. After he put together a season that included a .420 batting average, 24 home runs, 66 RBI and slugging percentage of .828, McCarty was suddenly on everyone's wish list. He was named *Baseball America's* College Player of the Year, then was the third pick overall in the '91 June Major League Draft by the Minnesota Twins. The only player in Stanford history who was selected higher in the draft that McCarty was Dunning, who was the second pick in 1970. McCarty's '91 batting average of .420 was the second best in school history and his 24 homers tied him for number-two on Stanford's single-season list. Along with being named the national Player of the Year, he was also Selected First-Team All-America, First-Team All-Pac-10 and Pac-10 Southern Division Player of the Year. He had an amazing 26-game hitting streak during the '91 campaign in which he hit .490 with 10 home runs and 32 RBI. "You can't consistently get him out with the same pitch," said Cardinal baseball coach Mark Marquess in 1991. "It's hard to fool him because his balance is so good." McCarty, who started 166 games at first base from 1989-91, including 133 straight in '90 and '91, finished his career with 41 home runs (tied for third all-time), a .359 batting average (second best ever), 44 doubles (sixth all-time) and 155 RBI (seventh all-time).

STANFORD NOTABLE

One of the most important authors of the 20th century, John Steinbeck grew up in the Salinas Valley as a farm laborer and studied intermittently at Stanford University from 1919-25, but he did not receive a degree. Instead, Steinbeck continued to work as a laborer and write, often with a sympathetic focus on the poor, the eccentric or the dispossessed. His first popular success was *Tortilla Flat*, written in 1935. *Of Mice and Men* was written in 1937. *The Grapes of Wrath*, which won him the 1940 Pulitzer Prize, was written in 1939. Other great Steinbeck novels include *Cannery Row* (1945), *The Pearl* (1947) and his most ambitious project, *East of Eden* (1952). Steinbeck received the Nobel Prize for literature in 1962. He died at the age of 66 in 1968.

1991-92

- September 9, 1991: Boxing champ Mike Tyson was indicted on rape charges by a Marion County (Indiana) grand jury.
- November 7, 1991: Basketball's Magic Johnson retired after announcing that he had tested positive for the HIV virus.
- December 25, 1991: Mikhail Gorbachev resigned his position as leader of the Soviet Union.
- May 1, 1992: President Bush ordered federal troops to enter riot-torn Los Angeles. The unrest was triggered when a jury acquitted four policemen charged with beating Rodney King.
- May 22, 1992: More than 50 million TV viewers tuned in to watch Johnny Carson's final appearance on "The Tonight Show."

Legendary coach Bill Walsh returned to Stanford in January, 1992, to become the school's head football coach.
(Stanford Athletics)

STANFORD MOMENT

Bill Walsh Returns to Stanford

It was called by many a "coronation." Indeed it was not the usual press conference to announce the next football coach. It was much more than that. Word had already leaked that Bill Walsh, legendary coach of the Super Bowl champion San Francisco 49ers, former head coach at Stanford, the *genius*, a future Hall of Famer, was coming out of retirement to become the head coach at Stanford University. It was only about a week before the official announcement on January 16, 1992 that Stanford Athletic Director Ted Leland was going through the normal process of searching for a replacement to Denny Green, who had left Stanford for the Minnesota Vikings, when someone threw out the name of a possible candidate—Bill Walsh. Several closed doors meetings between Leland and Walsh, and between Walsh and prominent Stanford alums, and some soul-searching by Walsh himself led everyone to Burnham Pavilion for a press conference that was more a celebration of the return of a coaching icon. Over 600 people jammed Burnham to get a glimpse of Walsh, the Stanford Band played and the Dollies danced, professors and staff took time out to attend, television cameras were everywhere, the press conference was broadcast live on local radio and ESPN carried the event live to a national audience. "I wanted to teach undergraduates," Walsh said at the news conference. "I missed coaching. I missed working with young men, being a part of something from the inside. But it really hadn't hit me until the Stanford opportunity happened."

TO WIN THE **TRIPLE CROWN** in collegiate tennis, one must be an exceptional talent and be surrounded by a great team. In 1992, Stanford's Alex O'Brien was just that. O'Brien, from Amarillo, Texas, had been an All-American his first three years at Stanford (1989-91) and had been a part of two NCAA championship teams. He considered leaving The Farm after his junior season to join the pro tour, but instead decided to stay for his senior year. "People told me this was going to be my year," O'Brien said after the '92 NCAA's. O'Brien became the first Cardinal since 1974— and third in school history —to win the Triple Crown, that is winning the NCAA singles, doubles and team championships in the same year. He finished his career with a 40-5 record in NCAA Tournament play, setting a new NCAA record. In four years at Stanford, O'Brien was a four-time All-American, two-time Pac-10 Player of the Year, NCAA singles champ and NCAA doubles champ while his teams won three national titles. "We've never had anyone do the kinds of things Alex has done," said his coach, Dick Gould. "Thank goodness he decided to come back for his senior season. He was the catalyst who sparked our team all year."

Stanford Stat . . .

Only once in the history of NCAA competition had a school won five team championships in a single season, but that's exactly what Stanford did during the 1991-92 campaign. In an astonishing show of dominance, NCAA championship trophies were won by the men's and women's swimming teams, women's basketball, men's gymnastics and men's tennis. The women's swimming team won Stanford's first title in '91-92 by scoring an NCAA-record 735.5 points, a feat duplicated a week later by the men's team's 632 points at the NCAA meet. The women's basketball team won its second title in three years in March, the men's gymnastics team won its first-ever national championship and the men's tennis team was crowned national champions for the 12th time.

STANFORD LIST

WOMEN'S SWIMMING OLYMPIC GOLD MEDALISTS

Name, Olympic Year: Gold Medal (s)

Ann Cribbs, 1960: 400 Medley Relay

Chris Von Saltza, 1960: 400 free, 400 medley relay, 400 free relay

Sharon Stouder Clark, 1964: 100 fly, 400 medley relay, 400 free relay

Kim Peyton, 1976: 400 free relay

Jenna Johnson, 1984: 400 free relay, 400 medley relay

Janet Evans, 1988: 400 free, 800 free, 400 IM
1992: 800 free

Lea Loveless, 1992: 400 medley relay

Summer Sanders, 1992: 200 fly, 400 medley relay

Jenny Thompson, 1992: 400 free relay, 400 medley relay
1996: 400 free relay, 400 medley relay, 800 free relay

Catherine Fox, 1996: 400 free relay, 400 medley relay

Lisa Jacob, 1996: 400 free relay, 800 free relay

Stanford LEGEND

Summer Sanders

Olympic and NCAA champion Summer Sanders won 10 NCAA titles in her two-year Cardinal career. (Stanford Athletics)

Here's a quick review of Summer Sanders' two-year career at Stanford: NCAA champion in all six events she swam, member of four NCAA-winning relay teams, two-time NCAA Swimmer of the Year, two-time Pac-10 Swimmer of the Year, member of one NCAA championship team (1992) and one second-place team (1991), set two American and three NCAA records. And that's not including her Olympic accomplishments. After missing the 1988 U.S. Olympic team by just .27 seconds in the 200 individual medley, Sanders, then a 15-year high school student from Roseville, California, realized that she was indeed at the same level as the other swimmers. She dedicated herself to making the 1992 team. Four years later and her Stanford accolades behind her, Sanders made the biggest splash at the '92 Olympic Trials. She won three events and placed second in another, thus becoming the first woman since the '76 Games to qualify in four individual events. In Barcelona, Sanders did not disappoint. She took home two gold medals (200 fly, 400 medley relay), one silver (200 IM) and one bronze (400 IM). "She has that special drive that separates good swimmers from great ones," said her '92 Olympic and Stanford head coach, Richard Quick. After her two seasons at Stanford and her Olympic performance in Barcelona, Sanders decided to forego her final two years of NCAA eligibility to accept commercial endorsements. "It was the most difficult decision I've ever had to make," she said at a news conference announcing her intention to leave Stanford, "but I feel like there are certain opportunities that come about once in a lifetime." Indeed, Sanders' stay on The Farm was a once in a lifetime opportunity for the Stanford community.

STANFORD LORE

Stanford observed the 100-year anniversary of its opening day on October 1, 1991 in a ceremony filled with music, speeches, cheers and what President Donald Kennedy called a hard but successful test of Stanford's core values. A flag-bedecked recreation of the Opening Day platform under the West Portal of the Inner Quad was the site of a planned stately culmination of four days of centennial festivities that drew more than 11,000 well-wishers to the campus. California Gov. Pete Wilson gave the keynote speech.

1991-92

- Stanford beat USC and UCLA in football in the same year for the first time since the 1971 Rose Bowl team.
- Senior Jeff Rouse was named the NCAA Male Swimmer of the Year after winning three events and leading his team to the NCAA title.
- Jair Lynch led the Cardinal men's gymnastics team to its first-ever NCAA championship.
- At the NCAA South II baseball regional in Tallahassee, Florida, Stanford won its first two games to put itself in position to advance to the College World Series, but two losses on May 23 to Western Carolina and Florida State eliminated the Cardinal.
- Stanford's reign of six consecutive women's tennis championships came to an end when Texas upset the Cardinal in the semifinals held at the Stanford Tennis Stadium.
- If Stanford were a country, it would have tied for 17th in the world with 19 medals at the 1992 Olympic Games in Barcelona. Stanford athletes won 10 gold medals, four silver and five bronze.

STANFORD MOMENT

Women's Hoops Win Second NCAA Title

Stanford won its second NCAA championship in women's basketball in 1992. *(Stanford Athletics)*

For the second time in three years, the Stanford women's basketball team came home with the NCAA championship trophy. The Cardinal finished the year 30-3 overall and 15-3 in the Pac-10 while winning its fourth straight conference title. After losing three key seniors from the previous year—Sonja Henning, Trisha Stevens and Julie Zeilstra—Stanford was not expected to contend for the national title in '91-92. An early season overtime win against defending champ Tennessee, however, gave Stanford confidence that it could play with the elite teams in the nation. Junior center Val Whiting earned First-Team All-America honors and was named the Pac-10 Player of the Year after averaging 18.5 points and 9.1 rebounds. Junior point guard Molly Goodenbour rose the occasion in the NCAA Tournament, earning Regional and Final Four MVP honors, while sophomore guard Christy Hedgpeth, freshman forward Rachel Hemmer and junior forward Chris MacMurdo also spearheaded Stanford's run to the national title In the Final Four, Stanford upset top-seeded Virginia 66-65 in the semifinal game to send it to the championship game against Western Kentucky. The Cardinal's 78-62 victory over WKU tied the record for the largest margin of victory in an NCAA women's championship game. Hemmer led the team with 18 points and 15 rebounds, Hedgpeth added 17, Whiting had 16 points and 13 boards while Goodenbour added 12 points and six assists.

STANFORD'S "NOW BOYS" entered the 1991 Aloha Bowl riding a seven-game winning streak, an 8-3 overall record and a number-17 national ranking. After winning its final seven games of the regular season, Denny Green had his Cardinal team in the midst of the longest winning streak on The Farm since 1951. But, on a sunny Christmas Day in Hawaii, Stanford let a 17-10 lead slip away in the final minute as Georgia Tech capitalized on a big play and beat the Cardinal, 18-17. "Touchdown" Tommy Vardell, who set school records with 1,084 yards rushing and 20 touchdowns, led the resurgent Cardinal to a second-place finish in the Pac-10 and its first bowl game since 1986. Vardell scored two TDs and rushed for 104 yards against Georgia Tech as Stanford built a 17-10 halftime lead. Vardell suffered a broken collarbone, was forced to leave the game early in the second half and watched as the Cardinal offense stalled. The Yellow Jackets' Willie Clay took a punt at his own six-yard line with 1:41 left in the game and promptly raced 63 yards to the Stanford 31. Eight plays later, QB Shawn Jones scored a TD from a yard out with 14 seconds left in the game, making the score 17-16. Georgia Tech's ensuing two-point conversion attempt was successful, giving them an 18-17 win.

Stanford Stat . . .

Kristin Klein was born to be an athlete. Her father, Bob, played in the NFL and her brother, Jimmy, was a football and volleyball player at Stanford. For Kristin, volleyball was her ticket. In four years on The Farm (1988-91), Klein was a four-time First-Team All-American, the 1991 National Player of the Year and the '91 Pac-10 Player of the Year. Her four Stanford teams went 103-21, including an 18-0 Pac-10 record her senior year. A member of the U.S. National team since 1992, Kristin earned a spot on the 1996 United States Olympic Team.

STANFORD LIST

Stanford Athletes won an amazing 19 medals at the 1992 Olympic Games in Barcelona. Below are the nine Cardinal medalists:

Name, Sport	Medals Won (Event)
Janet Evans	Women's Swimming
1 gold (800 free), 1 silver (400 free)	
Scott Fortune	Men's Volleyball
1 bronze (Team USA)	
Joe Hudepohl	Men's Swimming
1 gold (400 free relay), 1 bronze (800 free relay)	
Lea Loveless	Women's Swimming
1 gold (400 medley relay), 1 bronze (100 back)	
Pablo Morales	Men's Swimming
2 gold (100 fly, 400 medley relay)	
Kim Oden	Women's Volleyball
1 bronze (Team USA)	
Jeff Rouse	Men's Swimming
1 gold (400 medley relay), 1 silver (100 back)	
Summer Sanders	Women's Swimming
2 gold (200 fly, 400 medley relay), 1 silver (200 IM), 1 bronze (400 IM)	
Jenny Thompson	Women's Swimming
2 gold (400 free relay, 400 medley relay), 1 silver (100 free)	

Stanford ❦ LEGEND ❦

Adam Keefe

Adam Keefe held or shared 17 school records, including a Stanford-best 25.3 scoring average in 1991-92. (Stanford Athletics)

Adam Keefe's choice following his junior season in the spring of 1991 was clear: enter the NBA Draft where an estimated four-year, $4 million contract awaited, or return to Stanford for his senior season. To the elation of his coaches and teammates, Keefe chose Stanford. "Probably more than anything, staying here is going to mean friendships and keeping my friends. Being able to share this final year with my friends, and develop with them, is what's going to make it worthwhile," Keefe said in announcing his decision to stay in school. "If it's meant to be for me to be in the NBA, then it's going to be there next year. I don't think it's something requiring me to leave now to have happen." So Keefe stayed for the 1991-92 season, finished his career either holding or sharing 17 school records while leading his team to an appearance in the NCAA Tournament for only the third time in school history. He scored 734 points and grabbed 355 rebounds his senior year—both school records. His 25.3 points per game average in '92 was the best ever at Stanford and his 12.2 rebounds per made was the third best season on The Farm. Among all his records, he left The Farm with 2,319 points, number two at Stanford and number five in Pac-10 history, and 1,119 career rebounds, number one at Stanford and number four in the league record book. He was named First-Team All-Pac-10 for three straight seasons and was a Second-Team All-America selection as a senior. Keefe, who also played on the Cardinal men's volleyball team, was the 10th player chosen in the 1992 NBA Draft by the Atlanta Hawks. He married former Cardinal women's volleyball All-American Kristin Klein.

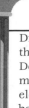

STANFORD NOTABLE

Dianne Feinstein was the first woman to represent California in the United States Senate, she was among the first women to be considered for selection as Vice President in 1984, and in 1990 she became the Democratic candidate for Governor of California, the first woman to be nominated for that position by a major party in California. A 1955 graduate of Stanford with a bachelor's degree in history, Feinstein was elected to a two-year term in the U.S. Senate in 1992, then re-elected for a six-year term in 1994. She became mayor of San Francisco in 1978 in the aftermath of the assassinations of Mayor George Moscone and Supervisor Harvey Milk. She served as mayor for an additional two terms.

1992-93

- November 3, 1992:   Bill Clinton won the presidential election, defeating incumbent George Bush and independent candidate Ross Perot.
- December 8, 1992:   The first United Nations-authorized troops landed in Somalia to assist the starving populace.
- February 26, 1993:   New York City's World Trade Center was bombed by terrorists.
- April 19, 1993:   Nearly 100 people perished in a fire to end the 51-day standoff of David Koresh's Branch Davidians against federal agents in Waco, Texas.
- June 20, 1993:   The Chicago Bulls defeated the Phoenix Suns, 99-98, to win their third consecutive NBA championship.

On its seventh trip to the Final Four, the Cardinal women's volleyball team finally won the national championship in 1992. (Stanford Athletics)

STANFORD MOMENT

Seventh Final Four A Charm

Six times before the Cardinal women's volleyball team had advanced to the Final Four. Three times before it had reached the championship match. But, on December 19, 1992, Stanford finally hit paydirt, exorcised its Final Four demons, winning the NCAA championship for all the great teams and greats players who left the Farm with everything but that magical trophy. For on this day, the underdog Cardinal, a team that was 30-2, was not supposed to beat the 33-0 Bruins. Many experts were calling UCLA the best women's volleyball team ever. They had already handed Stanford its only two losses of the season and the championship match was expected to make it official that the Bruins were the best team in the land. The Cardinal, however, had other plans. Led by All-Americans Bev Oden and Carrie Feldman, Stanford won the match 15-8, 15-9, 6-15, 15-10 in Albuquerque, New Mexico. Oden led the team with 21 kills, nine digs and a .452 hitting percentage, Cary Wendell had 16 kills and 12 digs while Feldman added eight digs, five blocks, two aces and a season-best 67 assists. Despite being labeled the underdog, the Cardinal was certainly no fluke. It finished the season winning 14 straight matches, during which time it lost only four games while winning 42, and its final record of 31-2 was the best in school history. In Stanford's 33 matches, only four times did an opponent win more than one game and in 22 of those matches, the Cardinal won in three straight games. Head coach Don Shaw, in his ninth season at the helm, fifth trip to the Final Four and fourth appearance in the championship match, finally had his championship ring.

NO SWIMMER IN STANFORD HISTORY was as versatile as Janel Jorgensen. You would need a road map to trace her success in all her individual and relay events. She was Stanford's workhorse from 1990-93. Sometimes overshadowed by the likes of Janet Evans and Summer Sanders, make no mistake about it, Stanford would not have won two NCAA team championships and finished second twice without Janel Jorgensen. In all four of her NCAA championship meets, Jorgensen competed in no less than three individual and three relay events each year. How impressive was she? Consider this: Jorgensen swam in 12 individual races in NCAA championship competition and finished first five times, second four times, third twice and fourth once. She was a member of 15 Cardinal relay teams in four NCAA meets, winning 10, placing second twice and third three times. That's 27 finishes in the top four in 27 races. That's 15 firsts and six seconds out of 27 races. She was named All-America on all 27 occasions—a Stanford record. Jorgensen also won a silver medal at the 1988 Olympic Games as a member of the U.S. 400 medley relay team. Quite impressive indeed.

Stanford Stat . . .

Bev Oden, the youngest of the three volleyball-playing Oden girls, followed in her sisters' footsteps by being named the nation's collegiate women's volleyball Player of the Year. Bev had some big shoes to fill as sister number three. Kim, the oldest, starred at Stanford from 1982-85 and was twice named Player of the Year (1984, 1985). Elaina, the middle sister, played at UOP from 1985-89, and was the National Player of the Year in 1986. And in 1990, Bev, in her sophomore season, was tabbed the Player of the Year. Bev earned First-Team All-America honors for four straight seasons (1989-92) and was a member of Stanford's first NCAA championship volleyball team in 1992.

STANFORD LIST

Most NCAA Team Championships by School
Stanford has been the most dominate athletic program in the nation over the last two decades. Since 1980, Stanford has won 56 NCAA team championships, far and away the most in the country. Below is how Stanford fares in the all-time NCAA championships list:

School	Mens'	Women's	Total
UCLA	61	15	76
USC	68	6	74
Stanford	48	22	70
Oklahoma State	42	0	42
LSU	12	19	31
Arkansas	29	0	29
Texas	12	16	28
Michigan	28	0	28
Yale	25	2	27
North Carolina	7	17	24
Penn State	20	3	23
UTEP	21	0	21
Wisconsin	18	2	20
California	20	0	20
Indiana	19	0	19
Denver	19	0	19
Ohio State	19	0	19

Stanford LEGEND

Val Whiting

Val Whiting graduated from Stanford as the school and Pac-10 leader in scoring and rebounding.
(Stanford Athletics)

Sports Illustrated wrote of Val Whiting in an article in November, 1992: "All-America and premed student doesn't begin to tell the story of Val Whiting. That description sounds too neat and ordered. The truth is, the boundaries blur, and each pursuit— books and basketball— constantly intrudes on the other, making her a sort of hybrid: Val Whiting, All-premed America." And that may have been an understatement. Perhaps no player in Stanford basketball history has earned the label "All-America" more than Val Whiting. Both on and off the court, Whiting was the consummate team player and leader, driven to success in every facet of her life. She was the 1989-90 national freshman Player of the Year, a First-Team All-American, Pac-10 Player of the Year and Naismith Player of the Year finalist in both 1991-92 and '92-93, and a member of both of Stanford's NCAA championship teams. During her four years on The Farm, her teams went 114-16 overall, 63-9 in the Pac-10, 62-1 at home in Maples Pavilion and 14-2 in the NCAA Tournament. She graduated with a degree in biology as the school and Pac-10 leader in points scored (2,077) and rebounds (1,134). She also set Stanford records for most games played (129) and most shots blocked (201). For four seasons, she averaged 16.1 points and 8.8 rebounds per game— numbers that may never be matched. Whiting, who said her "ultimate goal is to be a doctor" deferred starting medical school at U.C. San Francisco in order to play professional basketball overseas. In 1997, she played for the San Jose Lasers of the American Basketball League.

STANFORD LORE

At his inauguration speech on October 2, 1992, Gerhard Casper utilizes the "winds of freedom" theme— Stanford's unofficial motto—to discuss the freedoms and responsibilities that should guide universities. Stanford's ninth president offers an audience of 7,000 gathered in Frost Amphitheater a scholarly lesson on the derivation of the motto, mixed with low-key, self-deprecating humor. That wind, Casper said, must include the freedom to pursue knowledge, to challenge both established and new orthodoxies, to think independently and speak freely, and to find pleasure in the scholarly life.

·· SEASON HIGHLIGHTS ··

- The women's soccer team, led by All-Americas Julie Foudy and Sara Rafanelli, went 17-2-1 and reached the NCAA quarterfinals for the second straight season.
- Stanford swept the men's and women's swimming championships for the second consecutive year. It was the fourth NCAA title for the women and the sixth for the men.
- The Cardinal women's basketball team was upset in the NCAA West Regional semifinals, losing to Colorado 80-67. Stanford finished the year 26-6.
- For the first time since 1985, Stanford did not win a national championship in either men's or women's tennis. The women placed second while the men finished sixth.
- Forgettable seasons by the men's basketball and baseball teams resulted in a 7-23 record for the basketball team—the worst at Stanford since 1970-71—and a 27-28 record for baseball, the worst showing on The Farm since 1964.

The scoreboard tells the story: Stanford beat Notre Dame 33-16 in South Bend. (Stanford Athletics)

STANFORD MOMENT

Walsh vs. Holtz Ends in Classic Game

Bill Walsh had been to South Bend, Indiana for a football game on many occasions since retiring as head coach of the San Francisco 49ers. He had seen the Irish play many times, observed Lou Holtz on the sidelines numerous times and watched film of Notre Dame's offense and defense. That was all as a commentator for NBC's coverage of Notre Dame home games. Now, in his fifth game back in his return season as Stanford's head coach, Walsh once again sat in his office studying the Fighting Irish. And after the events of October 3, 1992, one would have to give Walsh a passing grade as he led his team to an improbable 33-16 win—Stanford's second consecutive upset win in South Bend. Stanford, 3-1 and ranked 18th nationally, went into South Bend to face a Notre Dame team that was 4-0 and ranked sixth in the country. What transpired was a magical moment for every Cardinal fan. Notre Dame sacked Stanford Cardinal quarterback Steve Stenstrom on the game's first play, then drove 55 yards on its opening possession and quickly led 9-0. A second-quarter TD put the Irish on top 16-0 and it seemed as though the rout was on. The Cardinal then reeled off 33 unanswered points and left no doubt who was the better team on this day. Stenstrom completed 21-of-32 for 215 yards, two touchdowns and no interceptions in a very efficient game while running back Glyn Milburn gained 119 yards and scored two TDs. But much of the credit was given to the Cardinal defense. The Irish, who gained 231 yards in the first half, was held to just 118 in the second half. Stanford forced five Notre Dame turnovers and held All-American quarterback Rick Mirer to a dreadful 13-of-38 afternoon. Cardinal free safety John Lynch was the spark on defense as he caused a fumble early in the second half that led to a Stanford TD, intercepted a pass in the end zone to thwart an Irish drive and put fear in the minds of Irish receivers who dared cross him.

THE CULMINATION of one of the greatest football seasons in Stanford history occurred on a New Year's Day, 1993 on a warm, overcast day in Miami. The Cardinal, co-champions of the Pac-10 for the first time in 21 years, played its first New Year's Day bowl game since the '72 Rose Bowl and came away with a resounding 24-3 victory over traditional power Penn State in the Blockbuster Bowl. Stanford finished the season 10-3 overall and ranked ninth in the final polls. It was the school's first 10-win season since 1940 and its highest final national ranking since 1970. The formula that had gotten the Cardinal to this point was once again deployed—a dominating defense and an effective offense. Stanford led 14-3 at halftime before its vaunted defense took over the game in the second half. PSU could muster just 29 rushing yards and 82 total yards while being shutout in the second half. Quarterback Steve Stenstrom completed 17-of-28 for 210 yards and two touchdowns, fullback Ellery Roberts gained 98 yards on the ground and running back Glyn Milburn's nifty 40-yard TD reception gave the Cardinal an insurmountable 24-3 lead late in the third quarter. Cornerback Darrien Gordon was named the game's MVP after his performance on Penn State's All-America receiver O.J. McDuffie. Gordon was credited with seven tackles and six pass break-ups.

Stanford Stat . . .

Stanford won four more NCAA team championships in 1992-93, bringing to nine the number of national titles won by Cardinal teams the past two years. The Cardinal won NCAA championships in women's volleyball—the first in school history—men's and women's swimming and men's gymnastics. Stanford was also named the NCAA's "Champion of Champions" for the seventh time in the last eight years, recognizing the school with the most NCAA team titles in a given year. During this eight-year span, Stanford teams won an unprecedented 27 national team championships.

STANFORD LIST

PACIFIC-10 CONFERENCE CAREER ALL-PURPOSE RUNNING

Three of the top 11 all-purpose runners in Pacific-10 Conference history are from Stanford, including two of the top three. The totals below include bowl games.

	Name, School	Years	Yards
1.	Charles White, USC	1976-79	7,226
2.	Darrin Nelson, Stanford	1977-81	6,885
3.	Glyn Milburn, Stanford	1990-92	5,970
4.	Napoleon Kaufman, Washington	1991-94	5,658
5.	Marcus Allen, USC	1978-81	5,657
6.	Anthony Davis, USC	1972-74	5,420
7.	Derek Loville, Oregon	1986-89	5,223
8.	Sean Burwell, Oregon	1990-93	4,972
9.	Russell White, California	1990-92	4,943
10.	Mike Garrett, USC	1963-65	4,828
11.	Vincent White, Stanford	1979-82	4,662

Stanford LEGEND

Glyn Milburn

Glyn Milburn earned the reputation as one of the most dangerous backs in college football. (Stanford Athletics)

While Denny Green and his staff struggled through a 3-8 season in 1989, a 5-9, 175-pound running back was waiting in the wings for his chance to play. Glyn Milburn, who played his freshman season at the University of Oklahoma in 1988, transferred to Stanford in 1989 and, by NCAA rules, had to sit out the season. He reminded Cardinal football followers of Darrin Nelson, another diminutive running back capable of scoring anytime he touched the ball.

Milburn was a spark, a human highlight reel, a menace to defenses who tried desperately to slow him down. But Milburn, who finished his career second at Stanford and third in the Pac-10 with 5,857 career all-purpose yards (not including bowl games)—he played just three years on The Farm from 1990-92—could run, catch, return punts and return kickoffs. In a word, he was fun to watch. In his first season as a Cardinal, Milburn set a school record with 2,222 all-purpose yards in 1990, which was also the second best season ever in Pac-10 history. He was a First-Team All-America selection in 1992 after gaining 2,121 all-purpose yards and leading Stanford to a 10-3 record and a Blockbuster Bowl win on New Year's Day. As a punt returner, Milburn was the most dangerous return man in college football in '92. He returned three punts for touchdowns and averaged 18.5 yards per return—both school records. He finished his career among the school's all-time best in rushing (third), receptions (tied for sixth), touchdowns (sixth), punt return yards (first), kickoff return yards (second) and all-purpose running (second). His 1990 Big Game vs. Cal in which he gained 194 yards rushing and a Pac-10 record 379 yards in all-purpose running will go down as one of the greatest offensive performances in Stanford history. Milburn was a second-round pick in the 1993 NFL Draft by the Denver Broncos.

STANFORD NOTABLE

It was during his sophomore year at Stanford University that Ted Danson became interested in drama. In 1972, Danson transferred to Carnegie-Mellon University in Pittsburgh, then began his journey to become an actor. Danson appeared in off-Broadway productions, daytime dramas a some feature films before landing the role of Sam Malone on NBC's hit comedy "Cheers," which ran for 12 years. Danson was nominated nine times for an Emmy Award for Best Actor in a Comedy Series and won twice. He also won two Golden Globe Awards playing Sam Malone.

1993-94

- October 6, 1993: Michael Jordan shocked professional basketball by announcing his retirement from the Chicago Bulls.
- October 23, 1993: Joe Carter hit a three-run home run in the bottom of the ninth inning of Philadelphia's Mitch Williams to give the Toronto Blue Jays their second consecutive World Series title.
- January 17, 1994: An earthquake in southern California killed 57 people.
- June 17, 1994: Former football star O.J. Simpson, charged with two counts of murder, led a convoy of police cars on a 60-mile chase before returning to his home.
- August 12, 1994: Major league baseball players went on strike. The balance of the season, including the World Series, was canceled on September 14.

Stanford won three aquatic championships in 1993-94, including women's swimming. *(Stanford Athletics)*

STANFORD MOMENT

Stanford Aquatics Sweep NCAA Championships

Stanford University turned the first aquatic hat trick in NCAA championship history in 1993-94: winning the NCAA title in water polo, men's swimming and women's swimming. DeGuerre Pool, home to all Cardinal aquatic teams, added three more championship trophies to an already full display. Dante Dettamanti led Stanford to its seventh national title in water polo in '93 after finishing with a 24-6 overall record. Five players earned All-America honors for Dettamanti's squad, including 1996 U.S. Olympians Jeremy Laster and Wolf Wigo along with Larry Bercutt, Antonio Busquets and Chris Wallin. Title number two in '93-94 belonged to Richard Quick's women's swimming team, who won the sixth championship in school history and third in a row under Quick. Jenny Thompson was once again the star for Stanford as she won the 100 free and 100 fly while anchoring two NCAA champion relay teams and taking second in the 50 free. Lea Loveless won the 100 back and took second in the 200 back and 200 IM. Stanford's men's swim team completed the hat trick by winning their third consecutive and seventh NCAA championship in school history. The Cardinal had five athletes win NCAA titles, including two by Brian Retterer (50 free, 100 back) and one each by Derek Weatherford (200 back), Tyler Mayfield (100 breast) and Kurt Grote (200 breast).

THE RISE OF THE STANFORD women's soccer program in the late 1980s and into the '90s can be traced to two players: Julie Foudy and Sara Rafanelli. Foudy came to Stanford in 1989; Rafanelli followed in 1990. The two were both four-time All-Americans and considered among the best players in women's soccer in the U.S. And they both brought Stanford to heights never before known. In 1993, Rafanelli, now a senior and without Foudy, led the Cardinal to its best finish ever—an 18-2-2 record and a trip to the Final Four. Rafanelli, who led Stanford in scoring three of her four seasons on The Farm, scored 59 goals in her career to go along with 34 assists and 152 points, all three Stanford records. During the '93 campaign, she scored 20 goals and accounted for 48 points, breaking two school records in the process. Stanford came within a penalty kick from advancing to the championship game in 1993 as the Cardinal lost a 1-1 tie-breaker with George Mason in the national semifinal game. In her four seasons, Rafanelli's teams went 67-9-4 and advanced to the NCAA Playoffs each season. Rafanelli was a member of the U.S. National Team in 1992-93 and an assistant coach at Stanford in 1994.

Stanford Stat . . .

Frank Brennan's record of success at Stanford is nothing short of phenomenal. Since his arrival in 1980, Brennan has transformed Stanford into, quite simply, the top women's tennis program in the United States. In 18 seasons at the helm, Brennan's teams have won an unprecedented nine NCAA team championships while recording a dual match record of 425-45—a winning percentage of .904. He has coached eight NCAA singles champions and led his team to four unbeaten seasons. He was named the NCAA Coach of the Decade for the 1980s after his teams won six national titles.

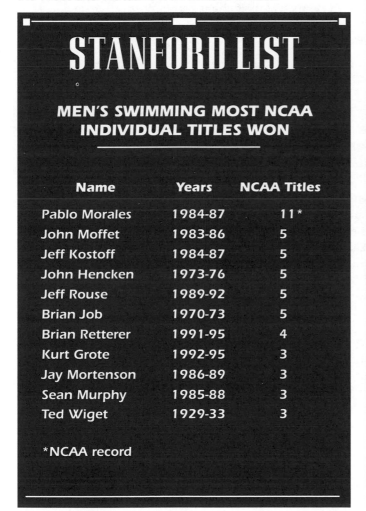

STANFORD LIST

MEN'S SWIMMING MOST NCAA INDIVIDUAL TITLES WON

Name	Years	NCAA Titles
Pablo Morales	1984-87	11*
John Moffet	1983-86	5
Jeff Kostoff	1984-87	5
John Hencken	1973-76	5
Jeff Rouse	1989-92	5
Brian Job	1970-73	5
Brian Retterer	1991-95	4
Kurt Grote	1992-95	3
Jay Mortenson	1986-89	3
Sean Murphy	1985-88	3
Ted Wiget	1929-33	3

*NCAA record

Stanford LEGEND

Jeff Rouse

Jeff Rouse was an Olympic champion, five-time NCAA champion and world-record holder. (Stanford Athletics)

Jeff Rouse had won an Olympic gold and silver medal, five individual NCAA titles, one NCAA team championship and was a world-record holder. But he wasn't satisfied. So, after his final season at Stanford in 1992, in which he led the Cardinal to the NCAA title and was named the Swimmer of the Year, and the '92 Olympic Games in Barcelona, Rouse dedicated himself to four more years of training. Why? Because his silver medal in Barcelona came in the 100 backstroke, an event in which he held the world record and an event he was favored to win. "I remember standing on the awards stand and listening to the anthem of Canada being played," Rouse said. "In my mind, it should have been the Star Spangled Banner. I remember committing myself right then to four more years. Winning the gold's been my dream for a long time." Four years later, in Atlanta, Rouse's dream came true. He won the gold medal in the 100 backstroke at the 1996 Games, and added a second gold in the 400 medley relay, giving him three golds and one silver in two Olympiads. His career was now complete. Rouse, who set the world record in the 100 backstroke while swimming the leadoff leg in the 400 medley relay at the '92 Barcelona Games, became the first swimmer in history to break the 55 second barrier in the 100-meter back. At the 1992 NCAA Championships, Rouse won three individual events (100 back, 200 back, 200 IM) and was a member of three national championship relay teams. Rouse continued to train at Stanford until his double-gold medal performance at the 1996 Olympic Games in Atlanta.

STANFORD LORE

Stanford graduate Amy Biehl was attacked and killed on August 25, 1993 in South Africa. Biehl, 26, was first drawn into study of African democratic movements while writing an honors thesis at Stanford. She was one of thousands of victims—and the first American to die—in the violence associated with South Africa's transition from apartheid to democracy. Biehl, 26, entered Stanford in 1985 and graduated in 1989 with a degree in international relations. She was a member of the Stanford diving team and captain her senior year.

·· SEASON HIGHLIGHTS ··

- Junior QB Steve Stenstrom broke John Elway's school and Pac-10 record by passing for 3,627 yards. He also tied Elway's school and conference record with 27 touchdown passes.
- The Cardinal women's basketball team suffered a rare loss at Maples Pavilion, but this one was costly. Purdue upset Stanford 82-65 in the NCAA West Regional finals, ending Stanford's bid for another Final Four appearance.
- Freshman Brevin Knight sparked the men's basketball team to a 17-11 overall record and an appearance in the NIT. He was named the Pac-10 Freshman of the Year.
- Stanford lost a heartbreaking 4-3 decision to USC in the NCAA men's tennis championship match.
- Freshman pitcher Jason Middlebrook tossed a no-hitter against UCLA on May 8, 1994 in the second game of a doubleheader. Middlebrook struck out 14 in Stanford's 3-0 win.

Stanford won its first NCAA men's golf championship in 41 years in 1994. (Allsport)

STANFORD MOMENT

Stanford Wins First Golf Championship in 41 Years

Stanford had six NCAA men's golf championships on its resume, but none since 1953. Forty-one years later, on June 4, 1994 at Stonebridge Country Club in McKinney, Texas, the Cardinal added number seven. Led by junior William Yanagisawa's final round 64, Stanford won the NCAA Championship by finishing the four-day event with a 23-under par 1,129, four strokes better than runner-up Texas. "This is the highest honor a team can give its coach," said Stanford head coach Wally Goodwin after winning his first NCAA title. "I've had a lot of kicks in life, but this is the greatest." Yanagisawa led Stanford with a 72-hole score of 277, which tied him for third in the tournament. Junior Notah Begay III shot 280, second best on the team and tied for fifth in the tournament. Casey Martin's 290, Steve Burdick's 292 and Brad Lanning's 299 rounded out the Cardinal scorecard. "This is a dream come true," said Begay, whose second day total of 62 set an NCAA Championship record and sent the Cardinal on their way to a 273, the lowest round of the tournament. "At times, I've imagined being the last man on the course, bringing the team in to win a national championship. But this is real. Today the dream came true," he said.

TWO OF THE GREATEST SWIMMERS in Stanford history could easily qualify as Cardinal legends: Derek Weatherford and Lea Loveless. Loveless, who transferred to Stanford in 1992 after swimming at Florida, won three straight NCAA championships (1992-94) on the Cardinal women's swimming team. Individually, she won four NCAA events, was a member of six NCAA championship relay teams and was named All-America 19 times. Loveless was a member of the 1992 Olympic Team and won one gold and one bronze medal in Barcelona. She set American records in the 100-yard back and the 100-meter back. Weatherford was a model of consistency during his four years (1991-94) on The Farm. He won two NCAA individual titles and was a member of five championship relay teams and was perhaps the team's most valuable swimmer during a career that included three NCAA team championships (1992-94) and one second-place finish (1991). He scored 184 points in NCAA competition, third all-time at Stanford behind Pablo Morales (235) and Jeff Kostoff (193). As a freshman in '91, Weatherford set an American record in the 200 backstroke and showed he would be a force for Stanford for years to come.

Stanford Stat . . .

By the time she began diving at the age of 14, Eileen Richetelli already had over 10 years of training in ballet and gymnastics. It was an easy transition to diving—one that Richetelli made easier by winning the U.S. Junior National one-meter championship at age 15. When she came to Stanford in September of 1990, she had already competed internationally and established herself as one of the nation's top young divers. She was twice named the NCAA Diver of the Year (1992, '93), won five individual NCAA diving championships and six Pac-10 championships while her teams won four straight NCAA titles. She is the only female diver in Stanford history to win an NCAA individual championship.

STANFORD LIST

STANFORD'S BEST GAMES UNDER BILL WALSH

Date	Opponent	Score
1977	UCLA	W, 32-28
1977	Cal	W, 21-3
1977	LSU	W, 24-14
1978	Cal	W, 30-10
1978	Georgia	W, 25-22
1992	Oregon	W, 21-7
1992	Notre Dame	W, 33-16
1992	UCLA	W, 19-7
1992	USC	W, 23-9
1992	Cal	W, 41-21
1-1-93	Penn State	W, 24-3
1993	Colorado	W, 41-37
1994	Washington	W, 46-28

Stanford LEGEND

Bill Walsh

A member of the Pro Football Hall of Fame, Bill Walsh is also one of Stanford's all-time great coaches. (Stanford Athletics)

Not only is Bill Walsh one of the great coaches in Stanford University history, but his name will forever live as one of the greatest coaches in football history. Walsh had three tours of duty at Stanford, one as an assistant coach (1963-65) and two as the Cardinal's head football coach (1977-78, 1992-94). In between his stints on The Farm, Walsh became the architect of the San Francisco 49ers for 10 seasons (1979-88), where he won three Super Bowl championships (1981, 1984, 1988) and was dubbed "The Genius" for his innovations that changed the game of football. He was named the NFL's Coach of the Decade for the 1980s and in 1993, Walsh was elected to the Professional Football Hall of Fame, becoming only the 14th coach in history to be elected to the Hall. Walsh was 46-years old when he took his first head coaching job at Stanford in 1977. He led the Cardinal to a 9-3 record and a victory in the Sun Bowl, then followed that with an 8-4 season and a Bluebonnet Bowl win in 1978. Walsh's two-year head coaching career at Stanford ended after the '78 season when the 49ers hired Walsh to turn their struggling franchise around. Four years after retiring from pro football following the 1988 season, Walsh returned to Stanford in '92 amidst a giddy celebration that had everyone on campus talking. The Walsh touch worked its magic once again in '92 as the Cardinal finished 10-3, beat Penn State in Blockbuster Bowl and finished ranked ninth in the nation, Stanford's first top-10 ranking since 1970.

STANFORD NOTABLE

Born August 15, 1938 in San Francisco, Stephen Breyer, Associate Justice of the United States Supreme Court, attended Lowell High School in San Francisco before matriculating to Stanford University, where he earned an A.B. degree in 1959. Breyer went on to Oxford University and the Harvard Law School, graduating magna cum laude in 1964. He was nominated by President Jimmy Carter on December 10, 1980 as a Judge for the U.S. Court of Appeals for the First Circuit. On August 3, 1994, Breyer was nominated by President Bill Clinton as an Associate Justice of the Supreme Court.

1994-95

- September 8, 1994:   USAir flight 427 crashed near Pittsburgh, killing all 132 on board.
- November 5, 1994:   Forty-five-year-old George Foreman became boxing's oldest heavyweight champion.
- November 8, 1994:   The Republicans won control of both houses of Congress for the first time in 40 years, rebuking Democratic president Bill Clinton.
- January 29, 1995:   The San Francisco 49ers won an unprecedented fifth Super Bowl title, beating the San Diego Chargers 49-26.
- April 19, 1995:   One hundred sixty-eight persons, including several children, were killed when the Federal Building in Oklahoma City was bombed. It was the deadliest terrorist attack ever on U.S. soil.

Freshman Kyle Peterson tied a school-record with 14 wins and led the Cardinal to an appearance in the College World Series. *(Stanford Athletics)*

STANFORD MOMENT

Baseball Team Returns to College World Series

Never before had a Stanford baseball team came from the losers' bracket, won two NCAA Regional games in the same day to stay alive before winning the regional final to advance to the College World Series. But on May 29, 1995 in Wichita, Kansas, the Cardinal did just that. Stanford had won its first two games in the Midwest Regional by one-sided scores of 10-3 over Arkansas and 8-1 over Lamar. But, game three vs. top-seeded Texas Tech put the Cardinal in the losers' bracket after a 3-1 defeat. In order to get to Omaha, Nebraska and the College World Series, Stanford was faced with winning three games in two days. First up came Lamar, who again proved no match for Stanford in a 16-9 Cardinal win. Later that day, Stanford forced a winner-take-all game by defeating Texas Tech 3-2, setting up a one-game playoff to decide the CWS participant. Eric Sees' two-out, RBI single in the bottom of the ninth made a winner of Mario Iglesias, who pitched a masterful game (complete game, two runs, five hits) against a Red Raider offense tabbed the best in the nation. With the May 29 sweep complete, the Cardinal rode the right arm of freshman Kyle Peterson and the explosive bat of Steve Carver to beat Tech 6-5 in the deciding game, sending Stanford to Omaha for the first time in five years. Peterson, named the Regional MVP, walked one and struck out 11 in tossing his second complete game of the regional. Carver, who had four home runs and 11 RBI in Wichita, had a home run and two RBI in the final game while Brian Dallimore, who hit .478 in the tournament, added two hits and a key RBI in the eighth inning which broke a 4-4 tie.

"**I'VE ALWAYS SAID** personal honors are not important. Volleyball is about teamwork, so the most important thing is how the team does. If I didn't get any honors and the team won the national championship, that would be fine with me." So said one of the great women's volleyball players to ever play on The Farm, Cary Wendell. During her four years at Stanford (1992-95), Wendell received both personal accolades and team success. Her four Cardinal teams won two NCAA championships (1992, 1994), two Pac-10 titles, went 114-13 overall and 64-8 in conference play. Wendell's athleticism, however, did not go unnoticed. She was twice named the National Player of the Year—in 1994 and '95—and was named First-Team All-America after her junior and senior seasons. As a sophomore, she was a Second-Team All-America and as a freshman, she was named the National Freshman of the Year. Wendell, a six-foot setter and outside hitter, graduated from Stanford in 1996 with degrees in political science and psychology.

Stanford Stat . . .

If there was a *Jeopardy* answer such as, "He is the greatest women's swimming coach in the country and one of the most respected in the world," the question would certainly be, "Who is Richard Quick?" Quick's teams have won 11 NCAA women's swimming championships in the last 14 years. He was the head coach of the 1988 United States Olympic Swim Team and the head women's coach of the 1996 U.S. Olympic Team. He has been Stanford's head women's swim coach for nine years (1989-97), during which time his teams won six NCAA titles, placed second on three occasions, won nine conference championships and went 67-1 in dual meets. Prior to coming to Stanford, Quick won five NCAA championships in six seasons as the head coach at Texas.

STANFORD LIST

CAREER PASSING LEADERS

1. Steve Stenstrom, 1991-94	10,531
2. John Elway, 1979-82	9,349
3. John Paye, 1983-86	7,669
4. Jim Plunkett, 1968-70	7,544
5. Guy Benjamin, 1974-77	5,946
6. Jason Palumbis, 1988-91	4,954
7. Mike Boryla, 1970-73	4,082
8. Dick Norman, 1958-60	3,737
9. John Brodie, 1954-56	3,594
10. Mike Cordova, 1973-76	3,556

Stanford LEGEND

Steve Stenstrom

During his four-year career, Steve Stenstrom re-wrote the Stanford record book. (Stanford Athletics)

Heading into the fifth game of the 1991 season, Cardinal head coach Denny Green found his team struggling with a 1-3 record when he turned to his redshirt freshman quarterback, Steve Stenstrom, and told him he would start the October 12 game against Cornell. Stenstrom, one might say, made the most of his opportunity. He proceeded to start the next 41 games for Stanford, break 11 school and seven Pacific-10 Conference records and become one of the most prolific passers in NCAA Division 1-A history. He threw for 10,531 career passing yards, placing him number-one in the Stanford and Pac-10 record book and number-seven on the NCAA's all-time passing list. He also set school and conference records for career total offense (9,825 yards) and was second to John Elway with 72 career touchdown passes. In his 41 games as the Cardinal's starting QB—a Stanford record—he threw for over 200 yards in a game 28 times, over 300 yards in 19 games and over 400 yards in three games. Once he was inserted into the starting lineup in '91, he led Stanford on a seven-game winning streak and an appearance in the Aloha Bowl. The next season, with Bill Walsh as his head coach, Stenstrom led the Cardinal to its first 10-win season since 1940 and its first New Year's Day bowl game since 1972. He followed that season in 1993 with a record-breaking campaign that included breaking Elway's school and conference record with 3,627 yards passing and tying Elway's records with 27 touchdown passes. Stenstrom earned his degree in political science in 1994, was selected in the fourth round of the NFL Draft by the Kansas City Chiefs and married Lori Heisick, a former All-American and NCAA champion swimmer at Stanford.

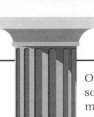

STANFORD LORE

On October 11, 1994, Stanford alums David Packard and William Hewlett provided the single largest gift in school history, $77.4 million, to complete a science and engineering quadrangle. Packard said the new mini-campus will enable Stanford to enter the 21st century with research facilities that rank second to none. Packard, who with Hewlett founded the pioneering Silicon Valley firm of Hewlett-Packard Co. in a garage in the late 1930s, said their success "was highly dependent on the research done at Stanford."

1994-95

·· SEASON HIGHLIGHTS ··

- Justin Armour broke Ken Margerum's school record for career receiving yards with 2,482. Armour became the second receiver in school history to surpass the 1,000 yard mark in a single season, accounting for 1,092 receiving yards.
- Wolf Wigo was named All-America for the fourth consecutive season as he led the water polo team to a 27-1 record and a second straight NCAA title.
- Stanford finished 30-3 and advanced to the women's basketball Final Four, where it lost to eventual champion Connecticut in the semifinals.
- Much-heralded freshman golfer Tiger Woods did not disappoint in his first season on The Farm, earning First-Team All-America honors and finishing fifth at the NCAA Championships.
- The men's golf team lost a one-hole playoff to Oklahoma State and settled for second place at the NCAA Championships.
- Freshman pitcher Kyle Peterson was named the National Freshman of the Year, Pac-10 Pitcher of the Year and First-Team All-America after going 14-1 with a 2.96 ERA.

Dion Cross' three-pointers helped the Cardinal beat UNC Charlotte for its first NCAA tourney win since 1942. *(Stanford Athletics)*

STANFORD MOMENT

Men's Hoops Win First NCAA Tourney Game Since 1942

It took Stanford 53 years to win another NCAA Tournament game, but on March 17, 1995, Stanford's 70-68 win over UNC Charlotte was the school's first since the 1942 NCAA championship game against Dartmouth. Guards Brevin Knight and Dion Cross and center Tim Young paved the way for the 10th-seed Cardinal, who upset the seventh-seeded 49ers at the Knickerbocker Arena in Albany, New York. Stanford, 19-8 overall entering the game, was making its fourth appearance in the NCAA Tournament and third under coach Mike Montgomery. The game was tight throughout, with UNC Charlotte holding its largest lead of nine points at 16-7 early in the game while the Cardinal's largest lead of seven points occurred with 14 minutes left in the game at 44-37. Neither team could pull away from the other. The Cardinal, led by Cross' three, three-pointers, led 30-26 at the half. After chipping away at Stanford's 44-37 lead in the second half, the 49ers took the lead at 66-65 with 1:34 left to play. Two free throws by Stanford's Andy Poppink and a layup by Bart Lammersen on a pass from Knight put the Cardinal on top 69-66 at the 1:03 mark. UNC Charlotte could not get another shot off until after David Harbour's free throw with 12 seconds left in the game put the Cardinal on top 70-66. Two days later, in the second round game, Stanford ran up against top-ranked UMass, which disposed of the Cardinal rather easily, 75-53.

STANFORD WON ITS FIRST Sears Directors' Cup after bringing home five NCAA team championships and having 21 teams finish in the top-10 nationally. In its second year of existence, the Sears Cup recognizes the nation's top overall athletic program. Stanford, which scored 971.5 points to runnerup North Carolina's 789.5, had an amazing year in '94-95. National championships were won by water polo, women's volleyball, women's swimming, men's gymnastics and men's tennis. It was the second time that Stanford won five team titles in one academic year (the other year was 1991-92) and only the third time in NCAA history that a school won five championships in one year. More impressive is the fact that 13 Cardinal teams finished among the top-five nationally and 21 were among the top-10. Stanford also won 14 conference titles, a school record. "I'm definitely proud to have played a part in this," said women's swimming coach Richard Quick. "It's very relevant and it's a pat on the back for the diversity of Stanford sports," said men's tennis coach Dick Gould.

Stanford Stat . . .

Brian Retterer did not know what to expect once he returned to the pool. It was during the 1992-93 season—his junior year—when Retterer suffered nerve and muscular damage to his shoulder. He was forced to redshirt the season and spend most of his time in the training room. When he did return to competitive swimming for the '93-94 season, Retterer was better than ever. He won two NCAA titles in '94 (50 free, 100 back), was a member of three NCAA-winning relay teams and helped his team win its third straight NCAA championship. Retterer broke the American record in the 100 back while swimming the leadoff leg of the 400 medley relay and his split in the 200 free relay was the fastest in history. Retterer won two more NCAA titles at the 1995 NCAA's (100 back, 200 back).

STANFORD LIST

NCAA WOMEN'S SWIMMING ALL-TIME TITLES WON

(the NCAA championship for women's swimming began in 1982)

Name, School	Individual	Relay	Total
Jenny Thompson, Stanford	9	10	19
Tracy Caulkins, Florida	12	4	16
Leigh Ann Fetter, Texas	7	8	15
Janel Jorgensen, Stanford	4	10	14
Marybeth Linzmeier, Stanford	8	3	11
Jill Sterkel, Texas	7	3	10
Jenna Johnson, Stanford	6	4	10
Summer Sanders, Stanford	6	4	10
Lea Loveless, Stanford	4	6	10
Kristin Quance, USC	8	1	9
Betsy Mitchell, Texas	7	2	9
Dara Torres, Florida	3	6	9

Stanford LEGEND

Jenny Thompson

Jenny Thompson's 19 NCAA championships is the most in collegiate history.
(Stanford Athletics)

Jenny Thompson is truly a legend in the sport of women's swimming in the United States. After her triple-gold medal performance at the 1996 Olympic Games in Atlanta, Thompson tied speedskater Bonnie Blair for the most Olympic gold medals in history (five) of any U.S. woman. Her total of six Olympic medals tied her for second behind Shirley Babashoff (eight) on the all-time U.S. list. She is a former world record holder, a 19-time NCAA champion and 26-time All-American—and those are just the highlights of an unparalleled career for the Dover, New Hampshire native. Thompson won gold medals in Atlanta as a member of three U.S. relay teams: 400 free relay, 800 free relay and 400 medley relay. At the 1992 Games in Barcelona, Thompson won a silver medal in the 100-meter freestyle and gold medals as part of the 400 free relay and 400 medley relay, which both set world records. She set a world record in the 100-meter free at the '92 Olympic Trials. On the collegiate level, her 19 NCAA championships (nine individual, 10 relays) is the most by any female in the history of the sport. Thompson won four straight NCAA 100 free titles (1992-95) while also winning the 50 free twice, the 100 fly twice and the 200 IM once. Her Stanford teams went 27-0 in dual meets and won four consecutive Pac-10 and NCAA championships. She was named the 1994-95 NCAA Female Athlete of the Year after completing another magnificent season in the pool. At the 1993 Pan Pacific Championships, Thompson won six gold medals, marking the second best individual performance at an international meet behind Mark Spitz's seven golds at the '72 Olympics. To call Jenny Thompson a legend in the sport of women's swimming is, indeed, an understatement.

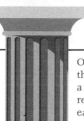

STANFORD NOTABLE

One of the most famous tandems in Stanford University history was William Hewlett and David Packard. Friends since their undergraduate days at Stanford, Hewlett and Packard formed a partnership on January 1, 1939 and, by the toss of a coin, named their new company Hewlett-Packard. Hewlett was born on May 20, 1913 in Ann Arbor, Michigan. He received a bachelor's degree from Stanford in 1934 and a degree of Engineer from Stanford in 1939. In between, he earned a master's in electrical engineering from M.I.T. in 1936. In 1940, HP recorded net revenues of $34,000 with three employees and eight products. By 1990, net revenue had reached $13.2 billion and the number of employees was 91,500.

1995-96

·· AMERICA'S TIME CAPSULE ··

- **September 6, 1995:** Baltimore Oriole shortstop Cal Ripken, Jr., played his 2,131st consecutive game before a sold-out crowd at Oriole Park in Camden Yards, breaking the record set by baseball legend Lou Gehrig in 1939.
- **October 3, 1995:** The "Trial of the Century" came to an end in Los Angeles when the jury, sequestered for 266 days, deliberated less than four hours and found O.J. Simpson not guilty of double murder.
- **April 3, 1996:** Federal agents seized the home of Theodore Kaczynski, thought to be the notorious Unabomber, sought for over 17 years in connection with a series of mail bombs that killed three and injured more than 20.
- **July 17, 1996:** TWA Flight 800, traveling from New York City to Paris, exploded and crashed into the Atlantic Ocean off the coast of Long Island, killing all 230 people aboard.
- **August 4, 1996:** The Summer Olympic Games, held in Atlanta, came to a close. Highlights included Carl Lewis' fourth consecutive gold medal in the long jump and Michael Johnson's victories in the 400-meter and 200-meter races.

Athletic Director Ted Leland is presented with the Sears Directors' Cup for the second straight year. *(Stanford Athletics)*

STANFORD MOMENT

Stanford Wins Second Straight Sears Cup

For the second consecutive year, Stanford University captured the Sears Directors' Cup and was once again labeled the best overall athletic program in the country. While Stanford won just two NCAA team championships in 1995-96 - compared to five in winning the Sears Cup in '94-95 - the overall depth of the Cardinal athletic program was simply overwhelming. Stanford finished with 961.5 points, well ahead of runner-up UCLA with 866. The two team championships went to Richard Quick's women's swimming team and Dick Gould's men's tennis team. Quick won his 11th NCAA title and sixth at Stanford while Gould placed championship trophy number 14 in his office. Stanford dominated the rest of the field by placing 23 teams among the nation's top-10 and 13 teams in the top-five - an impressive display of excellence by anyone's standards. Three Cardinal teams placed second in the nation (synchronized swimming, women's tennis, coed sailing) and three more took third place finishes (women's volleyball, women's basketball, men's gymnastics). Fourth place finishes went to men's swimming and men's golf while teams finishing in fifth place in the NCAA included men's cross country, women's golf and women's water polo.

Stanford SPOTLIGHT

THIS IS HOW THE 1995-96 SEASON was shaping up for the Cardinal women's basketball program before the year began: head coach Tara VanDerveer announced she would take a one-year hiatus to be the head coach of the 1996 U.S. Olympic Team, three starters were lost to graduation and the team's third-leading scorer, Kristin Folkl, announced she would stop-out of school to train with the United States National Volleyball team. For Amy Tucker and Marianne Stanley, named co-head coaches for the '95-96 campaign, the job ahead was indeed daunting. But, as with any great program, the winning tradition continued. All eyes of concern followed the team's season opening loss to UMass, but that was short-lived. The Cardinal proceeded to win its next six games and 29 of the next 30, including a school-record 23 straight, to win another Pac-10 title and advance to post-season play. Stanford reached the Final Four for the fourth time in six years, but lost to Georgia in the national semifinals to conclude its season 29-3.

Stanford Stat . . .

During his 11 years as Stanford's men's basketball coach, Mike Montgomery rebuilt a program that went 47 years between NCAA Tournament appearances and is now a regular in the 64-team field. Montgomery has brought his team to the NCAA Tournament five times during his tenure on The Farm, including three straight from 1995-97—a first at Stanford. His 1990-91 team did not make the 64-team NCAA field, but it won the 32-team NIT championship. Montgomery's 204-128 career record at Stanford makes him number two on the school's all-time list behind Howie Dallmar's 257 —a record that will likely fall during Montgomery's time on The Farm.

STANFORD LIST

STANFORD BASEBALL OLYMPIANS

1988 at Seoul, Korea (gold medalists)

Mark Marquess, Head Coach
Doug Robbins, C
Ed Sprague, 3B

1992 at Barcelona, Spain (fourth place)

Willie Adams, P
Jeffrey Hammonds, OF
Rick Helling, P

1996 at Atlanta (bronze medalists)

A.J. Hinch, C

Stanford LEGEND

A.J. Hinch

A.J. Hinch was a three-time All-American and a member of the '96 Olympic baseball team. (Stanford Athletics)

A.J. Hinch is one of the greatest players in Stanford baseball history and the best catcher ever on The Farm. After all, he is the only three-time first-team All-America and two-time Pacific-10 Conference Player of the Year in school history. He is the only player in Stanford history to be among the all-time top 10 in nine offensive categories, including games played (229), batting average (.351), home runs (31) and RBIs (191), among others. For four years (1993-96), Hinch started 228 games, most of them behind the plate. He was drafted out of high school and after his junior year at Stanford, but he turned down offers to play professional baseball both times to come to Stanford and complete his degree. He was team captain for the United States Olympic Baseball Team in 1996 that won a bronze medal in Atlanta. He was respected by his teammates both on an off the field. After being named the National High School Player of the Year, Hinch was selected in the second round of the 1992 Draft by the Chicago White Sox. He turned down their offer, accepted a scholarship to Stanford, hit .350 as a freshman and was named a freshman All-American. He hit .309 his sophomore season, .366 with nine homers and 58 RBI as a junior and .381 with 11 home runs and 59 RBI his senior year. He was twice named Pac-10 Player of the Year (1995, '96) and was a finalist for the Golden Spikes Award as the nation's top player in 1996. He was selected in the third round of the '96 Draft by the Oakland A's and began his professional career after the 1996 Olympic Games.

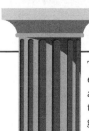

STANFORD LORE

The Rev. Jesse Jackson galvanized an enthusiastic crowd of 2,000 on November 14, 1995 in White Plaza, exhorting them to follow up the rallies and marches with affirmative political action in support of affirmative action. "It's not enough to have a big crowd and then have conservative action," Jackson told the gathering of Stanford students, faculty and staff and the community at large. "Young America, you have got to come alive," he said. "If you come alive, you can change the whole world. And when you come alive, don't glorify Woodstock, glorify Birmingham!"

1995-96

- The Cardinal women's volleyball team won 26-straight matches and advanced to the NCAA Final Four for the ninth time, but were upset by Texas on December 14, 1995 in the semifinal match.
- Stanford advanced to the second round of the NCAA men's basketball tournament for the second straight season, beating Bradley in the opening round and losing once again to UMass in the second round.
- Jessica Tong and Claudia Franco each won individual NCAA titles as the Cardinal women's swim team won its fifth straight NCAA championship on March 23, 1996.
- Stanford beat UCLA 4-1 on May 21, 1996 to capture its second straight NCAA men's tennis championship and 14th overall—all under head coach Dick Gould.
- A school-record 18-game winning streak by the baseball team ended on May 25, 1996 at the NCAA West Regional held at Sunken Diamond when Stanford lost two, one-run games to conclude its season with a 41-19 overall record.

First-year head coach Tyrone Willingham led Stanford to a berth in the 1995 Liberty Bowl. *(Stanford Athletics)*

STANFORD MOMENT

Cardinal Plays in 17th Bowl Game

Stanford entered the 1995 season picked to finish in last place in the Pacific-10 Conference, but first-year head coach Tyrone Willingham was not about to accept that prediction. In his first year as a head coach on any level, Willingham earned Pac 10 Coach of the Year honors after leading his team to a 7-3-1 regular season, a fifth-place finish in the Pac 10 with a 5-3 record and a trip to Memphis for the St. Jude Liberty Bowl—the 17th bowl appearance in school history. The Cardinal, however, did not play its best game on December 30 as East Carolina topped Stanford, 19-13. Still, the bowl game was nevertheless testimony to a tremendous season put together by Willingham and his squad. The Cardinal offense, which led the Pac 10 with a 30 points per game average, was less than effective against the Pirates. Stanford rushed for only 72 yards and turned the ball over four times while the defense kept the game close with one of its finest games of the year. ECU led 10-0 in the second quarter when fullback Adam Salina capped an 11-play, 69-yard drive by scoring from a yard out. Two field goals at end of the second quarter gave East Carolina a 16-7 halftime lead. With its offense struggling, the Cardinal's comeback hopes were contingent upon a big play by the defense or special teams—and they got one. Early in the third quarter, Stanford cornerback Kwame Ellis, named the game's MVP, scooped up a blocked punt and raced into the end zone from two yards out for a touchdown. Nicodemus Watts was credited with the blocked punt, which brought the Cardinal within a field goal at 16-13. But the Cardinal could muster no more points as ECU added a field goal and held on for a 19-13 victory.

KRISTIN FOLKL would sit atop any list of the most talented female student-athletes in Stanford history. Her accomplishments as a volleyball and basketball player on The Farm after her first three years puts her in a category all by herself. Kristin Folkl proved to be one of the nation's best volleyball players, while at the same time showcasing her skills on the basketball court despite playing part time. She led Stanford to NCAA volleyball titles as a freshman in 1994 and junior in 1996 while earning All-America honors each season. Following the '95 volleyball season, Folkl decided to stop-out of school to train with the U.S. National Team. She wound up being the first alternate for the 1996 U.S. Olympic Team. In basketball, Folkl played for the Cardinal her freshman season in 1995, but did not play in '96 because she was with the U.S. volleyball team. She was named a pre-season All-America in basketball prior to the '97 season even though she had not yet decided to play. She eventually did return to the basketball team in February of '97 and helped spark the Cardinal to another Pac-10 title and a trip to the Final Four. In only three years, Kristin Folkl had already established herself as one of the great athletes in Stanford history.

Stanford Stat . . .

Maureen McLaren's record of six NCAA team championships is one record that may never be broken. A 6-1 outside hitter on the women's volleyball team and a backstroker on the Cardinal women's swimming team, McLaren was a member of four straight NCAA championship teams in swimming (1993-96) and two in women's volleyball (1992, 1994). She became the first woman in school history to win two NCAA team titles in one academic year in 1992-93, then she matched that feat in 1994-95. McLaren was a three-time All-American in swimming and a key reserve for the women's volleyball team for four years.

STANFORD LIST

TIGER WOODS' CHRONOLOGY

- Appears on "Mike Douglas Show" with Bob Hope at age 2
- Appears on "That's Incredible" at age 5
- Wins International Junior World championship five times between ages 8-14
- Wins U.S. Junior National Championship at age 15, 16 and 17
- Wins U.S. Amateur Championship at age 18, 19 and 20
- Enters Stanford University at age 18 in the Fall of 1994
- Wins 1996 NCAA championship as a sophomore
- Named First-Team All-America and Pac-10 Player of the Year in both 1995 and '96
- Announces he is leaving Stanford and turning pro in August, 1996 at age 20
- Wins his third professional tournament
- Wins the 1997 Masters by a record 12 strokes at age 21—youngest champion in history

Stanford LEGEND

Tiger Woods

The rise to superstardom for Tiger Woods began at age two and culminated in the 1997 Masters championship. (Stanford Athletics)

The legend of Tiger Woods began at the tender age of two, when he appeared on the "Mike Douglas Show" putting with Bob Hope. By the time Tiger was 21, his legend had grown into one of international fame and fortune matched only by the likes of Michael Jordan. Indeed, Tiger's two-year stint at Stanford was memorable: two-time All-American, NCAA champion, two-time Pac 10 Golfer of the Year, NCAA Golfer of the Year—but it was after his departure from The Farm in 1996 that Tiger's meteoric rise began to unfold. When he came to Stanford in the fall of 1994, Tiger had become the youngest player ever to win the U.S. Amateur championship, which he did the previous summer as an 18-year-old. He proceeded to win the U.S. Amateur the next two years, in 1995 and '96, while also winning the 1996 NCAA championship. In his second year at Stanford, Tiger won eight tournaments, finished second three times and third once in 14 tournaments. After winning the NCAA's and his third straight U.S. Amateur, Tiger decided to leave Stanford in August of 1996 and join the pro tour. His first win as a professional came less than two months after he joined the tour as he won the Las Vegas Invitational in October. But it was his 14th pro event that catapulted Tiger-mania into overdrive. In a record-setting display of domination, Tiger won his first Green Jacket by winning the 1997 Masters by a record 12-strokes while becoming the youngest player to ever win the Masters. He won his next event as well, giving him five tour wins in his first 15 events. The legend of Tiger Woods will be written in the years ahead.

STANFORD NOTABLE

David Packard was an engineer with the General Electric Co. from 1936-38 before returning to Palo Alto, California to begin a partnership with his Stanford classmate, William Hewlett. Packard earned a B.A. from Stanford in '34 and a master's in electrical engineering in '39. The two began working part-time in the garage with $538 in working capital. Packard held the position of President of Hewlett-Packard Co. from 1947-64. He took a two-year hiatus from the company from 1969-71 to become the U.S. Deputy Secretary of Defense in the first Nixon Administration. He returned to HP in 1972 and was the Chairman of the Board until his retirement in 1993. He died on March 26, 1996 at the age of 83.

1996-97

- **September 14, 1996:** Troops for the United States and other countries monitored implementation of a peace accord between the three warring factions in Bosnia and Herzegovina.
- **September 26, 1996:** U.S. astronaut Shannon Lucid ended a 188-day stay in space, which was longer than any other American or any other woman in history.
- **November 5, 1996:** Bill Clinton was reelected to a second term as U.S. President, easily defeating former Kansas senator Bob Dole. Clinton won 31 states.
- **April 13, 1997:** Former Stanford golfer Tiger Woods, at the age of 21, became the youngest person in history to win the Masters' Golf Tournament. His 12-stroke victory was the largest in the history of the event.
- **June 2, 1997:** Timothy McVeigh was found guilty of the worst act of domestic terrorism in American history, the bombing of the Alfred P. Murrah Federal Building in Oklahoma City that killed 168 people in 1995.

Led by All-America point guard Brevin Knight, Stanford advanced to the "Sweet Sixteen" for the first time since 1942. (Stanford Athletics)

STANFORD MOMENT

Men's Hoops Advances to Sweet Sixteen For First Time Since 1941-42

The Stanford men's basketball program reached new heights during the 1996-97 season as it advanced to the Sweet Sixteen in the NCAA Tournament for the first time since the 1941-42 team won the national title. It was a special season on The Farm. A talented group of freshmen and sophomores and their 7-1 center rode the back of their 5-10 point guard to a 22-8 season and a near-miss into the Elite Eight. Brevin Knight, the lifeline of the team for four years, was the ringleader once again. He was the focal point for Stanford throughout the season—and he did not disappoint. Center Tim Young, only the second seven-footer in Stanford history (along with Rich Kelley), returned from a back injury in 1996-97 to give the Cardinal a legitimate inside game. Stanford finished tied for second in the Pac-10 with a 12-6 reading and earned its third straight trip to the NCAA Tournament. At the West Regional in Tucson, the Cardinal beat Oklahoma and Wake Forest to advance to the Sweet Sixteen. There, Knight almost willed his team one step further. His 22-point second-half performance against second-ranked Utah, which included a leaning three-pointer with 7.1 seconds remaining in regulation, allowed the Cardinal to tie the score at 67-67 and send the game to overtime. Unfortunately for Knight and Co., the Utes prevailed 82-77 and Stanford's Cinderella march to the Final Four ended, but not before concluding the best season on The Farm in 55 years.

1996-97 WAS A RECORD-BREAKING YEAR for Stanford Athletics as Cardinal teams won an unprecedented six NCAA team championships and took home the Sears Directors' Cup for the third straight season. Only three times before had a school won five NCAA titles in a single season—and two of them belonged to Stanford, in 1991-92 and again in 1994-95. In the fall, Stanford took home NCAA championships in men's and women's cross country, the first titles in those sports in school history and the first for head coach Vin Lanana. Don Shaw led his women's volleyball team its third title in five years in the most lopsided final match in history as Stanford swept past Hawaii 15-7, 15-3, 15-5. The Cardinal men's volleyball team won its first NCAA championship by beating UCLA 15-13 in the fifth game to give coach Ruben Nieves his first championship ring. Stanford tennis continued its domination as both the women's team and men's team won the national crown. Frank Brennan's women's team beat Florida 5-1 for the title while Dick Gould won his 15th championship as his men's team shutout Georgia 4-0 in the championship match.

Stanford Stat . . .

Stanford has had many notable baseball-football dual-sport athletes, but none who became the starting quarterback in a bowl game and starting pitcher in the College World Series. Enter Chad Hutchinson, who turned down a $1.5 million offer from the Atlanta Braves, who had made him their number-one draft pick, to come to Stanford and play both sports. Hutchinson redshirted his freshman season in football, but went on to be a freshman All-American in baseball. In his second year on The Farm, he was the football team's starting quarterback and was named the Offensive MVP in the '96 Sun Bowl. In the spring, as Stanford's number-two pitcher in the starting rotation, he started the opening game vs. Auburn in the 1997 College World Series in Omaha, Nebraska.

STANFORD LIST

CHAMPIONSHIP COACHES

Which Stanford coach has won the most NCAA team championships? Listed below are the coaches who have won at least two NCAA championships at Stanford.

Coach	Sport, NCAA Championships	
Dick Gould	Men's Tennis	15
Frank Brennan	Women's Tennis	9
Dante Dettamanti	Water Polo	7
Skip Kenney	Men's Swimming	6
Richard Quick	Women's Swimming	6
Eddie Twiggs	Men's Golf	5
Sadao Hamada	Men's Gymnastics	3
Don Shaw	Women's Volleyball	3
Dink Templeton	Men's Track	3
Mark Marquess	Baseball	2
Tara VanDerveer	Women's Basketball	2
Vin Lananna	Cross Country	2

Stanford LEGEND

Brevin Knight

Brevin Knight was one of the most exciting players in Stanford basketball history.
(Stanford Athletics)

When he came to Stanford in the fall of 1993 from Seton Hall Prep in New Jersey, Brevin Knight was an unheralded 5-8 point guard who was overlooked by college recruiters. Except at Stanford, where Knight proceeded to start 114 games over the next four years and become one of the all-time great basketball players in school history. He was the spark plug who quarterbacked his team to unprecedented heights—three straight NCAA Tournament appearances and a trip to the Sweet Sixteen his senior year. With Knight at the helm, Stanford became one of the most dangerous teams in college basketball. "Brevin's infectious," said Cardinal coach Mike Montgomery. "He just doesn't look at things as something he can't conquer. He did so much for our team and had to carry so much of the responsibility for four years. He's a very special player." Indeed his credentials put him in a category by himself. He finished his career as the Stanford record holder in career and season assists and career and season steals. His 1,714 points puts him third on Stanford's all-time scoring list. He was the Pacific 10 Conference Freshman of the Year in 1993-94, then earned first-team All-Pac 10 honors the following three seasons. Brevin was a first-team All-America in 1996-97, a finalist for the John Wooden Award as the nation's top player and winner of the Francis Pomeroy Naismith Award as the best college player under six-feet. Knight was a first-round draft pick in the 1997 NBA draft.

STANFORD LORE

In a nationally televised news conference on August 7, 1996, a NASA/Stanford research team announced that it found evidence that strongly suggests that microscopic life may have existed more than 3.6 billion years ago on the planet Mars. "For me, this touches on the fascinating question, "Are we alone?" said Stanford chemistry Prof. Richard Zare, who was asked by NASA some two-and-a-half years prior to analyze meteorite samples for organic compounds. Stanford researchers, led by Zare, detect the first organic molecules of Martian origin in a meteorite that scientists believe originated on Mars billions of years ago.

1996-97

·· SEASON HIGHLIGHTS ··

- Not only did Cardinal teams won a record six NCAA team championships, but Stanford had 20 teams finish among the nation's top-10, 15 among the top-five, four placed second in the nation and 16 teams won their league championship.
- Stanford teams won a national-best 26 NCAA team championships in a six-year period beginning with the 1991-92 season.
- Freshman Kerri Walsh was named the NCAA Final Four MVP after leading the women's volleyball team to the NCAA championship.
- Tara VanDeerver led her women's basketball to a 34-2 overall record and another trip to the Final Four, but lost a heart-breaking 83-82 decision to Old Dominion in the semifinal game.
- The Cardinal won the Pac-10 Southern Division championship, went 4-0 at the NCAA West Regionals held at Sunken Diamond and made its 10th appearance in the College World Series, finishing tied for third in the country.

QB Chad Hutchinson was named the Sun Bowl Offensive MVP after completing 22-of-28 passes for 226 yards. (Stanford Athletics)

STANFORD MOMENT

Cardinal Shuts Out Michigan State, 38-0, in Sun Bowl

It was the most lopsided bowl game victory in school history and it was every bit as one-sided as the score would indicate. Stanford's 38-0 win over Michigan State on December 31, 1996 in the Norwest Sun Bowl was not only the school's first shutout in 22 seasons, but it capped what has to be called the greatest comeback a Cardinal team has ever made in the 102-year history of Stanford football. There were not many people who counted the Cardinal as bowl contenders after Stanford saw its record dip to 2-5 on October 25. But, second-year head coach Tyrone Willingham somehow rallied his troops to four straight wins to end the regular season and finish in third place in the Pac-10, qualifying Stanford for a trip to El Paso, Texas and the Norwest Sun Bowl. The game was a complete dismantling by Stanford over the Spartans. The Cardinal scored touchdowns on offense, defense and special teams, led 21-0 at the half and never gave MSU a chance to get back in the game. Sophomore QB Chad Hutchinson (22-of-28, 226 yards, one TD) was named the game's Offensive MVP while junior defensive end Kailee Wong (10 tackles, three tackles-for-loss, two quarterback sacks) earned Defensive MVP honors. Stanford ended the season with five consecutive wins and a 7-5 overall record, which included a 42-21 win over Cal in the Big Game and a 38-0 win in the Sun Bowl.

MAKE NO MISTAKE ABOUT IT, Kyle Peterson is a "Legend" in Stanford athletic history. If there was a better, more consistent pitcher for three years on The Farm, you would be hard-pressed to convince many people. Simply put, Peterson was Stanford's best pitcher for three years (1995-97), led his teams to two College World Series appearances, broke Jack McDowell's career strikeout record (363) and Stan Spencer's single-season strikeout record (156), was a three-time All-America and three-time All-Pac-10 selection, was twice named the Pac-10 Pitcher of the Year, was the 1995 NCAA Freshman of the Year and was first-round selection (13th pick overall) in the June, 1997 Major League Baseball Draft by the Milwaukee Brewers. Peterson ended his career with a sparkling 35-9 record, matching McDowell's career win total and just two behind the 37 wins by Stanford record holder Jeff Ballard. He was also third all-time in innings pitched with 398.1. In his three seasons, Peterson went 14-1 as a freshman, 10-5 as a sophomore and 11-3 as a junior and is the only Cardinal pitcher—along with McDowell—to post three straight 10-win seasons.

Stanford Stat . . .

Freshman Lilia Osterloh became the seventh woman in Stanford history to win the NCAA singles crown when she beat M.C. White of Florida 6-1, 6-1 on May 23, 1997 at the Taube Family Tennis Stadium. Osterloh, from Columbus, Ohio, needed only 50 minutes to dispose of White. "I think I was in a zone," said Osterloh. "I had to play my game, worry about myself." Four days earlier, Osterloh led her team to a 5-1 win over Florida in the NCAA team championship match, giving Stanford its 10th overall national championship in women's tennis and first since winning six straight from 1986-91.

STANFORD LIST

WOMEN'S BASKETBALL PLAYERS IN THE PROS

Player, Years at Stanford	League	Team
Jennifer Azzi, 1987-90	ABL	San Jose Lasers
Molly Goodenbour, 1990-93	ABL	Richmond Rage
Christy Hedgpeth, 1991-94	ABL	Seattle Reign
Rachel Hemmer, 1992-95	ABL	Atlanta Glory
Sonja Henning, 1988-91	ABL	San Jose Lasers
Anita Kaplan, 1992-95	ABL	San Jose Lasers
Kate Paye, 1992-95	ABL	Seattle Reign
Charmin Smith, 1993-96	ABL	Portland Power
Kate Starbird, 1994-97	ABL	Seattle Reign
Katy Steding, 1987-90	ABL	Portland Power
Val Whiting, 1990-93	ABL	Seattle Reign
Jamila Wideman, 1994-97	WNBA	Los Angeles Sparks

Stanford LEGEND

Kate Starbird

Kate Starbird was named the 1997 College Basketball Player of the Year. (Stanford Athletics)

Watching Kate Starbird run the floor and drive to the hoop, or pull up for outside jumper, or knock down a three-pointer is like watching Picasso paint, or Sandy Koufax pitch, or Joe Montana play quarterback. Keep the camera rolling, show it to the youngsters and tell them this is how it's supposed to be done. For four years, Kate Starbird made more baskets and scored more points than any woman basketball player in Stanford history. She was a scoring machine, an opposing coaches' nightmare. As a senior in 1996-97, Starbird set a Stanford record by scoring 753 points, averaging 20.9 points per game and being named the Naismith Award winner as the nation's College Player of the Year. She was also a consensus first-team All-America and Pac 10 Player of the Year. In her four seasons on The Farm, her teams advanced to the Final Four three times, posted an overall record of 118-14 and a Pac 10 mark of 68-4, including back-to-back 18-0 conference records. She set the Stanford single-game scoring record her junior season in 1995-96 by scoring 44 points vs. USC. She scored 40 points, again vs. the Trojans, the following year and became the only Cardinal player to score more than 40 points in a game on two occasions. Following her senior season, Starbird was a first-round draft choice by the Seattle Reign of the American Basketball League.

STANFORD NOTABLE

Of Warren Christopher, President Bill Clinton said that "the cause of peace and freedom and decency have never had a more tireless or tenacious advocate than Warren Christopher. Today, if the children of the Middle East can imagine a future of cooperation, not conflict; if Bosnia's killing fields are once again playing fields; in no small measure, it is because of Warren Christopher," said Clinton at a ceremony on November 7, 1996 at which Christopher, the 63rd Secretary of State of the United States, announced his intention to return to the private sector. Christopher attended the Stanford Law School from 1946-49, held the position of Deputy Secretary of State of the U.S. from 1977-81 and Secretary of State from 1993-97.

tanford University has a proud and rich tradition of student-athletes who have earned varsity letters. Since the University was founded in 1891, thousands of Stanford students have earned recognition as varsity letter-winners. In this list, we have used all the resources available to compile the names of all those varsity letterwinners. Unfortunately, accurate and complete information simply does not exist for many sports and for many years. In fact, very little information exists prior to 1940. Therefore, this is a list of student-athletes who have earned varsity letters, not an all-time list and, admittedly, not without inconsistencies. Please contact the Stanford Media Relations Office if you discover an omission or error and it will be corrected for future publications.

Key for sport abbreviations:men's track = mtrk, men's water polo = mwp, football = ftb, men's gymnastics = mgym, baseball = bsb, wrestling = wrestling, men's crew = mcrew, men's volleyball = mvball, men's golf = mgolf, men's track = mtrk, men's basketball = mbsk, women's crew = wcrew, men's cross-country = mxc, women's cross-country = wxc, men's diving = mdive, women's diving = wdive, men's swimming = mswim, women's swimming = wswim, women's gymnastics = wgym, women's golf = wgolf, women's soccer = wsoc, men's soccer = msoc, synchronized swimming = syncswim, women's tennis = wten, men's tennis = mten,women's track = wtrak, women's volleyball = wvball, women's water polo = wwp, men's fencing = mfenc, women's fencing = wfenc.

Abbink, Matt mtrk	1995	Ahearn, Kerry mcrew	1967	Allen, Ronald mtrk	1950, 52
Abbott, Robert mwp	1983, 87	Ahlquist, Richard bsb	1946, 48	Allen, Thomas wrest	1963, 64
Abello, Tovi mtrk	1993, 94, 95	Ahrens, Tamara wcrew	1991	Allen, Tracy wsoc	1988
Abena, Tim D. ftb	1966, 67, 68	Ahumada, Albert mgym	1961	Allen, Wendy wtrack	1988, 89, 90
Abernatahy, William mgym	1957, 58, 59	Aimonetti, Steve ftb	1980, 82, 83	Allison, Jennifer wtrack	1989
Abraham, Jane wswim	1983, 84	Aimonetti, Steve mtrk	1980, 83	Allison, John mcrew	1961, 62
Abraham, Richard P. ftb	1945, 50, 51	Ainsworth, Lawrence mgym	1946, 47, 48	Alloo, Charles mten	1966, 67, 68, 69
Abrahamson, Arthur bsb	1951, 52	Akers, Kim wcrew	1990	Allsop, Brett mxc	1990
Abrams, Eric ftb	1992, 93, 94, 95	Alarcon, Ramon mtrk	1991, 93	Alstrom, John mvball	1988, 89, 90, 91
Accetta, Alex mtrk	1990, 91, 92	Albaugh, Brad mcrew	1989	Alustiza, Alfonso ftb	1937
Accetta, Alex, mxc	1988, 89, 90	Albers, Richard mgolf	1956, 57	Alustiza, Frank ftb	1933, 34, 35
Achenbach, Michael wrest	1972, 73	Albert, Frankie ftb	1939, 40, 41	Alustiza, John ftb	1969
Acker, Michael bsb	1953, 54	Albert, Seyon, ftb	1990, 91, 92	Alverado, Donald R. ftb	1971, 72
Adama, C.C. ftb	1892	Albertson, Kendall ftb	1928, 30, 31	Amado, Ralph mfenc	1951, 52, 53, 54
Adamek, Shawn mgym	1990, 91, 92, 93	Albertson, Macellus O. ftb	1929, 30, 32	Amaro, Ruben bsb	1984, 85, 86, 87
Adams, Barrett mcrew	1995, 96	Alborough, James mtrk	1986, 88	Ambler, Burton wrest	1967, 69
Adams, David bsb	1928	Alborough, James mxc	1985, 87, 88	Ammann, Kenny mbsk	1990, 91
Adams, Doug ftb	1971, 72	Albright, Bill mcrew	1977	Ammirato, Michael bsb	1967, 68, 69
Adams, Frederic L. ftb	1917, 19, 20	Albritton, Terry mtrk	1977	Amoroso, Dina wgym	1987, 88, 89, 90
Adams, Frederick mbsk	1920, 21	Alderman, Jessica wtrack	1992, 93	Amstutz, Mark mvball	1985, 88
Adams, John wrest	1955	Aldrete, Mike bsb	1980, 81, 82, 83	Anchondo, Robert mtrk	1967
Adams, Jon mtrk	1971	Alex, Mark wrest	1984, 85, 86	Anchondo, Robert mtrk	1969
Adams, P.A. ftb	1897	Alexander, Arthur wrest	1952	Anchondo, Robert mxc	1966, 68
Adams, Tess wtrack	1987, 88	Alexander, Charles mtrk	1983, 84, 86, 87	Andersen, Stanley mtrk	1938, 39, 40
Adams, William bsb	1939	Alexander, Charles mxc	1983, 84	Anderson, Arne R. mbsk	1934, 35
Adams, Willie bsb	1991, 92, 93	Alexander, Joe mcrew	1968	Anderson, Chris wvball	1977, 78, 79, 80
Adams, Woodrow G. ftb	1933, 34, 35	Alexander, William F. ftb	1969, 70	Anderson, Dana wswim	1986, 87, 88, 89
Adamson, Kelly wsoc	1995	Allaway, Darren mbsk	1993, 94, 95, 96	Anderson, Daniel mgolf	1966
Adelman, Samuel mgolf	1967, 68, 69	Allen, David mgym	1949, 50	Anderson, Dean mwp	1972, 73, 74
Adkins, Ann wbsk	1988, 89, 91, 92	Allen, Dusty bsb	1992, 93, 94, 95	Anderson, E. Martin Jr. ftb	1946, 47, 48
Adu, Florence wtrack	1992, 93, 94, 95	Allen, Ethan ftb	1992, 93, 94	Anderson, Edward W. mbsk	1925, 26, 27
Afflerbaugh, Jack K. ftb	1931, 32, 33	Allen, Harold K. ftb	1931, 32, 33	Anderson, Forrest A. mbsk	1940, 41
Agar, James bsb	1951, 52	Allen, Jack bsb	1962	Anderson, Frank mvball	1978, 79, 80
Aguilera, Chris mwp	1994	Allen, Jeff ftb	1995	Anderson, Frederick L. mbsk	1922, 23
Aguirre, Jimmy wrest	1992, 94, 95, 96	Allen, Jeff mtrk	1995, 96	Anderson, Gary mcrew	1967
Aguirre, Mickey bsb	1972	Allen, Robert mwp	1937, 38, 39	Anderson, Gary A. ftb	1973, 74, 75, 76

Anderson, Harold wrest	1964	Angove, Jerry mtrk	1954	Arnold, Ian mtrk	1967, 68
Anderson, Hillary wgym	1993, 94	Angove, Jerry C. ftb	1955, 56	Arnold, Mark mgym	1984, 85
Anderson, John mtrk	1971, 72, 73	Anhalt, Eric ftb	1989, 90	Arnold, Robert mwp	1976, 77, 78
Anderson, Karni wbsk	1985, 86, 87, 88	Annixter, Benjamin mtrk	1959	Arnstein, Timothy mten	1960
Anderson, Karen wvball	1987, 88, 89	Antonucci, Tonya wsoc	1986, 87, 88, 89	Arons, Jeff mten	1979, 80, 81, 82
Anderson, Ken mcrew	1959	Appleman, Nicole wvball	1988, 89,90, 91	Arrell, James L. ftb	1910
Anderson, Martha fh	1975, 76	Arce, William bsb	1947, 48, 49	Arrillaga, John mbsk	1958, 59, 60
Anderson, Martin mtrk	1945, 46, 47, 48	Arch, Dennis J. ftb	1966	Arriola, Dennis mtrk	1980, 81
Anderson, Nancy wten	1974, 75, 76, 77	Arch, Stephen mtrk	1962, 63, 64	Arterberry, Melvin Jr. mbsk	1973, 74, 75
Anderson, Ray ftb	1973, 74, 75	Archambeau, Lester ftb	1986, 87, 88, 89	Arthur, Albert bsb	1973, 74, 75
Anderson, Raymond bsb	1974	Archer, Elizabeth wtrack	1982, 83, 85	Artman, Corwin W. ftb	1928, 29
Anderson, Robert mgym	1972, 73, 74, 75	Ardell, Jon mgolf	1977, 78, 79	Artman, Jack wrest	1995
Anderson, Robert W. ftb	1946, 47	Argabrite, W.M. bsb	1912, 13	Arvanetes, Louis G. ftb	1979, 82
Anderson, Sarah wswim	1994, 95, 96	Argust, Jerry bsb	1974, 75, 76, 78	Asforis, Evon wbsk	1986, 87, 88, 89
Anderson, Stanley bsb	1932, 34, 35	Armand, Bernadette wtrack	1995, 96	Ashton, Becky wgym	1987, 88, 89, 90
Anderson, Stanley ftb	1932, 34, 37, 38, 39	Armistead, Matt ftb	1987	Askea, Michael V. ftb	1971, 72
Anderson, Thomas mtrk	1971, 72, 73	Armitage, Matthew ftb	1952, 53, 54	Asper, Lara wvball	1986, 87, 88, 89
Anderson, Todd M. ftb	1973, 74, 75	Armour, Justin ftb	1991, 92, 93, 94	Asplund, Kelly wswim	1980, 81, 82, 83
Anderson, Troy ftb	1988	Armour, Merrill A. ftb	1925	Atkins, LaMott ftb	1980
Anderson, Wilbert G. mbsk	1939	Armstrong, Darrell mtrk	1988	Atkins, William Tanner mten	1968, 69
Anderson, William E. ftb	1976, 77, 78	Armstrong, Darrell mtrk	1989	Atkinson, Brice mgym	1955, 56
Andreini, Gari mfenc	1957	Armstrong, Eric B. ftb	1940, 41	Atkinson, Franklin R. ftb	1961, 62
Andrew, Mark S. ftb	1984, 85	Armstrong, James mwp	1946, 47	Atkinson, George mcrew	1978, 79
Andrews, Gary R. mbsk	1951, 52	Armstrong, Jeff mgolf	1978	Atkinson, Herbert bsb	1940
Andrews, Harlan mtrk	1963, 64, 65	Armstrong, Jessica wgym	1986, 87	Atkinson, Herbert D. ftb	1954
Andrews, Robert B. Jr. ftb	1948, 49	Armstrong, Richard bsb	1936	Atkinson, Jeff mtrk	1983, 85, 86
Andrews, Robert W. ftb	1942	Arnaudo, Philip mtrk	1963, 64	Atkinson, Jeff mxc	1983, 84, 85
Andrews, Rupert mtrk	1949	Arnett, Richard W. ftb	1920	Atkinson, Lacy B. ftb	1974
Angelo, Thomas mwp	1976, 77, 78				

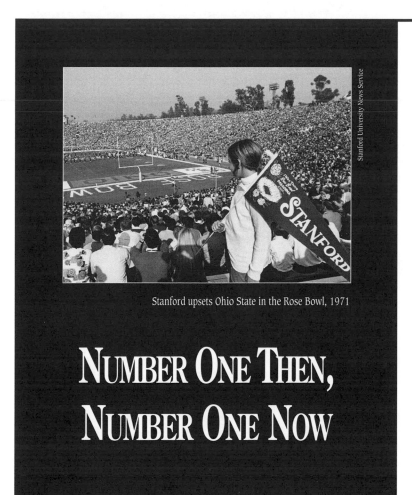

Atkinson, Robert mtrk	1959, 61	
August, Peter ftb	1942, 46, 47	
Austevoll, Elin wswim	1996	
Austin, Arthur mbsk	1923	
Austin, Charles bsb	1915	
Austin, Charles A. ftb	1913, 14	
Austin, Harry mbsk	1920	
Austin, Jeff bsb	1996	
Avant, Shaun R. ftb	1983, 84	
Avery, Brian mwp	1977	
Avery, George bsb	1957, 58	
Avila, Estevan ftb	1989, 90, 91, 92	
Awbrey, John C. ftb	1979, 80, 81	
Axtell, Allison wtrack	1991	
Axtell, Allison wtrack	1993	
Axworthy, Alan wrest	1973	
Azzi, Jennifer wbsk	1987, 88, 89, 90	
Babajian, Kenneth A. ftb	1961, 62, 63	
Bachrach, Ian mgym	1994, 95, 96	
Backer, Phillip T. ftb	1954	
Backstrand, James mtrk	1959	
Bacon, Barbara wswim	1976, 77	
Bacon, Hadley mwp	1941	
Badger, Brad ftb	1993, 94, 95	
Badger, Brandon mten	1996	
Baer, Katherine wsoc	1986	
Bagshaw, David mtrk	1973, 74, 75	
Bahlke, Adrienne wcrew	1980	
Bailey, Bruce wrest	1952, 53	
Bailey, Clark mfenc	1995, 96	
Bailey, Dick mcrew	1974, 75	
Bailey, Jeff ftb	1992, 93	
Bailey, Parker ftb	1991, 92, 93	
Bailey, Pete mtrk	1992	
Bailey, William mbsk	1931	
Baird, Darran ftb	1987, 88, 89, 90	
Baird, Kevin M. ftb	1980, 81, 82, 83	
Baise, Craig Callan mten	1965, 66, 67	
Baity, John mgolf	1875	
Bajala, Thomas wrest	1967	
Baker, Bonnie wcrew	1990, 91	
Baker, David bsb	1973, 74, 75	
Baker, George H. ftb	1922, 23, 24	
Baker, Julie wvball	1980, 81, 82, 83	
Baker, Julie wwp	1996	
Baker, Michelanne fh	1986, 87, 88, 89	
Baker, Phil H. ftb	1930, 31	
Baker, Philip L. mbsk	1931, 32	
Baker, Richard A. mbsk	1966, 67	
Bakkensen, Ralph mtrk	1971, 72, 73	
Bakst, Ken mgolf	1977, 78, 80	
Balkman, Jason mtrk	1996	
Balkman, Jason mxc	1995	
Ball, B.L. bsb	1910	
Ball, R.B. bsb	1903	
Ballard, Jeff bsb	1982, 83, 84, 85	
Ballinger, Steven G. ftb	1979	
Balthis, Douglass mgym	1942	
Banducci, Bruno ftb	1940, 41, 42	
Banducci, Thomas mtrk	1974	
Banks, Gordon mtrk	1977	
Banks, Gordon G. ftb	1977, 78, 79	
Bansbach, Louis P. ftb	1900, 02, 03, 04	
Banta, Susan wgym	1987, 88, 89, 90	
Barakaat, Dewar mfenc	1953, 54	
Barbe, Don mcrew	1987	
Barbe, Susie ennis	1980, 81, 82, 83	
Barbee, Troy W. Jr. ftb	1956, 57, 58	
Barber, Glen mtrk	1969	
Barber, William D. mbsk	1969, 70	
Barberio, Debbie wgolf	1979, 80, 81, 82	
Barbour, Lucien mten	1948, 49, 50	
Bardin, William J. ftb	1929, 30	
Bardsley, Doug wrest	1996	
Barker, Bruce C. ftb	1975, 76, 77	
Barkey, Jeanne wswim	1980, 81, 82	
Barkley, Richard mtrk	1965	
Barlow, Chris mtrk	1986, 87	
Barmeyer, Robert mtrk	1972	
Barnes, Andrea wtennis	1974, 75	
Barnes, Angie wgym	1981, 83, 84, 85	
Barnes, Benny J. ftb	1970, 71	
Barnes, Douglas mbsk	1979, 80	
Barnes, John D. ftb	1947, 48, 49	
Barnes, McKim mcrew	1967, 68	
Barnes, Michael E. ftb	1961	
Barnes, Molly wsoc	1984, 85	
Barnes, Ryan wrest	1994, 95	
Barneson, Harold J. ftb	1917	
Barnett, Audrey wcrew	1989, 90	
Barnhisel, Arthur H. ftb	1892	
Barnhisel, Peter wrest	1959, 60, 61	
Barnhisel, Walter B. ftb	1901, 02	
Barns, John W. ftb	1983, 84, 85	
Baroff, David mfenc	1980	
Barr, Edward mwp	1954	
Barrera, Catherine wsoc	1986	
Barrett, Daniel wrest	1963	
Bart, Jeremy mvball	1996	
Bart-Plange, Emmanuel ftb	1990, 91, 92	
Bartanan, Brad wrest	1977	
Bartell, Max J. ftb	1902	
Bartell, Thad mfenc	1978-79	
Bartels, Todd bsb	1993, 94, 95	
Barth, Charles mtrk	1961, 62	
Barto, Russell mcrew	1966, 67, 68	
Barton, Jeffrey S. ftb	1975, 76	
Barton, Robert mten	1953	
Baruck, Donald mwp	1948, 49	
Basham, David mten	1946, 47, 48	
Baskins, David mgolf	1972, 73, 74, 75	
Bassett, Jane wvball	1976, 77, 78, 79	
Batchelder, Arden mtrk	1960, 61, 62	
Bates, George Edward mten	1960, 61, 62	
Bates, John mwp	1959, 60, 61	
Bates, Kevin M. ftb	1978, 79, 81, 82	
Bates, Leonard mtrk	1957	
Bates, William F. ftb	1931, 32, 33	
Bateson, James mcrew	1976, 77	
Batson, Brian ftb	1993, 94, 95	
Batson, Tyler ftb	1989, 90, 91, 92	
Batson, Walter ftb	1987, 88, 89	
Battaglia, Kenneth mtrk	1940	
Battenberg, Jerry bsb	1979	
Baty, Gregory J. ftb	1983, 84, 85	
Baughman, Barbara wtennis	1983, 84	
Baum, Geoff wrest	1987, 88, 89, 90	
Baumgartner, Edward C. ftb	1910	
Baumgartner, Joe ftb	1974, 75	
Baur, Turner ftb	1988, 89, 91	
Bavinger, Markley fh	1990, 91, 92, 93	
Baxter, Andrea wgolf	1994, 95, 96	
Baxter, Georgia wdive	1982	
Baxter, Georgia wswim	1982	
Bazin, Karl wrest	1980, 81, 83	
Bea, Carlos T. mbsk	1954, 55, 56	
Beach, Jack bsb	1934	
Beale, Gregory A. ftb	1968	
Beardsley, George mcrew	1958, 59	
Beasley, Sam mwp	1967, 68, 69	
Beatie, Jerome wrest	1956	
Beatie, Jerome C. ftb	1955, 56	
Beattie, Robert wrest	1953, 54, 55	
Beaubien, Brian mwp	1994	
Beaubien, Layne mwp	1995	
Beaudet, Libbie wswim	1979, 80, 81, 82	
Beaudoin, Gerard wrest	1967, 70	
Beck, Barbara wswim	1976, 77	
Beck, Braden W. ftb	1963, 64	
Beck, Brian mwp	1961, 63, 64	
Beck, Jeffrey mwp	1963, 64, 65	
Becker, Bob wrest	1992	
Becker, Ricky mten	1993, 94, 95, 96	
Becker, Sue wcrew	1995	
Bedell, Robert G. mbsk	1964, 65, 66	
Bedford, Charles B. ftb	1977, 78, 79	
Bednar, William mgym	1960, 61, 62	
Beedle, Dale D. ftb	1935	
Beeger, J.A. bsb	1912, 13	
Beekman, Keith mgolf	1951	
Beernink, Kenneth mgym	1957, 58, 59	
Beers, John mgolf	1971, 73	
Befeler, Michael George mten	1964	
Begay, Notah mgolf	1991, 1992, 94	
Bei, Gary bsb	1974, 75	
Beischer, Tom mcrew	1989, 90, 91	
Beisser, Arnold mten	1946	
Bell, Donald mtrk	1960, 61, 62	
Bell, Duncan mfenc	1988, 89	
Bell, J. Ainslie ftb	1946, 47	
Bell, John bsb	1905, 06, 08	
Bell, Kenneth E. mbsk	1935, 36	
Bell, Willard mwp	1946	
Bellah, Jack mxc	1972, 73, 74, 75	
Belt, Robert mgym	1950	
Belton, Kimberly mbsk	1977, 78, 79, 80	
Bemis, Stephani wsoc	1983	
Benbrook, Brad mgolf	1987, 88, 89, 90	
Bender, Jeff mvball	1994, 95, 96	
Bender, Jeffrey mgym	1990, 91, 92, 93	
Benjamin, Guy E. ftb	1974, 75, 76, 77	
Bennett, Darron ftb	1986	
Bennett, F. bsb	1901	
Bennett, Stephen mwp	1951	
Bennett, Vickie wswim	1977	
Bennett, William mgym	1961	
Bennion, Dave mbsk	1995	
Benson, Boyd H. ftb	1948, 49, 50	
Benster, Dick mcrew	1974, 75	
Benton Light, Jessica wvball	1986, 87, 88, 89, 90	
Benton, Chandra wbsk	1995	
Bercutt, Larry mwp	1990, 91, 92, 93	
Berg, Chris ftb	1992, 93	
Berg, Harry bsb	1928, 29, 30	
Berg, Harry C. mbsk	1928, 29, 30	
Berg, Richard L. ftb	1963, 64	
Berger, Buffie fh	1976, 77, 78	
Bergeson, James mwp	1979, 80, 81, 82	
Berglund, Robert mwp	1952, 53, 54	
Bergren, John D. ftb	1980, 81, 82, 83	
Bergsteinsson, Nancy wcrew	1996	
Bergthold, Rudy G. ftb	1973, 74	
Berka, Chris mxc	1975	
Berka, Christsopher mxc	1972	
Berl, Warren mgolf	1939, 40, 41	
Berlin, Richard W. mbsk	1947	
Bernard, Amy fh	1981	
Bernard, Craig wrest	1969	
Bernard, David mten	1951, 1953	
Berner, Amy wcrew	1988	
Bernhagen, Lisa wtrack	1985, 86, 87, 88	
Bernharad, Harvey H. ftb	1942, 46	
Bernstein, Bobbi wsoc	1986	
Berra, Richard bsb	1964	
Berris, Beth wtennis	1993, 94, 95, 96	
Berry, Frederick wrest	1947	
Berry, Herbie ftb	1989, 90	
Berry, Robert M. ftb	1972	
Berry, Rod mtrk	1982	
Berry, Rod mxc	1978, 79, 80	
Berryman, Carol wsoc	1982, 83, 85	
Berryman, Robert P. ftb	1946	
Bertelsen, Geoffrey bsb	1959	
Berven, Sig mcrew	1987	
Berzins, Aimee wswim	1986, 87, 88, 89	
Besosa, Randy mgym	1984, 85, 86, 88	
Besse, Robert mtrk	1959, 60	
Bessen, Howard mgym	1971, 72, 73, 74	
Bessey, John D. ftb	1959, 60	
Beste, James Gilmore mten	1964, 65, 66	
Betts, Forrest A. ftb	1917, 19, 21	
Betzold, Kristina wxc	1995	
Bevier, George wrest	1948	
Beynet, Danielle fh	1990, 91, 92, 93	
Beynet, Michele fh	1988, 89, 90, 91	
Bezmalinovic, John mvball	1990, 91, 92, 93	
Bianchini, Gina fh	1991, 92, 93	
Bickel, John H. ftb	1951	
Bickenbach, Lee Pf. ftb	1941	
Bicknell, Becky wswim	1995	
Bicknell, Becky wswim	1996	
Biehl, Amy wdive	1988, 89	
Biehl, Amy wswim	1988	
Bielanski, Andrew bsb	1972	

Bigelow, Windsor D. ftb		1931
Biggs, Albert mbsk		1927
Bigler, Robert mcrew		1993, 96
Bigloe, David C. ftb		1898
Bihlman, George bsb		1916, 17
Bihlman, George H. ftb		1914, 16, 17, 19
Bilotta, Jodie wtrack		1989, 91
Bilter, Scott mtrk		1987, 88
Binley, Brook wvball		1985, 86
Birch, Sandra wtennis		1988, 89, 90, 91
Bird, Sue wswim		1979
Birk, Jodi wvball		1988, 89, 90
Birkhofer, Wendell mxc		1976
Birney, Brian mcrew		1986
Bishko, Dave wrest		1986
Bishop, Larry mgym		1954
Biszants, Allison wvball		1979, 80
Bitcher, Robert mgolf		1958
Bittner, Robert B. ftb		1966, 67, 68
Blabon, Kingdon Jr. mgolf		1949
Black, Ashley wtrack		1990, 91
Black, Robert H. ftb		1934, 35
Blackburn, J. Ramsey ftb		1975, 76
Blackburn, Robert mgolf		1953
Blackman, Duncan mvball		1989, 90, 91, 92
Blackman, Jimmy mvball		1990, 92, 93
Blackman, Martin mten		1988, 89
Blackman, Parker mvball		1987, 88, 89, 90
Blackstone, Bruce G. ftb		1972, 73
Blair, Neil mcrew		1986
Blaisdell, Jeff, ftb		1988
Blake, F.W. bsb		1902
Blanchard, John G. ftb		1972, 73, 74
Blanchard, Marcus ftb		1898
Blanchard, Mary wswim		1992, 93, 94
Blanche, Robert N. ftb		1976
Blankenberg, Robert mgolf		1969
Blankenhorn, David mwp		1989, 90, 92
Blankley, Laura wswim		1984
Blase, Roland R. ftb		1913, 14
Blayney, Doug mcrew		1972
Bleakley, Jennifer fh		1981, 82, 83, 84
Bledsoe, Julie wgym		1980, 81, 82, 83
Bleecker, John mwp		1940, 41
Bleecker, William mwp		1938, 39
Bleszynski, Ania wtennis		1995, 96
Blevins, Nik mfenc		1981, 82,83,84
Blitzer, Charles mcrew		1965, 66
Bloch, Melanie wtrack		1988, 89, 90, 91
Bloch, Melanie wxc		1987
Blodget, W.B. mbsk		1914, 15, 16
Blom, Pam wgym		1983, 84, 85, 86
Bloom, Jennifer wgym		1988, 89, 90, 91
Bloomer, Jennifer wsoc		1987, 88, 89, 90
Blue, Stephen mvball		1984, 85, 86, 87
Bluitt, Benjamin V. mbsk		1974, 75
Blum, Bob mcrew		1962
Blum, Erik mwp		1987, 88, 89
Blum, Robert mgolf		1975
Blunt, Robert L. ftb		1964, 65, 66
Bly, Cassius mtrk		1949, 50, 51
Board, Pam wtrack		1984, 85, 86, 87
Boatman, Bob bsb		1980
Boden, Roger ftb		1993
Boege, Sheldon Edward mten		1965
Boensch, Fred M. ftb		1942, 46
Boeschen, Doug mtrk		1992
Boggess, Brian mtrk		1987, 88 , 89, 90
Bogue, George R. ftb		1924, 25, 26
Bogue, Harris D. ftb		1929, 30
Bohlen, Curtis mfenc		1982
Bohner, Vince mtrk		1988, 89
Bokemeier, Matt bsb		1991
Boles, William sb		1965
Bolin, David M. ftb		1979
Bolton, Quinn mcrew		1990, 91
Bond, John E. ftb		1957, 58, 59
Bond, William B. mbsk		1955, 56, 57
Bondoc, Ron mtrk		1957
Bondurant, Scott mten		1979, 80, 81, 82
Bonetti, John E. ftb		1950, 51
Bonney, Fred L. mbsk		1917
Bonney, Fred L. ftb		1919
Booker, Cory ftb		1989, 90
Bookman, Anthony ftb		1994, 95
Bookman, Anthony mtrk		1995
Boone, Bob bsb		1967, 68, 69, 71
Boone, Elton bsb		1939, 40, 41
Boone, Kitty wtennis		1978
Boone, Rodney bsb		1972
Booth, Mark mgym		1991, 92, 93, 94
Boots, Suzie wsoc		1993, 94, 95
Borchers, Dick bsb		1969, 70, 71
Borchers, Harry mwp		1946, 47
Borchers, Leonard wrest		1967, 68, 69
Borda, Richard J. ftb		1952
Border, Brian mwp		1993
Bordoni, James mtrk		1973, 75
Boren, Frank H. ftb		1899
Bork, Derek mtrk		1993
Bork, Derek mxc		1990
Borkowski, Matt ftb		1989, 90
Boruck, Holbrook M. ftb		1949
Boryla, Michael J. ftb		1971, 72, 73
Bost, Roderick H. mbsk		1934, 35
Bostick, Tad mgym		1977, 78, 79, 80
Bostwick, William mtrk		1941
Bostwick, William mxc		1940
Bottomley, John mgolf		1965, 66
Bouchier, Robert mgolf		1965, 66, 67
Bouck, Craig mcrew		1986, 87, 88
Boughton, Robert S. ftb		1972
Boulware, George L. ftb		1919
Bounds, Roger mcrew		1962, 66
Bourne, Lloyd mten		1977, 78, 79, 80
Boutin, Frank mxc		1973, 74, 75, 76
Bowden, Robert Adkins mten		1956, 57, 58
Bowe, Patrick E. ftb		1977, 78, 79
Bowen, Jack mwp		1993, 94, 95
Bowen, Julie wgolf		1993, 94, 95, 96
Bowers, Richard L. ftb		1958, 59
Bowling, Clayton E. mbsk		1960, 61
Bowman, Kristen fh		1993
Bowman, Linda wgolf		1979, 80, 81
Boxold, James D. ftb		1977, 78
Boyce, Peter mtrk		1967, 68, 69
Boyd, Christy wtrack		1992, 93, 94, 95
Boyd, Cindy wgym		1984, 85, 87, 88
Boyer, Jan mcrew		1982
Boyette, Deanna wvball		1979, 80, 81, 82
Boylan, Barb wbsk		1977, 78
Boylan, Beth wbsk		1978, 79
Boyle, Theresa, fh		1980, 81, 82, 83
Brabyn, Phillip mtrk		1955
Bradach, Mary wbsk		1983, 84, 85
Bradberry, Carroll mfenc		1942
Braden, J.R. bsb		1916
Braden, Joseph R. ftb		1914, 15, 16
Bradley, Frank mtrk		1950, 51
Bradley, George mgolf		1940, 41
Bradley, Jeff wrest		1983, 84, 85, 86
Bradley, Pat mcrew		1989, 90
Bradshaw, Vincent mfenc		1985, 86
Bragdon, Susan wxc		1978, 79
Bragonier, Dennis S. ftb		1971, 72
Braheny, J. William ftb		1938, 39
Brammer, John David bsb		1995, 96
Brandin, Alf E. ftb		1934, 35
Brannon, Tom mfenc		1980,81
Branyon, Davis mtrk		1995
Bratz, Michael mbsk		1975, 76, 77
Braun, Chris mvball		1983, 84, 85, 86
Braun, Richard mxc		1940
Bray, C. Elwood mtrk		1950
Bray, Francis, mfenc		1939, 40
Bravin, Nick mfenc		1989,90
Brazel, Charles W. ftb		1952
Breckner, Robert mwp		1940, 41
Breen, Paul ftb		1972, 73
Brenner, John M. ftb		1938
Brenner, Karl mwp		1953, 54
Brent, Albert bsb		1935
Breschini, Leonard mtrk		1961, 63
Brewer, John mcrew		1959, 60
Brewster, Donald mvball		1979
Bridgeman, Jackie wtrack		1993, 94, 95
Briehl, Tom M. ftb		1982, 83, 84
Briggs, Stewart D. ftb		1892
Brigham, Samuel T.J. ftb		1936, 37
Brill, John Marty ftb		1965, 66, 67
Brinkman, Dean mten		1950, 51
Briscoe, Sandy wxc		1975, 76, 77
Britt, Chris bsb		1983
Brobston, Stan mfenc		1988,89,90,91
Brock, David mten		1938, 39, 40
Brock, Gregory mtrk		1968, 69
Brock, Gregory mtrk		1970
Brock, Gregory mxc		1967, 68, 69
Brock, John mgolf		1969
Brockberg, John ftb		1993
Brockmeyer, Neal H. mbsk		1958, 59, 60
Brodell, Ann wsmim		1975, 76, 77, 78
Broderick, John R. ftb		1950, 51, 52
Brodie, John mgolf		1955, 56
Brodie, John R. ftb		1954, 55, 56
Brody, David mfenc		1990,91
Broer, Bobbi wvball		1981, 82, 83, 84
Bronstein, Howard S. ftb		1933
Brooke, John bsb		1942
Brooks, Irving L. ftb		1921
Brookshire, Vija wsoc		1985, 86, 87
Broome, Richard D. ftb		1949, 50
Brothers, Charles mcrew		1958, 59
Broughton, Gregory J. ftb		1966, 67, 68
Brown, Arthur mxc		1973, 74
Brown, Barry R. mbsk		1954, 55, 56
Brown, Cory mvball		1978, 79, 80
Brown, David E. ftb		1942, 46
Brown, Delos E. ftb		1962, 64, 65
Brown, Donald mgym		1957
Brown, F.A. bsb		1900, 01, 02, 03
Brown, Floyd C. ftb		1907, 09, 10, 11
Brown, Fred golf		1952, 53, 54
Brown, Hartwell ftb		1990, 91
Brown, Isaiah ftb		1968, 69
Brown, Jackie R. ftb		1969, 70, 71
Brown, James mtrk		1986, 87
Brown, James A. ftb		1978, 79, 80
Brown, Jen wcrew		1995, 96
Brown, Ken bsb		1953
Brown, Mark W. ftb		1969
Brown, Mollie wgym		1991, 92, 93, 94
Brown, Ray mtrk		1938, 39, 40
Brown, Ricky mtrk		1977, 78
Brown, Robert bsb		1943
Brown, Robert L. ftb		1969
Brown, Steve mbsk		1982, 83, 84, 86
Brown, Steven L. ftb		1983
Brownell, Raymond mgolf		1941
Brownsberger, Keith mtrk		1953, 54, 55
Brownson, Lynn bsb		1946, 47, 48
Brownson, Lynn J. ftb		1946
Brubaker, E. William ftb		1942
Bruce, Duane mgym		1956, 57
Bruggman, Peggy wbsk		1976, 77, 78
Bruner, Gary mtrk		1979, 80, 81, 82
Bruno, Dennis mxc		1973
Bruton, Derek mbsk		1987, 88, 89, 90
Bruzzone, Rick bsb		1976
Bryan, Gaylord mtrk		1947, 48, 49
Bryan, Gaylord D. mbsk		1949, 50
Bryan, Robert mtrk		1949, 50, 51
Bryan, Robert E. ftb		1950
Bryant, B. mbsk		1927
Bryant, Laurie wsoc		1982
Bryant, Vaughn ftb		1990, 91, 92, 93
Bryla, Erin wsoc		1995
Bryson, Terri wvball		1982, 83, 84, 85
Buchan, Janet wswim		1980, 82
Buchanan, James mcrew		1991
Buchanan, Thad mgolf		1981
Buchrer, Cindy wswim		1994
Buchsbaum, Cindy wtennis		1987, 88, 89
Buck, Ronald mtrk		1949, 50, 51
Buckey, Jeff ftb		1992, 93, 94, 95
Buckingham, Gregory mwp		1966, 67

Buckley, Frederick O. ftb	1984, 85	
Buckley, Mike tb	1992	
Bucklin, James W. mbsk	1918	
Buckovich, Suzy wswim	1988, 89, 90, 91	
Buddie, Steve wrest	1988, 89, 90, 91	
Buddin, Chris mtrk	1995, 96	
Budge, Hamilton W. ftb	1947, 48	
Budinger, Stephen M. ftb	1977, 78	
Buechele, Steve bsb	1980, 81, 82	
Buehler, Charles E. ftb	1960, 61, 62	
Buehler, Donald mwp	1961, 62, 63	
Buehler, Donald wrest	1963	
Buehler, George S. ftb	1966, 67, 68	
Buell, Robert D. mbsk	1971, 72, 73	
Buese, Lisa wswim	1982, 83, 84, 85	
Bugge, John mtrk	1954, 55	
Bull, Herbert bsb	1939, 40, 41	
Bullwinkel, Clay mtrk	1976, 77, 78, 79	
Bunce, Donald R. ftb	1969, 70, 71	
Bunch, Tina wswim	1981	
Bunnett, Dave mcrew	1982, 83	
Bunyard, Guy G. ftb	1985, 86	
Burbank, D.W. bsb	1910, 11, 12	
Burch, Frederick W. ftb	1977, 78	
Burcham, Keith G. ftb	1977, 78, 79	
Burdick, Steve mgolf	1992, 93, 94	
Burford, Christopher W. mbsk	1958, 59	
Burford, Christopher W. ftb	1957, 58, 59	
Burgel, Joshua mcrew	1993, 95	
Burgess, John mfenc	1978,79,80	
Burget, Bill G. ftb	1956	
Burghardt, Joe mvball	1992, 93, 94	
Burgin, Elise wtennis	1981, 82, 83, 84	
Burk, James bsb	1958, 59, 60	
Burke, Christopher mfenc	1975, 76	
Burke, Douglas mwp	1975, 76, 77, 78	
Burke, Edward W. Jr. ftb	1946, 47	
Burke, John mtrk	1950	
Burke, Thomas R. ftb	1961, 63	
Burke, William ftb	1929	
Burke-Newsum, Joseph mtrk	1996	
Burkland, Phil V. ftb	1957, 59	
Burley, Frederick William mten	1961	
Burlingham, Sheri wswim	1978, 79	
Burmester, Russell mgym	1961, 63, 64	
Burness, Donald S. mbsk	1941, 42	
Burnett, Brady F. ftb	1893	
Burnett, Robert bsb	1937	
Burnett, Robert W. mbsk	1939	
Burnett, Roger bsb	1989, 90, 91	
Burnett, William W. ftb	1897, 99, 1900	
Burns, Randal mcrew	1991	
Burns, William mwp	1937, 38, 39	
Burns, William S. ftb	1914	
Burr, Leila wtrack	1994, 95, 96	
Burr, Leila wxc	1993, 94, 95	
Burrus, Susan wtrack	1981, 82, 83	
Bursch, Roy mtrk	1941	
Burt, Emily wsoc	1993, 94	
Burt, Emily wtennis	1994, 95, 96	
Burt, Robert John mten	1962, 63, 64	
Burtleson, Alfred mgolf	1956, 57, 58	
Burton, Kenneth mten	1951	
Burton, Kim wtrack	1994	
Burton, Mike mdive	1988, 89	
Burton, Sloan wxc	1981	
Busch, James bsb	1927, 28	
Buser, James mtrk	1971	
Bush, Clarence E. ftb	1930	
Bush, Krissie wswim	1981, 82, 83, 84	
Bush, Ronald J. ftb	1952, 53, 54	
Bushman, Julie wsoc	1994, 95	
Busquets, Antonio mwp	1992, 93	
Buss, Brian mtrk	1985, 86	
Buss, Rick mtrk	1977, 78, 79, 80	
Butler, Charles W. ftb	1961	
Butler, Greg mbsk	1985, 86, 87, 88	
Butler, John R. ftb	1959, 60, 61	
Butler, Lawrence A. ftb	1970, 71	
Butler, Rollyn mwp	1950, 51, 52	
Butt, Dale I. ftb	1919	
Butt, Dale J. mbsk	1918, 20	
Butterfield, Hayden G. ftb	1904	
Butterfield, Mark ftb	1992, 93, 94, 95	
Button, Sarah wgolf	1982	
Buvinghausen, Edward wrest	1946	
Byer, Evi-Lynn wswim	1995, 96	
Byers, Dan ftb	1990, 91	
Byrd, Jeff ftb	1995	
Byrer, James W. ftb	1957, 58	
Cabbage, Janeal wxc	1979	
Cable, Tory wsoc	1988	
Caddel, Ernest bsb	1930, 32	
Caddel, Ernest W. Jr. ftb	1930, 31, 32	
Cadwalader, D.P. bsb	1906, 07	
Cadwalder, Theodore R. ftb	1907, 08	
Cady, Carol wtrack	1981, 82, 83, 84	
Caffall, Mark ftb	1942	
Caglieri, Guido G. ftb	1929, 30	
Cain, Gary L. mbsk	1972	
Cain, Joseph ftb	1983, 84	
Cairns, Jim mwp	1989, 90	
Cairns, Walter S. ftb	1899	
Calderwood, John S. mbsk	1936, 37, 38	
Caldwell, Kent mbsk	1974, 75	
Calfee, Corie wswim	1996	
Calfee, Tsar N. Jr. ftb	1950, 51	
Callahan, Craig mgolf	1955	
Callaway, Claude P. ftb	1933, 34, 35	
Callaway, Ed mtrk	1984	
Callicoatte, Alison wtrack	1991, 92	
Calomese, David ftb	1992	
Calvelli, Anthony ftb	1936, 37, 38	
Camera, Paul C. ftb	1955, 56	
Cameron, Bruce bsb	1950, 51	
Camilli, Douglas bsb	1956	
Campanelli, Jim mgym	1982, 83, 84	
Campbell, Don mgym	1948, 49	
Campbell, Don mtrk	1947, 49, 50	
Campbell, Don L. ftb	1947, 48	
Campbell, Floyd bsb	1934	
Campbell, Floyd P. ftb	1919	
Campbell, Gordon bsb	1931, 32, 33, 34	
Campbell, Gordon ftb	1931, 32, 33	
Campbell, Howard F. ftb	1917, 19, 20	
Campbell, Jody mwp	1978, 79, 80, 81	
Campbell, John D. ftb	1921, 22, 23	
Campbell, L.G. bsb	1916	
Campbell, Lance mcrew	1981, 82, 83	
Campbell, Patty fh	1980	
Campbell, William E. ftb	1895	
Cannon, Phillip mtrk	1983, 84, 85, 86	
Cano, Matt wrest	1993, 94, 95, 96	
Canterbury, Christine wtrack	1985	
Canterbury, E.R. bsb	1909	
Carder, David ftb	1992, 93, 94, 95	
Cardinal, Bruce mgolf	1977	
Cardinal, Robert mgolf	1946, 47	
Cardinalli, Ben bsb	1947	
Cardinalli, Ray A. ftb	1974, 75, 76, 77	
Carey, Ann bsb	1986, 87, 88, 89	
Carey, Paul bsb	1987, 88, 89, 90	
Carico, David mvball	1979	
Carle, Nathaniel A. ftb	1895, 96, 97	
Carlisle, Kim wswim	1980, 81, 82, 83	
Carls, William mtrk	1957	
Carlson, Donald W. mbsk	1953	
Carlson, Harry J. Jr. ftb	1935	
Carlsten, Chris wrest	1991	
Carmack, Paula wvball	1978, 79, 80, 81	
Carmichael, Julie wgolf	1983, 84, 85, 86	
Carmody, Robert wrest	1956	
Carpenter, John ftb	1988, 89, 90	
Carpenter, John mwp	1946	
Carpenter, Sarah wtrack	1982, 83	
Carpenter, Scott ftb	1984	
Carpenter, William mwp	1946	
Carper, Mark bsb	1989	
Carr, Jenny wtrack	1996	
Carr, Kenneth mwp	1972	
Carrigan, Andrew J. ftb	1966, 67	
Carrigan, Casey mtrk	1971	
Carroll, Daniel B. ftb	1912, 13, 14, 15, 16	
Carroll, James J. III mten	1966, 67, 68	
Carroll, Jon P. ftb	1982	
Carroll, Livingston wrest	1968	
Carruth, Lowell mten	1957, 58, 59	
Carruth, Marlo wtennis	1990, 91, 92	
Carswell, Donn A. ftb	1954, 55, 56	
Carter, Cale bsb	1993, 94, 95, 96	
Carter, David bsb	1959	
Carter, Fred mtrk	1989, 90, 91, 92	
Carter, Fred mxc	1990	
Carter, Harley R. ftb	1921	
Carter, Jay mbsk	1975, 76, 77, 78	
Carter, Judy wbsk	1983, 84	
Carter, Kent F. mbsk	1958	
Carter, Kim mgolf	1976, 77, 79	
Carter, Pat mfenc	1983	
Carter, Ralph W. mbsk	1948, 49, 50	
Caruso, Aurelio bsb	1941, 42	
Carver, R.L. mbsk	1918, 21	
Carver, Steve bsb	1992, 93, 94, 95	
Casabona, Helen wswim	1980	
Casey, Carrie wvball	1976	
Casey, John R. ftb	1940	
Cash, Howard mfenc	1982, 83	
Cashin, Emmet mwp	1946	
Cashman, Patti wcrew	1979	
Cass, Bruce C. ftb	1968	
Cass, Darrell bsb	1984	
Cass, Louis bsb	1911, 12, 13	
Cass, Louis ftb	1909, 11, 12	
Cassady, Ralph bsb	1954	
Cassidy, Brian, ftb	1990, 91, 92, 93	
Castagnola, James D. ftb	1948, 49	
Castagnoli, James bsb	1949, 51	
Castellucci, Davis L. ftb	1951	
Castillo, Lori wgolf	1981, 82	
Cathcart, Alice wwp	1996	
Cathrall, Jeff mten	1987, 88, 89, 90	
Catlett, LaRue mgym	1956	
Caughey, Edgar R. ftb	1919	
Caughey, Reginald E. mbsk	1916, 19	
Cautley, Daniel mxc	1972	
Cavalli, Sue wcrew	1981	
Cavanaugh, Glen ftb	1990, 91, 92, 93	
Celms, Harold mtrk	1976, 78, 79	
Ceman, Canyon mvball	1992, 93, 94	
Cereghino, Alexander bsb	1940, 41	
Ceresino, Gordon J. ftb	1975, 76, 77, 78	
Cervenka, Andrea wcrew	1991	
Cevaer, Christian mgolf	1989, 90, 91, 92	
Chacon, Greg mtrk	1985	
Chaffee Roggeman, Jennifer wvball	1986, 87, 88, 89	
Chalberg, Thomas mwp	1962, 63, 64	
Chalmers, Alexander ftb	1903, 04, 05, 06	
Chalmers, Alexandra bsb	1904, 05, 06	
Chamberlain, Karen fh	1982, 83, 84	
Chambers, Victor mtrk	1941	
Chan, Bruce mfenc	1978	
Chan, Gayle wtennis	1980, 81, 82	
Chandler, Lore R. ftb	1917	
Chandler, Otis mtrk	1947, 48, 49	
Chang, Grace wfenc	1988, 89, 90, 91	
Chang, Jerry mgolf	1992, 93, 95, 96	
Chang, Tim mfenc	1996	
Changnon, Thomas bsb	1972	
Chapin, Christopher S. mten	1969, 1972	
Chapman, Chris P. ftb	1985	
Chapman, Kyle wxc	1978	
Chapman, Merilyn wgym	1981, 82, 84, 85	
Chapman, Michelle wbsk	1979	
Chapman, Michelle wswim	1986	
Chapman, Philip mwp	1951	
Chapman, Robert mgolf	1972, 73	
Chapman, Robert S. ftb	1977, 78	
Chapman, Scott wrest	1994, 96,	
Chapple, John mtrk	1963, 64	
Chapple, John L. ftb	1962, 63, 64	
Charles, Olive wcrew	1979	
Charnley, Donald mgym	1956, 57	
Chase, Andrew L. mten	1978, 79, 80, 81	
Chase, Cam wsoc	1982	

Chavalas, Gus J. mbsk	1948, 49, 50
Cheda, Gilbert E. ftb	1906, 08, 09, 10
Cheek, Andrea wtrack	1979, 80
Chen, Catherine syncswim	1996
Cheney, Allan mtrk	1954, 55
Chennell, Ward mgym	1946
Chenu, James bsb	1961
Chesarek, Donald mtrk	1957, 58, 59,
Chesarek, Richard mtrk	1962, 63, 64
Cheu, Elliott mfenc	1983, 84, 85, 86
Chez, Joe bsb	1950, 51, 52
Childs, Denny wrest	1981
Childs, Leroy bsb	1910, 12
Childs, Robert D. ftb	1947
Chiminello, Amy wtennis	1992, 93, 95, 96
Chitren, Steve bsb	1986, 87, 88, 89
Chitwood, Amalie fh	1984, 85, 86, 87
Choate, Christian mgolf	1960, 62, 63
Chokshi, Monal wtrack	1996
Chokshi, Monal wxc	1993, 94, 95
Chong, Stewart mvball	1994, 95, 96
Christ, H. mbsk	1927
Christensen, Don mgolf	1987, 88, 89, 90
Christensen, Frank mgym	1956, 57, 58, 60
Christensen, Norman mtrk	1939, 40
Christiansen, Gunnar E. mbsk	1954
Christiansen, William J. mbsk	1946
Christopher, Rob mvball	1975
Chukwudebe, Lawrence mtrk	1962
Chun, Linda gym	1993, 94, 95, 96
Chung, Mary fh	1983, 84, 85, 86
Chung, James mfenc	1996
Chung, Jeff mgym	1979, 80, 81, 82
Church, Gerald B. ftb	1973, 74, 75
Churchill, E. Perry bsb	1929, 30
Chutich, Peggy wbsk	1977
Claassen, Larry mcrew	1961
Claflin, Robert Mac mten	1969, 70, 71, 72
Clancy, Katie wgym	1992, 94, 95
Clapp, Jonathan mcrew	1968, 69
Clark, Chris bsb	1995, 96
Clark, Edgar bsb	1934, 35, 36
Clark, Ernest mtrk	1939, 40, 41
Clark, Frank mvball	1990
Clark, George H. ftb	1901, 02, 03, 04
Clark, Greg ftb	1995
Clark, Jo wswim	1979
Clark, John B. ftb	1956, 57
Clark, John E. ftb	1934, 36, 38
Clark, John V. ftb	1947
Clark, Kerri wcrew	1986
Clark, Paul mwp	1974, 76
Clark, Travis mtrk	1992, 93, 94, 95
Clark, William bsb	1939
Clark, William mcrew	1981, 82, 83
Clark, William N. mbsk	1926, 28
Clark, William N. ftb	1929, 30
Clarke, Alden mfenc	1996
Clarke, Ceci wswim	1982
Clarke, Doug mgolf	1978, 79, 80
Clarke, Jim mcrew	1978
Clay, Roger A. ftb	1965
Claypool, James bsb	1949, 50, 51
Claypool, John bsb	1948, 49
Cleaveland, Norman ftb	1922, 23, 24
Clegg, Richard bsb	1949, 50, 51
Clegg, Richard mbsk	1950
Clemans, Carl L. ftb	1892 (Spr.), 1892 (Fall)
Clemans, Charles mwp	1954
Clemans, William mwp	1952, 53, 54
Clemens, Brians mwp	1992, 93
Clemetson, Donald T. mbsk	1961, 62, 63
Clemetson, Douglas C. mbsk	1961, 62
Clevenger, Caroline, fh	1987, 88, 89, 90
Cline, Lee bsb	1980, 81
Cline, Tony ftb	1992, 93, 94
Clinton, Edgar M. ftb	1898
Close, Robin wgym	1984, 85
Closs, William R. mbsk	1968, 69
Clough, Kelley wswim	1979
Clover, Philip P. ftb	1913, 14

Cloyd, Carey fh	1995
Clymer, James J. ftb	1980, 81, 82, 83
Coachman, Kyle mtrk	1990
Coate, Jim bsb	1969, 70, 71
Cobb, Charles mtrk	1957, 58
Cobb, Mary wtrack	1996
Cobb, Mary wxc	1995
Cochrane, Guy H. ftb	1892, 93, 94, 95
Cocotos, Chris mten	1991, 92, 93, 94
Code, Thomas K. ftb	1892 (Spr.), 1892 (Fall), 93, 95
Codiroli, Mike bsb	1976, 77, 78, 79
Coe, Robert mxc	1969, 70, 71
Coelho, Joe wrest	1976
Coffin, Robbie L. ftb	1985, 86, 87, 88
Coffis, James bsb	1937, 38
Coffis, James T. ftb	1935, 36, 37
Cogan, Tony bsb	1996
Cohen, Jason mgym	1991, 92, 93, 94
Coie, Beth wcrew	1990
Coin, Harry mfenc	1981, 82, 83
Coker, Charles mtrk	1947, 48
Coker, Charles M. ftb	1947
Cokro, Sonya wtennis	1993
Colan, Doleen wtrack	1979
Colberg, Kent S. ftb	1962, 63
Colbert, John bsb	1904, 05
Colby, Thomas mtrk	1968, 69
Coldiron, Gene D. ftb	1937, 38, 39
Cole, Alfred W. ftb	1940, 41
Cole, Jimmy wrest	1972
Cole, Peter mwp	1950, 51, 52
Cole, Richard bsb	1951, 52, 53
Colehower, Kurt H. ftb	1984, 85, 86, 87
Coleman, Cappy fh	1974
Coleman, Richard R. ftb	1916
Colleran, Dave mtrk	1995
Collins, Charles D. ftb	1980
Collins, Jeff mcrew	1990
Collins, John bsb	1927
Collins, Michelle wswim	1995, 96
Collins, Raymond mwp	1968, 69, 70
Collins, Steven mgolf	1972
Collins, Timothy mtrk	1987, 88,89, 90
Colton, Allan wrest	1951, 53
Colvin, Donald L. ftb	1930, 31, 32
Colvin, Kenneth mgolf	1972, 73
Comanor, Katherine wswim	1990, 91, 92, 93
Comella, Greg ftb	1993
Compton, Robert mtrk	1942
Compton-Kherkher, Susan wvball	1981, 82, 83, 84
Conaway, Carlton D. ftb	1963
Condon, Wilson mcrew	1960
Cone, Jesse A. ftb	1949, 50, 51
Conklin, Roch M. ftb	1956, 58
Conklin, Roland mgolf	1951
Conly, Cheryl wvball	1987, 88, 89, 90
Conn, Michael mwp	1960, 61, 62
Connelly, Michael bsb	1965
Connelly, Michael O. ftb	1964, 65
Connolly, Adam mtrk	1995, 96
Connolly, Donald mcrew	1968, 69
Connolly, John mten	1990
Connor, Michael D. ftb	1975, 76
Connors, Katy wdive	1987, 88, 89, 90
Conolly, Brian mtrk	1985, 86
Conrad, Dennis mgolf	1971
Conrad, Robert L. ftb	1965, 66
Constant, Mark wrest	1991
Cook, Alex J. ftb	1927, 28, 29
Cook, Archibald B. ftb	1906, 07, 08, 09
Cook, Brad ftb	1987, 88
Cook, Donovan bsb	1965
Cook, Hart N. III, ftb	1948, 49, 51
Cook, Heather wcrew	1980
Cook, Mike ftb	1991, 92
Cook, Ralph bsb	1929, 30
Cook, Robert mgym	1964, 66
Cook, Ronald M. ftb	1951, 52, 53
Cook, Stacy wsoc	1993
Cook, Toi bsb	1984, 85, 86, 87

Cook, Toi w ftb	1984, 85, 86
Coons, Shane mwp	1990
Cooper, Amy wvball	1988, 89, 90, 91
Cooper, Ann wbsk	1978
Cooper, John mfenc	1941
Cooper, Kenneth F. ftb	1900, 01
Copeland, Caryn wtennis	1980, 81, 82, 83
Copithorne, Brad mcrew	1984, 85
Copp, W.W. bsb	1902
Copsey, Harlan B. mbsk	1939
Corbus, William ftb	1931, 32, 33
Cordes, Craig M. mbsk	1963.64.65
Cordes, William ftb	1971, 72
Cordingly, Bruce mgolf	1942
Cordova, Michael P. ftb	1974, 75, 76
Cordy, Thomas W. mbsk	1931, 32, 33
Corey, Craig mxc	1978, 79
Cornelius, Kay wgolf	1985, 86, 87, 88
Cornell, David bsb	1991, 92
Cornell, Warren Bradford mten	1967, 68
Cornett, Arnold mtrk	1939, 40
Cornew, Dan mcrew	1982, 83, 84
Cornish, Herbert James mten	1952, 53, 54
Cornwell, Al mcrew	1972
Correa, Cathy wfenc	1981, 82, 83, 84
Corse, John mten	1979, 80, 81, 82
Cortes, Alejandro mten	1976, 77
Cortes, Daniel wrest	1954
Cortright, Steven mtrk	1962, 63, 64
Corzine, H. Richard bsb	1951
Cosgrove, Charlie mvball	1977
Cosgrove, John C. mbsk	1932
Costello, Harold bsb	1940, 41
Costigan, Peter mfenc	1980
Cotten, J. Spencer ftb	1986, 87, 88
Cottle, Christopher C. ftb	1959, 60, 61
Cotton, David mgolf	1963
Cotton, S.W. ftb	1894, 95, 96, 97
Cottrell, Stephen G. ftb	1981, 82, 83
Cottrell, Steve bsb	1981, 82, 83, 84
Couch, John bsb	1912
Coull, Roderick mten	1983
Courtney, Mary wcrew	1984, 85, 86
Cowan, Roger D. ftb	1970, 71, 72
Cowart, James bsb	1959, 60, 61
Cowden, D.V. bsb	1900, 01, 02, 03
Cowden, William mbsk	1940, 41, 42
Cowgill, Andy mtrk	1995
Cowgill, Andy mxc	1994
Cowing, J. Emil mbsk	1934, 35
Cowles, Tim mcrew	1965, 66, 67
Cowley, Kelly mcrew	1972
Cox, Douglas mgym	1957, 58, 59, 60
Cox, Eric bsb	1989
Cox, James E. ftb	1942, 46
Cox, Robert bsb	1963, 64, 65
Cox, Roger mtrk	1966, 68
Cox, Roger mtrk	1968
Craft, Benjamin bsb	1927
Crahan, Jack L. ftb	1947
Craig, Bruce mwp	1973
Craig, Earle McKee III mten	1972
Craig, Gary H. ftb	1960, 61, 62
Cram, Laurence mgolf	1970
Cramer, Michael mfenc	1985, 86, 87, 88
Cramton, James mtrk	1988, 89, 90, 91
Crandell, Steven mbsk	1979
Crane, Robert L. ftb	1938, 39, 40, 41
Crane, Steve mcrew	1976
Crary, Heather wwp	1996
Crary, Sherman L. ftb	1929
Cravens, Robert I. ftb	1920, 22, 23
Crawford, C.H. bsb	1902
Crawford, David P. ftb	1905, 07, 08, 09
Crawford, Thomas H. mbsk	1959
Creasy, Robert mcrew	1988
Creighton, Robin mcrew	1969
Crenshaw, Terry wrest	1967, 68, 70
Crepeau, Richard A. Jr. ftb	1954
Crist, Frank L. (Skip) Jr. ftb	1950, 51, 52
Crocker, Helen wcrew	1979
Crocker, Helen wcrew	1980

Cromer, Barry ftb	1982, 83	Davidson, David G. mbsk	1947, 48, 49	DeSwarte, David ftb	1946
Cronin, Kevin bsb	1971	Davidson, E.E. ftb	1913	Detter, Tony bsb	1991, 92
Crooker, James mfenc	1946, 48	Davidson, Gwen wgolf	1974, 75	Dettinger, Tara wtrack	1996
Crooks, George A. ftb	1967, 68, 69	Davidson, Harry D. ftb	1947	Deubner, David mtrk	1965, 66
Croom, Noah mtrk	1985, 86	Davidson, Horace H. ftb	1927, 28	Deubner, David mxc	1964, 65
Crosby, Grant mwp	1994	Davidson, Kenneth W. mbsk	1939, 40, 41	Devens, Robert mten	1991, 92, 93, 94
Crosby, Jon bsb	1974	Davies, James M. mbsk	1920, 21, 22	Devine, Aubrey A. Jr. ftb	1946, 47, 48
Cross, Brookley mwp	1969	Davies, Julia syncswim	1996	Devine, Timothy mwp	1953, 54
Cross, Dion mbsk	1993, 94, 95, 96	Davies, Loring bsb	1979, 80, 81, 82	DeWeese, Armand mtrk	1959
Cross, Eric C. ftb	1970, 71, 72	Davis, Ashleigh fh	1994	DeWeese, Armand J. ftb	1955, 56, 57
Cross, James K. ftb	1967, 69	Davis, Branyon ftb	1993, 94	Dewey, Andrea wtrack	1980, 81
Crossland, Steve mcrew	1967, 68, 69	Davis, Bruce bsb	1976, 77	DeWitt, Richard wrest	1949, 50, 51
Crowden, John mtrk	1952	Davis, James mtrk	1961	deWitt, Wallace bsb	1937, 38, 39
Crowe, Becky wswim	1992, 93, 94, 95	Davis, James M. mbsk	1920, 21, 22	deWitt, Wallace W. ftb	1938
Crowe, Earle bsb	1920	Davis, James R. mbsk	1914	Dewitt, Ward mcrew	1960
Crowe, Rich bsb	1993	Davis, Joseph mgolf	1964	Dexter, Robert mcrew	1993, 95
Crowell, William mgym	1962	Davis, Karen wcrew	1980	Dey, Dena wsoc	1992, 93, 94, 95
Crowley, Bill mtrk	1987, 88, 89	Davis, Lewis mtrk	1949, 50, 51	Dey, Dena wtrack	1993, 94, 95, 96
Crowley, Bill mxc	1988	Davis, Mark bsb	1983, 84, 85, 86	Dick, Douglas W. ftb	1956, 58
Crowley, Stephen mtrk	1975, 77	Davis, Mark wrest	1972	Dickey, John mgolf	1985, 86
Crowley, Steve mxc	1973	Davis, Martin mwp	1975, 76, 77	Dickey, Lew mgolf	1981, 82, 83, 85
Crozier, Leslie wswim	1976	Davis, Michael mwp	1969, 70, 71	Dickson, Craig mgym	1968, 69
Crozier, Robert mgolf	1948, 49, 50	Davis, Ralph bsb	1947	Dietz, Rick bsb	1984, 85
Cruce, Richard wrest	1948, 49, 50	Davis, Scott mten	1981, 82, 83	Diffenbaugh, Daniel mvball	1996
Crumly, Jim mfenc	1975, 76	Davis, Stephanie wgolf	1989, 90, 91, 92	Diffenderfer, David mgolf	1955, 56, 57
Cuddeback, Murray W. ftb	1922, 23, 24	Davis, Stephen mtrk	1969, 70, 71	Differnbaugh, Noah mvball	1994
Culin, Edward L. ftb	1948	Davis, Steven bsb	1973, 74, 75, 76	Dillard, Marshall B. ftb	1983, 85, 86, 87
Culley, Grant mwp	1941	Davis, Timothy wrest	1963, 64	Dils, Stephen W. ftb	1977, 78
Cullison, Leonard wrest	1946	Davison, Michael wrest	1965, 66	Dinette, James wrest	1988, 89, 90, 91
Cumberpatch, Cathy wswim	1977	Dawkins, Rick mcrew	1966	Dingfelder, Clyde bsb	1947, 48
Cummings, Alan mxc	1973, 75	Dawson, Donald D. ftb	1958	Dinkelspiel, Lloyd mwp	1949, 50
Cummings, Edward A. ftb	1960, 61, 62	Dawson, Gaynor mcrew	1967, 68, 69	DiPietro, Bob bsb	1971, 72, 73
Cummings, Irving Jr. ftb	1937	Dawson, Grant mcrew	1995, 96	Dirksen, Emily wcrew	1990, 1991
Cummings, Thomas mwp	1972, 73	Dawson, Raymond E. ftb	1929, 30, 31	Dispalatro, Frank ftb	1979, 80, 83
Cummins, Anna wfenc	1993, 94	Dawson, Stanley mtrk	1950	Disston, Leeds mcrew	1965, 66
Cunha, William bsb	1942, 43	Dawson, Steve mtrk	1981	Ditlevsen, Robert F. ftb	1940
Cunliffe, William mtrk	1958, 59, 60	Day, D.M. bsb	1914	Dito, John bsb	1957
Cunliffe, William mxc	1959	Day, Richard mtrk	1973	Dittman, Seth ftb	1991, 92, 93, 94
Cunningham, Oliver mbsk	1987, 88	De la Forest, John M. ftb	1966, 67, 68	Dobson, George P. mbsk	1928
Cunz, Ken S. ftb	1982	De Los Reyes, Linda fh	1981, 82, 83	Docken, Terrence bsb	1965, 66
Curl, Kenneth mtrk	1972, 73, 74	De Sylvia, Terry ftb	1964, 65	Docker, Elizabeth wgolf	1976
Curr, Allan M. ftb	1962	De Young, E. William ftb	1948, 49	Doctor, Stephen D. ftb	1954, 55, 56
Curran, Terrance mgolf	1967, 68	Dean, Archie F. mbsk	1974	Dodds, Andrew mvball	1980
Curry, Julie wsoc	1980, 81, 82, 83	Dean, Bob mvball	1981, 82, 83	Dodge, Charles bsb	1934
Curtice, Aubrey A. ftb	1919	DeAnda, Abie wrest	1981	Doe, Charles W. ftb	1919
Curtin, Christa wtrack	1986	Deaton, Jeffrey S. ftb	1981, 82, 83, 84	Doelger, Maria wswim	1984
Curtin, Christine wxc	1984	DeBenon, Mike bsb	1983, 84, 85, 86	Doering Jr., Arthur mgolf	1968
Cusick, Joseph wrest	1950	DeBevoise, Kendall bsb	1963, 64	Doi, Suzanne fh	1982, 83, 84
Cuthberson, Anne wcrew	1981	Deckmann, Doug mcrew	1988	Dolan, Clare wgolf	1986, 87
Cutshaw, Mac bsb	1930	DeCosta, Bob bsb	1980, 81, 82	Dolan, O.D. mbsk	1915, 16, 17
		Dee, Larry mbsk	1942	Dole, Alfred R. ftb	1902
Dahl, Kristin wcrew	1986, 87, 88	Dee, Laurence mten	1940, 41, 42	Dole, Charles S. ftb	1895, 98
Dahle, David bsb	1948, 49	Deems, Howard E. ftb	1920	Dole, George E. ftb	1905
Dailey, Warren mgolf	1952, 53, 54	Deese-Dobson, Erica wsoc	1986	Dole, Kenneth L. ftb	1908, 09, 10, 11
Daka, Robert E. ftb	1937, 38	DeFabio, Richard bsb	1957, 58, 59	Dole, Norman D. ftb	1922, 23
Daley, Mark mwp	1983, 84	Deffebach, C.A. bsb	1923	Dole, Wilfred H. ftb	1902, 03, 04
Dallimore, Brian bsb	1993, 94, 95, 96	DeForest, Joseph G. ftb	1899, 1900	Dominick, Peter mcrew	1990
Dallmar, Howard bsb	1942, 43	DeGraw, Eric bsb	1988, 89	Domolky, George mfenc	1958
Dallmar, Howard mbsk	1942, 43	DeGroot, Dudley S. mbsk	1922	Donahue, Mary fh	1982, 83
Dalman, Chris ftb	1989, 90, 91, 92	DeGroot, Dudley S. ftb	1920, 21, 22	Donahue, Michelle wswim	1986, 87, 88, 89
Dalrymple, Tim mgym	1995	Dehlendorf, Christine wxc	1992	Donahue, Neil A. ftb	1937, 38, 39
Dalton, Jen wtrack	1994, 95, 96	Delaney, James Edward mten	1972, 73, 74, 75	Donahue, William F. ftb	1959
Dalva, Matt mcrew	1989, 90	Delaney, Patricia wtennis	1977	Donaker, Geoff mfenc	1993, 94, 95
Daly, David mfenc	1940	DeLellis, Anthony R. ftb	1961, 62, 63	Donald, Pamela wtrack	1980, 81, 82, 83
Daly, John S. ftb	1897	Delmare, John D. ftb	1979, 80	Donart, James mtrk	1970
Daly, Sharon wdive	1985	Delmas, Bert ftb	1931, 32, 33	Dondero, Harvey mwp	1968
Damico, Leonard mfenc	1989, 90, 91	DeLong, Donald bsb	1953, 54	Donester, Don ftb	1994
Damuth, Don wrest	1956	DeLong, Donald F. mbsk	1952, 53, 54	Donley, Michael mtrk	1967
Dana, I. Ross ftb	1942	DeMars, Susan wtrack	1992, 93, 95, 96	Donovan, Pat B. ftb	1972, 73, 74
Dana, Jack H. mbsk	1942, 43	Demorest, Margaret wtrack	1982, 83, 84, 85	Doo, Cheryl wgym	1986, 87, 88, 89
Dandurand, Thomas bsb	1953, 54, 55	Dempsey, Burke wrest	1981	Dooling, C.W. bsb	1914
Daniel, Robert mgym	1978, 79, 80, 81	Demree, Oliver mgym	1992	Dorlarque, Aaron bsb	1989, 90, 91, 92
Daniels, David ftb	1988	Denney, Carolyn wsoc	1985, 86, 87, 88	Dorn, Ernest F. III ftb	1953, 54, 55
Daniels, John mfenc	1957, 58	Denney, Denise wsoc	1988, 89, 90, 91	Dorst, Christopher mwp	1974, 75, 76
Daniels, Melinda wgolf	1992, 93, 94	Denney, Richard wrest	1959, 60, 61	Dose, Thomas W. mbsk	1962, 63, 64
Daniels, Tim wrest	1980, 81, 82	Dennis, Guy H. ftb	1922, 23	Doster, Guy L. ftb	1952, 53
Dapper, Samuel M. ftb	1978, 79, 80	Densmore, Gregg mtrk	1974, 76	Dotterer, Michael J. ftb	1979, 80, 81, 82
Darsie, William P. ftb	1912, 13	Dent, L.F. bsb	1913, 14, 15, 16	Dotterer, Mike bsb	1980, 81, 82, 83
Dauer, Arthur mgym	1956, 57	Derby, Richard ftb	1965, 66	Doub, William K. mbsk	1931, 32
Davalos, Gabriel mgym	1941	Derrig, William mwp	1964, 65, 66	Doub, William K. ftb	1930, 31, 32
David, Michelle wswim	1989, 90	Desilva, Sandra wtennis	1994, 95, 96	Doud, David mgolf	1941
David, Nelson B. mbsk	1925, 26, 27	DesJardins, Jeff bsb	1992, 93	Dougan, Paul mcrew	1958, 59

Dougherty, Carol wvball	1974	Edelen, Harold D. mbsk	1932, 33, 34	Eschelman, Scott ftb	1986, 87, 88, 89
Dougherty, Kelly wbsk	1991, 92	Edelman, Gabe mgym	1995, 96	Esgen Wienaienand K. mbsk	1919
Dougherty, Stephen mtrk	1971	Edelson, Bruce wrest	1958	Eshleman, Donald mtrk	1965, 66, 67
Doughty, R.M. ftb	1921, 22	Edelson, Roger wrest	1956, 57, 58	Eshleman, Michael mwp	1963, 64, 65
Douglas, Joe G. ftb	1921	Edie, Robert bsb	1968, 69	Esparza, Joline wcrew	1980, 81
Douglas, Jon mten	1956, 57, 58	Edman, Janell fh	1974	Esparza, Joline wvball	1976
Douglas, Jon A. ftb	1955, 56, 57	Edmonds, Brian wrest	1982	Esquer, David bsb	1986, 87
Dow, David bsb	1958	Edmonds, Duane W. mbsk	1936	Essegian, Charles bsb	1951, 52, 53
Dowd, Bernard G. Jr. ftb	1958, 59, 60	Edmunds, John mcrew	1961	Essegian, Charles A. Jr. ftb	1950, 51, 52
Dowling, Frank mwp	1938, 39	Edson, Dave bsb	1970, 71, 72	Estes, G.C. mbsk	1917
Downey, Dennis mtrk	1984, 85	Edwards, Ace mvball	1978	Estes, Herman bsb	1932, 33
Downey, Sheridan mtrk	1963	Edwards, Elise wsoc	1987, 88, 89, 90	Estrada, Art wrest	1975
Downing, Claud S. ftb	1892, 93	Edwards, Harry mbsk	1899, 1900, 01	Evans, Bruce mbsk	1914
Downing, P.R. bsb	1915	Edwards, Holly wswim	1976	Evans, Charles A. ftb	1976, 77, 78, 79
Downing, Paul M. ftb	1892 (Spr.), 1892 (Fall), 93, 94	Edwards, Jackie wtrack	1989, 90, 91, 92	Evans, Charles B. ftb	1908
		Edwards, James mdive	1992, 93, 94, 95	Evans, Don mcrew	1972
Doyle, Kent mtrk	1976	Edwards, Kari wswim	1996	Evans, Howard bsb	1953, 54, 55, 56
Doyle, Morris ftb	1928, 29	Edwards, LeRoy M. ftb	1906	Evans, Janet wswim	1990, 91
Draeger, Richarad mcrew	1957, 58, 59	Edwards, Lesley wsoc	1989, 90	Evans, Marlon ftb	1994, 95
Draft, Chris ftb	1994, 95	Edwards, Mary wswim	1991, 92, 93, 94	Evans, Richard Eckhardt mten	1969, 70, 71, 72
Dragovich, Darren mgolf	1993, 94, 95, 96	Edwards, Megan wswim	1975, 76	Evans, Sarah wbsk	1983, 84
Draper, Guy bsb	1917, 20, 22	Egan, Beth wsoc	1985, 86, 87, 88	Evans, Scott mcrew	1989
Dreissigacker, Peter mtrk	1971, 72, 73	Egan, Bill wrest	1976	Evenson, Sheri wgym	1986, 87, 88, 89
Dressel, Chris ftb	1980, 81, 82	Egan, David mwp	1977, 78	Everett, Danielle wvball	1990
Driano, Andrea wcrew	1991	Egan, Kathy wswim	1977	Ewing, Amy wtrack	1992
Driscoll, Thomas A. ftb	1928, 29	Eger, Greg mxc	1976	Ewing, Mike bsb	1969, 70
Driver, Walter mgolf	1965, 66, 67	Ehrhorn, Charles S. ftb	1930, 31	Ewing, Terry M. ftb	1968, 69, 70
Drown, Jack A. ftb	1933, 34	Eicher, Mike bsb	1988, 89, 90		
Druey, Kirk mgym	1981, 82, 83	Eick, Heidi wvball	1990, 91, 92, 93	Face, William H. Jr. ftb	1958, 59, 60
Druliner, David P. mbsk	1968, 69	Eikelman, John A. mbsk	1943	Fadil, Mark mtrk	1995, 96
Dubinsky, Kerre wgolf	1983, 84, 85	Einstein, Carolyn wsoc	1989, 90, 91, 92	Fadil, Mark mxc	1994, 95
Dubofsky, Frank N. ftb	1961, 62	Eisses, James wrest	1957	Fair, Lee wrest	1970, 71
duBray, Ernest mten	1950, 55, 56	Elder, John mcrew	1961	Fair, Lee P. ftb	1971, 72
Dudley, Ernest bsb	1905, 06	Eldredge, David P. ftb	1952	Fairchild, Peter mtrk	1969, 70, 71
Dudman, William wrest	1958	Eldredge, LeighAnn wtennis	1984, 85, 86, 87	Falberg, Mike mten	1981
DuFault, Scott wrest	1983			Falk, Oliver S. ftb	1917
DuFault, Scott G. ftb	1985	Eldridge, Etuan mcrew	1995	Fallon, Jamie wtrack	1988, 89
Duff, David Hopkins mten	1954, 55, 56	Elfving, William J. mbsk	1962	Fank, Frederick mtrk	1947, 48, 49
Duffy, Adriana wgym	1989	Elkins, Stephanie wswim	1982, 83, 84	Farb, Robert mgym	1975, 76
Duffy, Frank bsb	1966, 67	Eller, Jack R. ftb	1946	Farber, David J. mbsk	1934
DuFour, Thomas W. mbsk	1952	Ellestad, Denise wtrack	1980	Faris, James mtrk	1969
Duimistra, Peter mfenc	1988	Elliot, Blair wsoc	1986, 87, 88, 89	Farish, William mgolf	1960, 61, 62
Dukes, Pamela wtrack	1983, 84, 85, 86	Elliott, Grant mten	1994, 95, 96	Farley, Matt mxc	1994
Dukes, Peter mbsk	1990, 91, 92, 93	Elliott, John mgolf	1951	Farley, William F. mbsk	1966
Duncan, Gil bsb	1955	Elliott, Richard C. ftb	1955	Farmer, Jerome wrest	1991
Dunham, Robert mgym	1947, 48, 49	Elliott, Stuart mgym	1948, 49	Farnham, Anne wcrew	1986
Dunhill, Julie wgym	1988, 90, 91	Ellis, James mwp	1963, 64	Farrar, I.E. mbsk	1914
Dunlap, David mtrk	1949, 50	Ellis, Jamie mgym	1994, 95, 96	Farrar, Mike mcrew	1961
Dunlop, Manda wsoc	1986	Ellis, Kwame ftb	1992, 93, 94, 95	Farrell, George bsb	1936, 37, 38
Dunn, Curtis mten	1987, 88, 89	Ellis, Thomas mtrk	1976	Farrell, Jim mfenc	1988, 90
Dunn, Damon ftb	1994, 95	Elms, Steven mcrew	1984, 85, 86	Farrell, Robert mwp	1961, 62
Dunn, Dave mbsk	1956	Elson, Thomas mwp	1974, 75	Faulkner, George C. ftb	1908
Dunne, Tim mgym	1976	Elway, John bsb	1980, 81	Faville, Richard W. ftb	1921, 22, 23
Dunning, Steve bsb	1969, 70	Elway, John A. ftb	1979, 80, 81, 82	Fawcett, Randall ftb	1941, 42
Dunscombe, Kortney wtrack	1995, 96	Elzie, Jene wgym	1992, 94, 95	Fawcett, Vance mbsk	1929, 30, 31
Dunscombe, Kortney wxc	1994, 95	Emanuels, Kenneth mtrk	1962, 63	Fay, Peter ftb	1937, 38
Dupre, Patrick Marie mten	1973, 74, 75, 76	Emerton, Kelly wcrew	1989, 90	Fehlen, Philip mtrk	1955, 57
		Emory, Jerry mxc	1975, 76, 77, 78	Feinstein, Marc wrest	1973
DuQuette, Rusty bsb	1976	Emslander, Hilde wcrew	1984, 85, 86	Feldman Larsen, Carrie wvball	1989, 90, 91, 92
Duralde, Tom mvball	1977	Enberg, Donald M. ftb	1948, 49, 50		
Durket, Michael ftb	1947	Endo, Paul mfenc	1987	Feldman, Martin ftb	1946, 47
Dutton, Anona wcrew	1996	Engel, Dennis L. ftb	1979, 81, 82	Felix, Brian mwp	1980, 81
Dutton, E.R. mbsk	1914, 15	Engel, Eugene A. ftb	1977, 78, 79	Fendick, Patty wtennis	1984, 85, 86, 87
Duvall, Ron mcrew	1970, 72	Engen, Kip mvball	1979, 80, 81, 82	Fenster, L. Frederick mbsk	1953
Dvorak, Deidra wvball	1981, 82, 83, 84	Englehardt, Robert N. ftb	1986, 87, 88, 89	Fenton, K.L. ftb	1906, 07
Dwight, Herbert M. ftb	1923	Ennis, Greg C. ftb	1986, 87, 88	Fenton, Kenneth bsb	1905, 06, 07
Dwight, Robert bsb	1957, 58	Envela, Gus mtrk	1987	Ferguson, Carol fh	1976
Dwulet, Leon mgolf	1971	Epperson, David C. mbsk	1952, 53, 54	Ferguson, James J. ftb	1971, 72, 73
Dyck, Harry bsb	1942	Erb, Arthur L. ftb	1913, 14, 15	Ferguson, John mcrew	1962
Dye, Lowell A. mbsk	1957	Erb, Benjamin E. ftb	1908, 10, 11, 12	Ferguson, John ftb	1971, 72, 73
Dyer, Dave mxc	1994, 95	Erb, William M. ftb	1899, 1900	Ferguson, William mxc	1955
Dykstra, James C. ftb	1980, 81	Erck, Martin bsb	1966, 67	Ferko, Leo M. ftb	1936, 37
		Erickson, Scott mgolf	1982, 83, 84, 85	Fernandes, Ronald A. ftb	1958, 59, 60
Eadie, Ronald E. ftb	1950, 51, 52	Erickson, Stephanie wbsk	1977	Ferrazano, Richard bsb	1961, 62
Eagle, Walter E. ftb	1955	Erickson, Wayne C. ftb	1946, 47	Ferris, Harold H. ftb	1947
Eagleston, Richard mwp	1968, 69, 70	Erman, Julie fh	1982, 83	Ferro, Michael bsb	1935
Easter, James mtrk	1955, 57	Erndt, Nick mtrk	1984	Ferry, Ed mcrew	1961, 62
Eastham, Clarissa wfenc	1980	Ernst, Joanne wxc	1977, 78	Fetter, Margi wcrew	1980
Eastman, Tom mcrew	1967, 68	Ernst, William mwp	1946	Fetter, Margi wcrew	1981
Eaton, John wrest	1954	Ervin, Jarel mgym	1948	Fiala, Bruce bsb	1976, 77, 78, 79
Eaton, Mark mfenc	1974m 75	Ervin, Todd bsb	1977, 78	Fiander, William B. ftb	1984, 85, 86, 87
Eddington, Virginia wtennis	1986	Esbenshade, Richard wrest	1948, 49, 50	Fiatorone, Marie wfenc	1974, 75, 76

Fickert, Charles ftb	1894, 95, 96, 97, 98
Field, David wrest	1947
Field, Eric mfenc	1955
Field, Julian D. ftb	1947, 48, 49
Fields, Dodie wvball	1977
Fierro, Jose mtrk	1996
Figley, Jodi wgolf	1988, 89, 90, 91
Figueroa, Rudy bsb	1955, 56, 57
Filice, Michael bsb	1959, 60, 61
Filner, Katy fh	1989, 90
Filson, Lara fh	1991
Finch, Richard mfenc	1947, 48, 49
Finger, Chas. mgolf	1939, 40, 41
Finkelstein, Scott mgym	1996
Finklestein, David mfenc	1985, 86
Finkelstein, Stephanie fh	1995
Finley, John A. ftb	1975, 77
Finley, Warren mfenc	1951, 52
Finn, Barbara wvball	1974
Finn, Bridget syncswim	1996
Finney, Allison wgolf	1977, 78, 79, 80
Finney, Jay mcrew	1986, 87, 88
Fischer, Andy mbsk	1983, 84, 85, 86
Fischer, David mvball	1992, 93, 94
Fischer, Erich mwp	1984, 85, 86, 87
Fischer, Jessica wsoc	1992, 93, 94, 95
Fischer, Martin mwp	1983
Fish, Arthur mten	1952, 53, 54
Fishback, Nason mtrk	1951, 52, 53
Fishburn, Andy mvball	1977
Fisher, Ernest L. ftb	1983, 84, 85
Fisher, Forrest S. ftb	1896, 97, 98
Fisher, Jim mgym	1984
Fisher, Kelly wtennis	1991, 92
Fisher, Lynn fh	1991
Fisher, Ralph S. ftb	1899
Fisher, Richard Burt mten	1970, 71, 72, 73
Fisher, Robert wrest	1954, 55, 56
Fisher, Steven John mten	1972, 73, 74, 75
Fisher, Susan fh	1984
Fisher, William mgym	1966
Fishman, David mfenc	1987
Fishman, Susan fh	1994
Fisk, Jason ftb	1991, 92, 93, 94
Fiske, Amy wfenc	1976, 77, 78
Fitting, John W. ftb	1909
Fitzgerald, Robert mcrew	1991
Fitzmorris, Tyhce M. ftb	1961
Fitzner, Mark mbsk	1977
Fitzpaatrick, Casey wcrew	1989, 90
Fitzpatrick, Katie wgym	1996
Fix, Donald R. ftb	1947, 48, 49
Fix, Megan syncswim	1996
Fixler, Leslie mgym	1949
Flanagan, Michael mten	1991, 92, 93, 94
Flanagan, Thomas F. ftb	1964, 65
Flanders, William S. mbsk	1954, 55, 56
Flannery, Steven mtrk	1968, 69, 70
Flatland, Richmond (Jr.) bsb	1943, 46
Flatland, Richmond Jr. ftb	1946, 47
Fleischner, Chris mcrew	1993
Fleishhacker, Herbert Jr. ftb	1927, 28, 29
Fleming, Dana fh	1985, 86, 87
Fletcher, Charles mwp	1947, 48, 49
Fletcher, David mtrk	1953
Fletcher, Robert bsb	1955, 56, 57
Fletcher, Rod mvball	1977, 78, 79, 80
Flikke, Sean bsb	1996
Flinn, Douglass mfenc	1988
Flint, Robert mtrk	1975, 76
Flint, William mtrk	1954, 55
Flood, Randolph G. ftb	1918, 19
Flood, Raymond O. ftb	1924
Flowers, Monteville D. Jr. ftb	1919
Floyd, Dan B. ftb	1977, 78, 79
Floyd, Mary Ann wswim	1976, 77
Fluet, Greg mcrew	1991
Foley, Matt mfenc	1980, 81
Foley, Paul Stephen ftb	1978
Folkl, Kristin wbsk	1995
Folkl, Kristin wvball	1994, 95
Folsom, Myron mten	1938, 39, 40
Fontana, Laura wsoc	1986
Fontana-Harris, Barbra wvball	1983, 84, 85, 86
Fontius, John mtrk	1961, 62, 63
Forbes, Donn mtrk	1966, 67
Forbes, Frank A. Jr. ftb	1946
Forbes, Robert mten	1942, 1948, 49
Forbush, John mgolf	1955, 56
Ford Enthoven, Tucker wvball	1979
Ford, Eric mcrew	1990, 91
Ford, Gregory mtrk	1965, 69, 70
Foreman, Craig mbsk	1983
Forencich, Frank mwp	1974, 75
Forman, Adam mgym	1988, 89, 90
Forman, Mark wrest	1989, 90
Forood, Lisa wtennis	1976
Forrest, Stefanie wdive	1994, 95
Forsyth, Craig mvball	1987, 88, 89, 90
Forsythe, Raymond bsb	1934
Fortune, Scott mvball	1985, 86, 87, 89
Foster, Elie wsoc	1994, 95
Foster, Galen ftb	1989
Foster, John mtrk	1975, 76
Foster, Shelly wvball	1994, 95
Foudy, Julie wsoc	1989, 90, 91, 92
Fowler, John mtrk	1991, 93
Fox, Bradley S. ftb	1977, 78
Fox, Dennis bsb	1946
Fox, James mcrew	1987, 88, 89
Fox, Kenneth mwp	1947, 48, 49
Fox, Patrick mxc	1982
Foxworth, Jack mvball	1978, 79, 80
Fraioli, Claudio mfenc	1978
Franchetti, Michael mtrk	1957, 58
Francis, Charles mtrk	1969, 71
Francis, Dan R. ftb	1973, 74, 75
Francis, Jack P. ftb	1940, 41
Francis, Phillip K. ftb	1976, 77, 78
Franco, Claudia wswim	1995, 96
Frank, Alvin H. ftb	1910, 11
Frank, David mtrk	1982, 83, 84
Frankenheimer, Julius J. ftb	1892, 93, 94, 95
Fraser, Kenneth mtrk	1964, 65
Frawley, Matt mdive	1986, 87, 88, 89
Freccero, Francesca fh	1979, 80
Fredrickson, Terry mtrk	1966
Freebairn-Smith, Roderick mgym	1953, 54, 55
Freeberg, Melissa wxc	1993
Freeburg, Melissa wtrack	1992, 93
Freehafer, Susie wsoc	1986
Freeman, Charles G. ftb	1968
Freeman, Christopher ftb	1925, 26, 27
Freeman, Jody wvball	1982
Freeman, Lewis R. ftb	1898
Freeman, Victoria wswim	1978
Fregla, Darrell L. mbsk	1972
Freis, Joel H. ftb	1956, 57, 58
Freitas, Joan wcrew	1979, 80
Freitas, Mike bsb	1979
Frelier, Marc wrest	1973, 74
Fremouw, Edward mtrk	1954, 55
French, Todd bsb	1989, 90
Frentrup, Lud ftb	1927, 28, 29
Freuen, Regan wbsk	1995, 96
Frey, Marietta wgym	1988, 89, 90, 91
Friedman, Jeremy wrest	1992
Friedrichs, Charles mtrk	1951, 52
Friend, Anne wgym	1983
Fries, James mgym	1957
Frisbee, Robert D. ftb	1942
Frische, Eric mtrk	1963, 64, 65
Frizell, Porter T. ftb	1905
Froehlich, Charles mfenc	1950
Frojen, Robert mwp	1949, 50, 51
Frost, Carl D. mbsk	1972, 73, 74
Frost, David bsb	1972, 74
Frost, Jack mten	1954, 55, 56
Frost, John E. mten	1946
Frost, Rebekah wvball	1977
Frost, Scott ftb	1993, 94
Frost, Steve ftb	1994, 95
Frothingham, David mcrew	1960
Frye, Cheytom mtrk	1952
Frykman, Carl mcrew	1980, 81, 82
Frykman, Helen wcrew	1981
Fuentes, Martin K. ftb	1978
Fuerbringer, Matt mvball	1993, 94, 95, 96
Fujikawa, Ronald K. ftb	1969
Fukunagaa, Bert wrest	1983, 84
Fuller, Frank bsb	1923, 24
Fuller, Thomas G. mbsk	1943
Fulop, John mcrew	1960
Fung, Connie fh	1991, 92, 93
Funseth, Mark mgolf	1987, 88, 89, 90
Furlanic, Richard A. ftb	1954, 55
Furlong, Roger mfenc	1882
Furman, Fred (Jr.) bsb	1936, 37, 38
Gadd, Peter mwp	1969, 70, 71
Gaedtke, Richard J. ftb	1949, 50
Gage, Brian mgym	1984
Gail, William mtrk	1977, 78, 79, 80
Gaines, Catherine wswim	1978
Gaines, Chryste wtrack	1989, 90, 91, 92
Galbraith, Edwin bsb	1934
Galef, Stephanie wbsk	1976, 77
Galindo, Mike mcrew	1996
Gallagher, Frank mcrew	1970
Gallagher, Robert bsb	1967, 68
Gallagher, Zachary mwp	1992
Gallarneau, Hugh ftb	1938, 39, 40
Gallaway, Alan Hill mten	1957
Galt, Bruce wrest	1949, 50
Gamble, Greg mwp	1983, 84, 85
Games, David mgolf	1979, 80, 81, 82
Ganahl, Francis mtrk	1946, 47
Ganahl, Francis mxc	1946
Gandrud, Laura wswim	1991, 92, 93
Ganong, C.F. bsb	1908, 09, 10
Ganong, Carl F. ftb	1907, 08
Gansel, John mwp	1977, 78, 79, 80
Gant, Richard A. ftb	1952, 53
Gant, Vernon F. ftb	1968
Gantz, George mcrew	1972
Garber, Sidney J. ftb	1957, 58, 59
Garcia, Aaron mvball	1994, 95, 96
Garcia, Dave mgolf	1995, 96
Garcia, Rodrigo F. ftb	1971, 72, 73
Gard, F.J. ftb	1911, 12, 13, 14
Gardener, Greg C. ftb	1982
Gardiner, Jen wsoc	1990, 91, 92
Gardiner, Meg wtrack	1979
Gardner, Megan wdive	1994, 95
Garibaldi, Donald bsb	1926, 27, 28
Garner, Andrea wtrack	1992
Garner, Andrea wtrack	1993
Garner, Andrea wxc	1991, 92, 93, 94
Garner, Robert B. mbsk	1963
Garner, Rodney wrest	1951, 52
Garner, Rodney G. ftb	1950, 51
Garnett, David ftb	1989, 90, 91, 92
Garnett, Kevin ftb	1992, 93, 94
Garnier, Edward P. ftb	1936, 37
Garrard, Leslie wsoc	1990, 91, 92, 93, 94
Garrett, Brian mvball	1992, 93, 94, 95
Garrett, Chris mtrk	1990
Garrett, Paul mbsk	1990, 91, 92
Garrett, Robert D. ftb	1951, 52, 53
Garrett, Thornton mfenc	1953, 54
Garrett, Walter mtrk	1953, 54, 55
Garst, David wrest	1947
Garst, Stephen wrest	1949, 50, 51
Gartland, Laura fh	1985, 86, 87
Gash, John mtrk	1985, 86, 87, 88
Gaskin, Leroy wrest	1947, 48, 49
Gassner, Lindsay wswim	1995, 96
Gates, Diane fh	1974, 75
Gates, John mfenc	1957
Gates, Linda wtennis	1982, 83, 84, 85
Gates, Lloyd mten	1938, 39, 40
Gaughran, James mwp	1951, 52, 53
Gault, Frank bsb	1912
Gaumer, Kim wsoc	1979, 80, 81, 82
Gavin, Patty wswim	1983, 84, 85, 86
Gawthrop, Lynn wcrew	1986

Gaynor, T.J. ftb	1992, 93, 94, 95	
Gazis, Carrie wsoc	1980, 81, 82	
Gaztambide, Denise wtrack	1983, 84, 85, 86	
Gearhart, J.J. wvball	1979, 80, 81, 82	
Gebers, Mike wrest	1977	
Gebers, Richard mwp	1973	
Gebert, Robert R. ftb	1953	
Geddes, Donald ftb	1954, 55	
Gee, Steven wrest	1953	
Geenan, Nancy fh	1978, 79, 80	
Geer, Brad mgolf	1986, 87, 89, 90	
Geib, Katie wsoc	1989, 90	
Geiger, Josh mcrew	1991	
Geiken, Stacy mtrk	1976	
Geisler, Frederick mtrk	1971	
Geisler, Frederick mxc	1970	
Geisse, Amy wsoc	1983, 84, 85, 86, 87	
Geisse, Sally wsoc	1983	
Geissler, E.D. ftb	1910, 11	
Gelber, Marvin W. mbsk	1949, 50	
Gentry, George mten	1950, 51, 52	
George, Bill wrest	1983	
George, Fred mtrk	1952, 53, 54	
George, Laurence wgym	1986, 88, 89	
George, Ron ftb	1990, 91, 92	
Gerald, Gregory M. ftb	1915	
Gerardo, Charles mgym	1985, 86, 87, 88	
Gerfen, Earl mtrk	1977	
Gergen, Robert R. ftb	1953	
Gerrard, Jessie fh	1975, 76, 77, 78	
Gerring, Phillip mfenc	1979, 80	
Gerut, Jody bsb	1996	
Gervais, Richard P. ftb	1977, 78, 79, 80	
Getchell, Philip mgolf	1954, 55, 56	
Geyman, Cal mcrew	1981, 83	
Ghilotti, Robert V. ftb	1947, 48	
Giallonardo, Thomas M. ftb	1967	
Gibbs, Coy ftb	1991, 92, 93, 94	
Gibson, Gary mcrew	1979, 80	
Gilberg, Mark R. mbsk	1973, 74, 75	
Gilbert, John B. mbsk	1966, 67	
Gilfillan, S.W. bsb	1910, 11	
Gill, Stan P. ftb	1985	
Gillen, Christopher mfenc	1985, 88	
Gillespie, Lisa wswim	1987, 88	
Gillespie, Paul mtrk	1959, 60	
Gillingham, Chuck ftb	1987, 88, 89, 90	
Gilman, Charles E. ftb	1899	
Gilmartin, Adrienne wgolf	1985, 86, 87	
Gilmete, Joaquin A. ftb	1983, 84, 85	
Gilmore, John mgym	1952, 53, 54	
Gilmore, Rodney C. ftb	1979, 80, 82	
Gilstrap, William mtrk	1963	
Giovacchini, Paul mbsk	1977, 78, 79	
Girard, Joanna wtennis	1981, 82	
Girard, Marston mtrk	1939, 40	
Girard, Marston mxc	1939	
Giske, Grant mwp	1962	
Givens, Terr wtrack	1984, 85	
Gladden, Jason wrest	1994, 96	
Glasgow, Charles Jr. mbsk	1933	
Glass, Mike mcrew	1975, 76, 77	
Glathe, William mgym	1950	
Glazer, Nicole wwp	1996	
Gleason, Josh mtrk	1995, 96	
Gleichert, Marc mwp	1983, 84	
Glueck, Jennifer fh	1992, 93, 94, 95	
Godbold, Sheila wvball	1979	
Goedewaagen, Karen wbsk	1983, 84, 85, 87	
Goethals, Glenn mgolf	1974, 76, 77	
Goetz, Valerie wsoc	1988	
Gold, Claudia fh	1979, 80, 81	
Goldberg, Jerome L. ftb	1952, 53, 54	
Goldie, Dan mten	1983, 84, 85, 86	
Goldman, Craig mgym	1979, 80, 81	
Goldsborough, E.Scott mtrk	1948	
Goldsmith, Nancy wgym	1984, 85, 86, 87	
Goldstein, Max H. ftb	1971, 72, 73	
Goldstein, Paul mten	1995, 96	
Gomez, Mason wrest	1986	
Gompert, Kate wtennis	1982, 84	
Gong, Diane wxc	1980, 81	
Goode, John mtrk	1964, 65	
Goodell, Fred bsb	1932	
Goodenbour, Molly wbsk	1990, 91, 92, 93	
Goodman, Leslie wcrew	1980	
Goodman, Mary fh	1984, 85, 86	
Goodrich, Warren bsb	1952, 53, 54	
Goorno, Andy mfenc	1983, 84, 85, 86	
Gordon, Darrien ftb	1990, 91, 92	
Gordon, Jack S. ftb	1959, 60, 61	
Gordon, Lisa wtennis	1979, 80	
Gore, Debi wbsk	1979, 80, 81, 82	
Gorlin, Jed mcrew	1976, 77, 78	
Gorman, Kenneth mgym	1975, 76, 77, 78	
Gorter, Wytze mbsk	1934, 35	
Goss, David mvball	1990, 91, 92, 93	
Goss, Steven wrest	1971, 72	
Gould, Dick mten	1957, 59, 60	
Govea, John wrest	1975, 76	
Grabb, Jim mten	1983, 84, 85, 86	
Grable, Dave ftb	1991, 92, 93, 94	
Graff, Stanley R. ftb	1938, 39, 40	
Graham, Bill mxc	1979, 80, 81, 82	
Graham, Clark bsb	1941	
Graham, Debbie wtennis	1989, 90, 91	
Graham, Mark wrest	1989, 90, 91, 92	
Grame, Paul bsb	1978, 79, 81	
Grannis, William mgym	1939, 40	
Grant, Alan ftb	1986, 87, 88, 89	
Grant, Jeff wrest	1995, 96	
Grant, John mtrk	1941	
Grant, John E. ftb	1935, 36	
Grant, Whitney wtennis	1974, 75	
Gravely, Warren mbsk	1992, 93, 94, 95	
Graves, Jonathan ftb	1968, 69, 70	
Graves, Maury mtrk	1957, 58	
Graves, Maury mxc	1954, 55, 57	
Graviss, Chris mdive	1982, 83	
Gray, Carol wtrack	1987, 89, 90	
Gray, Carol wxc	1986, 87	
Gray, Garold mten	1952, 53, 54	
Grayson, Robert bsb	1934	
Grayson, Robert H. ftb	1933, 34, 35	
Greaney, Theresa wsoc	1981, 82, 83, 84	
Green, Frederick N. mbsk	1969, 70, 71	
Green, Gary mcrew	1962	
Green, George bsb	1921, 22	
Green, Glen mfenc	1977	
Green, Henry mtrk	1985,87, 88	
Green, Henry E. ftb	1985, 86, 87, 88	
Green, Ken bsb	1984, 85, 86	
Green, Lisa wtennis	1987, 88, 89, 90	
Green, Thomas S. mbsk	1952, 53	
Greenhut, Carl bsb	1947	
Greenlaw, David mtrk	1972	
Greenman, Obi mwp	1984, 85, 87	
Greenwood, Doug mtrk	1976, 78, 79	
Greer, Roger P. ftb	1975	
Greer, William L. ftb	1939	
Gregory, Richarad mwp	1961	
Greif, Sidney bsb	1959	
Greig, Katherine wcrew	1996	
Grenardo, Ozzie ftb	1991, 93, 94	
Gresser, Edward mgym	1981, 82, 83, 84	
Greve, F.H. mbsk	1917	
Grey, Alan mtrk	1939, 40, 41	
Grey, George C. ftb	1930, 31, 32	
Gribbin, Franklin P. ftb	1931, 32, 33	
Griffin, Donald B. mbsk	1967, 68, 69	
Griffin, Robert R. Jr. ftb	1949, 50, 51	
Griffin, Tim bsb	1988, 89, 90	
Griffith, Chris mvball	1995	
Griffith, Judy wbsk	1983, 84, 85, 86	
Griffith, William mtrk	1969, 70	
Griggs, Curge mcrew	1989	
Griglione, Michelle wswim	1987, 89, 90, 91	
Grimes, George mtrk	1946, 47, 48	
Grimes, George mxc	1946	
Grimes, Tom mvball	1977, 78, 79, 80	
Grimm, Thomas mtrk	1967	
Grimm, Trevor A. ftb	1959	
Grimsley, Jorn mxc	1995	
Grissum, Darrell W. ftb	1981, 82, 83	
Groff, Gayle mcrew	1980, 81	
Grolle, Fred mtrk	1979	
Grolle, Kenneth bsb	1973, 75	
Grosh, M.D. ftb	1892	
Groslimond, Gery W. mten	1970, 71, 72, 73	
Gross, Madison wfenc	1974, 75	
Gross, Richard mfenc	1950, 51, 52	
Grossberg, Linda wvball	1980	
Grossenbaugh, Mark mcrew	1974, 75	
Groth, Bob mgym	1984	
Grove Grolle, Margaret wvball	1980, 81, 82	
Groves, James L. ftb	1937, 39	
Grunseth, Eric wrest	1976	
Guardino, Tom bsb	1975, 76, 77, 78	
Guarria, Peter mcrew	1991	
Gueble, Jeff mfenc	1980, 81, 82	
Guess, Richard mgym	1967, 68	
Guglielmetti, Gary mtrk	1967	
Guillory, John L. ftb	1964, 65, 66	
Gumlia, Roxy wgolf	1982, 83	
Gunesch, Douglas wrest	1967	
Gunnerson, Lee mwp	1951	
Gurfein, Jim mten	1980, 81	
Gurley, John mten	1941	
Gust, Devens mfenc	1940	
Gustafson, Cheryl wsoc	1982, 83, 84, 85	
Gustafson, Jerry F. ftb	1953, 54, 55	
Guthrie, Franklin mtrk	1940	
Guyer, Peggy wtrack	1979	
Guzy, Pam wswim	1978	
Gwaltney, Doug bsb	1984	
Hachten, William A. ftb	1946	
Haddock, Steve mgym	1977	
Hadley, Mark mtrk	1976, 77, 78	
Haga, Richard G. mbsk	1957, 58, 59	
Hagan, Bernie mcrew	1981	
Hagey, Cari wtennis	1985, 86, 87, 88	
Hagey, James Stanford mten	1972, 74	
Hagey, Susan wtennis	1976, 77, 78, 79	
Hagstette, Margot wswim	1976, 77, 78, 79	
Hahn, Joy wtennis	1976	
Hahn, Piper wvball	1990, 91, 92, 93	
Hahner, Brooke wvball	1983, 84, 85, 86	
Haight, Mark mtrk	1970, 71, 72	
Haile, Jeffrey A. ftb	1980, 81	
Haine, Kisi wvball	1979, 80, 81, 82	
Haldeman, Bill mxc	1976, 77, 78, 79	
Hales, Tom mgolf	1977	
Haley, James mcrew	1967, 68	
Haley, Samuel M. ftb	1911	
Hall, Chip mtrk	1989, 91	
Hall, Efton Jr. ftb	1970	
Hall, Elwin B. ftb	1912, 13, 14	
Hall, Hilary wtrack	1979	
Hall, John bsb	1953, 54, 55	
Hall, Karen wgym	1979, 80, 83	
Hall, Michael mtrk	1973, 74, 75	
Hall, Mike ftb	1992, 93, 94, 95	
Hall, Robert mgym	1941	
Hall, Robert P. ftb	1942, 46	
Hall, Thomas Z. ftb	1977, 78, 81	
Halligan, William K. mbsk	1967, 68, 69	
Hallisey, Marianne wvball	1975	
Hallock, Sara fh	1990, 91, 92, 93	
Hallsted, Rick bsb	1977	
Halm, A.G. bsb	1912, 13, 14	
Halstead, Robert mbsk	1943	
Halstead, Samuel T. ftb	1915	
Hamacher, Danielle wsoc	1993, 94	
Hamilton, Dwain ftb	1983, 84	
Hamilton, Glenn bsb	1936, 37, 38	
Hamilton, Glenn H. ftb	1936, 38	
Hamilton, Kadar ftb	1994, 95	
Hamilton, Robert bsb	1934, 35, 36	
Hamilton, Robert A. ftb	1933, 34, 35	
Hamm, Peter bsb	1967	
Hammer, Jeffery mwp	1967, 68, 71	
Hammer, Kenneth mwp	1967	
Hammett, Raymond bsb	1941, 42	
Hammett, Raymond M. ftb	1940, 41, 42	
Hammonds, Jeffrey bsb	1990, 91, 92	

Hampton, Robert bsb	1973, 74, 75	
Hanan, Dan mvball	1987, 88, 89, 90	
Hancock, Dan mwp	1992, 93, 94, 95	
Hancock, John C. mbsk	1931, 32, 33	
Hancock, Ronald C. ftb	1971, 72	
Hand, Milton N. ftb	1930, 31	
Handley, Ray R. ftb	1963, 64, 65	
Handley, Stephen wrest	1957	
Handy, Jack mfenc	1974, 75	
Hanley, Mike mcrew	1961, 62	
Hanlon, William bsb	1941	
Hanna, Sherry wswim	1981, 82, 83, 84	
Hannaford, Kim bsb	1972, 73, 74	
Hanner, Allen F. ftb	1952	
Hanrahan, Noel wbsk	1983	
Hansel, Peter A. ftb	1971, 72, 73	
Hansen, Carl ftb	1994, 95	
Hansen, George wrest	1969, 70	
Hansen, Jed bsb	1992, 93, 94	
Hansen, Jeff ftb	1994	
Hansen, Johnna wtrack	1979, 80	
Hansen, Kent mtrk	1957, 58	
Hanslett, Don mgolf	1939, 40, 41	
Hanson, Mark ftb	1988, 89, 90	
Hanson, Tommy ftb	1994, 95	
Hanst, Curtis mwp	1982	
Hanweck, Gerald mgolf	1962, 64	
Harber, Eric wrest	1986, 87	
Harbour, David mbsk	1992, 94, 95, 96	
Harbour, L.B. Jr. mgolf	1941	
Harder, Theo bsb	1927, 28, 29	
Harder, Theodore ftb	1926, 27, 28	
Hardey, Alison wtennis	1981, 82, 83	
Hardgrave, Eric bsb	1980, 81, 82, 83	
Hardin, Tripp ftb	1982, 83	
Hardy, Arthur bsb	1929, 30, 31	
Hardy, Arthur C. ftb	1931	
Hargadon, Andy mcrew	1985, 86	
Haring, Vicky wsoc	1992, 93, 94, 95	
Hariton, Theodore wrest	1951	
Harlan, Richard mwp	1948, 49, 50	
Harlow, Charles mtrk	1952, 53	
Harlow, Jay mfenc	1974	
Harmon, Mark R. ftb	1981, 82, 83, 84	
Harmon, Robert wrest	1949, 50, 51	
Harms, M. William bsb	1942	
Harper, David mtrk	1969, 70	
Harper, Matt ftb	1993, 94	
Harpster, Howard mgolf	1970, 71	
Harrelson, William H. ftb	1893, 94	
Harrigan, P.F. ftb	1910, 11, 12	
Harrington, A. Tauasu ftb	1955, 56, 57	
Harrington, David mtrk	1967, 68	
Harrington, Robert mgolf	1973, 74	
Harrington,Tara wbsk	1994, 95, 96	
Harris Murray, Lane wvball	1975, 76	
Harris, Arthur C. mbsk	1966, 67, 68	
Harris, Charlie wrest	1970, 71	
Harris, Darrin mtrk	1987, 88, 89,90	
Harris, David bsb	1982, 83	
Harris, James mgym	1950	
Harris, John P. ftb	1975, 76	
Harris, Larry mbsk	1980	
Harris, Larry W. ftb	1977, 78, 79, 80	
Harris, Leo A. ftb	1925, 26	
Harris, Mark ftb	1993, 94, 95	
Harris, Marvin K. ftb	1961, 62, 63	
Harris, Ray wrest	1948, 50	
Harris, Richard mgolf	1966, 67, 68	
Harris, Sandy wvball	1977, 78, 79	
Harris, Walt bsb	1984, 85, 86	
Harris, Walter L. ftb	1984, 85, 86	
Harrison, Beth wxc	1978, 79	
Harrison, Bob mcrew	1961	
Harrison, Brian bsb	1976, 77, 78, 79	
Harrison, Courtney syncswim	1996	
Harry, Emile M. ftb	1981, 82, 83, 84	
Harshbarger, Jo wswim	1976, 77, 78	
Hart, H. Vernon mtrk	1941, 42	
Hartman, Jessica wtrack	1995	
Hartman, Stanley wrest	1955	
Hartranft, S. Glenn ftb	1921	
Hartvickson, Leon M. ftb	1967	
Hartwig, Charles M. ftb	1962, 63	
Harvard, Lomax mfenc	1942	
Harvey, Harold bsb	1918	
Harvey, Stephen wrest	1969	
Harvey, Will mcrew	1989	
Harwood, Charles mtrk	1973, 75	
Haserot, Karen wvball	1984	
Hashimoto, Mark ftb	1984, 85	
Haskins, Jon ftb	1994, 95	
Haslach, Margaret wswim	1978, 79	
Hasler, Sidney mbsk	1951	
Hassen, Howard L. mbsk	1966, 67	
Hasson, Grant mwp	1983	
Hatch, Robert mwp	1946	
Hathaway, Pierre mwp	1948, 49, 50	
Hatta, Robert wrest	1995, 96	
Hatton, Chris mtrk	1981, 83	
Hatton, Curtis mtrk	1980, 81, 82, 83	
Hatzenbuhler, Mark ftb	1990, 91, 92, 93	
Hauerwaas, John mwp	1940	
Haupt, Meredie wswim	1981, 82	
Hauser, Brad mxc	1995	
Hauser, Brent mxc	1995	
Hauser, Henry P. ftb	1917	
Hausladen, Bob bsb	1981, 82	
Hauverman, Cornelius D. ftb	1901, 02, 03	
Havskjold, Glenn mtrk	1966	
Hawkins, Chris ftb	1987, 88, 89	
Hawkins, Frederick H. mbsk	1929, 30	
Hawkins, Richard mgym	1958, 59, 60, 61	
Hay, David mwp	1994	
Hayes, A.S. bsb	1914, 15	
Hayes, Allen mtrk	1939, 40	
Hayes, Amy wvball	1985, 86, 87, 88	
Hayes, Jane wtennis	1974, 75	
Hayes, Sidney mgolf	1941	
Haygood, John T. ftb	1967, 68	
Hayman, Robert mtrk	1974	
Hayman, Robert mxc	1971, 73	
Haynie, John mtrk	1962	
Hays, Victoria wswim	1974, 75, 76, 77	
Hayward, Laura wtrack	1993, 94	
Hayward, Laura wxc	1992, 93	
Hazard, Jeff wrest	1983, 84, 85, 86	
Hazelrigg, Thomas R. ftb	1965, 66, 67	
Hazelton, John wrest	1966	
Hazen, Lisa wswim	1984, 85, 86	
Hazzard, William C. ftb	1894	
Head, Gordon E. ftb	1934	
Heads, Gina wtrack	1995	
Heagerty, Leo bsb	1936, 37	
Hearn, Arthur bsb	1934	
Hearney, Richard D. ftb	1960	
Heath, Charles M. mbsk	1937	
Heath, Tad mtrk	1995, 96	
Hebert, John ftb	1993, 94, 95	
Hecker, Toby mcrew	1961	
Hedgpeth, Christy wbsk	1991, 92, 93, 94	
Hedlund, Martin mtrk	1980, 81, 82, 83	
Heffernan, Robert E. ftb	1966, 67, 68	
Hegi, Peter mgym	1993, 94, 95, 96	
Heinecke, Walter ftb	1927, 28, 29	
Heinen, Jack bsb	1950	
Heinly, Donald ftb	1908	
Heinze, Kathy wswim	1974, 75, 76	
Heise, Michael mtrk	1980, 82, 83	
Heiser, Jeffrey mgolf	1969, 71	
Heiser, Peter E. ftb	1929, 30, 31	
Heisick, Lori wswim	1990, 91, 92, 93	
Held, Franklin mtrk	1947, 48, 49	
Helfter, Susan wtrack	1990, 91, 92	
Helling, Rick bsb	1992	
Helliwell, Donna wfenc	1978, 79	
Helliwell, Robert mfenc	1941, 42	
Hellman, Irving mgolf	1941	
Helm, Troy mtrk	1984	
Helser, Charles W. Jr. ftb	1920	
Hemmer, Rachel wbsk	1992, 93, 94, 95	
Henck, Pam wfenc	1981, 82, 83, 84	
Henderson, Amy wtrack	1995, 96	
Henderson, Courtney mten	1953	
Hendry, John L. mbsk	1959, 60, 61	
Heninger, David wrest	1946, 47	
Henley, Thomas H. III ftb	1983, 84, 85, 86	
Henlon, Vanessa wtrack	1987, 88, 89, 90	
Hennacy, Harold bsb	1953	
Henning, Sonja wbsk	1988, 89, 90, 91	
Henrion, Claudie wvball	1976	
Henry, Robert mtrk	1974	
Hensel, G.C. bsb	1916	
Henshaw, M.B. bsb	1911, 12	
Henton, John ftb	1993, 94	
Hepp, Virgil E. mbsk	1931	
Hepworth, Ted mcrew	1972	
Herasimchuk, David wrest	1962	
Heringer, Fred bsb	1933, 34, 35	
Herlands, Charles William mten	1967, 68	
Herman, Jeremy mgym	1995, 96	
Hermitte, Gene mcrew	1965, 66	
Hermiz, Rita wsoc	1994, 95	
Heron, Ivar C. ftb	1917	
Herrell, Dawn wfenc	1983	
Herrera, Kathy wxc	1977	
Herring, Ed ftb	1992	
Herrmann, Frank mtrk	1955, 57	
Herrmann, Zena wswim	1978, 79, 80, 81	
Herron, William bsb	1950	
Hertel, Caryn wtennis	1978, 79	
Hertel, Edward mtrk	1941, 42	
Hertz, Howard mtrk	1952, 53	
Herzog, Dick mcrew	1964, 65, 66	
Hestor, Donald mwp	1946, 47	
Hey, Clifford L. ftb	1924	
Hibbs, James bsb	1964, 65, 66	
Hibler, Michael K. ftb	1964, 65, 66	
Hibler, Paul J. ftb	1977, 78, 79	
Hickerson, Marcus mtrk	1988, 89, 90, 91	
Hickox, Charles mten	1951, 52, 53	
Hicks, Kenny mbsk	1990, 91, 92, 93	
Hidalgo, Loretta fh	1992, 93	
Higaki, Yuji mtrk	1993	
Higgins, John M. mbsk	1947, 48	
Higgins, John M. ftb	1946	
Higgins, Michael bsb	1972, 73	
Highsmith, William bsb	1955	
Hightower, Brad wrest	1982, 86	
Higson, Allison wswim	1994, 95	
Hilbert, Anne wsoc	1985, 86	
Hildebrand, Alfred P. ftb	1961, 62, 63	
Hildebrand, Kathy wtrack	1979, 80	
Hiler, Emerson mtrk	1941	
Hilgeman, Robin Dale mten	1958	
Hill, Cary mcrew	1977	
Hill, Corey ftb	1994, 95	
Hill, Donald K. ftb	1925, 26, 27	
Hill, Harrison W. ftb	1898, 1900, 01	
Hill, James L. mbsk	1946	
Hill, Jennifer wsoc	1984, 85, 86, 87	
Hill, L. Anthony ftb	1973, 74, 75, 76	
Hill, Mark N. ftb	1975, 76, 77	
Hill, Martin mxc	1964, 65	
Hill, Thomas mwp	1967, 68, 69	
Hillary, Ellin wxc	1984	
Hillman, Bob mvball	1991, 92, 93	
Hillman, Harry H. Jr. ftb	1929, 30, 31	
Hillman, John mwp	1985	
Hillman, John N. ftb	1931, 32, 33	
Hillyer, Russell mgym	1949	
Hinch, A.J. bsb	1993, 94, 95, 96	
Hinckley, Beckett ftb	1990, 91	
Hinckley, Kent B. mbsk	1963, 64, 65	
Hinckley, Robert W. ftb	1986, 87, 88, 89	
Hind, Robert mwp	1941	
Hindman, Holly wswim	1996	
Hines, Andre P. ftb	1978, 79	
Hing, Greg mten	1980, 81	
Hinojosa, Pepe bsb	1976, 77, 78	
Hinshaw, Chester J. ftb	1960	
Hinshaw, Dean S. ftb	1958, 59, 60	
Hinze, Richard mtrk	1946	
Hipp, Matt mcrew	1995, 96	
Hirsch, Kenneth mgym	1954	
Hirschbertg, Robert mtrk	1978	

Hirschfeld, Stuart mtrk	1984	
Hittner, Bernard bsb	1974, 76	
Ho, Melvin mtrk	1972, 73	
Hoaglin, Mark K. ftb	1974, 75, 76	
Hobday, Alistair mwp	1992	
Hoch, Morgan wfenc	1993, 94, 95, 96	
Hochgesang, Josh bsb	1996	
Hochstsetler, Mark mtrk	1993	
Hodge, Robert mfenc	1954, 55, 56	
Hodges, Jim mten	1977, 78, 79	
Hodges, John bsb	1968, 69	
Hodgkins, Samantha fh	1987, 89, 90	
Hodgman, Bradley Albin mten	1962, 63, 64	
Hoefer, Mike mvball	1994, 95, 96	
Hoegh, Robert L. ftb	1951, 52	
Hoel, Melissa wswim	1982	
Hoeveler, Charles mten	1995, 96	
Hoever, A.J. bsb	1916	
Hoff, Lawrence mtrk	1947, 48, 49	
Hoffman, Clifford P. ftb	1926, 27, 28	
Hoffman, Martha wcrew	1979, 80, 81	
Hoffman, Tad mvball	1995, 96	
Hoffmeyer, Shawn mgym	1982, 84	
Hoge, Anne wsoc	1989, 90	
Hogg, Charles H. ftb	1892 (Spring)	
Hoggatt, Monica wtrack	1993, 94, 95, 96	
Hogsett, Matthew mtrk	1974, 75, 76	
Hogue, Philip James mten	1955, 56	
Hoisch, Alan M. ftb	1942	
Hokanson, Charles mtrk	1950, 51, 52	
Hokanson, Charles R. ftb	1949, 51	
Holbrook, David bsb	1989, 90, 91, 92	
Holding, Ralph bsb	1956, 57, 58	
Holdren, Barb wswim	1981	
Holdridge, Jay F. bsb	1936	
Holiday, Albert mwp	1950, 51, 52	
Holland, J.P. mtrk	1982, 84, 85	
Hollberg, Leo mgym	1972, 73, 75, 76	
Hollingbery, Orin wrest	1967, 68	
Hollis, Jack bsb	1988, 89	
Hollister, Myron mtrk	1955	
Hollmann, Robert bsb	1962, 63, 64	
Holloway, Brian D. ftb	1978, 79, 80	
Holman, Darrell bsb	1936, 37	
Holman, John R. ftb	1906, 07, 08, 09	
Holman, Lisa wswim	1977	
Holmes, Eli wcrew	1988	
Holmes, Marvin mtrk	1975, 76, 77	
Holmes, Richard mtrk	1953	
Holt, Preston ftb	1919	
Holt, Rick mcrew	1981, 82	
Holt, Tyra wtrack	1994, 95, 96	
Holt, William bsb	1966, 67	
Holubar, Allen mtrk	1946, 47, 48	
Holwerda, Jacob J. ftb	1932, 33	
Holzman, Mickey bsb	1954, 55	
Hombrecher, Alexis mten	1990	
Honore, George L. ftb	1959, 61	
Hong, Richard mfenc	1996	
Hood, Thomas mbsk	1946	
Hood, Wilber K. mbsk	1918, 20	
Hool, Jason mcrew	1995, 96	
Hooper, Gregory F. ftb	1979, 80, 81, 82	
Hooper, William F. mbsk	1943	
Hoos, Earl M. ftb	1933, 36	
Hoover, Abby wtrack	1994	
Hoover, Shawn wvball	1975, 76, 77, 78	
Hope, Brandace wvball	1981, 82, 83, 84	
Hopkins, John ftb	1987, 88, 89, 90	
Hopkins, John mtrk	1988, 90	
Hopkins, Steven mtrk	1972, 73, 74	
Hopp, Ceci wtrack	1982, 83, 84, 86	
Hopp, Ceci wxc	1981, 82, 83, 84	
Hopwood, Tara wswim	1996	
Horn, Johan Jacob mten	1962	
Horn, Richard H. ftb	1949, 50, 51	
Horowitz, Steven C. ftb	1969, 70	
Horpel, Christopher wrest	1972, 73, 75	
Horton, Larry L. ftb	1905, 06	
Horwitz, Robert mgym	1971, 72, 74	
Hosley, Richard T. mbsk	1961	
Hothan, Harold wrest	1969	

Hotson, John mcrew	1967, 68	
Houck, George M. ftb	1922	
Houcke, Alexandre mfenc	1979	
Hough, Gordon mgolf	1940, 41	
Hough, Larry mcrew	1964, 65, 66	
Houkom, Kim wsoc	1995	
Houston, Holly wswim	1974, 75	
Hover, Wade mfenc	1946	
Hovley, Stephen bsb	1965, 66	
Howard, James mtrk	1973	
Howard, Robert P. ftb	1962, 63, 64	
Howe, Avery bsb	1912, 15	
Howe, John M. ftb	1952, 53	
Howe, Stephen J. ftb	1976, 77	
Howell, Rebecca fh	1979, 80, 81,82	
Howick, Jenny wsoc	1986, 87, 88, 89	
Hoyem, Steve fth	1990, 91, 92, 93	
Hoyt, Linvingston wrest	1947	
Hribar, John mvball	1990, 91, 92, 93	
Hromadka, Wendy wvball	1992, 93, 94, 95	
Hsu, Marjorie wtrack	1993, 94	
Huang, Milt mfenc	1981, 83	
Hubbard, Alysia wtrack	1988, 89, 90, 91	
Hubbard, C. William ftb	1975, 76	
Hubbard, Derek ftb	1995	
Hubbard, Frank mcrew	1961	
Hubbard, Philip mtrk	1972, 73	
Hucheon, Todd mgym	1975	
Huckestein, Ray C. ftb	1985, 86, 87, 88	
Huddleson, Darrol E. mbsk	1940	
Huddleston, A. Jack bsb	1936	
Hudson, Judy wswim	1977	
Hufbauer, Karl wrest	1957, 58	
Huffington, Roy mcrew	1969	
Hug, Steve mgym	1972, 73, 74	
Hugasian, Harry bsb	1949, 50, 51	
Hugasian, Harry ftb	1949, 50, 51	
Hugasian, Harry mbsk	1950	
Hughes Sloan, Liz wvball	1975, 76, 77, 78	
Hughes, Peter wrest	1949	
Hughes, Ross mten	1946, 47	
Hughes, Tracy wvball	1987, 88, 89, 90	
Hulbert, Ted mcrew	1959, 60	
Hulen, Ray J. ftb	1930, 31	
Hulick, Carl wrest	1954	
Hull, Stephen mwp	1961, 62, 63	
Hulvey, Kristin wsoc	1992	
Humphreys, Brad T. ftb	1985, 86, 87	
Humphreys, Philip M. ftb	1965	
Humphries, Scott mten	1995	
Hungerland, Christopher mtrk	1961	
Hunken, John bsb	1929, 30, 31	
Hunt, Albert B. ftb	1930	
Hunt, Barbara wbsk	1985	
Hunt, Charles mbsk	1984, 85	
Hunt, Helen fh	1976	
Hunt, Robert W. ftb	1923, 24	
Hunter, Errol mfenc	1993, 94, 95, 96	
Huntington, Patsy fh	1980, 81, 82, 83	
Hurlbut, John bsb	1959, 60, 61	
Hurst, Jerry Alton mten	1964	
Huss, Jon D. ftb	1966, 68	
Hustwick, David mtrk	1972	
Hutchings, Charles H. Jr. ftb	1980, 81, 82, 83	
Hutchings, Steve mgym	1991, 92, 93	
Hutchinson, Chad bsb	1996	
Hutchinson, James wrest	1953, 54	
Hutchison, Charles mten	1941	
Hutchison, James W. mbsk	1966	
Hyde, Blair mtrk	1940, 41	
Hyde, Clarence E. ftb	1904	
Hyde, David mgym	1980	
Hyde, Robert mtrk	1955, 57	
Hyland, Richard F. ftb	1925, 26, 27	
Hynes, William mwp	1954	
Hyvonen, Randall mtrk	1966	
Hyvonen, Randall mxc	1966	
Ifejika, Barbara wvball	1994, 95	
Iglesias, Mario bsb	1993, 95, 96	
Imbernino, David mwp	1983, 84, 85	
Ingard, Marianne wtennis	1977, 79	

Inge, Ron E. ftb	1973, 74, 75, 76	
Ingham, George W. ftb	1959	
Inglis, Bruce mgym	1956, 58	
Ingraham, Dave mxc	1974	
Ingram, Culton mgolf	1951	
Inouye, Ross mten	1996	
Ireland, Robert mgolf	1963, 64, 65	
Irsfeld, James bsb	1933	
Irvine, Rodger bsb	1953	
Irwin, Rob bsb	1976, 77, 78	
Irwin, Tom wrest	1996	
Irwin, William mgolf	1956	
Isaacs, Carl E. ftb	1955, 56	
Isaacs, John Manwaring mten	1962, 63, 64	
Isbell, Raymond mgolf	1968, 69	
Ishman, Reginald E. ftb	1971, 72, 73	
Issacs, Carl E. mbsk	1956, 57	
Iverson, Bruce A. mbsk	1950, 51, 52	
Iverson, Milton C. mbsk	1947, 48, 49	
Ivey, Noel wswim	1979	
Jacklich, Frank mfenc	1953, 54	
Jackson, Bill H. ftb	1985	
Jackson, Jay wrest	1991, 92, 94, 95	
Jackson, Jennifer wvball	1989, 90, 91, 92	
Jackson, Jodi wswim	1996	
Jackson, Katrinka wtrack	1995, 96	
Jackson, Michael mcrew	1960	
Jackson, Nancy fh	1976 78, 79	
Jackson, Rich mbsk	1994, 95, 96	
Jackson, Sue K wbsk	1976	
Jackson, Sukie fh	1976, 77, 78	
Jackson, Terence ftb	1981, 82, 83, 84	
Jackson, Tessa wtrack	1987	
Jackson, Valerie fh	1981, 82, 83	
Jackson, Vernell mtrk	1973, 74	
Jacob, Joseph C. ftb	1949, 50	
Jacob, Lisa wswim	1993, 94, 95, 96	
Jacobs, George C. ftb	1903	
Jacobs, Leah fh	1992, 93, 94, 95	
Jacobs, Michael mtrk	1967	
Jacobs, Quincy ftb	1993, 94, 95	
Jacobs, Regina wtrack	1982, 83, 84, 85	
Jacobs, Regina wxc	1982, 83, 84	
Jacobson, Lisa fh	1984	
Jacobson, Mark mten	1984, 85, 86, 87	
Jaeger, Susy wtennis	1981, 82, 83, 84	
Jaffe, David bsb	1979	
Jaia, Bernard mdive	1985	
James, Edwin W. ftb	1898	
James, Jeffrey D. ftb	1984, 85, 86, 87	
James, Kenneth wrest	1952, 53, 54	
James, Peter mgolf	1962	
Jameson, William bsb	1938, 39	
Jamieson, Gordon mwp	1940	
Jannsen, Bob mbsk	1922, 23	
Janssen, Clayton R. ftb	1922	
Jaqua, A. Richard mtrk	1953	
Jarvis, Sonia wbsk	1976	
Jasper, Travan mtrk	1991	
Jasper, Travis mtrk	1991	
Jauquet, Jennifer wtrack	1988, 90, 91	
Jayred, Wallace mbsk	1925, 26, 27	
Jeffrey, Clyde mtrk	1939, 40	
Jeffries, James Drake mten	1958, 59, 60	
Jeffries, Jerome mgym	1957	
Jeffs, A.S. ftb	1895, 96, 97	
Jen, Ed mfenc	1993, 94, 95, 96	
Jena, Douglas K. ftb	1972, 73	
Jenke, James A. ftb	1974, 75	
Jenneskens, Mary wcrew	1979, 80	
Jennings, Joe mcrew	1962	
Jennings, Katie wgym	1994, 95	
Jensen, Douglas mwp	1964, 65, 66	
Jensen, Kirk mwp	1982	
Jensen, Kristin wdive	1989, 90, 91, 92	
Jensen, Peter mgym	1956, 57	
Jensen, Robert mwp	1968, 69, 70	
Jensen, Stefanie wtrack	1994	
Jensen, Stefanie wxc	1993	
Jerich, Mike ftb	1992, 93, 94	
Jernigan, Tamy wvball	1979	

Jesperson, Michelle wswim	1994, 95, 96	
Jessen, Christopher F. ftb	1961, 62	
Jessen, Robert wrest	1952	
Jessup, Bruce mwp	1939, 40	
Jezek, Linda wswim	1979, 80	
Jiles, C. Norman mtrk	1951, 54, 55	
Jimmerson, Greg mtrk	1995, 96	
Jimmerson, Greg mxc	1994, 95	
Joe, Melissa fh	1989, 90, 91	
Johannessen, Edward L.H. ftb	1939, 41	
Johannsen, Alfred mbsk	1918	
Johannsen, Richard mwp	1974, 75, 76, 77	
Johnk, Carl mtrk	1976, 77, 78	
Johns, David mdive	1993, 94, 95	
Johnsen, Lester mtrk	1939, 40	
Johnson, Andrea wsoc	1991, 92, 93, 94	
Johnson, Brian bsb	1988	
Johnson, Brian ftb	1987, 88, 89	
Johnson, Brigham wrest	1981, 82	
Johnson, Bruce mtrk	1966	
Johnson, Chris wrest	1981	
Johnson, Craig Randall mten	1973, 74, 75, 76	
Johnson, Daniel bsb	1931	
Johnson, Dave mvball	1986, 87, 88, 89	
Johnson, Eric mtrk	1982, 84	
Johnson, Erwin mwp	1950, 53, 54	
Johnson, Franklin mtrk	1947, 48, 49	
Johnson, Gary mfenc	1980 81	
Johnson, Glen bsb	1970, 71, 72	
Johnson, Gordon mtrk	1947	
Johnson, Gordon mxc	1946	
Johnson, Grady mbsk	1984	
Johnson, James D. mbsk	1954	
Johnson, Jeffrey mgolf	1962, 63	
Johnson, Jenna wswim	1986, 87, 88, 89	
Johnson, Jill wswim	1988, 89, 90	
Johnson, Jimmie mtrk	1995, 96	
Johnson, Julia fh	1977, 79	
Johnson, Juliet wfenc	1988	
Johnson, Kara wcrew	1995, 96	
Johnson, Kylie wtennis	1989, 90, 91, 92	
Johnson, Lance ftb	1987, 88	
Johnson, Lance wrest	1991, 92, 93, 94	
Johnson, Martin mtrk	1952, 53	
Johnson, Marty mcrew	1981, 82, 83	
Johnson, Neil mbsk	1985, 86	
Johnson, Paul R. mbsk	1951, 52, 53	
Johnson, Ross mwp	1968	
Johnson, Stanley mwp	1971, 72, 73, 74	
Johnson, Susan wswim	1989, 90, 91, 92	
Johnson, Thor mdive	1983, 84, 85	
Johnson, Vernon bsb	1936, 37	
Johnson, Wendy wswim	1984	
Johnston, Charles F. ftb	1922, 23, 24	
Johnston, Jay mgolf	1975, 76, 77	
Johnston, Philip F. ftb	1932	
Johnston, Roger mwp	1960	
Johnston, Sharon wvball	1983, 84	
Johnston, Steve mcrew	1985	
Johnstone, Steve mvball	1995	
Jollett, Mikel mtrk	1993	
Jolley, Matt mcrew	1996	
Jolley, Missy fh	1987	
Jones, Ashley mwp	1950, 51, 52	
Jones, Christie wgym	1995, 96	
Jones, Donald mgolf	1946	
Jones, Karen fh	1985, 86, 87	
Jones, Keith mbsk	1981, 82, 83	
Jones, Kevin mtrk	1980, 81, 82, 83	
Jones, Kim wdive	1983, 84, 85	
Jones, Kim wswim	1983, 84	
Jones, Lawrence C. ftb	1970, 71	
Jones, Richard bsb	1956	
Jones, Richard V. Jr. ftb	1954, 55	
Jones, Robert mwp	1940	
Jones, Steffond wrest	1990	
Jones, Steven mtrk	1969, 70	
Jones, Thomas mtrk	1969, 70	
Jones, Vern wrest	1946, 47, 48, 49	
Jones, Winford M. ftb	1939	
Joneschild, Elizabeth wsoc	1988, 89, 90, 91	

Jonsson, Eric mcrew	1978	
Joondeph, Brad mgolf	1988	
Jordan, Barbara wtennis	1976, 77, 78	
Jordan, Judy wtennis	1980	
Jordan, Kathryn wtennis	1978, 79	
Jordan, Thomas mtrk	1971	
Jorgensen, Janel wswim	1990, 91, 92, 93	
Jose, Jamille wgolf	1992, 93, 94, 95	
Joseph, Jackie wtennis	1983	
Josephson, Kurt H. ftb	1984, 85, 86	
Josling, John mfenc	1996	
Jubb, Stephen W. ftb	1969, 70	
Judson, Olivia wfenc	1988, 89 90, 91	
Juillard, Catherine wvball	1993, 94, 95	
Julius, John mgolf	1980	
Juney, Norman bsb	1938, 39, 40	
Jurgens, Kathy wvball	1990, 91	
Kadziel, Ronald D. ftb	1968, 69, 70	
Kaffen, James P. ftb	1972, 73	
Kahle, Richard mgym	1956	
Kahn, Ronald J. mten	1968	
Kahn, Stella wdive	1989	
Kalbus, Randy mwp	1977, 78, 79	
Kalinowski, Cliff bsb	1994	
Kallam, Floyd bsb	1919, 20, 21	
Kamerschen, Rob bsb	1988, 89, 90	
Kammeyer, Bob bsb	1970, 71	
Kang, Lana wfenc	1990, 91	
Kanuka, Kerri wgym	1991	
Kaplan, Anita wbsk	1992, 93, 94, 95	
Karakozoff, Alex L. ftb	1973, 74, 75, 76	
Kardas, James mgolf	1959	
Kardong, Donald mtrk	1970, 71	
Kardong, Donald mxc	1968, 69, 70	
Karlgaard, Joe mtrk	1993, 95, 96	
Karmel, Clay mcrew	1981	
Karns, Norman Milton mten	1959, 60, 61	
Karsevar, Matt mtrk	1992, 93	
Kaspar, Bob mcrew	1970, 71, 72	
Kassulke, Kurt wrest	1984, 85, 86, 87	
Katz, Ed wrest	1982, 83, 84	
Kauffman, James mtrk	1969, 70, 71	
Kauffman, James H. ftb	1968, 69, 70	
Kay, Jon wrest	1962	
Kazanjian, John C. ftb	1927	
Kazazian, Sonya wtennis	1986	
Keare, Stacey wsoc	1985, 86, 87, 88	
Kearing, Jocelyln wswim	1979	
Kearing, Jocelyn wcrew	1980, 81	
Keataing, Robert wrest	1975	
Keblusek, Edward R. ftb	1946	
Keefe, Adam mbsk	1989, 90, 91, 92	
Keelin, Thomas mgolf	1970, 71, 72	
Keely, Colin mwp	1987, 88, 89, 90	
Keenan, Robert mten	1946	
Keesing, Felicia wcrew	1986	
Keesing, Roger mten	1955, 56	
Kegley, Carl S. ftb	1917	
Kehl, James A. ftb	1970, 71	
Kehrli, Bruce A. ftb	1963, 64, 65	
Keith, Dennis mcrew	1960	
Kelber, Phil bsb	1970, 71	
Kellar, William E. ftb	1974, 75, 76, 77	
Kellberg, Ernest Jr. mgolf	1947, 48, 49	
Kellenberger, Carl F. (Jr.) bsb	1943, 46	
Keller, Philip bsb	1968, 69, 70	
Keller, Richard ftb	1968, 69	
Kelley, Kerrie wgym	1991	
Kelley, Lawrence mtrk	1955	
Kelley, Richard R. mbsk	1973, 74, 75	
Kelley, Robert mxc	1965, 66	
Kellner, Stuart L. ftb	1966, 67, 68	
Kelly, Brendan mdive	1987	
Kelly, James bsb	1930	
Kelly, James B. ftb	1924	
Kelly, John mtrk	1958, 59, 60	
Kelly, Pat S. ftb	1985, 86	
Kelly, Paul mwp	1953	
Kelsey, Bobbie wbsk	1993, 94, 95, 96	
Kelsey, Christopher mwp	1978, 79, 80, 81	

Kelsey, Jane wswim	1994, 95, 96	
Kelsey, Mary wswim	1991	
Kemp, Audrey wxc	1977	
Kemp, Todd mwp	1985, 88, 89	
Kemper, Chris bsb	1991, 92	
Kemper, Steve A. ftb	1973, 74	
Kendall, Phillip wrest	1962, 63, 64	
Kennedy, Bess wcrew	1995, 96	
Kennedy, Don mgolf	1938, 39, 40	
Kennedy, Martin H. ftb	1892, 93, 94	
Kennedy, Tom wrest	1980	
Kent, Paul mtrk	1947, 48, 49	
Kent, Troy bsb	1995, 96	
Kenworthy, Dudley mgym	1950, 51	
Kenyon, Robert mgym	1940	
Kenyon, Robert mtrk	1939, 40	
Kephart, Murray mgym	1971	
Kerekes, George A. ftb	1976, 77, 78	
Kerkorian, Gary R. ftb	1949, 50, 51	
Kerman, John R. ftb	1939, 40	
Kern, A.E. bsb	1928	
Kern, Eugene mtrk	1941, 42	
Kern, Eugene F. ftb	1911, 12	
Kern, John mcrew	1991	
Kerr, d'Layne wtrack	1989, 90	
Kersemeier, Craig mtrk	1992	
Kershner, Karen wbsk	1982, 83, 84	
Kessel, John mtrk	1972, 73, 74	
Kester, Edgar C. ftb	1916	
Keusseff, Stephen E. ftb	1938, 39	
Kevan, Wendy wsoc	1989, 90, 91	
Key, Wanda fh	1984, 87	
Keyes, Missy wcrew	1995	
Keyser, Brian bsb	1987, 88, 89	
Keyser, Lynn fh	1978, 79, 80, 81	
Kidd, John D. ftb	1956, 57	
Kidder, Robert mwp	1951	
Kieburtz, Geoffrey B. ftb	1974, 75, 76, 77	
Kilburg, Joe bsb	1995, 96	
Killefer, Anne wbsk	1976	
Killefer, Anne fh	1975, 76, 77	
Killefer, Tom bsb	1936, 37, 38	
Killefer, Wade ftb	1969	
Kim, Eva mcrew	1995, 96	
Kim, Shane mvball	1982, 83, 84, 85	
Kimball, Robert mtrk	1952, 53, 54	
Kimelman, David mcrew	1976	
Kindler, Dorsey B. ftb	1946	
King, Alison fh	1976, 77, 78	
King, Gordon D. ftb	1975, 76, 77	
King, H. bsb	1926	
King, Leon, ftb	1950, 51	
King, Maxwell C. mbsk	1946	
King, Michael wrest	1976	
King, Thomas mcrew	1982, 84	
King, Wilford mtrk	1952, 55	
King, Wilford mxc	1952	
Kinkead, Libby wswim	1983, 84	
Kinnear, George mgym	1962	
Kinney, Paul B. ftb	1918	
Kinsman, Robert mgym	1942	
Kinsman, Shep mgym	1976, 77, 78	
Kircher, Alan bsb	1947	
Kirkland, Alfred D. ftb	1951, 52	
Kirkland, Weymouth mtrk	1963, 64, 65	
Kirkland, Weymouth mxc	1962, 63, 64	
Kirsch, William B. ftb	1937, 38	
Kirtman, Nathaniel ftb	1967	
Kirwan, Andre ftb	1993, 94, 95	
Kissin, Roy mxc	1975, 77, 78, 79	
Kite, Walter E. ftb	1932	
Kittell, Allan mgym	1939, 40	
Klabau, Theodore A. ftb	1927, 28, 29	
Klafter, Derron ftb	1991, 92	
Klass, Craig mwp	1983, 84, 85	
Klein, Adrian mfenc	1993, 94	
Klein, Bud bsb	1949, 50	
Klein, Bud D. ftb	1948, 49	
Klein, Jimmy ftb	1989, 90	
Klein, Kristin wvball	1988, 89, 90, 91	
Klein, Pat mvball	1996	
Kleinheksel, Leslie wdive	1985, 86, 87	

Kleinheksel, Leslie wswim — 1988
Klemperer-Johnson, Maria wcrew — 1995, 96
Klier, Richard mtrk — 1960, 61, 62
Klier, Richard mxc — 1960
Klinger, Francis bsb — 1966, 67, 68
Klingsporn, Greg mcrew — 1991
Klipper, L. Younger ftb — 1970, 71, 72
Kloos, Michael A. ftb — 1971
Klopp, Kenneth wrest — 1963
Kmetovic, Peter G. ftb — 1939, 40, 41
Knaebel, Stephen mgym — 1962
Knecht, Tommy ftb — 1991, 92, 93
Knight, Brevin mbsk — 1994, 95, 96
Knight, Courtland W. ftb — 1913, 15
Knight, Molly wdive — 1992
Knight, R.B. bsb — 1902
Knight, Robert B. ftb — 1901
Knight, Sherman mcrew — 1993
Knight, Theodore mgym — 1947, 48
Knosher, John mgolf — 1950, 51
Knott, Stephanie wfenc — 1979
Knowles, Nancy wsoc — 1982
Knudsen, Geoff mcrew — 1966
Kober, Frederick bsb — 1958
Koberlein, Earl mbsk — 1983, 84, 85, 86
Kobrine, Nicole wgym — 1989, 90
Koch, George mxc — 1973
Koehn, John P. ftb — 1970
Koerner, Henry mcrew — 1973, 74, 75
Koerner, William ftb — 1905, 06, 07, 08
Kohl, Tracey wgym — 1996
Kohlmoos, Michael ftb — 1987, 88
Kolderup, Karl mvball — 1984
Kole, Julie wswim — 1992, 93, 94, 95
Kolesnikow, Andy M. ftb — 1974, 77
Koll, Donald mwp — 1952, 53, 54
Kolotouros, Peter mtrk — 1987, 88, 89, 90
Kolp, Lisa wbsk — 1976
Koman, William mcrew — 1980
Kommers, Thomas mtrk — 1968, 69
Kondik, Stephanie wgolf — 1985
Kopolow, David wrest — 1972, 73
Kosanke, Raymond W. mbsk — 1964, 65, 66
Koshy, Anita wsoc — 1990, 91, 92, 93
Kosola, Kevin mfenc — 1982
Kostas, Kathy wgolf — 1983, 84, 85, 86
Kostoff, Jeff mxc — 1985
Kostohryz, James mtrk — 1989, 90, 91
Kovacevich, Richard bsb — 1963, 64, 65
Kovas, Ronald mwp — 1962, 63
Kozak, Kathryn wtrack — 1985
Kozel, Scott mtrk — 1989
Kraemer, Karen wswim — 1989, 90, 91, 92
Kraft, Warren H. ftb — 1921
Kraik, Spencer mcrew — 1987
Kramer, Jordyn fh — 1995
Kraus, Bambi wswim — 1977
Krause, Marc mdive — 1990, 91, 92
Krebs, Kenneth wrest — 1972, 73, 75
Krebs, Rodney mcrew — 1960
Kreigshauser, Cathy wswim — 1974, 75
Kreitz, R. Darrell mtrk — 1948, 50, 51
Kretz, Arvid mtrk — 1971,
Kretz, Arvid mxc — 1969, 70, 71
Kribel, Joel mgolf — 1996
Krickeberg, Roy W. ftb — 1953, 54
Kring, Kenneth mtrk — 1973, 74
Kroeger, George mwp — 1951,
Kroeger, John mwp — 1952, 53
Kroeker, Andrew ftb — 1995
Kruger, Thomas mten — 1941, 42
Kruse, Brad mtrk — 1985
Kuchenbecker, Stephen mbsk — 1968, 69, 70
Kueny, Rachel wsoc — 1984
Kuhn, James mcrew — 1985
Kuhn, Larry bsb — 1978, 79, 80
Kuller, Melissa wdive — 1989, 90, 91, 92
Kunkel, Kevin bsb — 1983, 84, 85, 86
Kunzel, Frederick mwp — 1951, 52, 53
Kupferer, Kim wbsk — 1980, 81, 82, 83
Kurfess, James wrest — 1946, 47, 48, 49
Kurth, Kristine wtennis — 1992, 93, 94

Kuschner, Aaron mgym — 1991, 92, 93, 94
Kwong, Karen wfenc — 1984, 85

La Brum, Frank bsb — 1948
La Combe, Emile A. ftb — 1931
La Prade, Loren H. ftb — 1941, 42
La Telle, Russell mwp — 1949, 50, 51
Laakso, Albert M. ftb — 1948, 49
Laborde, Henri J. ftb — 1932
Lacey, Laurcene A. wsoc — 1958, 59
Lachman, Don mcrew — 1971, 72
Lachmund, Otto G. ftb — 1913, 14
LaComb, Emile A. mbsk — 1932
Lacoste, Jeanette wgym — 1979, 80, 81
Ladue, William bsb — 1933
Lafaille, Leon L. mbsk — 1939, 40
LaFranchi, Richard bsb — 1937
Lahde, Bernhard mtrk — 1971
Lahde, Bernhard mxc — 1971
Laidlaw, Scott R. ftb — 1972, 73, 74
Laird, WIlliam bsb — 1928, 29, 30
Lallas, Peter mbsk — 1981
Lam, Cecelia wcrew — 1986
Lamanuzzi, Victor ftb — 1971, 72
Lamar, Kevin T. ftb — 1980, 82, 84
Lamb, Therese wxc — 1978
Lambert, Bethane wswim — 1987, 88, 90
Lambert, Debbie wvball — 1994, 95
Lambert, Elizabeth wswim — 1975, 76
Lambert, Greg mwp — 1979, 80, 81, 82
Lambert, Mike mvball — 1993, 94, 95
Lambert, Thomas B. mbsk — 1932
Lambert, Thomas B. ftb — 1930, 31
Lambie, Thomas mgolf — 1946, 47, 48
Lamey, Jack mgolf — 1959
Lammersen, Bart mbsk — 1992, 93, 94, 95
Lamoreaux, Phililp mtrk — 1961, 62, 63
Lamoure, James bsb — 1973, 74, 75
Lampert, Tom mwp — 1982
Lanagan, J. bsb — 1898, 99, 1900
Lander, J.A. bsb — 1916
Landis, Craig S. ftb — 1985, 86
Laney, Robert mtrk — 1973, 74
Lang, Bruce ftb — 1986, 87, 88, 89
Lange, Scott ftb — 1993
Langemach, Rich mcrew — 1961
Langevin, Aimee wxc — 1994
Langford, J. Michael ftb — 1974, 75
Langley, Raymond mfenc — 1980
Lanigan, Amy wswim — 1992, 93, 94
Laningham, Fred bsb — 1985
Lannin, Meegan wgym — 1992, 93, 94, 95
Lanning, Brad mgolf — 1992, 94
Lansberg, Justin mwp — 1985
Laord, William H. ftb — 1930
Larntz, Jessica wswim — 1988
LaRocca, Todd bsb — 1992, 93, 94
Larsen, David mtrk — 1971
Larsen, Neils T. ftb — 1934, 35
Larson, Cara wcrew — 1991
Larson, Carrie wswim — 1986, 87, 88
Larson, Meredish wsoc — 1995
Larson, Richard mtrk — 1972, 73, 74
Larson, William mtrk — 1946, 47, 48
Lasater, Richard W. II ftb — 1968, 69, 70
Lasley, J.J. ftb — 1989, 90, 91, 92
Lassen, Kristine wswim — 1986, 87
Lassen, Richard mtrk — 1958, 59, 60
Laster, Jeremy mwp — 1992, 93, 94, 95
Latham, Robert M. ftb — 1951
Latimer, Wendy wsoc — 1993, 94, 95
Latta, Bob mvball — 1975
Latting, John mcrew — 1985, 86, 87
Lau, Howard mfenc — 1984
Laubscher, Alan wrest — 1955, 56, 57
Laubscher, Wesley F. ftb — 1951
Lauchner, Craig mvball — 1982, 83, 84, 85
Lauer, Hilary wsoc — 1983, 84, 85, 86
Lauer, Mike mtrk — 1987
Laumeisteer, Clarence F. ftb — 1906
Laverty, Roger M. ftb — 1942
Lavoie, Celeste wbsk — 1988, 89

Law, Dennis Martin mten — 1965
Lawler, Russell K. mbsk — 1953, 54, 55
Lawrence, Amy wgolf — 1992, 94, 95
Lawrence, Harry bsb — 1960, 61, 62
Lawrence, Matt mtrk — 1993
Lawson, Andrew mwp — 1985, 87, 88
Lawson, Jack mxc — 1969
Lawson, James bsb — 1924, 25
Lawson, James W. ftb — 1922, 23, 24
Lawson, Roy bsb — 1959
Lawyer, Trayce wsoc — 1995
Layzer, Carolyn wxc — 1978
Lazetich, Peter G. ftb — 1969, 70, 71
Lazzarone, Albert bsb — 1938, 39
Le Vant, Simone wswim — 1984
Le, Tuan Van ftb — 1988, 89, 90, 91
Leachman, Josh mwp — 1992, 94, 95
Leahey, Mike mdive — 1982, 83, 84
Leahy, John G. ftb — 1959
LeBlanc, Charmaine wsoc — 1995
Leck, Brian Christopher mten — 1965, 66, 67
Leckrone, Susan fh — 1988, 89, 90, 91
Ledbetter, Stewart mgolf — 1953
Ledeboer, Frederick B. ftb — 1937, 38
Ledgerwood, Michael mbsk — 1961, 62
Lee, Anne wtrack — 1992, 93, 94, 95
Lee, Arthur mbsk — 1996
Lee, Clarence bsb — 1930
Lee, Dave wrest — 1985, 86
Lee, David mcrew — 1968
Lee, Ellen fh — 1987, 88, 89, 90
Lee, Horace B. mbsk — 1937
Lee, Howard S. ftb — 1899, 1900
Lee, James mwp — 1952, 53
Lee, Mike mgym — 1979, 81, 82
Lee, Peter mwp — 1941
Lee, Valeri wvball — 1978
Lee, Valerie wswim — 1977, 78, 79
Leeuwenburg, Richard P. ftb — 1962, 63
Lefcourt, Edwin R. mbsk — 1946
Leholzky, Daniel mwp — 1993, 94, 95
Leicher, Richard mwp — 1970
Leidig, Theodore bsb — 1935
Leighton, Julia wtennis — 1979, 80
Leiker, Tony W. ftb — 1985, 86
Leming, Josh wrest — 1990
Lemon, Steven R. ftb — 1980, 81, 83
Lemons, Roger mbsk — 1981, 82
Lenihan, Sheila wtrack — 1987
Lenth, Susan wswim — 1986, 87, 88, 89
Leonard, Danton mcrew — 1979, 80
Leonard, Lionel R. mbsk — 1957
Leonard, Thomas mgym — 1958, 59
Leone, Danielle wgym — 1990
Leopold, Robert bsb — 1957, 58
Leroux, Monique fh — 1995
Letterer, James mtrk — 1967, 68
Letterer, James mxc — 1965, 66, 67
Lettinich, Edward B. ftb — 1934
Letts, John mten — 1983, 84, 85, 86
Leuschel, Nannette wswim — 1974, 75
LeVant, Simone wdive — 1984, 85
Leverenz, Humboldt bsb — 1930
Levin, Elaine wbsk — 1976
Levin, Jacquie fh — 1991
Levin, J.M. bsb — 1928
Levinson, Kathy fh — 1974, 75, 76
Levinson, Laurie mcrew — 1976, 77
Levitan, Meagan wfenc — 1985
Levitan, Steve mfenc — 1984, 85, 86, 87
Levy, David N. ftb — 1919, 20
Levy, Gordon mtrk — 1948
Levy, Jon mgym — 1983, 84
Lew, Kevin wbsk — 1977
Lewczyk, Julie wcrew — 1995, 96
Lewin, Bruno mtrk — 1991
Lewinger, Beth fh — 1986, 87, 88, 89
Lewis, Craig mcrew — 1988, 89
Lewis, Dave mcrew — 1962
Lewis, David R. ftb — 1964, 65, 66
Lewis, Douglas bsb — 1928, 29
Lewis, Ellen wswim — 1981, 82

Lewis, Fred mten	1948, 49	Lindskog, Stanley V. ftb	1960, 61, 62	Longinotti, John F. ftb	1965
Lewis, Hiram bsb	1966	Lindskog, Victor J. ftb	1940, 41	Longley, Carl mcrew	1966
Lewis, John K. ftb	1955	Lindsley, Richard wrest	1966	Lonsinger, Donald B. ftb	1981, 83
Lewis, Kristin wswim	1978, 79	Linford, Robert mfenc	1955, 56	Look, David mvball	1988
Lewis, Laurence D. ftb	1926, 27, 28	Ling, H.J. mbsk	1914	Loomis, Frederick C. ftb	1923
Lewis, Rickey mbsk	1983	Linn, Allen mgym	1946, 49	Loomis, J. Vard bsb	1930
Lewis, Robert bsb	1905	Linville, Becky wswim	1979	Loomis, John S. mbsk	1973
Lewis, Robert mten	1947, 48, 49	Linzmeier, Marybeth wswim	1982, 83, 84, 85	Loop, Charles mgym	1987, 88, 89, 90
Lewis, Robert W. mbsk	1947, 48, 49	Lisle, Josh wrest	1987, 88, 89, 90	Loos, Greg mwp	1987, 88, 89
Lewis, Sidney (Jr.) bsb	1939, 40	Lister, Eric wrest	1995	Lopez, George bsb	1980
Lewis, Todd mxc	1989, 90	Littleboy, John mtrk	1977, 78	LoPresti, Joe bsb	1978, 79
Lewis, William R. mbsk	1949	Liu, Roger wrest	1993, 95	Loreen, Jon mcrew	1959, 60
Lewyn, Thomas mten	1950, 51, 52	Livermore, Douglas mcrew	1968, 69	Lorenz, Jack mwp	1977, 78
Leybold, Dennis mfenc	1975, 76	Livermore, Norman "Ike" bsb	1931, 32, 33	Lorenzetti, Greg bsb	1982, 83, 84
Liang, Jing,-Wei mgym	1993, 94	Lloyd, Norman mtrk	1958, 60	Lorimer, Delmar B. ftb	1972, 73
Lichti, Todd mbsk	1986, 87, 88, 89	Lobsinger, Tom mxc	1977, 78, 79, 80	Lorimer, Leslie wbsk	1986
Lifur, Gregory bsb	1918	Lockard, Brodie mgym	1978, 79, 80, 81	Lorraine, Andrew bsb	1991, 92, 93
Light, Holly wcrew	1991	Locke, Ann wtrack	1982, 83	Lortie, Joe E. ftb	1985, 86, 87
Light, Jeff bsb	1991	Locke, Ann wxc	1981, 82	Lorton, John mwp	1959, 60, 61
Lightfoot, Dan R. ftb	1968, 69, 70	Lockhart, Wayne C. mbsk	1953	Lorton, Robert mwp	1959, 60, 61
Ligotti, Pete mgolf	1993	Lodato, Jack D. ftb	1962, 63, 64	Lorton, William mwp	1961, 62, 63
Likins, Peter wrest	1955, 56, 57	Loeb, Alan Michael mten	1966	Lough, Betsy wbsk	1977, 78, 79
Liljenwall, Theodore J. ftb	1947, 48	Loehing, Eric B. mbsk	1965	Lough, Charles ftb	1989
Lilly, J. Kenneth mbsk	1919	Lofton, James D. ftb	1975, 76, 77	Lougheed, Herbert bsb	1897, 98, 99, 1900
Lilly, John K. ftb	1917	Logan, Phillip mfenc	1977	Louis, Jon mgym	1985
Limmer, Harlan mtrk	1959	Lohmann, Janet fh	1983	Love, Ralph mtrk	1955
Lin, Seppi mfenc	1994	Lohrer, Eva wfenc	1977, 78, 79, 80	Love, Ralph mxc	1955, 56
Linari, Frederick J. mbsk	1942, 43	Loitz, Greg mwp	1971, 72, 73	Loveless, Lea wswim	1992, 93, 94
Lincoln, James mtrk	1939, 40, 41	Lollie, Marcus mbsk	1990, 91, 92, 93	Lovelle, Nathan wrest	1993
Lind, Bradley, C. mbsk	1971	Lomnicky, Gregg bsb	1981, 82, 83, 84	Loveridge, Gary F. mbsk	1965
Lindberg, Colleen wtrack	1982, 83	Lonborg, James bsb	1962, 63	Lovvold, Nancy wbsk	1976, 77
Linde, Leonard bsb	1937	Loncar, Ken ftb	1994, 95	Low, Robert mten	1939, 40, 41
Lindeman, Terry bsb	1959, 61	Long, James mxc	1995	Lowe, Mark mvball	1983
Linden Straus, Jan wvball	1978, 79, 80, 81	Long, Joe E. ftb	1955	Lowe, Mike mvball	1988, 89, 90, 91
Linden, Blue mcrew	1985	Long, Leo mtrk	1952, 53, 54	Lowe, Tricia wsoc	1986
Lindfors, Paul A. mbsk	1962	Long, Margaret, wfenc	1974	Lowe, William mgolf	1948
Lindow, Jesse wrest	1994	Long, Robert W. ftb	1954, 55, 56	Lowell, Gerald wrest	1954, 55, 56
Lindsey, Robin M. mbsk	1934, 35	Long, Thomas mtrk	1971, 72	Lowen, Alyze wsoc	1993, 94

Lowenfish, Martin mcrew	1989, 90	
Lowenthal, W.B. bsb	1901, 02	
Lozano, Claudia wcrew	1991	
Lucas, Richard M. ftb	1949, 50	
Luce, Edgar mtrk	1945, 46	
Luceti, Ronald mgolf	1956, 57	
Lucich, Mark bsb	1971, 72, 73, 74	
Lucido, Caryn wgym	1981, 82, 83, 84	
Luckett, William E. ftb	1936, 37	
Ludeke, Frederick S. ftb	1921, 22, 23	
Ludeke, John M. ftb	1954	
Luhn, Larry bsb	1976	
Luisetti, Angelo (Hank) mbsk	1936, 37, 38	
Lull, Walter mwp	1946, 47	
Lum, Kim mvball	1977, 78, 79, 80	
Lund, Kirsten wswim	1985	
Lundblade, Rick bsb	1983, 84, 85	
Lundh, Bente wtrack	1979	
Lundh, Ulf mtrk	1959, 60	
Lundh, Ulf mxc	1959	
Lundstrom, Chris mxc	1995	
Lunn, Jason mtrk	1996	
Luo, Kay wtrack	1992, 93, 94, 95	
Luo, Kay wxc	1991, 92, 93, 94	
Lusiani, Craig bsb	1969	
Luther, Richard mwp	1972	
Luttrell, Emmet mtrk	1954, 55	
Lycette, Errol mten	1948, 49	
Lyles, Frank wrest	1985	
Lynch, Jair mgym	1990, 91, 92, 93	
Lynch, John bsb	1991, 92	
Lynch, John ftb	1990, 91, 92	
Lynn, Gary ftb	1975, 76, 77	
Lynn, Jack bsb	1969, 70	
Lynn, Susie fh	1975	
Lynn, Tom M. ftb	1974, 75	
Lyon Richard P. mbsk	1939	
Lyon, Richard mcrew	1959, 60	
Lyons, Alonzo mtrk	1947, 48, 49	
Lyons, Alonzo mxc	1946	
Lyons, Ellen wtrack	1982, 83, 85	
Lyons, Ellen wxc	1980, 83, 84	
Lyons, Oliver wrest	1952, 53, 54	
Lyons, Samuel mtrk	1957	
Lyons, Willard E. ftb	1905	
Lysaght, Kren wvball	1981, 82	
Lysaught, Karen wtrack	1982	
Lytle, Vicky wswim	1977	
Maas, Jake mtrk	1996	
Mac Kay, Andrew mgolf	1977	
MacAlpine, Archibald B. ftb	1920	
Macarthur, Amy wtrack	1994, 95	
MacArthur, Amy wxc	1994, 95	
Macaulay, John D. ftb	1978, 79, 80, 81	
Macaulay, Rob M. ftb	1983	
Macdonald, Duncan mtrk	1969, 70, 71	
MacDonald, Duncan mxc	1968, 70, 71	
MacDonald, Frank mwp	1948	
MacDonald, John W. ftb	1956	
MacGraw, Frank J. (Jr.) bsb	1947, 48	
MacGregor, Scott mwp	1964	
Machtolf, Mark bsb	1984, 85, 86, 87	
Machtolf, Mark A. ftb	1983, 84	
MacKay, Carrie wcrew	1991	
MacLean, Douglas mwp	1965, 66	
MacMillan, Kevin B. ftb	1979, 80, 81	
MacMurdo, Chris wbsk	1990, 91, 92, 93	
MacNair, Tracy wtennis	1974, 75	
MacPherson, Sara wsoc	1981, 82, 83, 85	
MacQuarrie, Jamie mcrew	1996	
Macrorie, John mtrk	1975, 76	
Madati, Jamil mtrk	1993	
Madden, James mcrew	1966, 67, 68	
Madden, Patrick wrest	1952, 53	
Mader, Paige fh	1994, 95	
Madigan, Richard B. ftb	1946	
Madsen, Josh ftb	1991, 94, 95	
Madsen, William mgym	1973, 74, 75, 76	
Maentz, Robert C. ftb	1933, 34, 35,	
Maganini, Robert mgym	1979, 80, 81, 82	
Magee, Michael bsb	1959, 60, 61	

Mager, Robert mtrk	1952	
Magnussen, Bernard mgolf	1957, 58, 59	
Maguire, William bsb	1926, 27, 28	
Maguy, Bill mwp	1992, 93	
Maguy, Chuck mwp	1988, 89, 90	
Mahon, John mgolf	1987, 88	
Mahoney, Anne wswim	1990, 91, 92, 93	
Mahoney, John V. ftb	1985, 86, 87, 88	
Mahoney, Philip A. ftb	1980, 81	
Maiocco, Robert mtrk	1979, 80, 81, 82	
Major, Barbara wswim	1980, 81, 82, 83	
Major, Edwin mwp	1947, 48	
Mallatrat, Gordon bsb	1933, 34, 35	
Mallatratt, Gordon W. mbsk	1934	
Maloney, Kathleen fh	1980	
Malueg, Debbie wtrack	1988, 89, 90, 91	
Mangan, Robert T. ftb	1936	
Mangini, Beth syncswim	1996	
Manley, Todd mbsk	1992, 93, 94, 95	
Mann, George mgym	1941, 42	
Mann, Lawrence mwp	1972, 73	
Mann, Michael O. mbsk	1972, 73, 74	
Manning, Brian ftb	1993, 94, 95	
Manning, Brian mtrk	1995	
Manning, Scott mfenc	1977, 78	
Mannon, William H. ftb	1942	
Mannon, Willie mvball	1975	
Manoogian, Norman V. ftb	1950, 51, 53	
Manoukian, Donald J. ftb	1954, 55, 57	
Manson, Andrew mgym	1993, 94, 95, 96	
Manwaring, Frederick mwp	1939, 40, 41	
Mapel, William mwp	1941	
Maple, Ray bsb	1913, 14	
Maragua, Rover mgolf	1986	
Maramatsu, Saundra wgym	1978	
March, Bob mvball	1982, 83	
Marchin, Jeff T. ftb	1985, 86	
Marciel, Ronald bsb	1955	
Marcoux, Sionainn wswim	1991, 92	
Marcus, Lenard ftb	1994	
Marcy, Theodore mgym	1973, 74, 75, 76	
Marfil, Amy	1993, 94, 95	
Marek, Jamie mtrk	1990, 91	
Marenghi, Matt bsb	1992, 93, 94	
Margala, Kenneth J. ftb	1971	
Margerum, Kenneth ftb	1977, 78, 79, 80	
Margerum, Lee Ann wtrack	1981	
Margerum, LeeAnn wbsk	1983, 84, 85	
Marguiles, Dan mgym	1978, 79, 80	
Mariani, Lisa wswim	1979	
Marienthal, Paul mten	1968, 70	
Marik, Rich mgolf	1985, 86, 87	
Markel, John mcrew	1984	
Markezich, Amy syncswim	1996	
Marks, Heather wswim	1991, 92	
Marks, John mgym	1967, 68, 69	
Marks, William P. ftb	1930, 31	
Marohnic, David J. ftb	1981, 82, 83, 84	
Maron, Dave mvball	1975	
Marquardt, Richard mgym	1948, 49, 50, 55	
Marquess, Mark bsb	1967, 68, 69	
Marquess, Mark E. ftb	1966, 67, 68	
Marra, John mgym	1979	
Marriott, Joseph S. ftb	1916	
Marron, Ralph mgolf	1961, 62, 63	
Marsal, Kalle mtrk	1992	
Marshall, Bob bsb	1969, 70, 71	
Marshall, Brian mtrk	1985, 86, 87, 88	
Marshall, Robert G. II ftb	1954, 55	
Martel, Mark wrest	1980, 81, 82	
Martin, Brent J. ftb	1981, 82, 83, 84	
Martin, Casey mgolf	1991, 92, 94	
Martin, Christine wsoc	1986, 87, 88, 89	
Martin, Dell mtrk	1966	
Martin, Edward D. mbsk	1967, 68	
Martin, Erin wsoc	1993, 94, 95	
Martin, Folrest S. ftb	1972, 73, 74	
Martin, Jason mtrk	1988, 91	
Martin, Jason mxc	1987, 88, 89, 90	
Martin, Joseph C. ftb	1972, 73	
Martin, Julie wswim	1989	
Martin, Lawrence mtrk	1969	

Martin, Loy mgolf	1965, 66, 67	
Martin, Lugene B. mbsk	1946	
Martin, Lugene B. ftb	1946, 47, 48	
Martin, Marcia wtrack	1981, 83, 84, 85	
Martin, Paul mtrk	1959	
Martin, Paul mxc	1956, 57, 58	
Martin, Sahlan wrest	1992, 93, 95, 96	
Martin, Wendy wcrew	1991	
Martinez, Dina wtrack	1979	
Martinez, Martin J. ftb	1981	
Martland, Richard mgym	1952, 53	
Marty, Douglas mbsk	1979, 80, 81, 82	
Marx, Amy wtrack	1991	
Mashima, Kyle mvball	1975	
Mason, Harry bsb	1943	
Mason, James bsb	1948	
Mason, John bsb	1964, 65, 66	
Mason, John F. ftb	1964, 65, 66	
Mason, Michelle wtrack	1985	
Mason, Michelle wxc	1981, 84, 85	
Mason, Reggie mtrk	1975	
Massell, Christina wsoc	1989, 90, 91, 92	
Massey, James bsb	1934	
Massey, Thomas mtrk	1968, 69	
Massey, Thomas J. ftb	1967, 68	
Massimino, John mwp	1969, 70, 71	
Mastalir, Eric mtrk	1987, 90 91	
Mastalir, Eric mxc	1987, 88	
Mastalir, Mark mtrk	1987, 88, 90, 91	
Mastalir, Mark mxc	1987, 88	
Masterson, Brian mtrk	1982, 83, 84, 85	
Mastin, Robert H. ftb	1941	
Matarangas, John mwp	1989, 90, 91, 92	
Mather, Ralph mgym	1958	
Matheson, Scott Milne mten	1972	
Mathews, Bryce mwp	1994, 95	
Mathias, Robert mtrk	1951, 52, 53	
Mathias, Robert B. ftb	1951, 52	
Matlock, Mike mcrew	1970	
Matta, Edwin bsb	1975	
Mattei, A.C. bsb	1917	
Mattern, Britt mdive	1994, 95	
Matthews, Robert bsb	1936, 37	
Matthews, Robert E. ftb	1935, 36, 37	
Mattson, Robert M. ftb	1980	
Matyas, Bela Tamas mgym	1978, 80, 81	
Matzek, Michael mgym	1985, 86, 87, 88	
Maurer, Darin mbsk	1983	
Maurer, Frederick mwp	1947, 48	
Maxeiner, Thomas Philip mten	1964	
Maxwell, J. Terry mtrk	1947	
May, Christie wcrew	1987, 88	
May, George mgym	1971	
May, J. Earle bsb	1923, 24	
Mayer, Alex mten	1971, 72, 73	
Mayer, Gene mten	1974, 75	
Mayers, Frank B. ftb	1907	
Mayotte, Tim mten	1979, 80, 81	
Mayrhofer, Leonard F. ftb	1952	
Maze, Bill mten	1975, 76, 77, 78	
McArthur, Peter bsb	1937	
McBeth, Brian wrest	1995	
McBride, Erin fh	1991	
McBride, Larry mcrew	1965, 66	
McBride, Michael mgolf	1974, 75	
McBurney, Raymond D. mbsk	1924	
McCabe, John Smith mten	1965, 66	
McCaffery, Brian mxc	1994	
McCaffrey, Edward T. ftb	1986, 87, 89, 90	
McCaffrey, J. Leo mbsk	1942, 43	
McCain, Warren E. ftb	1940, 41	
McCalla, Harry mtrk	1962, 63, 64	
McCalla, Harry mxc	1962, 63	
McCalmon, Ryan mtrk	1995, 96	
McCalmon, Ryan mxc	1995	
McCamant, James D. ftb	1954	
McCamant, Wallace mtrk	1951, 52	
McCandless, John B. mbsk	1927, 29, 30	
McCandless, William bsb	1923, 24, 25	
McCann, Erin wgym	1990, 91	
McCann, Eugene D. ftb	1976, 77	
McCarthy, Kathleen wgolf	1984, 85, 86, 87	

McCarthy, Paul mtrk 1976, 77
McCarty, David bsb 1989, 90, 91
McCarty, Jeff mtrk 1996
McClain, Sean mfenc 1995
McClintock, Colin H. ftb 1939
McCloskey, P.N. bsb 1913, 14, 15
McCloud, Charles E. ftb 1970, 71, 72
McClure, Timothy J. ftb 1968, 69, 70
McColl, Duncan B. ftb 1974, 75, 76
McColl, John mvball 1980, 81
McColl, Milton B. ftb 1977, 78, 79, 80
McColl, William F. ftb 1949, 50, 51
McConnell, Amy wtrack 1990
McConnell, Christopher mfenc 1984, 85
McConnell, Mark mxc 1971, 72, 73, 74
McCormick, Charles T. ftb 1961, 63
McCormick, Jen wtrack 1993, 94
McCormick, Robert mfenc 1977
McCreery, John H. ftb 1925, 26, 27
McCullough, Natalie fh 1991, 92, 93
McCurdy, John mtrk 1953
McDade, Sarah wtrack 1988
McDermott, John mvball 1 984, 85, 86, 87

McDevitt, Christy wsoc 1986, 87, 88
McDevitt, Kelly wsoc 1985, 86
McDevitt, Mary wswim 1985
McDonald, Andrew mwp 1973, 75, 76
McDonald, Bruce mgolf 1976
McDonald, Karin wsoc 1986
McDonough, John T. ftb 1939
McDougal, Damon ftb 1993
McDougall, John, mfenc 1953, 54, 55, 56
McDowell, Jack bsb 1985, 86, 87
McElhinney, Kim wxc 1992
McElroy, William D. ftb 1937, 38
McElwain, Malcom S. mbsk 1967, 68, 69
McElyea, John mgolf 1950, 51, 52
McEnroe, John mten 1978
McEnroe, Patrick mten 1985, 86, 87, 88
McFadden, John bsb 1935
McFadden, Leslie mtrk 1972, 73
McFadden, Leslie mxc 1972
McFadden, Ralph J. ftb 1900, 01, 02
McFadden, Thomas L. ftb 1899, 1900
McFarland, Donald mtrk 1941
McFarland, Jason mvball 1987
McFarland, Keith wrest 1958
McFarlane, James bsb 1982
McGann, Alison wgym 1985, 86, 87, 88
McGibbons, Kristin wsoc 1988
McGilvray, Alexander mten 1968, 69
McGilvray, A.B. bsb 1902
McGilvray, A.B. ftb 1902
McGinn, Dan mtrk 1993, 95
McGonigle, Patricia wgolf 1985, 86, 87
McGovern, Larry D. ftb 1974, 76
McGrath, Meredith wtennis 1990
McGregor, J. Keith mgym 1950
McGregor, Robert A. ftb 1978
McGuire, Denise wbsk 1980, 81, 82
McHose, John C. mbsk 1922, 23, 24
McHugh, John H. mbsk 1977, 78
McHulty, William mfenc 1952
McIntyre, Heather wsoc 1988, 89, 90, 91
McIntyre, Robert mtrk 1963, 64, 65
McIntyre, Terry wrest 1985, 86, 87, 88
McJennett, Patricia fh 1987, 88, 89, 90
McKay, Charles W. ftb 1951
McKay, Mhairi wgolf 1994, 95, 96
McKay, Peter mtrk 1951, 52, 53
McKee, Geordie mten 1984, 85, 86, 87
McKee, Stephen mtrk 1947, 48, 49
McKee, T. Downing mtrk 1948
McKeen, Mark mten 1981, 82, 83, 84
McKeever, Barry J. ftb 1985, 86, 87, 88
McKenna, Chris mfenc 1991
McKenna, John F. ftb 1956
McKenna, Thomas J. ftb 1955
McKenzie, Douglas B. ftb 1967, 68
McKenzie, Walter mtrk 1939, 40
McKie, Jay bsb 1943

McKittrick, Jack W. ftb 1947, 48
McKnight, James mcrew 1960
McLallen, Robert wrest 1955
McLaren, Maureen wswim 1994, 95, 96
McLaren, Maureen wvball 1992, 93, 94, 95
McLean, Douglas mtrk 1974, 76
McLean, Kia wsoc 1994
McLean, Laurie wswim 1987, 88
McMahon, Michele wtrack 1988
McMillan, Donald C. ftb 1936
McMillan, Frank L. ftb 1937
McMillan, George ftb 1893
McMillen, Jery L. ftb 1955, 56, 57
McMillen, Roderick E. Jr. ftb 1957, 58, 59
McNair, Keven mtrk 1969, 70, 71
McNair, Rick mwp 1987, 88, 89, 90
McNamee, Paula wvball 1994, 95
McPeek, Kevin mcrew 1989, 90
McPherson, John Clarke mten 1963, 1965, 66
McSweeney, Brian mbsk 1986, 87, 88, 89
Mead, Aaron mvball 1992
Mead, Reginald E. mbsk 1931, 32
Meagher, Leah wcrew 1995
Mears, James bsb 1930
Mears, James B. mbsk 1930
Mechem, Kirke mten 1947, 48, 49
Mecklenberg, Marvin bsb 1959, 60, 61
Medeiros, Sarah fh 1995
Medina, Ed wrest 1993, 94, 95
Medved, Anton J. ftb 1942
Mehaffey, Douglas mcrew 1982, 83
Mehoff, Lisa wswim 1978
Meier, Dave bsb 1979, 80, 81
Meigs, James R. mbsk 1940
Meigs, James mgolf 1941
Meihaus Clarke, Carol wvball 1976, 77, 78
Meiners, Arnold W.J. ftb 1939, 40, 42
Meinert, Scott mbsk 1985, 87, 88, 89
Melendez, Dennis mgym 1973, 74, 76
Melendez, Michael mtrk 1980
Melendez, Mike mxc 1979, 80
Melloway, Marvin L. ftb 1949
Melton, David bsb 1948, 49, 50
Melton, James mgym 1951
Melzer, Thomas bsb 1965, 66
Mend, Laurel wfenc 1988
Mendoza, Mary wxc 1987
Mennie, Carl ftb 1994
Menz, Charles mtrk 1969, 70
Menz, Charles mxc 1967, 68, 69
Mercer, Kim wbsk 1984, 85, 86, 87
Merchant, David mtrk 1959
Meredith, Allen mtrk 1970, 71
Meredith, Jack P. mbsk 1946
Merino, Karen wsoc 1981, 82
Merja, Chuck mvball 1975
Merlo, James L. ftb 1971, 72
Merlo, Richard M. ftb 1974, 75, 76
Merrill, James A. ftb 1970
Merrill, Robert mtrk 1976
Merriman, Lloyd bsb 1943, 46, 47
Merriman, Lloyd A. ftb 1946
Merritt, Ethan mfenc 1974
Merritt, Russ mcrew 1967
Mertz, Laurence L. ftb 1921, 22
Mervin, Daniel D. ftb 1947, 48, 49
Mescher, Kevin ftb 1987, 88
Mesick, Dennis mgym 1969, 70
Messer, Phillip H. ftb 1966, 67, 68
Messina, Joseph mgym 1941, 42
Messner, Harold bsb 1955, 56, 57
Messner, Steve mcrew 1976, 77, 78
Metz, Barb wswim 1988, 89, 90, 91
Metzger, Margaret wtrack 1980
Metzger, Meg wbsk 1980, 81, 82, 83
Metzger, Vivian wxc 1980
Meyer, Frederick D. ftb 1939, 40, 41
Meyer, Jean wdive 1982, 83, 84, 85
Meyer, Jean wswim 1982, 83, 84
Meyer, Jon mfenc 1983, 84
Meyer, Lang mbsk 1988, 90, 91
Meyer, Rachel wcrew 1988

Meyer, Rod bsb 1993, 94
Meyer, William mwp 1965, 66
Meyerhoff, Richard mfenc1939, 40,41 Meyers, Robert mtrk 1951
Meyers, Robert E. Jr. ftb 1950, 51
Meyers, William J. ftb 1971, 72
Miao, Clarence mgym 1995, 96
Miccichi, Tony ftb 1988, 89
Michael, Douglas mtrk 1979, 80, 81, 82
Michael, Phil mfenc 1973, 74
Michaud, Frederick mgym 1959
Michel, Doug mtrk 1993
Michel, Michael D. mbsk 1969, 70, 71
Michel, Michael W. ftb 1975, 76
Middlebrook, Jason bsb 1994, 95
Middlekauff, Pete bsb 1964, 65, 66
Middlekauff, Peter D. ftb 1964
Middleton, Joel D. ftb 1923, 24, 25
Middleton, Richard bsb 1942
Mignano, Brian bsb 1980, 81, 82
Milburn, Glyn ftb 1990, 91, 92
Miles, Richard bsb 1932, 33, 34
Millage, James H. ftb 1926
Millar, Dave mcrew 1961, 62
Millar, Walter mcrew 1968, 69
Millard, Junius mwp 1948, 49
Miller, Ann wbsk 1979, 80, 81, 82
Miller, Arthur bsb 1931
Miller, Arthur mtrk 1965, 66
Miller, Grover mten 1946
Miller, Harold mgym 1967
Miller, Heather wtrack 1995, 96
Miller, Jack bsb 1943, 46
Miller, Jim mten 1982
Miller, John D. ftb 1907, 08
Miller, Julie wswim 1985, 86
Miller, Kevin ftb 1995
Miller, Mark bsb 1961, 62
Miller, Matt mcrew 1995, 96
Miller, Michael R. ftb 1967
Miller, Ray wrest 1955, 56
Miller, Steve mtrk 1989, 90
Miller, Steve mxc 1988
Miller, Susannah wswim 1987, 88, 89, 90
Millham, Steve mwp 1987, 88, 89
Milligan, Robert F. ftb 1931
Milliken, Mike mgolf 1991, 92
Millington, Robert mtrk 1946
Mills, Aaron ftb 1991, 92, 93, 94
Mills, Bertrand C. mbsk 1920, 21
Mills, James M. ftb 1965, 66
Mills, Ralph mgolf 1949
Milner, Mark mtrk 1980
Miltz, Robert mtrk 1963, 64
Minegishi, Hiroyuki Y. mten 1961, 62, 63
Minna, John Dorrance mten 1962
Minock, Michael wrest 1958
Minstrell, Melinda wsoc 1991, 92, 93, 94
Minthorn, Pam wswim 1991, 92, 93, 94
Minturn, LeRoy ftb 1906, 07, 09, 10
Miott, Craig mfenc 1984, 85
Miraglia, Roger mgolf 1987
Mishima, Paula wbsk 1977
Mishima, Paula fh 1978
Mita, Roy mfenc 1980
Mitchel, Patrick ftb 1981, 82, 83, 84
Mitchell, Emery F. III ftb 1948, 49
Mitchell, Emory bsb 1920, 21, 22
Mitchell, Frank mwp 1940, 41
Mitchell, Howard L. mbsk 1925, 26
Mitchell, Howard L. ftb 1923, 24, 25
Mitchell, Kent mcrew 1959, 60
Mitchell, M.M. bsb 1908, 90, 10
Mitchell, Mark Steven mten 1973, 64, 75, 76
Mitchell, Matt mten 1976, 77, 78
Mitchell, Mike ftb 1993, 1995
Mitchell, Mowatt M. ftb 1907, 08, 09
Mitchell, Pat mtrk 1981
Mitchell, Phil, mfenc 1948, 49
Mitchell, Robert S. ftb 1941
Mitchell, Standish L. ftb 1909, 10
Mitchell, Thomas mwp 1993

Mitre, Anthony ftb	1977, 78	
Mittelstaedt, Brian mxc	1970, 71, 72	
Mitten, David mgolf	1950	
Mix, Greg bsb	1990, 93	
Miyamoto, Alan mgym	1963, 64, 65	
Miyamoto, Theodore mgym	1972, 73, 74	
Miyasaki, Nola wgolf	1978	
Modory, Steve mvball	1984, 85, 86, 87	
Moe, Roy mgolf	1948, 49, 50	
Moench, Lee bsb	1959, 60, 61	
Moffatt, Phil J. mbsk	1931	
Moffatt, Philip J. ftb	1929, 30, 31	
Moffett, Eugene V. ftb	1966	
Mogno, Leonard mtrk	1968	
Mohrman, Allen M. Jr. ftb	1965, 66	
Moiso, Cristy wvball	1985, 86	
Molfino, Albert A. ftb	1905, 06	
Moller, John M. ftb	1976	
Moller, Ron mcrew	1981	
Molsalve, Carlos A. ftb	1934	
Momsen, Robert mwp	1967	
Monahan, Keri wgym	1995, 96	
Mondragon, Fred mtrk	1985, 86, 87	
Mondry, Josh mgolf	1982, 83, 84	
Moncllo, Brctt mvball	1983, 84, 85, 86	
Money, Maxwell mgym	1950	
Monmouth, Michael mtrk	1977	
Monmouth, Reuben L. Jr. ftb	1972	
Monoukian, Donald wrest	1955	
Monroe, Doug mgolf	1984	
Monson, Chris S. ftb	1980, 81, 82	
Montague, James P. mbsk	1973, 74	
Montague, Ruth wbsk	1977	
Monteeth, Richard J. ftb	1952, 53	
Montgomery, Jerry mcrew	1987	
Montgomery, John mcrew	1977	
Monzingo, Robert mtrk	1959, 60	
Monzingo, Robert mxc	1956, 57, 58, 59	
Moody, Scott mten	1985, 86, 87	
Mooers, George mtrk	1949	
Moone, Erika wswim	1989	
Moore, Adele wgolf	1989, 90, 91, 92	
Moore, Brian mvball	1994, 95, 96	
Moore, Bryan S. mbsk	1935, 36, 37	
Moore, Charles mbsk	1968, 70, 71	
Moore, Daniel mtrk	1961, 62, 63	
Moore, Dennis J. ftb	1968, 69, 70	
Moore, E. Paul mtrk	1939, 40	
Moore, E. Paul mxc	1939	
Moore, Francis J. ftb	1925	
Moore, Hollis H. mbsk	1962, 63, 64	
Moore, Jack mtrk	1940	
Moore, Jack mxc	1939	
Moore, James mcrew	1986, 87	
Moore, Melissa wsoc	1994	
Moore, Miles N. ftb	1969, 70, 71	
Moore, Misty wgym	1995, 96	
Moore, Patrick S. ftb	1970, 71, 72	
Moore, Rob G. ftb	1980, 81, 82, 83	
Moore, Robert R. ftb	1968, 69, 70	
Moore, Sara wtrack	1995, 96	
Moore, Sara wxc	1995	
Moore, Sue wsoc	1980, 81, 82, 83	
Moore, Susan wsoc	1984	
Moos, Malcolm wrest	1972, 73	
Moos, Ryan mvball	1989, 90, 91, 92	
Morabito, Justin ftb	1993, 94, 95	
Morales, Pablo mwp	1985	
Moran, Matthew R. ftb	1981, 82, 83, 84	
Morehouse, Charles J. ftb	1960	
Moreno, Theodore mwp	1938, 39, 40	
Morgan, Brian mgym	1970, 71, 72	
Morgan, Craig mgym	1958, 59, 60	
Morgan, Daryle L. mbsk	1978, 79, 80	
Morgan, Gerald bsb	1956, 57	
Morgan, Elise fh	1992, 93, 94, 95	
Morgan, Jim mbsk	1991, 92, 93, 94	
Morley, Samuel R. mbsk	1953	
Morley, Samuel R. ftb	1951, 52, 53	
Morley, Vivirn A. ftb	1927	
Morris, Allyn E. ftb	1947	
Morris, Betsy fh	1974, 75	
Morris, Brandon mtrk	1995	
Morris, Brian M. ftb	1983, 84, 85, 86	
Morris, Carl G. ftb	1984, 85, 86, 87	
Morris, Greg mwp	1988, 89, 90	
Morris, Leslie mtrk	1985	
Morris, Mike mbsk	1990	
Morrison, Benjamin F. ftb	1942	
Morrison, Diane wtennis	1976, 77, 78	
Morse, Eric mgolf	1978, 79	
Mortenson, Eva wswim	1989, 90, 91, 93	
Morton, Dana wswim	1980, 81, 82	
Morton, Gary bsb	1974	
Morze, David S. ftb	1978, 79, 80, 81	
Moscrip, James bsb	1934	
Moscrip, James H. ftb	1933, 34, 35	
Mosher, John wrest	1946	
Mosich, Anthony J. ftb	1954, 55	
Mosk, Richard Mitchell mten	1958, 59, 60	
Mouchawar, Alan mwp	1978, 79, 80, 81	
Mouchawar, Marvin mwp	1983, 84, 85	
Mouchawar, Maurice mwp	1980	
Moulton, Alycia wtennis	1979, 80, 81, 82	
Moulton, Everts mbsk	1918, 19	
Mountain, Joanna wsoc	1982	
Mowat, John mwp	1948	
Moyer, David, mfenc	1975	
Moyer, Steve mwp	1982, 83, 84	
Mueller, Daniel wrest	1972, 73	
Mueller, Melissa fh	1993, 94	
Mueser, Erica wbsk	1984, 85, 86, 87	
Muir, Michael mgym	1969	
Mulchay, Roland bsb	1923, 24, 25	
Mulitauaopele, Naomi wbsk	1995, 96	
Mullen, Tom wrest	1981, 83, 84	
Muller, Donald F. ftb	1927, 28, 29	
Muller, Wes C. ftb	1933, 34, 35	
Mullin, Jack W. ftb	1939	
Mullins, Eric mtrk	1984	
Mullins, Eric D. ftb	1980, 81, 82, 83	
Mulroy, Vincent D. ftb	1976, 77, 78	
Mumby, Winston wrest	1947, 48	
Mungai, Annette wxc	1977, 78, 79	
Munger, Burton mgym	1951	
Munger, John R. ftb	1936	
Munoz, Claudia wtrack	1993	
Munro, David mgolf	1961	
Munroe, Richard P. ftb	1942	
Murakami, Amy wgym	1996	
Murfee, Eileen wvball	1993, 94, 95	
Murk, Larry mfenc	1984, 85, 86, 87	
Murphy Mariotti, Lisa wvball	1981, 82, 83, 84	
Murphy, Allen T. mbsk	1946	
Murphy, Carmel wsoc	1992, 93, 94, 95	
Murphy, Chester bsb	1898, 99, 1900	
Murphy, Chester G. ftb	1896, 97, 98, 99	
Murphy, Kathy wbsk	19 78, 79, 80, 81	
Murphy, Michael ftb	1925, 26, 27	
Murphy, Philip wrest	1959, 60, 61	
Murphy, Robert bsb	1951, 52, 53	
Murray, Brent mgolf	1974	
Murray, Gary S. ftb	1970, 71, 72	
Murray, Paul C. ftb	1922, 23	
Murton, David mwp	1951, 52, 53	
Mussina, Mike bsb	1988, 89, 90	
Muster, Brad W. ftb	1984, 85, 86, 87	
Myers, Brian bsb	1981, 82, 83, 84	
Myers, Glenn C. ftb	1963, 64, 65	
Myers, Theodore mten	1947	
Naber, Kenneth E. ftb	1977, 78, 79, 80	
Nafzinger, James ftb	1947, 48	
Nagano, Patrick bsb	1940	
Nagel, Otto A. ftb	1918	
Nahama, Dave wrest	1989	
Nakano, Erin wsoc	1985	
Napper, Lowell wrest	1947	
Narver, Richard mwp	1946, 47	
Nash, Dan ftb	1987, 88, 89	
Natcher, Stanlus Z. ftb	1926	
Nava, Robert bsb	1948, 49	
Navis, Ray mgolf	1975	
Navran, Leslie bsb	1946	
Naylor, Kelly fh	1994, 95	
Neal, Joe F. ftb	1962, 63, 64	
Neal, Ronald B. ftb	1910	
Neal, Sarah wvball	1995	
Neal, Tyler mvball	1995, 96	
Neale, Emery mten	1941, 42, 43	
Neely, Wendy wxc	1987	
Neff, Hector mgym	1972, 73, 75	
Neff, John R. ftb	1954, 55	
Neglay, Mark wrest	1995, 96	
Negrete, George mgym	1973, 74	
Neighbor, Robett wrest	1952	
Neil, Amy wgym	1995, 96	
Neill, Kerry wswim	1982	
Neill, Michael R. ftb	1979, 80, 81	
Neill, Philip S. ftb	1929, 30, 31	
Neill, William C. Jr. ftb	1923, 24	
Neils, Jamie mcrew	1961	
Neithardt, David mgym	1989, 90	
Nell, Theodore bsb	1942, 47, 48	
Nelsen, Jeremy mfenc	1990, 91, 92, 93, 94	
Nelson, Bernard mtrk	1955	
Nelson, Brad mvball	1985, 86, 87, 88	
Nelson, Brian mgym	1979, 80, 81, 83	
Nelson, Clarke bsb	1954	
Nelson, Darrin M. ftb	1977, 78, 80, 81	
Nelson, David bsb	1987	
Nelson, David E. ftb	1965, 66, 67	
Nelson, David Martin mten	1957, 58, 59	
Nelson, Harvey mgym	1959	
Nelson, Kenneth bsb	1972, 73	
Nelson, Margaret wbsk	1976, 77, 78	
Nelson, Marlin wfenc	1941	
Nelson, Mike bsb	1970, 71	
Nelson, Warren bsb	1959	
Nemcek, Albert mgym	1976, 77, 78	
Nemcek, John mgym	1981	
Nemcek, Paul mgym	1978, 79	
Nemcex, Albert mgym	1975	
Nesselrod, Jerrold mgym	1951, 52, 53, 54	
Nester, Leann wfenc	1977	
Neuman, James bsb	1934	
Neumann, Paul R. mbsk	1957, 58, 59	
Nevers, Ernest bsb	1924, 25	
Nevers, Ernest mbsk	1924, 25	
Nevers, Ernest A. ftb	1923, 24, 25	
Nevinny, Corinne wtennis	1978, 79, 81	
Newcomer, Douglas mgolf	1967	
Newell, Daniel mxc	1972	
Newell, Warren bsb	1962, 63	
Newhouse, F. mbsk	1926	
Newkirk, Joel bsb	1957, 58, 59	
Newsom, William bsb	1936	
Newton, James wrest	1957	
Newton, Michael E. ftb	1986, 87, 88	
Nguyen, Baochi fh	1993, 94, 95	
Nichols, Bart mcrew	1987, 88	
Nichols, Blaik bsb	1988	
Nichols, Robert G. Jr. ftb	1962, 63, 64	
Nicholson, Kathleen fh	1979, 80, 81, 82	
Nicholson, Robert S. mbsk	1972	
Nicholson, William H. ftb	1967, 68	
Nickel, Paul B. mwp	1989, 90, 91, 93	
Nickerson, Karen wtrack	1983, 84, 85, 86	
Nicolao, Luis mwp	1966, 67	
Nicolet, Robert A. ftb	1957, 58	
Nicoud, Trey mcrew	1978, 79	
Nieland, Kird mtrk	1957	
Nieland, Kirk wrest	1955	
Nielebeck, Monica wswim	1986, 87, 88	
Nielsen, Phillip mten	1949, 51	
Nieves, Ruben mvball	1980, 81	
Nikolai, Irvin ftb	1957, 58, 59	
Nilmeier, Conrad mgolf	1972, 73, 74, 75	
Nino, Kathy wgolf	1981, 82, 83, 84	
Nisbet, Thomas R. mbsk	1967	
Nissen, Eugene bsb	1926, 27	
Nissen, Richard wrest	1946	
Niu, Tina wtrack	1986	
Nixon, Carver mwp	1953, 54	

Nixon, Diane wgolf 1982, 83, 84
Noble, Michael F. ftb 1982, 83, 84, 86
Nobs, Kenneth A. mbsk 1934, 35, 36
Noga, Steve mxc 1973
Nonnenberg, Wade mgolf 1976
Nonoshita, Leni wsoc 1989, 90, 91, 92
Noonan, Carol wswim 1977, 78
Noonan, Tim mten 1971, 72, 74, 75
Noonan, W.F. bsb 1914, 16
Norberg, Henry F. Jr. ftb 1940, 41, 42
Nordland, Thomas R. mbsk 1961
Norgaard, Steve mcrew 1986
Norgard, Alar A. mbsk 1932
Norgard, Alvar A. ftb 1931, 33
Noriega, Jimmy bsb 1993
Norman, Richard M. ftb 1958, 59, 60
Normand Stinehart, Sherry wvball 1976, 77, 78, 79
Norris, George D. ftb 1978
Northrup, Tim mvball 1982, 83, 84
Northway, John mtrk 1960, 61, 62
Northway, John mxc 1959, 60
Norton, Helen wsoc 1981, 82, 84, 85
Norton, Jeff mxc 1976
Norton, Robert mten 1954, 55
Norton, Stephanie wswim 1985, 86, 87, 88
Norville, John mgolf 1978
Norwood, Toby ftb 1990, 91, 92, 93
Norwood, Toby mtrk 1991, 92, 95
Nottage, David mwp 1939, 40
Notter, Dave mcrew 1966
Nourse, John mtrk 1959, 60, 61
Nourse, Norman mtrk 1948, 49, 50
Novatny, Jerry mtrk 1976
Nowick, Dave wrest 1989, 90, 92, 93
Nowick, Phil wrest 1991, 92, 93
Nowlis, Mat wrest 1989, 90
Nussbaum, David A. mbsk 1980, 83
Nutter, Nathan mtrk 1996
Nutter, Nathan mxc 1994, 95
Nutting, Lowell bsb 1934
Nyarady, Steve mcrew 1972
Nye, Blaine F. ftb 1965, 66, 67
Nye, Tom A. ftb 1984, 85, 86
Nygaard, Vanessa wbsk 1995, 96
Nyweide, Kristin wswim 1995, 96

O'Meara, Francis wbsk 1976, 77
O'Brian, Alan bsb 1971, 72, 73
O'Brien, Alex mten 1989, 90, 91, 92
O'Brien, William A. mbsk 1946
O'Connor, Robert C. ftb 1933
O'Neill, Dennis T. mbsk 1969, 70, 71
O'Sullivan, John J. mbsk 1950, 51
Obear, M. bsb 1910, 12
Oberhelman, Amy wswim 1995, 96
OBrien, John mtrk 1966, 67
Ocasek, Gregory mwp 1983, 84, 85
Odegard, Philip John mten 1961
Odell, Tim mcrew 1974, 75
Oden, Bev wvball 1989, 90, 91, 92
Oden, Kim wvball 1982, 83, 84, 85
Odita, Peggy wtrack 1988, 89, 90, 91
Oeding, Jeff mwp 1985, 87, 89
Offen, George mfenc 1957
Ogas, Jay mvball 1988
Ogden, Richard Mitton mten 1959, 60, 61
Ogelsby, John wrest 1951, 52, 53
Ogle, William A. ftb 1964, 65, 66
Ogorek, Robert E. mbsk 1953
OHanlon, Kerry wswim 1994, 95, 96
OHara, Ryan mvball 1989, 90, 91
OKeefe, Marcia wtennis 1974, 75
OKeefe, Marcy wtennis 1976
Olenchalk, John H. ftb 1974, 75, 76
Olesen, Laura wvball 1985, 86, 87, 89
Olesen, Marc mtrk 1984, 85, 87, 88
Olesen, Marc mxc 1983, 84, 85
Oliver, Fred H. mbsk 1942, 43
Oliver, Rhonda wtrack 1990, 91, 92
Oliver, Richard E. ftb 1967, 68, 69
Olivia, David M. mbsk 1923, 24, 25

Olmstead, Nate bsb 1992, 93, 94
Olmsted, Clarence E. ftb 1910
Olmsted, Scott mvball 1981
Olsen, Alonzo mgym 1954
Olsen, Benjamin mten 1942
Olsen, Nathan ftb 1992, 93, 94
Olsen, Parker bsb 1957, 58
Olson, Diana wcrew 1988, 89, 90
Olson, Francis mtrk 1941
Olson, Greg mwp 1988, 89, 90
ONeil, Tom mxc 1977
ONeil, Tom mxc 1979, 80
Onesti, Silvio mwp 1946
Ong, George wrest 1956, 58
Ong, Mei-lin wswim 1974, 75
Orchard, John bsb 1962
Orehobl, William E. mbsk 1947
Orizzi, Edward bsb 1973
Orley, Thomas mfenc 1958
Orme, Charles H. Jr. ftb 1938, 39, 40
ORourke, Ron mcrew 1979
Orvick, Kenneth E. ftb 1980, 83
Osborn, W. Gregory mbsk 1969, 70
Osborne, Daniel mwp 1951, 52, 54
Osborne, Mary wtrack 1980, 81, 83, 84
Osenbaugh, Roger bsb 1951, 53
Osmera, Jeanne wbsk 1986
Osterloh, Rick mvball 1992
Ostrander, Clinton mtrk 1969
Ostrander, Dale H. ftb 1960
Ostrander, William R. ftb 1965
Ostrom, Sig R. ftb 1973, 74, 75
Osuna, Al bsb 1984, 86, 87
Otoupal, Vince ftb 1989, 90, 91, 92
Ott, Marshall wrest 1966
Ottmar, David A. ftb 1972, 73
Otto, Nikki wvball 1993, 94, 95
Ottoboni, Gina wswim 1985
Overman, Robert bsb 1960, 61, 62
Oviatt, Todd bsb 1924, 25
Owen, Chauncey bsb 1906, 07
Owen, Chauncey C. ftb 1906, 07
Owen, Heather wbsk 1995, 96
Owen, Stanley mten 1939, 40, 41
Oxenstierna, Anna wgolf 1985

Paadden, Dana wgym 1978
Paaso, Kristi wvball 1989, 90, 91, 92
Paccione, Angie wbsk 1979, 80, 82, 83
Pacillo, Joanne wgolf 1980, 81, 82, 83
Packard, David ftb 1933
Packard, David mbsk 1932
Packard, Zander mcrew 1990
Padden, Dana wvball 1976
Page, Alfred B. mbsk 1934, 35
Page, Philip bsb 1953, 54
Palacios, Josh mvball 1996
Palamountain, Bennett H. ftb 1932, 33
Palecek, Misha mten 1995, 96
Palin, Drew W. ftb 1973, 74
Palisoul, David bsb 1946
Pallette, Charles W. Jr. ftb 1919
Pallow, Rick ftb 1989, 91
Palmbush, Scott ftb 1987, 88, 89, 90
Palmer, Caroline wswim 1996
Palmer, E. Payne mbsk 1932, 33
Palmer, Jared mten 1990, 91
Palmer, Richard A. ftb 1940
Palmer, William A. mbsk 1968, 69, 70
Palmieri, Pamela wgolf 1974, 75, 76
Palmquist, Paul mgolf 1952
Palumbis, Jason ftb 1988, 90, 91
Pande, Albert mtrk 1942
Pande, Eliza wtennis 1974, 75
Pande, Liza wtennis 1976
Papathanassiou, Andrew ftb 1986, 87, 88, 89
Papathanassiou, Andy mtrk 1987, 88, 90
Pape, Terry E. ftb 1972, 73, 74
Pappas, Ted A. ftb 1973, 74, 75
Pardner, Wynn mfenc 1980
Parel, Stephanie wgolf 1989, 90
Parietti, Jeff mxc 1973, 74, 75, 76

Paris, Amy wgym 1995
Parish, Don E. ftb 1967, 68, 69
Park, Kaulana H. ftb 1982, 83, 84
Park, Linda wgym 1978, 79
Parker, Garth ftb 1897, 98, 99
Parker, John mwp 1966, 67
Parker, Melvin F. ftb 1918, 19
Parker, P.P. bsb 1901, 02, 03
Parker, Richard mtrk 1960, 61
Parker, Richard D. ftb 1977, 78, 79
Parker, Roderick J. ftb 1938, 40
Parker, Shannon wtrack 1990
Parker, Tyrone ftb 1990, 91, 92, 93
Parks, A. mbsk 1918, 20
Parks, Nathan ftb 1994, 95
Parks, Terry mtrk 1983, 84, 85
Parks, Walter mwp 1951, 52, 53
Parmely, Mark mwp 1965, 66, 67
Parr, Dan mvball 1982, 83, 84, 86
Parris, George mgym 1958, 59
Parson, Stacy wbsk 1987, 88, 89, 90
Parsons, Francis mtrk 1951, 52, 53
Parsons, Harry (Jr.) bsb 1940, 41, 42
Pasarell, Stanley Juan mten 1968, 69, 70, 71
Pascoe, Karin wxc 1978
Paskin, Wendy wswim 1976
Passanisi, Ariel wgym 1994, 95, 96
Patch, Donald mwp 1948
Patchett, Ernest L. ftb 1925, 26
Patel, Vimal mten 1991, 92, 93, 94
Patitucci, Anna wsoc 1992, 93, 94
Patitucci, Frank M. ftb 1961, 62, 63
Patrick John mbsk 1988, 89, 90, 91
Patrick, Chris mtrk 1981
Patrick, John C. ftb 1919, 20, 21
Pattersen, David E. ftb 1939, 42
Patterson, Edwin bsb 1921, 22, 23
Patterson, Timothy mbsk 1973, 74, 75, 76
Patterson, W. Thomas mgolf 1941
Patton, Bobby mbsk 1992, 93
Patton, Chester G. ftb 1939
Patty, Duncan mwp 1939
Patzwald, Dave mbsk 1986
Paul, Robert mgym 1946
Paulman, William H. ftb 1935, 36, 38
Paulsen, Troy bsb 1988, 89, 90
Pauly, Stephen mgym 1956
Pavelski, Rene wtrack 1994, 95
Pavko, Michael R. ftb 1965, 66
Pavlic, John W. ftb 1961, 63
Paye, John A. ftb 1983, 84, 85, 86
Paye, John Jr. mbsk 1984, 85, 86
Paye, John P. ftb 1962
Paye, Kate wbsk 1992, 93, 94, 95
Payne, Kevin N. ftb 1985
Payne, Marshall mcrew 1977
Payne, Walter bsb 1955, 56, 57
Paz, Socorro wcrew 1979
Pearlman, Marshall mwp 1948, 49, 50
Pearson, Bradbury mgym 1968
Pease, Maria wswim 1979, 80, 81
Pease, Norman mtrk 1959, 60
Peavy, Claude bsb 1922, 23
Pecci, Jay bsb 1996
Peck, Edward L. ftb 1913
Peck, Kendall ftb 1947, 49
Peck, Mike mgolf 1975, 76, 77, 78
Peck, Murray mfenc 1978
Peck, Russell mtrk 1941, 42
Pederson, Leigh wbsk 1982, 83
Pederson, Scott mvball 1988, 89
Pegelow, Frederic J. mbsk 1962
Pelluer, Arnold ftb 1986, 87, 88
Pelouze, Robert F. mbsk 1917, 19, 20
Pelouze, Robert F. ftb 1916, 19, 20
Pemberton, John R. ftb 1906, 07, 09
Pendergrass, Donald bsb 1942, 47
Penn, Robert M. mbsk 1940, 41, 42
Pentz, Raymond mten 1954
Perez, David bsb 1975, 76, 77, 78
Perkins, Doug wrest 1980, 81, 82, 83
Perkins, William mfenc 1942

Perreault, Pierre E.	ftb	1970, 71, 72
Perry, George	mtrk	1992
Perry, Ron	wrest	1987, 88, 89, 90
Perry, Wolfe	mbsk	1976, 77, 78, 79
Perscheid, Jason	mtrk	1995
Perscheid, Jason	mxc	1994, 95
Pershing, Richard S.	ftb	1919, 20, 21
Pete, Michael	wrest	1968
Peter, Donald G.	ftb	1959, 60
Peters, Frederick	mtrk	1957
Peters, Maurice	bsb	1947
Petersen, Karla	fh	1993, 94, 95
Petersen, James	mgym	1967
Petersmeyer, Gary S.	mbsk	1966, 67, 68
Peterson, Charles	mtrk	1957
Peterson, Dennis W.	ftb	1971, 72
Peterson, Kim	wsoc	1988, 89, 90, 91
Peterson, Kyle	bsb	1995, 96
Peterson, Lorne	mtrk	1963
Peterson, Nicholas	bsb	1972, 73
Peterson, Rob	mcrew	1986
Peterson, Robert	mvball	1987
Peterson, Robert L.	ftb	1956, 57, 58
Peterson, Rolf	mcrew	1957, 58, 59
Peterson, Thor	bsb	1939
Peterson, Thor	mtrk	1940, 41
Peterson, Thor J.	ftb	1938, 39, 40
Peterson, Todd	mtrk	1971
Petho, Julie	syncswim	1996
Pettigrew, Gary L.	ftb	1963, 64, 65
Pettigrew, Kenneth	mwp	1961, 62, 63
Pettinger, George	mgolf	1972, 73, 74, 75
Pettingill, Brian	mtrk	1982, 84, 85
Pettingill, Brian	mxc	1981, 82, 84, 85
Pettingill, Henry S. Jr.	ftb	1914, 15, 16, 17
Peus, Eric	mten	1987, 88, 89, 90
Pew, Jim	mcrew	1982, 83
Pew, John	wrest	1959, 60
Peyton, Kim	wswim	1977, 78, 79
Pflueger, John M.	mbsk	1957, 58
Pfyl, Monte	mtrk	1941
Pfyl, Monte (Jr.)	bsb	1939, 40, 41
Pham, By	wrest	1994, 95, 96
Phelps, Robert C.	ftb	1947
Pheney, William D.	ftb	1922
Philbrick, Heidi	wsoc	1982
Phillipi, Vincent	bsb	1928, 31, 32
Phillips, Damon	ftb	1993, 94
Phillips, Jack	mgolf	1942
Phillips, Michael	mgym	1977
Phillips, Ralph L.	ftb	1975, 76, 77
Phleger, Atherton M.	ftb	1946, 47, 48
Picard, Gregory	mgolf	1965, 66, 67
Picazo, Bob	wrest	1976
Pichon, Patty	wgolf	1978, 79
Pickering, Shaun	mtrk	1982, 83, 84, 85
Pickett, David	mtrk	1985, 86, 87, 88
Pierce, Eric	ftb	1988, 89, 90
Pierce, Peter	wrest	1954
Pierce, Robert	mgym	1954, 55, 56
Pigg, Jauron	mtrk	1996
Pigott, John S.	ftb	1976, 77, 78
Pike, Gary E.	ftb	1958, 59
Pillsbury, Ronald	mgym	1954, 55, 57, 58
Pimental, William E.	ftb	1983
Pinckney, Jon	ftb	1988, 89, 90, 91
Pincock, Norman	mgym	1957, 58, 59
Pinion, G. Keith	bsb	1943
Pitchford, Gary	ftb	1975, 76, 77
Pitchford, Mark B.	mbsk	1978
Pitchford, Thomas	mtrk	1976
Pitkin, William	wrest	1956
Pittinger, Lyndon	mgolf	1975
Pitts, Raymond	mbsk	1922
Pitzer, Gregory	mgolf	1967, 68, 69
Plain, Louis	mtrk	1957
Plain, Louis C. III	ftb	1956, 58
Plate, Horatio R.	ftb	1898
Platz, John	mbsk	1983, 84
Plaut, Amy	wgym	1983
Player, Stephen W.	ftb	1960, 61
Pleis, Mitchell F.	ftb	1977, 78
Plemel, Lee	bsb	1985, 86, 87, 88
Pligavko, Andra	wcrew	1996
Plumer, Patti Sue	wtrack	1981, 82, 83, 84
Plumer, Patti Sue	wxc	1980, 81, 83
Plunkett, James W.	ftb	1968, 69, 70
Poehler, Jennifer	wsoc	1991, 92, 93, 94
Poerio, Shelley	wtrack	1980, 81
Pokluda, Jennifer	wswim	1985, 86, 87, 88
Polich, Tyrone T.	ftb	1956
Pollard, James C.	mbsk	1942
Pollock, Dean Michael	mten	1972
Pollock, James	mtrk	1950, 51
Pollock, John	mwp	1941
Polte, Ernest	mwp	1949, 50
Poltl, Randall P.	ftb	1971, 72, 73
Pomeroy, Russell A.	ftb	1949, 50
Pool, Hampton J.	ftb	1938, 39
Poolman, Devin	mvball	1995, 96
Popejoy, David	mtrk	1991, 92, 93
Poppink, Andy	mbsk	1992, 94, 95, 96
Porcello, Anthony	bsb	1972
Porteous, Will	mcrew	1993
Porter, B.G.	wrest	1985
Porter, George	mtrk	1964, 65, 66
Porter, Gerald	mtrk	1969, 70
Poruri, Laxmi	wtennis	1991, 92, 93, 94
Post, Ellis	ftb	1926
Post, Gregory	bsb	1961, 62, 63
Post, Seraphim T.	ftb	1927, 28
Poteete, Rodney	bsb	1967, 68, 69
Poterbin, Walter	mwp	1965, 66, 67
Potok, Jennifer	wsoc	1989, 90, 91, 92
Poulson, Charles W.	ftb	1949, 50
Poulson, Ward E.	ftb	1924, 25, 26
Powell, Jerry	mcrew	1970, 72
Powell, Owen	bsb	1952
Powell, Owen M.	ftb	1950, 51
Power, Brad	mvball	1975
Powlison, Daniel	mwp	1970, 71
Prato, John	mcrew	1995
Prato, Lawrence	bsb	1946
Pratt, Frank	wrest	1965, 66
Pratt, Wilfred	mwp	1962, 63, 64
Preissler, Paul	mcrew	1970, 72
Preissman, Ronald Steven	mten	1963, 64, 65
Prelsnik, Charles J.	ftb	1931
Presley, G.J.	bsb	1906, 07
Presley, George J.	ftb	1906
Presley, Ross	mgym	1953
Preston, John B.	ftb	1927, 28, 29
Preston, Patrick P.	ftb	1967, 68, 69
Preston, Ronald	mgolf	1959, 60
Price, Dana	wtrack	1981
Price, Eric E.	ftb	1981, 82, 83, 84
Price, Fred V.	mbsk	1925, 26
Price, Fred V.	ftb	1925
Price, James	ftb	1986, 87, 88, 89
Price, Jim	bsb	1987
Price, John	mtrk	1992
Price, Richard	wrest	1951
Price, Robert L.	ftb	1960, 61, 62
Pridham, Dwight	mfenc	1978, 79
Priesler, Michael L.	mbsk	1965, 66
Prince, Robert	mten	1955, 56
Prindville, Michael	mxc	1995
Proctor, Carol	wswim	1980
Proctor, Glenn	mwp	1973
Prono, Daniel	mtrk	1963
Protiva, Eric V.	ftb	1956, 57, 58
Proudfoot, Duncan	mfenc	1978
Pruitt, Leroy	ftb	1993, 94, 95
Prukop, Tom A.	ftb	1984, 85
Pryde, Katherine	fh	1988, 89
Ptacek, Edward D.	ftb	1963
Puk, Kevin	ftb	1989, 90, 91
Pulskamp, Flint	wrest	1983
Pulskamp, Tori	wdive	1982, 83
Pulskamp, Victoria	wswim	1982, 83
Purcell, Thomas	mwp	1973, 74
Purkitt, Claude	bsb	1941
Purkitt, Claude H.	ftb	1940
Purpur, Patty	wtrack	1986, 87, 88, 89
Pursell, Frank D.	ftb	1958, 59, 60
Pursell, Stephen W.	ftb	1960, 61, 62
Purves, Sam	mcrew	1962
Puryear, Kris	fh	1988, 89, 90, 91
Pusch, Ann	wsoc	1988, 89
Putnam, Laura	wgym	1984, 85
Putty, R. Drew	mten	1947
Pyle, Brian	mwp	1992, 93, 94, 95
Pyle, H. Carter Jr.	ftb	1951, 52
Pyle, John	bsb	1978, 79
Pyle, John F.	ftb	1976
Pyle, Michael	mwp	1995
Quaccia, Luke	bsb	1996
Quade, William H.	mbsk	1936
Questsad, Larry	mtrk	1963, 65, 66
Quigley, Brett	ftb	1988
Quinn, Tom	bsb	1926
Quinn, Willie	mvball	1990
Quiring, Daro	bsb	1965, 66, 67
Quist, George	ftb	1946, 47
Raaka, Clayton	mtrk	1963
Raaka, Clayton L.	mbsk	1963, 64, 65
Radtke, John	bsb	1982, 83, 84
Radtke, Kenneth	mcrew	1980, 82
Rae, Chris	mtrk	1989
Rae, Chris	mxc	1989, 90
Rael, Jose	mtrk	1948, 49
Rafanelli, Sarah	wsoc	1990, 91, 92, 93
Rafanelli, Stephanie	wsoc	1987, 88
Raffetto, Estral J.	ftb	1925
Raftery, Michael R.	ftb	1955, 56
Ragsdale, Richard A.	ftb	1962, 63, 64
Rahn, Gilbert F.	mbsk	1937, 40
Raines, John	mcrew	1969
Raines, William	mtrk	1972
Raitt, C.B.	ftb	1899, 1900, 01
Ramee, Keith	mbsk	1983, 84, 85, 86
Ramirez, Malia	wsoc	1993
Ramos, David	mcrew	1988
Ramos, David	mtrk	1985, 86
Ramos, John	bsb	1984, 85, 86
Ramos, Leo	mcrew	1988, 89, 90
Ramstead, James B.	mbsk	1950, 51
Rand, Richard	mvball	1977
Randall, John	bsb	1940, 41
Randall, Laura	wswim	1987, 88
Rankin, Alexandra	wfenc	1987, 88
Rannells, Roland J.	ftb	1957
Ranney, Gilbert Kenneth	mten	1959, 60
Ransom, Andrea	wbsk	1986
Rapp, Jenny	wswim	1982, 83, 84, 85
Rapp, Susan	wswim	1984, 86, 87, 88
Rapp, William A.	mbsk	1938, 39
Rappaport, James	wrest	1974
Rasmussen, Neil Jr.	ftb	1936, 37
Rasmussen, Sue	wtennis	1979, 80, 81, 82
Rast, John	mten	1976, 77, 78, 79
Rath, Robert R.	ftb	1964, 65
Ratner, Ezra	bsb	1920, 22
Rau, Allen F. Jr.	ftb	1946, 47, 48
Ravn, Nick	mbsk	1992, 93
Rawlins, Brooks Grover	mten	1957, 58, 59
Rawn, Chantal	wswim	1996
Ray, Alvin	mbsk	1930
Ray, Conrad	mgolf	1995, 96
Raymond, Alonzo	bsb	1964
Raymond, Laura	wswim	1978, 79, 80, 81
Read, Amanda	fh	1975, 76, 77, 78
Read, John M.	ftb	1964, 65, 66
Read, Robin	mgym	1954
Reader, Richard	mfenc	1988, 89
Ready, Peter	mwp	1965, 66
Ready, William	mwp	1963
Reagan, Mark	mvball	1980, 81, 82, 83
Rebele, Andy	mcrew	1986, 87
Redell, Ron	ftb	1989, 90, 91, 92
Redle, Frank	wrest	1960, 61, 62
Redwine, David	mxc	1967
Reece, Bob	bsb	1970, 71, 72, 73

Reed, Bill E. ftb — 1982
Reed, Dan bsb — 1993, 94, 95
Reed, Harold E. ftb — 1907
Reed, Ian mtrk — 1951, 52
Reed, Richard mgolf — 1950
Reed, Richard Randall mten — 1966, 68
Reed, Robert mtrk — 1953, 54
Reeder, Rob mtrk — 1996
Reeder, Rob mxc — 1994
Reeder, Robert mtrk — 1993, 95
Rees, David mtrk — 1986
Rees, David mtrk — 1988
Rees, David mxc — 1988
Reeves, Frank W. ftb — 1910, 13, 14
Rehm, Francis E. ftb — 1914, 15
Reich, Lawrence mgolf — 1957, 58, 59
Reid, Alison wfenc — 1982, 83, 84
Reid, John bsb — 1990, 91
Reid, William J. ftb — 1972, 73
Reider, Jon mcrew — 1967
Reif, Ricly mgolf — 1984
Reilly, Michael mtrk — 1993
Reilly, Mike mxc — 1990
Reimer, C. Dale bsb — 1937
Reimers, John mcrew — 1989
Reimers, Tom bsb — 1994, 95, 96
Reinhard, Robert R. ftb — 1967, 68, 69
Reinhold, Amy Jo wswim — 1987, 88
Reis, Evan mfenc — 1986
Reisner, John A. ftb — 1933, 34
Reiss, Donald mtrk — 1942
Rembisz, Aaron ftb — 1989, 90, 91, 92
Remmelgas, Johan mgolf — 1990
Renfro, Charles mtrk — 1951, 52, 53
Renfro, Sarna wtrack — 1995, 96
Renfro, Sarna wxc — 1994, 95
Rennaker, Terry L. ftb — 1977, 78, 79
Rennert, Peter mten — 1977, 78, 79, 80
Reno, Nancy wvball — 1984, 85, 86, 87
Renshaw, Matt mvball — 1993, 94
Renteria, Amanda wbsk — 1993, 94
Renwick, Donn C. ftb — 1965, 66, 67
Repath, Charles J. ftb — 1918, 19
Replogle, Dee mgolf — 1941
Revak, Paul A. ftb — 1952
Revelli, John mbsk — 1981, 82, 83, 84
Reveno, Eric mbsk — 1985, 86, 87, 89
Reynolds, Barry R. ftb — 1971, 72
Reynolds, Craig wrest — 1975, 76, 77
Reynolds, Jackson E. ftb — 1894, 95
Reynolds, Kenneth M mbsk — 1929, 30, 31
Reynolds, Larry bsb — 1976, 77, 78
Reynolds, Larry D. ftb — 1975, 76, 77, 78
Reynolds, Robert C. ftb — 1933, 34, 35
Rhee, Jinny wgym — 1986, 87, 88
Rheim, James mgolf — 1963, 64, 65
Rhetta, Duane mcrew — 1968
Rhoads, Caroline fh — 1979, 81
Rhoads, Roger mgym — 1962, 63, 64
Rhodes, Ian mcrew — 1996
Rhodes, Stewart mgolf — 1952
Rhyne, Homer ftb — 1907
Rice, Arthur H. ftb — 1898, 99
Rice, Cara wcrew — 1995
Rice, Darren mcrew — 1993
Rice, Doug mgolf — 1976
Rice, Gordon ftb — 1949, 51
Rice, J. Bermingham ftb — 1896, 97
Rich, Ellsworth L. ftb 1892 (Spr.), 1892 (Fall)
Richards, Barry mten — 1987, 88, 89, 90
Richards, Dowell mbsk — 1928, 29
Richards, Martha wbsk — 1989, 90, 91
Richards, Martha wgolf — 1991, 92, 93
Richardson, Albert ftb — 1988, 89, 90, 91
Richardson, Bruce G. ftb — 1985, 86, 87
Richardson, Clement mgolf — 1970, 71
Richardson, Kevin L. ftb — 1985, 86, 87, 88
Richardson, Wendy wtennis — 1978
Richetelli, Eileen wdive — 1991, 92, 93, 95
Richmond, Carrol L. mbsk — 1920, 21, 22
Richter, Elmer mtrk — 1948
Riddell, Robert mgolf — 1967, 68, 69

Riddervold, Lesley syncswim — 1996
Ried, Gary mcrew — 1959
Riedl, Robert mcrew — 1986
Riegel, Gordon S. ftb — 1972, 73, 74
Rieke, Forrest wrest — 1962
Riese, Elmer bsb — 1925, 27
Righter, Cornelius mbsk — 1917, 19, 20, 21
Righter, Cornelius E. ftb — 1917, 19, 20
Riley, Michael mcrew — 1980
Rimi, Carmine mcrew — 1990
Rinderknecht, Robin mgym — 1962, 63, 65, 67
Ring, Craig mfenc — 1988
Rinker, Robert L. ftb — 1967
Rintala, Rudolph bsb — 1930, 31, 32
Rintala, Rudolph A. mbsk — 1931
Rintala, Rudolph A. ftb — 1930, 31
Rippner, Robert mten — 1967, 68, 69, 70
Risser, Randy ftb — 1980
Ritchey, Craig S. ftb — 1963, 64, 65
Ritter, Darrell mwp — 1941
Ritter, Russell, mfenc — 1976, 77
Robbins, Dave mcrew — 1964, 65, 66
Robbins, Doug bsb — 1986, 87, 88
Robbins, Mike bsb — 1993, 94, 95
Robbins, Rob bsb — 1991
Roberts, Andrew mten — 1942
Roberts, Donald mwp — 1971, 72
Roberts, Ellery ftb — 1990, 92, 93
Roberts, Frank mtrk — 1971
Roberts, Glynnis wsoc — 1990
Roberts, Jennifer wgym — 1980
Roberts, John mwp — 1972, 73, 74, 75
Robertson, Bruce mgolf — 1972
Robertson, Harold O. mbsk — 1934
Robesky, Donald A. ftb — 1926, 27, 28
Robesky, Kenneth L. ftb — 1939, 40, 41
Robinson, Benjamin bsb — 1958, 59
Robinson, Benjamin B. ftb — 1956, 57, 59
Robinson, Bruce bsb — 1973, 74, 75
Robinson, Chuck ftb — 1988, 89
Robinson, Jason mtrk — 1993
Robinson, John mfenc — 1985
Robinson, Neil mgolf — 1979, 80, 81, 82
Robinson, Noel J. ftb — 1955, 56, 57
Robinson, Paul mten — 1982, 83
Robinson, Tim mgolf — 1981, 82, 84, 85
Robison, Doug C. ftb — 1984, 85, 86, 87
Robnett, Timothy L. ftb — 1970, 71
Rochell, Steven mgym — 1969, 70, 71
Rodda, Harry bsb — 1958, 59
Rodello, Arturo mwp — 1995
Rodman, J. Thomas mbsk — 1946
Rodolph, Frank E. Jr. ftb — 1899
Rodriguez, Rene mtrk — 1993
Roeder, Edwin mcrew — 1986, 87, 88
Roessler, Kurt mtrk — 1979
Roger, Spencer mdive — 1982
Rogers, Charles O. mbsk — 1934
Rogers, Charles O. ftb — 1932
Rogers, Douglas K. ftb — 1978, 79, 80, 81
Rogers, John bsb — 1927
Rogers, Johnny mbsk — 1982, 83
Rogers, Pete wrest — 1983, 84, 85, 86
Rogers, Robert mwp — 1969
Rogers, William B. Jr. ftb — 1952, 53
Rogers, Wister mbsk — 1922, 23
Roggeman, Timothy ftb — 1986, 87, 88, 89
Rohlfing, Jeffrey bsb — 1967, 68
Rohrer, Gretchen wfenc — 1984
Rohrer, Robert L. ftb — 1947, 48
Roinestad, Gerald bsb — 1943
Roldan, Henry mtrk — 1955, 57
Roldan, John mtrk — 1995
Roldan, John mtrk — 1996
Rolley, Carina wtennis — 1989, 90, 91
Romeu, Laura fh — 1988, 89, 90, 91
Rominger, Joseph C. ftb — 1978
Roney, G.J. mbsk — 1917
Roosevelt, William K. ftb — 1901, 04
Root, John P. ftb — 1965, 66, 67
Root, Jon mvball — 1983, 84, 85, 86
Ropp, Andy mgym — 1986, 87, 88, 89

Rosberg, Robert bsb — 1946
Rosburg, Robert mgolf — 1946, 47, 48
Rose, A. Allan mten — 1940, 41
Rose, Christopher C. ftb — 1979, 80, 81, 82
Rose, Donald bsb — 1967, 68
Rose, Girard J. mbsk — 1959
Rose, Kenneth C. ftb — 1948, 49
Rose, Rollin wrest — 1950, 51
Rose, William G. mbsk — 1948, 49
Rosecrance, Robert mgolf — 1947
Rosekrans, John N. ftb — 1948
Rosen, Nick mtrk — 1988, 89, 91
Rosen, Rich mgym — 1980, 82, 83
Rosenberger, Richard mwp — 1960
Rosenfeld, Eric mten — 1983, 84, 85, 86
Rosenkrantz, David bsb — 1951, 53
Rosenthal, David mfenc — 1982
Rosenthal, Michael mwp — 1993, 94, 95
Rosenzweig, Lawrence A. mbsk — 1971
Ross, Duncan wrest — 1961, 64
Ross, Jerry wrest — 1971, 72, 73
Ross, Susan wtennis — 1984, 85, 86
Ross, Thomas L. ftb — 1963, 64, 65
Ross, William wrest — 1968, 69, 70
Rossides, Eleni wtennis — 1986, 87, 88, 89
Rostagno, Derrick mten — 1984, 85
Rostand, Sara wvball — 1980
Rotert, Denise wvball — 1991, 92, 93, 94
Roth, Almon E. ftb — 1909
Roth, Richard mwp — 1968
Rothenbucher, Tom mdive — 1983, 84, 85
Rothert, Harlow P. mbsk — 1928, 29, 30
Rothert, Harlow P. ftb — 1928, 29, 30
Rothman, Jeannie wxc — 1992
Rouble, Lawrence E. ftb — 1933, 34, 35
Rounds, George S. ftb — 1960
Rounsaville, Guy Jr. ftb — 1962, 63, 64
Rouse, Darryl mvball — 1988
Rowan, Michael mcrew — 1979
Rowe, Stuart mwp — 1970, 71, 72
Rowen, Hilary wfenc — 1974
Rowen, Keith L. ftb — 1972, 73, 74
Rowland, Jennifer wsoc — 1987, 88, 89, 90
Rowley, James mgolf — 1956, 57, 58
Rowley, Milton H. mbsk — 1930
Rowley, Phil mgolf — 1984, 85, 86
Royden, George mgym — 1954, 55
Royer, James mtrk — 1972, 73, 74
Royse, Larry L. ftb — 1960, 61
Royval, Jen wsoc — 1994
Ruark Hoff, Jeanne wbsk — 1979, 80, 82, 83
Rubin, Bruce wrest — 1981, 82
Rubin, Dale mtrk — 1965
Rubin, Dale F. ftb — 1965
Rubin, Donna wtennis — 1978, 79, 80, 81
Ruble, Robin mtrk — 1962, 63
Rucker, Tanda wbsk — 1992, 93
Rudd, Nancy wtennis — 1977, 78
Ruess, Isabel wswim — 1982, 83
Rugless, Jamie wswim — 1989, 90
Rule, Orville mwp — 1946
Rupp, William mtrk — 1954
Rusco, Patrick bsb — 1973
Rusco, Patrick D. mbsk — 1971, 72, 73
Rush Campbell, Kari wvball — 1980, 81, 82, 83
Rush Humphreys, Wendy wvball 1984, 85, 86, 87
Rush, John P. ftb — 1898
Rusher, William mgym — 1963, 64, 65
Russ, Dave mfenc — 1987, 88, 89
Russell, Bill mcrew — 1967
Russell, Dell mtrk — 1947, 48, 49
Russell, Earl bsb — 1959, 61
Russell, George wrest — 1952, 53, 54
Rutherford, Darilyn wcrew — 1981
Rutkowski, Dave mgolf — 1991, 92, 93
Rutledge, J.D. bsb — 1908
Rutledge, Robert mten — 1946, 47
Rutter, Richard mwp — 1953
Ruymann, Frederick wrest — 1956
Ryan, Jeffrey K. mbsk — 1978, 79, 80, 81
Ryan, Timothy mgym — 1989, 90, 91, 92

Rye, John G. ftb	1949, 50, 51
Ryersen, Barbara wcrew	1981
Ryker, Robin wswim	1977
Ryska, Tom A. ftb	1974, 75
Ryzewicz, Mark wrest	1995
Saad, Ramy wrest	1992, 94
Sackinsky, Brian bsb	1990, 91, 92
Sacks, Dave wrest	1990, 91, 92
Sacks, Wendy wtennis	1993, 94, 95, 96
Sadler, James D. ftb	1938
Saenger, Jeff bsb	1987, 88
Saeta, Dave mvball	1978, 79
Saeta, Steve mvball	1981, 82
Saftig, Tom mcrew	1978, 79
Sagel, Darrell mdive	1991, 92, 93
Saibel, Charles M. ftb	1969
Sakamoto, James mgym	1971
Sakowski, Vince bsb	1982, 83
Sala, Ralph mwp	1947, 48, 49
Sale, Mary Ellen wgolf	1976
Sales, Dudley bsb	1904, 05, 06
Salina, Adam ftb	1993, 94, 95
Salter, John bsb	1996
Salzenstein, Jeff mten	1993, 94, 95, 96
Sampson, C.E. bsb	1906, 07
Sampson, Ralph G. ftb	1969, 70, 71
Sanborn, M.H. bsb	1916
Sanchez, BJ wrest	1996
Sandborn, Thomas ftb	1909
Sande, John P. III ftb	1968, 69, 70
Sanderman, Fred A. ftb	1942
Sanders, Donald L. ftb	1951
Sanders, John mvball	1992, 93, 94
Sanders, Kraig mtrk	1984, 85, 86, 87
Sanders, Summer wswim	1991, 92
Sanderson, Reginald J. ftb	1970, 71, 72
Sandoval, Anthony mxc	1972, 73, 74, 75
Sanford, Allen mtrk	1967, 69
Sanford, Allen mxc	1968
Sappenfield, Joel W. ftb	1954, 55
Saras, James mtrk	1954, 55
Sargent, Gary A. ftb	1960, 61, 62
Sasse-Shulte, Linn wxc	1995
Satre, Philip G. ftb	1969, 70, 71
Sauer, Peter mbsk	1996
Saunders, Edward mgym	1948
Saunders, Rich mfenc	1973, 74
Saunders, William F. mbsk	1933
Savage, William mgolf	1946
Saviano, Nick mten	1974, 75
Savides, Stephanie wtennis	1984, 85, 86, 87
Sawchuck, Lanny mgolf	1982, 83, 84
Sawin, Laurie wvball	1989, 90, 91, 92
Sayler, Ann wswim	1950, 51
Saylor, Brent E. ftb	1976, 77, 78, 79
Saxenian, Michael mfenc	1978
Scanlon, John mgolf	1982
Scarffenberger, James bsb	1975
Schabel, Fred K., mbsk	1933
Schader, George mbsk	1976, 78
Schadler, Steve mtrk	1985, 86, 87, 88
Schadler, Steve mxc	1985, 87
Schaefer, John bsb	1949
Schaeffer, Jon bsb	1995, 96
Schaer, John mtrk	1979, 80, 81, 82
Schaer, John mxc	1978
Schaffer, Scott mgym	1986, 87, 88, 89
Schaklich, Timothy R. ftb	1970, 71
Scharfen, John mbsk	1948
Schatzman, Susie fh	1974
Schaub, Robert wrest	1954, 55
Schaum, Stephen wrest	1964, 65, 66
Schaupp, Karl L. ftb	1911, 12
Scheible, Ben mtrk	1974, 75
Scheidecker, William R. ftb	1953
Schellenberg, Don bsb	1969, 70
Scheller, Robert Sean ftb	1984, 85, 86, 87
Schembra, Charles mtrk	1967
Schembs, Robert mcrew	1986
Scherer, Charles mtrk	1964
Schickel, Lise wcrew	1991
Schimpf, Kerry A. ftb	1978
Schless, Guy mfenc	1949, 50
Schlicke, Paul mtrk	1963, 64, 65
Schlicke, Paul mxc	1962, 63, 64
Schlobohm, Dean mten	1966, 67, 68, 69
Schlukebir, Katie wtennis	1994, 95, 96
Schmalzried, Thomas mbsk	1977, 79, 80
Schmid, David mcrew	1985
Schmidt, Dan mvball	1975
Schmidt, George mcrew	1979, 80
Schmieder, Vincent mten	1949, 50, 51
Schmidt, Stephen mfenc	1988, 89
Schmidt, Tracy wfenc	1987, 88, 89
Schmitt, Earl mfenc	1951, 52
Schmitt, John mwp	1951, 52, 53
Schmitt, Laurence mtrk	1957
Schmitt, Lawrence E. ftb	1959, 60
Schneider, Frank mwp	1992, 93, 94
Schneider, Glenn mtrk	1986, 87,88, 89
Schneider, Philip D. ftb	1965, 67
Schnurpfeil, Kim wtrack	1980, 81, 82
Schnurpfeil, Kim wxc	1979, 80, 81, 82
Schoen, Bruce bsb	1970, 71
Schoenrock, Kurt mxc	1971, 72
Schoknecht, Kurt mcrew	1972
Scholfield, William R. ftb	1903
Schomaker, Michael bsb	1966, 67, 68
Schonert, Turk L. ftb	1977, 78, 79
Schott, Carl V. mbsk	1935
Schott, Carl V. ftb	1934, 35, 36
Schrader, Carl F. ftb	1962, 63, 64
Schreiber, Fred mgym	1953, 54
Schroeder, Arthur mgolf	1951, 52, 53
Schroeder, Becky wcrew	1988
Schroeder, Francis mten	1946
Schroeder, Frederick mten	1942
Schroeder, Steve mgolf	1978, 79, 80
Schubert, Cory wtrack	1984
Schubert, Cory wxc	1983, 84, 87
Schubert, Vincent mwp	1969
Schuchard, Robert mxc	1973
Schultz, Bryan ftb	1992
Schultz, Jack G. ftb	1968, 69, 70
Schultz, Jane fh	1974, 75
Schultz, Joseph bsb	1962
Schulz, Kathy wbsk	1979, 80
Schutzmann, Hal bsb	1960, 61
Schwager, Charles mbsk	1987
Schwaiger, Leo E. mbsk	1954, 55
Schwartz, Harvey wrest	1961
Schwartz, Martin mcrew	1993
Schwarz, Andrew mwp	1959
Schwarzenbeck, Francis mbsk	1918
Schwarzenbek, Francis ftb	1917
Schwarzer, Claudia wswim	1982, 83, 84
Schweitzer, Edward H. mbsk	1974, 75, 76
Scofield, Frank bsb	1912
Scott, Charles mgym	1951, 52, 53
Scott, Chris wsoc	1986
Scott, Errol R. ftb	1959, 60, 61
Scott, Gary bsb	1977, 78
Scott, Joseph K. ftb	1947
Scott, Julie wtennis	1995, 96
Scott, Kevin R. ftb	1983, 84, 85, 86
Scott, Kevin T. ftb	1987, 88, 89, 90
Scott, Leland bsb	1907, 08, 09
Scott, Leland (Jr.) bsb	1942
Scott, Leland S. ftb	1909
Scott, Malcolm wrest	1975
Scott, Olympia wbsk	1995, 96
Scott, Robert mtrk	1949
Scott, Robert E. ftb	1950
Scott, William D. ftb	1970, 71, 72
Scramaglia, Richard bsb	1952, 53, 54, 55
Scribner, Frederick F. ftb	1931
Scroggy, Logan mtrk	1950
Scudamore, Dave mtrk	1991, 92, 93
Scudamore, David mxc	1988, 89, 90
Seabright, Benjamin F. ftb	1896
Seabrook, Thomas mxc	1966
Seale, Kirby wsoc	1989, 90, 91
Seanor, William mgolf	1957, 58, 60
Sears, Andrew mtrk	1967, 68
Sears, Roger G. ftb	1959, 60, 61
Seaton, Mark mbsk	1996
Seaver, James mten	1938, 39, 40
Seavey, William mcrew	1981, 83
Sebolt, Sue wbsk	1984, 85, 86, 87
Seckler, James bsb	1963
Seebold, James mtrk	1955
Seed, Aubrey mtrk	1941
Seed, Aubrey mxc	1939, 40
Seeley, Carrol C. ftb	1900
Sees, Eric bsb	1994, 95, 96
Selix, Sherman mgolf	1940
Selleck, George A. mbsk	1954, 55, 56
Sellers, Janet wtrack	1986
Sellman, Roland ftb	1926, 27, 28
Semple, Jeremy mten	1982, 83
Sepeda, Jamie bsb	1990, 91, 92
Serjak, Chris wrest	1994, 96
Severin, Niles wrest	1950
Sevillian, Niki wbsk	1991, 92, 93, 94
Sey, Chris mgym	1991, 92, 93, 94
Seymour, Kent mbsk	1983, 84, 85
Seymour, Peter M. ftb	1967, 68, 69
Seymour, Robert J. ftb	1955
Shafer, Steve mfenc	1981
Shaffer, Lisa wsoc	1981, 82, 83, 84
Shanahan, Robert mgolf	1958
Shane, Mario ftb	1988
Shank, Harvey bsb	1967, 68
Shannon, Jennifer wswim	1986, 88
Shannon, Mary Beth wsoc	1986
Shannon, Tammy wswim	1993, 94, 95, 96
Shapiro, Peter mvball	1981, 83
Sharp, David B. ftb	1968, 69
Sharpe, Tom mtrk	1993
Sharpley, Lisa wvball	1994, 95
Shasby, Kim wtennis	1993, 94, 95, 96
Shaver, Benjamin wrest	1968
Shaver, Thomas mcrew	1980
Shaw, Allen bsb	1956, 57, 58
Shaw, Charles mtrk	1940
Shaw, Dan bsb	1971, 72, 73
Shaw, David ftb	1991, 92, 93, 94
Shaw, Thomas bsb	1950, 51
Shaw, Thomas L. ftb	1948, 49, 50
Shaw, Vaness syncswim	1996
Shea, Charles A. III ftb	1956, 57
Shea, Ryan ftb	1988
Sheats, Alan mtrk	1976, 77, 78
Shebelut, Lance bsb	1986
Sheehan, Dennis J. ftb	1969, 70, 71
Sheehan, Kathleen wcrew	1990
Sheehan, Timothy G. ftb	1965, 66
Sheehy, Ann wtrack	1994, 95, 96
Sheehy, Ann wxc	1993, 95
Sheerer, Gary mwp	1965, 66, 67
Shelby, Annette wtennis	1985
Shelby, Dana wvball	1983
Sheldon, Willard H. ftb	1919
Sheller, Willard N. ftb	1941, 42
Shellworth, Tom mtrk	1977, 78
Shelor, Brant mvball	1992, 93, 94, 95
Shenk, Kathy wcrew	1984, 85, 86
Shenkel, Jill wtrack	1990
Shepard, Jack bsb	1951, 52, 53
Shepherd, John Camp mten	1968, 69
Sherman, David mfenc	1982, 83
Shettle, Kim wswim	1978
Shields, Harvey H. ftb	1903, 04
Shipkey, Arthur H. ftb	1942
Shipkey, Harry H. mbsk	1924, 25
Shipkey, Harry H. ftb	1922, 23, 24
Shipkey, Theodore mbsk	1925, 26
Shipkey, Theodore E. ftb	1924, 25, 26
Shirley, Michael mgym	1962
Shlaudeman, Karl W. ftb	1919, 20
Shlaudeman, Robert ftb	1919, 20, 21
Shockley, Hillary E. ftb	1969, 70, 71
Shoemaker, William B. ftb	1966, 67, 68
Shore, Robert A. ftb	1966, 67, 68
Shortall, Richard bsb	1938, 39, 40

Shotts, Ronnie bsb	1967, 68, 69
Showalter, Jack mgolf	1938, 39, 40
Showley, Guy mgolf	1940, 41
Shroyer, James L. ftb	1961, 62, 63
Shryock, Greg mtrk	1993
Shuler, John mgolf	1946, 47, 48
Shull, Rod J. ftb	1985
Shulman, Joel bsb	1961, 62, 63
Shumway, Garrett mtrk	1979, 80, 81, 82
Shumway, Gary mtrk	1979
Shupe, Lewis H. mbsk	1963, 64
Shupe, Stacy wswim	1985, 86, 87, 88
Shupe, Steven J. mbsk	1972, 73
Sibert, Robert mten	1951, 52, 53
Sickmeier, Andrew C. ftb	1977, 78
Sidone, Paul Theodore mten	1971, 72, 73, 74
Siebel, Jen wsoc	1992
Siebert, Peter mwp	1966, 67
Siebert, Thomas T. mbsk	1938
Siegler, David mten	1980
Siemens, Jeffrey S. ftb	1974, 75, 76
Siemon, Jeffrey G. ftb	1969, 70, 71
Siguenza, Jane wfenc	1982
Silliman, Frank mgolf	1955
Silliman, Lynn mcrew	1979
Silva, John mtrk	1942
Sim, William C. ftb	1932, 33
Sime, Lisa wsoc	1988, 89
Similia, Alan W. mbsk	1962
Simkins, William bsb	1929
Simkins, William J. ftb	1928, 29, 30
Simms, Pam wbsk	1987, 88
Simon, Robert mtrk	1951, 52, 53
Simon, Robert mxc	1952
Simon, Robert mfenc	1955, 56

Simonds, Vance mwp	1965
Simone, Michael A. ftb	1970, 71
Simons, Alan W. mbsk	1962
Simons, Carlton B. ftb	1960, 61, 62
Simonton, Tyler mcrew	1987, 88, 89
Simpkins, William mwp	1970, 71
Simpson, Richard mtrk	1938, 39, 40
Simpson, S. bsb	1960
Simpson, Tina wcrew	1987, 88
Sims, Ford mtrk	1955
Sims, John ftb	1992, 93
Sims, R.E. bsb	1928
Sims, Robert mgolf	1953, 54
Sims, Robert F. ftb	1926, 27, 28
Sinclair, Andy L. ftb	1985, 86, 87, 88
Single, Douglas W. ftb	1971, 72
Singler, William D. ftb	1973, 74, 75
Sinnerud, James A. ftb	1958
Sivara, Dean L. ftb	1980
Skeels, Mark bsb	1990, 91, 92
Skerrett, Shawn mgym	1971, 72, 73, 74
Skilling, Jack mgolf	1979, 80, 81
Skillman, Harold bsb	1952
Skillman, Jane wswim	1993, 94, 95, 96
Skoog, Christian mtrk	1985, 86, 87, 88
Skrable, Burman mtrk	1940
Skrabo, Paul M. ftb	1974, 75, 76
Slachmuijlder, Lena fh	1986, 87
Slaker, Frank L. ftb	1900, 01
Slinkard, Brad mtrk	1976
Sloat, George bsb	1946, 47, 48
Sloat, George E. mbsk	1946
Slusher, Dale ftb	1905
Small, Brian mtrk	1986, 87
Small, Sami Jo wtrack	1995, 96

Smalling, Charles O. mbsk	1928
Smalling, Charles O. ftb	1928, 29
Smart, Charles mtrk	1966
Smiley, Arthur C. ftb	1970
Smimek, Suzy wsoc	1983
Smith Richardson, Teresa wvball	1984, 85, 86, 87
Smith, Alison fh	1985, 86, 87
Smith, Anne wgym	1979, 80, 81, 82
Smith, Barrett C. ftb	1951, 52, 53
Smith, Brian wrest	1967
Smith, C.E. wrest	1993
Smith, Charles mtrk	1964, 65, 66
Smith, Charmin wbsk	1994, 95, 96
Smith, Chris mgym	1981, 82, 83, 84
Smith, Chris mwp	1990, 92
Smith, Craig mwp	1959
Smith, Dean mtrk	1958, 59, 60
Smith, Edward mwp	1940, 41
Smith, Edward A. ftb	1899, 1900, 01, 02
Smith, Emily wswim	1996
Smith, F. bsb	1960
Smith, Ferrell W. ftb	1968, 69, 70
Smith, G.W. ftb	1903
Smith, Gary bsb	1963, 64
Smith, Gary mgym	1983, 84, 85
Smith, Gerald mwp	1949, 50, 52
Smith, James bsb	1961
Smith, James Z. ftb	1959, 61
Smith, Jim mtrk	1984
Smith, Jim mxc	1980, 81, 82, 83
Smith, Jody wswim	1988, 89, 90, 91
Smith, John K. mbsk	1943
Smith, Kathy wswim	1983, 84, 85, 86
Smith, Kathy wtrack	1985
Smith, Kathy wxc	1984, 85
Smith, Leonard wrest	1970
Smith, Louise wbsk	1979, 80, 81, 82
Smith, Lyle bsb	1983, 84
Smith, Lyle W. ftb	1933
Smith, Martin E. ftb	1976, 77, 78
Smith, Mike mtrk	1982, 83
Smith, Randy mvball	1979, 81, 82
Smith, Rea E. ftb	1896, 97, 98
Smith, Roy mtrk	1954
Smith, Russell bsb	1941
Smith, S.P. ftb	1901
Smith, Scott mcrew	1984
Smith, Sidney B. ftb	1947
Smith, Stephen mgolf	1960, 61
Smith, Steve ftb	1989, 90, 91
Smith, Steve mwp	1979, 80
Smith, Terry A. mbsk	1980
Smith, Trent wrest	1987, 88, 89, 90
Smith, Warren L. ftb	1910, 11, 12
Smith, Willard mtrk	1942
Smith, William mtrk	1948
Smith, William mvball	1994
Smitherum, Edgar ftb	1915
Smythe, James J. ftb	1974, 75
Snell, Pete mgolf	1975
Snelling, Robert mgolf	1959
Snelson, Eric W. ftb	1984, 85, 86, 87
Snider, Hank bsb	1969, 70
Snider, John E. ftb	1972, 73, 74
Snider, Malcolm P. ftb	1966, 67, 68
Snoke, Albert wrest	1960
Snook, Peter Franklin mten	1961
Snowden, Tina wgym	1992, 93, 94, 95
Snyder, Alan mtrk	1947
Snyder, James mgym	1967, 68
Snyder, Peter mwp	1972, 73
Sobieski, John bsb	1926, 27, 28
Soderhold-Difatte, Vivian wxc	1977
Soderlund, Matt D. ftb	1982, 83, 84, 85
Solander, Olaav bsb	1960, 62
Solis, Santiago mcrew	1995
Solomon, Fred bsb	1923, 25
Solomon, Fred F. ftb	1923, 24, 25
Solomon, Glenn mten	1988, 89, 90, 91
Solomon, Steve bsb	1989, 90, 91, 92
Sommer, Eric wrest	1976

Sommers, Robert H. mbsk	1962, 63
Sones, Thomas H. ftb	1970, 71
Soper, Harold C. ftb	1914, 15
Sorem, Michael mwp	1964, 65, 66
Sorensen, Loren R. ftb	1953
Sorenson, Loren mtrk	1953, 55
Sourlis, Virginia wbsk	1983, 84, 85, 86
South, Glenn bsb	1941
South, Glenn E. ftb	1939, 40
Southern, Vanessa wfenc	1990
Southwick, Scott mcrew	1987, 88
Southwood, Eric J. ftb	1949, 51
Soyster, Jane fh	1975, 76, 77
Spaeth, G. mgolf	1952, 53, 54
Spain, David mwp	1995
Spangler, Jim wrest	1977
Spaulding, Alfred B. ftb	1894, 95
Spayde, Erik mtrk	1993, 95
Spayde, Erik mxc	1994
Spees, Patricia wswim	1980, 81, 82, 83
Speigel, Arthur wrest	1959
Spence, Craig mxc	1990
Spence, Daniel H. ftb	1961, 62
Spence, Robert mwp	1959, 60, 61
Spencer, Robert wrest	1954
Spencer, Stan bsb	1988, 89, 90
Sperry, Michelle wgolf	1996
Spicer, Richard mtrk	1954, 55
Spiegel, John W. mten	1967, 68, 69
Spiekerman, Cindy wtennis	1985
Spies, Jessica wtrack	1983
Spilman, Elisabeth wfenc	1988, 89
Sprague, Ed bsb	1986, 87, 88
Sprott, Walter K. ftb	1902, 03, 04
Sproull, Henry F. ftb	1921
Spurgeon, William bsb	1956
Sright, Zak mtrk	1995
St. Geme, Edmond F. ftb	1981, 82, 83, 84
St. Geme, Joseph W. III ftb	1977, 78, 79
St. Geme, Joseph W. Jr. ftb	1950, 51, 52
St. Geme, Peter E. ftb	1980, 81
Stack, Christopher mtrk	1961
Stafford, W.J. bsb	1914, 16
Stahl, W. Fred ftb	1985, 86, 87
Stahle, Douglas C. ftb	1939, 40, 41
Stahler, John K. mbsk	1958, 59, 60
Staley, L. Martin bsb	1929
Stalla, Heidi wtennis	1995, 96
Stalwick, David K. ftb	1978
Stamm, Edward mtrk	1942
Stamm, Edward A. ftb	1940, 41, 42
Standlee, Norman S. ftb	1938, 39, 40
Stanford, J.N. ftb	1905, 06
Stanicek, Pete bsb	1983, 84, 85
Stanley, Grant mwp	1983, 84, 86, 87
Stanton, Emmett wrest	1973, 74
Stanton, John G. ftb	1952, 53, 55
Starbird, Kate wbsk	1994, 95, 96
Stark, Jonathan mten	1990, 91
Stearns, Laura wcrew	1988
Steding, Katy wbsk	1987, 88, 89, 90
Steele, Gordon D. mbsk	1923, 24, 25
Steele, Russell B. ftb	1956, 57, 58
Steffes, Kent mvball	1987
Steiglitz, Tracy fh	1986, 87
Stein, Josh mgym	1992, 93, 94, 95
Stein, Matt mcrew	1996
Stein, Richard B. ftb	1957
Steinberg, John C. Jr. ftb	1951, 52, 53
Steiner, Renee wbsk	1978, 79
Stenius, Vanja wcrew	1995
Stenstrom, Steve ftb	1991, 92, 93, 94
Stephan, Jennifer wsoc	1991, 92, 93
Stephen, Roy A. ftb	1957, 58
Stephens, Clare fh	1987, 88, 89, 90
Stephens, Darryl bsb	1980, 81, 82, 84
Stephens, James D. ftb	1977, 78
Stephenson, Andrew mfenc	1957
Stephenson, Leland wrest	1960, 61, 62
Sternfels, Bob mwp	1989, 90
Steuber, Harold A. ftb	1959, 60, 61
Stevens, B.L. bsb	1915

Stevens, James mgym	1953
Stevens, Kim wtrack	1986
Stevens, Kim wxc	1985, 86, 87
Stevens, Patrick L. mbsk	1971
Stevens, Trisha wbsk	1988, 89, 90, 91
Stevenson, Don V. ftb	1974, 75, 76
Stevenson, William B. mbsk	1951
Stewart, G. Stephen bsb	1956, 57
Stewart, Gerald bsb	1925, 26, 27
Stewart, James R. ftb	1952
Stewart, John mtrk	1954, 55
Stewart, John K. mbsk	1929
Stewart, John K. Jr. ftb	1953, 54, 55
Stewart, Lisa fh	1984
Stewart, Traccy wdive	1981, 82, 83, 84
Stewart, Tracy wswim	1982, 83, 84
Stewart, Warren mgym	1946, 48, 49
Stice, Robert H. ftb	1919, 20, 21
Stiling, Jeff mwp	1981, 82
Stillinger, Scott mtrk	1970
Stillman, Mark mtrk	1978, 79
Stillwell, Roger H. ftb	1972, 73, 74
Stimson, Dennis mwp	1954
Stinson, Jason mcrew	1989, 90
Stitt, John mcrew	1966, 67
Stivaletti, Kerry wsoc	1988, 89, 90, 91
Stoecker, Robert mtrk	1964, 66
Stoecker, Robert mtrk	1965
Stoefen, Arthur O. mbsk	1936, 37, 38
Stojkovich, Andrew ftb	1938, 39
Stokely, Herbert mwp	1948, 49, 50
Stokes, Jim mvball	1975
Stoll, Ryan mtrk	1985, 86
Stoll, Ryan mxc	1983, 84, 85
Stoltenberg, Blaise mcrew	1985
Stolz, Gary mtrk	1991, 92, 93
Stolz, Gary mxc	1990
Stone, Glen J. ftb	1971, 72, 73
Stone, Grant B. ftb	1936, 37
Stone, Hal Jr. mgolf	1940
Stone, Robert mtrk	1940, 41
Stonehouse, Paul ftb	1989, 90, 91, 92
Storek, Frederick mtrk	1969
Storey, Fred mcrew	1978, 79, 80
Storm, Rosemary wswim	1976, 77, 79
Storum, William mtrk	1950, 51, 52
Storum, William A. ftb	1950, 51, 52
Story, Donald bsb	1930
Story, Quentin wcrew	1988, 90
Stott, David (Jr.) bsb	1947, 48, 50
Stott, E.P. bsb	1906, 07
Stott, Edmund P. ftb	1904, 05, 06
Stotz, Dean bsb	1974
Stout, David bsb	1963
Stout, Mark mfenc	1986
Stowell, Pat mtrk	1991, 92
Strada, Vicky wgolf	1993, 94, 95, 96
Strahorn, Derrick wrest	1981, 82
Straight, Herbert R. ftb	1896
Strand, Justin ftb	1993
Strand, Justin mtrk	1995
Strang, Dave mxc	1989, 90
Strang, David mtrk	1988, 89, 90, 91
Stransky, George mwp	1962, 63
Stratton, John S. mbsk	1971, 72
Strauss, Kim wgym	1981, 83
Strohbehn, John mgym	1957
Strohn, Clarence bsb	1897, 98, 99, 1900
Strong, Charles mtrk	1954, 55
Strong, Charles mxc	1955
Strong, John mcrew	1968
Strong, V. David ftb	1975, 76
Stubblefield, Don P. ftb	1981, 82, 83
Stuhr Doane, Kerry wvball	1980, 81
Stump, Bill mcrew	1965, 66, 67
Stundell, Alfred L. ftb	1910
Sturgeon, John B. ftb	1939
Styrnad, Lyse fh	1974, 75
Sudaleff, Oleg bsb	1954
Sugarman, Jason bsb	1993
Sullens, Stephen ftb	1987, 88, 89
Sullivan, Brendan bsb	1994, 95

Sullivan, Kevin bsb	1974, 75
Sullivan, Michelle wsoc	1988, 89, 90
Sullivan, Mike bsh	1981
Sullivan, O.M. mbsk	1917
Summers, Alan ftb	1984, 85
Summers, John J. ftb	1978, 79, 80, 81
Summers, Jon ftb	1987, 88
Sundheim, George M. ftb	1973, 74
Supin, Pete mcrew	1970
Supple, Frederick E. Jr. ftb	1946
Surmon, Tod wrest	1993, 94, 95, 96
Sutcliffe, Henry mten	1954, 55
Sutherland, Darrell bsb	1961, 62, 63
Sutherland, Darrell W. mbsk	1961, 62, 63
Sutherland, Sam ftb	1985
Suttle, John wrest	1967, 68, 69
Sutton, Richard X. ftb	1937
Suzdaleff, Oleg mbsk	1951, 52, 53
Svitenko, Paul L. ftb	1985, 86, 87
Svoboda, Tammy wbsk	1988, 89
Swan, Betsy wsoc	1984
Swan, Frederick H. ftb	1924, 25, 26
Swan, Mary wcrew	1980
Swan, Richard bsb	1965, 66, 67
Swanholm, Keith H. mbsk	1919
Swanson, Pete ftb	1993, 94, 95
Swanson, Pete mtrk	1995
Swanson, Peter L. ftb	1957, 58
Swanson, Sandy bsb	1970
Swarts, Clifton R. ftb	1917
Swartz, Donald E. ftb	1966, 67
Swartz, Raymond bsb	1952, 53, 54, 55
Sweeney, David F. ftb	1984, 85, 86, 87
Sweetman, Robert wrest	1973
Sweetwyne, Kermit mtrk	1969
Swerdloff, Jon mwp	1987, 88, 89
Swigart, Theodore E. ftb	1915, 16
Swindells, Charles bsb	1898, 99
Swinton, Eliel ftb	1993, 94, 95
Swope, Sharyl wfenc	1974
Sydorak, Roman mten	1992, 93
Syer, Christina fh	1991, 92, 93, 94
Symonds, Nathaniel M. ftb	1926
Sypher, Clarence bsb	1926, 27, 28
Taguchi, Mark wrest	1976
Takimoto, Chris mgym	1976, 77, 78, 79
Takimoto, Corey mgym	1979
Talboy, Al mbsk	1953
Talboy, Alan bsb	1953, 54
Tallant, E.P. bsb	1908, 09
Tallman, Troy bsb	1989, 90, 91
Tam, John wrest	1967
Tam, Lindsay wwp	1996
Tam, Richard bsb	1937, 38
Tampeke, E. John mbsk	1929
Tan, Jackie wcrew	1981
Tan, Kiat mfenc	1994
Tanaka, Mike mgym	1975
Tandy, Ray E. ftb	1928, 29, 30
Tanner, Douglas mwp	1972, 73
Tanner, Edwin S. ftb	1951, 52, 53
Tanner, John mwp	1981, 82
Tanner, Leonard Roscoe mten	1970, 71, 72
Taplin, Russell mtrk	1967, 68
Tarango, Jeff mten	1987, 88, 89
Taranik, James mwp	1959
Targhetta, Paul ftb	1931, 32, 33
Tarkington, Carolyn wgym	1981
Tarpey, Paul A. ftb	1901, 02
Tarr, William H. ftb	1953, 54, 55
Tatarakis, James wrest	1974
Tatum, Frank mgolf	1940, 41
Taussig, Carl mcrew	1978, 79, 80
Taylor, Albert W. ftb	1921
Taylor, Angela wbsk	1990, 91, 92, 93
Taylor, Bryan bsb	1992
Taylor, Charles A. ftb	1940, 41, 42
Taylor, Clay mcrew	1984, 85
Taylor, Clyde mtrk	1950, 51, 52
Taylor, Edwin D. ftb	1950
Taylor, Gary ftb	1988, 89, 91

Taylor, Holly mfenc	1984, 85, 86, 87	
Taylor, J.B. mvball	1994	
Taylor, Jack R. ftb	1955, 56, 57	
Taylor, James R. mbsk	1940, 41	
Taylor, Kory fh	1993, 94	
Taylor, Michael S. ftb	1980, 81	
Taylor, Paul A. mbsk	1944	
Taylor, Perry bsb	1929, 30	
Taylor, Perry N. ftb	1929, 30	
Taylor, Rich mgolf	1952	
Taylor, Robert mcrew	1993	
Taylor, Robert mtrk	1961	
Taylor, Terry mbsk	1986, 87, 88, 89	
Taylor, Wilbur mtrk	1950, 51	
Taylor, Wilbur R. ftb	1949, 50	
Taylor, William mwp	1980, 81	
Teague, Milton bsb	1923	
Teel, Skip mcrew	1985	
Teeuws, John L. ftb	1985, 87	
Teeuws, Michael L. ftb	1979, 80, 81, 82	
Temby, Claudia wfenc	1975, 76	
Templeton, Debbie wtrack	1991, 92, 93, 94	
Templeton, Robert bsb	1940	
Templeton, Robert L. ftb	1915, 16, 17, 19, 20	
Templeton, Robert M. ftb	1939	
Templeton, William mwp	1954	
TenBruggencate, Al J. ftb	1974, 75, 76	
Tenn, David T. ftb	1973, 74, 76	
Tennefoss, Marvin ftb	1950, 51, 52	
Tenney, Richard mtrk	1971	
Terramorse, Drew mtrk	1949, 51	
Terriell, Chester C. ftb	1908	
Terry, Claude L. mbsk	1970, 71, 72	
Terry, Kenneth mwp	1968	
Terry, Zebulon bsb	1911, 12, 13, 14	
Test, Eric B. ftb	1973, 74	
Test, Jennifer wtrack	1996	
Thacher, George bsb	1963, 64, 65	
Thayer, Kendra wswim	1992, 93, 94, 95	
Theder, Richard R. ftb	1986, 87, 88	
Theile, William bsb	1907, 08, 09	
Thoburn, James H. ftb	1910, 12, 13	
Thomas Johnson, Dr. Nancy wvball	1977, 78	
Thomas, Arthur B. ftb	1922, 23, 24	
Thomas, Benjamin A. ftb	1896, 97	
Thomas, David wrest	1969, 70, 71	
Thomas, Eric ftb	1989, 91	
Thomas, Frederic mxc	1967, 68	
Thomas, Frederick mtrk	1969, 70	
Thomas, Jim mten	1993, 94, 95, 96	
Thomas, John M. ftb	1957, 59	
Thomas, Kat fh	1985, 86, 87	
Thomas, Mark mcrew	1995, 96	
Thomas, Randy mcrew	1975, 76	
Thomas, Robert mcrew	1967, 68, 69	
Thomas, Rooney ftb	1992	
Thomas, Ryan wtrack	1995	
Thomas, Ryan wxc	1994	
Thomas, Stuart mbsk	1987	
Thompson, Brewer mwp	1950, 51, 52	
Thompson, Byron mgym	1947, 48, 49, 50	
Thompson, Christopher mwp	1983, 84, 85	
Thompson, Cole mgolf	1983, 85	
Thompson, Doug mgolf	1981, 82, 84, 85	
Thompson, James G. mbsk	1928	
Thompson, James G. ftb	1929	
Thompson, Jenny wswim	1992, 93, 94, 95	
Thompson, John bsb	1920	
Thompson, John M. ftb	1940	
Thompson, Kelly mbsk	1975	
Thompson, Mark mbsk	1995, 96	
Thompson, Morley P. mbsk	1947, 48	
Thompson, Nancy wswim	1978, 79, 80, 81	
Thompson, Oscar wrest	1946	
Thompson, Quentin bsb	1939, 40, 41	
Thompson, Robert A. ftb	1901, 03, 04, 05	
Thompson, Robert N. ftb	1951, 52	
Thompson, Roger mcrew	1976	
Thompson, Savann J. ftb	1975, 76, 77, 78	
Thomson, David mtrk	1978, 79, 80 81	
Thorne, Gary wrest	1975	
Thorpe, Charles A. ftb	1906, 07, 09	
Thorsen, Don wrest	1977	
Thorson, Jay mtrk	1982, 83, 84, 86	
Thrower, Craig wrest	1981	
Thrupp, Ann wxc	1977, 78, 79	
Thuesen, Gerald J. mbsk	1958, 59, 60	
Thurber, Bernie mcrew	1970	
Thurber, Kent mcrew	1969	
Thurlow, Stephen C. ftb	1961, 62, 63	
Tiederman, William (Jr.) bsb	1958	
Tietjen, Robert mwp	1940	
Tilton, Lloyd I. ftb	1913	
Timbie, Rachel fh	1992, 9, 94	
Tingler, Matt mwp	1984, 85, 87	
Tipton, David L. ftb	1969, 70	
Tipton, Michael E. mbsk	1958	
Tipton, Richard mtrk	1969, 70, 71	
Tipton, Thomas ftb	1974, 75	
Title, Larry mcrew	1967	
Tittle, Kay wtennis	1985, 86, 87, 88	
Titus, Michael G. ftb	1946, 47	
Tobin, Donald J. ftb	1951	
Tod, Jay K. mbsk	1932, 33	
Tod, Jay K. ftb	1931, 32, 33	
Toda, Bobby wrest	1969	
Todd, Raymond W. ftb	1934, 35	
Tokola, Marla wfenc	1980	
Toledo, Suzanne wswim	1996	
Toliver, Derek mtrk	1973, 74	
Tollerud, David wrest	1971	
Tolles, Roy wrest	1974, 75, 77	
Tolley, William wrest	1953, 54, 55	
Tolliver, Michael T. ftb	1980, 81, 82, 83	
Tomerlin, Clemens ftb	1940	
Tomlinson, Daniel J. ftb	1971	
Tomlinson, Robert mgym	1969, 70, 71	
Tomsic, Ronald P. mbsk	1952, 53, 54, 55	
Tong, Jessica wswim	1994, 95, 96	
Toorvald, Philip S. ftb	1960	
Toothman, Mike bsb	1979, 80, 81, 82	
Topham, Matt wrest	1990, 91, 92	
Topic, Jim mcrew	1972	
Topp, Gregory A. ftb	1981	
Topping, W. Keith mbsk	1933, 34, 35	
Topping, William K. ftb	1933, 34, 35	
Torrens, Tilla wxc	1994	
Torrey, Denise wtrack	1979	
Toton, Jennifer wswim	1989, 90, 91, 92	
Toxby, Peter mgym	1959, 60	
Trabucco, James bsb	1950	
Tracht, Neil mcrew	1985	
Traeger, William J. ftb	1899, 1900, 01	
Trautman, Gerald bsb	1932, 33, 34	
Tremaine, Frank bsb	1934, 35, 36	
Tremaine, Nicole wsoc	1990, 91	
Trevino, Chris fh	1989, 90, 91	
Trevino, Rodrigo mfenc	1978	
Triefenbach, Marnie wvball	1992, 93, 94, 95	
Triggs, Kevin bsb	1976, 77	
Trimble, Dede wswim	1989, 90, 91, 92	
Tripaldi, Greg bsb	1990	
Triplett, Edward mtrk	1951	
Triplett, William bsb	1932, 33	
Tritch, W.E. bsb	1903	
Trobbe, Scott R. mbsk	1973, 74, 75	
Trombetta, Julius C. ftb	1926	
Trompas, Alexander G. ftb	1934, 35	
Trompas, Steven mgolf	1972, 73, 74, 75	
Trousset, Tony ftb	1988, 89	
Trout, William mtrk	1940	
Trout, William W. Jr. ftb	1939	
Trowbridge, Alfred bsb	1903, 04	
Truher, James mtrk	1955	
Truitt, Sarah wtrack	1993, 94, 95	
Truitt, Sarah wxc	1992, 93, 94	
Trupin, Beth wswim	1976	
Tsai, Vivian wswim	1994	
Tshionyi, Kamba mbsk	1995, 96	
Tsoutsouvas, Louis S. ftb	1936, 37	
Tucker, Mandy wsoc	1993, 94	
Tucker, S. Edward mbsk	1951, 52	
Tunney, Jono ftb	1987, 88, 89, 90	
Turbow, Dan mten	1988, 89, 90, 91	
Turner, Beth wfenc	1979	
Turner, Carol wswim	1978	
Turner, Charli wbsk	1985, 86, 87, 88	
Turner, Hillary wsoc	1986	
Turner, J. Howell bsb	1935	
Turner, J. Howell mbsk	1935, 36, 37	
Turner, Leslie wtrack	1979	
Turner, Ryan bsb	1990, 91	
Turner, William T. mbsk	1954, 55	
Turriziani, Alfred L. ftb	1948	
Tussing, Ford bsb	1922	
Tweedy, Anne wswim	1981, 82, 83, 84	
Tweet, Russell bsb	1968, 69	
Twist, Allison wtrack	1996	
Tyler, Amanda wsoc	1991, 92, 93	
Tyler, Andre M. ftb	1978, 79, 80, 81	
Tyler, Donald M. mbsk	1929, 30	
Uhrhammer, Mike mtrk	1985	
Ukropina, James R. ftb	1957, 58	
Ulrich, Carl mcrew	1959, 60	
Underwood, Philip mgolf	1960, 61	
Underwood, Robert mxc	1969, 71	
Unruh, Kathy wtrack	1991, 92, 93	
Upperman, Jeff mtrk	1986	
Upton, Kathleen wfenc	1982	
Urban, Joseph C. ftb	1912, 13, 14, 15	
Urdan, Jeffrey mcrew	1985, 86	
Utley, Rodney mtrk	1971, 73	
Utter, Barbara wcrew	1991	
Vahan, Randolph K. ftb	1960, 61, 62	
Vail, Stanley M. ftb	1907	
Valadez, Jeanine fh	1977, 78, 79, 80	
Valelly, Steve mten	1977	
Valli, Louis P. ftb	1955, 56, 57	
Vanderbilt, Doug mfenc	1994, 95	
Vanderweld, Lee mfenc	1974, 75	
Van Alstyne, Bruce E. ftb	1949, 50	
Van Brussell, Mark mwp	1971, 72	
Van Dellen, Elzo L. Jr. ftb	1933, 34	
Van Dervoort, Theodore Jr. ftb	1905, 07	
Van Dorn, Nicholas mgym	1942, 46	
Van Galder, Gary C. mbsk	1956, 57	
Van Galder, Gary C. ftb	1955, 56, 57	
Van Heusen, George mtrk	1949, 51	
Van Hook, Stuart G. ftb	1924, 25	
Van Linge, Charles mgolf	1954, 55	
Van Sant, Merritt mtrk	1950, 51	
Van Uum, Katherine wcrew	1990	
Van Zandt, Craig mwp	1973, 74	
Vance, Sandy bsb	1967, 68	
Vanderlip, Manford ftb	1955	
Vanier, Gary mgolf	1970, 71, 72	
Vaniman, Bryan wrest	1994, 95, 96	
Vannelli, Vince mwp	1981	
VanWagenen, Brodie bsb	1993, 94	
Vardell, Thomas ftb	1988, 89, 90, 91	
Varga, Patricia wtennis	1976, 77	
Varnado, Art mtrk	1979	
Vataha, Randall E. ftb	1969, 70	
Vaughan, Craig mtrk	1966, 67, 68	
Vaughn, Matt ftb	1993	
Vaughn, Susan wswim	1985	
Veach, Marlene wtennis	1974, 75	
Veit, Brian wrest	1987	
Velez, Jose Jaime mwp	1983, 84, 85	
Vella, Veronica fh	1979	
Verdieck, James E. ftb	1939, 40	
Verducci, John bsb	1983, 84, 85	
Verdurmen, Edmond (Jr.) bsb	1955, 56, 57	
Veris, Garin L. ftb	1981, 82, 83, 84	
Vermilya, Robert H. ftb	1928	
Vernallis, Kayley wswim	1979	
Vernallis, Nancy wswim	1980	
Vick, James A. ftb	1950, 51, 52	
Vickers, Leon ftb	1993	
Vidal, Kristina fh	1989, 90, 91	
Vierthaler, Albert mtrk	1946	
Vigby, Jack ftb	1917	
Vigil, Daniel mtrk	1986, 87	
Vigil, Loren wrest	1988, 91	

Vigna, Joseph A. ftb	1935, 36	
Villaret, Doug mtrk	1981, 82, 83, 84	
Villars, Denise wgym	1989, 90	
Vincent, Louis R. mbsk	1926, 27, 28	
Vincenti, Louis R. ftb	1927	
Violich, Paul mwp	1954	
Vlahov, Andrew mbsk	1988, 89, 90, 91	
Vogelpohl, William wrest	1966, 67, 68	
Vojvodich, Nicholas mbsk	1957	
Volastro, Christie wgym	1988	
Volmert, Lawrence E. ftb	1964, 65, 66	
Volpe, Jon ftb	1987, 88, 90	
Volta, Eric L. ftb	1984, 85, 86, 87	
Von der Ahe, Matt wrest	1995	
Von Kulgen, Evan mcrew	1982	
von Wronski, Arthur bsb	1957, 58	
Voorhis, Steve mcrew	1990	
Voorsanger, Conrad mgym	1987, 88, 89, 90	
Voss, Edward A. mbsk	1941, 42, 43	
Voss, Sally wgolf	1976, 77, 78, 79	
Vucinich, Milton bsb	1940	
Vucinich, Milton C. ftb	1940, 41, 42	
Wade, James mten	1940, 41, 42	
Wagner, Carl mgolf	1983, 84, 85, 86	
Wagner, Emily wbsk	1988, 89	
Wagner, Harold A. mbsk	1955, 56, 57	
Wagner, Ronald A. mbsk	1954, 55, 56	
Wagner, Willis mcrew	1977	
Waichler, Steve mgym	1977, 78, 81	
Wair, Kristen wsoc	1991	
Wakefield, Charles ftb	1942, 46	
Walburger, Andrew mwp	1994	
Waldo, John H. ftb	1918	
Waldvogel, Jerry A. ftb	1974, 75	
Walker, Alan wrest	1947	
Walker, Ann fh	1974, 75	
Walker, David ftb	1992, 93, 94, 95	
Walker, David B. ftb	1972, 73, 74	
Walker, Edgar L. ftb	1924, 25, 26	
Walker, Frank F. ftb	1915, 16	
Walker, Harold L. ftb	1947	
Walker, Kelly J. ftb	1973, 74	
Walker, Meagan wsoc	1984	
Walker, Willard wrest	1946	
Walkup, Ward bsb	1942, 43, 47	
Wall Doug mbsk	1984, 85	
Wallace, J.M. mbsk	1915, 16	
Wallace, John mgolf	1950	
Wallace, Thomas mgym	1955, 56	
Wallace, William mxc	1958	
Wallin, Brian mwp	1993, 94, 95	
Wallin, Chris mwp	1992, 93	
Wallin, Mark mwp	1989, 90	
Walquist, Doug mvball	1989, 90, 91	
Walsh, Chris ftb	1988, 89, 90, 91	
Walsh, James bsb	1951	
Walsh, James mtrk	1965, 66, 67	
Walsh, James P. mbsk	1950, 51, 52	
Walsh, Thomas J. ftb	1959, 60, 61	
Walston, Carl mgym	1951	
Walsworth, Don mgolf	1983, 84, 85, 86	
Walt, Steve mfenc	1975, 76, 77	
Walter, Carl mfenc	1953, 54, 55	
Walters, Bruce bsb	1976, 77, 78, 79	
Walton, H.A. ftb	1892 (Fall), 1893	
Walton, Jackson ftb	1934, 37	
Wandrey, William mtrk	1961	
Wang, Timothy mgym	1988, 89, 90, 91	
Ward, James mtrk	1966, 67, 68	
Ward, Jennifer wgym	1993, 94	
Ward, Mike mgym	1974	
Ward, Orlando mbsk	1979, 80, 82	
Ward, Tom bsb	1946	
Warde, Jock Jeffrey mten	1973, 74, 75	
Warden, Thomas mwp	1972, 73	
Ware, Janet wswim	1978, 79, 81	
Waring, Clinton J. mbsk	1956, 57	
Wark, Thomas L. ftb	1916, 17, 19	
Warnecke, John C. ftb	1939, 40	
Warner, Bonny fh	1982, 83, 84	
Warner, Morgyn wtrack	1987, 88, 89	
Warren, Douglas L.B. mbsk	1958, 59	
Warren, Lynnae wtrack	1981	
Warren, Robert mwp	1970, 71	
Warren, William B. mbsk	1950	
Wartnik, Neil wrest	1984, 85, 86	
Warwick, Gregory ftb	1978	
Warwick, Richard mtrk	1966, 67, 68	
Washburn, Edward bsb	1942, 43	
Washington, Demea G. ftb	1968, 69, 70	
Washington, Gene mtrk	1968	
Washington, Gene A. ftb	1966, 67, 68	
Washut, Beth wswim	1984, 85, 86	
Wasik, Todd R. ftb	1979, 80	
Wassenaar, Rob bsb	1984, 85, 86, 87	
Waters, Harry mcrew	1970	
Waters, Rich A. ftb	1974, 75, 76	
Waters, Ryan ftb	1993, 94, 95	
Watkins, Frederick B. ftb	1911, 13	
Watkins, Steven mwp	1970	
Watson, Donald R. ftb	1957, 58	
Watson, Jarvis P. ftb	1952, 53	
Watson, Kevin mwp	1992	
Watson, Louise wtrack	1993, 94	
Watson, Louise wxc	1992, 93	
Watson, Paul C. mbsk	1951	
Watson, Thomas mgolf	1969, 70, 71	
Watt, Mike mvball	1975	
Watts, Frank A. ftb	1918, 19	
Watts, Jennifer fh	1990	
Watts, Nicodemus ftb	1993, 94, 95	
Wayne, Peter mgym	1990	
Weaver, Clark E. ftb	1962, 63	
Weaver, J. Carrell mbsk	1930, 33	
Weaver, Jason mbsk	1991, 92	
Weaver, Richard C. mbsk	1965	
Webb, George mwp	1972, 73	
Webb, Jami ftb	1993, 94	
Webb, Jamie mtrk	1995	
Weber, Chris E. ftb	1983, 84, 85, 86	
Weber, John mcrew	1984, 85, 86	
Weber, Kathryn wgolf	1995	
Weber, Stephen ftb	1987, 88	
Wedge, Wesley E. ftb	1954	
Wedge, Winfred E. ftb	1952, 53, 54	
Weed, Kenneth mtrk	1969	
Weeden, Alan mwp	1946	
Weeden, Donald mwp	1948, 49, 50	
Weeden, Frank mwp	1938, 39, 40	
Weeks, Dana wtrack	1991, 92	
Weems, Kris mbsk	1996	
Wehat, Gilbert C. ftb	1923	
Weidmann, Chuck mtrk	1978, 79	
Weiershauser, Ray bsb	1936, 37	
Weill, David mtrk	1961, 62, 63	
Weingartner, Thomas A. ftb	1966, 67, 68	
Weinstock, Lisa wgym	1985	
Weiss, Michelle wtennis	1981, 82, 83, 84	
Weiss, Scott bsb	1989, 90, 91	
Weissbluth, Marc mgym	1963	
Welch, Andrea fh	1980, 81	
Welch, Brian wrest	1979, 80, 81, 82	
Welch, William mgolf	1961	
Weldon, Jon mtrk	1995, 96	
Weldon, Jon mxc	1994, 95	
Weldon, Richard mgolf	1950	
Weller, Milo J. ftb	1903, 04	
Wells, David mtrk	1977, 78	
Wells, Debby wtrack	1993	
Wells, Debby wxc	1993	
Wells, Eric mvball	1992, 93, 94	
Wells, Evan mgym	1992, 93, 94, 95	
Wells, Frank M. mbsk	1940	
Wells, Valana wswim	1976	
Wells, Vanita wswim	1979	
Welsh, Joseph mwp	1968	
Welsh, Lindsay wwp	1996	
Wendell, Cary wvball	1992, 93, 94, 95	
Wensel, Robert J. mbsk	1940, 41	
Wente, Karl mbsk	1996	
Wentworth, William A. ftb	1953	
Werdel, Alyce wtennis	1983, 84, 85	
Werdel, Marianne wtennis	1986	
Werhane, Hilary fh	1981	
Werle, Bob mcrew	1977, 78	
Werner, Bryan ftb	1994, 95	
Werstler, John E. ftb	1978	
Wessner, Dan mgym	1976, 77, 78, 79	
West, Byron F. ftb	1937, 38	
West, Laurie wgym	1991, 92, 93, 94	
West, R.F. ftb	1904	
Westerfield, Dan mtrk	1983	
Westerfield, Dan D. ftb	1982, 83, 84	
Westersund, Kristen wrest	1973, 74	
Westerwick, Kelly fh	1977, 78, 79, 80	
Westfall, Buck mcrew	1966	
Westphal, James D. mbsk	1953	
Westwater, Heather wcrew	1990	
Wetnight, Ryan ftb	1991, 92	
Whalen, John mtrk	1954	
Wheatly, Winston R. mbsk	1915, 16, 17	
Wheaton, David mten	1988	
Wheeler, Erica wtrack	1987, 88, 89	
Wheeler, Robert mgym	1942	
Wheeles, Darcy wsoc	1992	
Whelan, Peter mcrew	1962	
Whipple, John H. ftb	1947	
Whitaker Tokar, Cindy wvball	1976, 78	
White, Alison wxc	1995	
White, Alistair ftb	1995	
White, Amanda wswim	1994, 95	
White, Amanda wtrack	1994, 95, 96	
White, Amanda wxc	1993, 94	
White, Benita wtrack	1986, 87	
White, Charles H. ftb	1934	
White, David mfenc	1946	
White, Gilbert mten	1956, 57, 58	
White, Gordon W. ftb	1948, 49, 50	
White, J.J. mtrk	1995	
White, J.J. mxc	1994, 95	
White, Jason ftb	1992, 93, 94, 95	
White, John mgym	1972, 73, 75	
White, John wrest	1947, 48, 49	
White, Miles mcrew	1975, 76, 77	
White, Nancy fh	1976, 77, 78, 79	
White, Olivia wwp	1996	
White, Philip mgym	1964	
White, Philip mtrk	1961, 62, 63	
White, Randall mtrk	1969, 70, 71	
White, Richard mten	1950	
White, Robert mgym	1949, 50, 51, 52	
White, Robert W. ftb	1948, 49, 50	
White, Stephen F. ftb	1972, 73	
White, Steve mgolf	1987, 90	
White, Vincent D. ftb	1979, 80, 81, 82	
Whitehill, Wendy wvball	1985	
Whitehouse, Louis M. ftb	1893	
Whitehurst, Keenan mvball	1995, 96	
Whiteing, David mtrk	1970, 72	
Whiteing, David mxc	1971	
Whitfield, Bob ftb	1989, 90, 91	
Whiting, Bill mvball	1975	
Whiting, Val wbsk	1990, 91, 92, 93	
Whitlinger, John Thomas mten	1973, 74, 75	
Whitlinger, Tami wtennis	1988, 89	
Whitlinger, Teri wtennis	1988, 89, 90, 91	
Whitsitt, Novian mbsk	1984, 85, 86, 87	
Whitt, Scott ftb	1994, 95	
Whitt, Scott wrest	1991, 94	
Whittemore, John R. ftb	1892 (Spring)	
Whittle, Alexander mxc	1965	
Whittle, Derek W. ftb	1983	
Wichary, Hans mbsk	1981, 82, 83, 84	
Wickerham, N.W. bsb	1916	
Wickersham, James bsb	1946	
Wickersham, Jim mcrew	1974, 75, 76	
Wicks, Anne wvball	1991, 92, 93, 94	
Wideman, Jamila wbsk	1994, 95, 96	
Wiesen, Rachel wtrack	1986	
Wiggen, Scott wrest	1983, 84, 85, 87	
Wiggin, Paul D. ftb	1954, 55, 56	
Wightman, Brad mdive	1990, 91, 92	
Wigo, Wolf mwp	1992, 93, 94	
Wilbor, Jonathan mcrew	1967, 68	
Wilbur, John L. ftb	1963, 64, 65	

Wilburn, Albert T. ftb   1964, 65, 66
Wilcox, Chester bsb   1917
Wilcox, Chester A. ftb   1920, 21, 22
Wilder, Robert mfenc   1977
Wiley, Alison wtrack   1983, 84, 85, 86
Wiley, Alison wxc   1982, 83, 84, 85
Wiley, Craig mcrew   1986
Wiley, Keith mgym   1994, 95, 96
Wiley, William M. ftb   1972
Wilhelm, Bob bsb   1970
Wilhelm, Bruce mtrk   1965
Wilhelm, Bruce wrest   1965
Wilkes, Laura wsoc   1991, 92, 93, 94
Wilkin, John S. ftb   1963
Wilkins, Alfred mtrk   1946, 47, 48
Wilkins, Earl B. ftb   1916
Wilkins, Randall mwp   1969, 70, 71
Wilkins, Tyler mtrk   1964, 65, 66
Wilkinson, Dell wgym   1983, 84
Wilkinson, Michael P. ftb   1975, 76
Willard, Michael R. ftb   1967
Willard, William C. ftb   1937, 38, 40
Willens, Heather wtennis   1990, 91, 92, 93
Williams, Anre mtrk   1984
Williams, Bradley B. ftb   1973, 74
Williams, Brent mbsk   1991, 92, 93, 94
Williams, Charles bsb   1966, 68, 69
Williams, Charles R. ftb   1966, 67
Williams, Donald wrest   1949, 50, 51
Williams, Donald E. mbsk   1939, 40, 41
Williams, Fred mtrk   1981, 82, 83, 84
Williams, Fred L. ftb   1934, 35, 36
Williams, Gwen wtrack   1995
Williams, Gwen wxc   1994
Williams, Howard L. ftb   1967, 68, 69
Williams, Jody wrest   1982, 84
Williams, John mbsk   1984, 85
Williams, Justina fh   1995
Williams, Ken R. ftb   1982
Williams, Kraig mcrew   1976
Williams, Lewis I. ftb   1971
Williams, Nora wtrack   1985
Williams, R.A. bsb   1903
Williams, Thomas bsb   1971, 72
Williams, Thomas M. ftb   1895, 96
Williams, Thomas N. ftb   1958
Williams, Tom ftb   1989, 90, 91, 92
Williams, Vaughn ftb   1980, 81, 82, 83
Williams, Vincent M. ftb   1978, 81
Williamson, Craig mtrk   1938, 39, 40
Williamson, Frederick W. mbsk   1918, 19
Williamson, Michael bsb   1974, 75, 76
Williamson, Raymond mtrk   1957
Willis, Anthony ftb   1995
Willis, Robin mgym   1949
Wilner, Doug mcrew   1986, 87, 88
Wilson, Dawn wtrack   1986, 88
Wilson, Dean R. ftb   1977, 78, 79
Wilson, Elwood J. ftb   1929
Wilson, Geoff ftb   1995
Wilson, Gerald E. ftb   1973, 74, 75
Wilson, Jeff wrest   1983, 84
Wilson, John H. ftb   1892 (Fall), 1893
Wilson, Kirk mcrew   1977, 78, 79
Wilson, Paul mten   1942
Wilson, Phil bsb   1979
Wilson, Philip C. ftb   1952, 53
Wilson, Philip L. ftb   1898
Wilson, Philip L. Jr. ftb   1931
Wilson, Phillip E. ftb   1980
Wilson, Richard Douglas mten   1962, 63, 64
Wilson, Timothy bsb   1971, 72
Wilson, Valerie wtennis   1987, 88, 89, 90
Wilson, Wayne mwp   1968, 69

Wilson, William bsb   1942
Wilson, William A. ftb   1941
Wilton, Frank bsb   1927, 28, 29
Wilton, Frank S. Jr. ftb   1926, 27, 28
Wimmer, Gary E. ftb   1979, 80, 81, 82
Winden, Andy mcrew   1989, 90
Windsor, John T. mbsk   1960, 61, 62
Wines, Blaine L. ftb   1913, 14
Winesberry, John C. ftb   1971, 72, 73
Wing, George wrest   1946
Wingard, Jason mtrk   1995
Wingate, Deshon mbsk   1988, 89, 90, 91
Wingo, Scott mtrk   1975, 76
Winham, William P. ftb   1916, 17
Winnek, Phil S. ftb   1929
Winston, Daniel wrest   1946
Winston, Daniel wrest   1949
Winter, Jerry mtrk   1958, 59, 60
Winter, John bsb   1958, 60
Winterer, Sean mtrk   1979, 80, 82
Winterhalter, Ray bsb   1946, 49
Winters, Jerry E. ftb   1960
Winton, Kent mgolf   1959, 60, 61
Wirt, William bsb   1903, 07
Wirth, Harry Mackey mten   1955
Witmer, Rhonda wtrack   1996
Witmeyer, Ron bsb   1986, 87, 88
Witte, Bill mvball   1982, 83
Witte, Wesley mfenc   1978
Wittenau, Carl ftb   1929
Wittman, Billy ftb   1992
Wogulis, Mark mcrew   1985
Wohlberg, Shira wgym   1989
Wolcher, Sarah wsoc   1992
Wolf, Charles bsb   1941
Wolfe, Bruce mtrk   1974
Wollett, Joseph mtrk   1955, 57
Wolpert, Andrea fh   1983 84, 85, 86
Wolters, Ryan mten   1996
Wong, Dale Louis mten   1967
Dave Wong mfenc   1974
Wong, David wrest   1951
Wong, Kailee ftb   1994, 95
Wong, Rachel syncswim   1996
Wong, Randy bsb   1975, 76, 78
Wood, Casimir J. mbsk   1944
Wood, Gerald mtrk   1952
Wood, Gerald mtrk   1953, 54
Wood, John bsb   1964
Wood, Molly wdive   1993
Woodberry, John mwp   1985
Woodcock, Elbert C. ftb   1911
Woodhouse, Emma wtennis   1991, 92, 93, 94
Woodhouse, Sophie wtennis   1996
Wooding, Audrey wgolf   1989, 90, 91, 92
Woodruff, Daniel mtrk   1967
Woods, Tiger mgolf   1995, 96
Woodward, Tyler bsb   1922, 23, 24
Woodward, Tyleve F. ftb   1921, 22, 23
Wool, Michael mtrk   1966
Woolfolk, Chris mwp   1983, 84, 85
Woolley, James (Jr.) bsb   1933, 34
Woolley, Norman mtrk   1950, 51, 52
Woolley, Robinson mwp   1969, 70, 71
Woollomes, James P. ftb   1920
Worden, Bill bsb   1980, 81
Worden, Richard C. ftb   1927, 28
Worden, Vickey wgym   1983, 84, 85
Workman, Tom bsb   1913, 14, 15
Worley, Davie E. ftb   1951
Worrell, Steve bsb   1989, 92
Worthy, A.E. mbsk   1914, 15, 16
Wotherspoon, Ann wtrack   1980
Wotherspoon, Ann wxc   1979

Wrede, Chris mvball   1989, 90, 91
Wright, Barbara wgolf   1979, 80, 81, 82
Wright, Billy mten   1992, 93, 94
Wright, Gerald wrest   1957
Wright, Howard mbsk   1986, 87, 88, 89
Wright, John Alan mten   1969, 72
Wright, Josh ftb   1990, 91, 92, 93
Wright, Muirson bsb   1929, 30
Wright, Perry mten   1975, 76, 77, 78
Wright, Richard mgolf   1938, 39, 40
Wright, Vicky wxc   1977
Wrye, Mary Lynn wcrew   1986
Wulff, Russell mtrk   1938, 39, 40
Wustefeld, Amy wbsk   1993, 94, 95
Wustrack, Karl M. mbsk   1966
Wycoff, Robert mwp   1949, 50, 51
Wylie, James T. ftb   1914, 15
Wylie, Robert M. ftb   1959, 60
Wyman, David M. ftb   1982, 83, 84, 86
Wyman, Michael E. ftb   1981, 82, 83, 84

Yanagisawa, William mgolf   1994
Yancey, Mark wrest   1977
Yandle, John bsb   1975, 76, 77
Yanke, Jill wbsk   1986, 87, 88, 89
Yarbrough, Steve wrest   1987, 88, 89, 91
Yardley, George H. mbsk   1948, 49, 50
Yardley, Rich mvball   1978
Yarus, Alyson wfenc   1985, 86, 87
Yee, Carl mcrew   1988, 89
Yee, Jason mten   1990, 91, 92
Yett, Ronald bsb   1964, 65
Yoshida, Lester wrest   1976, 77
Yoshimara, Michael mcrew   1968, 69
Youd, James mwp   1962, 63
Youmans, Anne wsoc   1983
Youmans, Anne wsoc   1986
Young, Charles ftb   1993, 94, 95
Young, Charlie ftb   1987, 88, 90
Young, Chris M. ftb   1985, 87
Young, Dan mgym   1969
Young, Gordon A. ftb   1954, 55, 56
Young, Maia syncswim   1996
Young, Peter mtrk   1951
Young, Philip wrest   1957
Young, Ray bsb   1954, 56
Young, Roderick A. mbsk   1966
Young, Sheila wvball   1978, 79
Young, Tim mbsk   1995
Young, William B. ftb   1942
Yu, Jennifer wfenc   1983, 84, 85, 86

Zager, Peter G. ftb   1936, 37, 38
Zaltosky, Craig R. ftb   1972, 73
Zamloch, Archer bsb   1935
Zamloch, Archer W. mbsk   1935
Zander, Josh mgolf   1988, 89
Zandvliet, Tara wcrew   1990
Zaninovich, George mbsk   1952, 53
Zappettini, Donald M. ftb   1942
Zartler, Stacey wxc   1985
Zeilstra, Julie wbsk   1989, 90, 91
Zellmer, Craig A. ftb   1978, 79, 80, 81
Zenorini, Carissa wswim   1996
Zentner, John R. ftb   1985, 86, 87, 88
Ziegler, Robert mwp   1954
Zmijewski, Bryan mtrk   1996
Zmijewski, Bryan mxc   1994
Zock, Diana wswim   1983, 84, 85, 86
Zone, Robert J. mbsk   1936, 37
Zonne, Phil W. mbsk   1937, 38, 39
Zucker, Sasha mfenc   1995, 96
Zuercher, Mike bsb   1989
Zuvella, Paul bsb   1977, 78, 79, 80

■ Stanford Olympic Medalists ■

1996 Games at Atlanta

Athlete	Sport	Event	Medal
Jennifer Azzi	Basketball	Team USA	Gold
Julie Foudy	Soccer	Team USA	Gold
Catherine Fox	Swimming	400 Meter Freestyle Relay	Gold
		400 Meter Medley Relay	Gold
Chryste Gaines	Track	400 Meter Relay	Gold
Kurt Grote	Swimming	400 Meter Medley Relay	Gold
A.J. Hinch	Baseball	Team USA	Bronze
Joe Hudepohl	Swimming	800 Meter Freestyle Relay	Gold
Lisa Jacob	Swimming	400 Meter Freestyle Relay	Gold
		800 Meter Freestyle Relay	Gold
Jair Lynch	Gymnastics	Parallel Bars	Silver
Jeff Rouse	Swimming	100 Meter Backstroke	Gold
		400 Meter Medley Relay	Gold
Katy Steding	Basketball	Team USA	Gold
Kent Steffes	Beach Volleyball	Team USA	Gold
Jenny Thompson	Swimming	400 Meter Freestyle Relay	Gold
		400 Meter Medley Relay	Gold
		800 Meter Freestyle Relay	Gold

1992 Games at Barcelona, Spain

Athlete	Sport	Event	Medal
Janet Evans	Swimming	800 Meter Freestyle	Gold
		400 Meter Freestyle	Silver
Scott Fortune	Volleyball	Team USA	Bronze
Joe Hudepohl	Swimming	400 Meter Free Relay	Gold
		800 Meter Free Relay	Bronze
Lea Loveless	Swimming	400 Meter Medley Relay	Gold
		100 Meter Backstroke	Bronze
Pablo Morales	Swimming	100 Meter Butterfly	Gold
		400 Meter Medley Relay	Gold
Kim Oden	Volleyball	Team USA	Bronze
Jeff Rouse	Swimming	400 Meter Medley Relay	Gold
		100 Meter Backstroke	Silver
Summer Sanders	Swimming	200 Meter Butterfly	Gold
		400 Meter Medley Relay	Gold
		200 Meter IM	Silver
		400 Meter IM	Bronze
Jenny Thompson	Swimming	400 Meter Free Relay	Gold
		400 Meter Medley Relay	Gold
		100 Meter Freestyle	Silver

1988 Games at Seoul, Korea

Athlete	Sport	Event	Medal
James Bergeson	Water Polo	Team USA	Silver
Jody Campbell	Water Polo	Team USA	Silver

Janet Evans	Swimming	400 Meter Freestyle	Gold
		800 Meter Freestyle	Gold
		400 Meter Individual Medley	Gold
Scott Fortune	Volleyball	Team USA	Gold
Alison Higson (Canada)	Swimming	200 Meter Breaststroke	Bronze
Janel Jorgensen	Swimming	400 Meter Medley Relay	Silver
Craig Klass	Water Polo	Team USA	Silver
Tim Mayotte	Tennis	Singles	Silver
Jay Mortenson	Swimming	400 Meter Medley Relay	Gold
Anthony Mosse (New Zealand)	Swimming	200 Meter Butterfly	Bronze
Alan Mouchawar	Water Polo	Team USA	Silver
John Pescatore	Men's Crew	The Eight	Bronze
Doug Robbins	Baseball	Team USA	Gold
Jon Root	Volleyball	Team USA	Gold
Ed Sprague	Baseball	Team USA	Gold

1984 Games at Los Angeles

Athlete	Sport	Event	Medal
Doug Burke	Water Polo	Team USA	Silver
Jody Campbell	Water Polo	Team USA	Silver
Chris Dorst	Water Polo	Team USA	Silver
Jenna Johnson	Swimming	400 Meter Freestyle Relay	Gold
		400 Meter Medley Relay	Gold
		100 Meter Butterfly	Silver
Sheryl Johnson	Field Hockey	Team USA	Bronze
Drew McDonald	Water Polo	Team USA	Silver
Pablo Morales	Swimming	400 Meter Medley Relay	Gold
		100 Meter Butterfly	Silver
		200 Meter Individual Medley	Silver
Sussan Rapp	Swimming	200 Meter Breaststroke	Silver
Dave Schultz	Wrestling	163.5 pounds	Gold
Mark Schultz	Wrestling	180.5 pounds	Gold

1980 Games at Moscow, Soviet Union (Boycott)

1976 Games at Montreal, Canada

Athlete	Sport	Event	Medal
Mike Bruner	Swimming	200 Meter Butterfly	Gold
		800 Meter Freestyle Relay	Gold
John Hencken	Swimming	100 Meter Breaststroke	Gold
		400 Meter Medley Relay	Gold
		200 Meter Breaststroke	Silver
Linda Jezek	Swimming	400 Meter Medley Relay	Silver
Kim Peyton	Swimming	400 Meter Freestyle Relay	Gold

1972 Games at Munich, West Germany

Athlete	Sport	Event	Medal
John Hencken	Swimming	200 Meter Breaststroke	Gold
		100 Meter Breaststroke	Silver
Mitch Ivey	Swimming	200 Meter Backstroke	Silver
John Parker	Water Polo	Team USA	Bronze
Gary Sheerer	Water Polo	Team USA	Bronze

1968 Games at Mexico City, Mexico

Athlete	Sport	Event	Medal
Greg Buckingham	Swimming	200 Meter Individual Medley	Silver
John Ferris	Swimming	200 Meter Individual Medley	Bronze
		200 Meter Butterflly	Bronze
Mitch Ivey	Swimming	200 Meter Backstroke	Silver
Brian Job	Swimming	200 Meter Breaststroke	Bronze
Bill Toomey	Track	Decathlon	Gold
Larry Hough	Rowing	Pairs Without	Silver

1964 Games at Tokyo, Japan

Athlete	Sport	Event	Medal
Sharon Stouder Clark	Swimming	400 Meter Freestyle Relay	Gold
		400 Medley Relay Relay	Gold
		100 Meter Butterfly	Gold
		100 Meter Freestyle	Silver
Dick Roth	Swimming	400 Meter Individual Medley	Gold
Dave Weill	Track	Discus	Bronze
Kent Mitchell	Rowing	Pairs With	Gold
Dick Lyon	Rowing	Fours Without	Bronze

1960 Games at Rome, Italy

Athlete	Sport	Event	Medal
Paul Hait	Swimming	400 Meter Medley Relay	Gold
George Harrison	Swimming	800 Meter Freestyle Relay	Gold
Chris von Saltza Olmstead	Swimming	400 Meter Freestyle Relay	Gold
		400 Meter Freestyle	Gold
		400 Meter Medley Relay	Gold
		100 Meter Freestyle	Silver
Anne Cribbs	Swimming	400 Medley Relay	Gold
Kent Mitchell	Rowing	Pairs Without	Bronze
Dan Ayrault	Rowing	Fours Without	Gold

1956 Games at Melbourne, Australia

Athlete	Sport	Event	Medal
Nancy Simon Peterson	Swimming	400 Meter Freestyle Relay	Silver
Jim Walsh	Basketball	Team USA	Gold
Nancy Simons Peterson	Swimming	400 Meter Freestyle Relay	Silver
Ron Tomsic	Basketball	Team USA	Gold
Duvall Hecht	Rowing	Pairs Without	Gold
Jim Fifer	Rowing	Pairs Without	Gold
Dan Ayrault	Rowing	Pairs With	Gold

1952 Games at Helsinki, Finland

Bob Mathias	Track	Decathlon	Gold

1948 Games at London, England

Athlete	Sport	Event	Medal
Brenda Helser DeMoreles	Swimming	400 Meter Freestyle Relay	Silver
Bob Mathias	Track	Decathlon	Gold

1936 Games at Berlin, East Germany

Athlete	Sport	Event	Medal
Gordon Dunn	Track	Discus	Silver
Marjorie Gestring Bowman	Diving	Springboard Diving	Gold

1932 Games at Los Angeles

Athlete	Sport	Event	Medal
Frank Booth	Swimming	800 Meter Freestyle Relay	Silver
Austin Clapp	Water Polo	Team USA	Bronze
Hec Dyer	Track	400 Meter Relay	Gold
Ben Eastman	Track	400 Meters	Silver
Rothert Harlow	Track	Shot Put	Silver
Henry Laborde	Track	Discus	Silver
Harold McCalister	Water Polo	Team USA	Bronze
Bill Miller	Track	Pole Vault	Gold
Wally O'Connor	Water Polo	Team USA	Bronze
Calver Strong	Water Polo	Team USA	Bronze
Ted Wiget	Water Polo	Team USA	Bronze

1928 Games at Amsterdam, Holland

Athlete	Sport	Event	Medal
Pete Desjardins	Diving	Platform Diving	Gold
	Diving	Springboard Diving	Gold
Bob King	Track	High Jump	Gold
Bud Spencer	Track	1600 Meter Relay	Gold

1924 Games at Paris, France

Athlete	Sport	Event	Medal
Arthur Austin	Water Polo	Team USA	Bronze
Phillip Clark	Rugby	Team USA	Gold
Norman Cleveland	Rugby	Team USA	Gold
Dudley DeGroot	Rugby	Team USA	Gold
Robert H. Coleman Devereaux	Rugby	Team USA	Gold
Elmer Collett	Water Polo	Team USA	Bronze
Pete Desjardins	Diving	Springboard Diving	Silver
Charles Webster Doe, Jr.	Rugby	Team USA	Gold
Dave Fall	Diving	Springboard Diving	Silver
Linn Farrish	Rugby	Team USA	Gold
Reggie Harrison	Water Polo	Team USA	Bronze
Glenn Hartranft	Track	Shot Put	Silver
Richard Hyland	Rugby	Team USA	Gold
Wally O'Connor	Swimming	800 Meter Freestyle Relay	Gold
Wally O'Connor	Water Polo	Team USA	Bronze
John Patrick	Rugby	Team USA	Gold
Clarence Pinkston	Diving	Platform Diving	Bronze
		Springboard Diving	Bronze
William Rodgers	Rugby	Team USA	Gold
Al White	Diving	Platform Diving	Gold
		Springboard Diving	Gold

1920 Games at Antwerp, Belgium

Athlete	Sport	Event	Medal
Danny Carroll	Rugby	Team USA	Gold
Charles Webster Doe, Jr.	Rugby	Team USA	Gold
Morris Kirksey	Track	400 Meter Relay	Gold
	Track	100 Meters	Silver
	Rugby	Team USA	Gold
Feg Murray	Track	110 High Hurdles	Bronze
John Norton	Track	400 Meter Hurdles	Silver
John Patrick	Rugby	Team USA	Gold
C.E. Righter	Rugby	Team USA	Gold
Norman Ross	Swimming	400 Meter Freestyle	Gold
		1500 Meter Freestyle	Gold
		800 Meter Freestyle Relay	Gold
Clarence Pinkston	Diving	Platform Diving	Gold
		Springboard Diving	Silver
Dink Templeton	Rugby	Team USA	Gold
Heaton Wrenn	Rugby	Team USA	Gold

1912 Games at Stockholm, Sweden

Athlete	Sport	Event	Medal
George Horine	Track	High Jump	Bronze

Other Titles by Sports Publishing Inc.
a division of Sagamore Publishing

STANFORD: Home of Champions
(leather-bound edition)

Autographed by Stanford legends Jack McDowell, Janet Evans and Bob Mathias. This book is a limited edition of 500 copies and is sure to become a collector's item. Includes certificate of authenticity. $129.95 Available only through Sports Publishing, Inc. To order call 1-800-327-5557.

BILL WALSH: Finding the Winning Edge $24.95

A business-style book that illustrates the basic organizational, coaching, and system philosophies that Bill Walsh used throughout his career with the San Francisco 49ers. The coach of the decade for the 80s reveals how after being out of professional coaching for nine years he still has more influence on the NFL than any current coach.

BILL WALSH: Finding the Winning Edge
(leather-bound edition)

Autographed by Bill Walsh and other former players. Limited edition. Includes certificate of authenticity. $149.95. Available only through Sports Publishing, Inc. To order call 800-327-5557.

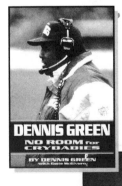

DENNIS GREEN: No Room for Crybabies $24.95

The life story of former Stanford coach and current Minnesota Vikings coach, Dennis Green. The Dennis Green story represents the millions of untold stories of people who have been denied their full American rights, but refuse to give up. Green reveals what life is like breaking taboos, living on the edge and crashing through glass ceilings. Candidly, he illustrates what it is like when "there is no room for crybabies and life tries to make you cry."

DENNIS GREEN: No Room for Crybabies
(leather-bound edition)

Autographed by Dennis Green and two former players. Limited edition of 250 copies. Includes certificate of authenticity. Only $59.95! Available only through Sports Publishing, Inc. To order call 800-327-5557.

Available at your local bookstore
or by calling 800-327-5557